Merry Christmas
Choccy

and Easter, too!

Happy the book,

I hope you enjoy the
especially the marked pages.

Chocy II

The Andrews Sisters

The Andrews Sisters

A Biography and Career Record

H. Arlo Nimmo

McFarland & Company, Inc., Publishers
Jefferson, North Carolina, and London

Frontispiece: This quintessential photograph of the Andrews Sisters captures their association with World War II. A publicity photograph for the film *Buck Privates* (1940), it has probably been reproduced more than any other photograph of the sisters (Author's collection)

LIBRARY OF CONGRESS CATALOGUING-IN-PUBLICATION DATA

Nimmo, Harry.
    The Andrews Sisters : a biography and career record /
  H. Arlo Nimmo.
      p.   cm.
    Includes bibliographical references, discography, filmography,
and index.

ISBN 0-7864-1731-5 (illustrated case binding : 50# alkaline paper)

    1. Andrews Sisters.   2. Singers—United States—Biography.
  I. Title.
  ML421.A47N56   2004
  782.42164'092'2—dc22   2003021124

British Library cataloguing data are available

On the cover: The Andrews Sisters (*from left: LaVerne, Patty* and *Maxene*) in the 1943 film *Always a Bridesmaid* singing "Thanks for the Buggy Ride" (*Robert Boyer Collection*)

Manufactured in the United States of America

McFarland & Company, Inc., Publishers
  Box 611, Jefferson, North Carolina 28640
    www.mcfarlandpub.com

To Robert Boyer, Everett Searcy,
Merle Smith, and John Tyler,
longtime Andrews Sisters fans
whose generous sharing
made this a much better book.

Contents

Preface

Thank God for the Andrews Sisters. When the going gets rough, when there seems to be no cause for joy in the world, here they come singing and bouncing their way into your heart.[1]

An early critic said they sounded like "Chinese puzzles set to off-key music."[2] They reminded another of "a group of banshees wailing in the closest possible harmony."[3] An alliterative record reviewer called them "the Throaty Threesome" and "the terrifying trio." When Groucho Marx learned they were on the same train with him, he quipped, "I thought they made all their trips by broom."[4] "The most frightening act in motion pictures" was the *Harvard Lampoon*'s assessment of their first movie appearance.[5]

Not so, said their loyal fans, who far outnumbered their detractors. "They're artists from the word go," proclaimed one, "both vocally and in showmanship."[6] "The greatest fem vocal trio in show business," assessed another.[7] Said still another, "They offer a stylized brand of throaty harmonizing and phrasing that's as easy and natural as breathing and as smooth as velvet."[8] A charmed Brit saw them on stage and concluded, "They are so wholehearted and unspoilt and determined to please that it is impossible not to like them."[9] "Let's face it," demanded a fan, "these dolls ARE show business."[10]

They were, of course, the Andrews Sisters—Patty, Maxene, and LaVerne—who topped the music charts for fourteen years during the late 1930s, 1940s, and early 1950s, and entertained America collectively and individually for sixty-five years. The three singing sisters from Minneapolis won the hearts of their nation and became an enduring part of Americana. They are still the most successful female singing group in history, and until the Beatles came along they

1

were the top-selling music group ever. In 1951, the Voice of America claimed that the Andrews Sisters were "the most listened to women in history."[11]

During their long career, the Andrews Sisters charted 113 of the 605 songs they recorded, made thousands of personal appearances, and entertained three generations of GIs. The Andrews Sisters personified swing and boogie woogie, but also tried romantic ballads, country, western, blues, polkas, waltzes, show tunes, hymns, Hawaiian, folk, Christmas, cha-cha, calypso, jazz and Latin; they even toyed with rock. They sang with some of the greatest show business names of the century, including Desi Arnaz, Nat Cole, Perry Como, Bing Crosby, Judy Garland, Bob Hope, Lena Horne, Burl Ives, Al Jolson, Danny Kaye, Dean Martin, Groucho Marx, Carmen Miranda, Les Paul, Frank Sinatra, The Supremes, Ernest Tubb, Rudy Vallee, and even Tallulah Bankhead, Gabby Hayes, Peter Lorre, and Sydney Greenstreet. Among the greats of the swing era who backed them were Bunny Berigan, Jimmy Dorsey, Tommy Dorsey, Duke Ellington, Benny Goodman, Woody Herman, Harry James, Gene Krupa, Glenn Miller, Buddy Rich, and Joe Venuti.

During their heyday, the Andrews Sisters were ubiquitous. From 1931 when they joined the vaudeville circuit until they retired as an act in 1968, they crisscrossed the country scores of times and traveled to Europe to entertain legions of fans at personal appearances. They appeared in eighteen movies during the so-called Golden Age of Hollywood and were regulars on radio during the Golden Age of that medium. They then joined television when it supplanted radio as America's home entertainment. Their faces were everywhere—on record dusters, magazine covers, record albums, matchbooks, movie posters, sheet music covers, and anywhere their manager could work them into a publicity stunt or story.

In the popular imagination, the Andrews Sisters are indelibly associated with World War II. However, they first gained national recognition in 1938 and were already household names when the war began. Their popularity continued throughout the war years and into the postwar period until 1951 when they charted their last hit. They performed together until LaVerne died in 1967, after which Patty and Maxene continued with another singer until 1968. The two remaining sisters then pursued solo careers, but reunited for the successful Broadway show *Over Here!* in 1974. Maxene performed until her death in 1995, and Patty currently lives in retirement in southern California.

The Andrews Sisters' popularity continues. Some sources claim they still sell over a million CDs annually. I found no documentation to back that claim, but their popularity is such that over one hundred CDs of their hits have been issued since 1987—not to mention the dozens of CD anthologies that include their songs. On any given day over 400 items of "Andrews Sisters" memorabilia appear on the Internet auction site eBay, often purchased at hefty prices by Andrews Sisters fans across the country and around the world. Singing groups imitate them to add verisimilitude to World War II era productions, and their recordings often provide background music for films and theater pieces depicting their era. Their songs continue to inspire choreographers, and few Halloweens, Mardi Gras, or drag shows transpire without an appearance of

A word about spelling. Spelling variations of the Andrews Sisters' first names occur in the literature. "LaVerne," "Maxine," and "Patricia" appear on the sisters' birth certificates. LaVerne was frequently spelled "Laverne" by the press. Maxine changed the spelling of her name to "Maxene" early in her career. Patricia was always known as "Patty," but sometimes the press spelled her name "Patti." For consistency, throughout this book I have used LaVerne, Maxene and Patty, the most common spellings and the ones the sisters preferred. I have even committed the "no-no" of changing the name spellings in quotations for the sake of consistency.

And finally, if you don't have one, go out and buy a "Great Hits of the Andrews Sisters" CD and listen to it before you begin reading this book. And while you're out, pick up a video or DVD of one of their movies. I hope you enjoy reading this book. I certainly enjoyed researching and writing it.

CHAPTER ONE

1887–1932

When my sisters and I began to sing together, we were young children living with our immigrant parents in Minneapolis. The music became the fabric that bound our family together and kept us strong during some very difficult times.

—Maxene Andrews[1]

Few people leave their homeland without regret, and such was probably the case with the maternal grandparents of the Andrews Sisters when they left Norway in the late 19th century. Norwegians had witnessed some bleak decades. During the middle of the century, overpopulation, food shortages, and mechanization led to farm foreclosures throughout the country. Some regions experienced actual starvation when crops failed and herring runs disappeared from the coasts. Spurred by these worsening conditions at home as well as glowing letters from friends and relatives in the New World, entire families left Norway for a new life in the rich forests and farmlands of Wisconsin and Minnesota.[2]

Among them was one-year-old Olga Sollie, the future mother of the Andrews Sisters, who in 1887 immigrated to the United States with her parents, Peter Peterson Sollie and Sophia Hoove Sollie, and her four siblings, Peter, Martin, Edward, and Petra.[3] As many before them, the Sollie family probably left their original surname at Ellis Island and adopted the more pronounceable Sollie, the name of their home region in Homalvik, Norway.[4] Forty-four-year-old Peter Sollie, his thirty-nine-year-old wife Sophia, and their five children traveled westward to join other Norwegians in Minneapolis, Minnesota.

The specific whereabouts of the family are unknown until 1889 when "Peter Soley" first appeared in the Minneapolis City Directory as a "laborer" residing at 803 22nd Avenue North, a poor immigrant section of the city. In 1890, little Olga Sollie acquired another sibling when her mother gave birth to her sixth child, a daughter named Elydia, and three years later another sister, Mable, was born. The 1900 United States Census documented the entire Sollie family living in a rented house in a section of north Minneapolis that housed many poor immigrants. Olga's father was a "day laborer," and her brothers Peter, Martin, and Edward held blue-collar jobs while her sister Petra was a "clerk in Commission House." Twelve-year-old Olga and her younger sisters Elydia and Mable were students.

The first decade of the new century was a tragic one for Olga and her family. Her brother Martin died in 1901 of unknown causes.[5] Olga's sister Elydia died in 1908 of "Acute Pulmo Tuberculosis" that was exacerbated by "exposure to cold."[6] Sollie family lore claims Petra died within days of Elydia from the same exposure that killed her sister.

In 1903, Olga's brothers Peter and Edward Sollie opened the Hiawatha Ice Cream Company in the small town of Mound, Minnesota, where they serviced the early tourist boats on Lake Minnetonka, which then as now was a summer resort for Minneapolitans.[7] Located some twenty-five miles west of Minneapolis, Mound was built on a peninsula in Lake Minnetonka surrounded by wooded hills and small farmsteads. The Indian burial mounds along the shores of the lake gave the town its name. When the Sollie brothers began their ice cream business, Mound was a favorite summer vacation spot and had a resident population of only a few hundred people. Olga's future daughters, LaVerne, Maxene, and Patty Andrews, would later spend summers and school vacations in Mound visiting their uncles.

Olga's father worked at various blue-collar jobs in Minneapolis between 1900 and 1910. Her brothers Peter and Edward spent summers in Mound selling ice cream to the tourist trade and winters at other jobs in Minneapolis. Olga probably joined the workforce after she left school at sixteen. She tried several occupations, including clerk, milliner, "trimmer," and "sorter" at a woolen mill. She is sometimes identified as "Olive," probably a mishearing of her nickname "Ollie."

The 1910 Census recorded the Sollies still residing in north Minneapolis where they shared a rented house with another family, a fairly common arrangement among the city's poor population. According to the census, Olga's father spoke no English[8] and worked as a carpenter. Olga was a milliner in a dry goods store.

In 1910, Olga's brothers Peter and Edward Sollie returned to Mound to live permanently. They operated their ice cream company until 1922 when they opened the Sollie Brothers Grocery Store, which remained in business until 1964.[9] Olga's parents followed their sons to Mound and lived with them in a house near their grocery store.

At the turn of the century, a Greek youth later known as Peter Andrews was sufficiently unhappy with his lot to seek solace in the United States. At age thirteen, Andrews ran away from his village near Athens and in 1900, at seventeen, he immigrated to the United States.[10] Why he left home and how he made it to America are unknown. His own daughters would know virtually nothing about his early years, which he was always reluctant to discuss. Although "Andrews" appeared on his citizenship papers,[11] it was doubtless an immigration officer's Anglicization of "Andreas," his original Greek name according to his daughter Maxene, who said her father could neither read nor write but was "sharp as a tack."[12]

It is unclear how Peter Andrews ended up in Minneapolis, which had few Greeks at that time. Perhaps friends or relatives offered a home there as he found his way in the new country. His daughter Maxene once claimed he went directly to Minneapolis upon arriving in the United States,[13] but he does not appear in the city directory until 1907. The language barrier and his minority status probably created problems in finding jobs, so he took what was offered—often menial ones.

When Peter Andrews arrived in Minneapolis, it was a city of 325,000, one of the largest cities in the Middle West. Over 16 percent of the city's population was of Norwegian descent while Swedes, Germans, and British comprised its other large ethnic communities.[14] In 1900, only seventy-five Greeks lived in the entire state of Minnesota, but by 1910 the Greek population had grown to 1,840, about a third of whom lived in the Minneapolis–St. Paul area.[15] As early as 1900, a small Greek Orthodox Church was established in rented quarters in downtown Minneapolis. In 1909, the small Greek community built St. Mary's Greek Orthodox Church, which served the Greek community for the next several decades.[16] In addition to serving as a community center, St. Mary's provided an afternoon school where Greek children studied Greek language and culture after their public school classes. Three of Peter Andrews' daughters would eventually attend some of these classes and one of his daughters would be buried in the church's cemetery.

Sollie family lore claims that Peter Andrews first became acquainted with the Sollies when he applied for a job at the Sollie brothers' ice cream company in Mound—perhaps as early as 1903. How the young Greek immigrant ended up in Mound, Minnesota, is unknown. After working for the Sollies in Mound, Peter Andrews accompanied them to Minneapolis where the city directory listed him as a roomer in their household in 1907. He worked at the Crescent Creamery Company where young Peter Sollie also worked as an ice cream maker.

Sometime during this period, Peter Andrews met and fell in love with Olga Sollie, once described by her daughter Maxene as "a very dark Norwegian … [with] a sense of rebellious freedom."[17] As most young people in love, Peter and Olga wanted to marry. Olga's family, however, opposed the marriage—most likely because Peter was Greek, a heritage that also included his Greek Orthodox religion. The Sollies were Lutherans and Norwegians. Immigrants, happy as they were to leave the Old Country, nonetheless usually wanted their children to marry within their own culture, or at least a closely related one. The Sollies were no exception.

Peter Andrews left the Sollie household in 1909—possibly because of his involvement with Olga—and moved to a large rooming house at 71 Western

Avenue (now Glenwood Avenue) where he still lived at the time of the 1910 Census, which claimed he was a "salesman" in a "store." However, much of the 1910 Census data on Andrews is dubious. For example, the census claimed that both he and his parents were born in Minnesota and that he could read and write, information that does not jibe with other data.

Although Peter Andrews left the Sollie household, he and Olga continued their relationship. Both were strong-willed individuals, and not about to let others dictate their marriage choices. Their daughter Maxene would later say, "my father … was a very staunch old-country Greek [who] married a very modern Norwegian woman who was as strong as he was."[18] Peter and Olga eloped, and married without her family's approval on July 6, 1910.[19] Olga was twenty-four years old and Peter was twenty-eight.

After three months of marriage, Olga became pregnant. The young couple was doubtless excited about the birth of their first child, which would seal their marriage and return them to the fold of the Sollie family. Exactly one year after her marriage—July 6, 1911—Olga gave birth to a daughter in her home at 826 Plymouth North Street, Minneapolis. She was attended by a midwife from the Scandinavian community where the young couple lived who was apparently not a close friend or relative since she misspelled the names of both Olga and Peter on the birth certificate—or perhaps her literacy was limited. The infant was identified as "Baby Andrew," a misspelling of the last name that would pursue the family throughout their lives. It is unlikely the child was named "Baby," but rather was identified as such until a proper name was bestowed at her christening, a tradition in the Greek Orthodox Church. The name "Baby," however, remained on the birth certificate until nineteen years later in 1930 when Olga altered the document to correct the spelling of the last name to "Andrews" and to change "Baby" to "LaVerne." She also corrected her own name at that time, which was misspelled "Alger Sallie."

Two years later on July 14, 1913, Olga gave birth to a second daughter whose name does not appear on the birth certificate, but she is later identified as "Angeline" on her death certificate. The Andrews family was still living in north Minneapolis, but now at 1013 14th Avenue North. The same midwife who delivered LaVerne delivered the new baby. Eight months later the little girl died in the house where she was born of bronchial pneumonia caused by "exposure," according to the doctor who signed her death certificate. She was buried a few days later in St. Mary's Cemetery, the burial place for Minneapolis' Greek population.

Peter and Olga Andrews' third daughter, Maxene, was born January 3, 1916. She also was born at home and attended by the same midwife who assisted the births of her older sisters, but the family had moved from north Minneapolis to 729 East 14th Street. Again the family's last name is misspelled "Andrew" on the birth certificate with an "s" obviously added later. Maxene's name is spelled "Maxine," but later she always spelled it "Maxene." Peter and Olga were hoping for a son, and Peter, whose Greek heritage favored sons, was especially disappointed. His niece remembered that Peter made Maxene somewhat of a "tomboy," but nonetheless he became angry if he caught her playing ball with the boys. To his niece, he always seemed "harder" on Maxene than his other two daughters.[20]

By the time their fourth child arrived, Peter and Olga had moved yet again and were living at 1501 11th Avenue South, Minneapolis, a few blocks from Maxene's birthplace. This child was also a girl, again to the disappointment of both parents. Patricia Andrews was born February 16, 1918, and was attended by a physician, perhaps reflecting a greater affluence for the family or a concern about the delivery. Peter's name is again misspelled "Andrew" on the birth certificate but this time it is not corrected. His daughter's last name, however, is spelled correctly. A young woman who lived next door to the Andrews family in the apartment house where Patty was born remembered her first visit to the Andrews: "Patty, who was about two years old and still in diapers, jiggled up and down in time to the music from the player piano Mrs. Andrews was playing. Patty had rhythm at that age."[21]

The Andrews Sisters' cousin Gladys Leichter always remembered the sisters' birth dates because each was born two days after a holiday: LaVerne two days after the Fourth of July, Maxene two days after New Year's Day, and Patty two days after Valentine's Day.[22] The Andrews Sisters' middle names are LaVerne Sophia, Maxene Angelyn, and Patricia Marie. An early writer claimed Olga chose the sisters' first names for her Norwegian side of the family and Peter chose the second names for his Greek side.[23] This is not entirely true since LaVerne's middle name, although a popular Greek name, is also the name of Olga's mother. On her memorial plaque, Maxene's middle name is spelled "Anglyn," but the name of her deceased sister after whom she was apparently named was spelled "Angeline." These middle names do not appear on the sisters' birth certificates, and were most likely bestowed at their christenings.

Nothing in the literature indicates that religion was important in the lives of the Andrews family, except for Maxene who became a born-again Christian in her later years. The sisters were all baptized into the Greek Orthodox Church, but they never discussed religion in their many interviews. When Lou Levy, their manager, first met them in the late 1930s, he said they "all wore crosses" and claimed they were Catholics.[24] Obviously, religion was not important to them since Levy knew them intimately and eventually married Maxene, but apparently never learned they were Greek Orthodox.

Ages are problematic in the literature on the Andrews family. The most common birth dates the sisters gave the press are 1915 for LaVerne, 1918 for Maxene, and 1920 for Patty. Their birth certificates, however, reveal that all these dates are incorrect. LaVerne probably sliced the years in order to make her age closer to her sisters, but why Patty and Maxene made themselves younger is unclear since they were quite young when they began their careers. I found only two published sources that correctly reported LaVerne's age,[25] which is even incorrect on her memorial plaque. The sisters consistently claimed they were younger than they were. Patty once told a reporter: "I've never kept my age a secret." But later in the interview, she said, "I was 16 in 1938 when we had our first hit record, 'Bei Mir Bist Du Schoen.'"[26] She was, in fact, a month shy of her twentieth birthday.

Olga Andrews' age also varies in the literature. Since her birth certificate is unavailable, only census reports and the birth certificates of her daughters are available to ascertain her age, but they reveal inconsistencies. At the time she died in 1948, obituaries reported her age as fifty or fifty-two, at least ten years younger than the ages recorded elsewhere. Her memorial plaque claims she was born in 1898, which would make her only thirteen when LaVerne was born, and is inconsistent with other reports of her age. Peter Andrews was probably born in 1883, but his memorial plaque claims 1890 as the year of his birth, at least seven years later than the age reported on his daughters' birth certificates and the censuses.

Peter Andrews tried a variety of jobs including ice cream maker, laborer, green grocer, and restaurateur before he eventually settled into managing pool halls in Minneapolis.[27] In interviews throughout their career, the Andrews Sisters claimed their father operated a Greek restaurant during their childhood. He actually operated a restaurant for only two years—possibly four, since Peter's profession is not provided in the city directory for the year preceding and following the two-year listing of his restaurant. Throughout most of his years in Minneapolis, however, Peter managed a pool hall, a business he shared with many others. In 1928 seventy-eight "Billiards and Pocket Billiard Rooms" were listed in the Minneapolis City Directory, obviously an important recreation for Minneapolitans. The five most common Greek businesses in Minneapolis in 1915 were confectionery stores, restaurants, shoeshine parlors, fruit stores, and billiard parlors.[28] If his job as an ice cream maker is included in the confectionery business, Peter Andrews explored four of these occupations of his countrymen.

Between 1910 and 1920, Peter and Olga Andrews moved six times and each of their four daughters was born at a different address. In 1920, the family moved to 1600 Lyndale Avenue North where they remained until they left Minneapolis in the early 1930s. They initially rented the house, but later bought it.

The 1920 Census provides a glimpse of the Andrews household at 1600 Lyndale Avenue North where Peter and Olga lived with their three daughters and Peter's cousin Garry (or Harry) whose last name is illegible on the census form. Peter was thirty-seven, Olga was thirty-two, LaVerne was eight, Maxene was three and a half, Patty was one and a half, and Peter's cousin was thirty-seven. The date of Peter's immigration to the United States is illegible, but Olga emigrated from Norway in 1890, three years later than the claim by her parents in the 1910 Census. Peter's cousin was a Greek alien, unable to read or write, who immigrated to the United States in 1906. Peter was also unable to read or write, but Olga was literate. All members of the household spoke English. Peter's profession was "Billiard & Pool Hall" where he was an "employer." Peter's cousin worked as a "maker" at an "ice cream company," probably one where Peter formerly worked.

In 1920, Olga Andrews' parents died in Mound, Minnesota. Seventy-six-year-old Peter Sollie died February 8[29] and his seventy-one-year-old wife Sophia died six months later.[30] Both were buried in Mound Union Cemetery, the small cemetery south of the town. Only Olga, her married sister Mable, and her two bachelor brothers Edward and Peter remained of the once large Sollie family.

The earliest known photograph of the Andrews Sisters. Maxene (left) is about three years old, Patty (center) is about one, and LaVerne (right) is about eight. This photograph probably was taken when the Andrews family moved to their home at 1600 Lyndale Avenue North in Minneapolis in 1920. (John Szforza Collection)

When the Andrews family moved to their home at 1600 Lyndale Avenue North in 1920, they invited Irene Wilmot, their young neighbor, to board with them. Years later Wilmot remembered the household: "The house was sparsely furnished. There were four bedrooms upstairs, four large rooms and one small one plus an entrance hall downstairs. A would-be artist painted the wall going up the stairway. If I remember correctly, he painted huge lions." She also remembered that Peter Andrews' cousin lived in the house and was in ill health. For a short time, Wilmot shared a room with Olga's sister Mable who was briefly separated from her husband.

Wilmot remembered that the household "had a lot of activity, excitement, noise and *music! music!* … Mrs. Andrews' sister Mable and I both played the piano and everyone sang." LaVerne took piano lessons "and played piano in stores where sheet music was sold, as was the custom then … for a would-be customer, if he desired to hear it." Wilmot thought "LaVerne had her father's nature and resembled him, while Maxene and Patty favored their mother." Olga Andrews had a good sense of humor "and was fun to be with." Mr. Andrews was "a very kind and a gentle man, but firm. They were good parents. We were a happy lot." Wilmot occasionally accompanied the Andrews family to Mound when they visited Olga's brothers and parents. When Mrs. Sollie died in 1920, she sang at her funeral.[31]

Maxene (left) and Patty Andrews, circa 1921. At this early age, Patty revealed
the personality that would later spark the Andrews Sisters' act. (Gladys
Leichter Collection)

The Andrews family lived in one of the poorer sections of Minneapolis. A classmate of Patty later remembered the neighborhood as an old part of the city occupied by people of modest incomes living in single family homes, duplexes, and occasional fourplexes. A nearby area to the east was considerably rundown, one of the most depressed areas of the city, and to the south was another "considerably deteriorated area."[32]

Tragedy visited the Sollie family again in July 1925 when thirty-two-year-old Mable Sollie Moberg died following the birth of her fifth child, a son. Serious complications had followed her fourth child's birth and she was advised to deliver any future children in the hospital. She was terrified of hospitals, however, and refused to go for the birth of her next child. After the child was born, it became apparent that the midwife could not handle the complications of the birth and Mable's husband Walter Moberg called an ambulance to take his wife to the hospital. She lost consciousness before the ambulance arrived and was dead upon arrival at the hospital, two days after the birth of her son.

Olga Andrews was devastated by her sister's death. They had always been very close, and became even closer after the deaths of their other two sisters. Mable spent much time at Olga's home, and after her marriage she lived within blocks of the Andrews family and the children of the two sisters frequently played together.

With five children to provide for, Walter Moberg had little time for mourning. The most pressing problem was the care of the infant. Olga Andrews helped him, and for awhile, Moberg thought the Andrews would adopt the little boy since Peter often expressed disappointment in not having a son. They declined to do so, however, and Moberg reluctantly allowed his infant son to be adopted outside the family. His children were heartbroken to see the baby leave, especially ten-year-old Gladys who loved her new baby brother. She begged her father to keep the child, and offered to stay home from school to care for him and the other children. Necessity demanded the baby's separation from the family, however, and he was adopted two weeks after his mother's death. Gladys went to live with the Andrews and her siblings were farmed out to other relatives.

Of the Andrews Sisters, Maxene was most saddened by Mable's death. She spent much time at the Mobergs playing with her favorite cousin Gladys and was very fond of her aunt. In turn, Mable favored Maxene of the three sisters and often said, "Maxene's going to be the singer. Mark my word."[33]

Gladys Moberg Leichter lived with the Andrews family for about a year after her mother's death. She remembered being somewhat afraid of Peter who was "always kind of big and gruff" but she was close to her Aunt Ollie who was "very good" to her. Every Saturday night, Peter hosted a poker game in the dining room for his cronies from the pool hall. Olga tolerated the sessions, but never approved of them. She sealed off the room by closing the double doors to the parlor and shutting the kitchen door. The house had two staircases, a main staircase from the dining room and another from the kitchen. While the poker games were in session, the family used the kitchen staircase to egress the upstairs.

To young Gladys, the Andrews house seemed huge. She remembered when Peter tried to administer the girls' periodic castor oil, they would run up one staircase and down the other to elude him. She, Patty, and Maxene slept together, but LaVerne had her own bedroom; another upstairs room was used as a combination playroom-sewing room. Peter and Olga Andrews were rather strict parents. Gladys remembered Peter once caught her and Maxene playing football with the neighborhood boys and angrily sent them home. Gladys went unpunished, but Peter used the razor strap on Maxene, which hurt Gladys as much as it did Maxene. Maxene was the only sister who ever received the razor strap. Gladys once asked her if it hurt very much and she replied, "Maybe, a little bit." Maxene would have a rocky relationship with her father her entire life.

Gladys spent summers with her Andrews cousins at the Sollie family home in Mound. Their grandfather always kept peppermints for his grandchildren, which he parsimoniously parceled out to them. Like most young people in Mound, the girls swam in Lake Minnetonka, picnicked on the beach, and roller skated at Chapman's Casino and Dance Hall, the local amusement center located only a couple blocks from the Sollie house. The young girls helped in the grocery store of their uncles Pete and Ed Sollie, who always checked their pockets when they left to be sure they weren't smuggling out candy. During their forays away from home, LaVerne was supposed to chaperone the younger girls, but she more frequently ditched them and spent time with her own friends, especially Florence Hannahan. Age mates Maxene and Gladys roamed together, often excluding the younger Patty who may have grown up resenting that exclusion. Gladys remembered that she and Maxene often teased LaVerne and called her "a big hippo." Tall, large-boned LaVerne seemed big to the two girls five years her junior.

During the school year in Minneapolis, the Andrews Sisters attended both public school and Greek school, which offered instruction in Greek religion and culture. A classmate remembered Patty as "the bossy one," Maxene as "the prettiest," and LaVerne as "the solid one."[34]

The Andrews Sisters' musical gifts came from their mother's side of the family—some may have come from their father's side, but nothing is known of his family. Olga Andrews' sister Mable loved the piano and played it from an early age. Before her marriage, Mable and one of her sisters, Petra or Elydia, occasionally sang at the Bijou Theater in downtown Minneapolis on weekends when the theater provided live entertainment between films. Mable also played the piano for silent films at the theater. After her marriage, she frequently visited the Andrews family to play their piano since she had none at her own home. LaVerne Andrews expressed an early interest in piano and Mable taught her the basics which she later expanded when she studied with a teacher.[35]

Olga Andrews also loved music, instilled that love in her daughters, and encouraged their latent talents. Maxene recalled, "There was always music in our home, but we never took music lessons and never learned to read music."[36] "Sometimes, mama would say, 'While I'm doing the dishes, sing for me.' So, we'd go into the living room and play. If LaVerne wasn't there with us, we had

Lake Minnetonka at Mound, Minnesota, circa 1926. Seated left to right, LaVerne, Olga, and Maxene. Patty is directly behind Olga. Others are unidentified. The Andrews family spent many weekends and summers at Mound where Olga's bachelor brothers Pete and Ed Sollie operated a small grocery store. (Robert Boyer Collection)

a player piano, and Patty and I knew how to put the rollers on. We'd share the little tiny seat, and each of us put both of our feet on the pedals and pumped away, and then we'd sing with the music."[37] Olga once said she encouraged her daughters to sing at home to keep them out of mischief.[38]

LaVerne was perhaps the most musically gifted of the sisters during their younger years. After learning the basics of piano from her Aunt Mable, she studied it for several years[39] and was the only sister who read music. She eventually rebelled against taking piano lessons, and played the music she liked which Maxene described as "a kind of jazz."[40] In her early years, she had aspirations of becoming a blues singer. Her cousin Gladys remembered her singing "low down blues songs."

To complement the musical talents of her daughters, Olga decided they should study dance. But money was tight and the family budget had no room for dancing lessons, so Olga arranged for LaVerne to play the piano three days a week at the Knickerbocker Dance School in the Orpheum Theater building in exchange for free lessons for the sisters. Years later, Sidney Stocking, owner of the Knickerbocker Dance School, remembered the semi-annual student reviews called the "Kidnight Follies" the sisters participated in at Minneapolis' Orpheum Theater. The show opened with a chorus line featuring everyone in the class, and individual dancers followed. Then several specialty acts appeared, including the Andrews Sisters who once sang "St. Louis Blues." The chorus line returned to close the show. Stocking remembered that LaVerne eventually became too tall for the show, but Patty and Maxene continued together—he specifically remembered a "high kick" dance they performed to a song called "Thrill Me." Patty was a very good dancer and sometimes danced without her sisters.[41] She sang her first solo "Ain't She Sweet" when she was about eight years old in a kiddie review at the Orpheum Theater. Her cousin Gladys Leichter remembered that Olga dressed her in a very short skirt to make her appear even younger and she stood on a box to sing. Although Patty was a natural at dance, Maxene hated it.[42] Later filmed performances of the sisters indicate that LaVerne had no great skills at dance, but her feelings toward it are unrecorded. The dancing lessons paid off when the sisters later perfected their act for the vaudeville circuit.

Sidney Stocking, the sisters' dance teacher, remembered that Peter Andrews operated a pool hall and the family was "very poor" and lived in a "very bad area" of Minneapolis. Some socially ambitious mothers resented the poor sisters' presence in the class, and the other children sometimes called them "dirty little Greeks." At the time, the sisters all had dark hair, including Patty who became a blond much later.[43]

Opinions conflict regarding Olga Andrews's role in shaping her daughters' musical careers. Maxene reiterated in several interviews that Olga was not a stage mother and did not push her daughters into entertainment.[44] "She was an encourager," remembered Maxene, though she also credited her mother for their success: "She was our guiding light and encouragement all the time."[45] "She loved music and she knew that we loved music at a very young age, so she would encourage us to sing and entertain for her friends, and that was the

Gladys Leichter (left) and Patty Andrews at Mound, 1930. The sisters' cousin Gladys lived with the Andrews family for about a year after her mother died in 1925. She was close to the sisters most of their lives, especially Maxene. (Robert Boyer Collection)

gist of it."[46] Olga told her daughters, "God gave you this wonderful gift [of music] and you have to share it." Maxene added, "We were fortunate having a mother who understood that and encouraged it."[47] The sisters' cousin Gladys Leichter concurred, noting that Olga was proud of her daughters but never "pushy."[48]

Nonetheless, the girls began performing in public at a very early age. Maxene sang her first radio broadcast in Minneapolis at age four: "I don't remember whether it was good or bad. I only remember it was the worst snowstorm Minneapolis had in the history of the city. Mama was determined I was going to make my debut and we walked from our home to downtown Minneapolis to do that radio broadcast."[49] The sisters' cousin Gladys remembered when she and her mother heard five-year-old Maxene sing at a women's club: "Here she was at five years old, singing with no microphone ... this kid got up and sang and rang out that whole auditorium."[50] At six Maxene entertained at Veterans' hospitals, for the mayor of Minneapolis, and at DAR luncheons.[51] LaVerne was playing the piano at six, and Patty was singing when she was seven. Twice a year they participated in kiddie revues at the Orpheum Theater in downtown Minneapolis.[52] The sisters' participation in these events at such a young age could only be the result of parental encouragement. Olga was probably more of a stage mother than Maxene realized. A schoolmate of the sisters remembered Olga as a "stage mother," but their father was "old fashioned" and "did not want his daughters in show business, but their mother persevered."[53] Another childhood friend recalled: "Mrs. Andrews did not indulge the girls in any foolishness. By that I mean Mrs. Andrews had the girls practice a great deal and they were kept busy with auditions and appearances."[54] A woman who boarded with the Andrews family remembered, "Ollie had a lot of determination and that's what it took to get her girls started in their singing careers."[55] Years later, swimming star Esther Williams remembered Olga as the Andrews Sisters' "crazy stage mother,"[56] perhaps echoing a view held by others in Hollywood.

Music was an important part of the Andrews Sisters' childhood. An early friend and neighbor of the sisters recalled those early years:

> We lived a few blocks from each other. Many times after school LaVerne and other friends came home with me. LaVerne played the piano and we all sang and had such good times.... We had after-school dances in the gym and one time LaVerne brought Maxene and Patty to school to sing for us. A teacher never let them finish and of course it sent LaVerne into tears and her friends were outraged. In later years when seeing them at the Chicago Theater I hoped that teacher might be in the audience to know how very wrong she had been.[57]

Another childhood friend of the sisters remembered: "We used to have amateur shows in our garage—probably charging a penny for admission—and then eat homemade currant jelly on rye bread."[58] A man who attended North High with LaVerne reminisced about their common musical interests:

> I must have been among her first accompanists: I played for LaVerne when she sang at school dances held late in the afternoon on Fridays. Our big number in

the spring or fall of 1926 was "The Girl Friend," from the musical of the same name, but we knew lots of others—in fact, no kids knew more songs than we did, chiefly because we had ears like radar and the girls' parents gave LaVerne carte blanche to buy all the latest hits.... We had the most marvelous times with music. We also cracked each other up. It all made for a devoted friendship.

Of course, I remember Maxene and Patty very well indeed; we saw each other constantly at their home, where LaVerne's music and dance loving friends were always made very welcome. My first recollection of their singing together was at a PTA meeting at Jordan Junior High, thanks to my asking LaVerne if they could because my mother, then president of the neighborhood PTA, was in need of providing entertainment at a modest fee—like for nothing. And I have erred already in saying that was the first time; the first times were in their home, Patty already at the ready, Maxene having to be coaxed or coerced.[59]

A school friend of Maxene remembered: "She was a classmate, my dancing partner in a Boy-Girl School Skit, my bunk partner and swimming buddy at a school sponsored lake outing, she and I carried the alto in the girls' glee club. We were two of a kind–tomboys."[60] A junior high classmate of Patty recalled her: "My recollection of Patty was that she had an outgoing, vivacious and personable temperament. She was ... bright ... and probably in the middle range of students. Her interest in song and dance was certainly marked. I recall being in a musical and dance program with her at Franklin [Junior High], which would have been in about 1929 or 1930."[61]

While still in high school, LaVerne played piano for silent films at the Princess Theater, not far from her father's pool hall. Maxene and her cousin Gladys often walked from the pool hall to the movie house where LaVerne played to accompany her home because Peter did not want her on the streets alone after dark.[62] LaVerne dropped out of high school, probably when she reached sixteen. In 1928, her name first appeared in the city directory as a "musician" residing at the Andrews family residence. In 1930, LaVerne appeared in the directory as an instructor at the Clausen School of Dancing where she probably played piano. The following year she left music, and appeared in the city directory as "driver Liberty Cabs"—the first and only mention of this surprising, short-lived career, if indeed it was a career and not an error in the city directory.

The first published mention I found of the Andrews Sisters as entertainers was in the *Minneapolis Tribune*, December 21, 1930. A photo of sixteen girls who appeared in the "Kid-Nite Follies" at the RKO Orpheum Theater included Patty, although she is misidentified as Maxene. Beneath a picture of two girls dressed in Spanish costumes is a lengthy caption about the cast of the Follies; "Patricia Andrews" is identified as a "tap dancer" and the "Andrews Sisters" are listed as a trio.[63]

It was LaVerne who first suggested the sisters form a singing trio, although in later interviews Maxene would sometimes take credit for it. During the sisters' childhood, the radio came into its own as America's foremost source of entertainment, and as most families, the Andrews listened to the radio reli-

Patty, Maxene, and LaVerne Andrews. Perhaps the earliest photograph of the Andrews Sisters as entertainers, circa 1930, it is inscribed "To Gladys from the Andrews Sisters" in the lower right hand corner. (Author's collection)

giously. Peter Andrews liked the news and information programs and tuned in his favorites regularly, but the girls and their mother preferred music and comedy programs.

Maxene frequently recounted how the sisters discovered the Boswell Sisters, their early idols and models. According to Maxene, in the early 1930s LaVerne heard a late afternoon radio show starring Bing Crosby and a southern trio named the Boswell Sisters. LaVerne was a devoted Bing Crosby fan and she soon became enamored of the trio of sisters who sang with him. Each afternoon, the sisters rushed home from school to listen to the singing Boswells. After the program, LaVerne went to the piano, played one of the Boswell Sisters' songs, worked out a three-part harmony and taught the parts to her sisters. The girls loved the Boswells and their music, and began imitating their harmony, complete with southern accents. Patty sang lead, Maxene sang a higher soprano, and LaVerne sang contralto, the arrangement that would persist throughout their singing career.[64] The first song they sang as a trio was "Dinah," but the first Boswell Sisters arrangement they copied was "Heebie Jeebie Blues."[65]

Appealing though Maxene's story is, it has problems. First, in the early

1930s, LaVerne was no longer in school. More importantly, the Boswell Sisters did not sing on the radio with Bing Crosby until 1934 when the Andrews Sisters were already traveling the vaudeville circuit. The Andrews Sisters certainly copied the Boswells, but it didn't happen quite the way Maxene remembered.

The Andrews Sisters were not the only fans of the Boswell Sisters who, in the early 1930s, were among the most popular singers in the country. Sister acts had a long history in show business and many preceded the Boswells. In the early part of the century, the glamorous Dolly Sisters starred in the Ziegfeld Follies, but were equally famous for their high lifestyle and multiple husbands. About the same time, the Cherry Sisters built an act around their bad voices and sang behind a net to avoid the vegetables thrown by the audience. The Duncan Sisters were best known for their Eva and Topsy act, which featured one sister in blackface. "Dainty June and Company" starred sisters June and Louise Hovick, who later became actress June Havoc and stripper Gypsy Rose Lee. Hundreds of other lesser-known sister acts filled the stages of American entertainment.

But the Boswell Sisters broke the mold of previous acts and set the stage for subsequent singing sister groups in that—as Maxene put it—they took the idea of jazz and did it vocally.[66] Many critics would concur they have yet to be surpassed, or even equaled. Martha, Helvetia, and Connee Boswell grew up in New Orleans where they studied the piano, violin, and cello respectively. Connee was crippled by polio in childhood and, consequently, was always seated during performances. Early influences on the Boswell Sisters' singing style included a family barbershop quartet, the black jazz of New Orleans, opera singer Enrico Caruso, and black blues singer Mamie Smith as well as the classical music of their early training. The sisters began singing harmony around New Orleans and came to the attention of Victor Records after winning a local radio contest. They left New Orleans in 1928 with a vaudeville tour and ended up on the West Coast where their broadcasts in Los Angeles and later San Francisco began attracting a national following of fans. In 1931, the Boswells moved to New York where they signed with Brunswick Records and joined musicians such as Tommy and Jimmy Dorsey, Bunny Berigan, and Joe Venuti who were contributing to the sounds that would eventually become the swing era. Successful records as well as radio and film appearances soon made the Boswells among the most popular singers of their time. The sisters all married in the mid-1930s. Helvetia and Martha retired shortly thereafter, but Connee pursued a successful solo career into the early 1970s.

Maxene Andrews once said the Boswell Sisters were the precursors of all harmony groups. From a broader perspective they were part of the ongoing syncretism of Euro-American music and African American music that contributed to American popular music. The Boswell Sisters were within the jazz tradition—as that tradition was interpreted by white singers—and they, with other black and white musicians, paved the way for the swing era of the mid-1930s.

The Boswells were not the only influence on the Andrews Sisters. Another important source of inspiration came from the Orpheum Theater, which was located near their father's restaurant and which Maxene once described as their nursemaid. "On weekends, when Mama would have to cashier at the restaurant, they'd put us in the theater and the theater manager would watch us and we'd sit there and watch the movies and the stage shows. So I sort of feel like I was raised on show business." The sisters' cousin Gladys Leichter recalled that Patty loved the dance routines and rushed home to copy the arrangements she saw on stage.[67]

Going to a movie was a major entertainment event at Minneapolis' Orpheum Theater in the late 1920s and early 1930s. The featured film was preceded by a vaudeville show, sometimes starring nationally known entertainers like George Burns and Gracie Allen. In addition to the major star, the program might include magicians, dancers, singers, jugglers, acrobats, clowns, a dramatic reading, a bicycle act, or even an animal act—dogs and chimpanzees were especially popular. Like most young people, the Andrews Sisters were captivated by the performances. Even before they learned about the Boswell Sisters, Maxene and Patty saw the two Duncan Sisters at the Orpheum Theatre and decided they wanted to become a singing act.

In early June 1931, a rotund vaudevillian arrived in Minneapolis with his traveling unit show and changed the course of the Andrews Sisters' lives.

Three-hundred-pound Larry Rich—sometimes he was described as two-hundred-and-fifty pounds—and his vaudeville show opened at Minneapolis' RKO Orpheum Theater on June 12 with the featured film *Everything's Rosie* starring Robert Woolsey. Rich's show was advertised as "Larry Rich And His 14 Oompahs!" with the "RKO Knickerbocker Kiddie Revue." A news story summarized the show: "Larry Rich acts as master of ceremonies, and has with him his 'Oompahs.' Marion Sunshine gives her impression of Maurice Chevalier and Ruth Etting and sings songs of her own, one of them being 'The Peanut Vendor,' for which she wrote the lyrics. Phil Rich is 'Old Man Goof,' and Edler and the Reed Brothers offer a 'Wave of Taps,' a dance set."[68]

Unit shows such as Rich's were part of vaudeville. Typically, vaudeville theaters in New York and other large cities hired six or eight individual acts diverse enough to satisfy the eclectic tastes of the men, women, and children from the various ethnic groups and social classes that made up the audience. A unit show, however, was a group of performers who toured together and provided an entire program of entertainment. The show included musicians, magicians, jugglers, dancers, singers, strong men, acrobats, comedians, animal acts, and sometimes even physically deformed persons whose handicaps appealed to the darker tastes of the audience. Unit shows simplified booking for the impresario because he dealt only with the show's manager rather than several individual acts. Frequently, unit shows were booked by theater chains, such as RKO Orpheum, and toured the country performing at theaters for a week at a time.

Larry Rich (originally Laurence Jossenberger) was a classic vaudevillian. Practically born in a trunk, he worked in a medicine show at six, in Schepp's Dog and Pony Circus as a teenager, spent time in traveling theater shows, acted in silent films, tried a minstrel show, and finally put together his own traveling vaudeville show.[69] Maxene would later say, "He had no particular talent, but he was show-biz wise."[70]

The Knickerbocker Kiddie Revue, which performed on the same bill with Rich at the Orpheum, was a semi-annual revue of "novel kiddie presentations" by students of the Knickerbocker Dance School where the Andrews Sisters studied and LaVerne occasionally played the piano. A story in *The Minneapolis Journal* summarized the Kiddie Revue: "A number of very clever bits have been woven into one of the most novel kiddie presentations. Specialty song and dance numbers, together with a number of comedy bits go to make up a very unusual performance by a group of clever youngsters.... Elaborate costumes and effects have been added to the show which give the clever kiddies an air of professionalism."[71] A list of the young participants included "Patricia Andrews" and an ad for the show beneath the story promised a program of "Ballet, Tap, Spanish and General Stage Dancing."

As often with the Andrews Sisters, stories conflict about how they came to Rich's attention. Maxene, the chronicler for most of this stage of their career, related different stories at different times. In one interview, she said they met Rich while performing in a kiddie revue on the same bill with him at the Orpheum Theater in Minneapolis. We know, however, only Patty was in the kiddie revue with Rich. In another interview, Maxene gave a different account:

> I must have been ten years old, Patty eight, and LaVerne 12. We were in a Kiddy Revue the dancing school put on during Easter Vacation when I heard that a man named Rich, who had a big show traveling on the RKO circuit, was in Minneapolis and was auditioning kids for a new show. I got on the phone and called him. I told him that we had the greatest trio in the world—and I wanted him to listen. We went right down and sang for him in his dressing room. He was a fat, jovial man, and looked something like Paul Whiteman. I remember how he sat there in his bathrobe, with a very pleasant expression, and he called his wife in while we sang "On the Sunny Side of the Street." LaVerne played the piano, Patty sat on the piano, and I stood between LaVerne and Patty. In my young mind, I knew he liked us. He said we'd hear from him; but when months and months went by and we never heard, the showbusiness dream began to fade.[72]

Maxene's story presents several problems. First, it is unlikely Peter and Olga would have allowed their three daughters, aged eight, ten and twelve to leave home and join a traveling show—especially since Peter was not enthusiastic about his daughters becoming entertainers. The ages of the girls provided by Maxene are way off. In summer 1931, LaVerne was twenty years old, Maxene was fifteen (almost sixteen), and Patty was thirteen (almost fourteen). It is much more understandable why Peter and Olga allowed their daughters to join Rich since LaVerne was an adult and Maxene and Patty were teenagers. In other interviews, Maxene consistently claimed the girls were much younger than they actually were when they began their careers.[73] Patty also sliced years from their ages. She once told a reporter she was eleven years old, 4'8" tall, and weighed seventy pounds when they went on the road[74]; she was, in fact, thirteen years old (almost fourteen) and doubtless taller than 4'8" and heavier than seventy pounds. It also seems unlikely that Maxene, a ten-year-old child, would make the arrangements for meeting Rich. As a fifteen-year-old teenager, it is more believable.

The details of the Andrews Sisters' audition for Rich are unknown, but they auditioned with other young hopefuls from Minneapolis. Then they waited to hear his decision.

While the sisters were waiting to hear from Rich, the hot summer of 1931 broke temperature records and took lives. *The Minneapolis Journal* kept them in touch with events of the world. Lynn Fontanne and Alfred Lunt were in town to star in the play *Elizabeth the Queen*. The Andrews Sisters probably noted with interest that the local Irvine triplet sisters, who frequently made the Minneapolis news, were special guests at a production of the Viennese operetta *Three Little Girls*. Probably with even greater interest they read that the four Aalbu Sisters returned home to Minneapolis for the summer after a successful vaudeville tour. It's likely the Andrews Sisters saw another sister act, "The Three Peppy Allison Sisters," in a vaudeville show at the Orpheum. Political observers predicted the Democrats would dominate the House of Representatives in the coming election. *Indiscrete* with Gloria Swanson, *Dishonored* with Marlene Dietrich, and *Dishonored Lady* with Tallulah Bankhead filled the movie screens with fallen ladies. For forty cents, Minneapolitans could dine on a small steak, French fried potatoes, rolls and butter, sliced tomatoes, strawberry shortcake, and good coffee at Wilmac Restaurant. A "Negro" laborer won $145,000 in the Irish Sweepstakes. News of the Japanese invasion of Manchuria was unsettling for some, but it was too far away to trouble most Minnesotans. George Burns and Gracie Allen appeared in a vaudeville show at the RKO Orpheum while the French were preparing poison gas safeguards in the event of another war. "Tarzan," "Buck Rogers," and "Gasoline Alley" provided fantasy and amusement in the comic pages. Al Capone was linked to a big still near Minneapolis where fifty gallons of "moonshine" were seized. Dorothy Dix offered daily advice to the lovelorn and others in need of her somewhat prudish wisdom while Will Rogers provided earthy, homespun commentary as he deflated sacred cows in his newspaper column. Amelia Earhart crashed her autogiro in Texas shortly after take-off while Charles Lindbergh and his wife Anne prepared for their proposed trans–Pacific flight.

According to Maxene, the sisters were in Mound at Lake Minnetonka visiting their uncles, Ed and Pete Sollie, when Rich returned to Minneapolis later in the summer and approached their parents about the sisters joining his show. Peter Andrews was "dead set against showbusiness" for his daughters, but Olga Andrews saw it as "a marvelous opportunity."[75] Maxene said, "Our mother encouraged it. She figured that we weren't doing so well in school and that it couldn't be any worse on the road."[76] A few months later, Rich invited the sisters and six other Minneapolis youths to travel by bus to join his show in Atlanta. But, according to Maxene, there was one problem: he did not want Patty because he thought she was too young. LaVerne and Maxene refused to go without Patty, and eventually Rich gave in even though it meant a tutor would have to accompany them. The sisters' cousin Gladys Leichter remembered the story somewhat differently. She claimed that Rich was only interested in Patty because she was such a fantastic dancer; Olga, however, would not let Patty go without her sisters.[77]

Maxene said Rich offered them $250 a week, an amount that seems much too high for the time, the depths of the Great Depression. Another writer claimed Rich paid the sum to the entire group of young Minneapolis entertainers[78]—a salary somewhat more in keeping with the times. One writer suggested it was the salary that persuaded Peter and Olga to let their daughters go with Rich.[79] Financial concerns were likely behind some of their decision. Even if no salary were involved, they would be eased the support of their three daughters at a time when money was extremely scarce. Maxene once said their father had been ill, and presumably out of work, when Rich offered them the job—doubtless another incentive for letting the sisters try their luck on the road. And there was the added possibility the sisters might succeed as entertainers. Their dancing teacher claimed Peter and Olga "sold their piano and other furniture to finance the trip" to join Rich.[80]

Maxene once said, "The only kind of encouragement we got from our family was that they let us go."[81] Frequently, she said their father did not approve of them going into show business. "Our father, being Greek, did not think it was honorable to have female relatives in show business. He never said it to us directly, but it showed in his disapproval. He thought his daughters should go back to school and become private secretaries, which was the furthest thing from LaVerne's mind, from Patty's mind, and from my mind."[82] Elsewhere, she said their father was happy to have them sing at home, but he "was against us going into show business. He was adamant about it ... which may have been the way fathers felt in those days, but our father had an edge over those other fathers. He was Greek."[83] In still another interview, she said, "Our father hoped we would fail [in show business] so that we'd finish our schooling."[84]

It may very well have been the financial possibilities that changed Peter's mind about his daughters going into show business. Once on the road, however, according to Maxene, the sisters received only a dollar a day for the three of them, the amount Rich claimed he owed them after their expenses were deducted. Rich's deductions seem extreme, but it was not uncommon for entertainers to receive considerably reduced salaries after theater owners or impresarios deducted charges for props, costumes, dressing rooms, stage hands, musical accompaniment, and other costs of putting on an act. Such abuses by management led to the unionization of entertainers in New York in the early part of the century.

Maxene said, "When the offer came to perform, our mother went to the mayor, and he thought it would be a great opportunity. We were then on the road and had a tutor with us."[85] Elsewhere, Maxene said jokingly, "The mayor said he thought that travel was going to be more beneficial to us, which I think meant that he was reading our report cards."[86] It was apparently necessary to obtain the mayor's permission to take Maxene and Patty out of school since education was (and still is) compulsory until the age of sixteen in Minnesota. Maxene claimed they soon got rid of the tutor. Their departure from Minneapolis was the end of the sisters' formal education. LaVerne left high school when she turned sixteen, and Patty and Maxene never again attended school after they joined Rich's show at thirteen and fifteen respectively. Maxene once told a reporter, "We're ignorant, but we never forgot what Mom told us. She said what you don't know, you won't miss."[87]

CHAPTER TWO

1932–1934

The three Andrew [sic] Sisters ... kill the tuneful qualities of songs and make them sound like Chinese puzzles set to off-key music.[1]

The young Andrews Sisters could not have chosen a more inauspicious time to join the world of show business, especially the world of vaudeville.

Most show business historians agree that vaudeville's greatest years extended from the turn of the century to the mid-1920s. Early silent films presented some competition to vaudeville's live performances, but it was the introduction of sound films, the "talkies," and the growth of radio that seriously challenged the entertainment that reigned supreme in America for two and a half decades. Perhaps the final nail in traditional vaudeville's coffin was the stock market collapse of 1929. As Americans tightened their financial belts, entertainment was one of the first items eliminated from personal and family budgets. People stayed home and read, or listened to radios—if they had them. By 1932, vaudeville had declined 70 percent from the previous five years.[2] Movie attendance had dropped by 40 percent in 1931 and fell even lower in 1932. Panicked Hollywood executives concocted schemes to lure people back into the theaters.[3] "Give-away nights" gave customers free dishes when they bought their tickets, and if patrons attended regularly, they could collect a complete set of dinnerware—the so-called "Depression Glass" sought by collectors today. One theater offered two-for-one tickets as well as coupons entitling female customers to free hair permanents. Bank nights were introduced: If no winner was drawn, the pot was increased for the following week and as the amount grew higher, more and more people flocked to the theater in hopes of holding the lucky ticket. Many impresarios provided live entertainment before the featured film to entice audiences into the theater; the Andrews Sisters traveled the RKO circuit with Larry Rich in such an attempt. It was also during this period that the "B" movie was introduced to mark the beginning of the double bill. The B movies were cheaply made movies shown before the featured film to woo patrons back with the promise of two films for the price of one. The B movies not only increased audiences, but they also provided the studios a testing ground for their unproven talents—actors, directors, script writers, camera men, the entire production crew—as well as a retirement pasture for their fading stars. Much of the future film career of the Andrews Sisters would be spent in these films.

Outside the world of entertainment, the early 1930s were an angry, hungry, turbulent, and frightening time for America. The nation was on the move as thousands of unemployed men and women rode the rails, hitchhiked, or walked the country in search of jobs. A veteran's march on Washington, D.C., in 1932 turned violent when desperate veterans were forced from their encampment by soldiers led by the likes of Dwight Eisenhower and Douglas MacArthur who would become heroes in the approaching war. Food riots, including one in the Andrews family's hometown, erupted when desperate people broke through doors and windows of grocery stores to steal food for their hungry families. The three young Andrews girls faced a bleak, unhappy, and disillusioned nation when they took to the road in the fall of 1931.

Maxene remembered when they left Minneapolis on November 5, 1931, to join Rich with six other youths chosen to perform in his show.[4]

> I'll never forget the day we left. I really wanted to be in showbusiness, but, suddenly, when it came to leaving Mama, she had a terrible time getting me on the bus. Once on our way, it was pretty exciting. We'd never been out of Minneapolis or the local countryside.... I remember getting to Cincinnati and then crossing the Mason-Dixon Line [where she had the driver stop at 5 a. m. so she could put her foot on it]. I don't know how many days we were on that bus, but, finally, we got to Birmingham and started rehearsals.[5]

Maxene's memory was a bit off. It was actually Atlanta where the sisters joined Rich. Shortly after they arrived, Maxene wrote a letter to her parents reporting that the sisters found a hotel room that cost them $1.50 apiece per night. She told of their trip, during which they met a brother and sister bound for Bermuda who befriended them and bought their meals. Maxene was impressed by the southern accents of a group of young sailors, headed home to Nashville, who boarded the bus in Chicago. She was also impressed by the many blacks in Atlanta and appalled at how badly they were treated. She discovered the South was much colder than she expected.[6]

LaVerne also wrote her parents when they arrived in Atlanta. She, too, was excited by their venture into new territory, but unlike Patty and Maxene had been unable to sleep on the bus. She was unimpressed by Chicago and decided there was no place like Minneapolis. She detailed the states and cities they traveled through, and admitted she was not all that thrilled by what she saw. She assured her parents that they were fine, eating properly and enjoying themselves, and thought it was a wonderful experience for them to be on their own and try to make it in show business. She, too, was impressed by the southern accents in Atlanta. She reminisced about the big crowd that saw them off in Minneapolis and asked her parents to buy Patty a new dress because her clothes looked shabby. She concluded by urging her mother to write a long letter about all the news at home.[7]

On the same day she wrote her parents, LaVerne also wrote the first of many letters she would write to her close friend Florence Hannahan. She admitted to tiredness after the long trip of two days and three nights, but despite her sadness at leaving home and friends, she was not the least bit homesick. They arrived in Atlanta at six A.M., checked into a hotel and slept until evening. She told Florence that the people all talked like "Negroes" and treated Negroes like slaves. She described their itinerary, wished Florence was with her, and urged her to visit her mother.[8]

Five days later, LaVerne wrote again to her friend Florence and told her about the sisters' exciting venture into show business and their crushes on new boyfriends.

> Dear Florence,
>
> How are you Hannahan? We are having a marvelous time down here. The city is beautiful, and the weather is warm.
>
> We have been rehearsing every night after the show till 3:30 in the morning and then sometime we have morning rehearsals.
>
> We don't associate with the other girls at all. They surely are a jealous mob. Now for the big news.
>
> We got the best break of anybody from Minneapolis, wait till you see our show. Larry Rich has a band just like Duke Ellingtons, his brother is music arranger for Duke Ellington and all those famous Broadway bands, and I am playing with the band. We are singing six trio numbers. A song Mr. Rich wrote, "Huckleberry Finn," and we are singing it. "It's the Girl," "Mississippi Roll On," "St. Louis Blues," "Save the Last Dance for Me." A challenge trio with a boy trio. Maxene and Patty are doing a song and do we have to work. Audrey and Katharine are doing no harmony. Audrey is whistling a chorus of Huckleberry Finn and singing a chorus, we sing two choruses of it. We arranged it. Then Audrey is whistling another chorus. They dance (Audrey, Katherine, Fern, Ruby) a chorus number and we all do a lineup number. Katherine Heinz does a little talking about 6 words. Fern is playing one chorus on her banjo (who got the break?). Clarice and Joe are in an act and they dance one number. We also dance altogether. On the Grand Finale the orchestra is on the stage playing St Louis Blues. My piano is in the middle (3 pianos). We are dressed like the orchestra singing St. Louis Blues answering Larry Rich. Everybody lined on steps on the sides. When we sing "It's the Girl," Fern, Audrey, Katherine and Ruby push me out on a little piano, then we sing. The orchestra plays for us on "Mississippi Roll On." We wear old fashioned costumes. If you want further information my mother has got it all.
>
> We are staying at a lovely hotel with radio in it. We are leaving for Birmingham, Alabama Friday nite. We broadcasted last night. We sang "Huckleberry Finn" and "It's the Girl" with the show. We were the only new ones that broadcasted from Minneapolis.
>
> Well, there is a boy trio with us and I have sort of a crush on one. He is from Texas and he is handsome, talks southern and sings like Nick Lucas. Has beau-

tiful auburn hair and is 21 years old. Patricia has a crush on Larry Rich's nephew from Australia and Maxene on Huey, one of his former actors who is 16 years old....

Please go over and see mother and dad after you get this letter and mother will explain to you what we are doing....

PS Send me all the news about everything since I left and don't tell anyone I got a new crush. Ha Ha.

Your Pal,
LaVerne

PS We have 30 people in our new show. PS Do you miss me? I miss you.[9]

The young LaVerne was perhaps overly exuberant when she compared Rich's band to Duke Ellington's, and it is unlikely Rich's brother was doing arrangements for Ellington and "all those famous Broadway bands." The radio broadcast mentioned by LaVerne is probably the sisters' first of the many they would eventually do. Rich's drummer was less enthusiastic than LaVerne about the Andrews Sisters' debut in Atlanta. He bet a saxophone player five dollars that the sisters would not last two nights.[10] Five dollars was a lot to lose during the Great Depression.

An ongoing problem in their early days on the road was hiding Patty's age from the Gerry Society, a watchdog group that enforced laws to prevent minors under sixteen from performing professionally. When the sisters joined Rich's troupe at Atlanta's Georgia Theater, he plucked their eyebrows, drew on pencil lines, beaded their eyelashes, and applied heavy makeup in an attempt to age Patty and Maxene.[11] The sisters soon discovered their promised salary was considerably reduced after room, food, costumes, and transportation were deducted. "He [Rich] gave everyone a dollar a day but he gave the three of us a dollar.... From that time on, everyone thought of us as one."[12] But Rich and his wife liked the three young sisters and took them under their wings. Maxene remembered:

Because we were so young, every city we went to, we'd have a connecting room with he [sic] and his wife, and we had to be in at a certain hour. After the theater, we were allowed to go out and eat with some of the cast, but then we had to go right back to the hotel and go to bed, and they knew we were in when we locked the doors between our room and theirs and the door into the hallway. He thought that we were very industrious because we always wanted to rehearse, and so he made it a point to teach us about the theater, how to walk on the stage and when to get off of the stage. He taught us about the scenery, about the lighting, about the respect of whoever the star was on the bill, and the importance of the time that you come into the theater. You never came into the theater after a half-hour was called, you had to be in before a half-hour.[13]

Rich taught the sisters the basics of show business they would build upon the rest of their careers. Maxene remembered that he taught them to empathize with their audience: "You've got to bring them into you ... you have to try to get something back from them."[14] Elsewhere, she elaborated:

[Rich] taught us theatre discipline and he also taught us the meaning of the word empathy and how that applied to our audience, and that you had to do

Maxene, LaVerne, and Patty, September 1932. This photograph, an interesting contrast to the preceding one (page 24), reveals the transformation that occurred after the sisters joined Rich's traveling unit show. Rich aged Patty (who was only 13 when she joined Rich's show) to elude the Gerry Society, a watchdog group that enforced laws that prevented children under 16 from performing professionally. (Robert Boyer Collection)

something more than just get up on the stage and sing. You had to learn to perform, and so I guess we were very willing students because everything he ever said to us stuck ... those are the years I call serving our apprenticeship.[15]

Larry Rich and his wife were impressed by the girls' love of singing, their hard work and constant rehearsals.[16] With or without a piano, the sisters rehearsed every day. Maxene remembered, "We would work all day until we perfected new songs in our own new, bouncier style. It was then we realized we had something special to offer."[17] They had no music and no arranger and therefore no special act so they copied the Boswell Sisters' arrangements, even their southern accents. LaVerne played the piano, Patty sat on it, and Maxene stood in front of it. In addition to songs, Maxene said, "you did everything, you told jokes, you sang songs, you did dances. If one didn't work, the other one was bound to."[18] "We got a dollar a day," remembered Patty, "and even if there were three people in the audience, we performed as tho it was a full house. We learned discipline, timing, and respect at an early age."[19]

In addition to stage experience, the young sisters gained firsthand knowledge of a large portion of their country during the eleven months they traveled with Rich. They performed in at least forty different theaters (perhaps as many as fifty-four, their itinerary is not always clear) and traveled to Atlanta, Birmingham, Louisville, Indianapolis (where the Andrews Sisters' name first appeared in Rich's ad, albeit misspelled "Andrew"), Rockford, Des Moines, back to New York, and then westward to their hometown Minneapolis. From Minneapolis, they traveled on to Tacoma, Washington, down the coast to San Francisco and Los Angeles, back east via Denver, Omaha, and Chicago to New York, Washington, D.C., and New Jersey—a total of thirty-three (maybe forty-four) cities, eighteen states, and thousands of miles. Sandwiched between movies, they did at least three shows a day—and frequently more—six days a week. They probably racked up close to a thousand performances during their tour with Rich. The young Andrews Sisters became seasoned performers in short order.

In late December 1931 when they'd been on the road a little over a month, the Andrews Sisters' picture appeared in the *Des Moines Register*—perhaps their first professional photo—when they made a special appearance with Larry Rich at a Christmas program for state employees. Wearing bell-bottomed pastel pants suits with open jackets, white blouses and white ties, they are seated together. A slightly plump, reserved LaVerne is in the center with a very young, irrepressible Patty on the right and a take-charge, youthful Maxene on the left—personae that would persist throughout their lives.[20]

After an engagement in Davenport, Iowa, the troupe was stalled—whether by a broken vehicle or financial problems is unclear. Rich succeeded in booking an engagement in White Plains, New York, and the sixty-member troupe piled into a bus designed for twenty-five passengers and made the trek across country in time for a New Year's Eve date. Maxene and Patty rode in the overhead baggage rack most of the trip.[21]

In late January, New York City's Hippodrome Theater hosted the Rich entourage. A reviewer for *The Billboard* liked their show, and the Andrews Sisters' names appeared for the first time in the premier publication of the entertainment industry. The review conveys the nature of Rich's show:

> The usual eight-act show is not on hand this week, with Larry Rich's unit taking the place of seven acts, and Falls, Reading and Boyce booked as the eighth. Latter act is sandwiched in the Rich affair. Whole show runs 75 minutes ... Shapes up as delightful entertainment, the kind at which audiences evidence thoro enjoyment. The first show found a full lower floor and well-tenanted balconies. Screen fare was James Dunn in "Dance Team," supplemented by the Jack Dempsey flicker, "The Lure of the Ring."
>
> The show gets going nicely with an effective overture from the house crew, augmented by a few of Larry Rich's bandsters. Rich makes his entrance amid a shooting fest, and immediately sings and gabs his way into the audience's favor. For 15 minutes he and some of his stooges ply comedy, and Hughey O'Donnell and Phil Rich bring in their effective specialties.
>
> Falls, Reading and Boyce are spotted here for four minutes of their punchy acrobatics and legwork. The two boys are clever hand-to-hand balancers as well as floor workers. Girl does o. k. acro bits and tap routines. They took their leave to a heavy mitting.

Publicity photograph for Larry Rich's unit show. Rich is standing to the far left with his wife, Cheri. Standing beside them is Fern Schuettler. Patty is third from the right. Standing beside her is Maxene, and seated is LaVerne. Other members of the troupe are unidentified. (Author's collection)

Rich gets back to his unit again by doing his familiar singing bit with Cheri. This is good for laughs. Toma Genaro is spotted for neat acro dancing, and a Chinese lass, England Ong, goes big with native and modern warbling. Quite a bit of time is taken by Rufe and Al, hillbilly boys, whose excellent talent warrants the many minutes they stay on. They are outstanding mimics and light comedians.

The rest of the unit is practically an all-musical, singing and dancing affair, with not enough comedy brought in to hold up the early laugh spasms. Rich leads the 18-piece band capably, and a few of the band boys double to specialties, with Joe Bohn and Joe Bell showing up well in their respective hoofing and warbling numbers. Others working in front are Murray Wood, the half-pint [midget] with a big and melodious voice; Andrews Sisters, harmony trio, and Tommy Long, funster. Rich announced at this show that Miss Genaro and Bell would be married on the stage Tuesday night. The unit has been staged, routined and dressed excellently.[22]

Variety saw the show also and thought it needed tightening, but gave it a good review anyway. The Andrews Sisters were not mentioned by name, but their performance was reviewed favorably, albeit briefly: "Second half of the show brings on the band, with a harmony trio (girls) spotted in it for numerous numbers that come over very nicely."[23]

Sometime during their stay in New York, Maxene met her idols the Boswell Sisters:

> The first year we were out with this big band in New York and the bass player was from their home town and knew them. He knew how crazy I was about the Boswell Sisters.... "When we get to New York," he kept saying "I'll introduce you." He called me up one night about 11:00. "You want to meet the Boswell Sisters? ... Get dressed." And I met him and he took me over to a place called Lindy's Restaurant ... and there they were ... sitting at a table with four or five songwriters.... And I sat at the end of this table and I remember Connee sat in her wheel chair. Martha sat at the very top.... I never remember meeting Vet. She was there but she never said anything. They were talking about something. And I just sat there and looked ... if they had said anything to me I couldn't have answered them.[24]

During that same visit to New York, Maxene and LaVerne saw the Boswell Sisters perform at the Paramount Theater on the same bill with Bing Crosby:

> I never forgot that time [I saw Bing Crosby and the Boswell Sisters]. We were in New York... The show had moved up to White Plains, but [LaVerne and I] were sent down to Manhattan to pick up some things for the stage ... with one of the stagehands. Patty couldn't go because she was ... too young. So, we got to the corner of 44th and Broadway and there was the wonderful Paramount Theater. And it was freezing cold... And I looked up on the side and the billing was Bing Crosby, the Boswell Sisters and the Ritz Brothers [Rio Brothers]. And I ... said to my sister LaVerne, "We've got to go in." We didn't have a dime in our pockets... So while we were standing there ... the throngs of people going into the theater ... pushed us in... We didn't have to pay. So there we were and I said to LaVerne, "We're going to see them. We're really going to see them." And so, they came on just before Bing Crosby ... and they sang ... stationary at a piano ... into ... the microphone decorated like a flower bouquet. And I'm telling you, all I can remember is just closing my eyes. Like you just want[ed] to get every bit of breath. When we went out, I stood there and I looked at LaVerne and said, "Close your eyes and just visualize Bing Crosby and the Andrews Sisters." I said, "Someday, LaVerne, we're going to be working at the Paramount Theater." And she said, "You and your crazy ideas."[25]

In early February, Rich's show was in Providence, Rhode Island, where a local paper described it as "a blend of comedy, dancing and singing" and noted the Andrews Sisters among the performers.[26] Later that month, Rich opened in Newark where the trio was advertised as "Andrews Sisters, The Harmonious Family."[27]

In a letter dated February 5, 1932, New York, LaVerne wrote to her friend Florence Hannahan at some length about clothes she bought at prices that challenge the sisters' claim they received only a dollar a day from Rich. She also answered her friend's questions about their new career.

> Dear Florence:
>
> Received your letter and thought I would answer it right away. We are leaving tonight for Providence, Rhode Island for one week so write me at the RKO Vaudeville there, c/o Larry Rich. By the way, call my mother up and tell her it's Rhode Island instead of Long Island. Right away.

From left to right, LaVerne, unidentified woman, Fern Schuettler, and Patty, 1932. The furs worn by LaVerne and Patty challenge their claim that they received only one dollar a day from Larry Rich. Rich successfully aged Patty—she is only fourteen years old in this photograph. (Robert Boyer Collection)

That letter Helen and you sent me from the lake was great. It was so entertaining. If you don't mind do things like that some more. I like surprises. It makes me feel I have some real friends. I can just imagine the two of you sitting in the store writing those letters. What's happened to good old Cullen Smith? ... I wonder if he still belches like he used to. Ha! Ha! Those were the good old days.

I got a terrible throat again and am frantic about today's shows. Last night we worked a benefit at the N.V.A. here in N.Y. for actors you know. The Aalhu Sisters were there. They left their regards for me in the theater I am playing now. We are working a beautiful theater now ... The first half of the week we worked in Patterson, N.J. We crossed the Hudson everyday on a ferry. It was lots of fun. All the steam liners leave from there. So there was a new thrill in them.

I bought Maxene a beautiful new Lopin jacket, and did I chew the Jew down. It was marked $39.50. Clothes are very cheap here you know, and before you know it, he sold it to me for $16.95. I surely got a kick out of it. Say, by the way, I am coming back here next Saturday and we will be at the same place here for two weeks. So if you kids would like me to get you something, send me money and I will buy something. I am going to get you gifts here too, but I am not going to give them to you until I come back home. It will be more fun. I thought if you kids would like for yourself, shoes or something, you could send money and I will buy them. Genuine reptile shoes are all $2.95 and $3.95 all over Broadway and even 5th Ave. You can get beautiful dresses for $5. Beautiful net hose for $.88. That's all I wear now. Gorgeous kid gloves from $1.00 up. Hats and dresses are very reasonable too.

Publicity photograph for the Huckleberry Finn number in the Rich unit show, 1932. Maxene (third from left), LaVerne (sixth from left), and Patty, standing next to LaVerne. The young woman with the banjo is Fern Schuettler, one of the youths from Minneapolis who joined Rich with the Andrews Sisters. The barefooted young man is Huey O'Donnell. Others in the photograph are unidentified. (Robert Boyer Collection)

Now to answer your questions:

What kind of sensation do I get when the curtain goes up. Answer: It is just like a routine now. Smiling, personality, even though, sometimes you don't feel anymore like working than the man in the moon.

Did all the new sights thrill me? Answer: At first they did, but I've seen so much now. It seems funny myself, but I am so accustomed to new things that it just seems natural.

Have the kids changed much? Answer: Yes and No. Patty wears gray reptile shoes, net hose and fineries now, but is still unaffected. Of course, it's different in the theater, it is natural to be conceited in your work. Larry Rich taught us that. Patty has very thin eyebrows. Wears her hair in a long bob, is the same height as Maxene and is the pride of all the band boys and the love of Murray Woods, the midget. Maxene has the same temper, is just as much shorter than I am. Has her eyebrows plucked thin. Wears clothes like a model and is claimed by Larry to be the beauty of the show. Bawls the wardrobe mistress out, almost killed her for something the other day. Larry hates anyone to argue with him, but of course, Maxene insists, and he has the worst temper of anyone I've ever seen in my life. One day he hit his negro valet for nothing. But we still like Larry Rich.

What kind of songs are we singing? The midget and us are featured in the overture. He singing Larry Rich's own tune, "When I Grow to Be a Man," and we do Larry's other new number "Huckleberry Finn." Then next we are in Huckleberry Finn act in which Huey O'Donnell is Huck Finn and we do music accompaniments real soft. Our costumes are beautiful. White organdy, old fashioned. Next we are used as a background for an acrobatic dance, with the rest of the kids. Patty isn't, but he had to use us, Maxene and I cause he hadn't enough girls. Then, next we are featured in the band act, the main thing. The first number we do parts and breaks of Duke Ellington's Heat Waves, Nobody's Sweetheart and Tiger Rag. Next we do and introduce "Sleepy Time Down South," sing a chorus and two introductions and then a little negro dances to it. Next we introduce Joe Bell, we sing a chorus of "Faded Summer Love," and then he sings and a girl dances. Then we sing "Ida" while Joe Bohn dances. Then we do our number, "It's the Girl." Next is the midget who works alone. Then we have a snake-hip dance and we sing a chorus of "Dinah" to this dance. That's all.

Yes, I think of people back home often enough. But I have forgotten completely of people who didn't mean anything to me.

I have bought only one new hat, a brown felt hat, braided in orange feathers. Very smart.

No, I don't like most of the people I meet. I am not friendly with everyone like I used to be. You can't trust anyone in this game.

Whenever I want to think of pleasant things and to feel good I think of you and Helen.

My heart is really full when I say this and I know we will have many more great times together...

Answer soon.
Your Pal, LaVerne

During the next two months, Rich and his show played in the New York City vicinity with trips to New Jersey, Rhode Island, and upstate New York. In early April 1932, they began moving westward. LaVerne wrote to Florence from Cleveland about people who joined and left the show and places they played. She also admitted to an involvement with a twenty-two-year-old married man. She expressed relief that he had left for New York City to be with his wife and concluded: "Thank Heavens. I can't have these heavy affairs, which could cause trouble."[28]

As the Rich troupe moved away from New York, Maxene's worldview continued to expand, but sometimes conflicted with her Middle West values. Many of the show's musicians had wives in New York and spent their off-hours with them while in the city. However, as they moved beyond New York and their wives, the musicians pulled out their little black books and hooked up with women along the way. Years later, Maxene said, "And I thought that was terrible."[29]

In May, the Rich entourage arrived at the Andrews Sisters' hometown Minneapolis. Olga saw her daughters perform and was so impressed by their plucked eyebrows that she plucked her own.[30] A small story in a local newspaper noted: "Miss Fern Schuettler, LaVerne, Maxene and Patricia Andrews all Minneapolis girls and pupils of the Knickerbocker Dancing School joined the R.K.O. circuit … last fall and have played in all principal cities in the east during the past season."[31] The other Minneapolis youths who joined Rich with the sisters are not mentioned; perhaps they had left the show.

After Minneapolis, the sisters traveled westward to Seattle where they opened in late May. LaVerne described the trip in a letter to her friend Florence:

> I had the most beautiful trip of my life from Minneapolis to Seattle. I spent most of my time in the observation car and the dining car, of course.
>
> I took a boat trip day before yesterday across Puget Sound. Stopped for a half hour at naval headquarters across the bay, had lunch and came back … I've attended every theater in town. Maxene attended a big boxing [match] with Larry Rich the other night.
>
> Our show seems fresh and new after the lay-off and it is a pleasure to work. We have different costumes, and we do our new number. It is on the end of the bill and goes great. We got some wonderful write-ups. Mother has them and will show them to you.
>
> Have you got a position yet? It is too bad you don't live in a progressive town like this one. You wouldn't have any trouble…[32]

The Rich show moved down the coast through Tacoma and Portland. In Portland, the Andrews Sisters were reunited with their cousin Vernon Moberg who had lived there with relatives since his mother's death some seven years previously. In early June the sisters saw San Francisco for the first time, and a reviewer spent almost as much space detailing Rich's girth as she did reviewing the show. Although not named, the Andrews were singled out as "a trio of synchronizing sisters, whose ballads were well received." The reviewer praised Rich's band and noted that it offered "the late dance numbers and ballads, as well as more than one novel jazz arrangement of their own."[33]

On June 8, LaVerne Andrews wrote to her friend Florence about her enthusiasm for San Francisco:

> Arrived in San Francisco this morning. The train took us to Oakland, Ca., and then we took a ferryboat here. The trip was a thing of unusual beauty. The train climbed 4,000 ft. We had to have two engines on our train. The mountains and plateaus were so beautiful I couldn't talk. The mountain lakes were divine.
>
> We had a nice time in Portland. We saw Vernon all the time we were there. They took us on a beautiful automobile trip in the Mts. Sunday to see the waterfalls. Vernon has grown so and certainly is a wonderful boy.
>
> We went swimming in the ocean this afternoon and was it glorious… The sand on the beach is almost white. The waves are like big walls closing in on one. They have huge sand dunes here. It is like a picture. I love it.
>
> When I think of stinky Minneapolis I shrink from the very thought of it. You certainly would love it here. The city itself is a fast moving town. People buzzing around like a bunch of bees.
>
> We are going to be here for two weeks and a half, which makes me very happy. My happiness would be complete if mama and papa were here. They'd love it.
>
> Did you have a nice time over Decoration Day? We had a parade and worked as usual. It was gloomy anyway so I didn't mind…
>
> We have a week and a half lay-off now and work a week here. So write soon a nice long letter as I enjoy them a great deal.

Love (to a little pal)
LaVerne
Also Maxene and Pat[34]

Later the same month, LaVerne again wrote to Florence from San Francisco with an account of clothing purchases that again challenges Maxene's claim that they received only one dollar a day.

> We have been working five shows a day, both in "Frisco" [and] Oakland, Cal., which was exceedingly tiresome. Then we had to take a ferry back and forth every day, while in Oakland so our spare moments were very measly.
>
> Well, had the chance to meet George Bancroft, and was he grand. We worked a big Shriner's benefit here at the Palace Hotel. He and Claudette Colbert were present. After all the doings were over we were in our dining room and Larry brought him in. After we were introduced, he remarked about us being "cute" sisters. Hmm! Maxene, Pat and I passed a remark about us not wanting to wash our hands after shaking hands with him. He got a big laugh when Larry told him about it, and said he would be sure and see us in Los Angeles. He certainly is a wonderful man nevertheless.
>
> One night last week Larry took us to a "Cotton Club." We had a fairly good time. Louise had us out to her home for dinner one night and guess who follows me out there. Joe Rio—now, now.
>
> I love it here and have also made many friends too. There is no place like the coast.
>
> We are heading for Los Angeles Wednesday morning. We are going to reside at the Hollywood Plaza, in the heart of Hollywood. I am really quite thrilled.
>
> I bought myself a good looking orange bathing suit, cap & slippers, beach sandals, although white bathing suits are now commonly worn here. Today I bought myself a good-looking white knitted skirt & sweater dress. Also, a hat. I bought my white shoes in Tacoma, Wash. I also got Maxene a beautiful orange striped sweater trimmed in white angora and bought Patty some brown beach slacks of real woolly material. It is too bad you can't be here. People seem so alive and happy. I love it.
>
> Did you see the hat I bought mother? Does she look nice in it? It sold for $15.00, and I the old bargain hunter of course didn't pay that much, but it is beautiful....[35]

Los Angeles was the next stop. Rich was announced as "Big Time Vaudeville" at the Orpheum Theater and billed as the "Heavyweight Champion of Fun and His 22 Enemies o' the Blues." The show was not reviewed in Los Angeles, but while there the sisters learned that Franklin Delano Roosevelt won the Democratic nomination for the presidency of the United States.[36]

The Rich troupe headed eastward and made a stop in Denver where a local critic liked their show and concluded his review: "A grinning black boy, a well-formed Chinese lass, three singers of the Boswell Sisters type and other hard-working entertainers help, too, to make the vaudeville bill very pleasing."[37]

The next stop was Omaha in late July where LaVerne complained to Florence about the heat and the difficulties of adjusting to the "thin" air in Denver. She said they were doing a new number called "We Got the South in Our Soul" and recommended a book called *Thirteen Women* she'd recently read. She liked their hotel: "We are staying in a popular little hotel here. A crowd of band boys who play at lake resorts stay here—in fact I caught two peeking in my bedroom door tonight. Quiet please. The café 'Jack and Jill' caters to the social younger set, which is fun for us after all this show business."[38]

The Billboard reviewed Rich's show in August when it played Chicago's Palace Theater: "Rich has a versatile gang and an act chock-full of entertainment ... The Andrews Sisters, a vocal trio, do "The South in My Soul" and a tap dance ... A succession of specialties follow, including band numbers, singing and dancing, and only lack of space prevents listing them. All in all the routine wowed them and put them over for a hit."[39]

In late September, Rich and his troupe were back in New York, this time at the Orpheum Theater where a *Variety* reviewer noted the opening day was "one of the poorest at the box office in weeks." He thought the show was too long, but acknowledged Rich was a good showman and had a decent show if he would tighten it up and eliminate some technical problems, which especially plagued the Andrews Sisters' segment: "Andrew [sic] Sisters, one of those femme singing trios, didn't stand a chance here because of a p. a. system that wouldn't function. Maybe they can sing. It'll remain to be tested in another theatre."[40]

Shortly after this engagement, the Andrews Sisters left Rich for unclear reasons. A few months later, Rich dissolved his unit show—possibly he was beginning to downsize at the time the sisters left. A letter dated October 19 from LaVerne to her friend Florence suggested the parting was not amiable.

> We've certainly been through a lot since I last wrote you.... Our show closed two weeks ago yesterday, but we had already been offered to do an act for the Loew Circuit. Well, Larry wanted to put us out on our own, so he got two fellows who did comedy, but they were terrible to my estimation. Well, we went to Larry one day and told him we had an offer from the Loew office. He is also being booked by the same office, but a different agent. Well, he took it calmly, but went down to our office and told them we were under contract to him and all that sort of stuff. They called us down later and told us about him. I sent my folks a telegram and he intercepted it. Nevertheless, he had us near a nervous breakdown.[41]

LaVerne's letter does not explain how the conflict with Rich was resolved, but apparently he released them from their contract. Why he was holding them to a contract when he dismissed them from his show is not clear, unless he was expecting some sort of remuneration while they were under contract to him.

In later years, Maxene and Patty both fondly remembered Larry Rich and his wife, Cheri, how they looked after them and taught them important, basic lessons of show business. However, in a 1938 interview with the Andrews Sisters, one of their first for a national publication, they remembered the experience less fondly, claiming Rich misled them regarding their salary. LaVerne attributed her inferiority complex to the experience, while Maxene said her combative powers were enhanced by it.[42]

Patty, Maxene and LaVerne Andrews toured with Larry Rich's unit show for approximately eleven months, most of them in 1932. When they left Rich in New York City, he told them to return to Minneapolis. The show business bug, however, had bitten the young Andrews Sisters and Minneapolis was not the future they had in mind.

After leaving Rich, the Andrews Sisters telephoned their parents and told them they wanted to stay in New York and continue their fledgling career. Apparently the home front was looking none too promising. Peter and Olga Andrews consented.

Olga traveled by bus to New York to join her daughters and Peter hooked up with them a year later.[43] LaVerne wrote Florence: "I suppose you know mother is coming in. It will be wonderful. I wish papa could come, but it will be impossible so you'll have to take good care of him. Be his secretary in other words."[44] It was probably "impossible" for Peter to come because of his pool hall business and perhaps LaVerne asked her friend to be Peter's "secretary" because of his limited literacy.

Peter's consent to a separation from his family is somewhat surprising, considering the control he maintained over them most of his life. Eventually, the prospects of his daughters' show business career must have looked more promising than the pool hall business. Or if Peter lost the pool hall, as some sources claim, he probably had little choice but to see what the sisters could make as a singing act since jobs were scarce during the Great Depression years. Maxene offered a more romantic explanation: "It wasn't that Pop had changed his mind about show business ... he just loved Mama, and where Mama went, he went."[45]

LaVerne claimed she and her sisters joined vaudevillian Joe E. Howard after they left Rich. According to her, Howard was playing on the same bill with Rich, and Murray Wood (the midget singer with Rich who befriended the sisters) told the girls he was looking for a "girl trio." They tried out for Howard and he signed them to a contract.[46]

Maxene told the story somewhat differently. According to her, a "hillbilly" comedian from the Rich troupe, named Rufe Davis, helped the sisters find their first job in New York after they left Rich. Davis would go on to a successful radio and film career playing rube characters, but at the time he was struggling with other young hopefuls like the Andrews Sisters. He loaned the sisters money to hold them over, and introduced them to a woman who made their stage wardrobe, the black velvet pajamas they wore during this period. Maxene explained: "Pajamas ... because we couldn't let Patty show her legs—everyone would have known how young she was. In Larry's show there'd been one little midget, and the Child Welfare people came backstage every week and pulled him offstage, thinking he was a little boy. We couldn't let that happen to Patty. Besides, the pajamas made us look taller and made LaVerne look thinner."[47]

The job Rufe Davis helped the sisters find was a short stint in a vaudeville theatre where they shared the bill with Joe E. Howard, an old time vaudevillian who was probably in his early seventies—biographers are uncertain of his birth date—when the sisters teamed up with him. He was well known in vaudeville, having written eighteen musical comedies and over 200 songs, the best known of which was "I Wonder Who's Kissing Her Now?" His salad days were wilting when the Andrews Sisters came along, but he was still a big name.

Maxene explained: "Joe was looking for some girls and Mama was familiar with his name through sheet music. He gave us $150 a week and off we went on tour. Mama loved the act because we did numbers with big hats with feathers and long skirts. Then we'd change and come back in our black velvet pajamas and do our own routine." [48]

Shortly after the sisters joined Howard, they participated in a benefit with Broadway luminaries for Eva Tanguay, the once popular vaudeville singer, who was on the skids following an illness. LaVerne wrote Florence that they were the only "not famous ones" on the bill that included Sophie Tucker, Fannie Brice, Paul Muni, and Jack Dempsey. Their act went over big and they were encored. LaVerne also claimed they auditioned and were signed by NBC at this time and would begin "training" within a week for appearances on a small station which would evolve into a regular spot on *The Beachnut Hour* radio show with Joe E. Howard. [49]

I was unable to locate any evidence of the NBC radio deal. LaVerne may have been overly optimistic about their audition, although it is possible they sang on a small affiliate station. The hookup with Joe E. Howard on *The Beachnut Hour* never materialized. In the same letter, LaVerne said her boy friend from Mound, Gordon Edlund, had proposed marriage. [50]

The sisters were unnamed in their first review with Howard when they appeared with him at the Academy Theater in New York in early October 1932, but two weeks later they and their black pajamas were unfavorably reviewed when they joined Howard at the Grand Opera House in New York:

> Joe E. Howard the deucer with the 3 Andrews sisters. The customers here do not care much for harmonizing trios. They would swap all three for an encore from the comedian. When the girls wear black pyjamas instead of snappy costumes, they'll toss in trading stamps to boot. These girls wear black. They gave Howard two chances to catch his breath and they went off to a slim hand each time. Not very strong at best. They never got a chance until the finish when they sang with Howard some of his old timers and then it was the songs. [51]

The sisters next appeared with Howard in Providence, Rhode Island in early November where their act was advertised as "The Popular Musical with JOSEPH E. HOWARD with the Three Andrews Sisters, Radio Stars, in SONGS OF TODAY AND YESTERDAY." Their billing as "Radio Stars" suggests they sang on NBC as claimed by LaVerne, or perhaps it was media hyperbole.

The most significant event for posterity stemming from the Andrews Sisters' time in Providence was a ten inch 78 RPM vinyl RCA Victor home recording they made, probably at a local radio station. The recording was never released commercially although it may have been aired on radio. It was discovered in the mid-1980s by a collector who dubbed it onto tape and it has since circulated among Andrews Sisters devotees. How or why the recording was made is unknown, but handwritten on the label are the song titles followed by "Andrews Sisters, 11–10–32." Written on the reverse label is "Providence, R. I." The five songs on the record (all associated with the Boswell Sisters) are "Sentimental Gentleman from Georgia," "Cabin in the Cotton," "Music Hath Charms for Me," "Hand Me Down My Walking Cane," and "Go on Satan."

The voices are hardly recognizable as the Andrews Sisters known to later fans, but the recording confirms the sisters' claim that they imitated the Boswell Sisters during their early years. The sound quality is very bad, and the nondiscriminating ear might mistake the sisters for the Boswells. This is the first known recording made by the Andrews Sisters.

Years later, Maxene described their act with Howard from the sisters' side of the lights:

> You know he drank a lot…. We did this thing where LaVerne was over there and I was here; Patty and Howard right next to each other. They had to face each other at close range and Patty would gag at the smell of gin and garlic. He must have been nearly 70 then and after every show, there was a bunch of 15 or 16 year old girls waiting for him. You know, he had a beautiful wife, too.[52]

LaVerne remembered Howard's womanizing also: "He was pretty old when we knew him, but there was always some young chick waiting in the wings." Patty added: "He wrote 'I Wonder Who's Kissing Her Now.' Only you didn't have to wonder—it was Joe."[53] She said their act consisted of Howard singing songs in a traditional style and then the Andrews Sisters would "jazz them up" in their own style.[54]

In mid–November, the sisters were in Philadelphia with Howard. When they returned to New York, LaVerne wrote Florence, again mentioning an offer from NBC radio. Her letter detailed their busy schedule, her optimism about their career, and an admonition that Peter Andrews not be told about the sisters' many "offers" from boy friends.

> Received your sweet letter but really have been working hard and steady.
> We have a wonderful act and are now playing over on Staten Island at the St. George Theater, a beautiful place and only two shows a day. Saturday we open in Lowell, Massachusetts and play out of town all next week. We had a little trouble though. We received a telegram last Saturday in Philadelphia telling us that as soon as we returned to New York to see Tom Kennedy, who is the biggest man on NBC. He heard us sing and wanted to sign us up immediately, but we are under contract to Howard. Well, nevertheless it caused a great deal of trouble, but we are in between the devil and the NBC. We have an apartment now and bought a 13 pound turkey for tomorrow. It will seem good to have a home-cooked meal for a change…. Honest, Flo, we are being weighed down by friendships—don't tell daddy—also offers. Our improvement has built a reputation now and sisters are in big demand. We may get in a couple of big shows, because vaudeville is collapsing all around us. Larry Rich's act is breaking up Friday. I guess he's all washed up here. I got a couple of new pairs of shoes yesterday, so did Mom. How is Daddy getting along? We had a beautiful engagement in Philadelphia last week, but we worked with a band act, although we headline, and they presented us all week.[55]

Maxene claimed they were with Howard for seven months, but left because they wanted to sing with a band.[56] They were actually with Howard only about six weeks and probably left him in early December 1932.

Howard later discussed with fondness his time with the Andrews Sisters in his autobiography. He hired the sisters because he was told he could get some vaudeville dates around New York if he teamed up with a trio. "They were a good bet because they were a great trio having a style of their own." He said "the managers did not like the Andrews Sisters' style of singing, so we broke up after playing the six weeks. The trouble was that the girls were ahead of the time with their jazz singing but they really had the goods and they proved it later on." He said that after the sisters left him they got "a job with a band playing around Chicago and stayed with it the rest of the season." He concluded: "They deserve all [the success] they got because they came up the hard way and no praise is too high."[57]

Years later, the sisters assessed their time with Howard: "He taught us how to sing the lyrics and not mess up a song with a lot of fancy stuff. He made us realize that we had to sing in the same style that a trumpet player plays the trumpet, clear and true."[58]

It is unclear where the sisters went after leaving Howard. Sidney Stocking, their childhood dance instructor, remembered that he booked Emil Velasco and his orchestra for the Marigold Ballroom in Minneapolis in late 1932 and was surprised to discover the Andrews Sisters were vocalists for the orchestra.[59] I found no evidence of them singing with Velasco.

LaVerne wrote to Florence Hannahan sometime in early January 1933. The letter is undated and the first page is missing, but the letterhead is Hotel Chesterfield, New York. LaVerne expressed concern about her friend's recent "sorrow" and related that her boyfriend from Mound sent her a picture of himself for Christmas. She also said her mother planned a surprise trip home to visit Peter Andrews the following month and would bring a gift for Florence from LaVerne. As often in her letters, she said she missed her friend's companionship and expressed concern about her father's wellbeing. She said Christmas seemed "meaningless" since she was away from home. As usual, she sent greetings from Maxene, Patty, and her mother.[60]

The first half of 1933 is a major blank in the Andrews Sisters' career. This was probably one of those lean periods Maxene often mentioned in later interviews when the sisters moved from city to city taking whatever jobs they could find. In mid-summer 1933, the Andrews Sisters hooked up with Ted Mack, who would later achieve national fame when he took over Major Edward Bowes' popular *Original Amateur Hour* radio show in 1946. Mack eventually took the show to television for a twenty-two year run during which such hopefuls as Maria Callas, Ann-Margret, and Pat Boone made their national debut. However, when the sisters teamed up with him, Mack was working the Middle West with what he called "an entertaining orchestra." The orchestra played for dancing and then later in the evening, everyone in the orchestra participated in a stage show.

The Andrews Sisters joined Mack at the Waukesha Beach Ballroom on Pewaukee Lake near Milwaukee, probably in mid–July, after he lost his "girl trio."[61] He paid them $35 a week plus expenses.[62] LaVerne remembered their stay at the Waukesha Beach resort: "When we weren't working, we were swarming all over the roller coasters and rides ... Boy, did we have fun."[63] Years later, Maxene recalled their rather lean time with Mack:

> I don't think he was very impressed with the Andrews Sisters, because from the
> very beginning the only thing that the Andrews Sisters could copy from the

Boswell Sisters were their arrangements, because we sang loud and we moved a lot. Harmony groups never moved, but we never could contain ourselves. When we heard music, we had to bounce with the tune. We traveled around, mostly in the West, with Ted's orchestra.... And it was just a case of year after year and day after day of just rehearsing. We used to rehearse sometimes six and eight and ten hours a day. We would do it on an empty stomach. It was better than sitting around saying we have nothing to eat.[64]

During this period, the sisters began to develop their distinctive style. Maxene recalled:

Technically, I can't explain it ... because I don't have the technical knowhow to tell you how it's done. I always sang harmony to Patty, then LaVerne would find her harmony to me. To this day we don't read music, we just hear it. We were just doin' what came naturally. When we were going through our years of apprenticeship we would spend six, eight, ten hours a day just rehearsing, even if we didn't have a job. It was constant, constant, constant rehearsing. And we'd listen to musicians, the way they'd play, and we'd try different things until finally we decided which way we wanted to go. For awhile we thought we'd like to sing so all the musicians would think how great it was, but we learned that was a lotta hogwash. We found it was more fun singing the things that the audience enjoyed hearing, because as we'd sing to them, we would get something back from them which stimulated us.[65]

The sisters' next engagement with Mack was in Indianapolis, but I could find no review of the show.[66] After Indianapolis, Mack and the sisters were at the Silver Slipper nightclub in Memphis, Tennessee, from November 11 through early December 1933. A local newspaper ran a photo of the sisters with a caption that noted they had "recently shone brightly in the radio firmament." [67]

After Memphis, Mack took his show to Cleveland for a short gig and then on to Colorado where he opened in mid–December at the Denver Theater. A photo of the Andrews Sisters in the *Rocky Mountain News* identified them as the "Three Rhyhmets, blues-singing trio with Ted Mack."[68] A review noted that Mack's singing and comedy dominated the show, but claimed "He is run a close second, however, by his supporting artists, particularly a trio of charming girls who harmonize in a most pleasing manner."[69] Another reviewer wrote: "With him are three girl blues singers who sound quite a bit like the Boswell sisters. They are second only to Mack in popularity."[70] Although the Andrews Sisters were well received by the Denver audiences, they remained unnamed in the press coverage of their engagement.

While in Denver, LaVerne wrote Florence that she was pleased with their reception in Denver and optimistic about their career. She also revealed that her long distance affair with her Mound boyfriend continued:

I have been working terribly hard and making some terribly big jumps. We went from Memphis, Tenn. to Cleveland, which is one thousand miles and from Cleveland to Denver which was 1,500 miles. We are at the Denver Theater from two to four weeks. It is most successful, believe me, and we are having a glorious time. Our band broke up in Cleveland. The musicians union was death against traveling bands and then the Denver musicians association wouldn't let

Ted bring in any outside men, so he almost had to reorganize a whole new organization. I certainly felt bad for the boys who lost their jobs before Xmas....

Yes, Flo, I hear from Gordon almost regularly. We have built up a beautiful correspondence, one which is sort of precious to me.

I have been working so hard. We are improving every day and have some fine things in view for the coming year. I will not mention them until I know definitely. We expect to do big things this coming year.

Patty is bigger than I am. She certainly has grown to be a beautiful young lady. Maxene is the choicest.

We have got quite a few lovely gowns, sport coats, sweaters recently.

Mother is with us now and we certainly have lots of fun. She never seems to change. Gets younger and more attractive every day. It certainly makes me happy when I see her.

Well, Flo, I have four shows tomorrow and will be rather busy so I must retire early ... To you I send my love. Merry Christmas dear from all of us.[71]

The sisters left Ted Mack in Denver for unknown reasons. Maxene once said Mack stranded them in Denver and another story claimed their father went to Denver to take them back to Minneapolis.[72]

After the Andrews Sisters left Mack in Denver, they went to Chicago with their parents. LaVerne remembered: "We moved to Chicago and lived in a hotel on the North Side, working in night clubs and waiting for a real break. Our father brought us to work and waited until we were ready to go home."[73]

In mid–January, Florence Hannahan received letters from Olga Andrews and LaVerne, suggesting the family was having some tough times with illness. The sisters had not worked for four weeks and LaVerne was anxious about their career: "I'm lonesome lately. I don't know what's wrong with me. I'm so restless. I guess I'm too much in a hurry to be successful. I get so angry. Our trio really rates A-1, but it is more difficult to climb the ladder being good than bad. It is the truth. It's not egotism knowing." They were scheduled to appear with Olive Borden, "famous movie star," for a short stint. LaVerne also wrote of their new dog and their plans to buy a Doberman and raise prize dogs—a plan that never materialized.[74]

The Andrews Sisters took whatever jobs they could find, often in dives such as a Chinese restaurant in Cleveland that landed them in a police raid. Maxene remembered: "That was the first time we ever saw a stripper. At some point during her routine her G-string came off and was flapping between her legs, the police came and pulled her off the floor and raided the joint." Patty continued: "The bandleader got us off the stage as fast as possible. I remember we were standing in the kitchen and when she came off she was stark naked, just with the fans ... she took the fans, stuck them under her arms and walked right through the kitchen stark naked."[75]

Maxene later remembered some lean times, possibly the months after they left Mack:

He [Peter Andrews] drove us everywhere. Anyone who hired us had to pay the expense for the whole family. Most of the time, in those early days, we'd stay in some little apartment where Mama could cook. I think Pop thought we'd get this out of our systems and go back home and go to school. His dream was that we'd be private secretaries.[76]

I can't tell you how many jobs we had—and how many jobs we got fired from. We survived it because we were young, and we really started to enjoy what we were doing. Then the idea of becoming successful grabbed hold and became the most important thing.[77]

Years later, Patty and LaVerne recalled some tough times in the Chicago area, where their hotel had a ping-pong table in the basement. Patty had become a good player and a young man challenged her to a game with a twenty-five cent wager. Patty won the game, collected the money, and hurried out to buy food for her and her sisters who had not eaten in two days. She later learned her defeated partner was the ping-pong champion of Chicago.[78] In another version of the story, the sisters said Patty used the money to buy cigars for their father and a can of dog food for their dog.[79] LaVerne remembered a discouraging audition at which an agent advised them to go home and forget about singing. Walking dejectedly down the street, she spied an envelope in the snow containing twenty dollars. "Boy, did we eat!" she remembered.[80]

The sisters may have had some tough times, but their enthusiasm for show business was undiminished according to Maxene: "[We were] thrilled to be in show business. We wanted to replace the Boswell Sisters ... and we had plenty of drive to do it. It's funny, but even with all the hard work, the problems, the uncertainty about whether we'd eat the next day, we had fun. We never thought about the kind of fun other teenagers had that we were missing—we had a different kind of fun of our own." [81]

In spring 1934, the sisters' cousin Gladys Leichter remembered the Andrews family unexpectedly showed up in Mound, Minnesota, for her high school graduation. To the surprise of all, Peter, Olga, Patty, Maxene, and LaVerne arrived in the crowded 1929 Buick with their suitcases and two dogs. They stayed a few days and then moved on to their next engagement.[82]

In mid–July 1934, the Andrews Sisters joined Bob Chester's band in Detroit for an "indefinite stay" according to a local paper.[83] In early August, they returned to Chicago. The Windy City was wrapping up its two-year Century of Progress Exposition Fair that had provided a boon to Chicago's depression-shattered show business. It was probably this boon that brought the sisters to Chicago along with Clayton Moore, who would achieve TV fame as the Lone Ranger, and the Gumm Sisters, one of whom would become known as Judy Garland. Sally Rand was there, too, wagging tongues with her ostrich-feather fans that left enough flesh exposed to assure her both notoriety and fortune. The Andrews Sisters auditioned for George Jessel who was opening at the Oriental Theater, one of Chicago's premiere theaters that had recently reinstated vaudeville. According to Maxene:

> We went with a dozen other acts, down in the basement of the Oriental, and finally our turn came and we went in and we auditioned for Mr. Jessel, who I thought at the time was very rude because he was so busy smoking his cigar and telling jokes and walking in and out of the room that I felt that he never heard us sing. Of course at that time, I was a real cocky kid—what was I? About 14 or

15 years old [she was actually 18]—and I was sure that we were the best singing trio in the world. And I was highly incensed that Mr. Jessel wouldn't give us his undivided attention ... But we got the job and we played that week in Chicago and I couldn't wait until the "Billboard" review came out ... It said, "The Andrews sisters, a singing trio who sound like a Chinese jigsaw puzzle set to off-key music..." and that was the one review that set us straight. Our mother had said to us one time, pertaining to our lives, "One day the time will come when you will come to a crossroad in your life, and you will have to make a choice, and the choice will be yours." Well, we very unconsciously applied that to music. You'll either sing for the musicians or you're going to sing for the general public and make a living so we went that way.[84]

Even though it lasted only a week, it was no small feat for the sisters to land a job with George Jessel, one of the country's leading entertainers. They appeared at the Oriental Theater with him on a bill that included a comedian on a unicycle, a woman piano-accordion player, a ukulele-playing comedy team, and a "Night Club Revue" in which the sisters appeared with Jessel as master of ceremonies and "the Alton Girls in scant costume," an acrobatic tap dancer with "somersault twists and flip-flops," a female exotic dancer who did a "Black Panther" dance, and a couple who performed "eccentric dances." *The Billboard* review noted by Maxene appeared August 18, 1934, and understandably caused the sisters to rethink their style. They were the only act in the show that received a bad review:

> The three Andrew [sic] Sisters were next. They are not yet ready for stage appearances before critical audiences, who are bound to compare them unfavorably with better harmony trios. These girls could be much better if they would junk the peculiar arrangements they are now using, which kill the tuneful qualities of songs and make them sound like Chinese puzzles set to off-key music.[85]

It is unclear what "peculiar arrangements" the sisters were using, but according to Maxene, they were trying to "sing for the musicians," which she said they stopped doing after *The Billboard*'s review and began singing for the general public. *Variety* reviewed the show also and rather prudishly dismissed the "Black Panther dance" as "another meaningless strip dancer." The Andrews Sisters were merely mentioned with the rest of the cast which the reviewer thought "summed up to a highly satisfactory lineup."[86]

Next to the sisters' review in *The Billboard* was a small ad for their old boss Larry Rich, "Star of Vaudeville and Musical Comedy," who was appearing at the RKO Palace in New York. He had apparently abandoned his unit show to try it on his own. A year later he would die of cancer and diabetes at the age of forty-one, having shed 130 of his famous 300 pounds.

During the week the Andrews Sisters worked for Jessel, they met the young Judy Garland who was singing with her sisters as the Gumm Sisters. Maxene remembered:

> The only friends we ever made was when we were in Chicago in 1934, at the end of the world's fair. We met three girls who had a trio. Their mother played piano for them, and they were terrible. They were staying at the same hotel

because they had worked at the Streets of Paris at the fair, and they didn't get paid for the last week. They were on their way back to California.

We got first dibs on the rehearsal room, which was an old rug storage room, but anything where there was a piano so we could rehearse, which we did about four, five, six hours a day. We couldn't do anything else because we hadn't had anything to eat. So, that encouraged our practicing.

One day they came knocking at the door, and we were rehearsing. One of the sisters was a little chubby girl about 12 years old. They wanted us to sing a song for them, which we did. Then they said, "We're a girls trio," and we said, "Can you sing for us?" Their mother wasn't there to play for them, but the little girl said, "I want to sing for you." So, LaVerne helped lift her up and put her on the piano, and she sang "He's Just My Bill." LaVerne played for her, and we stood there with tears in our eyes, she was so great, so wonderful.

We were finishing a week with Georgie Jessel at the Oriental Theater, and we knew that we were being booted out for the second week. We left because we got a job with some little orchestra out of Chicago. He came to us and said, "Do you know of another girls trio?" and we thought of the kids at the hotel. After that evening, we came back to the hotel. I got a hold of the little one, and I said, "Baby, tell your mother to take you over to see Georgie Jessel first thing in the morning. He's looking for a girls trio." Well, they went over there, and of course he thought the trio was not good, but he loved the little girl, and Georgie was the one that gave her her name. He named her after two of his girlfriends. One was Judy and one was Garland.[87]

William Ruhlmann notes that Maxene's story about meeting Judy Garland conflicts with other evidence. According to a Garland biographer, the Gumm sisters were staying at the St. Lawrence, a "first-class hotel" and they played at the Old Mexico Café and not the Streets of Paris. After they lost their job, they moved from the hotel into an apartment. A trumpet player named Jack Cathcart directed them to Jessel. Another biographer claimed the Gumms were hired because Jessel had fired his other trio because it "was so bad." He changed their name to "Garland," borrowing the name from a New York theater critic, and little Frances eventually chose the name "Judy" after Hoagy Carmichael's song of the same name.[88]

It seems unlikely Maxene made up the story as Ruhlmann implies, especially since Patty told essentially the same story in a 1942 interview[89] and later in 1974.[90] Also, in a March 1938 letter to her friend Florence Hannahan, LaVerne mentioned that Judy Garland visited them in Chicago when they were doing their first radio show—obviously they had met before. Beyond details such as the name of the club where the Gumm Sisters previously worked and how Judy Garland got her stage name, the chief difference between the two stories is Maxene's claim that she and her sisters directed the Gumm Sisters to Jessel as opposed to Ruhlmann's evidence that a trumpet player called Jessel's attention to them. Another account claimed that both the trumpet player and the Andrews Sisters recommended the sisters to Jessel.[91] As Ruhlmann noted, the intriguing question is whether the Andrews Sisters were the trio that was fired because it was so bad.[92] Perhaps so, if we believe *The Billboard*'s review.

After the week with Jessel, the sisters were back on the road looking for jobs. Peter became increasingly adamant that they give up their show business dreams, return to Minneapolis, go back to school and become private secretaries. Patty, Maxene, and LaVerne were not ready for that. Olga sided with them and insisted they give it more time.[93] The women won out.

CHAPTER THREE

1934–1937

...the Andrews Sisters, broke and unknown, nobody knew them from a head of cabbage.[1]

The Andrews Sisters' itinerary is unclear after they left Jessel, but the family had some bleak weeks, and even months, as they bounced around the Middle West in search of jobs. Maxene remembered:

> We went hungry at times, like anyone else starting out in show business. Mama and Papa traveled with us, helping to save money by cooking meals in our hotel room and doing laundry.
>
> I complicated the act every once in a while because of my love for dogs. I've always had a dog traveling with me ... in our first years of performing every dog I owned was named Peter in honor of Papa.... When we were playing in Boston, Peter the cocker spaniel, got into some rat poison and died. For several days after that, every time I opened my mouth to sing, all I could think of was poor Peter and I would burst into tears. It didn't do a thing for our act....
>
> But we were on our way. We learned the responsibilities and the disciplines of life in the theater—show up early, work hard for your audience, and never peek through the curtain. We worked hard at it every day, rehearsing our own Andrews Sisters style and sound.... We worked on perfecting it every spare moment we had, mostly in the back seat of my father's 1929 Buick.... We never got to drive, either. Papa was Old World Greek and as chauvinistic as most men in those years: women weren't allowed to do anything. The Andrews sisters, three innocent and naïve girls from the Midwest with a Greek father and a Norwegian mother, knew our place....
>
> [W]e appeared in every club and theater, large or small, that was willing to book us for a few dollars a night. In the years of the Great Depression you

couldn't get picky. We sang anything the audience wanted to hear, doing three shows, piling back into the family car and heading for the next town.

Travel by car took a lot longer than it does today.... We didn't have tape decks or four-speaker stereo systems to entertain us during the long automobile trips, and while only a few cars had radios, that was one luxury we enjoyed. We listened to a lot of music in that car, and thanks to the two most popular radio comedians, Jack Benny and Fred Allen, we got plenty of laughs to relieve our boredom.[2]

In later years, Patty was asked if there was a particular point when the sisters realized they were going to make the big time. She replied: "I don't think ... that we had any different thought in our minds than we were going to make it big. When we were kids, we always said we were going to take the Boswell Sisters' place."[3]

In September 1934, the Andrews Sisters joined a floorshow at the Paramount Club on the north side of Chicago.[4] At the end of the month, the *Toledo News Bee* announced they were appearing with SIGI (Sigmund Boguslawski) and his Hollywood Band at the Travertine Room in the Commodore Perry Hotel in Toledo. They were still there when LaVerne wrote Florence in mid–October and told her their future engagements. She hoped they would make it back to Minneapolis for a few days the next month. They had "new white satin sport dresses and hats" made for their dancing act which she wanted Florence to see because it was "a very cute act." LaVerne was happy with the direction of their career and said, "This year holds something for us in our work which is going to make us I know." She also said they paid fifty dollars for a pedigree English Setter dog.[5]

The sisters returned to vaudeville to play at the Lyric Theater in Indianapolis where they were billed as the "Queens of Harmony." Sharing the bill with them was a promising young ventriloquist named Edgar Bergen who someday would have a mannequin named Charlie McCarthy and a daughter named Candace. Following Indianapolis, the sisters moved on to the Hollender Hotel in Cleveland where they stayed two weeks. In early December, LaVerne again wrote Florence, this time from Louisville, Kentucky. She had not heard from her friend in several weeks and expressed displeasure:

I don't know if you're just lazy, neglectful or busy, but you have really lost me as a friend. I write you a letter from Cleveland, go back to Chicago and work for two weeks, come down to Louisville, Kentucky for two weeks, also, send Stella's baby a little remembrance and so I never hear from you.... Now I am down South and it's snowing.... We are having a grand time down here and are working at a swanky gambling club. This is our second week. I suppose we will be back in Chicago Saturday.

Before we came down here we have been working at the elegant Opera Club in Chicago. O! Were we ever. I'll say.

We might come home around Xmas. And you better have some pretty nice night spots rounded up and show me the town.[6]

The sisters returned to Chicago in early December for another engagement at the Paramount Club, which according to *Variety* lasted until early February 1935. LaVerne wrote a long letter to Florence in mid–December from the New Lawrence Hotel in Chicago and revealed that she and her hometown boyfriend had terminated their relationship. She also mentioned that the sisters were suing Larry Rich for reasons that are not explained. I found nothing further about the suit.

> Well, it's about time you answered. I really thought you'd dropped off somewhere. Really, I've been working steady for 12 weeks and working late nights and traveling all night to be at work the next day, so we're taking a vacation this week and rest up.
>
> Nope, don't think I can come home for Xmas, but will try afterward, I mean after New Year's before we head for New York. We are sick of Chicago. In fact we've wasted too much time in this "hick" town. "Youssah!" I've been down south for two weeks and have acquired a southern accent. Do tell! I'll say!...
>
> We visited Father Coughlin's church when we were in Detroit and what a gorgeous spectacle that is. My father lives for his Sunday speeches. A great man, Father Coughlin. I'm sorry you didn't see Edgar Bergen too. He is such a grand fellow. He probably would have taken you out. Too bad...
>
> My dear, we bought a radio and didn't miss one of Minnesota's games...
>
> My father was in Minneapolis the week Larry Rich played there. We are suing him. Dad didn't get much time to visit and so was unable to visit Helen or you.
>
> Today I went downtown to buy engraved cards, but it was too late to have that done, so I have just written and sent out 125 cards, and is my wrist weak.
>
> I hate to go shopping here so if you and Helen are two weeks late in receiving a little token from me—don't worry. It'll come bye and bye, and please don't send me nothing. I have everything. Now LaVerne quit bragging, but truly don't.
>
> Yes, show business is always good, if you're good. No bragging, but we are turning out to be a fine trio, and believe it or not my voice is slowly changing operatic imagine, so I'm going to study next year.
>
> No dear, Gordon and I correspond no more. It is all over and forgotten and it is better that way. He's not my type. He's too slow and kind of dumb. Not that I'm brilliant, but we'd never make a go of it. I like life, people, and he's a lonesome sort. You see...
>
> Mom, Pop, Patty, Maxene and "our dog" "Peter" send their best.[7]

LaVerne's reference to Father Charles Coughlin and Peter's devotion to him are revealing. Coughlin was one of the first "electronic" ministers. A Canadian born Catholic priest from Detroit, he began broadcasting sermons tinged with social commentary in the early 1930s and amassed a huge radio audience. He initially supported President Franklin Roosevelt, but later renounced his policies and became increasingly reactionary, ultimately expressing anti–Semitic views as he supported Hitler's rise to power. As his views became increasingly controversial, the church exerted pressure and he eventually left the air. At the time Peter Andrews was attracted to Coughlin, he was not yet so reactionary. Peter probably became disillusioned with him—as did much of the country— when he became so vehemently opposed to Roosevelt, whom Peter greatly admired. If the anti–Semitic rhetoric appealed to Peter, he had to clean up his act before six Jewish men came along to shape the lives and careers of his daughters.

In early January 1935, the Andrews family was still in Chicago. LaVerne wrote to Florence. The Christmas gifts mentioned by LaVerne suggest the family was not short on money.

> Thank you for the handkerchiefs and Maxene's birthday card. Maxene is 19 to us and 18 on the stage. Funny how time flies isn't it. It seems like yesterday we were all children but now we're all grown up young ladies with burdens on our shoulders and business to take care of.
>
> We had a lovely Xmas. We got each a complete set of satin underwear, hats and scarf sets, each a separate set of lounging pajamas, satin ones. Maxene got a Parker automatic pen and pencil set from [indecipherable] on her birthday she received 19 roses from the Edgewater Beach Hotel florist. Ted Taft gave Maxene a beautiful scarf and we gave her a dark tweed traveling suit trimmed in genuine beaver. Very smart. Mama got a satin nightgown from us and black chiffon velvet for a dress. Dad got a white angora sweater trimmed in white kid and a heater for the car.
>
> Maxene had pneumonia, terribly ill, but has recovered fully. Mother has been ill with the flu. Now I have it. It's an epidemic here and I do feel badly.
>
> We just got back from Cincinnati, Ohio to see about our radio program, we made it but the money is quite bad so our agent wouldn't allow us to accept unless they raise the anti [sic]. So, we are waiting. The station is WLW, largest in the world, 500,000 watts.
>
> We worked in at the Pere Marquette Hotel, New Years Eve in Peoria, Ill. We had a grand time, beautiful hotel, except we were all rather ill. I had two dinners in the course of two hours. I still have my appetite regardless...
>
> We received about 55 cards this year. Gordon Edlund sent me one too—my. I must have broke his heart.
>
> I am glad you liked Ted and Mary. They are very fine dancers.... Of course, Mary is no beauty, but she does have a nice figure in her dancing costumes. Beautiful legs. Did you think Ted was effeminate? But he isn't a pansy.[8]

The Andrews Sisters are next heard from in Vancouver, British Columbia, in early March 1935. It is unclear how they got there, but they were apparently with a band on a West Coast tour. Patty Andrews wrote to Florence and her letter is the only documentation of this leg of their career I could find. Patty didn't care much for Vancouver, but thought the mountains were beautiful and liked the English accents of the people. She said LaVerne enjoyed the city because of the beautiful English tweed clothes. Patty mentioned her new boyfriend, also in show business, who kissed her on her seventeenth birthday and said he loved her. She said she didn't take him seriously, but he was a lot of fun. She asked Florence to tell no one about her boyfriend because Maxene and LaVerne would tease her, and her father would think she wanted to marry him. The boyfriend was taking care of their dog because it could not be taken into Canada, but they would rejoin him in Los Angeles in two weeks.[9]

Sometime during this period, the Andrews Sisters probably auditioned for Fred Waring, a popular orchestra leader of the time. Later, during the war years when the sisters were among the top singers in the country, Waring introduced them at the Stage Door Canteen in New York and said: "I had three girls audition for our group three years in a row, and each time I told them no. Twice I even told them to go home. If I had hired them, I could have had the Andrews Sisters for seventy-five dollars a week." Maxene remembered that he told them "our voices were too husky, and we were too young to develop his kind of 'sound' for his shows. Each of those rejections was a blow to us. We were three cocky kids, and we thought we could compete with anybody, including his own group, The Smoothies."[10] It is understandable that the raucous, aggressive style of the Andrews Sisters did not blend well with a group called "The Smoothies."

The next documentation I found of the Andrews Sisters appeared in July 1935 when *Variety* reported they were at the Hi Hat Club in Chicago with a performer named Dick Huges.[11] Patty once told a reporter they received $65 a week for the stint.[12]

In an undated letter, probably mid–July, LaVerne told Florence of their activities and mentioned they had been at the Hi Hat for six weeks. One evening when they were guests of radio star George Givot at the Royal Frolics, they met Leon Belasco, a fairly well-known bandleader of the time. He had heard the sisters sing and called Maxene over to his table and told her, "It was a pleasure to see three such clean and refreshing young girls with such extremely fine talents." LaVerne said someone named Rubinoff wanted them to join his show in the fall, but they were more interested in radio. She acknowledged her recent birthday and said she was twenty-one years old "professionally"—she was actually twenty-four. She anticipated going home soon to spend time with Florence in Mound.[13]

In mid–August, 1935, the Andrews Sisters joined the Chicago-based Maurie Sherman orchestra.[14] Well known in Chicago music circles, Sherman played at the Hotel Sherman for ten years, directing the so-called afternoon "tea dances" in the College Inn. The sisters' first month with Sherman was a tour of one-nighters beginning at Fox Lake, Wisconsin, and including St. Paul, Sioux City, and Sioux Falls. After the month of barnstorming, the Sherman entourage moved on for a five-week stay at the Hotel Jefferson in St. Louis with local radio broadcasts. On November 8, 1935, they opened at the Ringside Café in Fort Worth, Texas, for a month stint where the Andrews Sisters were advertised as "Three Charming Sisters of Song and Dance." A caption beneath their picture in a local paper noted they "sing in the manner of the Boswell Sisters."[15]

Olga Andrews wrote to Florence Hannahan in mid–November from Fort Worth. She said the Andrews family was very happy and enjoying the mild climate of Fort Worth where they planned to be the rest of the winter. She thanked Florence for coming to the sisters' engagement in Minneapolis and expressed pleasure that so many friends were there. She said her daughters were exhausted by the "one-night trips" which had, however, paid off in experience and subsequent bookings.[16]

The Andrews Sisters rang in New Year's Eve at the Washington-Youree Hotel in Shreveport, Louisiana, where they appeared through January 18, 1936. They probably left Maurie Sherman after this engagement.

The first half of 1936 is another major blank in the Andrews Sisters' career. This was probably another lean period for the Andrews family. Peter drove them from job to job in the 1929 Buick while the sisters rehearsed in the back seat. Some jobs they learned about from other entertainers, others they found on their own. Frequently, money was short and food was scarce. Maxene remembered:

> [W]e had no money, and we'd pick up jobs. We'd find some little agent, or some act on the bill would recommend somebody, and we would get a little job here and a little job there and it was tough in those years because it was the Depression.[17]
>
> We starved.... But I'll tell you something that I'm very proud of. After we started making money, we went back to every one of those hotels that we owed money to and paid them off. The three of us had to do that, because we wouldn't have rested easy. They weren't big hotels like you have now. They were little. In those days, you could get into little hotels that had cooking facilities and they were like little apartments. They were called hotel apartments. When we were getting ready to leave, my poor mother and dad had to go down to the desk and tell them that we couldn't afford to pay what we owed, but we would pay as soon as we could afford to, and they said okay.[18]

In summer 1936, a promising new band out of Chicago led by a young violinist named Leonard Keller, sometimes billed as the "Tone Poet," hired the Andrews Sisters. Keller was an accomplished violinist with an academic background in classical music who was receiving good press in the Chicago area. His interest in the sisters said something about their growth as singers. They first appeared with him at the Lowry Hotel in St. Paul, across the Mississippi River from their hometown.[19]

Preceding the Andrews Sisters at the Lowry was the orchestra of Leon Belasco, whom the sisters had met the previous summer. Belasco was fairly well known, having played such prominent venues as the St. Loritz Hotel in New York City and the Chez Paree nightclub in Chicago. He caught their opening night at the Lowry. The next morning, the sisters found a telegram under their hotel room door from Belasco asking them to audition with his orchestra. They, of course, jumped at the chance to audition and impressed Belasco enough to land a job at $150 a week, a rather respectable salary in the middle of the Great Depression. Belasco was on tour from New York and his next stop was the Mayfair Club in Kansas City where he asked the Andrews Sisters to join him. Maxene told him their parents came with the act, and he agreed to take on the entire family. Leon Belasco, like Larry Rich before him, would change the course of the Andrews Sisters' career.

The Mayfair Club was the sisters' first gig at what Maxene called "a real high-class supper club," which featured "panels of mirrors on walls and ceilings, a circular bar with revolving fountain and a terraced restaurant" as well as "an extensive gambling layout."[20] The Andrews family piled into the 1929 Buick and headed for Kansas City, thinking this might be the break that would put the sisters' struggling career on the way up. The sisters owned two sets of gowns (made by Olga), six publicity photos and no music—since their act still consisted primarily of LaVerne playing the piano by ear as they sang songs copied from the Boswell Sisters. Billed as "The Showplace of the West," the Mayfair was Kansas City's leading nightclub and had recently opened its doors to the public with the indomitable Sophie Tucker. The club policy, as with

Maxene, Patty, and LaVerne circa 1934. In this publicity photograph, the Andrews Sisters emulate the sultry, seductive look of the era—a far cry from the wide grins and sparkling eyes that characterized their later personae. (Robert Boyer Collection)

many nightclubs, was to book a band for a long run and change the floorshow every two weeks.

Nightclubs had become the focus of American live entertainment. Some claim they grew from the "speakeasies" of the Prohibition Era, and while there's some validity to the claim, the combination of entertainment, eating, and drinking goes back to earlier times. The end of prohibition coincided with the decline of traditional vaudeville, and some historians suggest that vaudeville simply left the stage of the theater and moved into the more intimate atmosphere of the nightclub. A columnist for *The Billboard* noted: "About the only difference is that now the customers wait impatiently for their soup, while in vaude, waited impatiently for the feature picture."[21]

The nightclub usually featured tables around a dancing area backed by a small stage for the orchestra, a nearby bar, and sometimes a casino in an adjoining room. Soft lights and music accompanied dinner, and the décor created the current image of romance. French, Latin, and tropical themes were especially popular. Benny the Bum's, one of Philadelphia's classiest clubs, vied for distinction by featuring midget waiters.

When the Andrews Sisters began touring the nightclub circuit, the entertainment setting was already established, but the music was changing. "Swing" was coming in. The nightclub band, or "orchestra" as the big bands were often called, provided background music during drinks and dinner. After dinner, the music became more danceable and patrons took to the dance floor in front of the orchestra. Swing attracted a younger audience and increasingly the nightclub scene appealed to the twenties set. Following several dance numbers, usually featuring a "boy" or "girl" singer, a floorshow was presented with the band director often acting as emcee.

Some of the floorshow acts were straight from vaudeville. Dr. and Madame Hudspeth, "mentalists," featured Mickey Boy, the "wonder dog"; Princess Wee-Wee, an African American midget, had "no talents of any kind" but depended "entirely on her size and appeal ... altho she [was] no thing of beauty in tights"; the Nelson Sisters engaged in a vocal duel with "all the earmarks of a cat fight"; Hazel Ariel danced with a seven-foot python until it almost choked her to death one night in front of her audience; the Three Chocolate Chickens were juvenile "colored" dancers; John Tio was a talking parrot; fan dancer Loma Smith was fined $20.80 for "excess exposure." The judge was unmoved when she pleaded: "Your honor, these fans are hard to hold anyway and if one of them got away from me, could I help it?"[22] A husband and wife knife-throwing act ended in divorce after the wife was pinned to the board one evening by her tipsy husband. The ultra-swank St. Regis Hotel in New York once featured jugglers, fencing champions, and a skating monologist. Dancers of all types were popular, and a common blue nose complaint was that "art dances" were no more than a slightly cleaned up version of striptease. An emcee who doubled as referee for a female wrestling act quit his job because "he was tired of tossing 350 and 400-pound women around to amuse night clubbers." Female impersonators enjoyed periods of popularity much to the consternation of the blue nose watchdogs.

The upscale establishments, of course, featured better food, better drinks, better big bands, and better-known entertainers for the floorshow. Pretty cigarette girls, frequently scantily clad, moved among the patrons to satisfy nicotine needs during this era when liberated women enhanced their glamour with cigarettes while men relied on pipes, cigarettes or cigars for their images. *The Billboard* reported in late 1936 that over $100,000 in jewelry and cash had been stolen from New York nightclub patrons in recent months. Consequently, plainclothes policemen were planted in some of the plush clubs to curb the rash of thefts.[23]

Entertainers frequently complained about the nightclub scene. Some resented having to entertain an audience that was more interested in dinner and conversation than the performance. Occasional tipsy patrons created distractions. Musicians disliked the accompaniment of kitchen noise and the distraction of wandering waiters. Dressing rooms were non-existent in some clubs; closets, storage rooms, and even kitchens often filled in.

The Mayfair Club was a club of this sort, where the Andrews Sisters joined Leon Belasco and his orchestra in Kansas City. Like many nightclub shows, theirs was broadcast nightly over a local radio station. A local newspaper advertised it:

And Now THE MAYFAIR ... Brings You Plantation Chicken Dinners
As Prepared and Served by Aunt Lydia and Aunt Jemima
In the famous style of the old Southland. $1.50. No Cover Charge.
SUPERB ENTERTAINMENT
LEON BELASCO
And his Internationally famous dance band
MILES AND KOVER
THE HOLLYWOOD HORSE
NELSON'S MARIONETTES
THREE ANDREWS SISTERS
And 12 MAYFAIR DANCING GIRLS
Scientifically Air Conditioned for your Comfort[24]

A typically staccato *Variety* review revealed the nature of the show, which the reviewer thought was sparked by the Andrews Sisters:

> Present bill is par for the course, though opening is weak. Line of 12 girls start things in a routine manner. Stamm and La Rue don't add much in an adagio dance dressed in leopard skins. Three Andrew [sic] Sisters' harmony and rhythm singing really got things started. Doctor Chas. Hoffman works fast with his cocktail gadgets and pours some vari-hued liquids from same shaker and scores with his water to beer gag.... The big hand is a toss-up between Lee Morse and Pierce and Harris, latter hoofers. The customers liked the torcher. The mixed dance team sells easily.[25]

The sisters were at the Mayfair for about a month when their big break turned to disaster: the club caught fire and burned to the ground. Everything was lost—the musical arrangements and instruments, the sisters' gowns, and even their publicity photos. The sisters were certain this was the end of their career. Peter Andrews was becoming more and more disillusioned with the ups and downs of show business and wanted his daughters to return to Minneapolis, finish school, and become secretaries—less glamorous jobs, perhaps, but more reliable. Minneapolis was only a few hundred miles away and it threatened to be their next and final stop. Belasco, however, was impressed with the sisters' potential. He persuaded Peter and Olga to remain in Kansas City with their daughters while he went to New York to refurbish the orchestra. He gave the Andrews family an allowance and left for New York.

While waiting for their instruments to arrive, Belasco's band played a one-nighter in Kansas City's Fairyland Park with instruments borrowed from a local music company.[26] The Andrews Sisters were probably part of this engagement since they were still on salary. Belasco was soon back with new music and new instruments, and most importantly for the career of the Andrews Sisters, a nineteen-year-old youth named Vic Schoen who played the trumpet and arranged music. Years later, Vic Schoen remembered his meeting with Belasco:

> Well, there was a place—in those early days—where musicians looking for work would gather in a cluster somewhere in New York City between 49th Street and 54th Street on Broadway. And anybody looking for a musician would be sure to find him there. One day this weird little guy walked up to me and said, "Are you Vic Schoen?" I said, "Yeah." He said, "Do you want a job?" I said, "Sure." He said, "Alright, be ready to go to Kansas City tomorrow morning."[27]

The youthful Schoen was known for his swing arrangements, and Belasco was convinced that swing was the wave of the future. Belasco had decided to revamp his orchestra around the singing style of the Andrews Sisters. Previously his orchestra was a "society orchestra" that played for the slow, traditional ball-room dancing of the period. Vic Schoen's job was to bring the Andrews Sisters and the orchestra together with swing arrangements.[28] Schoen remembered:

> I developed a totally new style for them away from the Boswells. I wasn't want-ing to copy anyone.... As a matter of fact, I didn't come in with any other ideas than being contemporary. Or, being myself, whatever that was at the time. I didn't know contemporary from anything else. But what I wanted to be was original and, you know, myself.... So, it took time to develop that. And it did radically change the way they [Andrews Sisters] sang and therefore their voic-ing became different and I had to point those things out on the piano. And I'm not a pianist, so we struggled around and all of that. But it enabled me to give them sounds that they had not experienced.... They copied the Boswell Sisters. And that was all that they could generate for creating ideas. Because they just didn't have that ability.... Anything that I came up with must have sounded terrific, because it was new to them. They had never done this kind of music before. They were, you know, strictly hotel, one step above Lombardo. You know those types of bands. So, what I brought in was different. If it was good, so much the better.[29]

When Belasco returned from New York with Schoen, he remained in Kansas City and opened in late July at the Muehlebach Grill. A *Variety* reviewer liked Belasco's band and thought the Andrews Sisters had style (thanks to Vic Schoen), but didn't particularly like their voices: "Featuring a sophisticated style, with a sprinkling of hot and sweet, the band is surefire. Andrew [sic] Sis-ters, swing trio, have that something that spells click for the hot hymnals. Voices aren't particularly good, and again it's style that does the selling job."[30]

In late September, the Belasco entourage left Kansas City and opened a two-week engagement at Hotel Peabody in Memphis where *Metronome* noted: "Leon Belasco's return engagement to the Peabody was the result of his pop-ularity during his last engagement.... He features the Andrews Sisters and Smith Howard."[31] On October 10, they were at the Pavillon Caprice in the Nether-land Plaza Hotel in Cincinnati where a local reviewer liked the act—and was one of the few who thought the Andrews Sisters were good looking. He noted: "Accompanying Leon and his orchestra are three charming damsels, the

Maxene, LaVerne, and Patty, circa 1937. Publicity photograph when the sisters were singing with Leon Belasco. (Robert Boyer Collection)

Andrews Sisters, who form a vocal trio that is not only pleasurable to the ear, but to the eyes as well. Strangely enough, these three girls are "honest to goodness sisters, and not just traveling under this cognomen as part of their act."[32] A month later, Belasco and the sisters traveled to Detroit and the New Book Casino in the Book-Cadillac Hotel where they broadcast nightly on local radio. In early December, the sisters were back in their hometown with Belasco at the Minnesota Terrace in the Hotel Nicollet where they remained until mid–January. During their stay, they broadcast nightly over local station WCCO.

Sometime during 1936, the Andrews Sisters appeared for the first time on sheet music. "You're Here, You're There" featured a photograph of the sisters and a note identified them as vocalists with Belasco's band. Their photographs would eventually appear on over 200 pieces of sheet music.[33]

In early March 1937, Leon Belasco and the Andrews Sisters arrived in New York City where Belasco had new gowns designed for the sisters in anticipation of their opening at the Terrace Room in the Hotel New Yorker. The sisters were thrilled to be back in New York City, the capital of the entertainment industry, and hoped for the break that would make their career. However, the hotel's manager didn't like the Andrews Sisters' act. In an early interview, the sisters admitted the engagement was a disaster. "The band played one way and we sang another and we never did get together."[34] The manager told Belasco the sisters had to go if he wanted to continue on the hotel circuit.

But Belasco refused to fire the sisters, and apparently the manager demurred, since the sisters continued with Belasco.

The Billboard gave a lukewarm review of their Hotel New Yorker show—which also included a juggler, a dance team, and some guitar-playing Hawaiians—without mentioning the sisters: "Belasco's Orchestra, working show and dance, is so-so, undistinguished as to style and not overly strong as to dance rhythms."[35] *Metronome* published a much longer review of the band, and thought it was not good—despite some good musicians, who however, weren't playing too well together. Regarding Belasco: "[T]heir leader ... loses much dignity ... by flitting around in front of his boys like a molested moth trying to find a place to alight." The sisters were briefly and enigmatically mentioned: "The Andrews Sisters sit in front of the band for eye appeal; they alone could and should suffice."[36]

While in New York, Belasco approached RCA Victor Records for a recording date with the Andrews Sisters, but after hearing them sing, the agent told Belasco: "I'll take the middle sister [Patty] and make another Martha Raye out of her."[37] The sisters, however, were unwilling to break up the act. Belasco eventually arranged a recording session with Brunswick Records on March 18, 1937, in New York. "There's a Lull in My Life" features an almost unrecognizable Patty in a ninety-second soft solo midway through the slow swing number. "Jammin'" reveals the Boswell Sisters' influence on the Andrews. It has a fast paced 20s jazz sound dominated by the sisters' scat and harmony singing with the band performing a mere fifteen-second solo. "Wake Up and Live" is an unremarkable swing number with the sisters harmonizing a short chorus and a bit of scat and then returning with an even shorter finale. The singers are certainly recognizable as the Andrews Sisters, but they have not yet developed the distinctive swing style typical of their early Decca recordings. The fourth side of the session was "Turn Off the Moon" sung by Wes Vaughn and backed by Belasco's orchestra.

Both *Variety* and *The Billboard* noted the recordings, *The Billboard* commenting, "Leon Belasco gives way to the Andrews Sisters, harmony trio, whose tricky rhythmic disposition of 'Jammin'" listens beaucoup well[38] ... Leon Belasco distinguishes himself again with 'There's a Lull in My Life' and 'Wake Up and Live,' the vocal dispositions of the Andrews Sisters on the later side an added asset."[39] None of the songs went anywhere on the charts, perhaps because better known artists had versions out.

From New York, the Belasco troupe moved on to the Roosevelt Hotel's Blue Room in New Orleans where they opened on April 15 for a month's stay. New Orleans liked the show, and the sisters received a good, prophetic review, one of their first extensive ones:

> The Andrews Sisters are not only featured vocalists in the Belasco band, they are show stoppers on the floor too. Tall, charmingly personable and possessed of voices that harmonize nicely, and a sense of singing rhythm that should take them to the peak of success, they offer a series of song arrangements both new and delightful. They have a grand sense of comedy too, no slapstick or corny buffoonery, but neatly modulated clowning that adds greatly to their success, both on the band stand and on the floor.[40]

Another reviewer liked the show also and wrote: "Sparkling is the harmonious chanting of the three Andrew [sic] Sisters, received in appreciative fashion."[41] The Andrews Sisters had come a long way from their "Chinese puzzle" days and were evolving into top-flight entertainers.

From New Orleans, Belasco's band went to the Adolphus Hotel's Century Room in Dallas, Texas, where they opened May 23. Once again the show was well received and a picture of the sisters and Belasco appeared in the *Dallas Morning News.* "There are the Andrews Sisters, Patty, Maxene and LaVerne, a peppy and thoroughly capable trio of the Boswell tradition. Patty goes it solo now and then, as well she can." Vic Schoen's arrangements were lauded as well as his performance on the trumpet.[42]

After Dallas, Belasco and company opened in Memphis where they appeared the first week of July at the Cascades Roof Garden in the Hotel Claridge. I found no review of their show, but a picture of the sisters appeared in a local newspaper, which reported they were scheduled to sing on a local radio swing show.[43]

After the Memphis engagement, Belasco decided to disband his orchestra because he claimed the strenuous tour was about to give him a nervous breakdown.[44] He would eventually go to Hollywood where he pursued a successful career as a character actor. Although the sisters' time with Belasco is usually glossed over in most accounts of their career, these very significant months groomed the sisters for their explosion onto the national scene a few months later. Maxene acknowledged Belasco's important influence on their career by bringing them into the big band era. Before Belasco, she said (and she should have included Vic Schoen), "the Andrews Sisters didn't know what they were doing, they were just singing." Patty once told a reporter: "Being with Leon [Belasco] … taught us a lot about show business. He was a smart leader, and the experience we gained under his direction proved invaluable to us."[45] Years later, Leon Belasco reminisced about the Andrews Sisters' stint with his band:

> The Andrews Sisters … came to me, three very young, very thin, almost emaciated, girls whose wardrobe consisted of two outfits made by their mother (not a paragon of stylish couture) and three arrangements, "Night and Day," "Dixieland Jazz Band," and one of those doo-wah doo-wahs, the name of which I don't recall. But I recognized their talent and so did most enthusiastically, the boys in my orchestra. Unfortunately, business started to pick up, they held us over and just four days before the 4th of July the Mayfair Club at night burned to the ground. I lost my violin, my library, and of course the entire band all their instruments. I went to New York and hired another emaciated character with his front tooth missing, who played trumpet and trombone, but whose main task was to reconstruct and make new arrangements. His name was Vic Schoen. They all were with me until (at the advice of a very good doctor) I gave up my band and went to Hollywood. I gave the Andrews Sisters all orchestrations which Vic Schoen made as well as a release of the contract they had with me. Those orchestrations did not come easy. To put it bluntly, the girls were lazy. They did not want to sing any pop tunes. Only Dixieland. When I displayed them at the New Yorker Hotel everybody (agents, producers, etc.) wanted only Patty ("to make another Martha Raye").[46]

Leon Belasco, 1937. When the sisters joined Belasco in late 1936, he revamped his band around the Andrews Sisters with arrangements by Vic Schoen. The tutelage of Belasco and Schoen groomed the sisters for their explosion onto the national scene in 1938 with "Bei Mir Bist Du Schoen." (Robert Boyer Collection)

When the sisters left Belasco, Peter Andrews had other plans for his daughters. In his eyes, the Belasco engagement was another connection that looked promising but led to nothing. The sisters had had their chance to break into show business and it hadn't happened, so it was back to Minneapolis and the dreaded secretarial courses. Even Olga could not persuade him otherwise.

Minneapolis and secretarial school were not what the Andrews Sisters had in mind. Miserable in Minneapolis, they wanted another stab at New York, the heart of the entertainment industry. They told their parents, they wanted to return. Maxene explained:

> I knew that the longer we stayed in Minneapolis, the less chance we were going to have to go back into show business. So finally one day my sister Patty and I were talking. We were both very disgruntled, and so we decided that one of us would have to speak to Papa and see if we couldn't get a chance to go back to New York. So we drew straws, real straws, and I got the short end, so it was my turn to talk to Papa. I waited until I was able to handle it, and I said it real fast: "Papa, we want to go back to New York. Can we go back to New York?" And I waited, expecting the worst, and I was very surprised when he said, "Well, let's wait 'til dinner and we'll talk to Mama about it." And it was decided that night that we would go back and make one more stab at New York.[47]

Once again Olga was their ally, and they all packed into the car (this time a 1931 Packard) with their dog and a hundred dollars borrowed from Olga's brothers, and drove to New York.[48] Significantly, the sisters still sought their father's permission, even though by now LaVerne was twenty-six, Maxene was twenty-one, and Patty was nineteen.

When the Andrews family returned to New York, they discovered that most of the entertainment industry had vacated the city for the summer. Nonetheless, they started making the rounds of agents and music publishers for jobs. After the sisters auditioned for the William Morris Agency, an agent told Olga, "Mrs. Andrews, take your daughters back home and put them in school. They sing too loud, they move too much, and they'll make people nervous!"[49] Undaunted, the sisters persevered.

They connected with a music publisher named Bernie Pollack who let them use his office and piano at the New Yorker Hotel to rehearse as he helped them find jobs. The family stayed at a nearby cheap hotel while the sisters went to Pollack's office every morning at nine and rehearsed until the building closed at six. "Brother, was it a funny place!" Maxene remembered years later. "Downstairs in the lobby, or even right outside on the street, the comics would be doing their routines to nobody at all, like crazy people, just hoping that an agent would come along and book them into the Catskills."[50] Olga gave them fifteen cents a day for lunch. They went to Hector's Cafeteria at 50th and Broadway where they divided one sandwich and a cup of coffee three ways. Maxene remembered that LaVerne lost weight, which she never regained.[51]

Meanwhile, Pollack spread word about the sisters to his contacts. Several arrangers and band leaders came to hear them, but few offered them jobs because, according to Maxene, "in those days it was a single girl singer or boy singer, nobody wanted a trio"[52]—which was not entirely true since many bands featured trios. They landed a few jobs, but for the most part nothing significant. In late September, a *Daily Mirror* columnist hyperbolically announced that "The Famous Andrews Sisters, sensational girl trio" were scheduled to appear on the *Daily Mirror Road to Fame*, a radio program sponsored by the newspaper which featured new talent: "Their recent appearances on WOR [New York] have the agencies buzzing with excitement."[53] Hyperbolic as his comments were, "buzz" did seem to be mounting, and soon thereafter the sisters had their first feature story. It appeared in the *New York Daily Mirror* October 4, 1937, and contained the misinformation that many future stories would repeat:

> The Three Andrews Sisters, LaVerne, Maxene and Patty ... [ellipses in original] born in Minneapolis, Minnesota ... LaVerne came first, then Maxene and finally Patty ... their dad ran a restaurant in Minneapolis ... girls did the dishes ... they got in the habit of harmonizing in the kitchen ... clink of dishes made a nice background ... patients (I mean customers) stayed for second helping of everything inspired by the girls' singing ... went into vaudeville and were instant hit ... broke into radio on WCCO Minneapolis ... CBS brought them to New York last March and featured them over its network from the New Yorker with Leon Belasco for six weeks ... they are now heard over WOR ... all are single and all tall, rangy beauties ... mixture of Norwegian and Greek ... girls look like athletes but go in for photography, painting and books ... they have two show dogs, Pete an English setter who looks like Gene Carroll of Gene and Glenn, and Gypsy a gorgeous wire-haired terrier ... girls have been so successful that dad gave away the restaurant and travels with them ... they do their own arranging ... LaVerne plays the piano and sings bass ... Patsy [sic] sings lead and Maxene, tenor ... you'll hear of this trio ... It has plenty on the ball.[54]

In early October, the sisters were featured in "The Gay and Sparkling Riviera Follies" at the Riviera Club.[55]

Despite these minor victories, however, Peter was growing increasingly unhappy with the New York venture and was adamant that at the end of three months, if no breakthrough occurred, they would return to Minneapolis. The deadline was drawing near.

Soon thereafter, the sisters received a visit from Vic Schoen, who had recently picked up a job with the Billy Swanson orchestra at the Edison Hotel. Maxene, always the aggressive one, said: "Vic, you go tell the bandleader that you can't take the job unless he hires the Andrews Sisters." Schoen told her the bandleader was not interested in a "girl trio," but after badgering from Maxene and her sisters, he promised he would see what he could do. A few days later Schoen reported that Swanson would give them an audition.[56] Their last weekend (probably October 2) in New York was approaching, and Peter announced they would leave for Minneapolis the following Monday. Maxene told the story:

> So we auditioned for ... Billy Swanson, and there was nobody in the room, but in a booth at the far end of the room sat a lone woman. Billy thanked us and said, "It was very nice and you were very good, but I can't use you. I have a girl singer." So dejected, we started to walk out, the three of us on the verge of tears, and this woman called us over. She said, "Are you going to sing with this orchestra?" And we said, "No, he didn't hire us." She said, "Well, sit down here." She said, "My name is Maria Kramer. I own the hotel." ... And so she said, "I want you to sing with the orchestra." You know, he [Billy Swanson] had a coast-to-

coast hookup on Saturday night, 15 minutes, and that was the thing we wanted to get on because I knew that if somebody heard us, they were going to like us, and I just couldn't imagine all of those years of rehearsing that somewhere it wasn't going to pay off. And Maria kept saying, "They're going to sing." And Billy said, "You know I can only pay them $5 apiece," and we said, "Well, that's fine." We'd have worked for nothing. And we thought, "Oh dear Lord, you spared us." Saturday night came and Papa and Mama had gotten everything packed, because Monday we were on our way back. We got to the hotel and Maria Kramer was not there. Maria had gone down to Brazil because her husband was ill. And of course Mr. Billy Swanson knew that, so instead of our singing the whole arrangement of "Sleepy Time Down South," he cut us down to one chorus. As soon as we were done, he said, "Here's your pay, you're fired." So there went our big chance.[57]

Dejected and in tears, the sisters returned to the hotel where their parents had packed their belongings. Their fate seemed sealed. It was back to Minneapolis and the dreaded secretarial school on Monday. The next morning, Vic Schoen called and invited them to the hotel for a farewell lunch. Only Patty and Maxene joined him. Maxene remembered: "[W]e got a sandwich and we split between us. We were so used to splitting food, it never dawned on us to order one a piece. And we had some ice cream and a soda."[58]

As they were eating their farewell lunch with Schoen, a young man dressed in flashy clothes named Lou Levy approached and asked Schoen if he was with the band that had a girl trio on the air the previous night. Schoen replied affirmatively. Maxene remembered their first meeting with the man who would become their manager and eventually her husband:

> Then this fellow walks in, and says his name is Lou Levy. He was this much above being a zoot-suiter. He had pointed-toe shoes, with the wide snap-brim hat, and the pockets in the back of his jacket. We were terrified of zoot-suiters. But he told us that Dave Kapp, who, with his brother Jack, founded Decca Records, had been at a Tommy Dorsey opening at the Hotel Commodore and over the radio in a taxi on the way home had heard us singing on the broadcast from the Edison, and he wanted to sign us to Decca.[59]

Patty and Maxene let Levy know they were two-thirds of the Andrews Sisters and would be more than happy to audition for Decca. They rushed back to the hotel to help LaVerne and their parents unpack, and to rehearse for the audition the following morning.

An early interview with the Andrews Sisters claimed they did "two radio shots a week with Billy Swanson,"[60] and in a later interview, Maxene said they were fired after two shows.[61] Patty once told an interviewer that Swanson played nightly, but he could only afford them on the two nights a week when he had "broadcast outlets." It was one of these broadcasts that Dave Kapp heard.[62] Vic Schoen also told the story differently:

> We [Billy Swanson Orchestra] had a half-hour three times a week. I suggested to the band leader that it would be a welcome addition if we could bring three girls on that I knew and that I'd written for and it would give them an additional sound, and he agreed. So, the Andrews Sisters—broke and unknown, nobody knew them from a head of cabbage—were hired for three broadcasts a week,

and they each received $5 per show, so that each of them made $15 a week, and that was okay. They survived on that.[63]

Patty Andrews claimed Dave Kapp, the vice president of Decca, came directly to the hotel the night he heard the Andrews Sisters on the cab radio and asked them to audition the following Monday.[64] Vic Schoen had yet another version. He said Dave Kapp knew Lou Levy and sent him down to see Schoen about the sisters. Schoen introduced Levy to the sisters and they made a management deal.[65] However it happened, the Andrews Sisters auditioned for Decca the following Monday, and shortly thereafter Lou Levy became their manager.

What the sisters didn't know was that Jack Kapp, president of Decca Records and brother of Dave Kapp, was probably looking for someone to replace the Andrews Sisters' early idols, the Boswell Sisters. When the Boswells retired as a trio in 1935, Decca lost one of its most popular recording groups. It may very well have been the imitation of the Boswells that the Andrews did so well that attracted Dave Kapp when he heard them on the cab radio.

The following Monday, the Andrews Sisters went to Decca Studios for their audition. Patty and Maxene remembered the audition differently. According to Patty:

> The three of us went up there, and we sang for Jack Kapp.... We only had one song we sang for him, and it was very funny because it was "Night and Day," and instead of singing the melody, we sang our take-off chorus, our second chorus, thinking that that would make us different than anybody else. But it was because of that he signed us up to make our first record.[66]

Maxene remembered, perhaps more accurately:

> He [Jack Kapp] was a quiet man ... and he stayed at the round end of the piano, and he listened intensely. He said, "Sing a song for me." So, we started to sing. We finished one, he said, "Another." We sang seven songs for him, and then he said to us, "How would you like to record for Decca?" That's how we got our break. We went to Decca. They gave us our first recording session.[67]

On October 14, 1937, Patty, Maxene, and LaVerne Andrews recorded their first two songs for Decca Records, "Why Talk About Love?" and "Just a Simple Melody." The contract they signed was a flat fee of $50 without royalties for each two-sided record they made—a not uncommon arrangement at that time. Vic Schoen, as their arranger, got $25 a record.[68] Maxene was elated with the agreement: "Well, I figured that we could make a record every day. That was nothing. We'd be rich!"[69]

The Andrews Sisters' first Decca record set the pattern for the style that would eventually bring the sisters their great success. William Ruhlmann describes this best:

> [T]he single introduced a musical approach that would provide the Andrews Sisters' biggest hits. Schoen arranged their voices in distinctly rhythmic style, giving Patty short solos that contrasted with the close harmony and having the sisters sing with phrasing that emphasized the melody over the meaning of the words. In fact, they start out "Why Talk About Love?" singing "doodley-dee" rather than actual words, and at any moment they may extend syllables of words

or launch into other nonsense syllables. The effect is like having two complementary horn sections (especially in "Just a Simple Melody," where the singers and the horns answer each other), and the arrangements are constantly surprising. Using Dixieland and swing elements, but mixing and varying effects, Schoen has invented a fresh new approach to vocal music.[70]

Original though the Andrews Sisters' first record may have been, it did not sell well. This was not the big break the sisters hoped for and they were convinced Decca would drop them because of the disappointing sales. But Jack Kapp was not ready to abandon his new trio. He called them in on November 24 for their second recording session.

The song chosen for the A-side of the record was "Nice Work If You Can Get It" by George and Ira Gershwin from the movie *A Damsel in Distress* where it was sung by Fred Astaire. Several other versions of the song were out and Decca hoped to cash in on its popularity, a common practice in those days. The B-side, or throwaway side, was an obscure Yiddish song called "Bei Mir Bist Du Schoen." It is impossible to determine from the literature where this song came from because every person involved in its recording had a different story about its origins. Sammy Cahn, who wrote the English lyrics for "Bei Mir Bist Du Schoen," claimed that he first heard the song performed by a black act at the Apollo Theatre in Harlem, and later found the sheet music in a store in the Jewish Lower East Side of Manhattan. At that time he shared an apartment with Lou Levy, who was now managing the Andrews Sisters. One day at the apartment, Patty Andrews noticed the music and thought it was a Greek song. Cahn played the song for the sisters; they liked it and recorded it. Vic Schoen claimed he found the song in a collection of folk songs in a small shop in the lobby of a Yiddish theater on Second Avenue. He gave it to Lou Levy who in turn gave it to Sammy Cahn and Saul Chaplin who wrote lyrics for it. Lou Levy said he bought the song for fifteen cents in the Lower East Side, and eventually passed it on to the sisters to record and sing at various Jewish clubs and functions.[71] Maxene had her own version of the song's origins:

> We had no place to rehearse, so this young man [Lou Levy] whom we had gotten to know quite well had offered us his apartment that he was sharing with a songwriter by the name of Sammy Cahn. And he came in one day and said, "I got the song for you." He said, "New York has a very big Jewish population, and if you girls sing this song, you'll be the hit of New York City." We said, "Well, what is the song?" And he said, "I don't have any music, but it goes like this," and he started to sing it and it was terrible. It was in Yiddish and his voice was terrible. So Vic [Schoen] said, "Let's see if I can figure it out." He one-fingered it on the piano and it was so melodious that it was almost immediate that we could sing it as a trio number. But then we had a problem because there were no English lyrics. So Lou taught us "Bei Mir Bist Du Schoen" in Yiddish phonetically.[72]

However the song got there, it became the B-side of "Nice Work If You Can Get It." During the recording session (which was piped into Jack Kapp's office), Kapp heard the song being recorded in Yiddish, interrupted the session, and told them he wanted it in English. Conflicting stories relate how the

English translation came about. Cahn claimed he didn't want to do a translation, but eventually did after a couple of days. Maxene also claimed that it took two days to get an English translation. Levy maintained the translation was done within a few minutes in the recording studio.[73] In another interview, he said the translation was made over the telephone.[74]

Vic Schoen arranged the song and directed the studio musicians who backed it. Schoen and Bobby Hackett played trumpet, Al Philburn was on trombone, Don Watt on clarinet, Frank Froeba on piano, Dave Barbour on guitar, and Stan King on drums. All were unknown at the time, but several would go on to illustrious careers. When Jack Kapp heard the record he reportedly told the sisters: "You'll either be the biggest hit or the biggest flop."[75]

Sometime during this period, Lou Levy became manager of the Andrews Sisters. He loaned them money to hold them over until their career began to take off. He booked them anywhere that would take them, including Jewish women's clubs where they sang "Bei Mir Bist Du Schoen" and other Yiddish songs he taught them.[76] They also appeared on a Sunday morning swing radio show on WNEW with Martin Block and his band and did other dates with him around New York City.[77]

But times were still lean for the Andrews Sisters. Maxene remembered that in order to buy Christmas presents for their parents, they borrowed $25 from a friend: "[W]e went to this big drugstore on Broadway and we bought a box of powder for our mother, a box of White Owl cigars for our father, and a can of Red Heart dog food for the dog."[78]

The Andrews Sisters' second Decca record was released in December 1937 and to the surprise of all involved in its production, it was the B-side, "Bei Mir Bist Du Schoen" that hit the charts. Maxene's recollection of their realization that they had a hit song was like a scene from the B movies the sisters would later make:

> You know, in your lifetime there is always one big thrill, and after that, it never quite reaches that height. One morning we were asleep in our little apartment at the Whitby and were still there because we were still getting only $50 a recording session ... But we were so grateful for anything. So we were sound asleep one morning and my father shook me real hard and he woke up my sisters and he kept saying something about a record. So we got dressed and we walked down towards Broadway, and there was a little music shop right around the corner on Broadway and 45th Street ... They had the speaker pointing out to the street, and the street from 7th Avenue to Broadway was nothing but people. All traffic was stopped, and all they played was that record ["Bei Mir Bist Du Schoen"], over and over, and the people would say, "Play it again, Play it again." And I walked through some of the crowd and I wanted to say to them, "That's me, That's me!" And of course, you never do. Every time I hear "There's No Business Like Show Business," I think of that line, one night you're nothing and the next day on your dressing room they hang a star. But it wasn't really, because we had put in our years of apprenticeship.[79]

Maxene and her sisters did not know that Lou Levy paid the music store to promote the song, an illustration of Levy's business savvy that would serve the Andrews Sisters' career so well. Years later, Levy said: "I *paid* to have that damn record played in the street outside of the music store, and when her father heard it, they ran to see what was going on. Everybody was in front of the store listening to the first Yiddish song that became a big, big hit that anybody could sing."[80]

The lyrics of "Bei Mir Bist Du Schoen" are no better or worse than most songs of the time. The sisters' singing is appealing and the band is good, but from the distance of sixty-some years, it is difficult to understand why the song was such a huge hit. Various explanations have been offered. One writer suggested:

> [I]ts singable melody ... was set in a bittersweet, minor key, reflecting the mood of a world on the cusp of crushing economic depression and World War ... Internationalism was in the air. So a Yiddish title to a song containing Italian and German had a cosmopolitanism not reserved solely for the upper classes ... "Bei Mir" had the universal appeal of a love-song that ignored politics and poverty ... the Andrews Sisters' imprimatur was never topped. The energetic young women sang with eagerness, optimism and perfect vocal harmony. To a world full of dread and anticipation, it simply cheered people up.[81]

Perhaps. I personally think the A-side of the record, "Nice Work If You Can Get It," is a more interesting song, both musically and lyrically. Others obviously felt differently. "Bei Mir Bist Du Schoen" catapulted the Andrews Sisters to overnight fame:

> Of all the boys I've known, and I've known some,
> Until I first met you I was lonesome.
> And when you came in sight, dear,
> My heart grew light, and this whole world seemed new to me.
> You're really swell I have to admit you
> Deserve expressions that really fit you.
> And so I've racked my brain, hoping to explain
> All the things that you do to me.
> Bei Mir Bist Du Schoen,
> Please let me explain,
> Bei Mir Bist Du Schoen means you're grand.
> Bei Mir Bist Du Schoen, again I'll explain,
> It means you're the fairest in the land.
> I could say bella, bella even say wunderbar.
> Each language only helps me tell you how grand you are.
> I've tried to explain, Bei Mir Bist Du Schoen,
> So kiss me and say you understand...

Word soon spread about the new song and fans flooded record stores with requests for "the new French song," "Buy a Beer, Monsieur Shane," "Mr. Barney McShane," "My Dear Mr. Shane," and "My Mere Bits of Shame."[82] They may not have known how to pronounce the title, but they bought the record. A woman's leg was broken when she was knocked down by a crowd that mobbed a record store to buy copies.[83] The song even reached the Navajo Indian reservation in Utah where it was chanted by Navajo and Ute Indians at a "squaw dance" to aid polio victims in a ceremony celebrating President Roosevelt's birthday.[84]

"Bei Mir Bist Du Schoen" entered the charts on January 1, 1938, and hit number one for the first of five weeks on January 22. It sold 100,000 copies in its initial release, and by the end of January had sold a quarter million copies. Bing Crosby was the only other Decca artist with records surpassing the 100,000 sales mark. "Bei Mir Bist Du Schoen" became a hit before it was published as sheet music, a rare phenomenon in those days. Twelve other artists, including Ella Fitzgerald and Kate Smith, recorded the song in hopes of cashing in on its popularity. The American Society of Composers, Authors and Publishers (ASCAP) named "Bei Mir Bist Du Schoen" the most popular song of 1938.[85]

The original composer of "Bei Mir Bist Du Schoen," Shalom Secunda, had sold its rights to song publishers J. and J. Kammens for only $30 a few months before the song was recorded by the Andrews Sisters. The Kammens sold the rights to Harms, Inc. to publish the English version. After much publicity about Secunda receiving nothing for the enormously popular song—including an item in Walter Winchell's column—the Kammens gave Secunda 20 percent of the royalties they collected from Harms.[86]

A columnist for *The Billboard* noted: "Not since the days of the 'Music Goes Round and Around' has any tune received the publicity that 'Bei Mir Bist Du Schoen' has. In the past few weeks columns have been devoted to the interesting human-interest story behind this tune in newspapers and magazines all over the country."[87] The song became such a national sensation that *Life*, the leading photo-news magazine of the day, published a photo essay on January 31, 1938, giving its version of the song's history—including a very unflattering photo of the Andrews Sisters.[88]

The three "dirty little Greeks" from Minneapolis, the homely daughters of poor immigrant parents, made it to the most popular newsmagazine of the nation with their runaway best-selling record. The Andrews Sisters were on their way, and they would not stop until they reached the very top.

CHAPTER FOUR

1938–1939

Less than a year ago, Patty, LaVerne and Maxene Andrews were obscure vocalists in an overcrowded entertainment world—but today—as if by magic—the name "Andrews Sisters" is a household word throughout the nation.[1]

The year 1938 was a heady one for Patty, Maxene, and LaVerne Andrews. After wandering the United States for six years, singing in any dive, nightclub, or theater that would hire them, sometimes living high but often living low, staying in cheap hotels and occasionally foregoing food, they finally made the big time they dreamed about when they began singing together as kids back in Minneapolis. Within a matter of weeks, they skyrocketed from obscurity to the ranks of the best-known singers of the nation where they would remain the rest of their lives. Few could begrudge them their success for they had certainly paid their dues.

However, despite the big sales of "Bei Mir Bist Du Schoen," the Andrews Sisters were still short on cash. The $50 they received for that first hit record didn't go far. Maxene remembered: "Today ... you make a hit record and you're a millionaire. But we still couldn't pay the rent then. So we got a job in Boston."[2] That job was at Boston's Metropolitan Theater in early January 1938 for a record-breaking week.

For the engagement, the sisters purchased three black metallic dresses for $5 apiece and found shoes on sale for $3.50 a pair. They bought some magenta fabric, which their mother cut into their initials and sewed onto their dresses. They borrowed $40 from a friend and took a bus to Boston.[3] "We only knew three songs," Patty recalled, "so we sang 'Bei Mir Bist Du Schoen' 10 times, and they were screaming for more. All we did was sing that song, and we got $500 a week."[4] Given the many years they had been singing, they surely knew more than three songs, but as Maxene pointed out: "[T]he only thing people wanted us to do, six shows a day, was 'Bei Mir Bist Du Schoen.'"[5]

The sisters' growing popularity beckoned them to radio and they made a guest appearance on CBS's popular *Saturday Night Swing Session*.[6] After their Boston engagement, they joined the same network's Sunday evening radio program in Chicago, *Double Everything*, which aired until March 20. Sponsored by Wrigley's Doublemint Chewing Gum, *Double Everything* featured an "all double cast," including double announcers, double male singers, a double male sextet, a double piano team, twin "girl" singers, and a double ten-piece orchestra conducted by Carl Hohengarten. Two sticks of Doublemint Gum were distributed to guests as they left the studio after the show.[7] Somehow the producers rationalized the Andrews threesome in this show of twosomes.

LaVerne wrote her friend Florence Hannahan about the show after Helen Hayes was the guest star.

> Have you been listening to our program? You know Wrigley renewed our contract for eight weeks so we'll be here in Chicago. Hope we can drop home for a couple days soon. We're flying to New York for two days to make our new record next week. We may open at the Chez Paree Feb. 11 with Jimmie Durante here so we'll be plenty busy doubling....
>
> Did you see our picture in Life magazine this week? Hope you did. Write and tell me how you like our programs. Wasn't Helen Hayes good on our last week's show? She is the grandest person. She has a terrible complexion. Holes in her face...
>
> Mama and Papa have been here for a week and a half now and we have moved back to the New Lawrence Hotel. It's grand ... I'm sending you a little clipping of us. Would you mind sending it back as it's the only one I have.[8]

The Andrews Sisters broadcast the Chicago shows live and flew to New York in February and June for weekend recording sessions. Patty remembered, "[I]t took us seven hours to get to New York by plane. By the time we got to our recording sessions, we were so hoarse that the records came out flat. We started to cry, but the records were hits. We learned then and there that the public does not expect perfection."[9]

Billed as "Radio Swing Singers," the Andrews Sisters sang at the Chez Paree from March 4 through March 24 while they did their radio show. LaVerne described to Florence the new fur coats the sisters and Olga bought: money was beginning to roll in. LaVerne mentioned a visit from Judy Garland, already a Hollywood star, but soon to be an even greater one when *The Wizard of Oz* hit the theaters the following year. Florence was married now and had a new baby. LaVerne hoped to be the baby's godmother.

> Received your note and am so glad you are well and happy. I am so anxious to see your baby, and really I should be its Godmother, don't you think so. Wouldn't that be something?
>
> I am planning on flying home to Minneapolis to have my teeth fixed but it will have to be on a weekend as we broadcast every week day and most of our weekends will be spent in rehearsing. Ho-Hum what a life.

Hope you can come and visit us this summer and please try. Will have lots of fun I know and it will be a very good vacation for you as you'll need it.

We're still in this Chez Paree club and we are working ourselves ragged. I am so knocked out all the time I don't know whether I'm coming or going.

We are getting ourselves beautiful furs, mine is a silver fox cape, Maxene and Patty got red fox coats and mama is getting two silver fox furs. Ho-hum.

We make it, but it goes out as fast as it comes in what with our manager, two publicity men, arranger, and our big manager...

This letter is most boring to you, but I just want you to know I do think of you.

Judy Garland was down to see us last night and consequently we didn't get to bed till six A.M. So, therefore, I am really tired so excuse the letter.[10]

Sometime in early 1938, the Andrews Sisters' contract with Decca was renegotiated with Jack Kapp. Maxene remembered:

Mr. Jack Kapp was a very honest man ... and six months after "Bei Mir Bist," he called us in the office and said, "Bring your mother and father," and they came, and he tore up our contract and gave us a new contract and it went retroactive to the very beginning. See, after we did "Bei Mir," we came in and I think we did six records, or we had six dates, and he made that all retroactive. I thought that was a very fair thing to do.[11]

Patty claimed they got five cents a record, an amount matched only by Bing Crosby at Decca,[12] but *Newsweek* reported royalties of two cents a record. Another writer claimed that a year after "Bei Mir Bist Du Schoen" became a hit, the sisters were receiving five cents per record and that among recording artists they were preceded only by Bing Crosby in receiving royalties rather than a flat fee. Whatever the case, their new contract gave them considerably more than the $50 per record of their original contract. Their musical director, Vic Schoen, who with Lou Levy was perhaps most responsible for their success, did not share their good fortune. He remembered with a touch of bitterness:

I received the sum of $25 for scoring "Bei Mir Bist Du Schoen" ... we had ... six or seven quick hits, and again all I received was $25. I think it was somewhat after we had our seventh or eighth hit that they raised me to $35. Meanwhile, they [the Andrews Sisters] were making money hand over fist. I was at the bottom of the barrel. What I did wasn't considered that important, although they didn't see how they could do it without me, but it's the way things were.[13]

It is unclear when Lou Levy became their manager. Since their contract was renegotiated with their parents, according to Maxene, it would appear that they were still an important part of the act. Other data suggest Levy became their manager at the time they first began recording for Decca. Maxene once claimed it happened when their contract was renegotiated with Decca at the suggestion of Jack Kapp.[14]

The sisters' *Double Everything* radio show was so successful that Wrigley signed them for another thirteen-week CBS program called *Just Entertainment* that aired in Chicago Monday through Friday.[15] The orchestra for this show was also conducted by Carl Hohengarten, but one date featured special guest conductor Shalom Secunda, composer of "Bei Mir Bist Du Schoen," who had recently presented the song's original manuscript to the Andrews Sisters.[16] CBS broadcast the program coast to coast, Canada and Hawaii. When it began broadcasting, a columnist reported that "Radio editors and press agents went strictly social here this week, attending blowouts for the Andrews Sisters' new show."[17]

Just Entertainment did not excite the local or national critics much: *Variety* wrote, "It's a show without fanfare. Jack Fulton is all right; the Andrews Sisters are all right. The Andrews trio, of course, sings every song exactly alike as if afraid to change from the pace they clicked with in 'Bei Mir Bist Du Schoen.' But even that's all right. In fact, the trouble, paradoxically, with the show is that it's just 'all right.'"[18] A later review was more positive, reporting that "A nice juggle stunt is achieved once per program by having the girls swing out on a wholly jive arrangement of a tune after Fulton gives it straight rendition"[19]—a routine reminiscent of the sisters' days with Joe E. Howard. *The Billboard* thought crooner Jack Fulton appeared "pale in the shadow of so dynamic a harmony group."[20]

When the Andrews Sisters returned to New York City in early July 1938 at the conclusion of their radio show in Chicago, they entered the capital of what later generations would call the Swing Era. "Swing" has been differently defined by almost every person writing about it, but most agree that it was part of the ongoing syncretism of African American jazz and European American musical traditions, which gave rise in the 1930s to one of the most creative periods of American popular music. During this decade, jazz dominated the pop music sound, and never before or since has it been such an integral part of American popular music. One writer claimed "swing" was distinguished by the performer's timing, inflection and energy, rather than anything in the way it was written: "The same tune could swing or not swing, depending entirely on who played or sang it; given a swing rendition, the most familiar music could be transformed into something almost unrecognizably new—even Bach was made to jump and jive."[21] Swing was created all over the country, but especially in New York City.

Some pinpoint August 21, 1935, as the beginning of the Swing Era when Benny Goodman and his band appeared at the Palomar Ballroom in Los Angeles. Goodman had made it to L.A. after an exasperating cross-country tour during which his music was only moderately successful with audiences. Tired of trying to please the tastes of the provincials, Goodman and his band pulled out the stops and played for themselves when they reached L.A. The youthful audience, familiar with Goodman from his records and radio hookups, danced with abandon to the swing sounds of the band and crowded the stage to be closer to the musicians. Swing had arrived.

Obviously, it was not quite that simple. Swing's history stretched back several decades to the beginning of jazz. Most jazz historians trace the origins of jazz to African American musicians in New Orleans at the turn of the century. By the 1920s jazz had begun to influence mainstream American popular music, thus the twenties' sobriquet, the "jazz age." What was passing as jazz, however, was a very watered down version of black jazz offered by white jazz bands, such

Publicity photograph, 1938, perhaps the closest the Andrews Sisters (from left: LaVerne, Patty and Maxene) ever came to cheesecake. By now the sisters were regulars on the radio show *Just Entertainment* and had several hit records that skyrocketed them to national prominence. (Robert Boyer Collection)

as Paul Whiteman, and white jazz singers, such as Bing Crosby, to white dancers and audiences. It was still white music, but dressed up in black sounds. Appropriately, the most popular singer of the age was Al Jolson, a white man who performed his version of African American music in black face.

This syncretism of black and white music continued into the 1930s and resulted in the swing era of the big bands. Swing especially appealed to young people and it ushered in the youthful demographics that still dominate popular music. Although firmly segregated with few exceptions, both black and white bands participated in swing, but more doors were open to white performers in 1930s America. Duke Ellington, Chick Webb, Louis Armstrong, and Count Basie were among the big names that set the pace of the era among black musicians while on the white side of the ledger were such names as Benny Goodman, Tommy and Jimmy Dorsey, Artie Shaw, Woody Herman, and Harry James. Vocalists performed with the bands, but with a few exceptions they were mere window dressing—pretty "girls" or cute "boys" whose vapid styles did not compete with the sounds of the big bands. Most musicians would have preferred no vocalists, but audiences liked them. They typically sat on stage as the band opened the show, moved to the mike to sing a few harmless stanzas midway through the show, and then returned to their seats as the band completed the show.

On any given night in New York City during the late 1930s, one could hear several of the above mentioned big bands, many of which had radio hookups that broadcast locally and sometimes nationally. Members of the big bands read like a "Who's Who" of jazz and included such legendary musicians as Bunny Berigan on trumpet, Lionel Hampton on vibraphone, Peanuts Hucko on alto saxophone, Billy Butterfield on tenor saxophone, Teddy Wilson on piano, Jimmy Blanton on bass, Peewee Russell on clarinet, Joe Venuti on violin, and Gene Krupa on drums. Many historians consider Duke Elllington the greatest composer of the era—if not of the century—but others such as George and Ira Gershwin, Cole Porter, Johnny Mercer, Harold Arlen, Jerome Kern, and Irving Berlin also contributed to the sounds of the period. New York was home base for most of the bands, but much of their year was spent on grueling cross-country tours to their many fans in the hinterlands who knew them from radio and recordings.

Less talented musicians used gimmicks to find a niche on the big band bandwagon and formed midget big bands, black and white big bands, singing big bands, family big bands, and even a big band composed of sets of twins complete with twin female vocalists. Olympic champion Jesse Owens conducted a big band for awhile and a Philadelphia wrestler gave up the mat for the more lucrative bandstand. The sexism of the day excluded most women from the bands, so they formed their own, such as Ina Ray Hutton and her Melodears, Rita Rio and her Swing Girls, and the Harlem Playgirls.

All big bands had vocalists, but except for a few, such as Ella Fitzgerald, Billie Holiday, and Mildred Bailey, they were unknowns like Helen Forrest, Merv Griffin, Dick Haymes, Peggy Lee, and Frank Sinatra—many of whom would someday become top singers in the country. With a few exceptions, vocalists were innocuous and unobtrusive, and relegated to a few stanzas midway through the band number. Swing was a man's world that consciously and unconsciously denigrated vocalists by calling them "girl singers" or "boy singers." Female singers were further kept in place with epithets like "canaries," "thrushes," "warblers," "chirpies," and "sparrows."[22] A swing historian observed: "For many musicians and enthusiasts, female big-band vocalists (and most males as well) were regarded as unfortunate concessions to commercial taste, ornaments who added nothing to the music and usually detracted from it."[23] An October 1939 *Down Beat* headline proclaimed "The Gal Yippers Have No Place in Our Jazz Bands."[24] Another *Down Beat* article asked "Are Vocalists Unnecessary?" and concluded that most of them were.[25] *Metronome* interviewed "girl" vocalists about sexism and sexual harassment they received from orchestra members, managers and agents[26]—and most received plenty. It was not until September 1942 that *Metronome* featured a woman on its cover, Dinah Shore.

Given that most female singers were hired as window dressing, their looks were frequently considered more important than their talent. From the mid-1930s until 1948, *Metronome*, subtitled *The Review of the Music World*, published each month a "Heart Throb of the Month," a cheesecake photograph of a "girl" singer showing lots of leg, cleavage, or both. *Music and Rhythm*, a short-lived rival to *Down Beat* in the early 1940s, featured sexist cartoons of scantily clad women as well as cheesecake photos of "girl" singers. The closest the Andrews Sisters came to cheesecake was a comic photo on the back of *Down Beat* where they showed leg with the Ritz Brothers when they made their first film *Argentine Nights*.[27] Obviously, the sisters were not cheesecake material, which was probably one reason the boys in the big bands so frequently put them down.

White males not only dominated mainstream popular music during the swing era, but they also dominated the covers of *The Billboard*. Each week the magazine's cover featured a photograph of a popular musician. As late as 1941 when the Andrews Sisters were flying high on the charts, thirty-eight of the fifty-two covers were white male musicians, almost all big band leaders. Five covers featured women (one was the Andrews Sisters), four featured men and women, and five featured cartoon drawings. Not one non-white musician appeared on the cover, even though Count Basie, Louis Armstrong, Duke Ellington, Lionel Hampton, Cab Calloway, Ella Fitzgerald, Maxine Sullivan, the Mills Brothers, and the Ink Spots were big stars with many hit records.

The Andrews Sisters began to seriously participate in swing when they joined Leon Belasco, who saw the coming trend and changed his band from "sweet" (traditional ballroom music) to swing. Previously the sisters had sung with Maury Sherman's band, which was probably participating in the new swing sounds too. The bands of Sherman and Belasco were the stars, the sisters hired hands to help out with the singing. The only Andrews Sisters recordings from this period are the three sides they did with Belasco in March 1937 for Brunswick Records which doubtless reflect the music they were doing on the road with him. "There's a Lull in My Life" featured Patty in a brief soft solo midway through the band number. The sisters' singing dominated "Jammin'" but it is mostly scat that complements the band sounds. "Wake Up and Live" featured the sisters with some short solos and more scat singing.

As products of vaudeville, the Andrews Sisters never forgot that their chief function as singers was to entertain. Maxene once told a reporter: "The only things in our minds then and now is pleasing people. We don't want to educate the public; we just want to entertain them."[28] Their mother frequently told the sisters when they were young: "One day the time will come when you will come to a crossroad in your life, and you will have to make a choice, and the choice will be yours." Maxene continued: "Well, we very unconsciously applied that to music. You'll either sing for the musicians or you're going to sing for the general public and make a living, so we went that way."[29] The Andrews Sisters' decision to aim for the popular audience was later reinforced when they hooked up with Lou Levy and Jack Kapp who packaged them for commercial success. Their early Decca records helped popularize swing, and they were frequently advertised as "America's Number One Swing Trio." One writer described their musical style as "jazz-and-water: a somewhat toned-down version of swing that general audiences could enjoy."[30] Another said, "The Andrews Sisters helped carry [swing] from the ballrooms known to jazz aficionados into every living room in the United States."[31]

From the beginning, the Andrews Sisters built their act with Patty singing lead, Maxene singing higher harmony to Patty, and LaVerne singing lower harmony to Maxene. "LaVerne had a beautiful voice," Maxene remembered, "but we decided if it was going to be a trio, we couldn't all sing solos so we made the decision that Patty would do all the solo singing."[32] Patty explained: "By having only one voice, our sound was always consistent and identifiable.... Unlike most vocal groups, we never interchanged parts."[33] And Maxene added, "We were, at our best, one voice."[34]

Maxene elaborated: "When I listen to music, I listen in harmony. That's what I hear. LaVerne did too, and the interesting thing about LaVerne is that she played melody on the piano and sang third-part harmony at the same time. And any musician will tell you that's virtually impossible.... LaVerne's voice was the foundation of the trio. Many times you couldn't pick her voice out, but you felt it there."[35] Maxene claimed that Patty sang lead because she could not sing harmony.

> We purposely set up the act with Patty in the middle because Patty could never sing harmony, and with a harmony group the girl who sang lead had to be in the middle, 'cause that was where the mike was. We never hanged parts, almost from our first year in show business. To us, the lead had to predominate ... so it was decided more and more to give the intros and solos to Patty until it just naturally took its head, and we were satisfied to let Patty do it.[36]

Patty may not have been able to sing harmony, but she sang lead because she had the most expressive and most distinctive voice of the trio, as well as a great stage presence and a natural gift for comedy and dance. An early writer said, "[H]er voice has a polite foghorn texture that is priceless."[37] Patty added, "I've been hoarse like I have a bad cold ever since I was eleven."[38] Patty contributed most to the Andrews Sisters' distinctive sound, and without her, there would have been no Andrews Sisters. Maxene once said, "Patty was a hell of a singer ... had she wanted to go out on her own, I think she would have made a big name for herself."[39] Singer Mel Torme admired the Andrews Sisters greatly, especially Patty, and wrote:

> She stood in the middle of her sisters, planted her feet apart, and belted out

solos as well as singing the lead parts with zest and confidence. Whether doing one of the girls' many novelty hits ... or singing on her own ... Patty exuded an eyes-closed, smile-on-her-face persona that was irresistible. The kind of singing she did cannot be taught; it can't be studied in books, it can't be written down. Long experience as a singer and wide-open ears were her only teachers, and she learned her lessons well.... All in all [the Andrews Sisters were] one of the great acts, with fine three part harmony, clever staging, and, above all, the singing voice of Patty Andrews.[40]

When asked about the Andrews Sisters' style, Maxene once said: "We don't read music.... We'd just get together and work it out. I think our style just developed out of the way our voices sounded together. What came out was strictly a product of the ear and the heart, not the eye."[41] When asked where the Andrews Sisters got their unique sound, Patty once flippantly replied, "From our parents, of course!" While much of their sound was due to the physical qualities of their voices, a great deal of work went into it as well. Although they occasionally denied it, the Andrews Sisters studied voice at various times. Early in their career, after the success of "Bei Mir Bist Du Schoen," they independently strained their voices and thereafter studied breathing techniques for greater volume and projection. Intermittently throughout their career, the sisters studied with noted voice teacher Helen Fouts Cahoon in New York City.[42]

What was the sound the Andrews Sisters created to entertain the public? Their earliest recordings are frequently called imitations of the Boswell Sisters, and from the beginning the Andrews Sisters acknowledged their great debt to the three Boswells. The first known recording of the Andrews Sisters, made in a Providence, Rhode Island, radio station in November 1932, sounds very much like the Boswell Sisters and is almost unrecognizable as the Andrews Sisters. But what was the sound of the Boswells that the Andrews imitated? While most writers simply describe it as "southern," focusing on the fact that the Andrews Sisters copied their southern accents, there was more to it than that. Granted the Boswells were southern, New Orleans in fact, but that sound called "southern" was from African American New Orleans jazz, as the Boswells themselves acknowledged. As all white singers of the era, the black influence on the Andrews Sisters—whether via the Boswell Sisters or African American musicians—was great. Maxene once said: "The Boswells had broken the barrier between semiclassical and New Orleans Jazz for white singers. We imitated them—even their accents." Patty added: "We copied the Boswell Sisters so much ... that we developed southern accents. If you listen to our first record "Bei Mir Bist Du Schoen," we sound like shrimp trawlers."[43] Elsewhere she said, "We copied them so much, you would have thought we were straight from the plantation.... We sound[ed] just like a Yiddish Scarlet O'Hara!"[44]

Those "accents" the sisters imitated were the sounds of African American jazz and blues dressed up for white consumption. The most blatant imitation of black sounds is perhaps the sisters' version of "Shortenin' Bread"—in fact, Patty's solo is an almost embarrassing caricature of black dialect. "Bei Mir Bist Du Schoen," "Nice Work If You Can Get It," "Says My Heart," "Pagan Love Song," "Billy Boy," "Hold Tight," "From the Land of the Sky-Blue Water,"

"Long Time No See," "Begin the Beguine," "Beer Barrel Polka," "The Jump-ing Jive," "Well, All Right"—almost all the hits of the Andrews Sisters' early years reveal a strong black influence either from jazz or swing.

In addition to black phraseology and intonation, the sisters used a lot of scat singing in those early songs—nonsense words and sounds that follow the melody of the band. Although not restricted to black jazz, scat singing is an important ingredient in that tradition. Scat allowed the sisters to use their voices as musical instruments within the big band setting. A good example is "The Jumping Jive," a Cab Calloway song the sisters covered:

> Boy! Oh boy!
> Palomar Shalomar Swanee Shore.
> Let me dig, dig, dig that solid jive some more.
> Boy! Oh boy!
> The Jim Jam Jump is a jumpin' jive
> Makes you get your kicks on the mellow side.
> Hip, hip! (hip, hip, hip, hip) Hip, hip! (hip, hip, hip, hip).
> The Jim Jam Jump is a solid jive
> Makes you nine foot tall when you're four foot five
> Hip, hip! (hip, hip, hip, hip) Hip, hip! (hip, hip, hip, hip).
> Don't be that ickeroo,
> Get hep and follow through
> And get your steady foo
> Make the joint jump like the gators do...

In print, the lyrics of the song seem pure nonsense, but when vocalized by the sisters, they became part of the band sound.

In 1939, a writer for *The Billboard* recognized the influence of black music on the Andrews Sisters and other white singers:

> They [African American musicians] have the happy faculty of being able to add improvisations into any available material. A colored performer rarely sticks to the written note but sings and plays ad lib versions around the melody.... With the advent of swing, the white performer has learned this secret of the colored race and has hurriedly climbed aboard this band wagon with such leading expo-nents as Benny Goodman, Tommy Dorsey, the Andrews Sisters.... These per-formers have learned that expressions can be captured with the voice as well as the face and they insert these expressions that suit their personality and blend with their talents into their recordings.[45]

Indeed, it was by using their voices as instruments within the band that the Andrews Sisters became part of the big band sound. Patty once remembered early influences on her style: "I was listening to Benny Goodman and to all the bands.... I was into that feel, so that would go into my own music ability. I was into swing. I loved the brass section."[46] Maxene said when they were traveling with Ted Mack, "I used to sit on the bandstand and I would listen to the three trumpets, and I would say to my sisters, 'That's the way we should sing, like those three trumpets play.'"[47] Elsewhere she credited LaVerne for the state-ment,[48] and still elsewhere, Patty claimed it. Obviously, it was a consensus. If they couldn't compete with the big bands, they would become part of them. They also survived the big band scene by doing vocal covers of the bands' instrumental hits. Their first successful cover was "Begin the Beguine." Then came "Tuxedo Junction," "Pennsylvania 6-5000," "Daddy," "Elmer's Tune," "Chattanooga Choo-Choo," and others. In some cases, their covers became as popular as the original big band instrumentals.

In fall 1938, the Andrews Sisters published a series of three articles in *Swing* magazine entitled "So You Want to Start a Trio?" in which they gave advice to singers aspiring to become trios. Whether or not the articles were actually written by the sisters, they reflect their views on music. The first article, bylined by Patty, maintained that all members must be committed to the trio and not use it as a stepping stone to individual success, "get trio members, not soloists." She emphasized that intense rehearsal is necessary for success and pointed out that it is necessary to occasionally give up "a few personal pleasures" for the good of the trio. She added that the three voices should blend naturally and always sing with "absolute ease." She advised potential trios to be original and not copy other trios—apparently overlooking their imitation of the Boswell Sisters. Patty noted that it may help if one of the members occasionally acts as a soloist in order to vary the ensemble. Good accompaniment is critical to the success of a trio—Patty thought she and her sisters never sounded better than when they sang with Jimmy Dorsey at the Paramount Theater. She recommended the trio identify with "one tune"—one that nobody else is doing.[49]

The following month's article, bylined by Maxene, described the sisters' rehearsal patterns and arrangements. As in many interviews, they said they rehearsed constantly, never "less than five hours a day." Their rehearsal room contained only a piano, three chairs, and "music galore." "LaVerne, being the piano player, always has a half dozen tunes set aside that she has previously gone over and which she thinks might be suitable." They select the one they find most appealing and work out a "plot," by which they mean "a story or a definite idea" for the song which leads to an arrangement that "must make sense and not sound like a musical jig-saw puzzle, disconnected and liable to distract attention." Maxene emphasized that the song should be commercial, that is, "Know that whatever your trio is singing the audience can readily understand ... and will be able to sing right along with you." She concluded: "One more thing: It is important and essential that the musical background emphasizes the trio and does not take attention away from it. In other words, the thing to do is to enhance the trio, not the band"[50]—perhaps one of the reasons the sisters became unpopular with the boys in the big bands. The third article in the series, called "3 Kinds of Swing," provides less insight into the sisters' approach to music, but offers their views on the difficulties of defining swing.[51]

The Andrews Sisters brought more to popular music than just singing. Maxene often said they were the first trio to move about on stage: "Until we came along, all harmony groups put their heads together to get a blend. We never worried about a blend, and because music was such a part of our lives, we had to move! We were the first harmony group that ever moved on stage."[52] Patty pointed out that in doing so, they "started a whole new style. We felt the rhythm, the music, and we always moved and danced."[53] She later added: "We just kind of put all that stuff together ourselves.... We'd say, 'How about if we all do this when we come to that part?' Since we were performing on stage, we thought there had to be movement."[54] Their lessons from vaudeville were apparent.

And those lessons brought attention. A writer from *The Billboard* noticed early on that the sisters did more than just sing. A column in the magazine called "Possibilities" alerted producers, bookers, and agents to newcomers in the entertainment business. In early October 1938, the column called attention to the Andrews Sisters:

> Andrews Sisters—radio girl trio, among the tops in harmony, especially in swing singing. Team's stage appearances have displayed the girls' ability in that direction. They're not limited to straight mike singing, either. Patty Andrews is an okeh hoofer, while all three can handle dialog, being especially strong on comedy lines. Would be an invaluable asset to a revue; and, because of handling of lines, would also fit handily into a book show. Despite their reputation for singing, they're more than just specialists in song.[55]

The Andrews Sisters' success was not achieved without competition. "Girl" trios, and most commonly sister trios, were standard fare for many of the big bands that dominated the pop music scene of the era. The only sister act that ever offered the Andrews Sisters much competition—albeit never too threatening—during their early career was the King Sisters, a quartette of Mormon sisters from Utah. Their family name was originally Driggs but they adopted the less Dickensian first name of their music teacher father for their stage name. Like the Andrews Sisters, they idolized the Boswell Sisters and were influenced by their musical style. The Kings began as a trio, but became a quartette when one sister left to marry and two more joined the act. After a stint with Horace Heidt in San Francisco, they joined guitarist Alvino Rey and his orchestra. Recordings, radio, and personal appearances helped the King Sisters gather fans as they charted hits such as "The Hut-Hut Song" and "It's Love, Love, Love." They were already familiar names when the Andrews Sisters began to chart hit records.[56]

A survey of *Variety* for 1938 revealed fifty-three different female singing groups working the New York area, most of them sister trio acts. Among them were a trio that billed itself as "over 600 pounds of music," a Chinese quartet that combined acrobats with their songs, a white trio that performed in black face, several African American trios, a singing skating trio, and a duo of singing tap dancers, also called the Andrews Sisters. These were exceptions, however; most trios were pretty, petite, sweet, melodious, Anglo-Saxon, soft and feminine. This was not the Andrews Sisters. They were tall, homely, Greek-Norwegian, loud, and raucous. An early reviewer said they sang "like Chinese puzzles set to off-key music." Fred Waring told them their voices were "too husky" for his orchestra.[57] *Newsweek* once described their act as "a combination of cheerleading and jive stepping [that] sounds like a group of banshees wailing in the closest possible harmony."[58] Their earliest film appearance in *Argentine Nights* captured the raucous, aggressive, almost klutzy exuberance of their early act that led an observer to say they had more enthusiasm than talent.

And yet, it was precisely this boundless energy and enthusiasm that set them apart from other "girl" trios and brought them their great success: as they moved all over the stage, they brought a fresh, new approach to popular music that America loved. They became the personification of swing and their voice became part of musical Americana.

After concluding their contract with Wrigley, the Andrews Sisters were back on the East Coast for a tour of movie theaters. In the middle of June, they opened at the Paramount Theater in New York with Jimmy Dorsey and his orchestra, their first date on Broadway and a realization of an early dream.

The Paramount, the Roxy, and the Palace were the premiere theaters of New York City, and heading the bill at any of them was a sure indicator of success. The sisters shared the bill at the Paramount with *Professor Beware*, a Harold Lloyd film. Also appearing on the bill was Rufe Davis, their old friend from the Larry Rich days.[59] *The Billboard*'s reviewer wrote: "The Andrews Sisters and Davis do so well that the Dorsey band is overshadowed somewhat.... The Andrews Sisters, three brunets [Patty was not yet blond] in lovely white gowns trimmed with blue ribbons, socked across their harmony singing. Their warbling ... is vivacious, swinging and ear-catchy. The patrons loved them and just wouldn't let them go."[60] The sisters literally stopped the show. The feature film that followed their act was halted because the audience would not stop applauding the Andrews Sisters. The stage lights were turned up and the sisters sang another encore before the audience quieted down.[61] Their one-week engagement was extended to two, and a return engagement was booked for December at $2000, twice their original salary.

After the Paramount, the sisters headlined the Capitol Theater in Washington, D.C., where a reviewer wrote: "They're generous with their clever swing arrangements of ditties of today and yesterday and it is nice indeed to have them here."[62] Next stop on the tour was the Stanley Theater in Pittsburgh where Bunny Berigan and his orchestra backed them. *The Billboard* liked their show and noted: "The Andrews Sisters are theater from the soles up. Despite their incessant machine-gun rhythm, they held youngsters and old folks alike."[63] A local reviewer was even more enthusiastic:

> If we must have that swing music, I want the Andrews Sisters to supply my share. Here's a trio that really harmonizes beautifully and makes even those infernal inane ditties sound almost bearable. The girls steal first honor in the stage presentation with some of the best harmony work we have heard in a long time. They're newcomers in the theater circuits and overnight sensations of the airwaves but I've an idea they'll be popular when the swing craze is ancient history.[64]

A few weeks later, the Andrews Sisters headed a new vaudeville program at the Brooklyn Strand Theater and the attendance soared to record highs. A reviewer wrote: "That the [jitterbugs] were there was clearly evident when the Andrews Sisters unlimbered their rhythm harmony in the closing slot. Talented trio had a rough time getting off, when caught, even after five tunes."[65] Their busy schedule impressed *Variety* enough to note that after concluding their September engagement at the Brooklyn Strand, the sisters flew to Cleveland for an opening the following day at the Palace Theater.[66] Such movement is nothing today, but given the novelty and state of air travel in the late 1930s, it was newsworthy.

In October, the sisters were back home in Minneapolis where they played the Orpheum Theater with Jimmy Dorsey and his orchestra for the biggest box office-take of the season.[67] This was their first hometown performance since they hit the big time. A local reviewer noticed the southern drawls the sisters acquired in their imitation of the Boswells: "First of all, there's the Andrews sisters, who, we are informed, are Minneapolis girls, despite a practiced southern accent. These gals are good in their field and we think Dorsey is right when he says they're tops today. Patty—the one in the center—is the dynamo of the three."[68] In early November, "Pansy, the comic horse" shared the Andrews Sisters' bill at Akron's Palace Theater where they all received rave reviews.[69] The next week they and Dorsey were together again at the Earle Theater in Philadelphia where a reporter noted: "Andrews Sisters are back at the Earle for the second time in four months, highly unusual, but fully merit the encore. Nicely dressed, lookers warble swing stuff to perfection and exhibit considerable showmanship."[70] In mid–December, the sisters' busy schedule caught up with them, at least with Patty. After two nights of a four-week engagement at the Glass Hat Lounge in New York with Joe Venuti and his orchestra, Patty came down with laryngitis and the trio canceled the booking, after receiving good reviews.[71]

The Andrews Sisters wrapped up 1938 back at the Paramount Theater in New York with Glen Gray's Casa Loma Band where they received a subdued review in *Variety*: "Andrews Sisters ... are back for their second Paramount stage date in about six months. Trio offer the usual group of three numbers ... then encore with a fair swing version of 'Old Man River.'"[72] *The Billboard*'s reviewer was more enthusiastic about their performance and wrote, "their four numbers were hardly enough to satisfy either the audience or this listener."[73]

Down Beat's December 1938 issue published its readers' choices for top musicians of the year. In the category "Trio and Quartet," the Andrews Sisters scored number four out of thirty groups listed. The three above them were all instrumental groups.[74] The sisters were giving the boys in the bands a run for their money.

The Andrews Sisters recorded twenty-one songs in 1938. After the success of "Bei Mir Bist Du Schoen," its flip side, "Nice Work If You Can Get It," hit the charts for three weeks. "Joseph! Joseph!," another Yiddish song, was their next recording. If the public wanted Yiddish songs, the Andrews Sisters and Decca would provide them. The flip side was a Latin number called "Ti-Pi-Tin." Both hit the charts, "Joseph! Joseph!" for one week and "Ti-Pi-Tin" for four weeks. Other chart makers for the year included "Says My Heart," (five weeks), "Tu-Li-Tulip Time" (four weeks), "Lullaby to a Jitterbug" (three weeks), "Shortenin' Bread" (two weeks) and "Sha-Sha" (one week).[75] Within a six-month period in 1938, Decca sold over 250,000 Andrews Sisters records,[76] a phenomenal number in those years. The sales not only established the Andrews Sisters as a major new name in popular music, but also helped establish Decca Records as a major record company.

In late January 1939, the sisters were back at the Paramount, but this time in Newark, New Jersey. The good reviews continued: "Andrews Sisters deliver … in a manner only associated with this trio. Their voices are perfectly pitched for each other and they make any song stand out. Radio and disc prestige gave 'em an ovation on entrance."[77]

Following the Paramount engagement, the Andrews Sisters joined *Honolulu Bound*, an updated half-hour, weekly version of the old *Phil Baker Show* on CBS in New York. Baker's comedy-variety show, a radio staple since 1933, was reworked in a Hawaii format for the new sponsor Dole Pineapple and featured new cast members with announcer Harry Von Zell. *The Billboard*'s reviewer was impressed by the Andrews Sisters but not much else: "It had its spots, such as an announcer burlesque by Baker and the Andrews Sisters' top harmonizing, but not much else…. Andrews' handling of *Begin the Beguine* was jim dandy…. The Andrews Sisters who have been going places, arrived and held their own in fast company, with their unique swinging style…. The swingsterettes issue a gilt edge policy on the musical end."[78] The sisters joined the show in January and left the following October.

While doing the weekly radio show in New York, the sisters continued personal appearances at theaters and clubs. In mid–February, they joined a four-week vaudeville review at the Casa Manana nightclub in New York that included comedians, dancers, jugglers, acrobats, and the Ozzie Nelson band with vocalist Harriet Hilliard. Nelson and Hilliard would later achieve television fame with their two sons as the perfect family of the 1950s. Regarding the Andrews Sisters' performance, *The Billboard* wrote: "Their lively attention-getting delivery of swing arrangements of these tunes socked them over solidly."[79] In March, the sisters helped Jimmy Dorsey celebrate his fifteenth anniversary as a professional musician at the New Yorker Hotel. The Andrews cut the cake at the party, which was attended by such musical luminaries as Guy Lombardo, Glen Gray, Johnny Mercer, Mildred Bailey, and Helen O'Connell.[80] Later that month, the sisters were at the Flatbush Theater in Brooklyn where a reviewer noted: "Andrews Sisters, hit of the show and draught at the b.o. [box office], are doing a flock of numbers for show-stopping results. All in white, the trio run through three pops, then do an arrangement of 'Ole Man River' and 'Bei Mir Bist.'"[81]

When fans went to see the Andrews Sisters, their evening out was more than simply a performance by the sisters. The great movie palaces of the 1920s and 1930s were in their heyday, and most of the theaters that hosted the sisters' shows were visual feasts. These architectural wonders incorporated bits and pieces of décor and color from around the world and throughout time to provide patrons an escape into a world of fantasy. The street façade of the theater distinguished it from the mundane commercial structures that neighbored it. A brilliantly lighted marquee announced the current film, but the featured live entertainment frequently received greater prominence than the film title. Lines often stretched for blocks braving rain, snow, and heat to see their favorite swing trio. Once inside the theater, the lobby offered hints of the surprises within. Often an elaborate staircase or a long hall led to the majestic interior

In spring 1939, the Andrews Sisters joined *Honolulu Bound*, a radio variety show broadcast from New York City. Here they are pictured with Lyn Murray, orchestra director of the show. While doing the weekly show, they sang engagements in the New York area with Murray's orchestra. (Author's collection)

that seated perhaps 5,000 patrons and transported them into a fantasy world of Arabian nights, Oriental splendor, Greek grandeur, or European pageantry.

The program began with a number by the orchestra, which was often one of the major big bands of the country such as Glenn Miller, Jimmy Dorsey, Harry James, Joe Venuti, or Woody Herman. If the audience was youthful, as it always was with the Andrews Sisters, the band numbers brought dancing in the aisles by some of the more exuberant "jitterbugs" as the young devotees of swing were called. By the late 1930s, the jitterbugs were not considered the threat to youthful morals they were a few years earlier when some states, such as Iowa, prohibited their dancing in ballrooms while colleges, such as Brooklyn College, banned jitterbugs because they detracted from "real swing music."[82] Theaters initially welcomed them to their shows and sponsored jitterbug contests on stage. Many, however, became disillusioned with them when they stayed through four or five shows and occasionally trashed the theaters. During the band numbers, a "boy singer" or "girl singer" sometimes vocalized, but for the most part it was an instrumental prelude to the show. A dancer, or perhaps a team of them, might follow with instrumental backing from the band. Next a comedian, possibly headlining his own show in a few years, introduced laughs to the house. The Andrews Sisters, as the featured act, were reserved for the final spot. Their announcement brought pounding applause from the youthful audience as the swelling sounds of the band ushered them on stage. With the sisters' opening number, the "gators," or jitterbugs, filled the aisles once again as the sisters fed them their "gator meat" and remained there until the sisters' final number closed the show. The entire show was less than an hour, and as the applause quieted and dancers returned to their seats, the film portion of the program began. Newsreels, previews, cartoons, and short subjects preceded the main feature. A popular act like the Andrews Sisters pulled in the audiences, so the management often ran a run-of-the-mill film. Popular films with big name stars featured lesser-known live entertainers since the films had enough drawing power to attract an audience. An intermission followed the film and the theater emptied for the next show. Some enthusiastic patrons remained to see the show again. Five or six live shows were presented each day, starting as early as 9 A.M. and sometimes ending after midnight.

The programs were a delight to audiences, but they were grueling for the Andrews Sisters and their peers. Occasionally, they had a day off, but for the most part their days and nights were crammed with performances that left little time for anything except waiting for the next show. The sisters sometimes slipped out for lunch between shows. One fan spotted them at a lunch counter near the Chicago Theater with their hair in rollers devouring sandwiches between shows. Another was surprised to see them rushing into a back theater entrance in Baltimore as she hurried for a place in line at the Hippodrome where they were performing. Several times, Maxene mentioned the boredom of waiting between performances, occasionally interrupted by playing cards[83] or Patty's comic antics.[84] After a week or two of such demanding days and nights, the sisters moved on to the next city for a repeat of the same schedule.

In April 1939, the Andrews Sisters captured the number eight slot (out of thirty-seven) in *The Billboard*'s survey of favorite female singers on U. S. campuses as chosen by college editors.[85] A photograph of the Andrews Sisters appeared on the June 10 cover of *The Billboard*, the same magazine that in 1934 described their singing as "Chinese puzzles set to off-key music." The short piece accompanying the picture outlined their rise to fame and claimed they were "at the top of the entertainment heap." LaVerne's quiet smile and the broad grins of Maxene and Patty seem to say: "We always knew we could do it."

The sisters returned to New York's Paramount for their third date in early July 1939 with the Gene Krupa band, one of the top bands in the country. The by-now predictable rave reviews continued:

> With Krupa, the rhythmic Andrews Sisters are socko. The femme trio has cat-apulted to fame in short order, chiefly via their Decca disks…. They almost had to do the entire book before begging off, and only eased out via a rhythmic scat piece of business paced by Patty Andrews. The gals are becomingly costumed in blue-red contrast and are palpably a draw here, judging by the entrance salvo.[86]

The sisters boosted the Paramount box office to one of the best of the year.[87]

Shortly after their Paramount engagement, they joined Lyn Murray and his band for one-night engagements and college dates. Several name bands were reportedly interested in tying up with them, but they chose Murray because of their successful association on the *Honolulu Bound* radio show. They continued, however, to perform with other bands for their major theater engagements.[88]

In July, the National Swing Club of America held a big jazz jamboree at the Hippodrome in New York City. The Andrews Sisters were presented a trophy award and a silver disc record in recognition of their "combined contribution to American jazz."[89] This is the closest the sisters would ever be to the jazz community.

On August 12, they appeared with Lou Breese's band at Caleron's Pier Ballroom in Jamestown, New York, to 1,900 people, breaking an attendance record set by Louis Armstrong a few weeks earlier.[90] In late September, they were back in the vaudeville review at the Brandt Theatre in Brooklyn: "For the marquee draw as well as a stage sock, the Andrews femmes also are what the doctor ordered."[91] Late October found the sisters at the Baltimore Hippodrome with Woody Herman and his orchestra: "Closing spot is reserved for the Andrews Sisters and they obligingly provide a socko finish, their performance here adding to their already high rating as one of the top sister teams."[92] A few days later, they sang with Bob Crosby and his band in Scranton, Pennsylvania, at the annual firemen's ball where the proceeds went to a widows and orphans fund.[93] They moved on with Woody Herman to the State Theater in Hartford where a reviewer reported: "Next on are the Andrews Sisters, who are the top applause-getters. Harmony trio sing three numbers, encore with two others and have to beg off."[94] The Colonial Theater in Dayton hosted them next with the Mal Hallett band: "The Andrews Sisters, with the blond Patty in constant animation, deliver good and plenty."[95] Patty had become the blond she would remain the rest of her life. Following a performance at the Shubert Theater in Cincinnati, a reviewer reported: "Andrews Sisters turn in an excellent account of themselves…. They're artists from the word go, both vocally and in showmanship."[96]

The sisters were increasingly featured with the major big bands. The addition of the sisters to the big bands in the theater circuit was a surefire draw that brought big bucks to the theater coffers. The marriage was happier for the impresarios, however, than it was for the big bands. Although "boy" and "girl" vocalists were now part of the personnel of most big bands, the bands would have preferred going it alone. With few exceptions, most of the bands disliked playing background accompaniment to three sisters whose singing they didn't much care for. The Andrews Sisters invariably appeared last on the program— the choice spot—and closed the show with thunderous applause and encores. Like it or not, many of the major bands took back seat to the sisters.

One of the earliest feature stories about the Andrews Sisters offered a glimpse of their personal lives in fall 1939 when they were living in New York— or at least the glimpse they wanted the public to see:

> Papa and Mamma now head the household in New York. They have a big old-fashioned apartment on the Upper West Side which is constantly filled with visiting cousins and girl friends from the Middle West.
>
> "We sleep three in a bed but the meals are swell," says Maxene...
>
> Meanwhile they are unmarried and extremely fond of the shag [a current dance]. Maxene is the businesswoman of the trio, paying the bills, keeping the books and looking at contracts with a keen eye. She is also the bounciest of the gang, snapping her gum so loudly at radio rehearsals as to blast the sound engineers out of the booth. All Patty cares about are singing and dancing, being so good at the latter that she could go into a show as a hoofer. She would rehearse her singing ten hours a day if her mother didn't come in and threaten her with a dish mop.
>
> So now Broadway belongs to them. Patty and Maxene are addicted to mannish-looking suits and bandannas; LaVerne is more on the fluffy side. When they aren't riding in their new car, they're bouncing through the streets around Times Square, going to rehearsal, coming from rehearsal, meeting people, signing contracts. People yell at them from all sides and they answer in the same spirit.[97]

In early September 1939, the Andrews Sisters made their first recording with Bing Crosby, Decca's top moneymaker and the most popular singer in the nation. The sisters, like much of America, had been fans of Crosby for many years, and recording with him was a validation of their success. Maxene remembered that first session:

> Jack Kapp called us into his office and he said, "I have a favor to ask." He said, "How would you girls like to record with Bing Crosby?" That was the favor he wanted from us ... and that was like saying to us, "How would you like to meet God?" So we walked out of there on Cloud Nine. That was another tremendous thrill. I'll never forget, I kept worrying about how I was going to react when I came face to face with Bing Crosby.
>
> What do you do when you come face to face with someone like that? And as I remember, I was afraid to look at him. On that first date, it was Joe Venuti's orchestra—wild Joe, I loved—and we got the date over, and I had heard Bing really wasn't keen about working with us—he loved the Boswell Sisters, but he wasn't too keen—see, we had a very driving style and he was really—well, they didn't use the expression in those days, but he was really laid back, a laid-back singer. We did one side called "Yodelin Jive" and the other was "Ciribiribin," and that was our first gold record. That was the first million seller, and after that Bing said, "Anything the Andrews Sisters want to record, it's all right with me." He never turned down anything that we would suggest.[98]

Patty disagreed with Maxene and claimed, "The rhythmic drive is what he loved about us."[99] She also remembered their first session with Crosby: "I was so nervous I didn't think I'd be able to sing. He was on one side of the mike and we were on the other, facing him. But I knew that if I looked at him I wouldn't be able to open my mouth.... He never did snap his fingers when he sang. He had a thing with his foot. He would move it right-to-left, right-to-left and so on—just like a metronome."[100] Elsewhere Maxene said: "That first session with him, he must have thought we were the three dunces. We just stood there looking at him with our mouths open."[101]

The two songs from the session, "Ciribiribin" and "Yodelin' Jive," were arranged by Vic Schoen and backed by jazz violinist Joe Venuti and his orchestra. Both songs were hits, but not million sellers as Maxene claimed. "Yodelin' Jive" was on the charts twelve weeks while "Ciribiribin" charted for three, and was later recorded by Harry James to become his theme song. The songs stand out from the many later songs the sisters would record with Crosby. Their parts are less integrated with that of Crosby who almost sounds uncomfortable singing with the sisters, especially in "Ciribiribin" where the Andrews' sound comes across like bees attacking Crosby's baritone. In "Yodelin' Jive" Crosby mostly yodels while the sisters sing the song. To my ear, the sisters carry both songs and Crosby seems along for the ride. The recording was favorably reviewed in *The Billboard*'s "Record Buying Guide" for jukebox operators:

> *Yodelin' Jive.* It's a pretty even toss-up, according to reports sent in to this department this week, between this side and the reverse since they were both recorded by Bing Crosby and the Andrews Sisters, a prize combination in any man's phonograph. Mating Crosby and the singing sisters on one disk was an inspirational thought, and it's already bearing fruit in bigger and bigger returns to ops from this record. Take your choice of sides; one is as good and as potent as the other.[102]

Metronome also predicted the record would be a big seller and added: "Bing, of course, steals the show on both, with Joe Venuti doing some neat fiddling."[103] *Down Beat* liked the recording too and concluded: "Quite a combination of stars, and well worth hearing as a novelty."[104] In a discussion of the best recordings of 1939, *Metronome* noted: "Bing Crosby— *Yodelin Jive*: One of the cheeriest records of the age, with the Andrews Sisters as additional rays."[105]

Maxene claimed Crosby was content to leave decisions regarding their future songs and arrangements to the sisters and Vic Schoen, albeit with his final approval. Although they eventually recorded many successful songs with Bing Crosby, it would be four years before they again sang with him, apparently because he was on the West Coast most of the time while the sisters were working the East Coast.

After an early December engagement at the Buffalo Theater, the Andrews Sisters were back in Chicago, their old headquarters during the bleak years before they hit the big time. They appeared on a bill at the Chicago Theater with Harry James and his orchestra and a new "boy" singer named Frank Sinatra who was beginning to make waves in the music business. A good review with some critical pointers resulted from their opening show:

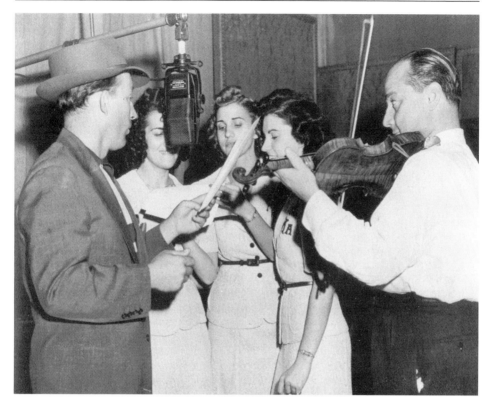

On September 20, 1939, the Andrews Sisters made their first Decca recording with Bing Crosby, "Ciribiribin" and "Yodelin' Jive." Backed by jazz violinist Joe Venuti, both sides made the charts. The sisters' collaboration with Crosby marked the beginning of one of the most successful combinations in recording history. (Robert Boyer Collection)

> [T]he Andrews Sisters finally are working at this theater, and at show caught scored a dynamite click. This smash scoring, however, almost hurt 'em at the last show Friday, when they stayed on and on, though in actual response to heartening applause. Should have scrammed while the mob out front still wanted more.... However, they warble solidly, working hard and earnestly. Slammed home four songs for their regular turn when reviewed, and then came back for two encores, winding up with the middle sister almost tiring the audience with some Suzi-Q business. That wardrobe also is not headline stuff.[106]

The Billboard's reviewer was more impressed by their show: "[T]he three rhythm gals with swing in their voices had little trouble stopping the show.... They take scientific pains in the delivery of each tune and the result is unusually wholesome."[107]

The Andrews Sisters ended 1939 with a new radio show with Glenn Miller and his orchestra called *Moonlight Serenade*, sponsored by Chesterfield cigarettes and named after one of Miller's hit records. Miller was beginning to gather a following, but he was still relatively unknown to much of America. To insure an audience for the program, the popular Andrews Sisters were hired on a thirteen-week contract for the fifteen-minute show that aired at 10 P.M. in New York on Tuesday, Wednesday, and Thursday. The first show, thirty minutes long, aired December 27 to a favorable review in *The Billboard*:

> Miller shares the show with the Andrews Sisters, who are on for the first 13 weeks only and who leave for theater work after that. Their first program was a jitterbug's delight, with Miller playing his standard clicks, such as "Little Brown Jug," "In the Mood" and "Londonderry Air," among others. Andrews did the song that made them, "Bei Mir Bist Du Schoen," and "Ciribiribin," and as always they socked....[108]

Fifteen minutes (twelve minutes after commercials) was a short time for so much musical talent. Typically, the Andrews Sisters sang one song, a band soloist sang another, and the band played an instrumental piece. The show was successful and shortly after its beginning, Glenn Miller's popularity soared. However, tensions began to develop on the show. Larry Bruff, the program director, recalled:

> Although scripts were cut to the minimum, with most song introductions made over music, it was a struggle for Glenn. The Andrews Sisters resisted making even minimal cuts in their numbers, insisting they be performed exactly as recorded. So, all the give fell on Glenn's shoulders. In truth, we had too much talent to showcase properly in twelve minutes each night and friction mounted. To add to the problem, the sisters were battling each other. After a few weeks the girls weren't even talking to each other—they'd gotten into a fight or something—and so we were having a helluva time trying to figure out what they wanted to sing.[109]

The tension of the show reached a point where something had to give, and Bruff claimed it was eventually agreed the Andrews Sisters' contract would not be renewed. Maxene claimed their original contract was for only thirteen weeks and they left the show, as planned, to fill engagements contracted before the show began,[110] a claim also supported by *The Billboard* review above.

In later years Maxene remembered their time with Miller:

> We did 13 weeks with Glenn, and it was interesting. We had tremendous respect for the man's ability but we did not find him a very friendly person to work with. Maybe that's unfair because of our limited [experience with him]. I'll tell you one thing: When that man got on the podium, it didn't matter if he liked your music or didn't like it, it was played right, and all the musicians that worked for him had tremendous respect. You know, musicians are like little kids, and they get up there and they jazz around and they tell jokes and they laugh, and if somebody doesn't control them, you know, they'll carry it right on through a program or whatever. But the minute Glenn came on, he didn't even have to tap his stick—silence.[111]

Maxene told another reporter: "I loved working with Glenn. He didn't dig our kind of music, but he was such a perfectionist when they played his music.... He wouldn't allow anyone to walk on that stage smoking anything but a Chesterfield."[112] Elsewhere, she added: "[D]uring those weeks we came to know Glenn as a thorough professional, a quiet man who went to extremes to make sure his band performed to its maximum potential and that every member of

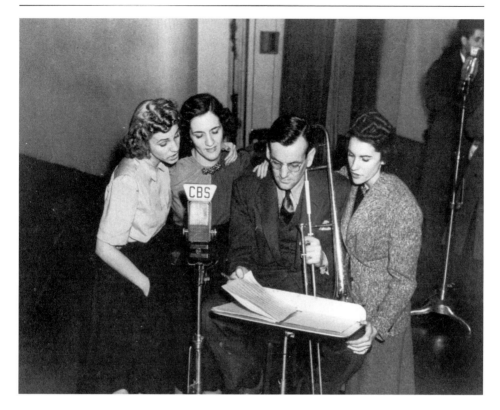

At the end of December 1939, the Andrews Sisters joined Glenn Miller's *Moon-light Serenade* radio show for thirteen weeks in New York City on CBS. The sisters' close harmony singing and Miller's big band music were among the sounds that defined the era. (Author's collection)

it conducted himself in a one hundred percent professional manner."[113] Maxene told another reporter that Miller always treated her and her sisters with respect and never demanded anything from them "except perfection" in their performances.[114] Patty added: "The one thing I remember about Glenn Miller is that he didn't like Dixieland music and that everything we sang was too beat. But we did the Chesterfield Program with him and we also worked the Paramount Theater with him a couple of times. He was a very fine musician."[115]

Glenn Miller may not have been overly fond of the Andrews Sisters' style, but they made some great music together, as illustrated by a recent CD that featured selections from the *Moonlight Serenade* radio program. Miller's big band sound and the Andrews' close harmony would soon become synonymous with the 1940s.

During 1939, the Andrews Sisters recorded fourteen songs. Eight hit the charts, four of which made the top ten, namely "Well All Right" (fifteen weeks), "Hold Tight, Hold Tight" (eleven weeks), "Beer Barrel Polka" (seven weeks), and "Yodelin' Jive" with Bing Crosby (twelve weeks).[116]

"Hold Tight, Hold Tight" and "Beer Barrel Polka" were the sisters' first encounters with the blue nosed watchdogs of the day. Popular columnist Walter Winchell prudishly reported that "Hold Tight, Hold Tight" contained suggestive, off-colored lyrics. Apparently, the refrain "Want some seafood, mama?" was the offensive phrase. At the height of the song's popularity, "Want some seafood, mama?" was adopted by the Fishery Council of New York and the Mid-Atlantic States as its advertising theme. Shortly thereafter, however, NBC and other local stations banned the original song and substituted innocuous words for the offensive phrase. *Swing* magazine reported NBC "banned the song because the lyrics were believed to be 'suggestive Harlemese.'"[117] The story claimed at least a half-dozen people (including Patty Andrews) contributed to the lyrics of "Hold Tight" and whatever obscenity the song had was accidental and in the imagination of the listener.[118] Maxene remembered the fuss: "So, it was banned from the airwaves, which increased the sale of the records because people wanted to know what was terrible in the song. Of course, to us there was nothing bad in the song, but Winchell did that with a lot of artists."[119] A man who remembered the controversy from his teenage years told me that he and his young peers thought the song was about cunnilingus. Needless to say, the controversy contributed greatly to the record's sales. It became the sisters' second major hit after "Bei Mir Bist Du Schoen."

"Beer Barrel Polka," also known as "Roll Out the Barrel," is perhaps the sisters' best-known song from this period, but they recorded it reluctantly. Maxene remembered:

> See, we grew up in the Midwest, so when we heard "Beer Barrel Polka," we said, "My God, we're not gonna sing a polka." ...That's all we heard when we were kids. We kept saying, "Oh, we don't think we're gonna do it," and we kept putting it off and putting it off.... Finally, one day Jack [Kapp] put it to us.... He called up, and he said, "I guess you don't want to record anymore," and I said to him, "What gives you that idea?" He said, "Well, you don't want to do 'Beer Barrel Polka.'" I said, "Jack Kapp, we're going to do 'Beer Barrel Polka' immediately," which we did.[120]

Vic Schoen didn't like the song either: "I hated 'Beer Barrel Polka' and arranged it as badly as I could, but it turned out to be their biggest hit. So I gave up trying to do anything musically worthwhile."[121] Given the many successful songs he subsequently scored for the trio, his last statement is questionable.

Variety announced in early August that "Beer Barrel Polka" was on its way to establishing "an eight-year high for the sale of a freak [novelty] tune" and exceeded the sales of "Bei Mir Bist Du Schoen." At that time, the Andrews' version had hit 200,000, second only to an RCA arrangement. The story further noted that the word "beer" was deleted by NBC when announcing the song, conforming to its policy against promoting alcohol on the air. They allowed the original lyrics on the air, however.[122] Prohibition sentiments were still strong and references to alcohol were taboo on the major networks. Some listeners rejected the song because they thought it was German (it was Czech) and wanted nothing to do with music from Nazi Germany.[123] *The Billboard* reported that some establishments grew so tired of hearing the song they removed it from their jukeboxes: "[T]he disc is out of nearly all spots in the Cleveland territory, due to pressure from locations, who were turning off the machines rather than hear it again. Spots practically demanded the removal of either the record or the machine, preferring a rest from the 'Barrel' to income from the boxes."[124]

The flip side of "Beer Barrel Polka" became a hit too: "Well, All Right!" made the charts for eleven weeks and was the first song published by Leeds Music, a new music publishing firm established by the Andrews Sisters' manager Lou Levy that would become one of America's major music publishing companies. Other chart makers of the year were "Chico's Love Song" (five weeks), "Ciribiribin" with Bing Crosby (three weeks), "Pross-Tchai" (one week), and "You Don't Know How Much You Can Suffer" (one week).[125]

CHAPTER FIVE

1940–1941

When our parents were alive, they traveled with us all over the country—and when the show was over, we were Papa's and Mamma's girls at home. No dating in high school, no parties or proms.[1]

—Maxene Andrews

The tension among the Andrews Sisters noted on the Glenn Miller show was the tip of a very threatening iceberg. Major problems were fermenting in the Andrews family.

Following the sisters' tour with Larry Rich, Olga Andrews joined her daughters in New York, and after settling his business affairs in Minneapolis, Peter Andrews joined his family a year later. From then on, the sisters were chaperoned by their parents wherever they went. In several interviews, Maxene remembered their overprotective parents:

> After that first year [with Larry Rich], our parents traveled with us.... On stage we were the Andrews Sisters. At home we were just the kids. Mama wanted to be sure success never went to our heads.[2] ... Although we played a lot of dives, we were extremely naïve about everything that was going on. We were raised very, very strictly. We weren't allowed to go out with boys.[3] ... Our Norwegian mother was very discouraging about boyfriends. If a boyfriend wanted to take one girl out, he had to take us all.[4] ... I don't know how any of the guys ever put up with us. If the guys were going to take us out on a date, there was Mama and Papa and LaVerne and Patty and Maxene and whoever the boy friends were. This was the whole routine. You can see how glued we were. There had to be a breaking point.[5]

That breaking point came on January 28, 1940.

When the Andrews Sisters joined the Glenn Miller show, LaVerne was twenty-eight years old, Maxene was twenty-four, and Patty was about to turn twenty-two. The top singing group in the country and among the most popular of all singers, they had charted hit records, starred on major radio shows, dominated the juke boxes, and were about to embark on a movie career. But they still lived with their parents in a suite at the Piccadilly Hotel on West 45th Street in New York and were chaperoned by them wherever they went. A writer claimed, "The girls were not allowed to go out at night unless the parents had a full report of what they planned to do, with whom they were going out, and what time they planned to return."[6] Their boyfriends had to meet the approval of their parents, and most of them did not. Maxene claimed none of the sisters was allowed to date without the accompaniment of the other sisters and their parents. Little is known about the love life of the Andrews Sisters during these years—perhaps because they had none. All I discovered was an item in *Metronome* for May 1939 that reported, "Maxene Andrews is deserting her musician boy friends for Ezra Stone, popular Broadway star"[7] and a mention of LaVerne's boyfriend in Minneapolis.[8] The Andrews Sisters were earning several thousand dollars a week, but Maxene told an interviewer "the checks were going to Mama"[9] and they were receiving five dollars a week for spending money.[10] Parental approval was necessary for any major expenditure.[11]

Maxene believed her father's controlling nature was partly explained by his Greek ancestry: "My mother was so proud to be an American, and so was my dad, that everything had to be American. But I think when it came to another part of my dad, he reverted back to the way the Greeks thought: You don't let go of your daughters until they're 40 or 50 years old, then you have to bring the boy home so they can meet him, or else they arrange [the marriage]." [12] An anthropologist's discussion of traditional Greek views of marriage sheds light on Peter's behavior—if not Olga's: "Free choice in mate selection with its stress upon personal interaction and romantic love was viewed as deleterious to the solidarity of the [Greek] family; it would have meant a diminishing control over the individual, particularly the female, and a weakening of the obligatory bonds that held the family together."[13] The anthropologist could have been writing about Peter Andrews.

Maxene and Patty wanted no part of Greek tradition and were ready for some different rules. At the time, Patty was dating the sisters' musical director Vic Schoen, and Maxene was dating their manager Lou Levy. Peter, Olga, and LaVerne did not think the sisters should mix business and romance. According to one story, when Patty and Maxene began dating Schoen and Levy, their parents became fearful that marriage would follow and terminate the sisters' act. Consequently, they forbade them to see their boyfriends. To get around their parents' interference, Maxene and Patty left the apartment together, parted to meet their respective dates, and then met again at a prearranged place to return home together.[14] The parents learned of the subterfuge, an argument ensued, and Patty and Maxene moved out of the family apartment Sunday night, January 28, 1940. Two days later, the police received a call reporting a loud quarrel in the apartment during which someone threatened to use a gun. When police investigated, they discovered Peter Andrews had a .38 revolver for which he had no permit. Peter acknowledged the family squabble but claimed he had no intention of using the gun. He said he had owned the gun for fifteen years and didn't realize he needed a permit.[15] He was arrested and taken to jail. Later that night Olga bailed him out, and the next day stories of the incident appeared in several New York newspapers, including one in the *Daily Mirror* in which Patty minimized the incident by claiming their father did not object to the sisters dating Levy and Schoen "because we aren't in love."[16]

Another version of the incident claimed that friends of the sisters were fearful Peter "might cause trouble" the night of the scheduled Tuesday night *Moonlight Serenade* broadcast and arranged for a police guard at the CBS studio. When the police heard someone mention "pa's gun," they went to the Andrews apartment and found a revolver in a shoebox under a dresser.[17] It is difficult to sort out what actually happened. Perhaps the best summary is from Vic Schoen who told the New York *Daily News* at the time: "You know how parents are. They think their daughters are still just kids. They felt that the girls shouldn't mix business with love affairs. I suppose they've forgotten that they had to run away from their parents to get married when they were young."[18]

Several dynamics were obviously at play. Maxene and Patty increasingly resented the restrictions of their parents. Olga and Peter told *Down Beat* that when the sisters' career took off after "Bei Mir Bist Du Schoen," they promised they would not marry or "get serious" with boyfriends for five years.[19] Perhaps the parents were concerned the sisters' marriages would terminate their act— as had happened with their early idols, the Boswell Sisters. Obviously, Peter Andrews had long ago given up his disapproval of his daughters' show business career in the face of their success. Indeed, the sisters had supported him and Olga the previous seven years. Maxene offered insights:

> I was the rebellious one ... I said to [my father], "You're not gonna pick out the man for me to marry," and so consequently my dad and I didn't see eye to eye on many things.... I think the story itself was blown so much out of what it really was. The gun had nothing to do with it, and I never knew who reported. The whole thing was, my dad slapped me. He'd never slapped me before, but when he slapped me for no good reason, I think that I just had made up my mind I wasn't gonna take it anymore. That started the whole ruckus.
>
> I knew my dad had a gun. We all knew he had a gun, because he used to drive us from place to place and always have it in the glove compartment.... And then I found out it was Patty who told Lou [Levy] or somebody that my dad had a gun, and they were the ones that called the police. Somebody [called], and then they came up to the apartment and wanted the gun—from what I understand, because after that I never went back and lived with my folks.[20]

Comments by Lou Levy some fifty-five years later suggest that Peter Andrews pulled the gun on him because of Maxene's intent to marry him. Peter apparently opposed the marriage partly because Levy was a Jew. Levy's rambling narrative hints at several dimensions to the situation:

The Andrews Sisters (from left: Maxene, Patty and LaVerne) with their mother Olga Sollie Andrews, circa 1940. The sisters were extremely close to their mother, whom they often credited with launching their career. Olga Andrews, known as "Ollie" to her friends and family, wore very thick glasses and was probably legally blind. She always removed the glasses, however, for photographers. (Robert Boyer Collection)

You mean the whole big story when I was going to marry Maxene and he chased me with a gun? It's goddamned true, but they made it sound like a press story. It's true.... The girls will deny it, but I'm not denying it. Sure he did, so what? I was marrying his daughter. I was a Jew. Who the hell gives a ——? A Jewish song made them, a Jewish record company made them, a Jewish picture company made them. What the hell has Jews got to do with it? Jewish songwriters, a Jewish manager. I was born a Jew, I don't work at it....

That story, that's not a story. That to me is a father. What father doesn't want to—chase me with a big gun? The gun was about as big as I was, and when I came out at the time, I said, "Oh, it was a publicity stunt." I don't know what the hell I told everybody, 'cause it wasn't right, not right. You don't go shooting people if a girl wants to marry me. You know, what the hell, I should have told her father, "I didn't ask your daughter to marry me, she asked me to marry her." Would that be any different? I should have done it that way.... It's a father wanting to hold his brood in. He sounded like he was a tough guy. He wore a diamond stickpin. That was him. I used to play cards with him, poker every Saturday night. I went there to lose, not to win. We all played cards every Saturday night.

But to say the old man ran with a gun, it's like, somebody says, "I'll kill you, you bastard." They don't mean they're gonna kill you in cold blood. The whole thing is just misinterpretation of feelings. Look, if he had to lift up the gun, the gun was too heavy for him to pick up to begin with. Everybody asked me, many years ago, did he chase you with a gun? Yes, he chased me with a gun. Was it loaded? I don't know. Everybody makes a big thing out of it. I married his daughter.[21]

The sisters were so upset the Tuesday night Peter Andrews spent in jail that they missed the first broadcast of *Moonlight Serenade*. Patty showed up alone for the second broadcast to sing "I Love You Much Too Much." Maxene visited her father in jail:

Of course, I was hysterical seeing him behind bars, but the desk sergeant was the guy who got me. Here we were, making 10, 12,000 dollars a week, and the checks were going to our parents and we were getting $5 apiece for spending money each week, and this guy, in great profanity, is reading me out, telling me that if I was his kid he'd beat the you-know-what out of me. I just ran from the police station because I just figured, there'd never been any kind of scandal in our family, and I didn't want to prolong it.[22]

After the story hit the newspapers, the sisters' fan mail increased ten-fold. Several airlines offered to fly Patty and Schoen and Maxene and Levy anywhere in the world if they wanted to elope.[23]

One version of the story claimed LaVerne was responsible for bringing the family back together: she escorted her parents to the hotel where Patty and Maxene had moved, a reconciliation occurred, and Peter and Olga agreed to allow the sisters more independence.[24] The trio was back together for the Wednesday and Thursday broadcasts as well as for a recording session the following week. Rumors that the sisters might break up because of the incident persisted into March.[25] One story claimed Patty and Maxene were rehearsing another singer to take LaVerne's place. However, Lou Levy later announced the Andrews Sisters would definitely not break up, and said the dissension stemming from "family and financial matters" was "practically settled." However, in late February, *Variety* reported that Peter Andrews had hired an attorney "in his proposed fight to control the threesome's income." Patty and Maxene had offered to split the trio's income four ways with each of the sisters receiving a quarter and their parents receiving the remaining quarter.[26] This arrangement was apparently not agreeable to Peter.

Maxene said she never again lived with her parents after the incident. Perhaps, but it would be two years before she eloped to marry Lou Levy, and she then kept her marriage a secret from her parents and LaVerne for almost two more years. Patty never married Vic Schoen and would continue to live with her parents until she married in 1947. LaVerne would not marry until 1948, after Olga's death, and then Peter lived with her and her husband.

Despite this personal turbulence, the Andrews Sisters' career continued to soar. During their radio tenure with Glenn Miller, the sisters appeared with him at the Paramount Theater in New York in early March, their fourth engagement at the theater. Because of illness, however, Miller missed opening night and Tommy Dorsey filled in for him. The Andrews Sisters were in good form, apparently having heeded the Chicago reviewer's criticism of their wardrobe: "Andrews gals, resplendent in dignified new gowns, tee right off socko and hold that groove throughout.... Their unusual handling and nifty harmonizing of even these comparative oldies give them an entirely fresh touch."[27] *The Billboard*'s reviewer didn't care for their selections, but noted: "Singing Andrews Sisters clicked, as they always do, and seemingly there is no audience reaction in connection with their recent publicized domestic troubles."[28] The show topped the city's box offices[29]—perhaps the chief incentive for the sisters to continue as a trio.

The Andrews Sisters played one of their more off-beat venues when they gave a Sunday afternoon swing concert for inmates at Sing Sing Prison February 11 with Glenn Miller. I couldn't discover the whys or wherefores of the concert, but LaVerne later by-lined an article about her impressions of the outing for *Swing* magazine. She said the sisters were initially apprehensive about appropriate material for the prison audience, but once they got on stage "we were greeted by wild applause and shouted requests for the numbers we had done in the past.... In fact, we had to do each tune at least twice and some of them three and four times." The sisters were surprised at the inmates' knowledge of current pop music and impressed by the large number of music periodicals and books in the prison library. LaVerne concluded: "And, readers, they really know what it's all about. None of the mushy, sweet stuff goes with them. They like their music torrid and in the groove."[30]

The Andrews Sisters didn't pack them in everywhere they went. In March, a Rochester, New York promoter brought the sisters and the Harlan Leonard Rockets, an African American band, to his hometown for a one-nighter and ended up losing money on the deal when only 400 people showed up. This was the first time the sisters appeared with a black band. When they were interviewed on a local radio station by the local swing club president, "a few hefty razzberries were heard over the air as he introduced them."[31] The *Down Beat* story reporting the incident offered no explanation for the sisters' failure to pull in a crowd. Possibly the racial mix was a factor—something most promoters of the time avoided even in the northern states.

In spring 1940, the Andrews Sisters, Jimmy Dorsey, and other Decca artists protested the record company's recently imposed ban on playing their records on radio. Decca believed if its records were played on the airwaves their sales would drop, since people wouldn't buy them if they could hear them on the radio for free. The Andrews Sisters and others reasoned that airplay would publicize their new releases and actually increase sales. The sisters' manager Lou Levy claimed their recording of "Beer Barrel Polka" sold only half as well as an RCA release of the same song because RCA allowed its record on the air whereas Decca did not. The sisters were further concerned that since they had concluded their radio show with Glenn Miller and were about to embark on a long summer tour, they would be reaching a much smaller audience that would hear their songs and buy their records.[32] Not surprisingly, artists with radio shows reaching mass audiences, such as Bing Crosby, supported the ban. Decca relented somewhat and allowed stations to play records of artists who were performing in their area; thus New York stations were allowed to play Andrews Sisters' records when the sisters played theaters in the area. Decca's fears seem ludicrous today, given the way promoters fight to air their records. After about six months of the ban, Decca and other recording companies caved in and allowed their records on the airways[33]—in fact, they eventually wooed disc jockeys to play their records.

In April 1940, the Andrews Sisters signed a contract with Universal Studios to appear in a film called *Argentine Nights*, a musical comedy scheduled for production in mid–May. Since their East Coast engagements made it impossible for them to go to Hollywood for screen tests, Universal bent a few rules and gave them tests in New York. The contract was for one picture with an option for more.

After completing contracted commitments in New York, the sisters and Lou Levy headed west for Hollywood with a stop in Chicago for a two-week engagement.[34] At the Chicago Theater, they shared the bill with a new comedian named Red Skelton and African American actress Hattie McDaniels who "was to the liking of this mob with her two quick readings from 'Gone with the Wind' and her round of vocalizing." The reviewer noted that the sisters' wardrobe had improved and they "generally impress with bright showmanship and pipes."[35] *The Billboard*'s reviewer added: "The always popular Andrews Sisters have gone a long way since they used to work around Chicago with Maury Sherman, and their singing session brought continuous rounds of applause.... The girls have excellent voices with plenty of volume and put their numbers across in showmanly style."[36]

Jack Kapp, president of Decca Records and a good friend of Nate Blumberg, president of Universal Studios, instigated the Andrews Sisters' movie career. According to Maxene, "Jack convinced him [Blumberg] that doing a series of inexpensive pictures with the Andrews Sisters would make him a lot of money; and it did. They cleaned up."[37] Lou Levy later claimed he was the one who took the sisters to Universal Studios "where they didn't make 'em good but they made 'em by Tuesday."[38] Maxene said she knew from the beginning that their contract with Universal was a mistake. When asked why, she replied:

> Because it was terrible. I mean, they were so cheap and all they were interested in was making money. They did nothing for you. We got no decent wardrobe. The makeup man, though he was a genius at making up the Wolf Man, Frankenstein, and that sort of thing, he was just a terrible makeup man for the rest of us.... And we found making movies very boring ... the first picture we made was called "Argentine Nights." It was with the Ritz brothers. It was a very sad experience, because we had never been in front of a camera before, and so we knew none of the things that you had to learn.[39]

In *Argentine Nights*, the sisters received second billing to the popular Ritz Brothers. The weak comedy starred the brothers as three con men who took their all-female orchestra (which featured the Andrews Sisters) to Argentina in order to escape creditors in the United States. While there, they helped resurrect a defunct hotel in the hinterland by putting on a show that attracted customers who showed up out of nowhere. George Reeves (one of the Tarleton twins in *Gone with the Wind* and later the first TV Superman) played the romantic male lead. The Andrews Sisters sang four numbers (all arranged by Vic Schoen) and had minor roles in the silly plot. LaVerne was the only one who developed a character, a rather simple man-hungry woman—a role she would later resurrect for their radio show. Their opening number, "Rhumboogie," (their first boogie woogie recording) was performed in dresses split up the front and layered in Carmen Miranda-like ruffles. The second number, "Hit the Road," was energetically sung from the deck of the liner en route to Argentina. "Oh, He Loves Me" featured perhaps the most outrageous costumes of their film career—and that is seriously outrageous. For reasons unclear from the plot, they wore blond wigs, epaulette shoulder-padded blouses featuring a prominent nipple-like circle on each breast, boldly patterned gaucho pants, and high boots. In the same costumes, they joined the Ritz Brothers in the final number "Brooklynonga." Performed with rousing, cheerleader-like exuberance, the numbers illustrate the raw energy that characterized the Andrews Sisters' early act. One of the most entertaining numbers is the Ritz Brothers' lip-synching of the sisters' "Rhumboogie" in Andrews Sisters drag, perhaps the first of the many drag impersonations of the trio.

The film provides glimpses of the sisters' popular image at the time. In the opening scene when the all-female orchestra fails to attract the audience, one of the Ritz Brothers says: "We gotta get the Andrews Sisters on quick!" Another replies in anguish: "Do we have to go through that?" Two scenes play on the unattractiveness of the sisters. In one scene the Ritz Brothers are about to kiss them until they open their eyes, realize who they are kissing, and run away. In another, when other women are told to bring in the men they have rounded up, the sisters are told to bring in the horses. When they return, they have only the harnesses explaining that even the horses ran away from them.

The *Harvard Lampoon* called the Andrews Sisters' performance in *Argentine Nights* the "most frightening act in motion pictures in 1940."[40] The sisters took it in good spirits and said, "Those Harvard boys are all right—but we'd like to sing at one of their proms—we'd show them how we really can scare people."[41] "Frightening" is perhaps not the appropriate adjective for their performance, but it certainly did not portend a great acting career for the sisters. A *New York Times* review suggested they "never should have attempted to become comediennes."[42] A *Variety* review was more generous and concluded that the film had a "series of gags and musical numbers that dovetail fairly well."[43]

The Andrews Sisters told a *Newsweek* reporter that the first time they saw themselves on screen in *Argentine Nights* they looked like three zombies.[44] Patty recalled their reaction to the film: "We went to the premiere at the Fordham Theater in the Bronx, and we looked like the Ritz Brothers in drag. Our make-up was done by the man at Universal who did the make-up for Frankenstein. We were so ugly that Maxene walked all the way back to Manhattan from the Bronx in tears."[45] Maxene's memories were, not surprisingly, also bad. She told a reporter:

The "most frightening act in motion pictures in 1940" was the *Harvard Lampoon*'s assessment of the Andrews Sisters' movie debut in *Argentine Nights*. In perhaps the most outrageous costumes of their film career, the sisters sang the final musical number "Brooklynonga." (Author's collection)

> "Argentine Nights" was the first one, and it was a disaster! We'd never been in front of a camera before, and it's deadly to see yourself—you have one idea of what you look like, and then you see yourself up there.... The studio didn't help much. The make-up department, the hair and wardrobe departments had no idea what to do with us, so we were just shuttled back and forth. At that time, Deanna Durbin was queen of the A's at that studio, so everyone wore Deanna Durbin hairstyles. It didn't matter whether or not it looked good on you, you wore it.[46]

In later years, when Patty and Maxene were asked "Which movie was the most distasteful to do?" Patty quickly replied: "*Argentine Nights* … You know, being the first picture and working with the Ritz Brothers who were very, very experienced doing pictures and they kind of made it rough for us." Maxene added: "It was incredible. They pulled every trick in the book to upstage us. They were overbearing, they were rude...." Patty continued: "There's one thing I did find out later on though … at that period we were so hot in the business, and they [Universal Studios] had a picture deal they *had* to do with the Ritz Brothers; so to get them off the hook with the Ritz Brothers they put us in the picture together."[47] An interviewer once asked Patty if the sisters ever dated the Ritz Brothers; she emphatically replied "Hell no!"[48]

Although many Andrews Sisters fans probably saw *Argentine Nights*, the film did not fare well at the box office and Universal was about to drop the option on the sisters' contract. However, interest in the film suddenly picked up after a showing in Argentina was hooted off the screen and almost caused a riot in the theater.[49] Maxene claimed it was then banned in Argentina because of its offensive portrayal of Argentines and their country. But the publicity generated by the incident sparked interest in the film in the United States and large numbers lined up to see it. As the money began to roll into the box offices, Universal offered to renew the sisters' option, and over Maxene's objections, they accepted the renewal.[50]

While the sisters were in Hollywood making *Argentine Nights*, they joined other celebrities in a fundraiser for the Red Cross. The wars in Europe and Asia were depleting Red Cross funds and the organization appealed to Hollywood to help raise money. Hollywood's Bronson Avenue was renamed "Avenue of Mercy" for the public performance on Sunset Boulevard near the Warner Brothers sound stage. The Andrews Sisters appeared with other celebrities as part of a two-hour radio show that was broadcast over Los Angeles local stations as well as NBC and CBS. This was the first of many public service events the sisters would join during the approaching war.

On June 1, the Andrews Sisters participated in a huge extravaganza at the Los Angeles Memorial Coliseum called the first annual Southern California Music Fiesta. The Fiesta was sponsored by the *Los Angeles Times*, which contributed the net proceeds to the P.T.A Milk Fund. Some 6,000 entertainers including bands, drum and bugle corps, drill teams, riding clubs, accordion bands, and special units were part of a four-mile long parade. Other events included the national anthem sung by a chorus of 3,500 accompanied by a 2,500-piece band, Hungarian folk dancers, 500 Spanish dancers, and a thousand voice male chorus. Celebrities included Orson Welles, Gene Autry, the Sons of the Pioneers, and the Andrews Sisters in their "premier performance" on the Pacific Coast "singing songs that their recordings have made internationally popular," backed by the Johnny Richards band.[51] The sisters had, of course, performed on the West Coast during their road days with Larry Rich before their rise to fame with "Bei Mir Bist Du Schoen."

In July before leaving California for an East Coast tour, the Andrews Sisters played the Paramount Theater in Los Angeles and the resulting review in *The Billboard* revealed they were as popular on the West Coast as on the East Coast:

> Paramount steps into big time this week by offering one of the most popular musical attractions now in show biz: namely, the Andrews Sisters. The gals prove conclusively that they are as good a draw in a vaude house as they are in a night spot.... Their stuff is so far above the average run-of-the-mill efforts of femme trios that they are definitely in a class by themselves.[52]

Before leaving California, they broke attendance records at the Casa Manana in Culver City with Johnny Richards' band.[53] At Detroit's Michigan Theater with Gene Krupa they topped the weekly box office, and at Atlantic City's Steel

Pier with both Jimmy Dorsey and Mitch Ayres, "they pulled one of the biggest week-end mobs in years."[54]

By late summer, the sisters were back in New York for theater and one-night dates prior to another engagement at the Paramount in late September. It was rumored they would become regulars on Bob Hope's radio show in the fall, but the rumor never materialized.[55] In mid-August they played the Hippodrome in Baltimore where they were "socko from the teeoff" and did an "Encore with 'Beer Barrel Polka,' a persistent request from the stubholders on hand. Came back at this showing for a bit of jam, set to offbeat hand-clapping from the audience ... and a strong closing spot with the Andrews gals giving out with 'I Am an American,' all climaxed with the dropping of a big American flag."[56]

A week later the Steel Pier hosted the sisters again where a reviewer noted, "Gals continue to have plenty of harmony and zip, and got a noisy reception ... when crowd calls for favorites the blonde member explains (putting in a plug for their forthcoming film) that they can't sing such numbers until pic is released."[57] Early September found them at Newark's Adams Theater on the same bill with Joe Venuti and his orchestra featuring Bunny Berigan and an unknown singer named Kay Starr, who would eventually top the charts on her own. When they left the stage, they had "the house in their collective pocket.... Two songs the crowd seemed to favor with more whistling approval than others were 'Rhumboogie' and 'Hit the Road,' both from their new Universal flicker, 'Argentine Nights.'"[58]

Their fifth appearance at the Paramount with Jan Savitt and his orchestra in late September received a lukewarm review in *Variety*: "Vocal trio are on their fifth trip at this house, and prove inconsistent in comparison to their other showings here."[59] *The Billboard* was more enthusiastic: "Andrews Sisters swing out in top form. Patty is still the topnotch entertainer, domineering in voice and showmanship. Maxene and LaVerne fill in nicely with harmony and lend admirable fullness to the turn. It's a polished, well-timed act from beginning to end and boasts some of the snappiest arrangements of pop tunes on record."[60]

One of the sisters' memorable shows during the Paramount was when Tom Therault made his stage debut. Little Tom, two-and-a-half year old son of the sisters' cousin Gladys, was backstage watching the show with his mother. Prior to the show, one of the musicians befriended Tom and let him play his trumpet. Tom saw his new friend on stage and proceeded to walk out to greet him before his mother could stop him. His appearance on stage brought down the house. The sisters stopped their number. Patty picked up Tom, introduced him to the audience, and asked if he'd like to join the act. After more repartee, she returned him to his mother and the show continued.[61]

It was during this visit to New York that Gladys learned of Maxene's intention to marry. Maxene confided to her cousin that she wanted to marry but was afraid her father would "kill her" if she got married. Gladys advised her "to follow her heart" and do what she wanted to do. A few days later, Lou Levy encountered Gladys on Broadway and asked her, "Would you like me for a cousin?"—and Gladys realized who Maxene planned to marry.[62]

**A fan took this picture of Patty Andrews (possibly LaVerne is seated behind her)
on the beach in Atlantic City when the sisters were appearing at the Steel Pier
in September 1940. (Courtesy Paul Yasenak)**

Following the Paramount engagement, the sisters appeared with Glen
Gray's Casa Loma orchestra at the Earle Theater in Philadelphia. A reviewer
described the noisy session in typical *Variety*-ese:

Maxene and LaVerne were relaxing between shows at the Steel Pier on the beach in Atlantic City when a fan took this photograph in September 1940. (Courtesy Paul Yasenak)

Between Glen Gray's Casa Loma crews and the Andrews Sisters the jive devotees are having a field day at the Earle this semester. It's like old times again, with the alligators sitting in their pews and beating it out with their dukes and stomping their feet in time to the swingeroo dished by Gray's boys and the

Andrews gals ... the sisters were forced to deliver five numbers before they could leave the stage.[63]

A week later the sisters pulled in the city's highest box office in Washington, D.C.[64] At the end of October, they returned to the Flatbush Theater in Brooklyn, again with Joe Venuti and Kay Starr, making a big hit despite a bad sound system.[65] After a week at the Windsor Theater in the Bronx in early November, they brought in a record box office at the Metropolitan Theater in Providence with Gene Krupa and his orchestra, which included a midnight performance on the eve of Armistice Day.[66] Atlanta was next on their tour where they scored big with Bunny Berigan and his orchestra:

> The trio was so well received they had to resort to a novelty—a fantasy of songs they have made famous—in order to leave the stage. They slipped into the wings before the spell-bound audience realized they were gone.... Patty is featured as soloist at times, taking the melody while the other two back away from the mike, and her mannerisms are a special attraction. She even converses with the audience, paying special attention to people in the loge, which she called "the shelf."[67]

As this review suggests, the sisters were beginning to alter their act. Their previous theater engagements were strictly musical and included four, at the most five of their songs. Their lessons from vaudeville began to surface as they added comedy and eventually dance to their act and interacted more intimately with the audience. The medley of past hits would become an ongoing feature of their act.

In early December, following an engagement in Atlanta, the sisters cancelled the remaining cities on their tour in order to return to Hollywood to begin work on a new film for Universal Studios. Film contracts had priority over other contracts—an arrangement understood in the entertainment industry.

Seven of the Andrews Sisters' songs hit the charts in 1940: "Ferryboat Serenade" (fourteen weeks) celebrated the joys of ferry travel; "Beat Me, Daddy, Eight to the Bar" (fourteen weeks) related the story of a Texas piano player in boogie-woogie beat; "The Woodpecker Song" (twelve weeks), originally from Italy, was a big band cover; "Say Si, Si" (ten weeks) explored the different ways of saying yes; "Rhumboogie" (nine weeks), from *Argentine Nights*, introduced the sisters to boogie-woogie and won its composers, Don Raye and Hughie Prince, an ASCAP award for the outstanding novelty song of 1940; "Down by the O-HI-O" (one week) told of musical escapades along the Ohio River; and "Hit the Road" (one week), was another song from *Argentine Nights*.[68]

The year 1941 was busy for the Andrews Sisters. They made four more movies—three with comedians Bud Abbott and Lou Costello, perhaps their best-remembered ones. The sisters had appeared on the same bill with Abbott and Costello at the Steel Pier in Atlantic City, and consequently were not strangers to one another when Universal paired them in a film.

Abbott and Costello, like the Andrews Sisters, had made a previous movie of moderate success. The sisters were now big stars and among the top-recording artists of the country, while Abbott and Costello were collecting a popular

This photograph, taken December 1940 in Hollywood, accompanied a bundle of Christmas gifts the Andrews Sisters sent their cousin Gladys' son Tommy: a bicycle, a wagon, a toy duck, a top, bedroom slippers, a suit, and tools. (Gladys Leichter Collection)

following on radio. Universal was apparently unconvinced that either act could carry a film alone so they cast them together in *Buck Privates* to cash in on fans of both acts. The film was a big box office hit, launching Abbott and Costello on their successful career. It reportedly grossed four million dollars[69] and was shot in twenty days at a cost of less than $200,000.[70]

A comic romp about two bungling army draftees, *Buck Privates* served as patriotic support for the newly installed military draft. In addition to Abbott and Costello's antics, the film featured a second plot about a spoiled upper class playboy who got his comeuppance during basic training and emerged a man worthy of Uncle Sam's army. A film historian wrote, "The War Office couldn't have wished for a better 84 minutes of recruitment propaganda than this, especially with the Andrews Sisters as a trio of Pied Pipers doing their close-harmony best for the war effort."[71] The humor and plot of the film have not worn well and it probably would not be watched by too many today were it not for the songs of the Andrews Sisters. *Buck Privates* has some of the sisters' best film musical numbers. Dressed in WAC uniforms, they wander in and out of the plot to sing the rousing, patriotic "You're a Lucky Fellow, Mr. Smith," the romantic "In Apple Blossom Time," the frenetic, defining song of the approaching war "Boogie Woogie Bugle Boy," and the jitterbugging "Bounce Me Brother with a Solid Four," accompanied by The World Champion Boogie Woogie Dancers.

Two of the songs most commonly associated with the Andrews Sisters, "Boogie Woogie Bugle Boy" and "In Apple Blossom Time," were almost eliminated from the movie because, according to Maxene, the studio execs didn't think the Andrews Sisters were up to singing boogie woogie and they didn't want to pay the $200 publisher's fee for "In Apple Blossom Time." Maxene's claim about "Boogie Woogie Bugle Boy" is questionable since the sisters had already charted three boogie-woogie numbers. "In Apple Blossom Time" was retained partly because the sisters paid the publisher's fee themselves.[72] Ironically, the two are among the best remembered of the sisters' songs. "In Apple Blossom Time" became their signature song and "Boogie Woogie Bugle Boy" received an Academy Award nomination for "Best Song" and today is probably their best-known song. The movie also received an Academy Award nomination for "Best Scoring of a Musical Picture,"[73] and while it didn't win any awards, the nominations speak highly of peer recognition of the sisters' talents. Universal would not hire a choreographer for the sisters' dance routines, so Patty choreographed their numbers, which they rehearsed at night because the tight shooting schedule allowed no time for daytime rehearsals.[74] In commenting on the tight budget of the film, a later critic wrote: "Nonetheless the Andrews Sisters make the picture swing. Watching them belt out "Boogie Woogie Bugle Boy" makes you want to enlist. The musical numbers are crisp and snappy. If the movie was made on a shoestring budget, these production numbers certainly don't show it."[75]

The film was well received by the critics, as was the Andrews Sisters' performance. *Variety* wrote: "Aiding considerably is the appearance of the Andrews Sisters, who do their regularly competent harmonizing of several tuneful melodies."[76] *The Billboard* reported that the Andrews Sisters were "Treated a great deal more kindly by the make-up and lighting departments ... [and they] received the benefit of proper handling that shows them in a light that will do much to erase the mistakes of 'Argentine Nights.'"[77] The *New York Times* critic, never a fan of the Andrews Sisters, grudgingly wrote: "The songs ... should cause a noticeable increase in new volunteers, and the Andrews Sisters do hectic things with a tune. They're good. But please, Sergeant, even when it's good we don't like agony singing."[78]

The college boys at Yale didn't like the Andrews Sisters any better than their rivals at Harvard. An undeserved, vicious review of "Boogie Woogie Bugle Boy" and "Bounce Me Brother with a Solid Four" appeared in *The Yale Record*: "This gang of hags is pretty much the world's corniest set. The stuff is phony, which is the big thing. Corn is corn until it's phony; then it's time to blast. The Andrews Sisters have one excuse for existing—that's the take-off the Revuers do on them at the Village Vanguard ... in which two beat chicks carry on without the third member of a trio. The absent member sings lead!"[79] The boys at Yale had no idea that "Boogie Woogie Bugle Boy" would become one of the

The sisters donned khaki for their roles in *Buck Privates* (1941), their first film with Bud Abbott and Lou Costello. Although this film is often regarded as a World War II musical comedy classic, it was actually filmed prior to the United States' entry into the war. In this scene, the sisters swing out "Bounce Me Brother with a Solid Four." (Author's collection)

enduring songs of the coming war as well as the quintessential Andrews Sisters song.

While in Hollywood making *Buck Privates*, the sisters teamed up again with Johnny Richards and his band for several one-nighters.[80] January 31, 1941, the day *Buck Privates* opened in New York, the Andrews Sisters were back at the Minneapolis Orpheum, the hometown theater where they had performed in talent shows as kids. They were traveling again with Joe Venuti and Kay Starr, but had added the Three Stooges to the show. A local critic wrote, "When someone in the audience called 'I Hear a Rhapsody' to the Andrews as a request, Patty answered 'Not from us, you don't!'"[81]

The sisters had never been pleased with their reception in Minneapolis. Prior to the 1940 release of *Argentine Nights*, they told a reporter when asked if they had one wish: "We've never been able to make any dent on the folks in our home town.... If we had just one wish, we'd ask to have the picture premiered there, and maybe we could make a personal appearance."[82] Lou Levy apparently decided to pull out the stops to let the locals know the Andrews Sisters were back in town. The day after they opened at the Orpheum, their picture appeared in the *Minneapolis Star Journal* with Mayor George Leach who "welcomed them back to Minneapolis."[83] Patty and LaVerne sported long fur coats, hats, and muffs while Maxene opted for a cloth coat. The next day two large photo ads appeared in the paper. One featured five photos of the sisters at a pinball machine, "America's newest national pastime," dressed in "military costumes from their newest picture 'Buck Privates.'"[84] The ad was a photo essay on the excitement of the pinball machine, and was probably sponsored by the pinball machine industry. Elsewhere in the same newspaper, the sisters appeared in ads for a dairy, an Italian restaurant, a bowling alley, a radio store, and an automobile dealership.[85]

Happily, the sisters' wish for a warm reception in their hometown was fulfilled: *Variety* reported that "They received warm welcome from the outset and generated by far the greatest audience enthusiasm of any act on the bill. Their nifty harmony makes ... a real experience for those whose tastes run to swing vocalizing. They're great show closers, with the customers unable to get enough and plenty noisy in their efforts to bring the gals back for more." [86]

After Minneapolis, the sisters moved on to the Chicago Theater where they topped the week's box office with Gene Krupa.[87] The enthusiastic reviews continued:

> And probably the best of [the] lot, according to the applause-meter, is the Andrews Sisters trio.... They walloped 'em here, and deservedly so, for there is no trio anywhere comparable with these girls. They have a tonsil flavor that is outstanding and unique and a method of selling a song that must satisfy all types of audiences.[88]

Next stops were the Riverside Theater in Milwaukee and the Lyric Theater in Indianapolis, and then on to the Stanley in Pittsburgh, still with Joe Venuti, where they drew an overflowing crowd despite a snowstorm:

> Snow was so thick at noon today that an autoist couldn't see his radiator cap; temperature was around zero and traffic just wasn't because of the icy streets. Yet, the Stanley was packed to the rafters and there were a couple of hundred cash customers behind the ropes at the break. Only one answer to all that—the Andrews Sisters. It was a jukebox crowd—that much was apparent from the audience, which kept yelling for the trio's best-known waxes, and they would have been happy and contented if the rest of the show had forgotten to show up so the Andrews gals could have had the stage to themselves.[89]

A local reviewer wrote: "There's a lilt and a rhythm to their singing that will intrigue even the most outspoken enemies of swing. They even sound good to one who has heard the sisters' arrangements in the juke boxes till he's been driven to distraction."[90] Their show again topped the city's box offices.[91]

During their Pittsburgh stint, a local variety store proprietor arranged an autograph session with the sisters. He placed ads in the local papers about the Andrews Sisters' coming appearance, and then bought up all their records from other stores in town. When the sisters showed up for the autograph session, police were called to handle the mobs that came to see them. In less than thirty minutes, they autographed some 2,000 records and the store claimed it could have sold at least that many more.[92]

The Andrews Sisters were scheduled for three weeks at New York's Paramount in late March with popular female band leader Ina Ray Hutton, but they canceled two of the weeks when Universal Studios called them back to Hollywood to begin *In the Navy*, another film with Abbott and Costello.

As soon as *Buck Privates* was completed (and before its distribution), Universal began production of *Oh Charlie!* (later changed to *Hold That Ghost*), another Abbott and Costello vehicle. Halfway through production, box office returns began coming in for *Buck Privates*. The figures were so great that the studio shelved *Hold That Ghost* and began production of *In the Navy* to cash in on the public's enthusiasm for *Buck Privates*.[93] *In the Navy*, another patriotic comic romp, was released a few months later with almost the same cast as *Buck Privates*, but with the addition of singer Dick Powell who portrayed a crooner who joined the Navy to escape his adoring female public. The Andrews Sisters played themselves as musical camp followers and performed numbers throughout the predictable plot. "Gimme Some Skin," teamed with energetic jitterbugs, was perhaps their best number followed by the patriotic "You're Off to See the World." Their Hawaiian number, "Hula Ba-Luau," is best remembered for their campy costumes—shimmering blouses above bare midriffs, aloha print skirts, bongo drums on hips, hibiscus in hair, and floral anklets above strapped high-heeled shoes. The sisters' sang "Starlight, Starbright" with Dick Powell and joined the entire cast with "We're in the Navy" to wrap up the film.

Because scenes of the film were shot at the San Diego Navy base, the Navy Department insisted on approving the final version. After viewing the film, they refused to allow its distribution because of a scene where Lou Costello impersonated an admiral to impress the Andrews Sisters and almost destroyed the entire fleet. The Navy brass felt the scene made them look like buffoons. To please the brass, Universal turned the scene into a dream by Costello rather than a "real" sequence. The Navy was satisfied and the film was released. It, too, was a box office hit, and the careers of Abbott and Costello and the Andrews Sisters continued to soar. *Variety* liked the Andrews Sisters in *In the Navy* and wrote: "Andrews Sisters handle three numbers in their usually capable, rhythmic fashion."[94] The *New York Times* reviewer was predictably less impressed: "Certainly the Andrews Sisters ... with their flat songs, would not be missed. They simply get in the way."[95]

Hold That Ghost was completed and released after the successful run of *In the Navy*. Despite an unoriginal plot set in a haunted house with disappearing bodies and hidden money, its comedy holds up perhaps best of all the Abbott and Costello films. The Andrews Sisters had no roles in the plot, appearing only in two nightclub scenes wearing long white evening gowns. They sang "Sleepy Serenade" and "Aurora," backed by Ted Lewis and his orchestra. The musical numbers were added after the sisters' popular reception in the earlier two films.[96] *Variety* wrote of their performance: "The Andrews then deliver a socko arrangement of 'Sleepy Serenade,' which is geared for pop attention. Finale brings on the band and the girls again, with the Andrews Sisters singing 'Aurora' (already a pop tune in the juke-boxes)."[97] The *New York Times* conceded that the Andrews Sisters' songs "are entertaining of themselves, [but]

Patty flirts with Lou Costello in a scene from *In the Navy* (1941) as Maxene, LaVerne and Bud Abbott look on. After the great success of *Buck Privates*, Universal rushed together *In the Navy* with almost the same cast. It made even more money at the box office as the careers of the Andrews Sisters and Abbott and Costello continued to soar. (Author's collection)

they tend to slow up the film's pace."[98] A *Chicago Tribune* reviewer was unimpressed by the Andrews Sisters' performance: "The Andrews sisters have their following, I am told, tho I have a blind and deaf spot where they are concerned, especially when the middle Andrews sister [Patty] endeavors to imitate a few of Carmen Miranda's gyrations."[99]

Years later when asked about working with Bud Abbott and Lou Costello, Maxene replied:

> We knew Lou better than we knew Bud, because Bud had a big drinking problem. We knew Lou's family so we would spend Saturdays and Sundays at their house. On the set we never saw them because Universal gave them a big trailer, and they sat in there and gambled between every scene. They let me watch, and there was never less than $30,000 in the pot with nothing less than one hundred dollar bills.[100]

Patty added, "Lou had a dominating type of personality.... And Bud was the second banana, as far as Lou was concerned. They were not like their on-screen personas at all. Anne, Lou's wife, was just a lovebug."[101] After their filmmak-

The Andrews Sisters were not originally in *Hold That Ghost* (1941), their third film with Bud Abbott and Lou Costello. However, after their popular reception in *Buck Privates* and *In The Navy*, opening and closing scenes featuring the sisters were added to the film. Above they sing "Sleepy Serenade" as Ted Lewis and his orchestra back them. (Author's collection)

ing association, the Andrews family continued to socialize with Costello and his family. Maxene remembered:

> Bud was kind of in a world of his own…. We were quite close to Lou and Anne and the kids. We'd go over to their home on many weekends. None of us could afford a swimming pool, so we'd use theirs … oh, and the good food they would put out for us! When you get around Italian families, honey, mostly they're full of love—they're very tactile—and they love to feed you.[102]
>
> One of the great tragedies in Lou's life was when he came down with rheumatic fever. Here's a man with all of this ambition and energy and desire, and who's at the threshold of probably his greatest success in movies, flat on his back for about a year…. One time, while I sat and just observed him … I thought, what a tragedy! We were watching some movie in the little theater in his house. And here was this little funny man laid up like this. I really had tremendous affection for that man.[103]

The sisters' cousin Gladys Leichter had fond memories of Lou Costello as well. She became friends with him and his wife through her cousins and visited their home for pool parties with her two sons who were about the age of

Costello's two daughters. He often joked about adopting one of her sons since he had only girls. He later had a son, and Gladys remembered his devastation when the little boy drowned in the family pool.[104]

The year 1941 was a good one for the Andrews Sisters' movie career. *In the Navy*, *Hold That Ghost*, and *Buck Privates* (in that order) were Universal Studios' top moneymaking films of the year, and the Andrews Sisters appeared in all three films.[105] The sisters were enthusiastic about their movie career after the string of successes. Patty told a reporter:

> We've received more fan letters as a result of our film work than from any other type of job. Movies opened up an entirely new field for us, gave us an entirely new audience. The camera, I need hardly point out, is very different from live audiences. Movies are made in front of about four people who don't even blink an eyelash. Yet it's fun to do pictures when we realize that we come to life on a thousand screens all over the hemisphere.[106]

After completing *In the Navy* and *Hold That Ghost*, Universal asked the sisters to begin work on another film tentatively called *50 Million Nickels Can't Be Wrong*, a story built around the jukebox industry. The sisters demurred, however, citing a committed schedule for the summer, but agreed to do the film in the fall.[107] Universal apparently changed its mind about the film since it was never made, at least by that name.

The sisters also made a brief film appearance in a short "two-reeler" released in mid–October 1941. Entitled *Milton Berle Throws a Party*, the nine minute short was set at the turn of the century, and the Andrews Sisters appeared in period swimming suits for a brief skit with Berle and a rendition of "In Apple Blossom Time."[108]

As the sisters racked up film successes, they also explored new musical avenues. Maxene remembered: "[In 1940] the Andrews Sisters began a new style of music, or, more accurately, reintroduced a very old style from the Deep South—boogie woogie, with its eight beats to each bar of music."[109] Maxene was correct in noting that boogie woogie had been around for awhile, but not entirely correct in claiming the Andrews Sisters reintroduced it.

Some music historians date boogie woogie back to the African American "ring shouts" of early New Orleans that gave rise to jazz, and trace its rhythm to the waterfront saloons of that city where a piano was the only instrument available. "The essence of this style was the use of insistent left-hand patterns based on blues chord progressions, underscoring syncopated melody lines or block chords in the right hand. This contrast demanded skillful hand independence on the part of the pianist."[110] Boogie woogie was essentially a way of playing music, as opposed to a way of writing it. Like swing, almost anything could become boogie woogie if interpreted properly. By 1938, over seventy-five boogie woogie numbers had been recorded, virtually all by black musicians.[111] Although big band numbers such as Tommy Dorsey's "Boogie Woogie" (1938), Ray McKinley's "Beat Me Daddy Eight to the Bar" (1940), and Count Basie's "Basie Boogie" (1941) introduced boogie woogie to mainstream popular music, the Andrews Sisters were the most popular vocalists of the genre.

In the popular imagination the Andrews Sisters are synonymous with boogie woogie, but in reality, it is a small portion of their discography. "Rhumboogie" (1940) was their first venture into boogie woogie, and its success was followed by "Beat Me Daddy Eight to the Bar" (1940), a cover of Ray McKinley's swing version, "Scrub Me Mama with a Boogie Beat" (1941), "Boogie Woogie Bugle Boy" (1941), and "Booglie Wooglie Piggy" (1941). They resurrected boogie woogie in 1952 for "Carmen's Boogie," one of their last Decca recordings.

As Maxene noted, the Andrews Sisters' style began to change in the early 1940s at the time of these boogie woogie recordings. Increasingly, their style became louder, more raucous, and more aggressive. They were not about to get lost in a big band—rather they put on the show and the big bands played behind them, which is probably why many big band leaders put them down whenever they could. A music historian noted, "The Andrews Sisters had verve and a jazzy, shrill kind of sound, leaning toward numbers that swung, but they also achieved appealing harmonies in the ballads."[112] George Simon, record reviewer for *Down Beat* and never a fan of the Andrews Sisters, once said: "Theirs was strictly a straight-ahead, middle-of-the-road, no frills approach that may have driven some musicians up the wall."[113] Indeed, it did.

When bandleader Stan Kenton first met the Andrews Sisters he said, "It's nice to know you, but I can't stand your singing." Never at a loss for words, Maxene responded, "It's nice to know you, but I can't stand your music."[114] Maxene once complained about Artie Shaw's band: "If Artie's guys didn't like a certain passage we were singing, they'd play it out of tune, or miss it entirely.... They hated us because we were the stars and they had to be background music for us."[115] Although Glenn Miller always treated the sisters with respect, Maxene claimed he didn't care much for their music. Patty Andrews remembered: "We took Gene Krupa on the road for the first time. We hired Harry James. But the musicians all wanted to be stars, and they didn't really dig the kind of harmony we sang."[116]

In the early years of their career, the jazz and swing musicians liked the Andrews Sisters—an affair that did not last. In summer 1939, the sisters received awards at the jazz jamboree of the National Swing Club of America in New York City's Hippodrome for their "combined contribution to American jazz."[117] Several prominent names in jazz, including Chick Webb, Billie Holiday, Cab Calloway, and Ella Fitzgerald, received similar awards.[118] As late as October 1941, a *Down Beat* reviewer wrote: "It's not easy to shrug these chicks off—not so long as they remain the greatest fem vocal trio in show business. ...[A]ll the others are second-raters to the Andrews, and not a small share of their popularity must go to Vic Schoen, their arranger."[119] By the following May, however, *Down Beat* was tiring of the sisters: "When the Andrews Sisters first started, I, along with a few other million nickel-pushers, liked them. Now they've got so many little tricks, tasteless slurs, and sing so inconsistently out of tune that I can't even listen to their records long enough to review them properly."[120]

The music magazine *Metronome* was never a fan of the sisters either. Throughout most of the sisters' career, Leonard Feather and Barry Ulanov reviewed records for the publication, and they had little love for the sisters. *Metronome* first reviewed an Andrews Sisters record in December 1939 when their first pairing with Bing Crosby was released, "Ciribiribin" and "Yodelin' Jive." The sisters were not even mentioned in the review. The next *Metronome* review of an Andrews Sisters record ("When Johnny Comes Marching Home" and "East of the Rockies") did not appear until April 1943, despite the fact that they had been the top singing group in the country for five years: "Typical Andrews Sisters fare, with the background winning the plaudits for taste and skill in the Dixieland manner and the Sisters shouting as usual." Two months later in a review of an album of reissued Boswell Sisters songs, *Metronome* didn't pass a chance to put down the Andrews Sisters: "[T]hey [Boswell Sisters] sound better than anything ever done by the Andrews Sisters, whether from the standpoint of vocal blend, instrumental accompaniment or just all-around musical worth."[121] A review of "There'll Be a Jubilee" grudgingly conceded: "Nonetheless it jumps, after a fashion, which is less raucous and offensive than most Andrews productions."[122] *Metronome* complained that "'Tico Tico' reveals for the umpteenth time the handicaps of three-part harmony, especially as sung in the Andrews' shout style."[123] Throughout the remainder of their recording career, *Metronome* gave the sisters only one unreserved positive review, a collaboration with Bing Crosby: "'Apalachicola, Fla.' is a very humorous side thanks to both Bing and the Andrews Sisters."[124] It is perhaps relevant to note that *Metronome* was no fan of rock and roll either—it described it as "the scourge of American civilization"—and in 1956 offered the short-sighted prognostication that "rock 'n' roll is on the way out, as anyone could have predicted it would be, as early as the beginnings of its popularization, and this time next year will quite definitely see no more than the most barren vestiges of its current flavor."[125]

The editors of *Swing* magazine, a short-lived music magazine of the late 1930s and early 1940s, also fell out of love with the Andrews Sisters after initially giving them good press. A reviewer called their records "rowdy shout numbers."[126]

Down Beat, the major competitor of *Metronome* as the magazine of popular music, reviewed the Andrews Sisters' records more frequently. The early reviews, most by Michael Levin, were enthusiastic, but grew increasingly critical over the years. *Down Beat*'s first review of the sisters was "Ciribiribin" and "Yodelin' Jive" with Bing Crosby: "Quite a combination of stars, and well worth hearing as a novelty."[127] Regarding "Beat Me Daddy Eight to the Bar" and "Pennsylvania 6-5000": "Vic Schoen's studio band backing almost overshadows the girls shouting.... The girls are in top form on both."[128] A few weeks later, the sisters' recording of "Mean to Me" and "Sweet Molly Malone" was reviewed: "The gals change their style ... to go into a sweet groove.... It's a clever move inasmuch the A-chicks were beginning to get monotonous with their yelling, jumping harmonies."[129]

The sisters received few good reviews in subsequent issues of *Down Beat*. Levin seemingly spent more time creating clever alliterative epithets for them than he did listening to their records: "the terrifying trio," "the tremulous trio," and "the Throaty Threesome." Prefacing an unfavorable review of "Shoo Shoo Baby" and "Down in the Valley," he went literary: "The weird sisters are with me again, inevitable in their pursuit as the furies to Orestes or the sirens to Ulysses or the harpies to Aeneas or the witches to Macbeth."[130] In a review of an album of the sisters' hits, Levin reported: "There are those who say the girls don't always sing in tune and that their arrangements get a shade wearying, which includes me in, I'm afraid."[131] In an obfuscated review of "Malaguena" and "Hohokus, USA," he wrote:

> The fact that the Andrews Sisters are liked by many, many people merely is a demonstration of the virility of a democracy. These sides are very close to Justice Holmes' famous "line of clear and imminent danger." The harmony is essentially barbershop, with the top flatted and the bottom sharpened, a radical combination as anyone can see. But then again, lots of people like it, which is amoozin' as well as confoozin'.[132]

While *Down Beat*'s reviewers may not have liked the Andrews Sisters, its readers gave the sisters high scores throughout most of their career. Each year, *Down Beat* conducted a readers' poll to determine the most popular musicians of the year. From 1938 through 1940, the sisters were rated the number one "Vocal Group." In 1941 and 1942 they came in number two. In subsequent years through 1950, they ranked from five to ten.

After some short engagements around Los Angeles in spring 1941 following their movie making, the Andrews Sisters left Hollywood in June for a long tour that began in San Francisco and ended in Cincinnati. A reviewer saw their show at San Francisco's Golden Gate Theater on June 18 and liked what he saw:

> [T]hose Andrews Sisters are in town just ajivin' and ajumpin' in a bright white spot at the Golden Gate Theater, and man, they are really sendin' it!
> Patty—that's the middle one, and the personality gal of the trio—gives out with the derriere routine, atruckin' and Susy'Q'in', while LaVerne and Maxene clap their hands and blend their voices in that distinctive style of "scat" singing that has made these young ladies popular successors to the Boswell Sisters.
> They are generous with their talents, and the act is a natural for that Golden Gate audience. Yesterday Patty announced the singing of "Boogie Woogie Bugle Boy," one of the more frequently played nickel machine discs, and the applause was deafening; so, too, with "Rhumboogie" and "Apple Blossom Time." It must be fame when you get applause even before you do the number.
> There are times when the nose-wrinkling and general mugging which seems to be a necessary part of that style of vocalizing becomes just a bit uncomfortable, but there isn't much doubt of the fact that these Andrews Sisters are at the peak of their specialty right now.
> Except that, with all due respect to their theatrical wisdom, they're far from being ... sharp ... in that "Sonny Boy" routine. Better junk it, kids—you really don't need it. The act is solid as it stands.

The sisters shared the bill with "The Titans," "two magnificently muscled gentlemen," a marionette act, two African American dancers "with the unashamed vigor of a pair of wild horses," a clown, a short film feature about women's hair styles, and the featured movie *The Big Boss*.[133]

Variety reported that the sisters' Golden Gate Theater appearance topped the city's box offices,[134] a now familiar pattern wherever they went. San Francisco theaters had recently introduced cut-rate prices for military personnel, but the Golden Gate delayed the policy while the Andrews Sisters were pulling in such big audiences.[135] The sisters earned more at the Golden Gate than they originally asked. Unsure of their drawing power, the manager rejected their request for $3,500, offering them $2,500 with a fifty-fifty split over a gross of $17,500. He underestimated their popularity and they walked away with $5,000. The sisters' tight schedule necessitated a police escort from the theater to the airport where a plane waited fifteen minutes so they could make connections to New York and then on to Philadelphia the following day for an opening.[136]

In Philadelphia, back with Joe Venuti and his orchestra at the Earle Theater, the Andrews Sisters received more rave reviews and again managed to top the city's boxes for the week.[137] Their finale went over well:

> The trio is currently hotter than a Fourth of July firecracker, and only a plea of exhaustion enabled them to bow off.... Dolled up in cool-looking evening gowns, the sisters came on in the closing spot to a terrific reception.... The trio has found a clever trick for bowing off. They get the audience to clap hands in unison while they swing-sing "My Bonnie." As the beat becomes louder they ease behind the wings while Patty Andrews trucks slowly off.[138]

The sisters continued to top box offices wherever they went. At Pittsburgh's Stanley Theater with Gene Krupa, they scored the second largest box in the theater's history. The manager announced the theater was "rolling again" after the sisters' engagement and was so grateful that he gave them an additional $500 and booked them for a return at $500 more than their usual fee.[139] In mid–July they joined Joe Venuti and his band at the Palace Theater in Akron where *The Billboard* reported: "The Andrews Sisters have perfectly blended voices for the 1941 pop songs, and are mistresses of rhythm without equal among the gal trios."[140]

Maxene took time out from their busy schedule to secretly marry Lou Levy on July 28, 1941, at Elkton, Maryland, a town known for its quickie marriages. Little is known about Lou and Maxene's courtship, but when a reporter asked about it, Levy replied: "I chased her ... but she brushed me. At the time the girls didn't go in for heavy dates. They thought if any of them got married, it would break up the act. The Andrews Sisters always came first. Why LaVerne even sat down and delivered me a talk—no romance."[141] Peter and Olga Andrews apparently had not changed their minds about their daughters marrying. Maxene revealed her marriage to Patty only and kept it a secret from her parents and LaVerne for almost two years.[142] Elsewhere, Maxene said none of her family knew about the marriage, but Patty and LaVerne told a reporter they were aware of it. She later confided: "I loved Lou ... I loved Lou because he was the first young man I met that had get up and go. If he wanted something he went after it."[143] When a reporter later asked Levy about their elopement, he said: "Greatest hide and seek act the world has ever known.... We could hide better than Hitler. Patty and LaVerne spent all their time looking for us."

Maxene remembered: "We were on the road most of the time, playing theaters.... Wore out more hotel carpets—running up and down stairs."[144]

In early July while at the Steel Pier, the Andrews Sisters did their patriotic bit when they appeared at a local music store and autographed free records for the first twenty-five patrons who brought aluminum articles for recycling for the approaching war effort.[145] In early August, the sisters were back at the Chicago Theater where they again topped the city's box office—first with Lou Breese and his orchestra and the following week with Gene Krupa and his orchestra. A reviewer from *The Billboard* saw their show with Breese: "The Andrews Sisters are in the closing inning and, as usual, stop the show.... Patty is still the center of attraction, boasting the best voice and most forceful salesmanship."[146] *Variety* was enthusiastic about the show too: "Each time the Andrews Sisters make an appearance, the box office receipts get bigger, the reception louder and the customers acclaim more sockeroo! Solidly show-wise, trio remains tops in the fem vocal group field. They were little short of sensational with these customers."[147] Since last playing the windy city, their salaries had doubled to $8,000 for their two-week engagement.[148]

While in Chicago, the sisters made two appearances on *The Holland Furnace Show*, an NBC radio show featuring Benny Goodman and his band.[149] This was the only time the sisters sang with Goodman. A writer for *Radio Life* claimed that by August 1941, the Andrews Sisters had logged an estimated 700 hours on the air. The hours seem exaggerated, but they nonetheless convey the great number of radio appearances the sisters made. The writer continued, "You'd have to be a hermit to escape them."[150]

At summer's end, the sisters again played the Steel Pier in Atlantic City, their third trip to the resort that summer. The holiday crowd was so big the shows were extended to ten a day.[151] Years later, Maxene remembered (somewhat inaccurately) that weekend: "We used to do seven shows a *day*, 45 weeks a year. One Labor Day at the Steel Pier in Atlantic City we did 11 shows, each 25 minutes long with 15 minutes between shows."[152] A publicity contest—doubtless drummed up by Lou Levy—during the Andrews Sisters' Steel Pier engagement offered a date with the sisters to the winning contestant. Participants (eighteen years or older) submitted a one-hundred-word letter stating why they wanted a date with the Andrews Sisters. The winner had dinner with the sisters at the Hotel President, attended their show at the Steel Pier, and then escorted them to the Paradise Club, a "Harlem hotterie." If the winner could sing, he would appear on stage at the Steel Pier as a vocalist with the sisters. The twelve runner-ups received free tickets to the sisters' show.[153]

After the Steel Pier engagements, the sisters went to Minnesota for a rest with friends and relatives at Mound, interrupted by a one-night stand at Minneapolis' Excelsior Park with Joe Venuti and his orchestra where billboards announced "The Andrews Sisters are Minnesota's own."[154] The turnout for their performance was disappointing, perhaps because the admission was high at $1.10 or because their show was on the eve of the opening of the Minnesota State Fair.[155] While in Mound, Maxene told her cousin Gladys Leichter that she had married Lou Levy, but begged her not to tell her parents.[156]

Throughout their touring years, the sisters usually managed a summer break to visit family and friends at Mound. One reporter claimed the visit was always three weeks,[157] but more often it was shorter and interrupted by career dictates. The sisters' mother, Olga Andrews, was always concerned about the well-being of her two bachelor brothers, Pete and Ed, the only remaining members of her once large family. After their parents' deaths, the two brothers continued to live in the family home and operated their nearby grocery store where pictures of the Andrews Sisters increasingly adorned the walls as their fame grew. When the Andrews family prospered, Olga shared their good fortune with her brothers. She replaced the outhouse and well with indoor plumbing and a new kitchen. She frequently bought her brothers furniture and appliances, painted the house, and sent them gifts. Years later when the brothers died, the family found many of the gifts in closets, unused, and sometimes unopened.[158]

After their respite in Mound, the Andrews Sisters were back on the road topping box offices again. In early September, they topped at the State Theater in Hartford, Connecticut, with Joe Venuti and his orchestra.[159] A week later at Baltimore's Hippodrome they topped again.[160] In early October, they capped Boston's box offices where a reporter noted: "Standees and huge throngs awaiting seats were regular sights in front of the house."[161] Because of delayed air flights, Maxene didn't make the opening show in Boston, and the "result was that a mob of hep boys and girls stayed over to see the second show, with Maxene rejoining the act for a terrific round of numbers, each received by a barrage of whoops, whistles, and plaudits."[162]

While in New York in October, the Andrews Sisters recorded "Any Bonds Today?" an Irving Berlin song written at the invitation of the U.S. Treasury Department to drum up public support for the military mobilization of the United States. "Any Bonds Today?" was unashamedly patriotic, if not propagandistic, and remained a popular song throughout the approaching war. Maxene remembered: "It is a sign of those times that the number was a big hit. Americans enjoyed singing it. Nobody regarded it as forced government propaganda or a boring attempt at motivating us. It was popular because Irving Berlin wrote a good song, and because it struck a responsive chord in all America."[163] Eventually, Bing Crosby, Kay Kyser, Barry Wood, Jimmy Dorsey with vocals by Helen O'Connell and Bob Eberly, and even Bugs Bunny (Mel Blanc) recorded the song.

When the sisters made their seventh appearance at the Paramount in late October, a review in *Variety* suggested they needed some new numbers:

> Andrews Sisters, as usual, went big with the customers at show caught. Nonetheless, they stand in need of at least one or two fresh novelties for picture house dates … [and their] comedy interpolations could well be replaced. The Sisters continue to pack rhythm, pep, distinctive delivery, currently representing greater marquee value than ever as a result of their film appearances.[164]

Despite the reviewer's misgivings, the trio managed to bring in the largest box office for the nation that week.[165] Patty soloed the last two shows on Thursday because "grippe and high fever" forced Maxene out of the act and since "two of the girls wouldn't blend vocally, LaVerne was also dropped." LaVerne also came down with a cold, but the next day they were all singing again while a doctor and nurse attended Maxene between shows.[166]

In mid–November, the sisters appeared with Joe Venuti and his orchestra again—this time at the Adams Theater in Newark where "they got the loudest audience response and they deserved it when caught."[167] Thanksgiving week caught them back at the Stanley Theater in Pittsburgh with the Johnnie Scat Davis Band and once again they led the city's box offices.[168] In mid–December, the Andrews Sisters made the cover of *Down Beat* for the first and only time. The holiday issue featured a photo of them in performance with manager Lou Levy dressed as Santa Claus. The caption reported they were making $5,000 a week in theaters, the highest sum ever paid a singing act.[169]

The Andrews Sisters had ten chart hits in 1941, including "In Apple Blossom Time" (seventeen weeks), from *Buck Privates* which soon became their signature song; "Aurora" (eleven weeks), the story of a Rio café dancer featured in *Hold That Ghost*; "Jealous" (nine weeks), a song of almost psychopathic jealousy; "Boogie Woogie Bugle Boy" (eight weeks), also from *Buck Privates* and destined to become everyone's favorite Andrews Sisters song; "Scrub Me, Mama, with a Boogie Beat" (eight weeks), "The Irish Washer Woman" set to boogie woogie; "I, Yi, Yi, Yi, Yi" (six weeks), a forgettable number about south of the border; "I Wish I Had a Dime" (two weeks); "Sonny Boy" (one week), a Jolson number redone for laughs; "The Nickel Serenade" (one week), and "Sleepy Serenade" (one week), also from *Hold That Ghost*.[170]

On Friday, December 5, 1941, the Andrews Sisters opened at Cincinnati's Shubert Theater with Joe Venuti and his orchestra. An enthusiastic reviewer reported:

> The present stint of the trio calls for them to purr songs, whisper 'em, kid 'em and stand up and sing out sweet and straight in a manner that ignites old favorites with a new blaze of life. In putting over their songs the girls offer a stylized brand of throaty harmonizing and phrasing that's as easy and natural as breathing and as smooth as velvet. No animated wooden Indians on a stage, the girls intersperse their numbers with rhythmic business that contributes no little to a nicely paced act.[171]

After filling the house the first two days of their engagement, the sisters arrived at the theater on December 7 for their first Sunday performance. They sensed a strange pall about the theater. Maxene remembered the day:

> I noticed something different when LaVerne, Patty and I arrived at the Shubert Theater. We had been packing them in throughout our engagement there, and the management told us we were attracting such large audiences every afternoon and night that we were about to break the theater's attendance record for a single engagement.
>
> I believed it. Every day when we arrived, there was a long line of people standing on the sidewalk in front of the box office to buy tickets for our first show. It didn't make any difference how cold it was—and in Cincinnati, it gets plenty cold!—or how much snow we might get, people were lined up for blocks. But on that Sunday in 1941, the sidewalk was empty.

From a vantage point of fifty years, it's clear to see that the absence of a line in front of the theater that day was symbolic. We went inside and started down the center aisle toward the stage. But instead of seeing the lights up as usual and people busily preparing for another day's performance, the theater was dark. As we walked farther down the aisle, we could see that the doorman and the stage-hands were gathered in a small cluster on the stage, huddled around a small table model radio. There was only a bare light bulb illuminating that one small spot at center stage. When we came within hearing distance, a radio announcer told LaVerne, Patty, and me what the workers on the stage already knew: Pearl Harbor, a place we'd never heard of, had been attacked.

I looked at the doorman and asked the question that millions of other Americans were asking each other that day: "Where's Pearl Harbor?"

He said he wasn't sure, but that the voice on the radio was saying we were finally in the war.

Suddenly the empty sidewalk outside the theater symbolized a stark reality: The world was different now and would be for the rest of our lives.[172]

CHAPTER SIX

1942–1943

Everywhere they appeared—on records, on radio, in movies, on USO tours in Europe and in nightclubs and theaters across the land—they made the air smell a little sweeter and the world look a little brighter.[1]

When World War II began, the Andrews Sisters were top names in the entertainment industry of America. Veterans of four nationally broadcast radio shows and guests on many others, they had appeared in five films—three of them hits—and set attendance records at almost every theater where they performed. Their Decca record sales totalled more than eight million and they reigned as "queens of the juke box." They held the record for an act at New York's Paramount Theater where they appeared seven times for a total of fifteen weeks during the previous three years.[2] A reviewer remarked, "In case you have never heard a radio, don't know what a phonograph looks like, have never been to a moving picture show, or aren't breathing, the Andrews Sisters are what makes the juke-box industry such a whale of a business."[3] America was on first name basis with Patty, Maxene, and LaVerne Andrews, and the only singers who matched their popularity were Kate Smith and Bing Crosby—and a couple of fast rising newcomers named Dinah Shore and Frank Sinatra.

Although much of the world had been enmeshed in the turmoil of war for some time, most Americans thought they would be spared battle and were reluctant to support America's entry into the conflict. That changed dramatically after the Japanese simultaneously attacked Pearl Harbor in Hawaii and Manila in the Philippines, virtually destroying the Pacific defenses of the United States. America responded by declaring war on the Japanese Empire and the

Axis powers of Europe. Young men lined up in droves to enlist in the various branches of the armed forces—and those who didn't volunteer for service were soon drafted. The nation rapidly converted its industrial complex to wartime production. As young men left jobs for military duty, older men and women filled their roles in war-related industries. Job opportunities in industrial cities attracted workers from throughout the nation, creating population shifts that would forever alter the face of America.

With the rest of America, Hollywood joined the war effort. Big names like Kate Smith, Bing Crosby, Bob Hope, and the Andrews Sisters appeared at bond rallies to raise money to finance the war. Movie studios began cranking out patriotic, propagandist films to help maintain public support for the war and provide escapist fare so people could forget the horrors of the conflict for a few hours. Some months prior to the Pearl Harbor attack, the YMCA, YWCA, National Catholic Community Service, National Jewish Welfare Board, Salvation Army, and National Travelers Aid Association joined forces to create the United Services Organization, better known as the USO. Financed by voluntary contributions, the USO established "canteens" throughout the country where servicemen could relax during off hours or en route to new assignments. Hosts served refreshments while local and nationally known performers provided entertainment for military personnel. The best known of these canteens were the Stage Door Canteen in New York City and the Hollywood Canteen in Los Angeles.

The music industry responded to the U.S. entry into war with a spate of new songs, including such fortunately forgotten titles as "You're a Sap, Mr. Jap," "Let's Knock the Hit Out of Hitler," "We're Gonna Have to Stop the Dirty Little Jap," and "Put the Heat on Hitler, Muss Up Mussolini and Tie a Can to Japan."[4] Happily, no one talked the Andrews Sisters into recording any of these.

After Christmas the sisters headed back to the West Coast to fulfill the next chapter in their contract with Universal Studios. Shortly after arriving in Hollywood, they learned their record "In Apple Blossom Time" was among the five top-selling Decca records of 1941. Of the twenty-five top titles listed by the five major record companies for 1941, only three were *not* big band numbers, namely those by the Andrews Sisters, Bing Crosby, and the Ink Spots.[5] The sisters were number eight among the top thirteen most popular recording artists played on juke boxes in 1941; all others on the list, except Bing Crosby, were big bands.[6] Big bands still dominated pop music but the Andrews Sisters were giving them some stiff competition.

As the nation was reeling from the Pearl Harbor attack, the Andrews Sisters' new film for Universal was released. It was a departure from their previous three movies in that they did not share the screen with Bud Abbott and Lou Costello. Universal apparently thought both teams were now big enough to carry films on their own. Initially called *Wake Up and Dream*, then *What's Cookin', Soldier?*, the film was eventually released as *What's Cookin'?* Film historian Clive Hirschhorn succinctly summarized the plot: "Those curious enough to find out 'What's Cookin'?' left the cinema with very little on their plates. Really a jam session by the Andrews Sisters, Woody Herman and His

Orchestra, Jane Frazee, and the Jivin' Jacks and Jills, it was another quickie from Universal about a group of youngsters ... determined to make it into show business."[7]

What's Cookin'? was the beginning of a string of weak films by the sisters. The comedy is bad, except for a short scene where the Andrews Sisters were stacked to be sawed in half by an amateur magician. Some of the musical numbers were good, such as "Woodchopper's Ball," a swing number by Woody Herman accompanied by the energetic dancing of the Jivin' Jacks and Jills, but some were awful, such as "Il Bacio (The Kiss)," an unlikely duet between the Andrews Sisters and Gloria Jean, Universal's B-answer to Deanna Durbin. A soldier occasionally wandered in and out of the meandering plot to remind the audience that a war was going on. Although the Andrews Sisters received top billing, it was the music of Woody Herman and the dancing of the Jivin' Jacks and Jills that made this film worth watching. A very young Donald O'Connor, who would later become one of Hollywood's popular song and dance men, made an early film appearance.

Most critics didn't like the film. *What's Cookin'?* was described by a *New York Times* critic with a culinary flair as "a highly incidental dish of nonsense knocked together by Universal out of a little bit of this (the Andrews Sisters) and a little bit of that (Gloria Jean), all oozing with jam provided by Woody Herman's orchestra and a gang of rug-cutting kids. Cinematically speaking, it's as dull as a plate of stale hash and has no more form or consistency than a bowl of jelly dropped upon the floor."[8] But the critic grudgingly admitted that the film had "a few rather juicy plums" of music. Typically, *Variety* was kinder and praised the new, young talent in the film, as well as the "plentiful display of the showmanly presentations by the Andrews Sisters and the Herman band."[9] *Metronome*, which usually liked nothing associated with the Andrews Sisters, gave *What's Cookin?* a surprisingly good review; however, most of it praised Woody Herman's band.[10]

The last three films of the Andrews Sisters had been box office hits and contributed significantly to their career, thanks partly to the rising popularity of Bud Abbott and Lou Costello. *What's Cookin?* was no big hit at the box offices, but it pulled in many of the sisters' fans. Unfortunately it set the pace for their remaining pictures at Universal, silly predictable plots sprinkled with musical numbers. Universal apparently realized the Andrews Sisters' name could pull in audiences for any film, and consequently didn't waste money on script writers.

After finishing *What's Cookin'?*, the sisters left Hollywood for another grueling cross-country tour. In early February, the Golden Gate Theater in San Francisco hosted them again as they surpassed the box office of their earlier visit[11] and made $5,900, their highest weekly salary.[12] A reviewer noted: "Warblers are even hotter now than they were on their previous tour."[13] Later in the month, the Andrews Sisters were back at the Chicago Theater for five shows a day (six on Saturday) starting at 9:30 A.M. and ending at 10:30 P.M. They again led the city's box offices.[14] A reviewer was impressed by their act:

Gloria Jean and popular band leader Woody Herman joined the Andrews Sisters in *What's Cookin'?* (1942), an inane musical comedy romp about kids trying to break into show business. (Robert Boyer Collection)

> The [Andrews Sisters] improve with age in showmanship, singing ability and drawing power. They handle swingaroos and ballads equally well, with Patty still in front with an interesting voice and a face that is a natural for mugging. Patty, too, is great on handling noisy jitterbugs, and they were many at the first show.[15]

Their astute manager, Lou Levy, negotiated a guarantee of $4,000 and a split of the gross, or $7,750 for the first week, again their top weekly salary.[16] While in the city, Patty celebrated her 24th birthday (she claimed it was her 22nd) and threw a party for the press and radio executives in the Radio Room at the Chicago Theater.[17] Detroit's Michigan Theater was their next stop where they again topped the city's box offices[18] and walked away with $8,200 to make them the highest paid vocal group in the business. From Detroit they moved on to the Palace Theater in Cleveland, predictably pulling in the city's highest theater gross, after which they were called back to California for more movie-making.[19]

The sisters received top billing in *Private Buckeroo*, their second movie of 1942, released in late May and an obvious contribution to the war effort. The diffuse plot of this rambling film seems pieced together with cuttings swept from Universal's editing room floor. The only reason for watching it today are the musical numbers by the Andrews Sisters and Harry James and His Music Makers, and the jitterbugging Jivin' Jacks and Jills. The limp plot about an orchestra leader (Harry James) drafted into the army with his musicians provided excuse for a series of musical numbers. Inexplicably wandering in and out of the plot, the Andrews Sisters sang six songs, including "Three Little Sisters" (wearing gowns that look like they were made from their dressing room drapes, complete with nipples that were surely unintended), "Six Jerks in a Jeep" (in WAC uniforms in the back of a jeep, one of their more forgettable numbers), "That's the Moon My Son" (a rare film appearance when they don't wear matching outfits, although they share gigantic shoulder pads that make the Green Bay Packers look wimpy), and "Don't Sit Under the Apple Tree" (back in khaki again with comic assistance from Shemp Howard, one of the original Three Stooges). They send the boys off to battle with a rousing "Johnny Get Your Gun Again" and conclude the film with "We've Got a Job to Do," sung over scenes of war preparation on the home front. The film was intended as war escapism with a heavy dose of patriotism to boost the morale on both the home and fighting fronts. It probably succeeded.

Advertisements of the film promised it was as good as *Buck Privates*. The critics didn't think so. A *New York Times* reviewer began: "For consistent ineptness, for frantic dullness, for the sheer impertinent waste of film at a time when Hollywood supposedly is seeking ways of saving raw stock 'Private Buckeroo' ... deserves some sort of prize." He continued: "[The cast includes] those Andrews Girls whose close harmonies continue to remind this corner of the effect of a nail scratched on a slate blackboard."[20] *Variety* was kinder: "Despite total lack of plot structure, 12 musical numbers are spotted along the route of sufficient merit in both rendition and setup to make this one a strong filmusical programmer." Regarding the Andrews Sisters: "[They] deliver in their regular expert style."[21] A later critic described *Private Buckeroo*: "As ridiculous as a zoot suit and just as shapeless."[22] Nonetheless, the popularity of the Andrews Sisters and the first movie appearance of Harry James managed to attract a sizeable audience. It was a hit at the box office.

After finishing *Private Buckeroo*, the sisters were back on the road. Before leaving Los Angeles in early June, they headlined the Orpheum Theater where they pulled in a full house: "When [Al] Lyons announced the Andrews Sisters, the audience welcomed them with thunderous applause.... Audience gave them a swell reception for a swell performance. Show ended with the playing of 'Star-Spangled Banner.'"[23]

Later that month, the sisters almost lost their manager Lou Levy to the war when he was slated for induction into the army. He arranged for his brother to manage his music publishing business, and Marty Melcher (who would play a later role in the Andrews Sisters' lives) was scheduled to manage the trio.[24] However, after Levy's physical examination revealed tumors on his arm, he was exempted from military service and resumed his civilian activities.[25] The tumors were later successfully removed.[26]

While traveling from Minneapolis to an engagement in Davenport, Iowa, in late June, Patty was taken from the train in Rock Island, Illinois, for an emer-

Private Buckeroo (1942) was another of the Andrews Sisters' war-themed films from Universal Studios. This was the first film appearance of Harry James, but the sisters previously sang with him in the movie theater circuit. (Author's collection)

gency appendectomy. The Davenport engagement was cancelled, as was a scheduled three-week date at New York's Paramount Theater.[27] Her sisters and manager Lou Levy remained with her, and Peter and Olga Andrews drove in from California. Olga was so exhausted by the trip, she was confined to a bed in Patty's room. A *Down Beat* story claimed Patty's appendectomy cost the trio $40,000 in cancelled bookings.[28]

The sisters' first appearance after Patty's surgery was at the Hippodrome in Baltimore where she was "as good as new, giving out with the solid jive and sending to the very limit to vociferous audience response." The sisters, billed as "America's No. 1 Singing Trio" gave the theater one of its biggest weeks.[29] A teenage fan of the sisters named Joyce DeYoung was thrilled when she saw the sisters entering the theater during this engagement. She later saw their show and never dreamed that one day she'd be one of the Andrews Sisters.[30] Despite a heat wave in Boston, their next stop, the sisters pulled an audience into the RKO Theater that once again topped the city's weekly box offices.[31] *The Billboard* reviewed their show: "For a call-back [they] do a new number called 'Strip Polka,' a sure-shot hit. Patty emulates a burlesque queen's routine, her two sisters coming in on the comedy. Draw terrific laughs and crowd clamored for more but to no avail."[32]

The Andrews Sisters, like most of America, were unashamedly patriotic after the bombing of Pearl Harbor and bursting to do all they could for the war effort as they began performing at military camps and installations near their theater dates. Maxene remembered:

> Our parents, in their early fifties, were super patriots who supported the war and FDR with enthusiasm. That rubbed off on LaVerne, Patty and me, and we were able to project our Americanism to our audiences. Our feeling was that we had beaten the Depression, and now we were going to beat the enemies. Americans could beat anything and anybody, and if you didn't believe it, the Andrews Sisters would make a believer out of you.
>
> Patty, LaVerne, and I wore our patriotism on our sleeves in the khaki clothing that became popular, especially for us in our wartime movies. The response to our enthusiasm became so great that the Air Corps crews began naming their fighter planes and bombers after our song titles.[33]

In summer 1942, Leeds Music Corporation published an anthology of sheet music entitled *The Andrews Sisters' Army, Navy and Marines Song Folio.* The publisher's foreword claimed that the songs were the ones most requested by servicemen at the various camps where the sisters sang: "We felt that the Andrews Sisters were so closely allied with the building of morale based on their activities in Hollywood, on the radio, in personal appearances and on records that they should have the privilege of selecting these songs."[34] More likely Lou Levy, the sisters' manager and owner of Leeds Music Corporation, selected the songs; nonetheless, the inclusion of the Andrews name in the title illustrates the sisters' popular association with entertaining servicemen and supporting the war effort.

On August 1, 1942, the Andrews Sisters' recording sessions came to an abrupt halt. The American Federation of Musicians struck against the record companies, claiming the recording industry was ruining the jobs of over 60 percent of the AFM membership.[35] Juke boxes and radio disc jockeys were replacing live music and thus the jobs of AFM members. Virtually all recording artists honored the strike. For months the AFM negotiated with record companies to get more money, but they were unable to reach agreeable terms until September 1943 when Decca was the first company to record again. Decca, like all record companies, anticipated the strike and consequently backlogged recordings for release during its duration. None of the companies, however, anticipated the great length of the strike, and consequently eventually exhausted their backlogs.

The Andrews Sisters' third film of 1942 was completed in thirteen days in early September. Although the Andrews Sisters received top billing, *Give Out, Sisters* was about a young heiress (Grace McDonald) trying to break into show business as a dancer over the objections of her guardians, three prudish spinster aunts. The predictable but entertaining, fast-paced plot included a segment with the Andrews Sisters disguised as the three maiden aunts. The talented cast included such Universal staples as Charles Butterworth, Walter Catlett, Donald O'Connor, Peggy Ryan, and the Jivin' Jacks and Jills. Two of the sisters' co-stars would move on to greater roles. Dan Dailey, the male romantic lead, became a popular song and dance man in 20th Century–Fox technicolor extravaganzas with the likes of Betty Grable, Ethel Merman, and Marilyn Monroe. William Frawley, already middle aged, played the nightclub owner and a decade later achieved television immortality as Fred Mertz in *I Love Lucy*. Film buffs will recognize the sisters' old boss from their pre "Bei Mir" days, Leon Belasco, who had a small role as a waiter.

The Andrews Sisters sang four songs in *Give Out, Sisters*, including "New Generation," sporting peculiar caps perched precariously atop their heads; "You're Just a Flower from an Old Bouquet," looking glamorous in powdered colonial wigs and gowns; "Who Do You Think You're Fooling?" wearing horizontal black and white stripes over shoulder pads that would chill the heart of a linebacker; and "Pennsylvania Polka" in their old maid disguises. Patty sprained her ankle during the "Pennsylvania Polka" number, but Universal had a schedule to meet so a doctor put a cast on her foot and within hours she was back in the studio to finish the scene.[36]

Most critics were unenthusiastic about *Give Out, Sisters*. A film historian later wrote: "The tone of the reviews might better have been directed toward Hitler."[37] *Variety* reported that "the Andrews Sisters are here starred in a musical whose only appreciable virtue is the singing of several songs by the harmony trio ... Popularity of the Andrews threesome is all that recommends the picture for boxoffice purposes."[38] The *New York Times* was less generous: "There is nothing as exasperating as a bad musical film, and Universal appears to have missed on all bets in making 'Give Out Sisters.'"[39] Other reviews were more positive. *Daily Variety* liked the film: "Here is an all-out comedy, expertly built and played for laughs.... The Andrews Sisters justify their entertainment repute."[40] *Motion Picture Herald* opined: "This is without question the best of the minor musicals which have rolled in unspectacular succession from the sound stage of Universal."[41] I personally think *Give Out, Sisters* holds up better than most of the sisters' Universal wartime films. The supporting cast is strong, the musical numbers are fun, the dances are lively, and the pace is fast. A great film it is not, but fun escapist fare it is—complete with dance, romance, music, and comedy.

Shortly after the release of *Give Out, Sisters*, the Andrews Sisters told the press they were unhappy with their movies. "Universal has made us look so bad in pictures, it must be an art. They must study it nights, like homework." They went on to say that others in Hollywood were getting glamorous makeovers, but they were given roles and costumes that made them look like "underfed goats." They claimed they tried to buy their contract from Universal, but the studio wasn't interested in selling. Patty told the *New York Post*, "[T]he critics were right about that last turkey [*Give Out, Sisters*] of ours. To say anything nice about it, a critic would have to be practically a relative." The sisters claimed that when they first went to Universal, only one person on the board of nine directors had ever heard of them. They were told: "Your necks are too long, your faces are thin, your eyes are sunk in, and you walk like football players. Maybe your singing will put you over, but you girls are really ugly." Maxene added: "But they made us look so ugly, I was ashamed to walk out on

Disguised as prudish spinsters, the Andrews Sisters receive a disapproving glance from butler Leonard Carey in *Give Out, Sisters* (1942). (Author's collection)

the street. When I saw one of the pictures up in the Bronx, I ran out crying. People were laughing at us." LaVerne said: "You go in and tell them, 'Look, we're not happy,' and they pat you on the fanny and say 'Oh, now it's all right,' and that's all that happens. They've patted me so much I've lost 15 pounds."[42]

The Andrews Sisters may have been unhappy with their films, but they didn't harm the trio's popularity. Fans were still flocking to their movies, buying their records, lining up for their personal appearances, and dropping nickels to hear their songs.

In late September, the sisters were back at New York's Paramount for four weeks where they once again brought in the city's biggest box offices[43]: "Andrews Sisters, back from a picture-making jaunt to Hollywood, reveal plenty of professional skill and poise."[44] The sisters sold war bonds in a "Dressing Room Bond Canteen." Patrons who purchased a $100 bond at the theater were taken backstage to the sisters' dressing room where they met the Andrews Sisters and received an autographed hit record from them.[45]

After closing at the Paramount, the sisters moved on to Philadelphia's Earle Theater where a reviewer thought Hollywood had taught them some new tricks: "Fresh from the Hollywood lots, trio has learned a glamour trick or two, and look plenty appealing to the eyes. In their customary professional eclat, pitch

Looking glamorous in powdered wigs and colonial gowns, the Andrews Sisters sing "You're Just a Flower from an Old Bouquet" in *Give Out, Sisters* (1942). (Author's collection)

their voices for the swing ditties identified with their disking."[46] While there, they almost doubled the average box office.[47] From the Earle, they went to the Chicago Theater for two weeks and again led ticket sales for their best tally in the city.[48] A reviewer noted: "[T]he Andrews Sisters ... live up to their motion picture enhanced reputation of providing sock harmonics.... Their rendition of 'Strip Polka' highlights a sock performance, closing the show."[49]

"Strip Polka," one of the Andrews Sisters' big hits of late 1942 and early 1943, was written and originally recorded by Johnny Mercer. After it caught on, several covers were made, including one by the sisters which, of course, was panned by *Down Beat* who thought it lacked the "sprightliness" of some of the other versions and was "unconvincing."[50] Fans felt otherwise, and the Andrews' version eventually surpassed the Mercer recording in popularity and sales.[51] Like "Hold Tight" and "Beer Barrel Polka," "Strip Polka" had problems with some of the blue-nosed watchdogs of the times. The lyrics about a stripper named Queenie who danced in a burlesque hall seem mild today:

> There's a burlesque theater where the gang loves to go
> To see Queenie, the cutie of the burlesque show.

From the time they achieved national fame in 1938 and throughout the war years, the Andrews Sisters performed regularly at the Paramount Theater in New York City. Here fans line up to see the sisters who shared the bill with *The Major and the Minor* starring Ginger Rogers and Ray Milland. 1942. (Author's collection)

> And the thrill of the evening is when out Queenie skips
> And the band plays a polka while she strips.
> "Take it off, take it off," cries a voice from the rear.
> "Take it off, take it off," soon it's all you can hear.
> But she's always a lady even in pantomime,
> So she stops and always just in time.
> She's as fresh and as wholesome as the flowers in May,
> And she hopes to retire to the farm someday.
> But you can't buy a farm until you're up in the chips,
> So the band plays a polka while she strips.
> "Take it off, take it off," all the customers shout.
> "Down in front, down in front," while the band beats it out.
> But she's always a lady even in pantomime,
> So she stops and always just in time...

The major radio networks decreed the lyrics "vulgar," "in bad taste," and "not in the best interests of their listening public," and allowed only the instrumental versions of the song on the air. E. H. Morris and Company, publishers of "Strip Polka," responded that the song did not flaunt bad taste, but rather was about an accepted phase of American life and noted it was included in stageshows and floorshows at the Paramount Theater, Roxy Theater, and other "respectable establishments" in New York. Needless to say, the controversy greatly enhanced the song's sales and popularity. *The Billboard* claimed it was the first song to become a "smash hit" without benefit of film, musical comedy, or radio.[52]

In late November 1942, the sisters performed at the Ambassador Theater in St. Louis where "The early birds were lined up for half a block before the house was lighted on opening day and they kept this 3,000 seater jammed.... The Andrews Sisters are reserved for the windup, and just the mention of their name ... was enough to set the mob off."[53] A local critic liked their show and thought "They were lustiest, however, in their rendition of 'Praise the Lord and Pass the Ammunition,' into which the audience joined with much loud clapping of hands." The youthful audience "yelled, whistled, clapped and stomped their lusty approval."[54] The sisters were scheduled for a 2:25 A.M. "War Workers Show" but cancelled for unspecified reasons.[55] Their grueling schedule during the war years sometimes began with shows at 9 A.M. and continued into the wee hours of the following morning.

Years later, Maxene remembered that date in St. Louis. By then she and her sisters routinely entertained at military bases near their theater dates. After a long day in St. Louis when they were dead tired from performances, the sisters were asked to sing at nearby Fort Jefferson:

> We were playing St. Louis when an army officer who had been a script writer in Hollywood called and asked if we could visit Fort Jefferson. He said the boys there were homesick and trying to adjust to a new life. Many of them had left the family farm for the first time. I hesitated, I said, "Gee, I don't know. It's been a long tour. I don't know if we can make it. We're exhausted." But while I was saying it, I was remembering a popular saying of the day: "Don't you know there's a war on?" While I was in the process of changing my answer from no to yes, the officer told me how important his request was. "You've got to come, Maxene," he said. "We have boys out there who have never seen a pair of shoes or taken a bath in a tub." Then he added, "Besides, it will be a whole new kind of audience for you."
>
> From what he was saying, I was sure of that. Besides, I knew that it wouldn't be a long trip out to Fort Jefferson and one more show wasn't going to kill us. So we went.
>
> I can't say our responses were always a cheerful, "Sure, let's go get 'em." There were times when we were dog-tired and wanted to beg off, so we growled when we shouldn't have. Doing six shows a day was grueling, and when someone asked us to get in a car and drive out of town to some remote location and do a seventh show that day, it was not always easy to smile and say okay.[56]

From the time they hit the big time with "Bei Mir Bist Du Shoen" in early 1938, the Andrews Sisters' schedule was staggering. Movie-making, recording sessions, radio appearances, and personal appearances at theaters kept them moving across the country. Their 1942 schedule was a typical year:

January: Movie-making at Universal Studios in Hollywood (*What's Cookin'?*).

January 26: Recording session in Los Angeles.
February 2: Personal appearance in San Francisco, California.
February 21: Personal appearance in Chicago, Illinois.
March 14: Personal appearance in Buffalo, New York.
March 21: Personal appearance in Detroit, Michigan.
March 28: Personal appearance in Cleveland, Ohio.
April: Movie-making at Universal in Hollywood (*Private Buckeroo*).
April 4: Recording session in Los Angeles, California.
April 23: Recording session in Los Angeles, California.
May 28: Recording session in Los Angeles, California.
June 6: Personal appearance in Los Angeles, California.
June 26: Personal appearance in Minneapolis, Minnesota.
June 27: Tour interrupted by Patty's emergency appendectomy.
July 17: Recording session in New York.
July 22: Recording session in New York.
July 29: Personal appearance in Baltimore, Maryland.
August 1: Personal appearance in Utica, New York.
August 21: Personal appearance in Boston, Massachusetts.
August 28: Personal appearance in Providence, Rhode Island.
September 6: Personal appearance in Atlantic City, New Jersey.
September: Movie-making at Universal in Hollywood (*Give Out, Sisters*).
September 26: Personal appearance in New York City.
October 24: Personal appearance in Newport, Kentucky.
October 31: Personal appearance in Philadelphia, Pennsylvania.
November 14: Personal appearance in Chicago, Illinois.
November 25: Personal appearance in St. Louis, Missouri.

The personal appearances were theater engagements of one or two weeks with five or six twenty-minute shows a day, beginning mid-morning and often running into the following morning to accommodate defense workers coming off the swing shift at local factories. Not listed are the many appearances the sisters made on radio, at bond drives, and at military bases and hospitals. In a forty-eight hour period, the sisters once rehearsed for two movies, made two records, rehearsed and aired a radio broadcast, and made a personal appearance at the Hollywood Canteen.[57] Years later, Patty reflected on their hectic schedule:

> All we knew is that we had a job to do ... we'd close at this theater and the next night we were opening in another theater. And then we'd finish an eight-month tour and then we'd fly out here and do pictures. And I can really honestly say that we didn't really enjoy it. It was like frantic all the time. We worked 52 weeks out of the year. For years and years and years and years.[58]

Maxene remembered those tiring years also:

> [W]e worked too hard ... We never took time out to vacation except Christmas holidays ... we never took time away from our work, to sit back and look at it. You know, you get on that treadmill and you go. And you go and you don't dare get off because if you can—if you're free to get off—that's the end of your career.[59]

The Andrews Sisters closed 1942 with a special one-hour *Command Per-*

formance radio show on Christmas Eve aired to U.S. military personnel through-out the world. The show was one of the few *Command Performance* broadcasts also aired to civilian audiences and according to emcee Bob Hope, it reached over a billion people in thirty different countries, one of the largest and most wide-spread radio audiences of the time. The star-studded variety show included a mix of comedy and songs by such luminaries as Fred Allen, Jack Benny, Edgar Bergen, Bing Crosby, Bob Hope, Kay Kyser, Charles Laughton, Dinah Shore, Red Skelton, and Ethel Waters. The Andrews Sisters sang one of their charted songs of the year, "Pennsylvania Polka," from their film *Give Out, Sisters*.

In 1942, the Andrews Sisters recorded seventeen songs. Of these, seven made the charts as well as two from 1941: "Three Little Sisters" (seventeen weeks), a patriotic song about three sisters and their military boy friends from *Private Buckeroo;* "Strip Polka" (nine weeks), the controversial polka about a stripper who longed for a quiet country life; "The Shrine of St. Cecilia" (seven weeks), a religious song about a shrine that survived a storm was recorded in 1941; "Pennsylvania Polka" (three weeks), from *Give Out, Sisters*, one of the sisters' enduring songs, which did not begin as a big hit; "That's the Moon, My Son" (two weeks), another song from *Private Buckeroo*; "Mister Five by Five" (two weeks), a musically clever, but politically incorrect ditty about a pound-enhanced man; "Here Comes the Navy" (two weeks), "Beer Barrel Polka" with new lyrics for the war; "I'll Pray for You" (one week), love on the saccharine side with a touch of religion was recorded in 1941; and "Don't Sit Under the Apple Tree" (one week), from *Private Buckeroo*—another of the sis-ters' enduring songs that did not begin as a big seller.[60] Decca reported that the sisters were their third highest money-makers in 1942 at $48,300, surpassed only by Jimmy Dorsey and the perennial top earner Bing Crosby.[61]

The Andrews Sisters were frequently called "Queens of the Jukebox," not only because their records often made the jukeboxes but because their career coincided with the rise of the jukebox as a source of entertainment and distri-bution of records.

Today's jukebox is only one of many ways in which popular music is dis-seminated, and a relatively minor one. When the Andrews Sisters' career began, radio was not dominated by disc jockeys, and some record companies did not allow their records played by the few disc jockeys on the air. The phonograph was not yet a standard fixture in most American homes and consequently, fans of popular music relied on jukeboxes to hear their favorite songs and singers. Jukeboxes were ubiquitous. Wherever people congregated, jukeboxes were found—restaurants, cafeterias, coffee shops, drugstores, bars, train stations, and bus depots. Young people had their popular hangouts and central to them was a jukebox, usually with enough space for dancing. This period setting is caught in Glenn Miller's 1943 swing hit "Juke Box Saturday Night."

Moppin' up soda pop rickeys	Juke Box Saturday Night.
To our hearts' delight.	Goodman and Kyser and Miller
Dancin' to swingeroo quickies,	Help to make things bright.

Makin' hot licks with vanilla,
Juke Box Saturday Night.

They put nothin' past us,
Me and honey lamb.
Makin' one Coke last us
Til it's time to scram.

Money, we really don't need bad.
We make out alright.
Lettin' the other guy feed that
Juke Box Saturday Night.

After sippin' a soda, we got a scheme.
Somebody else plays the record machine.
It's so easy to say pet names
When you listen to the trumpet of Harry
    James.
We love to hear that tenor croon
Whenever the Ink Spots sing a tune…

Money, we really don't need it.
We'll make out alright.
Lettin' the other guy feed that
Juke Box Saturday Night.

In 1938 when the Andrews Sisters' career was taking off, sales to jukebox operators accounted for 60 percent of all record sales, three-quarters of which were Decca records—primarily because of the thirty-five cent record Jack Kapp sold when other companies sold theirs for seventy-five cents. No one really knew how many machines were in operation, but estimates ranged from a quarter-million to a half-million.[62]

For much of America, the jukebox was the chief purveyor of popular music. Some singers had radio shows, such as Bing Crosby and Kate Smith, and bands routinely broadcast from hotel ballrooms—and a few, such as Benny Goodman and Glenn Miller, had their own radio shows. Singers sought guest slots on the major radio shows to introduce their latest records to the public. Major entertainers without radio shows, such as the Andrews Sisters, toured the country to reach audiences, but even with packed houses they reached a small portion of the population. Thus it was the jukebox, ultimately found almost everywhere people congregated, that spread popular music to the masses.

Jukebox operators owned the machines and placed them in public places where the proprietors received a cut of the profits. Operators bought their records from a middle man, or jobber, alert to the musical tastes of the area he covered, who relied on record reviews in trade publications such as *The Billboard* and *Variety*. In the early years of the jukebox, significant regional differences in musical taste prevailed to which the operator had to be sensitive. For example, a jukebox catering to patrons in a Missouri tavern would offer different musical selections from one catering to a high school crowd in Brooklyn. Songs censored by radio networks, such as the Andrews Sisters' "Hold Tight" and their later hit "Rum and Coca-Cola," became huge hits on the jukeboxes where they were played without censorship.

Jukeboxes were a multimillion-dollar industry whose benefactors included record manufacturers, recording artists, music publishers, songwriters, nightclubs, restaurants, taverns, as well as jukebox operators and manufacturers.[63] In 1940, *The Billboard* reported it took 720,000 records per week to fill the jukebox demand[64]—most of these were Decca records, and many were by the Andrews Sisters.

After a dark year of adjusting to the new war when it seemed each headline brought more bad news from both the European and Pacific fronts, the tide began to change for the United States and its allies in early 1943. In January, Allied victories over the Japanese in the Pacific at Guadalcanal and New Guinea stopped the southern expansion of Japan. The British defeated Rommel in the deserts of northeast Africa as American forces landed in northwest Africa to thwart the tide of German advancement. Meanwhile, the Russians stood against the Germans at Leningrad and eventually turned them back. Everyone knew the war was far from over, but the possibility of an Allied victory became increasingly likely.

In late January 1943, Patty, Maxene, and LaVerne Andrews filed an injunction in New York supreme court to restrain two dancing sisters, Lillian and Vivian Andrews, from using the "Andrews Sisters" billing. The singing sisters charged that the dancing sisters were trying to cash in on their popularity in the entertainment field. A few days later, the dancing Andrews Sisters filed a counterclaim against the singing Andrews Sisters, as well as their manager Lou Levy and their agency General Amusement Company, charging them with "attempting to force them to change their name; also with conspiracy, by spreading false rumors about them." They also claimed the singing sisters had interfered in their careers and their attempts to get work.[65]

The charges seem a bit silly. No one would mistake the act of the attractive shapely blonde dancers for that of the singing trio. The judge apparently thought so too. He examined affidavits and birth certificates presented to the court by dancer Vivian Andrews and singer Maxene Andrews as proof that the name "Andrews" was actual and not assumed. He then denied both claims and dismissed the case.[66]

The following year in late November, the two dancing Andrews Sisters and the three singing Andrews Sisters were back in court. The dancers claimed they had used the name "Andrews Sisters" since 1937, before the singing Andrews Sisters achieved popular name recognition. More importantly, the dancers claimed the singing sisters and their agent had let it be known in the trade that if the dancers advertised under the name "Andrews Sisters" they would take retaliatory action.[67] No follow-up story appeared. Apparently the case was again dismissed.

In early 1943, the sisters were back in Hollywood doing yet another ten-day wonder for Universal Studios. This one was originally called *Solid Senders*,[68] but was released as *How's About It?* in late January. The Andrews Sisters hang about the film to provide musical interludes in a story of weak comedy and predictable romance. The sisters play a trio of elevator operators in a music publishing building who are trying to make the big time. Mary Wickes, a B-version of Eve Arden, wisecracks one-liners to considerably aid the comedy. Shemp Howard plays his usual stooge role. The best musical number in the film is "East of the Rockies," which includes dance routines by the sisters and three jitterbugs. Patty shows off her not-inconsiderable dance skills with three young hoofers, especially Bobby Sheerer who also livens up the opening number, "Going Up," with his spirited steps. The final scene includes an energetic drum solo by Buddy Rich whose orchestra then backs the sisters on "Here

Comes the Navy"—new lyrics to their old arrangement of "Beer Barrel Polka." The film ends in a burst of patriotism with the Navy going off to war as the skies fill with fighter planes spelling "U.S.A." in formation—probably the same footage that concluded *Private Buckeroo*. The film was intended as wartime escapist fun with a dose of patriotism for good measure. Certainly it was not a great film, but it was not intended to be. It is still an entertaining period piece with some good dance and musical numbers.

The *New York Times* did not bother to review the film, and *Variety* could find little to recommend it except the music of the Andrews Sisters: "'How's About It' is a lightweight programmer that will have to carry through the dual supporting spots mainly on the strength of the Andrews Sisters. Aside from the five songs capably delivered by the trio, picture is lightweight."[69]

After their movie-making stint at Universal, the Andrews Sisters embarked on a four-month tour of movie houses from coast to coast with Mitch Ayres and his orchestra. At Oakland's Orpheum Theater, the sisters netted $10,500, one of their highest salaries.[70] While in Oakland, they signed records at a local department store and told a local reporter: "Our only goal is to entertain. We love to sing and if singing makes good entertainment, then we'll sing through every medium we find available." When asked about their movie career, Patty said, "Why kid ourselves? ... We know we'll never be the greatest stars in Hollywood. We like Hollywood. It's our home now. It's an exciting place to be and we get just as much of a kick out of meeting famous players as anyone else would." [71]

In early March, the sisters arrived in Omaha where they packed the Orpheum Theater.[72] They took a quick side trip to nearby Fort Cook where they entertained the soldiers with Mitch Ayres and his orchestra who joined them for the remainder of their tour. They then moved on to hometown Minneapolis where they led the city's box offices[73] and were "better than ever,"[74] despite a cold wave and late blizzard that tied up traffic for four days.[75] While in Minneapolis, they sang for the USO on Friday, visited a Red Cross canteen the following day, made a Sunday appearance at a veteran's hospital, entertained Monday at a nearby naval base, sang at Fort Snelling on Monday night, and dropped in on a WAC reception at a local hotel on Wednesday—all this sandwiched between five shows a day at the Orpheum Theater.[76] Next on the itinerary was the Lyric Theater in Indianapolis[77] where they led the theaters' coffers: "The three singing sisters, with their distinctive style, smart sense of rhythm and their individual flair, call it personality if you wish, make their appearance a special and entertaining time. Their charm and hearty spirit infuses their singing."[78]

In later years, Maxene reminisced about the sisters' cross-country tours during the war years:

> I learned a lot about my country during World War II, and not just its geography. I learned about the American people, too, and the variety of their preferences. The response to our songs was different because the people and their backgrounds were different.
> A song that was well received in one town might not go over in another. Then

The Andrews Sisters join drummer Buddy Rich in a publicity shot for their film *How's About It?* (1943), another lightweight film from Universal Studios about three elevator operators trying to make it as a singing trio as they aid and abet romance in the office building where they work. (Robert Boyer Collection)

we had to change our act and work in several new songs to take the place of those that weren't going over well. When we came away from the East Coast, we switched our routines to meet the taste and personality of our Midwestern audiences. When we left the Midwest, we switched our routines again to appeal to the people who made up our audiences on the West Coast.

When "Bei Mir Bist Du Schoen" came out, it took about a year to convince

Shemp Howard joins the Andrews Sisters in this scene from *How's About It?* (1943) Howard was one of the staples at Universal casting and appeared in five films with the sisters. He is best remembered by film buffs as one of the original Three Stooges. Bobby Sheerer is seated behind Patty (right). (Robert Boyer Collection)

the people in California that it was a big hit, yet through all that time it was a smash in the east. It took a long time for that song to get around the country, and I don't think it ever was popular in the Midwest. But if you sang a polka in the Midwest—like the hits we had with "Beer Barrel Polka" and the "Pennsylvania Polka"—you were a smash. When you worked the South, you learned that the folks down there loved Dixieland and sentimental music.[79]

At Detroit's Michigan Theater, "The Andrews socked over five numbers at the opening which left the audience howling for more."[80] In mid–April, they were at the Stanley in Pittsburgh where an enthusiastic reviewer reported: "The smash they clocked at opener Friday could have been detected blocks away.... Gals are nattily attired in tailored, pink suits and there isn't a minute of their 15 or thereabouts that isn't red hot and rich in vocal vitamins."[81] Cleveland was next on the tour and headlines again announced topped box offices.[82] The same was true in Boston at the RKO in mid–May[83] where a reviewer noted: "Maxene, Patty and LaVerne Andrews teed-off the current season at this spot back in August ... but it's still as potent as it was then, and their names on the marquee haven't cooled off a bit."[84] They led the box office at Erlanger Theater in Buffalo[85] and were later in Providence where they brought the Metropolitan Theater "a near season high."[86] Years later, Maxene remembered those gruelling weeks on the road:

While we were on the road in the war years, it was easy to fit into our gowns and costumes. That was the result of the food shortages and the rigors of our schedule. Fast foods restaurants didn't exist, so we always looked for the closest restaurant. Usually it was a "greasy spoon," and it didn't always resemble a restaurant, either. We tried to be careful with what we ordered, so we lived mostly on sandwiches—egg salad and tuna salad. And the coffee was more like colored water.

One of our constant fears was illness. Our tours were long, and fatigue often set in. We wanted to say yes to every request, but we always had to remain aware of our health. We couldn't afford to get run down and then catch a cold or the flu. If one of the three of us got sick, it would be disaster. People didn't want to see two of the Andrews Sisters. They wanted to see all three.

Our fears were real because the threat was real. Our bronchial tubes were sensitive to infection when we became tired and run down from our tours, something we forced ourselves to guard against constantly. But it still happened from time to time. Patty once strained her vocal chords so badly you couldn't hear anything she said for a week. She had to write everything on a piece of paper.

This scared all three of us, so we sought advice and took a series of exercises in breathing and "voice placement," which helps to get the voice out of the throat without straining it. The exercises were not easy, and they weren't fun, either. We'd get dizzy and see black spots in front of our eyes and almost pass out. At times I wondered if the cure was worse than the cause, but the exercises were ultimately helpful and we were able to hold lost time by any of us to a minimum.[87]

By the end of June 1943, the sisters were back in their now-familiar stomping ground, the Paramount Theater in New York, for a six-week stay, where they had a standoff with the management when they insisted Mitch Ayres and his band accompany them rather than the band scheduled by Paramount. The sisters won and opened to predictably big box offices despite a heat wave.[88] A *Variety* reviewer was impressed by their growing showmanship, poise and appearance. The Andrews Sisters had become more than a singing trio. They were an entertainment:

> The Andrews Sisters have become standard now, not only as topflight name thrushes but as a boxoffice entity.... However, it's not just the super-jive vocalization that gets 'em. Their showmanship is undeniable. First of all they've glamorized themselves anew with good coiffing and couturriering. The gals were always of good figure and on them the long, slinky gowns look good.... But there's also now added poise and self-assurance that's compelling. The middle gal [Patty] sparkplugs the whole works with a fine sense of comedy values. The end looker [Maxene] is OK for contrast, while the older sister [LaVerne], on the other hand, is fine basic balance. They know pace and tempo and manifest innate showmanship.[89]

The Billboard's reviewer was also impressed by the sisters' evolving showmanship: "They have come a long way since their Broadway debut here.... Now they have so much more poise, and their voices blend better and have infinitely more quality."[90] A reviewer from *Metronome* magazine, which never liked the Andrews Sisters, begrudgingly said a few good things about their showmanship, but, of course, not much good about their music:

Credit the Andrews Sisters with some slick showmanship. Handling hecklers, segueing from one song to another, the stagewise girls almost made one forget how annoying their yelling delivery could be—and was... "Send Me a Man, Amen," though not especially well done, had all the earmarks of a tremendous success—even as the shouting, music-routing Andrews.[91]

A young sailor was killing time in New York as he awaited his assignment to a ship in the Brooklyn naval yard. Years later, he remembered seeing Frank Sinatra and later the Andrews Sisters at the Paramount:

> My most memorable matinees and evenings were at the Paramount Theater for two great features. The first one was Frank Sinatra, one-and-a-half hours of driving the bobby sockers wild. The second one was those three Andrews Sisters— two hours of song, dance, and jokes with the servicemen in the audience. They sure cranked up the place. I don't think those gals left one song undone from "Boogie Woogie Bugle Boy" to "Don't Sit Under the Apple Tree." The place was mobbed and it was impossible to try to meet them, which was my only regret. After the matinee, I got to thinking maybe a person could pull it off. I retired to the gents' john in seclusion for about an hour and then mingled with the evening show. It worked. I saw it all over again.[92]

During their Paramount engagement, *The Billboard* featured the Andrews Sisters on its cover for the third time. The accompanying story revealed little new about them, but noted that during their recent nationwide tour, they played "shows at service camps and hospitals in every city."[93] A feature story about the sisters appeared in the *New York Post*, for which all three sisters and Lou Levy were interviewed. They reportedly made $300,000 the previous year and were currently earning $7,500 weekly at the Paramount. A good portion of the story was about LaVerne's eight fur coats and her circular bed, Maxene's sixteen dogs, and the home the sisters' recently bought their parents in California.[94]

Wherever the Andrews Sisters performed, they visited nearby military bases or hospitals to entertain servicemen. Performing at veterans' hospitals was not entirely new to them: when they were kids, they sang at a Minneapolis veteran's hospital. During a trip back home to Minneapolis during the war, they visited Snelling Veterans Hospital and were touched when some veterans of World War I and even a few from the Spanish-American War remembered that Maxene had sung for them when she was four years old. She later speculated: "It made me think, not entirely with joy, that I might be one of the few entertainers of my generation who had sung for veterans of America's wars as far back as 1898. For all I know, there could have been some veterans of the Civil War who were residents in that hospital when I sang there as a toddler in the early 1920's."[95]

The sisters were affectionately called "the three jive bombers" by their servicemen fans and reportedly played more Army, Navy, Marine, and Air Force bases than any other vocal group during the war.[96] Maxene remembered: "We worked very hard ... at hospitals, camps—six shows a day and, between shows, the USO centers. We'd even go to factories and sing for—what were they called?—the 'Rosie the Riveters.'"[97] Elsewhere she added: "My sisters and I didn't just go when asked. We went when we weren't asked, too. We always told the people handling our schedule in the next city to find some soldiers, sailors, and marines who would like to see and hear the Andrews Sisters in person."[98] In the cities they visited, the sisters invited three servicemen to dinner each night. On nights when other commitments interfered, they asked the manager of a chosen restaurant to give free dinners to the first three servicemen who came through the door and charge it to their account.[99] When they played the Paramount in New York, they made frequent appearances at the Stage Door Canteen to entertain the military personnel there. Maxene remembered that they also visited Times Square to help sell war bonds: "There was a big stage right there in the middle of the Square, and thousands of people would line up to buy war bonds and listen to us sing while they waited. We'd sing for two and three hours at a time. Then we'd hurry back before we were due in the theater again."[100]

Maxene remembered entertaining a shipload of troops in Seattle as they left for overseas.

> I remember we sang ... up in Seattle when a whole shipload of troops went out. We stood there on the deck and all those young men up there waving and yelling and screaming. As we sang "Don't Sit Under the Apple Tree," all the mothers and sisters and sweethearts sang with us as the ship went off. It was wonderful. The songs were romantic. It was a feeling of—not futility. It was like everybody in the United States held on to each other's hand ... I felt we were invincible. Right is right and we were right and we were gonna win. But the news was not encouraging. [101]

Sometime in 1943, the Andrews Sisters entertained new recruits at a naval base in Long Beach, California. The sailors had just finished basic training and Patty, who emceed the program, was asked to present a dress navy uniform to a sailor from the audience as part of the transition ceremonies from boot camp. She scanned the audience and saw a cute young recruit named Jerry Myhr a few rows from the stage and invited him to join her. Reluctantly the young man came forward, a bit embarrassed by the attention, and accepted the uniform to the applause of his fellow swabbies. The show went on, and the sisters forgot the incident. Jerry Myhr did not and would reenter the Andrews Sisters' lives after the war.[102]

After the exhausting but successful tour—during which Allied troops invaded Sicily to begin the liberation of German-occupied Europe—the Andrews Sisters returned to Hollywood for yet another bout of movie-making at Universal where Mitch Ayres and his band joined them. The sisters worked well with Ayres on tour and were eager to continue the association.[103] The two movies, *Always a Bridesmaid* and *Swingtime Johnny*, were released later in the year.

Because of their contract with Universal Studios, the sisters began spending more time on the West Coast. The Andrews family liked the California lifestyle and climate, especially Peter who was enamoured of the mild California weather that reminded him of his native Greece. According to an early 1943 story, the sisters lived in a "Hollywood apartment suite" with their parents; Patty

In 1943, the Andrews Sisters bought their parents a home on an acre of land in Brentwood, a fashionable section of Los Angeles where many Hollywood celebrities lived. The sisters pose for a photographer on the front steps. (Author's collection)

and Maxene shared a lower suite and LaVerne lived with her parents upstairs.[104] The story claimed Maxene was engaged to Lou Levy, but she was in fact married to him, unbeknownst to the rest of the family.

Sometime during this period the Andrews Sisters bought their parents a home on an acre of land at 430 North Saltair Avenue in Brentwood, a fashionable suburb of Los Angeles. Maxene said that they purchased the home from a woman who feared a Japanese invasion and sold it "for a fraction of what it cost her to build."[105] Patty and LaVerne moved in with their parents. Their neighbors included such film luminaries as Gary Cooper, Tyrone Power, Caesar Romero, Nelson Eddy, and Deanna Durbin.[106] Joan Crawford was another neighbor, and Maxene sounded like a star-struck fan when she described her first meeting with Crawford: "And she's a real person.... She's glamour—but she's homefolks, too. When she found that our house was only two blocks from her own, she invited herself over."[107] Unlike many female stars she encountered, Crawford was apparently not threatened by the Andrews Sisters.

The Andrews home was "a formal, substantial stone house with an acre of ground," according to a reporter. LaVerne added that it was "a nice neighborhood … Lovely people, real home people. We meet them all out on the road before dinner walking their dogs. Our doberman pinscher is in love with Deanna Durbin's cocker spaniel." The reporter described the home as "intensively decorated" and said she'd never seen a neater house. This pleased LaVerne who told her they had no servants and their mother did most of the cleaning and cooking, although she and Patty maintained their own rooms. She added: "We love our home, we're an ambitious family—we don't lay around." The reporter continued: "The girls' [Patty and LaVerne] bedrooms were luxurious—embroidered satin bedspreads, white fur rugs scattered on top of the carpets, elaborate dressing tables, delicate china lamps and glass tables. LaVerne's was the most eye-filling—with over a hundred perfume bottles, a collection of miniature glass animals and her perfectly round bed—six feet across."

LaVerne showed the reporter her "clothes-packed closets" and impressed her as "one who has an honest respect for hard-earned cash and also a normal interest in the pleasures that money can buy." LaVerne said that during their early years on the road, they had no place or money for possessions. But when they began making good salaries, they bought themselves annuities first and then treated themselves to extensive wardrobes and "little personal things for our rooms."[108]

The sisters told another reporter the house was filled with items their parents "always wanted and never dreamed of ever really owning"—such as a "massive" clock that stood in the entry hall. She described the bedrooms of Patty and LaVerne as "done in soft pastel shades and furnished with frills to delight the most feminine heart." LaVerne's circular bed was central to her mirrored bedroom and "arranged on the end tables and soft furry scatter rugs are the kitten statuettes which she avidly collects." Patty's room was similar to LaVerne's but lacked the circular bed, and instead of cats, Patty collected china elephants. At the time she was taking an art class and showed the reporter one of her charcoal drawings.[109]

The house also had a den where the sisters rehearsed: "a small cheery room comfortably furnished with colorful modern furniture, its walls lined with books and photos showing the girls at various stages during their career…. A fireplace is on one side of the den, and above it a large tinted portrait of the girls." The den and the basement "where Mr. Andrews and the male contingent like to play poker served to accommodate the large gatherings of family and friends that periodically collect in the Andrews home." The Andrews had no domestic staff and Mrs. Andrews did most of the cooking. "Oh, what a wonderful cook we have at our house," said Patty.[110]

Peter Andrews, affectionately called "Pete the Greek" by his daughters, was definitely the patriarch of the household. He jokingly called his wife and daughters "my harem."[111] At a time when smoking was fashionable, none of the sisters smoked because their father would not allow it. He still handled the financial affairs of his daughters, invested their money, kept the books, and took care of income tax matters. LaVerne said, "Everybody loves our parents…. They've been strict with us but not unreasonable—I think it's good to have strict parents." Patty added, "We've always been one of those ideal families … even when

The sisters relax on LaVerne's round bed circa 1943. A reporter once described LaVerne's room as "eye-filling—with over a hundred perfume bottles, a collection of miniature glass animals and her perfectly round bed—six feet across ... and her clothes-packed closets." (Robert Boyer Collection)

we were kids in Minneapolis, sitting around the piano after dinner, singing and dancing." When asked about marriage, Patty responded: "I wouldn't even consider marrying a guy who'd upset my life ... the act comes first. You don't give up something as big as this. It only happens once in a lifetime to a few people."[112] LaVerne said she and Patty were both engaged, she to a musician and Patty to an agent, but they had not yet set a wedding date.

Thus was the family image the Andrews Sisters projected to their public.

The sisters' cousin Gladys Leichter remembered the Andrews homelife a little differently. Peter Andrews had a poker room in the basement where he entertained his friends on Saturday night—as he had back in Minneapolis. Olga didn't like the poker games back in Minneapolis and she didn't like them in Brentwood either. While Peter and his friends were in the basement, the sisters frequently entertained friends in the upstairs den. Neither Peter nor Olga drank and did not approve of their daughters drinking. Peter smoked cigars, but forbade his daughters to smoke. Nonetheless, the sisters all drank and smoked— but not in his presence. When the sisters smoked in the house, they went to the bathroom and blew the smoke out the window so he could not smell it.[113]

The sisters establish a domestic scene for photographers at the Andrews home circa 1943. Patty and LaVerne were still living with their parents, but Maxene lived on a small ranch in Cold Water Canyon with husband Lou Levy. (Robert Boyer Collection)

In late May, Maxene's marriage to Lou Levy became known to the rest of the family—and the general public.[114] One day at the family home, Peter announced that he planned to buy Maxene a diamond ring for her birthday. Levy saw his opportunity and said: "You don't have to buy Maxene rings ... I'll take care of that. Already she has a diamond, four carats, I bought her." The family continued talking and then slowly realized what Levy was telling them. When asked if they were angry, Levy responded, "Deep inside, they all knew it had to happen."[115] The sisters' cousin Gladys Leichter remembered that when Peter found out about the marriage "he wasn't too happy."[116]

Maxene and Lou Levy bought a home in the Hollywood Hills, which a reporter described: "The Levy hilltop home ... is furnished mainly with modern pieces in solid bright colors that blend into a warm and cheerful pattern, accented by the built-in shelves of books and records which line the walls. The living room is done in a Chinese motif with a large pastel Oriental mural.... The Levy abode also boasts a swimming pool, and a guest house that includes a spacious game room."[117]

Tom Therault's memories of the Levy home centered around a bulldozer that ended up in the swimming pool. Tom and his brother Terry, sons of the sisters' cousin Gladys, were visiting the Levys with their mother, who now lived in Los Angeles. Lou and Maxene were in the midst of a landscaping project and the contractors left the bulldozer in the backyard over the weekend. The boys were playing in the backyard while the adults were inside. An older neighbor boy came over, climbed onto the bulldozer, and discovered a key in the ignition. He turned the key, the engine started and Tom and Terry jumped on for the ride. As the horrified adults emerged from the house, the bulldozer headed for the swimming pool. The boys jumped off but the dozer ended up in the pool. Levy successfully sued the contracting company for leaving the keys in the dozer and was reimbursed for the damage to the pool.[118]

Maxene and Levy later purchased a small ranch in Cold Water Canyon in the San Fernando Valley. Maxene now had plenty of space for dogs, and she began raising them in serious fashion. At one point, she had seventy-five dogs—boxers, Dobermans, and cocker spaniels. She once helped deliver thirty-five boxer pups during a break from the road. With an additional two hundred chickens, four cows and two calves, she was in her element. She rationalized her venture as a way to provide food to the rest of the family during the wartime shortages.[119]

Maxene always took a dog with her when the sisters were on tour. She once recalled an unrehearsed incident that brought down the house in Baltimore:

> We were playing the Hippodrome Theater in Baltimore during the war, and Tyrone [named after Tyrone Power], as always, was with me. I took him on every trip we ever made for the entire fifteen years of his life....
>
> Tyrone got tired of waiting, or of our act, and walked onto the stage. After we finished our number and before we went into our next one, the three of us just stood there looking at him—and he sat there, head cocked and tail wagging, looking at us.
>
> Finally, Patty put her hands on her hips and said to Tyrone for the first time in his life, "Now what would you do if Der Fuehrer [Hitler] walked in here right now?"
>
> That little thing got right up from where he was sitting in the middle of the stage, walked to the front, straight to the floor microphone, lifted his leg, and wet the base of the mike. The applause was deafening.[120]

In late September 1943, the next Andrews Sisters film, *Always a Bridesmaid*, was released in New York at about the time Italy surrendered to the invading Allied forces. The tide of the war was continuing to move against Germany but its end was still distant.

If the Academy of Motion Picture Arts and Sciences gave an Oscar for the worst movie of 1943, *Always a Bridesmaid* may have won—certainly it would have been a close runner-up. The Andrews Sisters received top billing, but they had minor roles in this film about two detectives, played by Patrick Knowles and Grace McDonald, who independently investigated a lonely hearts club radio show where the sisters worked. They exposed a swindler and his moll who tried to sell stocks in a bogus synthetic rubber company—and fell in love in the process. Patty had somewhat of a role in the plot, weak beyond weak, but LaVerne and Maxene did little more than join her in some of the most unin-

The Andrews family poses for a picture within a picture at their home in Brentwood circa 1943. The black cocker spaniel is one of the many dogs the sisters had throughout their lives. (Robert Boyer Collection)

spired songs of their movie career. They wore variations of the same long white gowns throughout the film, except in the opening scene where they sported pastel shoulder-padded suits. An early scene suggested the sisters might have had acting skills had they been provided a script. The jitterbugging Jivin' Jacks and Jills invaded two scenes to provide the only respite in this dreary film. Even the sisters' numbers added little to the plodding plot.

The *New York Times* declined to review the film, but *Variety* wrote: "Bunch of capable people are wasted in this trite, little musical.... Even the Andrews Sisters do not fare too well because forcibly injected, with their singing, into proceedings.... The Andrews look and sing better than usual."[121]

The fourteen-month music strike ended September 20 for Decca Records, and the Andrews Sisters and Bing Crosby were in the recording studios in Los Angeles shortly thereafter, the first singers to record after the strike. Decca agreed to pay the American Federation of Musicians one-quarter cent for each thirty-five cent record it sold with proportionately more for higher priced records. The money would be used by the union to support unemployed musicians. Other record companies would make their peace with AFM in the weeks to come. Decca had long since exhausted the recordings they stockpiled for

Always a Bridesmaid (1943) was perhaps the dreariest Andrews Sisters film cranked out by Universal. Here the sisters liven it up with "Thanks for the Buggy Ride." (Robert Boyer Collection)

the strike that lasted much longer than anyone anticipated. Jack Kapp flew out from New York and Crosby's brothers Everett and Larry were also on hand for the recording session that was covered by the press and photographers.[122]

This recording date was the renewal of an association between the Andrews Sisters and Bing Crosby that began with their two-sided 1939 hit, "Ciribiribin" and "Yodelin' Jive," and the beginning of a string of hits that one observer called "a career within a career." The A-side of the record was a cover of an enormously popular song called "Pistol Packin' Mama," recorded by a "hillbilly" (country) singer named Al Dexter almost two years prior to its popularity. The song was already a million seller by the time Crosby and the Andrews Sisters recorded it, and its scarcity because of a shellac shortage had created a black market for copies.[123] The song was banned by the major radio networks because of the lines "dancing with a blonde when my wife came in" and "drinking beer in a cabaret." The ban doubtless contributed to its popularity, and was lifted only when more acceptable lines were substituted for the offensive ones.[124] Maxene explained the song:

> The song didn't have anything to do with the war.... It came from a story about a woman who owned a honky-tonk joint and whose husband operated a whiskey

still in the mountains of Kentucky. A songwriter, Al Dexter, met the woman in his travels and learned that she carried a pistol for protection from both the moonshiners and the "revenooers." She told Dexter that at night, she'd go looking for her husband in the hills, hollering his name into the dark. "Lay that pistol down, Ma, or I ain't comin'," she said he'd call back.[125]

PIC magazine carried a two-page spread about the recording session and noted that "Pistol Packin' Mama" took less than an hour to record, and the B-side, "Vict'ry Polka," was made "without mishap after a couple of quick reharsals."[126] Decca took out a full-page ad in *The Billboard* to announce the new record and released it in its "Personality" series, priced at seventy-five cents—forty cents higher than normal records. The higher price was "due to the coupling of Crosby and the Andrews trio, which means paying a double royalty."[127] *Down Beat* didn't like the record, but nonetheless predicted its success:

> Decca asks six bits for this galaxy of stars and pairing of favorites. "Pistol Packin' Mama" and "Vict'ry Polka" both receive the ultimate at the hands of Vic Schoen and throats of the Groaner and the terrifying trio! Without any help from your disc-digger, this particular disc will hit the jackpot, Therefore, it will not need the help I would feel forced to withhold in any event.[128]

Metronome, of course, disliked the song also, and in an unusual gesture, panned Vic Schoen's arrangement which it usually considered the only worthy feature of the Andrews Sisters' recordings.[129] *Metronome* may have disliked the song, but America loved it.

> Lay that pistol down, babe, lay that pistol down.
> Pistol packin' mama, lay that pistol down.
> Drinking beer in a cabaret and was I having fun
> Until one night she caught me right
> And now I'm on the run.
> Oh lay that pistol down, babe, lay that pistol down.
> Pistol packin' mama, lay that pistol down.
> I'll see you every night babe
> And I'll woo you every day
> I'll be your regular mama
> And I'll put that gun away
> Lay that pistol down, babe, lay that pistol down.
> Pistol packin' mama, lay that pistol down...

The Crosby-Andrews recording of "Pistol Packin' Mama" topped the charts almost overnight and the song had such a renewed run of popularity that Decca couldn't fill the flood of orders that came in from record stores and juke box operators.[130] A New York radio station banned the Crosby-Andrews version because of the objectionable line "drinking beer in a cabaret"; unlike most versions of the song, Decca did not use the revised line "Singing songs in a cabaret."[131] The enormous popularity of the song brought nationwide comment. An unhappy editorial writer for an Alabama newspaper wrote:

> For a generation which may be forced to grow up believing that a juke box squalling, "Put that pistol down, babe," represents the ultimate in the tenderest

Decca was the first record company to reach agreement with the American Federation of Musicians to end the 14 month strike in September 1943, and the Andrews Sisters and Bing Crosby were the first singers back in the studio. This recording session produced "Pistol Packin' Mama," the sisters' first Gold Record. (Author's collection)

> and sweetest of all arts we'd like to suggest compulsory musical appreciation courses in our schools.... We get our music nowadays from the juke box or the radio, and the miserable caterwauling that assails the American ear on every side is nothing more or less than a reflection of the decadent taste of the American adult.[132]

A *Billboard* editorial about the song concluded more positively:

> There has been much chatter, (and too much concern, we believe), about the lack of inspirational songs in this war. It doesn't matter *what* we sing, so long as we *sing*! ... We do all right with "The Star Spangled Banner" for formal occasions, and when it comes to the strictly informal intercourse with the enemy, we believe our boys will make out just as well with "Pistol Packin' Mama."[133]

The song made the news again when a group of women workers at the Hudson Motor Company in Detroit wrote lyrics relevant to their wartime work and renamed it "Piston Packin' Mama":

Working hard in the packing room
But we are having fun;

We know if we do our work well
The war will soon be won.

| Don't lay that piston down, babe, | They're for our rootin', tootin' Yanks, |
| Don't lay that piston down; | Don't lay that piston down. |

The company reported that production went up with the new song, and the women elected a "Piston Packin' Queen."[134] Needless to say, all this publicity helped sell even more records.

"Pistol Packin' Mama" became the sisters' first million seller. Its flip side, "Vict'ry Polka," was an optimistic anticipation of victory and struck a happy chord for war-weary Americans. It, too, made the charts.

The Andrews Sisters subsequently enjoyed a string of hits with Bing Crosby that made them and the popular crooner one of the most familiar associations in the music world. One writer noted: "Crosby's humor and timing and his baritone voice proved a perfect complement to the sisters' zesty delivery and close harmony."[135] Another was impressed by "how much fun they seemed to have together, and how playful so many of the numbers are."[136]

Bing Crosby and the Andrews Sisters eventually recorded forty-six songs together, half of which made the charts. They were Decca's most popular recording artists and the combination attracted legions of fans. Their songs included swing, jazz, country, Christmas, Latin, Broadway, western, and mainstream pop. Most of the songs were light and fun, but some were love ballads, and many were westerns. Typically Crosby began the song, the sisters took a chorus, Crosby joined them, the band had a few licks, Patty and Crosby duetted, Crosby soloed, Patty soloed, and LaVerne and Maxene joined Crosby and Patty for a conclusion—a lot of musical activity for the three minutes that comprised most recordings.

The sisters liked Crosby. Maxene once told a reporter he was "probably the sweetest guy in the world—*we* think."[137] Although they saw one another frequently in the recording studio, Maxene claimed they never socialized with him.[138] She remembered: "The first thing that you learned about Bing was that he was the epitome of the perfect singing companion. The second thing you learned that though he was a great-great gentleman he could be just a little moody. If that hat was planted firmly on his head, don't kid around; if that hat was real jaunty—why, then you could kid him."[139] Maxene remembered recording with Crosby as both productive and pleasant:

> Bing's conduct during the recording session was ... thoroughly professional—so we could produce the best record possible. Cutting a record with Bing wasn't at all like the recording sessions we had with Al Jolson and Danny Kaye. They broke up the joint any time we recorded with them. There was a touch of irony where Jolson was concerned. Bing idolized Al and wanted to be just like him as a performer. He tried to sing in a deeper voice, and even insisted that we record in the morning so his voice would be deeper, but he wasn't the clown in the studio that Jolson was.... Bing wasn't worried about getting laughs from the band and the crew in a recording studio at ten o'clock in the morning. That wasn't why he was there. It was strictly business with Bing....
>
> He immediately became our favorite performer to sing with. He was the complete pro. He was always prepared, a fantastic artist. His main concern was to make the record a good one, and he didn't do it by demanding perfection. Some-

times perfection can ruin a performance, so he made sure everybody got it right, but had a good time while doing it.[140]

Patty also had positive memories of their recording sessions with Crosby:

> We loved recording with Bing. It was always so exciting. He always used to do a little something unexpected, like the time he sneaked in that line at the end of "Pistol Packin' Mama"—"Lay that thing down before it goes off and hurts someone." He broke us up. We were a complement to each other ... Bing would always record at eight in the morning ... I guess he used to vocalize in the car on the way to the studio—and he always wore his golf clothes. He claimed his voice had a husky quality in the morning ... Bing believed you had the best enthusiasm the first time [and therefore never did a second take], although I secretly believe he did it so he could get out on the golf course earlier.[141]

The sisters once told a reporter when asked about Crosby:

> He's so relaxed he makes you feel easy, and so unconcerned he doesn't even bother to wear his toupee in public. He strolls on stage in the most garish clothes, stands there hand in pocket, and just sings. Often he forgets the words, but nobody cares, least of all Bing. On record sessions he's just the same; usually arrives knowing only half the number he's going to sing. Like us, he doesn't read music and learns his songs by ear. Occasionally, he gets them wrong in some small detail; and when he does, it's hard to shake him off a note he feels is right.[142]

Although the sisters spent a lot of time in the recording studio with Crosby, their relationship with him was never intimate. Patty once said: "I would honestly say that I don't know Bing.... When he'd walk in the studio you'd get to know what mood he was in. I would look at him and if I thought he was unapproachable that day I wouldn't say anything to him and we all felt that way."[143] Elsewhere, Patty said, "We had a happy marriage together.... We loved singing with Bing, just so much fun."[144] Crosby echoed her sentiments when he succinctly told an interviewer, "I like singing with them ... It's fun."[145]

Vic Schoen, the sisters' arranger, remembered the sessions with Crosby also: "We never had any problem with Crosby. I never did. And I took some risks. I took a lot of risks in the way I wrote for them. But he loved it, so I went on doing it. I never had any indication to stop doing it or to change it." Schoen explained the way Patty and Crosby worked together:

> [Patty] didn't have the ability to improvise. I used to write parts for [the Andrews Sisters] even though they couldn't read it, but they could read the words, of course, and those things that one would call improvisation were actually written for her and the same with Crosby, except he would take what I wrote and enlarge on it most of the time. The magic thing that happens there is he took what I wrote for him and added himself to it, which changed it. Sometimes it wasn't even what I had written for him, but what I had written gave him another idea.[146]

The sisters' manager, Lou Levy, told a writer years later that he encouraged the duets with Crosby: "I believe, and always believed in duets 'cause I believed in vaudeville.... I believed in entertainment, and I was for it from the very first day we started to cut material with Crosby."[147]

While Patty suggested all their recordings with Bing Crosby were done in one take, the evidence reveals otherwise. In 1996, MCA released a CD set of their complete recordings together which included four "bloopers." In all four songs it was Crosby who botched the session, not the sisters.

In the fall of 1943, the Special Services Division of the Army Service Forces began producing "V-Discs," or Victory Discs. These twelve-inch vinyl 78 RPM records featured the prominent musicians of the nation and were sent to U.S. Army forces. The Navy, Marines, and Coast Guard soon joined the program and each month during the life of the program, V-Discs were shipped to military posts throughout the world. The shipment included one hundred phonograph needles and twenty records containing about forty musical numbers.

As their contribution to the war effort, the American Federation of Musicians and the major movie and recording studios cooperated with the War Department for producing and distributing the V-Discs as a morale booster to American troops overseas. Musicians and singers contributed their talents to special recording sessions held in studios, concert halls, sound stages, military bases, and nightclubs across the country. The talents ranged from Fats Waller and Arturo Toscanini to Benny Goodman and the Andrews Sisters. The recording sessions occurred whenever and wherever the performers were available, often in the wee hours of the morning after concert or nightclub appearances.[148] Some V-Disc songs were recorded during the radio show *For the Record*, which aired weekly on Mondays over NBC for seventeen weeks beginning July 31, 1944. The show was based on requests from servicemen. The Andrews Sisters appeared on the show in September 1944 and two of their songs ended up on V-Discs.[149] The Andrews Sisters recorded a total of seventeen songs for V-Discs[150]; all were remakes of earlier hits and one was with Bing Crosby. Some were recorded specifically for V-Discs while others were tracks from radio shows.

Prior to the Andrews Sisters' nationwide tours, Lou Levy published a booklet entitled *The Andrews Sisters Publicity* and sent it to venues where the sisters' performances were scheduled. I located only one of these publicity booklets, *Press Book. Fall–Winter, 1943–44*. According to the preface written by Levy, this edition was condensed and "streamlined" because of "war conditions and paper shortage."

The twenty-two page mimeographed booklet featured a picture of the sisters on the cover and contained suggestions to impressarios for advertising the sisters' engagements. "Billing" suggestions included "The Andrews Sisters—Maxene, Patty, LaVerne—The Top Trio of the Nation" and "The Andrews Sisters—Maxene, Patty, and LaVerne—The Belles of Fire." "Catch Lines for Andrews Sisters Billing" suggested "Singsational Stars of Screen, Stage, Radio & Recordings," "Those Three Slick Chicks," and "Meet the Queens of the Music Machines."

"Helpful Hints on Promotion and Exploitation" proposed that the impressarios "Contact your local Decca Distributors ... arrange for Special Window Display Blow-Ups of Andrews Sisters in leading Music Stores." Other suggestions included screening "the latest Andrews Sisters pictures previous to or in conjunction with their stage appearance," placing a sticker advertising their appearance on juke boxes, and introducing the "Andrews Sisters Swing Sundae" through local drug stores "stating Ice Cream keeps them Thin, Healthy." The booklet also included a list of the sisters' current hit records as well as "a list of the songs that the Andrews Sisters will sing, on the current Theatre Tour." A brief biography summarized their career and noted that they lived three months of the year in California.

The booklet included several feature stories for publication in local papers. One story plugged their recent best seller "Pistol Packin' Mama" with Bing Crosby and made the dubious claim that no arrangements were used for the recording and "Bing and the sisters adlibbed throughout." A story called "Versatile Sisters" claimed Patty was "a juvenile tap-dancing champion in her home state," Maxene "of the sweet smile" was "offered several jobs as a single by bandleaders," and "LaVerne was just beginning to win acclaim in the Middle West as a concert pianist when she gave up her concert career to sing with her sisters." (LaVerne played in silent movie houses for a short time. The claims for Patty and Maxene are equally dubious but, of course, were designed to herald the sisters' talents.) Other suggested stories for local papers were: "Swingtime for Johnny" (*Swingtime Johnny*) about their recent film; "Hard Work—But Fun," claiming the sisters recently "worked continuously for forty-eight hours straight without a rest (recordings, movies, radio broadcast, and a personal appearance at the Hollywood Canteen) before they launched their current personal appearance tour"; and "Pistol Packin' Sisters," another plug for their recent record with Crosby. Additional stories included their new association with Mitch Ayres, their recent selection as the "three best-dressed girls in Hollywood," their favorite recipes—Spanish spaghetti for Maxene, corn fritters for Patty, and Lazy Daisy cake for LaVerne, their support of war bonds to help "Uncle Sam in his current drive to free the world of Fascism and Nazism," and the "Three Sisters Kennel," a dog kennel they reportedly operated in Hollywood that specialized in cocker spaniels but would eventually train seeing-eye dogs. "Synchronized Sisters" discussed the division of labor within the trio: Patty handled "promotional and publicity details" and provided their latest recordings to radio stations; Maxene, the "business head," took care of "correspondence, fan mail, traveling details and various other business activities"; and LaVerne, "who specializes in clothes as a hobby," managed the wardrobe.

A section called "Column Notes" was geared to local columnists and claimed that the sisters managed a prizefighter named Al Medrano (currently in the Coast Guard), Maxene had a vegetarian dog, a gym in their home kept them in shape, and their Victory garden specialized in "swing beans, challots and jives and pure unadulterated corn."[151] Such was the image of the Andrews Sisters that Lou Levy presented to their public.

In early December, Decca released another record by the Andrews Sisters and Bing Crosby, this one for the holidays. "Jingle Bells" and "Santa Claus Is Comin' to Town" were recorded in subdued swing. "Jingle Bells" was another million seller, and both songs were destined to become classic Christmas fare for America.

Swingtime Johnny (1943) was about a group of entertainers who left their night-club jobs to work in a war munitions factory where a saboteur was at work. The weak plot soon got lost in a series of musical numbers, including the above where the Andrews Sisters participate in an old time melodrama, "Was There Ever a Woman as Wretched as I?" An evil banker tries to foreclose the mortgage on Patty and her aged mother (Maxene) and her child (LaVerne). (Author's collection)

Later that month, *Swingtime Johnny*, the Andrews Sisters' third film of 1943, hit the theaters. The film's meandering plot was about a group of night-club entertainers who alternated as workers in an organ factory converted to war production where a saboteur was at work. Linda, the band's "canary," was played by Harriet Hilliard who later became TV's perfect mother and wife on *The Adventures of Ozzie and Harriet*. The sisters had active roles in the silly plot that fortunately soon became buried by the many musical numbers. They sang "I May Be Wrong but I Think You're Wonderful" wearing long pastel gowns and sporting the "big hair" styles that became their wartime trademark. They joined Mitch Ayres' jamming band for a brief, but lively "When You and I Were Young, Maggie." "Boogie Woogie Choo Choo," performed in a night-club setting, was perhaps the weakest number in the film. Wearing bib over-alls, they sang "You Better Give Me Lots of Lovin', Baby" as they helped Harriet Hilliard romance her boss. At an amusement park, the sisters sang a brief "Boogie Woogie Bugle Boy" when they heard the song from a sidewalk radio, but couldn't convince anyone they were the Andrews Sisters, including a man who told them, "Everytime three dames get together, they think they're the Andrews Sisters." With her child (LaVerne) and elderly mother (Maxene),

Patty confronted an evil banker who attempted to foreclose the mortgage as the sisters spoofed an old time melodrama with "Was There Ever a Woman as Wretched as I?" The film concluded with the sisters in period gowns for a medley of Gay Nineties songs with the entire cast.

Swingtime Johnny was described by a *New York Times* critic as "one of those tired and tiresome musicals with the Andrews Sisters swinging the downbeat cantatas ... we suggest that the film be very quietly hidden away.... It's pictures like 'Swingtime Johnny' that bring out the Scrooge in us."[152] The film is certainly not one of the Andrews Sisters' best efforts, but some of its musical numbers are still entertaining.

The sisters wrapped up 1943 with an appearance on an Armed Forces Radio show called *Christmas Package*, a variety show hosted by actress Linda Darnell. In addition to the Andrews Sisters, who sang "Sing," the program included singers Ginny Simms and Lena Horne. Comedy was provided by Bob Hope and Fibber McGee and Molly who reworked "The Night Before Christmas" for laughs. Army and Navy chaplains from Washington, D.C., read special Christmas messages to members of the armed forces of the Allies.

In 1943, after the musicians' strike was settled, the Andrews Sisters recorded six songs, three of them with Bing Crosby. Four of the recordings made the charts: "Shoo Shoo Baby" (twenty-one weeks), a big seller for the sisters and one of the defining songs of World War II about a sailor leaving his wife and baby as he goes to fight the war; "Vict'ry Polka" (thirteen weeks), an optimistic polka with Bing Crosby that anticipated an Allied victory; "Pistol Packin' Mama" (eleven weeks), the popular song the sisters recorded with Crosby about a trigger-happy girlfriend; and "Jingle Bells" (one week), a swing version by Crosby and the sisters that became a Christmas classic. "East of the Rockies" (one week) from the sisters' film *How's About It?* was recorded in 1942, but didn't chart until 1943.[153]

Meanwhile, Allied forces on the Pacific front were pushing the Japanese out of the southwestern Pacific in their drive to liberate the Philippines. The tide of the war was definitely turning against Japan, but it was far from over. The Pacific battles were brutal and many of the casualties ended up in the military hospitals on the West Coast. In late 1943, the Andrews Sisters visited one of those hospitals, Oak Knoll in Oakland across the bay from San Francisco, where they were deeply moved by the injuries of the men they entertained. Maxene remembered:

> No matter how many shows a day we did, we always went to the camps. We always made the hospitals when they started bringing the boys back. We were the only girls allowed in Oak Knoll Hospital when they were brought back from the Solomon Islands. They were known as basket cases.
>
> We were working the Golden Gate Theatre, in San Francisco, when a Red Cross nurse asked us if we'd come out and do a show. She kept us outside for a while. She said it would be something different from whatever we'd seen. The most important thing was that we must not break down. The last thing the boys needed were tears.
>
> We walked into the first ward and it was very quiet. When we were announced, there wasn't any applause at all. It was a very long ward. We were ushered into

the middle. There were beds in front of us, beds behind us. We finally looked. The sight was terrible. We saw boys with no arms or legs, with half faces. The three of us held on to each other, because we were afraid we were going to faint. The terrible thing was to hold back the tears.

We sang for about forty-five minutes. I think some of the fellas realized how we were feeling. One of the boys, all clothed in bandages, started to cry. He was crying throughout the numbers. Finally, one of the fellas yelled, "Don't pay any attention to him, he's just dreaming about his girlfriend." We stayed there for about three hours, going from ward to ward.

As we were leaving, a male nurse came over to us: "I have a young patient who would love to hear you sing." He asked us to sing something soft. Nice and easy and relaxed. We went down a long hallway and stopped in front of a door that two male nurses were guarding. We were ushered in. We were in a padded cell. The two guards closed the door behind us. We were alone.

In the corner we saw a figure facing the wall. We started to sing "Apple Blossom Time." About halfway through we began to hear this hum. It was discordant and got louder and louder. When we came to the end of the song, we didn't stop. We just kept singing. We repeated it and repeated it. The figure turned around. He couldn't have been more than nineteen years old. His eyes were looking at us, but he wasn't seeing us. He was lost in another world. He was humming and humming. He was so handsome and young.

A few months later, at the Golden Gate Theatre, the doorman came to us; "You have a visitor." We were just about to do our last show. In walked a serviceman. On his back was another serviceman, with no arms and no legs. One we had seen in the ward. He had his artificial arms on. He said, "I never asked you for your autograph, because I said that one day I was going to give you mine." He leaned over on the dressing table and he signed his name: it was Ted.[154]

In later years, in a plea for public support of the proposed memorial for World War II veterans on the Washington, D.C., Mall, Patty also reflected on their visit to that hospital:

My sisters and I were innocent too, but not for long. We cheered the boys as they left for war but we also welcomed back the wounded and shattered. Those are some of the faces I will never forget. In one San Francisco [Oakland] hospital ward we were briefed about what we were about to see, and we were told not to show too much emotion. Behind the doors of that dire ward were young faces contorted with pain or frozen and mute. The sight of these boys—no different than the thousands of others we entertained except that they had been chewed up and spat out by the maw of war—brought home to me the absolute horror of war and the enormity of our debt to them.

In that frightful infirmary we talked, sang and tried to do something—anything—to bring a moment of pleasure, maybe a smile or a look of hope that life will somehow be better. I tried but could not begin to match their contribution. None of us can ever fully repay those boys who sacrificed their youth so we could forget such horror existed. But we need to try.[155]

Their encounters with military men on bases and hospitals in the United States and later in Morocco and Italy during their USO tour matured the Andrews Sisters considerably and left Maxene with anti-war sentiments. She later remembered: "I don't think that I can convey to you the feeling that you get when you stand on a stage and look out on 10,000 young boys and know that half of them will not be coming back.... It made me *very* anti-war."[156] She told another reporter: "The more my sisters and I saw as we performed for the troops, the more we knew what was happening was no solution. War is a waste. It's so unnecessary. And then in 15 or 20 years, somewhere in the world, we do it all over again. People just don't learn."[157]

CHAPTER SEVEN

Interlude: A Closer Look at the Sisters

"Never let it bother you that you're not beautiful. You all have ... wonderful personalities."[1]

—Olga Andrews

America fell in love with the Andrews Sisters during World War II. The three singing sisters from Minneapolis had already caught the fancy of the nation before the war began, but the affair was consummated during the war. As Universal Studios cranked out movies featuring the sisters happily singing the boys off to battle or camping it up in comedy escapist fare, the faces of the Andrews Sisters became increasingly familiar to the nation. Their upbeat songs filled the jukeboxes and distanced their listeners from the tragedies of the war. Live performances at military bases and appearances on the Armed Forces Radio Service personalized them to thousands of enlisted men at home and overseas. Civilians flocked to their theater engagements and saw them at war bond rallies. The Andrews Sisters were part of the family everyone had left somewhere during the unsettling times of the war—the sisters back home, the girls next door, the singers of happy songs. Their wide grins, sparkling eyes, corny jokes, unpretentious glamour, and self-deprecating humor threatened no one and endeared them to the nation at war.

The description of the Andrews Sisters I remember hearing as a child during the war years was "tall, skinny, and homely"—said with affection, not derision. The sisters' plain physical features were part of their public personae,

173

albeit one not entirely warranted. Once they learned the secrets of cosmetology and fashion, they were as attractive as most women in the entertainment business. Some of their alleged unattractiveness was doubtless because they did not fit the prevailing image of Anglo-Saxon femininity. Looking more Greek than Norwegian, they were three tall, strong, angular women whose unorthodox features were not easy to pigeonhole.

Today the Andrews Sisters would not be considered tall women, but sixty years ago they were. Since then America has become taller. A press release from Universal Studios during the early years of their career reported LaVerne was 5'6", 125 pounds with brown hair and eyes; Patty was 5'6", 110 pounds with brown eyes and "Titian" hair; and Maxene was 5'4", 115 pounds with hazel eyes and brown hair. In 1947, *Metronome* published a list of "girl singers" which included height and weight, and of fifty women listed, only three were as tall as Patty and LaVerne and only four were taller.[2] Height was not considered desirable for women back then, and many a tall woman ruined her posture by slumping to appear shorter. The sisters did not slump, and thus appeared tall on stage and film, frequently taller than the men in their films.

They were not particularly "skinny," although they lacked the voluptuous figures favored by the image-makers of the time. If anything, they were a bit on the strong side of the figure-scale. Maxene once told a reporter: "We are all very healthy, in fact we are as strong as horses." All three sisters had brown eyes, but their hair changed hues over the years. Early photos reveal naturally dark hair for all of them, with Patty's perhaps a bit lighter than her sisters'. Patty became a blond early in her career—an ungallant film historian once referred to her "usual, bad blonde dye job."[3] At one time, both Maxene and LaVerne were redheads.[4] Throughout most of their career, however, Maxene retained her brunette color while LaVerne kept her hair auburn—at her death she was described as the "red headed sister."[5]

Although they shared dark hair and eyes, the Andrews Sisters did not resemble one another—unlike such sister acts as the Boswells, the Fontanes, and the McGuires, who looked almost like triplets. Maxene once told a reporter: "What I mean about our being different—well, we don't even look alike. LaVerne and I are dark. Patty is the blondest. Our eyes are pretty much alike—they've been described as 'Greek eyes.' Patty has a lovely classic face with regular features, LaVerne has our mother's determined chin, while I—I have the sort of smallish round face that goes with short dark hair."[6]

A reporter who first met the sisters in the late 1930s remembered them as "three uniformly unattractive girls."[7] Another called them "A popular sister act, more famous for their crooning than their looks" and reported that when Groucho Marx learned they traveled by airplane, he quipped "I always thought they traveled by broomstick."[8] Maxene later claimed Marx made the quip when he learned they were on the same train with him.[9] A reviewer who saw them in San Francisco observed that they were a "little on the lean and angular side."[10] Another said they "get by on sound but are still short on sight."[11] When they returned home to Minneapolis in 1942, a reporter wrote, "No one has ever accused these three of being good-looking."[12] A *Coronet* writer observed: "In a business absolutely requiring glamour, they have gone to the top—without good looks ... the Andrews Sisters just aren't good looking, and everyone knows it."[13] Singer Mel Torme, a great fan of the Andrews Sisters, once wrote: "The sisters were not particularly attractive. LaVerne ... was presentable if not beautiful. Maxene was the best looking of the three sisters, with regular features, a petite nose, and a good figure. Patty was cute, that's all there is to it. She had a gamine kind of personality, a piquant face, and expressive eyes."[14]

In 1943, the sisters' press agent revealed that LaVerne had cosmetic surgery on her nose, and the sisters were making a conscious effort to upgrade their physical appearance: "I don't know if you have seen the girls recently ... but they have been rejuvenated ... Oh, they're young enough, but they have been around an awful long time. Well, they have a hair stylist who travels around with them. LaVerne had a little something done to her nose; and their wardrobe is all new and something to dream about."[15] The reporter described their hair as "wonderfully and precariously styled." This was when they began wearing the elaborate rolled hairstyles frequently associated with them during the war years. A later writer noted: "The girls are no Elizabeth Taylors when it comes to beauty but they are far from frightening. All three have large dark eyes with heavy black lashes, nice figures, pretty legs and loads of personality."[16]

The Andrews Sisters themselves had no illusions about their looks. A *Newsweek* reporter wrote: "The girls are deadly serious about their singing, but they don't kid themselves about their looks. The first time they saw themselves on the screen, the horrified sisters discovered they looked 'like three zombies.'"[17] Maxene once told a reporter "even though God didn't give us looks he gave us personality, and that makes me feel better."[18] She explained:

> From the beginning, we were the girls next door, the kid sisters. We were never glamorous, never great beauties, but we had a wonderful thing about us. When we went overseas during the war, the fellas would say, "Gee, you're just like my kid sister." Or, "It's so good being with you because you remind me of my family." That kind of feeling has stuck with the Andrews Sisters.[19]

As Maxene put it, "we were never the kind [servicemen] put up as pin-ups, on the planes or anything. I'd say that they might have a picture of the Andrews Sisters up next to a picture of their own girl, or their mom. It didn't bother us one bit. We were adorable—we wanted to be adorable."[20] Patty once jokingly said: "Betty Grable was [the servicemen's] dream—we were their reality." Maxene added, "We wanted to please people. We wanted people to like us."[21] And in another interview, the always loquacious Maxene added: "You know, we didn't care if we were beautiful or not. We knew we sang well. People would tell me that we made them feel happy. Our songs were all upbeat."[22] "We were never considered sex symbols anyhow," she said elsewhere. "We had the girl-next-door image, and that suited us just fine. When we were beginning to sing around Minneapolis at the start of the 1930s, our mother told us, choosing her words the way only a mother can: 'Never let it bother you that you're not beautiful. You all have'—then she'd pause—'wonderful personalities.'"[23]

Part of the sisters' act was self-deprecation of their looks. Late in their career they appeared on *The Tonight Show* with Johnny Carson and told him about the time they were in North Africa and unofficially taken off a plane bound for Italy to do a USO show. Patty joked, "You know how desperate they were to kidnap the Andrews Sisters!"[24]

The barbs about their looks occasionally hurt, however. Patty remembered that after they saw their first movie, *Argentine Nights*, Maxene cried all the way home because they "looked so ugly." Regarding their movie appearances, Patty said that "We laugh at it now, but, brother, it was heartbreaking at the time."[25]

In addition to favoring their Greek side physically, the Andrews Sisters identified more closely with their Greek ancestry than their Norwegian. They were baptized into the Greek Orthodox Church and attended Greek church school after public school in their early years. Maxene once said that they never received letters from fans who identified as Norwegian, but received many from Greeks who expressed pride in sharing their ancestry.

The Andrews Sisters always insisted they had totally different personalities. Others thought so too. A writer who knew them during their early days in New York claimed, "They were as different as three sisters could possibly be."[26] Maxene told a reporter: "We are three complete individuals, we have different tastes in men, clothes, just about everything, but we get on swell for sisters who have been thrown together so much and who are so different."[27] Elsewhere, she added: "I would take care of our music. LaVerne was Miss Clothes Horse and Patty had a great comedy trait."[28] One writer described them as "the fun-loving Patty, the calculating, aggressive Maxene, and the seemingly sober LaVerne."[29] Another said: "Tall, dark LaVerne, 25, is a sort of baritone, and the one who worries about getting places on time. Tomboy Maxene, 23, a soprano of sorts, handles the Andrews checkbook. Blonde, merry Patty, 22, likes to clown."[30] The ages are off and LaVerne was not a baritone, but otherwise the sketch fits. A reporter described them at an interview: "LaVerne was in dignified street dress, Patty, the youngest, was in bright blue silk slacks, pink waist, high heeled shoes, a large and fluffy blue net bow on her yellow head. Maxene was comfortable in a cotton house coat, rolled socks, battered brown and white sneakers."[31] A fan magazine once listed their hobbies as: LaVerne, "Clothes, home"; Maxene, "Outdoor sports"; Patty, "Knitting, painting."[32] One of the King Sisters told me Maxene was the "pretty one," LaVerne was the "most friendly and sociable," and Patty had "the best voice."[33]

Another reporter summed them up this way: "LaVerne is the balance wheel. She's as near to being serious as any of them ever get. Maxene is frivolous but surprises an interviewer with rare insight into human nature and good hard common sense. Patty ... is the fireball. In front of a microphone, an audience, a camera, or a luncheon companion, she is strictly a madcap."[34] In later years, Maxene reflected on the sisters' differences:

> I think we were very interesting girls because we were all so different.... So often sisters that work together are very much alike, and we were nothing alike. Our

greatest love was the thing that we shared for each other. Of course, there was always difference of opinion, but that's the way it should be. That kept you from being in the cookie cutter and [made] you individual, which we were. But we got a reputation of being fighting sisters, which was unfair. We loved each other very much. The things that we disagreed on [were]: We didn't like each other's boyfriends, we didn't like each other's individual clothes, our friends were different. But that had nothing to do with our relationship with each other.[35]

A reporter who interviewed them was impressed by the sisters' closeness to one another: "The Andrews Sisters are devoted to one another. They have arguments, like all sisters, but their affection is a bond you can see and feel. To outsiders, they praise one another lavishly."[36] The same reporter said the sisters were "unabashedly generous" and always gave their unused wardrobe to their cousins. The sisters said their act came before anything else in their lives, and that is why they survived.

When asked if the Andrews family didn't become tired of being together so much, Maxene replied: "Never ... We like being together—you'd have to meet our mother and father to understand. Our family is a sort of closed corporation—lots of our relatives moved out here [California]. We have aunts and uncles and cousins; they all come over to my parents' house on Sundays. My best friends are my cousins ... we've never been any place long enough to make really good friends." [37]

Maxene exaggerated her extended family. At the time, only the sisters' cousin Gladys Leichter, her husband, and three children lived in California. They had no aunts and their only uncles were Olga's two bachelor brothers in Mound, Minnesota. In a postwar interview, Maxene presented a rather idyllic picture of their domestic life:

> As sisters, brought up under the same rules, we like the same sort of food—the good, hearty kind. Singers need a lot of food, you know. When we're at home in California we always have the good, old-fashioned, family Sunday dinner at our parents' home. Patty and LaVerne live at home with Mother and Father, and I live not far away with my husband.... We're a united family, you see, and when we're all at home, we plan a big Sunday family dinner just like most of the families all over the U.S.A.[38]

Over the years, the press has spilled much ink about the alleged fights of the Andrews Sisters. These reports are greatly exaggerated. The sisters doubtless had many disagreements over the years, but their first major estrangement did not occur until 1940 when Maxene and Patty demanded more independence from the family and briefly considered continuing the act without LaVerne. Rumors of a possible split of the act surfaced again in 1948, but nothing materialized. The sisters split briefly in spring 1953 and then again for two and a half years in January 1954. A major estrangement separated Maxene and Patty in their later years after LaVerne's death.

The wonder is not that they had occasional disagreements, but rather that they were able to remain together as long as they did. From childhood until LaVerne's death in 1967, the sisters were always together—except for their two-and-a-half-year separation in 1954. During their early career, they were together virtually twenty-four hours a day as they traveled together, rehearsed together, ate together, performed together, socialized together, lived together, and sometimes even slept together. Anyone who has siblings will marvel that such intimacy lasted thirty-seven years with only three major blow-ups.

Maxene once told an interviewer, "We got along beautifully except during rehearsals. We would get angry and might yell at one another, but give us five minutes and it was all over with."[39]

LaVerne was five years older than Maxene and seven years older than Patty, a significant age difference, especially during childhood when a year or two make important differences in maturity. According to Maxene, LaVerne was afraid of being alone. When they were kids, LaVerne had her own bedroom. Patty and Maxene shared a room and bed, and they frequently awakened at night to find LaVerne between them.[40] Of all the sisters, LaVerne was the closest to her parents, a closeness no doubt fostered by the death of the family's second child when the infant LaVerne became the object of the grieving parents' affections. Maxene once observed: "But LaVerne adored them [Peter and Olga Andrews], and of course, they adored her. She was very close to my mother and father. It was just one of those things. If any problems came up, she never took Patty's [or my] part, she always sided in with mom and papa."[41] Elsewhere Maxene said: "LaVerne was very much Mama and Papa's girl. She didn't get married until after Mama died, and even after she married she had Papa living with them until he died."[42]

LaVerne was often described as the reserved sister whereas Patty and Maxene were much more vivacious. A reporter once described LaVerne:

> LaVerne, in her late twenties [she was actually 35], is the eldest and friendliest of the very friendly three.... She adores candy and eats it by the box with apparently little damage.... She has many hobbies—clothes, food, ice hockey, and staying home head the list. She also loves fur coats, and according to a studio blurb, "bestirred by memories of wintry days in Minnesota," she has invested in eight fur coats. She was voted "Most Constant Fan" of ice hockey in Los Angeles and presented the cup to the championship team this season.[43]

LaVerne's great love throughout her life was clothes, and she more than her sisters enjoyed the Hollywood life. According to Maxene, "LaVerne was the swinger of the group offstage. She was a great dancer, was very fashion conscious—for ten years she was voted one of the ten best-dressed women, and she had a beautiful figure. She had a great sense of humor, and she loved people. But on stage she was just Miss Quiet Dumdum. Never wanted to say or do anything. She was just happy to sing." [44]

Elsewhere Maxene said: "LaVerne was the one who wanted to be the movie star. LaVerne was the one who wanted to be one of the ten best-dressed women in the world. LaVerne was the one who wanted to have the money ... LaVerne loved the glamour. LaVerne loved the adulation ... those things didn't matter to me. I just wanted ... to sing."[45] Maxene told a reporter: "LaVerne loves clothes and has beautiful ones. She keeps them in sparkling order—there's never a loose snapper or anything. She's meticulously neat about everything she owns. She's the only one who can read music—she studied piano for ten years."[46] In

A publicity photograph circa 1943 revealing the hair styles associated with the Andrews Sisters (left to right: LaVerne age 32, Maxene 27 and Patty 25), during the war years. (Robert Boyer Collection)

a late interview, Maxene said without elaboration, "LaVerne had a great sense of humor, but she was a pain in the neck."[47]

LaVerne apparently had a weight problem when young. When Maxene mentioned the pajama-like outfits the trio wore in their early years, she said they not only made Patty look older, but made LaVerne look slimmer. During their hungry days in New York before their big break, Maxene remembered: "LaVerne began losing weight and never did put it back on. She had a beautiful figure."[48]

In filmed segments of their act, LaVerne sometimes looked uncomfortable on stage. In an interview, Maxene expressed concern about LaVerne: "I know how to relax but LaVerne's been getting very nervous lately. Show business has begun to catch up with her, I'm afraid." When asked about her "nerves" LaVerne said she became nervous about her lines on their radio program. To relax for the program, she went to bed at 8:30 the night before: "First I take a warm bath but I toss and toss thinking about my lines."[49] In later years, LaVerne began drinking to relax for performances. Toward the end of her life, her drinking got out of hand and she developed a serious alcohol problem.

Maxene was the organizer of the group, the most aggressive, and the one with the greatest drive. She told a reporter that she had "a drive inherited from our Norwegian mother for success."[50] An early friend recalled that "Maxene was the main gear and handled most of the trio's business dealings.... And she drove a car like a racer."[51] When an interviewer asked Patty which sister was the leader of the group, she responded:

> I think Maxene had that drive in her ... LaVerne was the least like that. At rehearsals, LaVerne would love to sit and look at magazines and read the newspaper and things like that. Maxene was the leader in the way of setting up the rehearsals and forcing rehearsals and getting the rehearsals together. And then I was the one that had the ideas of what to do musically.[52]

It was Maxene who urged Vic Schoen to get them the spot on the radio show that led to their discovery by Dave Kapp. And it was she who first challenged their parents' control over their personal, professional, and financial lives—a challenge that resulted in the altercation that landed Peter Andrews in jail and newspaper headlines. Commenting on that incident, she said: "I was the rebellious one. I said to [my father], 'You're not gonna pick out the man for me to marry,' and so consequently my dad and I didn't see eye to eye on many things."[53] While Maxene had difficulty getting along with her father, she later attributed her "level-headed approach to success and its pitfalls" to her Greek father and Norwegian mother who reared their children in "the Old Country way."[54]

Maxene was called "Maggie" by her family and friends in the early years of her career,[55] but was known among friends as "Mackie" toward the end of her life. She was often described as a "tomboy." She once said, "I'm the one who likes tailored clothes ... I wear slacks or suits or whatever I feel like wearing. I never wear a hat nor the elaborate costume jewelry Patty and LaVerne like to wear."[56] One writer called her "sports minded" and said she liked to swim, bowl, ride horseback, play golf, and bicycle ride.[57] Another described her as having a "winsome, pixie smile and direct, straight-from-the-shoulder manner."[58]

Maxene had a passion for dogs all her life. When the family first hit the road in the 1929 Buick, a dog always traveled with them. When she and her husband bought a home in California, it was large enough for a sizeable kennel where they raised dogs.[59] In later years when she toured her one-woman show, she was never without one. Several times Maxene said she was shy in crowds: "I always wished I could do what Patty did. She was very outgoing. I grew up shy and never felt I could talk. But Patty always had wonderful rapport with audiences."[60] Maxene was usually considered the prettiest of the sisters. A reporter described her first impression of Maxene: "She had a pretty smile, looked slim and athletic in slacks. No make-up."[61]

Patty is perhaps the least known of the sisters, despite her prominent role in the act. She is always described as the comic, the light-hearted one. In early interviews, she played up the "dumb blond" image popular in those years. She told one reporter, "I'm happy because I got no brains. Say, I don't know from nothing."[62] Maxene once said: "Patty is the happy-go-lucky one—she disregards worry or gloom.... LaVerne and I listen to the radio now and then—Patty makes a career out of listening. She hears every musical program and notes every number played—new or old."[63] Maxene told another interviewer: "Patty is crazy about music, jive bands and just about anything that will give her a laugh."[64] Elsewhere, though, she provided a different image of her sister: "Patty is just the opposite [of her stage personae] offstage—shy, very quiet, and socializes very little. Not at all, really."[65] When they were young, Patty and Maxene were close. After the altercation with the police in 1940 and the subsequent family strife, they considered dropping LaVerne from the act.[66] When Maxene eloped, Patty was the only one in the family she told and the two kept the secret from the others for two years.[67] Commenting on Patty's sense of humor, Maxene said:

> Patty probably would have drawn seams [on her leg makeup] if LaVerne and I had let her, and she might have made them intentionally crooked. Patty was the fun one of the group, the clown who kept us laughing during those endless periods of backstage boredom between shows when we were doing five and six shows a day. Patty was wonderful. She helped not only LaVerne and me but the rest of the acts in our show and the members of our orchestra keep our sanity. I don't know who helped her, but she sure helped us.[68]

A reporter who interviewed the sisters in 1943 described Patty as "a pleasant, gracious creature with her feet definitely on the ground, and pretty definite ideas of what course those feet should follow." When talking about her enthusiasm for Hollywood, Patty said: "Personally, I guess I'm just a jerk but I buy all the fan magazines the day they come out and spend most of my spare time at the movies."[69]

Patty was the most talented of the sisters and her personality dominated the act. From the beginning of their career, she was singled out as the sparkplug that paced the trio. She was an accomplished dancer, a great comedienne, a good actress, and a sensational singer. She probably could have had a successful solo career in her younger years, an unlikelihood for either Maxene or LaVerne.

Patty's goddaughter, Patricia Kurzawinski (daughter of the sisters' cousin Gladys Leichter), remembered her Aunt Patty as the most caring of the sisters toward her when she was young. Patty was comforting and nurturing, whereas LaVerne was lost in her own world of glamour, clothes, and Hollywood while Maxene seemed somewhat brusque and brash. As an adult, she knew Patty less well and Maxene became one of her favorite aunts.[70]

Although on stage Patty seemed the free spirit of the sisters, she was perhaps the most controlled of the sisters, not only by her parents (and perhaps her sisters) but also later by the men she married. She once told an unmarried friend: "I don't know how you can live your life as a single person ... I don't know how you can go it alone. I need to have a man in my life."[71]

Gladys Leichter, the Andrews Sisters' cousin, knew the sisters their entire lives. When asked to describe their personalities, she said:

> LaVerne was happy-go-lucky.... LaVerne liked dressing up, going out and partying. She was a party girl.... She was a very good dresser. She was sweet, nice. She was always smiling and happy. LaVerne seemed to be a happy person.

They always said Maxene was the strong one.... She was the manager. Not that she liked it. She always told me, 'I don't know why they think I'm the strong one, when I just hate doing it.' She did it because someone had to do it ... and, I think, Maggie did have more strength ... Maggie loved animals ... she loved collecting ... she collected dishes, Copenhagen dishes ... She was a great reader ... Maggie was very friendly. She loved people. I think Maggie was a little bit on the lonely side. I saw it more in the older years. She loved my kids. They called her "Aunt Mag."

Patty was the showgirl ... She really loved show business. She was the comedian on stage. Patty was aloof off-stage. She clung to the two men she had ... Patty was easily controlled ... Pat was more like her father ... She held grudges.[72]

Radio Life carried an article entitled "The Andrews Sisters Answer Twenty Questions." Several of the sisters' responses reveal a great deal about their personalities.

When each sister was asked to describe her sisters in a word, Maxene called Patty "talented" and LaVerne "gracious"; LaVerne called Patty "vivacious" and Maxene "vital"; and Patty called LaVerne "clothes-happy" and Maxene "horse-happy."

When asked, "What inanimate object is the dearest possession of each of you?" Patty replied, "My home movie projector, I guess. We have double features in our living room about once or twice every week." Maxene replied, "My new fireman-red Cadillac convertible—when I'm not on my horse, Golden Sis, once or twice a week." LaVerne replied, "The circular bed I have in my room is beautiful, and all our guests comment on it. Besides, it's comfortable."

When asked the low point and high point in their career, they concurred: "Before and after Lou Levy, 'Bei Mir Bist Du Schoen,' and all that followed."

When asked what careers they would pursue if they weren't singers, Patty responded, "I like to draw. As an artist of sorts, I imagine." Maxene said, "Dramatics thrill me. If I had the ability to be an actress, I would have liked to be one." LaVerne replied, "Since clothes delight me so, a dress designer, naturally."

In response to "What's the nicest compliment you've received?" they said, "Our mother's sacrifice and Lou Levy's drive for the benefit of the Andrews Sisters' career."

When asked if they relied on one person for choosing a song to record, they unanimously responded, "The answer to this is a big Y-E-S! Our manager—and 'our husband' (he's married to Maxene)—Lou Levy. He sings like Andy Devine with a cold—but he can tell a hit a mile away."

When asked about a good luck charm or special formula for success, they said: "We've been in the business long enough to know that the only way to have luck is to work hard for it, and keep working."[73]

The Andrews Sisters liked their fans and their fans liked them. Despite their meteoric rise to fame and the adulation they received wherever they went, they never became prima donnas. After interviewing them, one reporter exclaimed "...and the Andrews Sisters are but wonderful." He continued:

If I haven't made myself clear, let me hasten to tell you that the Andrews Sisters have taken their Nation-wide fame in their stride. With all the attention lavished upon them in the last few years, they have kept their feet on the ground. None of this phony "Please don't get too near me—I'm a star now" baloney for them. At least, none I could detect.

The success kids from Minneapolis like to kid around too much—they're living for laughs. Oh, they may kick up a little fuss every now and then—when things go off-beat a bit—but who doesn't? Most of the time, they're very regular gals, very regular indeed.[74]

Another reporter noted that "There's something tremendously homey and earthy about this trio."[75] An interviewer impressed by their friendliness reported: "They greeted us with the largest display of teeth and the heartiest handshakes we have had in a long while."[76]

> When you meet them, it's the great warmth and friendliness, the direct manner, the enthusiasm that you notice and remember. As far as looks go, they're rather like the girl down the street—neither beautiful nor homely, with pretty good figures. Okay in slacks. Their speaking voices are low and pleasant, with the hard edges and distinct articulation you get in their singing. Along with the general good humor that apparently emanates from all of them all of the time, Patty and Maxene throw off an extra portion of vitality and bounce. By comparison, LaVerne seems languid.[77]

Interviewers were impressed by the sisters' outgoing personalities: "All three girls have a rare and welcome quality of vivacity and a lack of boredom which makes them look alive. Work or play, they have fun, and that quality of enjoyment projects itself into their songs."[78] "Admittedly, none of the wide-mouthed sisters, America's most famous musical trio, is Hedy Lamarr. But when you meet them you are so engaged by their child-like friendliness that it doesn't matter."[79] "These harmonizers are the friendliest girls you ever could meet. There is nothing stagy about them, yet they reflect self-confidence."[80]

When Patty was asked what accounted for their popularity, she said: "We loved to sing … and we were honest."[81] Elsewhere, she added: "We were such a part of everybody's life in the Second World War…. We represented something overseas and at home—a sort of security."[82] And still elsewhere, she said: "People thought of us as members of their family … almost as their own sisters."[83]

Maxene felt they "were blessed with one great gift, the gift of giving. When we perform on the stage—and it's always been this way—our feeling has always been to make them happy, to make you happy…. What we do, it's a kind of giving."[84] When asked why they were so popular during the war years, Maxene replied: "We were like morale builders. We were happy. We had a great desire to please people. We wanted to sing things that would make them like us."[85]

Reflecting on the early part of their career, Maxene said: "I can't tell you how happy we'd always been. Success and all that didn't change us very much. We lived two lives. When we performed, we were stars; when the performance was over, we were just Mama and Papa's kids. We all lived together in a lovely house in Brentwood. Until four years before they died, Mama and Papa traveled with us."[86] Maxene suggested it was their presence that kept the sisters grounded: "Mama and Papa always made sure we never let our success go to our heads."[87]

Shortly before her death in 1995, Maxene waxed philosophic about their popularity: "I think it was our time … I think when your time is due, if you're not prepared, you're going to miss it and if you are prepared, it is going to happen."[88] Elsewhere she said: "We never analyzed where we fit in the big picture…. We just did what came naturally to us. We loved to sing, and we had developed a style over a period of years of serving our apprenticeship, and it caught on."[89]

Certainly part of the sisters' popularity came from the pleasure they derived from singing. Several times, Maxene said that when they performed they wanted something returned, something she called "empathy." It was important to the Andrews Sisters to receive their audiences' good will. Maxene told a reporter:

> We enjoyed our work. And that is the greatest satisfaction in living—keeping busy at something you really enjoy doing…. We all enjoyed singing, dancing, and entertaining…. People have always come backstage to tell us how much they've enjoyed themselves. This audience rapport means so much to me, and always will…. The most wonderful reward for performing is that you can feel the warmth and pleasure radiating from the audience when they're having fun along with us.[90]

Fans tell many stories of the sisters' warmth. Going out of their way for fans was not unusual:

> In Chicago in 1942, at the age of fourteen, my mother sat through six consecutive performances of the Andrews Sisters. She sat in the same seat in the front row every night. When a messenger was sent to ask if the sisters could do anything for her, Mom said that she'd love to meet them backstage—a wink during the show would let her know it was okay. Maxene Andrews winked, Mom went backstage, and a great friendship was begun. Maxene brought my mother to California and arranged for her to meet the right people to begin a modeling career. Years later Maxene became my godmother.[91]

Another fan reminisced: "I remember fondly the many times I saw them on stage back in the forties—they never failed to entertain, were never pretentious and kidded themselves unmercifully…. They were much more attractive in person [than in their photos and films] … Above all, they were FUN!"[92]

A school friend of the sisters remembered that when they achieved fame, "[T]hey remained good friends and unpretentious. Whenever they were at the Chicago Theater I would catch their show then go backstage and visit with them. Later years I would take our young son with me and they would give him an autographed picture, we still have them."[93]

I located over a hundred requests for photographs of the Andrews Sisters written by fans to Universal Studios, most of them dated April 1943. The writers were predominantly girls in their early teens and younger, and the postcards were possibly in response to an ad in a girls' magazine. Some included personal notes, such as the following, which are verbatim:

> You girls will bring cheer to any sad or down harted individual just to hear you sing. You are my favoriat trio singers. You girls were wonderful in "Hows About It."

I have heard you sing on the radio and I think you are wonderful. Just listening to you makes the thought of war so far away.

I enjoyed you's in Give out Sisters and I thought you's acted grand. You's made me laugh & how I enjoyed your acting.

I would like to have a picture of you all very much … Well you girls are certainly a swell team. Their is a question I would like to know. If you girls are really sisters.

I would be proud to have your picture in my home and I enjoy your heavenly voices very much.

I saw you in person at the Steel Pier in Atlantic City, N. J. You were very good.

I received your picture and wish to thank you very much. You all came out nice. All three of you are cute. I am going to see "Hows About It" in a couple days. I'm sure I'll enjoy it.

I have seen you in many movies and think that you are some of the best actors I have seen.

I think your singing are nice in what's cooking. Every time use come play in the show I go see it. I saw all your pictures in the show. Use sing very nice.

During my research for this book, I placed a notice in newspapers and magazines across the United States asking people to share their memories of the Andrews Sisters. I received almost a hundred responses, and what impressed me most about the letters was the great warmth and affection these people held for the sisters. Many told stories of meeting the Andrews Sisters and remembered how they went out of their way to make them feel comfortable.

The Andrews Sisters liked their fans, and their fans certainly liked them.

CHAPTER EIGHT

1944–1945

Reduce World War II to three voices, and the choices are obvious: the rant of Hitler, the rumble of Churchill ... and the single, seamless sound blended from the warble of the Andrews Sisters.[1]

Traveling to and from engagements was a serious problem faced by the Andrews Sisters and other entertainers during World War II. Most passenger trains were reserved for war-related travel and air flights were even more restricted. That left overcrowded buses and automobiles, but even they were complicated because tires and gasoline were rationed. To ease the problem the sisters tried to arrange their itinerary with no more than 500 miles between performances. Universal Studios convinced someone in power that the sisters' travel was essential to the war effort and managed to obtain gasoline ration stamps for their road trips. Maxene remembered that Peter Andrews was still driving them to most of their engagements:

> Papa was able to finesse his way through each challenge and conserve enough gas to get us and our '39 Buick to the next city on our tour. But we had to be smart about it. When we arrived, we tried to leave the car parked until the end of our engagement except for driving to a gas station for our weekly ration of gas. We walked from our hotel to the theater whenever it was possible or took a taxi. Anything to save gas.
>
> The other challenge was to get to our engagements on time. The closest call we ever had came when we finished one of our runs at the Paramount Theater in New York City. After our last show, we had to jump in the Buick and head west toward Cleveland for a rehearsal at nine o'clock the next morning.... We made it, but only because Papa was able to weave his way across New York, New Jersey, Pennsylvania, and Ohio and take certain liberties with that national "vic-

LaVerne, Patty and Maxene polish their father's 1939 Buick, the automobile that
transported them to and from many of their engagements during the war years.
Throughout most of the sisters' early career, Peter and Olga Andrews accompanied their daughters on tour. Circa 1944. (Author's collection)

tory speed" of thirty-five miles an hour all night long while LaVerne, Patty and
I slept in the backseat.[2]

The Andrews Sisters were back on the road in January 1944. In mid-month,
they were topping the box office again at the Chicago Theater with Mitch Ayres
and his orchestra.[3] *The Billboard* noted: "The Andrews Sisters are the hit of
the show, putting their numbers over in great style and getting hand after
hand."[4] While in Chicago, the sisters joined Cab Calloway and Duke Ellington
to entertain servicemen convalescing at Gardiner General Hospital.[5] They then
moved on to Detroit for a late January engagement where they again made the
city's highest box offices.[6]

While they were in Detroit, *Variety* and *The Billboard* concurrently ran a
three page spread that included a list of entertainers "who during 1943 gave
so generously of their time and talent to the men and women of the Armed
Forces of the United Nations" at the New York Stage Door Canteen, the Club
for Merchant Seamen, and the Servicewomen's Tea Dances. The Andrews Sisters were on the list.[7]

Columbus, Ohio, and the Palace Theater were next on the tour and then
on to the Albee Theater in Cincinnati where the sisters again capped box

offices.[8] From Cincinnati, they went to Cleveland and then to the Adams Theater in Newark for a mid-March engagement. An enthusiastic reviewer wrote:

> At the Adams this week patrons are plentiful and plenty satisfied. There's little doubt but that the Andrews Sisters deserve major credit for the boffo boxoffice totals.... LaVerne, Maxene and Patty, looking nice in striking pink costumes with checked tops, give out ... exiting while those out front clamor for more. This potent trio has had imitators here by the score. That's probably one reason why the mccoy gets such joyous response from the audience.[9]

After Newark, the sisters moved on to Boston's RKO Theater to top a post–Easter box office[10] where a reviewer wrote: "The Andrews girls, same as ever, do five numbers and fill with usual comedy biz. Still kill the customers, of whom there were plenty."[11]

During their stint in Newark, the sisters' latest film, *Follow the Boys*, was released in nearby New York City. *Follow the Boys* was a tribute to the performers who participated in the Hollywood Victory Committee to entertain U.S. military forces. The sprawling two-hour film by Universal Studios had an all-star cast that reads like a "Who's Who" of the Hollywood war years, including the Andrews Sisters, Dinah Shore, Marlene Dietrich, Orson Welles, Sophie Tucker, W. C. Fields, Jeanette MacDonald, Lana Turner, Louis Jordan, Donald O'Connor—and even a dog act. The acts are loosely pulled together by a weak plot about a former vaudevillian (George Raft) rejected by the military because of a bad knee who then organized entertainment for the troops.

The Andrews Sisters made two cameo appearances. They sang a medley of their hit songs on an outdoor stage at a naval base wearing pastel shoulder-padded tailored suits, white blouses, and bows atop their classic big-hair pompadours. A very blond Patty displayed her comedic talents in the "Strip Polka" segment as she began a striptease routine that Maxene and LaVerne interrupted. Later in the film, en route to Australia in the hold of a troopship wearing the same outfits, they entertained the boys—as well as George Raft and Sophie Tucker—with "Shoo Shoo Baby" accompanied by Freddie Slack's orchestra until a torpedo from an enemy submarine interrupted their number. Happily, they survived, but even more happily the hero did not and the dreary plot was concluded. The story line was awful and the acts were spotty. As usual, the sisters added sparkle to an otherwise tedious film and are one of the few reasons for watching it today. *Follow the Boys* was a box office success.

Although the public liked the film, most critics weren't wild about it. *Variety* applauded the effort but acknowledged the weak plot and suggested: "A number each by the Misses [Jeannete] MacDonald and [Dinah] Shore could be dropped for instance; ditto the Andrews and Miss [Sophie] Tucker. Not that all aren't expert, but it soon surfeits."[12]

Twice during 1944, the Andrews Sisters were featured on the *The Radio Hall of Fame*, a program that honored outstanding performers for their "Superlative Performance in the Field of Entertainment" as chosen by the editors of *Variety*. The show was "conceived as a kind of weekly Academy Awards of radio, with those judged worthy that week invited to perform in an all-star hour of music, drama, comedy and news."[13] On March 5, the Andrews Sisters

The Andrews Sisters made two cameo appearances in *Follow the Boys* (1944), a star-studded salute to entertainers who entertained the troops during World War II. Freddy Slack's orchestra backs the sisters for "Shoo Shoo Baby," one of their most popular wartime songs. (Author's collection)

shared the program with Danny Thomas and musical director Paul Whiteman, who provided the orchestra for the program each week. They sang "Rhumboogie" and a medley of their past hits. On October 1, they appeared on the show again, this time sharing the spotlight with Ed Wynn, and sang "Is You Is or Is You Ain't My Baby?", their current hit with Bing Crosby.

At Chicago's Oriental Theater in early May, the sisters drew their highest salary ever, a guarantee of $15,000 plus a split of everything over $35,000.[14] This marked their first trip back to the Oriental since their brief appearance there with Georgie Jessel in 1934 when *The Billboard* panned their act and said they sang like "Chinese puzzles set to off-key music." After the Oriental, they filled the Orpheum in hometown Minneapolis where a local reviewer wrote: "The Andrews Sisters seem to improve with age.... The Andrews girls have added a lot of comedy and poise to the rhythm and close harmony which have marked their performing.... The girls got a solid reception which was well deserved."[15]

The sisters' visit to their hometown was marred by a burglar who broke into their automobile and made off with $1,255 worth of clothing and equipment.[16] But the loss was soon forgotten, as the sisters joined the rest of the nation in celebrating the Allied liberation of Rome on June 5. The next day Allied troops landed on the beaches of Normandy for the long awaited D-Day, the massive invasion of Europe that would ultimately defeat Germany.

In early August, when the sisters were visiting Minneapolis, a local new-story announced that they had recently settled 25 percent of their earnings on Peter and Olga Andrews for their lifetimes, an amount that would total over $100,000. The news "recalled to [the Andrews Sisters'] friends here that the mother and father made many sacrifices so that the three daughters could attend the town's best dancing school and receive other educational advantages. The years of hard work and the sacrifices by the parents now are paying off." The folks back home apparently forgot that LaVerne had paid for the sisters' dancing lessons by playing piano for the classes, the sisters had dropped out of public schools, and they had supported their parents since LaVerne was in her early twenties and Patty and Maxene were in their teens. The story concluded: "The father operated a café here. He and his wife left their old-fashioned home to travel with the girls who, a few years ago, bought them a modern home, in Brentwood, near Hollywood."[17] No mention was made of the pool halls that provided Peter's livelihood during most of his years in Minneapolis. When asked about the sisters' settlement for their parents, Maxene said:

> They've earned it.... So often kids who've grown up working in show business forget that their parents put them where they are. Our father invested money in us when we weren't doing well and he gave up 12 years of his life traveling with us. In the early days we weren't rich enough to go by train. He drove us in an old jalopy—all of us and two dogs. Think of the time, effort and aggravation invested in us![18]

In early September, *Moonlight and Cactus* was released—the sisters' twelfth film for Universal and the only one with Lou Levy as associate producer. This was the only Andrews Sisters film I was unable to view, but thanks to a fan, I saw clips of its musical numbers. I rely on a film historian for the plot synopsis:

> Patty, Maxene and LaVerne Andrews starred in "Moonlight and Cactus," a short ... but tuneful programmer whose plot ... told the uncomplicated story of a rancher who returns to his ranch after active service with the merchant marines to find that, in his absence, all the cowhands have been replaced by women. Believing that a woman's place is in the home, and not on his land, he resents their invasion of his property, but soon changes his tune when his lady foreman proves to him that women can be as efficient as men. The Andrews Sisters served little purpose other than to sing....[19]

The film has some good musical numbers. "Wahoo" featured the sisters on horseback in cowgirl drag with their "big hair" styles. "Down in the Valley" put them before the camera in fluffy pinafores and aprons. Shemp Howard donned the same costume for an amusing Patty-drag in the sisters' "Sweet Dreams" number. "Send Me a Man, Amen" was a good bluesy number while "Home" was a bit on the sacharrine side with the sisters back in cowgirl outfits. "Sing" and "The Hand-Clapping Song" featured the sisters in white gowns for the finale.

The Andrews Sisters donned western outfits and rode horses in *Moonlight and Cactus* (1944), a film about a man who returned home from wartime duties to discover a group of women operating his ranch. (Robert Boyer Collection)

Variety thought the film was an entertaining musical, but had no illusions about its merits beyond that.[20] *Hollywood Reporter* called it "an outdoor showcase for an array of pleasant musical numbers, plus a dash of comedy and a western twang ... the Andrews Sisters [are] in excellent voice and abetted ably by the vocalists and instrumentalists of Mitch Ayres and his orchestra."[21]

About the time *Moonlight and Cactus* was released, *The Billboard* published results of a poll conducted among GIs to determine their favorite musicians. The Andrews Sisters were voted the favorite singing group. Favorite orchestra was Harry James, favorite female vocalist was Dinah Shore, and favorite male vocalist was Bing Crosby.[22] Among high school students, the Andrews Sisters placed second to the Ink Spots.[23]

Later in September, the Andrews Sisters were back at the Paramount Theater in New York for their twelfth engagement. Their first show opened to a cool start but soon moved into the tempo their fans expected:

> Andrews trio, the star act, walked into one of those things all turns do at one time or another—a cold spot. They follow on the heels of comedian Pat Henning, who takes the audience with him when he goes. Combined with a rather lifeless (for them) arrangement of "Lullaby of Broadway" to start, the situation

requires a couple of songs before the trio get their listeners back, but after that they're a pushover.[24]

Metronome offered one of its rare reviews of their show, and perhaps one of its cruelest. After bemoaning that the Mitch Ayres orchestra had only two numbers in the show, the reviewer continued:

> As for the Andrews gals, I have known them for years, I like them personally, and they seem to like me, despite what I always write about their work from the musical standpoint. So I'll go on record again as saying that I find them musically vulgar, tonally raw, and generally of no service to the community, save as a means of causing large sums of money to change hands among large numbers of people. Moreover, I think the lyrics of "Corns for Our Country" [sic] are in bad taste. Patty, Maxene and LaVerne—do you still love me?[25]

New Yorkers obviously didn't agree with *Metronome*. Once again, the sisters' show capped the city's box offices, this time at $94,000—$4,000 higher than Frank Sinatra's box office a week later.[26]

At the end of September, the Andrews Sisters announced a new muscial format, a concert tour that would debut in the symphony hall at Evansville, Indiana, and continue to Fort Wayne, Grand Rapids, Detroit, Ottawa, Rochester, and other stops to be announced. The sisters were guaranteed $20,000 a week plus a percentage of the gross. A *Variety* story explained the composition of the show:

> Sisters will be accompanied on the tour by Albert Ammons and Peet Johnson, boogie-woogie pianists, and a couple of longhair artists not yet bought in an endeavor to balance the production between jive and serious music. They will be getting regular concert prices and for the first time since becoming names intend going into Canadian bookings. Vic Schoen and a six-piece orchestra will play their music.[27]

The sisters were among the first pop singers to undertake concert tours. The concert format appealed to performers because they could make as much money in concert as in theater engagements but with considerably less work— one or two concerts a day compared to the five or six daily performances sandwiched between movies.[28]

The Andrews Sisters liked the concert format. They made $10,300 for three dates in Evansville, Nashville and Louisville—one show nightly, a routine considerably less grueling than their movie theater circuit. After concluding their tour in Ottawa, they announced that they planned seventy-five concert dates yearly.[29] But the sisters were overly optimistic about their new format. For unclear reasons—probably financial—they did not pursue it again.

After their concert tour, the Andrews Sisters celebrated their "twelfth anniversary in show business" at the Chicago Theater on November 7 where a reviewer reported they "have the crowd with them all the way in some new numbers and a goodly share of oldies…. None of the old power is missing; in fact, that 12-year patina doesn't show a bit."[30] The sisters had actually been in show business thirteen years. Predictably, their show topped the box offices for the week.[31]

Meanwhile, across the Pacific Ocean, General Douglas MacArthur had landed on Leyte Island to join Filipino resistance fighters for the liberation of the Philippines.

In early December, Warner Brothers released *Hollywood Canteen*, a film based on the popular entertainment center for military personnel in Hollywood. Inspired by the success of *Stage Door Canteen*, a film about Broadway luminaries and their interaction with servicemen in New York, *Hollywood Canteen* featured an all-star cast that outshone *Follow the Boys*, including the Andrews Sisters who were loaned by Universal Studios for the movie.

The predictable plot was about two GIs (Robert Hutton and Dane Clark) who ventured into the canteen where one of them found love with Joan Leslie, and they both ended up meeting most of Hollywood, at least those with Warner Brothers contracts. Stars featured in cameo appearances included Jack Benny, Eddie Cantor, Joan Crawford, Bette Davis, Sydney Greenstreet, Paul Henreid, Peter Lorre, Roy Rogers and Trigger, S. Z. Sakall, Barbara Stanwyk, Jane Wyman, Jimmy Dorsey and his band, and many others. The Andrews Sisters sang the title song "Hollywood Canteen" over opening credits, and then appeared in the canteen for two numbers, "I'm Getting Corns for My Country," a comic number that showcased a very blond Patty, and "Don't Fence Me In," which Roy Rogers also sang in the film. LaVerne and Maxene wore unflattering white skirts with dark aprons that made them appear rather hippy beside a svelte Patty in black who strummed a guitar she could not play in the "Don't Fence Me In" number.

The *New York Times* critic, of course, did not care for it, noting—among other things—that the stars seemed a bit condescending in their interaction with the common soldiers. *Variety* liked the film: "There isn't a marquee big enough to hold all the names in this one, so how can it miss? Besides, it's basically solid. It has story, cohesion and heart ... withal, a dandy filmusical for anybody's theater." Regarding the Andrews trio: "There are a flock of ... tunes. Cole Porter's "Don't Fence Me In" gets a two-ply plug, best via the Andrews Sisters."[32] Joan Crawford, who agreed to a cameo appearance in the film only after she learned that names would appear alphabetically and hers would precede her nemesis Bette Davis, reportedly called the film "a very pleasant pile of shit for wartime audiences."[33] The public liked the movie and packed theaters to see their favorite stars and made it the fourth largest box office hit of the year. Warner Brothers contributed an undisclosed portion of the profits to the Hollywood Canteen.[34]

As *Hollywood Canteen* was playing the theaters, Decca relased "Don't Fence Me In," another record by Bing Crosby and the Andrews Sisters. This pastoral longing for wide-open spaces struck a chord in wartime America. *The Billboard*'s reviewer predicted its success: "This Cole Porter disking, on the sweet side, with a little touch of the wide-open spaces, stands a good chance of joining 'White Christmas' as a platter that will ride in and out of jukes for a long, long time. The balance between ork and voices, between the groaner and LaVerne, Maxene and Patty is damned near perfect."[35] *Down Beat* liked the song and Crosby, but, of course, did not like the Andrews Sisters: "I doubt that Bing

Dane Clark encountered the Andrews Sisters when he dropped into the Hollywood Canteen in the film by the same name. *Hollywood Canteen* (1944) was another star-studded film about stars entertaining GIs during World War II. Above the sisters sing "I'm Getting Corns for My Country," a comic number about a dedicated hostess at the canteen. (Author's collection)

needs the help of the Throaty Threesome to put anything across, but perhaps they can use his help. *Don't Fence* from *Hollywood Canteen*, is quite a song ... Vic Schoen is right there with the backing!"[36] The public agreed with *The Billboard* and the record was a million seller—as was its sheet music:

> Oh give me land lots of land under starry skies above,
> Don't fence me in.
> Let me ride through the wide open country that I love,
> Don't fence me in.
> Let me be by myself in the evening breeze
> And listen to the murmur of the cottonwood trees.
> Send me off forever, but I ask you please,
> Don't fence me in...

"Don't Fence Me In" was a departure from Cole Porter's usual fare. He had reportedly bought the song from a Montana cowboy many years previously, then reworked it and forgot about it until it was resurrected for Crosby and the sisters and the film *Hollywood Canteen*. It was reputedly one of President Roosevelt's favorite songs (his favorite was "Home on the Range"), and Bob Hope joked on radio that it was dedicated to unorthodox First Lady Eleanor Roosevelt who seemed unfenced by the usual constraints of her position. One writer called it "man's insatiable longing for freedom of spirit" while others saw it as "an affirmation of individual freedom in the midst of the totalitarian powers of the world war." Kate Smith presented a watch to Cole Porter on her radio show "in recognition of his contribution to national morale in writing the song." In February 1945, when a shipload of wounded and disabled servicemen arrived in New York City, they disembarked to the recorded strains of "Don't Fence Me In" sung by Bing Crosby and the Andrews Sisters.[37] A month later on the West Coast, the shattered survivors of the Bataan Death March disembarked in San Francisco to a cheering crowd and a brass band playing "Don't Fence Me In."

Posterity served the song well. Years later, in 1998, "Don't Fence Me In" by the Andrews Sisters and Bing Crosby was inducted into the Grammy Hall of Fame.

The Andrews Sisters were among the most popular singers of the war years. Their songs filled the jukeboxes, movies, and airwaves, and made *The Billboard* chart of top songs almost every week. Maxene once said of their wartime songs, "[T]he songs of the Andrews Sisters were intended—and arranged—to give the American people the fun and upbeat feelings they needed during this awful war, to help America smile."[38] Arranger Vic Schoen agreed: "It was the consensus of opinion then that happy music was the best thing to do.... We reached for a lot of material that wasn't too heavy.... We did happy and bright things that were supposed to take your mind off the war, not relate to it."[39] Whether the songs were altruistically chosen for those reasons is questionable, but they certainly did lighten America's heart. More likely, the proven commercial success of such songs dictated their selection.

The sisters chose few of the songs they recorded. Recalling the war years, Maxene said: "We sang happy songs and novelty tunes, which were selected for us by Jack Kapp, the president of Decca Records, and Lou Levy, our manager."[40] Patty told a reporter that all their songs and arrangements were selected by Dave Kapp, the Artists and Repertory Director of Decca.[41] Lou Levy said he picked 90 percent of the songs they recorded, "Not only mine [published

Nightclubbing in Hollywood circa 1945. Left to right: Olga Andrews, Patty Andrews, Vic Schoen, LaVerne Andrews, Frank Ryan, Milton Therault, and Gladys Leichter, the sisters' cousin who was then married to Therault. (Gladys Leichter Collection)

by his firm], but songs that would fit them, songs that would catch the ear of the public."[42] Levy was in a good position to find songs for the sisters through Leeds Music, his music-publishing firm that was quickly becoming one of the largest in the nation. Maxene also acknowledged Levy's role in finding songs the public would buy:

> Lou remained the guiding genius behind these [record] successes. He couldn't read music any better than we could ... but he had a unique talent, and instinct, for what was good and would be commercially successful. He especially had a gift for knowing exactly what would be a perfect fit for the Andrews Sisters' style of music.... He always emphasized the importance of singing songs with clear, strong melodies and avoiding those that featured a heavy beat and not much else.[43]

The songs Lou Levy found for the Andrews Sisters were songs that appealed to the public—commercial commodities that could be hummed and whistled, songs that had a melody. He told a reporter that when he first met the sisters their arrangements were "out of this world," meaning long on harmony and complicated licks but short on melody. He claimed the sisters were the darlings of the jazz cultists but were starving to death. He convinced them if they wanted to hit the big time, they would have to go commercial, stick to melody and avoid complex arrangements that confused the general public. He claimed Bing Crosby and Guy Lombardo were perennially successful because they stuck to the melody. He added, "We don't want to go over the people's heads—the public buys this kind of music because they wanna sing it. They oughta be able to copy our musical phrases and hot licks."[44]

Levy said if he was unable to sing the melody of a song all the way through with the sisters during rehearsals then something was wrong with the arrangement. When asked if the sisters always agreed with him, he replied: "Aw, we always sit and argue. Patty's a hepcat you know—anywhere she hears there's a hot three-piece band, she'll go. LaVerne will sing anything you tell her to and Maxene, well, you see ... she likes symphonies. As for me, I'm a jazz kid, like Patty. I love hot, out-of-the-world jazz. But it isn't commercial."[45]

Also with an obvious concern for commercial success, Decca president Jack Kapp always insisted that artists stick to a melody when recording for him. Maxene remembered:

> Decca's studios in New York City were a long, rectangular room. At the far end was a large picture of an Indian maiden, standing up and holding her hand in the air, as if signaling that she had a question. In the "dialogue balloon" she was asking: "Where's the melody?"
>
> As you were recording at the opposite end, you couldn't help seeing that question. It was staring you in the face the entire time you were singing. At Decca under Jack Kapp's insistence, you played and sang the melody, and never mind a whole lot of improvising, or you didn't record for Decca again.[46]

At one point during the sisters' tenure at Decca, someone added a second dialogue balloon beside the Indian maiden, "Remember the Bank of America"— a further reminder that melody had commercial value.[47]

Patty once said she and her sisters liked to experiment with songs: "We were always looking for the different type of thing to do. 'Apple Blossom Time' was a waltz and we put it in fox trot. When we recorded 'Jingle Bells' with Bing [Crosby], we did it as a jazz thing."[48] In later years, Patty described the sisters' approach to music:

> Throughout the years we recorded country songs and folk songs, Latin and Calypso, polka and swing, religious and Christmas songs—we did them all. We tackled anything and everything they put before us and tried to come up with a new and fresh interpretation of the songs. Waltzes became 4/4 beats, fox trots became boogie woogie, traditional songs became swinging rhythms and it was a "ball" doing it. We took the submitted song and turned it upside down and inside out until it came out the way we hoped.[49]

The Andrews Sisters were, of course, not alone in redoing traditional music. Many big bands rearranged traditional music for swing—even some of the classical European art music—often to the chagrin of purists.

In interviews the sisters emphasized the importance of rehearsals, the many hours they rehearsed, and their dedication to their work. Maxene said:

> The only catch to success in the entertainment world is that you must work, work, work—and then work some more. Then when you've hit it once you have to work harder than before to stay there. There's plenty of room at the top in show business, but you have to be good to be tops and that means years of hard labor.
>
> Speaking for ourselves, we rehearse longer hours and oftener now than we

The Andrews Sisters (from left: LaVerne, Maxene and Patty), during a long rehearsal session with arranger Vic Schoen at the piano circa 1945. (Author's collection)

ever did. Our personalities may be different, but our ambition is strictly harmonized. We want to be better than we are, hoping that someday we'll be among the best. If work will do it—we'll be there.[50]

A reporter once described a rehearsal session with the sisters and Vic Schoen: "I found the girls hunched around an upright piano, singing. They made faces, beat their feet while their bodies jumped and swayed. Even the arranger's derriere wiggled madly on the piano seat. The whole room jumped, and I sat at the desk, chin in hand, catching the wail in their voices, the contagious rhythm and excitement."[51]

Lou Levy always worked to improve the Andrews Sisters' act: "All the years I went with them on the road, I'd have a pad ... I'd be out front saying, 'Patty, stop scratching your bottom,' 'LaVerne, you're playing with your brassiere.' I never came backstage if I didn't have 10, 12 changes for them. I believed in having a perfect act, and performers never know what they do onstage. They think they do, but they don't."[52]

Throughout the Andrews Sisters' long career, Patty was always lead singer and sang all the solos. Occasionally, Maxene and LaVerne harmonized together to back Patty, but for the most part they harmonized Patty's lead. Maxene and LaVerne soloed on only two recordings. On "The Twelve Days of Christmas" with Bing Crosby each sister soloed on one of the days, and on "Fugue for Tin Horns," one of their last recordings for Decca, all three sisters soloed. Except for the occasional radio or stage performance, the pattern of Patty singing the solos persisted throughout their career. Successful though this was, it placed limitations on their act and never fully realized the talents of LaVerne and Maxene.

Vaudeville left its imprint on the Andrews Sisters. They cut their show business teeth with Larry Rich's vaudeville show where they sang, danced, joked—anything it took to entertain the audience. When they began the movie theater circuit, their performance was three or four songs around the mike in front of a band. In the early forties, they added comedy and dance routines with Patty the star and Maxene and LaVerne as straightmen. While other sister singing groups huddled around the mike and sang, the Andrews Sisters were all over the stage with their musical antics. Reviewers often noted if you hadn't seen the Andrews Sisters perform, you didn't know what they were all about.

In 1944, the Andrews Sisters recorded twenty-three songs. "Bei Mir Bist Du Schoen," "Rhumboogie," and "In Apple Blossom Time" were slightly different versions of earlier hits. Of the twenty new ones, six made the charts. "Don't Fence Me In" (twenty-one weeks) with Bing Crosby was a million seller and a number one charter for eight weeks. "A Hot Time in the Town of Berlin" (fourteen weeks) also with Crosby, anticipated Allied victory over Germany. "Straighten Up and Fly Right" (thirteen weeks) was a novelty hit by Nat Cole, which the sisters covered to make a hit of their own. "Is You Is or Is You Ain't My Baby?" (twelve weeks), was an Andrews-Crosby cover of a rhythm and blues number by Louis Jordan. "Tico Tico" (one week) was a Latin song, as was "Sing a Tropical Song" (one week). "Down in the Valley" (one week), recorded in 1943 but charted in early 1944, was a haunting song of separated lovers, a departure from the sisters' usual upbeat fare.[53]

After years of radio guest appearances and sharing the bill with others, the Andrews Sisters finally got their own radio show in late December 1944 when they joined a rich array of programs and entertainers on the airways. Radio still reigned supreme as America's number one source of home entertainment and offered something for everyone with a twist of the dial. Large floor models made of the finest hardwoods graced the living rooms of those who could afford them while less expensive console models were more typical of most homes. Many independent stations flourished across the country, but the two major networks, the giant NBC and CBS, set the pace for what America listened to. In 1945, NBC was forced to dismantle its near monopoly of the airwaves and ABC was one of its spin-offs.

The radio day began with early news programs, weather reports, and farm reports as background for America's breakfast. As the nation settled into the workday, programs were tailored for housewives who listened to the radio as they

As many Hollywood celebrities, the Andrews Sisters routinely visited the Hollywood Canteen to entertain the military personnel that gathered there. 1944. (Ray Hagen Collection)

pursued household chores. Don McNeill's *Breakfast Club* was a popular morning show out of Chicago that featured talk, guests and music—a precursor to the many current morning television shows. Other wake-up shows on local stations offered a similar format for regional tastes. As the day wore on, soap operas began to appear, but then, as now, they more thoroughly populated the afternoon airways. Noon brought more news, stock, weather, and farm reports.

The soaps began in earnest in the afternoon. The long-suffering *Ma Perkins* jerked tears routinely from her faithful listeners. *One Man's Family* stretched traumas to weeks and even months. *Our Gal Sunday, The Romance of Helen Trent,* and *Stella Dallas* were only a few of the heroines who daily wrenched the hearts of their listening audience. As children returned home from school, adventure programs took over. *Sergeant Preston of the Yukon* transported young listeners to the excitement of the far north while *Jack Armstrong, the All-American Boy* combined traditional American values with on-going adventures. The trials and tribulations of *Little Orphan Annie* kept young listeners rapt and *Buck Rogers in the 25th Century* carried them to distant planets and galaxies aboard space ships. Hopalong Cassidy, Tom Mix, Gene Autry, and the Lone Ranger were a few of the cowboys who maintained law and order in the American West.

During and following dinner, evening news programs kept the family abreast of local, national, and world events. Most families eagerly awaited news of the war fronts, sometimes broadcast live by the likes of Edward R. Murrow and Lowell Thomas. Following the news, the family settled into the evening for some adult entertainment—albeit programmed for the sensitive ears of the youth who might be listening. The racy one liners of Bob Hope were carefully watched by the censors. Fibber McGee and Molly opened their famous overstuffed closet each week to the same raucous clamor. The parsimonious Jack Benny and his predictable but always funny cast of characters were into their second decade of making America laugh. Even longer running was the perennially popular *Amos 'n' Andy,* who brought a slice of African American humor to the living rooms of America, albeit embarrassingly racist and stereotyped by today's standards—as well as to the enlightened segment of the listening audience of the times. The squeaking hinges of the opening door of *Inner Sanctum* assured chills for a half-hour, and *The Shadow* weekly battled "the evil that lurks in the hearts of men." Dramatic programs, such as *Lux Radio Theatre* and *The First Nighter,* brought original plays and sometimes movie dramatizations to the air often starring leading actors of Hollywood and Broadway. Baseball, football, and basketball games were eagerly tuned in by sports buffs as were horse races and boxing matches. Classical music fans routinely heard Arturo Toscanini conduct the NBC Symphony Orchestra, and with a switch of the dial, they could hear Leopold Stokowski with the CBS Symphony Orchestra. Opera buffs knew that Saturday would always bring the Texaco broadcast of the Metropolitan Opera season in New York. *The Bing Crosby Show* and *The Kate Smith Hour* were the longest running popular music programs—although Kate increasingly became the commentator and more opinionated. Each Saturday night, *Your Hit Parade* featured the most popular songs in the nation. And Sunday morning provided a variety of religious programs for those who preferred to take their religion at home. It was this diverse, eclectic world of radio that the Andrews Sisters joined at the end of 1944.

Radio shows were eagerly sought by most performers. Not only did radio offer a more accessible audience, but it also allowed performers to live in New York, Chicago, or Los Angeles throughout the radio year and hit the road only in the summer for public appearances. As satisfying as it was to perform live before adoring audiences, it was equally satisfying to return home after a radio show rather than to a hotel room for a week or so before moving on to the next city. The radio show allowed a home life and a social life for the Andrews Sisters they had not enjoyed since they left Minneapolis thirteen years previously.

Variety's last issue of 1944 featured a full-page ad for the sisters' new radio show called *The Andrews Sisters Show*, subtitled *Eight-to-the-Bar Ranch*. The show was built around the fictitious Eight-to-the-Bar Ranch the sisters inherited from their "Uncle Ed Andrews" who stipulated in his will that the sisters must operate it themselves. They turned it into a dude ranch, thus setting the stage for their many guests. Other members of the cast included George "Gabby" Hayes, the grizzled character actor perhaps best remembered as Roy Rogers' comic sidekick, who played the ranch foreman, "Pigmeat" Martin, an African American comedian who played the cook, Foy Willing and his Riders of the Purple Sage who were singing ranch hands, Vic Schoen and his orchestra, announcer Marvin Miller, producer Lou Levy, and the sisters' first guest, "The Number One Dude Rancher of the Week," Bing Crosby.[54] The new program premiered Sunday, December 31, in Los Angeles from 1:30 to 2 P.M. on the Blue Network (later ABC), sponsored by Nash-Kelvinator, makers of Nash automobiles and Kelvinator kitchen appliances.[55] A pilot of the show was aired earlier and featured Frank Sinatra as guest and Wild Bill Elliot as ranch foreman. It was essentially the same show as the opening one with Bing Crosby but was broadcast on the Armed Forces Radio Service.

The western theme of the show is somewhat puzzling. The Andrews Sisters enjoyed a few western hits, such as "Pistol Packin' Mama" and "Don't Fence Me In," but they certainly were not considered western or country singers. Lou Levy told a reporter in the early days of the show, "100 million people love hillbilly [country] music—regardless of what the professional musicians say."[56] The always savvy Levy perhaps thought he might add another audience to the sisters' multitude of fans if he widened their repertoire.

The sisters' fans tuned in to hear *The Andrews Sisters Show* and probably liked most of what they heard, but the critics were less impressed. A *Variety* reviewer was critical of the script as well as Gabby Hayes, the "bewhiskered comic from horse opera B pictures." At the time of the review Bing Crosby and Eddie Cantor had already guest-starred on the show.

> Sooner or later, the Andrews gals and Hayes have got to deliver on their own.... The Andrews Sisters, of course, are like Martinis, you either like 'em or can't stand 'em.... Judging from first two programs the girls are relying on the tunes which gather the nickels in the nation's juke boxes and there's no denying they do these ditties in fine style—if you like their style. Script burdens haven't been heavy and the sisters handle this dept. okay. But without the guests, the show is just the rhythm trio, backed by a sock orch. and an old pappy guy with whiskers. You can't see those whiskers but you can get awful tired hearing about them.[57]

The Billboard review when Rudy Vallee guest-starred on the show was enthusiastic about the sisters' singing and thought the show had potential despite shortcomings of its scripts.[58] The *New York Times* gave a cautiously positive

On New Year's Eve 1944, the Andrews Sisters premiered their new radio show *The Andrews Sisters Show*, subtitled *Eight-to-the-Bar Ranch*. Each week the western-themed show featured a special guest who appeared with the sisters and the regular cast, which included Foy Willings and his Riders of the Purple Sage, pictured above with the sisters. (Robert Boyer Collection)

review of the show, but thought the sisters needed more variety in their musical selections.[59] Surpisingly, *Metronome*, which almost never had a good word for the Andrews Sisters, liked the show and had a few back-handed compliments for them:

> The Andrews talk as much as they sing on this show. They handle their several roles very well: Patty, alert and vivacious, as she is actually; Maxene, serious-minded, as she really is, and therefore responsible for Red Cross and Bond appeals, and such; LaVerne, a good-natured comedienne, playing dumb. They work well with their guests each week … and, somehow, when the Andrews sing on this show they don't sound quite as gross or grunty or grimly obstreperous as usual. Maybe it's because the thing is literally ethereal and not made permanent on record grooves. In any case, it's an amusing half-hour at times, sharply paced, with the yells and the caterwauls of the Andrews restrained, their personable sides well revealed, and even Vic Schoen's choppy Dixieland in hand.[60]

I heard seven of *The Andrews Sisters Show* radio programs; the music is good, but the scripts are terrible, badly written with corny, predictable jokes. All three sisters have dialogue with Patty handling the lion's share. LaVerne plays a dim-witted, man-hungry dunce. On one show, she says "I have a secret." Patty asks, "What is it?" LaVerne replies, "I don't know, it's a secret." On another show, Patty asks her, "Why are you so late getting up?" LaVerne replies: "I forgot to wind the rooster." This is typical LaVerne fare. Gabby Hayes has an ongoing crush on Patty, which she continually rebukes. He is invariably jealous of the male guest stars and much of his interaction with them is insults. He preferred to work without his false teeth and his dialogue was written so he could pronounce it sans teeth. "Pigmeat" Martin was unable to read and his lines were consequently kept short so he could easily memorize them.[61]

It is amazing the show lasted as long as it did without major changes. The musical numbers are its only saving grace. The show gave fans a chance to hear the Andrews Sisters sing songs they never recorded, such as "The Trolley Song," "Saturday Night Is the Loneliest Night," and "I'm Beginning to See the Light." They also sang with singers, such as Frank Sinatra and Rudy Vallee, they would otherwise not have joined because of competing record contracts. Comedians such as Eddie Cantor, Marjorie Main, and Bob Hope helped them through some feeble comic routines.

Probably the most bizarre combination of talent occurred when actors Peter Lorre and Sydney Greenstreet appeared on the show in late January 1945—perhaps to promote the film *Hollywood Canteen* in which the sisters, Lorre, and Greenstreet all had cameo roles. The plot featured Lorre and Greenstreet checking out the ranch as a possible site for their next picture. Suspecting sinister deeds from them, the sisters and Hayes eavesdropped and heard them talk about carving a roast chicken which they misinterpreted as dismembering a body. All ended well with the most unlikely singing combo of the Andrews Sisters' entire career when Lorre and Greenstreet joined them in a chorus of "Together."

Perhaps the most forgettable of the several forgettable routines on the show was a "hillbilly" song called "The Old Square Dance" when Gabby Hayes and radio comedienne Vera Vague joined the sisters. It's a tossup as to which was worse—the song, the arrangement, or the singers.

Nash-Kelvinator, sponsor of the show, was apparently none too happy with the program either. In early March, the show's writers were released, and two new ones were hired, both formerly with Milton Berle and Bob Hope.[62] In June, the sponsors, still dissatisfied, announced the show would be renewed for another year, but with less comedy and more songs.[63] Lou Levy and the sisters wanted to keep the original western format, but the sponsors were adamant.

The Andrews Sisters began reaching an even larger audience in early 1945 when the Armed Forces Radio Service initiated radio broadcasts to military forces around the world. Some broadcasts were short-wave radio transmissions, but many were transcriptions of music and radio programs on 33⅓ phonograph records that were sent to military bases for local broadcast.

Shortly after the program began, AFRS began producing records called the "Basic Musical Library" which included music ranging from popular to jazz and classical. The most popular series was the "P" (popular) series, which comprised songs by the popular singers of the day. For unclear reasons, these selections were frequently from rehearsals of radio programs (such as the Andrews Sisters' *Eight-to-the-Bar Ranch*) or alternate takes of commercial titles issued by record companies. Consequently, some of the songs were never heard on radio and some of the takes were never issued by record companies. Each 33⅓ record usually had five songs per side, either all by the same artist or by several different artists.

The Andrews Sisters began contributing to the "P" series in early 1945 and all these early songs came from their radio program. Thereafter, until the end of 1947, their "P" series songs were alternate takes of their Decca releases. I located forty-eight titles by the Andrews Sisters (some with other singers, such as Bing Crosby and Dick Haymes) on sixteen different records, but there were probably others since my source listed only the first 1000 "P" series recordings.[64]

In January 1945, *Her Lucky Night* was released, the Andrews Sisters' final film for Universal.

The plot involved the attempt of a young woman (Martha O'Driscoll), who worked in a studio where the Andrews Sisters recorded, to find a boyfriend through a fortuneteller. She ended up meeting an elderly millionaire who hired her to locate a long-lost nephew (Noah Beery, Jr.) so he could take over his uncle's business. She, of course, fell in love with the nephew who, after a series of misadventures, was reunited with his uncle. The sisters helped out their friend (O'Driscoll) and posed as maids in one scene to provide some laughs. The Andrews Sisters had more active roles in the plot than usual, and also displayed some of their best film singing, including such songs as "Straighten Up and Fly Right," "Sing a Tropical Song," and "Is You Is or Is You Ain't My Baby?" They used hand puppets of themselves in the "Dance with a Dolly" routine for an interesting diversion. Some of the comedy scenes hold up fairly well and Noah Beery, Jr. (later to become better known as James Garner's father on the popular television series *The Rockford Files*), portrayed an appealing Will Rogers–type country bumpkin.

Movie critics didn't care for the film. *Daily Variety* called it a "run-of-the-mill musical, plus farce comedy … having no standout entertainment enticements."[65] *Hollywood Reporter* was less kind: "The story is stupid and impossible and the script is worse, consisting almost exclusively of a mass of very tired clichés … it is a pity that so good a cast should have been wasted so completely, not to mention the waste of film…. The sole redeeming feature is the singing of the Andrews Sisters."[66]

Universal Studios was apparently running out of ideas for the sisters' films. *Hollywood Reporter* noted that a scene from *Her Lucky Night* was lifted from Harold Lloyd's silent film *The Freshman*. Lloyd saw the film and thought the comic routines were familiar. When he discovered the scriptwriter was one of his former directors, Lloyd went to court and successfully sued Universal for plagiarism, and ruined the career of the guilty scriptwriter in the process.[67]

Maxene claimed she was responsible for getting the sisters out of their Universal contract, but if the contract was as she claimed, it's unclear why she needed a lawyer:

Her Lucky Night (1945) was the Andrews Sisters' final film for Universal. In this scene, the sisters are disguised as maids as they try to convince George Barbier that his country bumpkin nephew is a suitable heir to his fortune. (Robert Boyer Collection)

> Our father, being Greek, was friendly with Spiros Skouras, who was then at 20th Century–Fox, and one day I said, "You do all those marvelous color musicals over at 20th, and the only Greeks you use are the Condos Brothers—why not use us?" And the offer came. But it didn't come to us, it came through Universal, and they refused to let us go! They said they'd be foolish to let us go to 20th Century Fox because we were making so much for Universal. And that made me mad, because we weren't being paid a lot of money, and we were constantly upset by the way they treated us there … so I took the contract to a lawyer. And it was this lawyer, for $25, who found the error in the contract. It said thirteen movies or 7½ years. We still had a few years to go on the contract, but we were already in our thirteenth movie. So I just went in with our manager and announced that this was our last picture!… At that time … Dan Kelly, who was the man I had to approach, pulled out a sheet of paper and said that they'd be a fool to let us go because our pictures never made less than a million-dollar profit for them.[68]

Maxene's proclivity for hyperbole appears to be surfacing here, as it seems unlikely their string of movies each made a million dollars' profit, a huge amount in those years. For many years, Maxene had bad memories of their film career at Universal:

It was terrible ... Making those movies was really unpleasant—movies to me were always a big bore. I could never even watch those pictures for years and years. It's only been in the last 3 years that I could watch them. At the time we made them I'd get so embarrassed, but that was basically because I knew how crummy Universal was. I always did my best, but I felt so self-conscious. But now when I see those movies I think, My God, those girls are good! My God, those girls move![69]

Patty seconded Maxene's opinion when asked about Universal:

[W]e really weren't happy ... that they never ever spent any time with us. When we'd come off the road to do a picture, everything was done in two weeks. And they never gave us a choreographer. And it would be like a rush thing all the time and almost ... thrown together. And we never liked doing things that way. We were never happy with wardrobe. They never gave us that much attention toward hairdressing or make-up or anything like that. And we really felt that we didn't come off looking as well as we would have liked to have looked.[70]

Elsewhere Patty joked about their make-up at Universal: "They asked us if we'd object to the same man who made up the Frankenstein monster and I said: 'We'll take him if he doesn't consider it a comedown.'"[71] Maxene told a reporter: "Universal was one thing ... Were you blonde and blue-eyed and cutesy-poo? And none of us were blonde, blue-eyed or cutesy-poo. But we could sing a helluva song."[72]

In January the sisters began paying back their radio guests. On *The Eddie Cantor Show*, they participated in a comic skit with Cantor about life on the Lower East Side as three tough sisters wooed by three equally tough streetsters. Cantor later joined them in their comic rendition of "Sonny Boy." In mid-month, they joined Rudy Vallee on *The Drene Show* for a couple of unremarkable skits but a good rendition of "Blues in the Night." They also sang the predictable "Bei Mir Bist Du Schoen" and joined Vallee for "Veini Veini." At the end of the month, they appeared on *The Kraft Music Hall* with Bing Crosby and sang their current hit "Don't Fence Me In," their whimsical "One Meat Ball," and a delightful version of "Ain't It a Shame About Mame?"

The Andrews Sisters appeared most frequently on radio as on records with Bing Crosby. Their appearances on his show usually featured a recent recording with him, or if no song was current, one of their past hits. The pattern of their radio appearances with Crosby was typical of most musical programs of the time. After their introduction, they joined Crosby in some banter, Patty always taking the lead, which segued into a song together, usually a current release. After a commercial and perhaps another song by Crosby or another guest, the sisters returned for a skit or more comic chit-chat that introduced another song, again a recent release. The show concluded with another Crosby-Andrews number. Their radio encounters with Crosby exuded the same friendly, relaxed mood typical of their many recordings with him. Although they never interacted with Crosby off the air or outside the recording studio, their sessions with him conveyed an ambiance of good friends getting together to sing songs they all enjoyed.

In late April, the sisters guest-starred on *The Abbott and Costello Show* with

The Andrews Sisters recorded 46 songs with Bing Crosby, half of which made the charts, and they were frequent guests on his radio show. Here they clown with Crosby on his show in February 1950 as the Firehouse Five Plus Two provides Dixieland music. (Author's collection)

their old buddies from their early movie-making days. Two weeks previously, Abbott and Costello aired an episode about a shady agent who tried to talk the comedy duo into hiring a group called the Andrews Brothers who sang a couple of the sisters' songs. The sisters' appearance featured a skit about their "lawsuit" against Abbott and Costello for slander. They sang a good "I'm Beginning to See the Light" and closed the show with their comic version of "Sonny Boy"—this time with Lou Costello.

Shortly before going on the air with Abbott and Costello, the sisters learned that President Franklin Roosevelt had died. They joined the nation in mourning the loss of the patrician father figure who led the nation out of the Great Depression and through the current world war. A few days later Adolf Hitler committed suicide, and on May 4, 1945, Germany surrendered to the Allied nations. The European war was over, but on the other side of the world the Pacific war still raged.

The Andrews Sisters were not great fans of their radio sidekick Gabby Hayes, at least Maxene wasn't. She remembered when President Roosevelt died and Hayes was given a eulogy to read on the air:

We did a radio show with Gabby Hayes, who was such a phony and a really crabby old man.[73] All of us except FDR's bitterest political enemies felt we had lost a true friend [when Roosevelt died] … One of those enemies was our own Gabby Hayes. He despised President Roosevelt and never made any secret of it, but—wouldn't you know it?—after the writers of our show came up with a beautiful eulogy of FDR, our producers gave it to Gabby, of all people, to read on the air. That struck me as the height of hypocrisy. The producers clearly should have given it to someone else, even a staff announcer, but not someone who absolutely hated the man and was so vocal and public about it. And Gabby should have turned it down and suggested that someone else read it instead. But he didn't. He did a convincing job of acting. He even got all choked up. It was a long time before I was able to forgive the producers and Gabby for that.[74] I wanted to hit him on the back.[75]

In early January 1945, Decca published a half-page ad aimed at jukebox operators in *The Billboard* for the Andrews Sisters' new record "Rum and Coca-Cola":

> Here's the low-down—and we mean lowdown—on GI Joe and his Yankee dollars and the Trinidad gals and other stuff. Patty, LaVerne and Maxene give it the works—Calypso style—on this new Decca record. It's a song that'll keep the coins rolling into your machines. Everyone will want to hear it again and again to find out exactly what Patty is saying in that undertone patter that runs through the song.[76]

In the middle of the month, Decca carried another ad, this time in *Variety*, for "Rum and Coca-Cola," "sensationally recorded by Andrews Sisters and Vic Schoen and His Orchestra."[77] The song was entering the charts and the country would soon hear much more of it. A week later, *Variety* carried a full-page ad for Leo Feist, Inc, the publisher of "Rum and Coca-Cola," which claimed the song was the "Most Spectacular Song Success of the Music Business" and it "Stopped Every Show at Paramount Theatre for Five Weeks" and was the "Biggest Decca Sell-Out Disc [for] Andrews Sisters."[78]

"Rum and Coca-Cola" was a calypso song about GIs in Trinidad and their interaction with the local women "working for the Yankee dollar." The song was obviously about sex and prostitutes, which Maxene claimed the sisters did not realize at the time they recorded it—a claim that taxes credibility: "People can't believe that we didn't know what that was about. It wasn't until we found out it was banned in some places that we started asking why, and they'd say, 'Well, dummies, it's about prostitution.' Young people today can't believe that people were so naïve in those days. We were very infantile."[79]

The Andrews Sisters may not have known what the song was about, but the rest of the country did. That's why so many people bought it and why so many others wanted to ban it. Maxene said the demand for the song was so great that Decca did not have enough shellac to press the record and had to borrow from RCA to fill orders.[80]

Ironically, "Rum and Coca-Cola" was recorded only because the sisters had time to fill at the end of a recording session. As Maxene recalled, "We'd already done four songs and had about 20 minutes left. LaVerne's [future] husband, trumpet player Lou Rogers, helped us, and we faked "Rum and Coke."

It became the biggest thing we ever did."[81] Patty remembered the recording session also: "We had a recording date, and the song was brought to us the night before the recording date.... We hardly really knew it, and when we went in we had some extra time and we just threw it in, and that was the miracle of it. It was actually a faked arrangement. There was no written background, so we just kind of faked it."[82]

The lyrics to the song follow. Patty spoke the words in parentheses sotto voce between stanzas. On the 78 rpm records of the time, the words were almost inaudible and led to the rumor they were off-color. As a nine-year-old kid, I remember playing the record over and over in an attempt to hear the reputed naughty words Patty was voicing.

> If you ever go down Trinidad, they make you feel so very glad.
> Calypso sing and make up rhyme, guarantee you one real good fine time.
> Drinking rum and Coca-Cola, go down Point Kumana.
> Both mother and daughter, working for the Yankee dollar.
> (Oh beat it, man, beat it.)
> Since the Yankee come to Trinidad, they got the young girls all going mad.
> Young girls say they treat them nice, make Trinidad like paradise.
> Drinking rum and Coca-Cola, go down Point Kumana.
> Both mother and daughter, working for the Yankee dollar.
> (Oh you vex me, you vex me.)
> From Chica-chi-carry to Mona's Isle, native girls all dance and smile.
> Help soldier celebrate his leave, make everyday like New Year's Eve.
> Drinking rum and Coca-Cola, go down Point Kumana.
> Both mother and daughter, working for the Yankee dollar.
> (It's a fact, man, it's a fact.)
> In old Trinidad I also fear, the situation is mighty queer.
> Like the Yankee girl, the native swoon when they hear Der Bingle croon.
> Drinking rum and Coca-Cola, go down Point Kumana.
> Both mother and daughter, working for the Yankee dollar.
> Out on Manzanella Beach, GI romance with native peach.
> All night long make tropic love, next day sit in hot sun and cool off.
> Drinking rum and Coca-Cola, go down Point Kumana.
> Both mother and daughter, working for the Yankee dollar.
> (It's a fact, man, it's a fact.)
> Rum and Coca-Cola, Rum and Coca-Cola.
> Working for the Yankee dollar.

Almost immediately after the song's release, the major radio networks objected to it, contending the lyrics were unsuitable for the listening audience. "Rum" was banned because of the traditional prohibition against promoting alcohol on the air. Shortly thereafter the watchdogs decided the Coca-Cola Company was receiving a free plug, so that part of the title was banned also. The song was banned from all the major radio networks, but it soon became the best-selling record in the country, which according to one commentator proved "once again that jukes [jukeboxes] can and do make a tune."[83] Another said the song was "born in the jukeboxes and wet-nursed by platter jockeys over indie [independent] stations, into a hit."[84]

In mid–February, *Variety* reported that "Rum and Coca-Cola" would probably become Decca's biggest selling record, despite the radio ban on it. Decca had produced 850,000 copies of the recording, and sheet music sales were close to the 500,000 mark. The Andrews Sisters sang one of the two airings of the song on their radio show, but substituted "lime" for "rum." Shortly thereafter, the major radio networks banned all vocal arrangements of the song, but instrumentals were occasionally allowed.[85]

The publishers of "Rum and Coca-Cola" complained to *The Lucky Strike Hit Parade* for not including the song on their radio show despite its great popularity on jukeboxes, records sales, and sheet music sales. The *Hit Parade* apparently excluded the song because of the airwave ban.[86] As the song grew in popularity, many underground versions appeared with increasingly obscene lyrics. *The Billboard* reported that employees at a restaurant in Phoenix grew so tired of hearing the song that they removed it from the jukebox, only to have the Andrews Sisters again dominate the jukebox with Bing Crosby singing "Don't Fence Me In" and "Ac-Cent-Tchu-Ate the Positive."[87] A veteran of World War II told me that when he shipped overseas, the song was played almost twenty-four hours a day on the P.A. system. Another told me he broke his barracks' record of the song because he got so tired of hearing it. A sailor once told Patty that he became so tired of hearing the song on board his submarine that he vowed if he ever met the Andrews Sisters he would kill them: "We played that song until it wore out. I never want to hear that song again!"[88] After the success of the Andrews song, Decca released a two-sided version with ten additional verses by Wilmoth Houdini and his Royal Calypso Orchestra.[89]

At the end of February, CBS announced that instrumental versions of "Rum and Coca-Cola" were no longer banned from the network, although the ban against "Rum" and "Coca Cola" still stood. It could be announced as "R. and C.C." The Blue Network (ABC) allowed the song but insisted it be called "Lime and Coca Cola." NBC continued to ban both the song and its title,[90] but later conceded the correct title could be used for instrumental playings; no lyrics were allowed, however. CBS also permitted the announcement of the correct title, but allowed no lyrics. Mutual Network allowed the song to be played as "In Trinidad."[91]

Metronome reviewed the record and begrudgingly did not pan it entirely: "The pseudo-Calypso atmosphere on "Cola," with ac-cents on the wrong syllab-les, comes off fairly well, but the simple theme becomes a little too repetitious toward the end. And even here Vic Schoen can't resist the temptation to stick in one of those Vic Schoen endings."[92] As if to compensate for its less than scathing review, *Metronome* later published a lengthy diatribe from a reader who thought its review was too kind and the sisters' recording an "abomination" because it was so removed from true calypso.[93]

"Rum and Coca-Cola" ultimately outsold all other Andrews Sisters recordings. I found no final sales figures for the song, but several writers claimed it was second only to Bing Crosby's "White Christmas" for the 1940 decade. Long after it faded from the jukeboxes, "Rum and Coca-Cola" continued to make headlines because of the litigation that followed its enormous popularity.

Morey Amsterdam, publisher of the song, originally heard the calypso melody in Trinidad. Believing it was in public domain, he adapted it for American audiences and then published it with his own lyrics. After the song became a major hit, Maurice Baron sued Amsterdam, claiming the song had been lifted from an album of Carribbean songs, published and copyrighted by him. Judgment was granted to Baron and heavy damages were fined. Amsterdam appealed the decision, but lost the appeal.[94] It was not until 1950 that the case finally concluded. The Andrews Sisters were not involved in the litigation.

The Andrews Sisters were flying high during the first half of 1945. The top three songs on the jukeboxes were theirs, "Rum and Coca-Cola," and "Don't Fence Me In" and "Ac-Cent-Tchu-Ate the Positive," both with Bing Crosby.[95] A survey of the most popular musicians conducted by a St. Louis radio station gave first place to the Andrews Sisters among female vocalists.[96] On June 9, *The Billboard* announced the results of a poll of high schoolers' favorite musicians: the Andrews Sisters were the top singing group. The same poll revealed that high schoolers' favorite song was the Andrews Sisters' "Rum and Coca-Cola" followed by "Don't Fence Me In."[97] A month later *The Billboard's* music poll among GIs placed the Andrews Sisters as their most popular singing group. A college students' poll, published a month later, ranked the Andrews Sisters number two favorites on America's campuses, second only to the Ink Spots.[98]

Throughout the war years, as well as the postwar years, the Andrews Sisters regularly appeared on the War Department's radio show *Command Performance*. The show was lauded by *Time* magazine as "the best wartime program in America," but few Americans at home ever heard it. The War Department produced *Command Performance* for direct short-wave transmission to troops overseas. All talent was donated, including the production staff. Both CBS and NBC gave free use of their network studios. Such stars as the Andrews Sisters, Bing Crosby, Bob Hope, Red Skelton, Judy Garland, Fibber McGee and Molly, Ethel Waters, Spike Jones, Dinah Shore, Frank Sinatra, and Charles Laughton appeared on the program. *Command Performance* continued until 1977, short-waving specials to American servicemen all over the world. In all, more than 400 shows were produced, ranging from the regular half-hour programs to two-hour specials.

The show came about when the War Department asked its Radio Division to develop a format for entertaining troops overseas. The program developers decided to let the troops choose their own fare and make the program a "command performance." The first shows were put together from verbal requests, but letters were soon flowing in from military personnel with requests. One soldier wanted to hear Lana Turner fry a steak. Another requested that Charles Laughton instruct Donald Duck in elocution. The show's engineers were once sent to record the sounds of birds chirping in a soldier's Indiana hometown, and for another show, the sounds of a nickel slot machine paying off a jackpot were recorded. Among the show's highlights were a special Christmas Eve broadcast in 1942; an all-jive show with the orchestras of Tommy Dorsey, Lionel Hampton, Count Basie, and Spike Jones; and a "fiddle fight" between Jascha Heifetz and Jack Benny.[99]

The Andrews Sisters appeared on nineteen broadcasts of *Command Performance* from May 1942 through April 1949, including three special programs "Christmas Command Performance" (December 1942), "Dick Tracy in B Flat" (February 1945) and "Army Day Command Performance" (April 1946). They participated in an all western music show (June 1944), acted as emcees on a show (December 1945), and joined Bing Crosby and Judy Garland to sing the "All Time Flop Parade" on a show called "Highlights of 1944" (October 1944). Entertainers who shared the bill with the sisters included Bob Hope, Bing Crosby, Benny Goodman, Doris Day, Jack Benny, Harpo Marx, Dinah Shore, Judy Garland, Lauren Bacall, Frank Sinatra, Nelson Eddy, Jimmy Durante, Jo Stafford, Bud Abbott and Lou Costello. The programs were truly a "Who's Who" of the entertainment world. At times *Command Performance* used a variety show format with an emcee announcing a series of entertainers. Typically the performances were recorded tracts pasted together for the show. At other times, the entertainers performed ensemble and interacted with one another in dialogue or skits.[100]

In later years, Maxene told a reporter that one of her most embarrassing moments on stage occurred during a *Command Performance* show with Bing Crosby and Bob Hope:

> We'd just finished a song with Bing ... he bowed; I bowed and started backing off stage. I slipped, made a wild grab at Patty, and yanked her skirt 'way down to her knees. Then I fell and kicked my legs in the air. The audience—all servicemen—howled. Bing was helpless, too; he just stood there and rocked. Bob rushed on stage and made things worse by cracking "If only the Andrews would fall for me like they fall for Bing."[101]

On February 15, 1945, *Command Performance* produced a "comic strip operetta" called *Dick Tracy in B Flat,* or *For Goodness Sake, Isn't He Ever Going to Marry Tess Trueheart?,* based on the comic strip characters of Chester Gould and featuring an ensemble that *Variety* called a "Dream Cast." The cast included some of the top names in the entertainment business: Bing Crosby as Dick Tracy; Bob Hope as Flat Top; Frank Sinatra as Shakey; Dinah Shore as Tess Trueheart; Frank Morgan as Vitamin Flintheart; Judy Garland as Snowflake; Jimmy Durante as Mole; the Andrews Sisters as the Summer Sisters; Cass Daley as Gravel Gertie; Harry Von Zell as Old Judge Hooper; and Jerry Colonna as chief of police.[102]

The plot was about Dick Tracy's attempt to marry Tess Trueheart. Each time the wedding ceremony was almost concluded, Tracy was called away to fight a criminal—first Flat Top (Bob Hope), then Mole (Jimmy Durante), then Shakey (Frank Sinatra), and then Gravel Gertie (Cass Daly). Among exaggerated sound effects and occasional off-color dialogue, the characters sang songs associated with them with cleverly rewritten lyrics that carried the plot along. For example, the Andrews Sisters as the Summer Sisters (May, June, and July) sang a version of "In Apple Blossom Time" and Judy Garland as Snowflake sang "Somewhere Over a Barrel" as she was terrorized by Flat Top (Bob Hope). The singers frequently broke character and obviously had a good time doing the show which was carried along by "Happy, Happy, Happy Wedding Day," the show's theme that was later recorded by Bing Crosby and the Andrews Sisters. After many interruptions, the wedding was finally concluded. The show was an hour long and broadcast only to armed forces. Consequently, most Americans never heard the program and it is available today only on copies of *Command Performance* programs, many of which are pirated. It is a clever pop music operetta sung by some of the top singers of the time, in some of the most popular music of the day. A small classic, the operetta deserves greater distribution than it currently enjoys.

The Andrews Sisters also made appearances on *Mail Call*, which began each broadcast with "Stand by Americans. Here's *Mail Call*. One big package of words and music and laughter delivered to you by the stars from whom you want to hear in answer to the requests you send to Armed Forces Radio, Los Angeles." The program was less successful, and its format so similar to *Command Performance* that one wonders why it was aired.

The Andrews Sisters took their radio show to the stage of San Diego's Orpheum Theater May 15 for a week run. The cast was the same as the radio show (minus the weekly guest), and differed from most movie house entertainment which typically offered a series of unrelated acts. Patty acted as emcee and the Andrews Sisters were in and out of the show from the beginning to the end. The sisters made a hefty $18,000 one-week salary at San Diego, their share of a 50-50 split.[103] The following week they took the show to the Orpheum Theater in Los Angeles for another successful run. Their Sunday radio show still aired, and the theater engagements were apparently warm-ups for their engagement at the New York Paramount scheduled for the following fall.

On June 10, the Andrews Sisters participated in the Seventh War Loan Drive at Warner Brothers' Wiltern Theater in Hollywood. Emceed by popular radio announcer Don Wilson, the two-and-a-half-hour show was broadcast nationally and featured a cast of such strange bed fellows as Bing Crosby, Lou Costello, Rise Stevens, Paulette Goddard, and Eddie "Rochester" Anderson. Admission was by bond purchase of $100 or more.[104] Carl Hoff and his orchestra provided music for the program that included Crosby singing "You Belong to My Heart," Rise Stevens with an aria from *Carmen*, phone calls from Rochester as he made his way across country to join the show, a "radio play" with Paulette Goddard called *The Most Beautiful Girl in Missouri*, "Who's on First" by Lou Costello assisted by Sydney Fields who replaced an ailing Bud Abbott. The Andrews Sisters sang the inevitable "Bei Mir Bist Du Schoen" and later joined Bing Crosby in their current hit "Don't Fence Me In."

On the personal front, 1945 brought a big change to the lives of Maxene and her husband Lou Levy.

Maxene once told a reporter that she and her sisters were biologically unable to have children.[105] Whether that is true is unknown, but none of the sisters had children of their own. In their younger years, they told their cousin Gladys Leichter that if she had children, they wanted to be called "Aunt" by them because they would probably not have children. Gladys eventually had two sons and two daughters who were close to the sisters when they were young and called them "Aunt." Gladys' first daughter was named "Patricia" at the request of Patty, who was her godmother.[106]

Maxene was unable to have children because she had a hysterectomy shortly after her marriage[107]; subsequently, she and her husband, Lou Levy, decided to adopt a child. Maxene told a reporter that she and Levy waited a long time to find a baby to adopt, but were unprepared when they were told a six-weeks-old girl was available for them in late June.[108] Maxene explained: "No clothes, no equipment, no experience with little babies. It was rugged at first ... but we wanted her for selfish reasons. We wanted a baby to love. I wash the diapers, we both feed her. When we're out, Lou's father takes over. Next week we get a nurse—we hope."[109]

Maxene did not mention that when the baby arrived, she and her sisters were on the road and Levy was in New York. The baby was taken to Maxene's cousin Gladys Leichter. When the new baby arrived, Gladys nicknamed her "Duchess," and although the little girl was eventually named Aleda Ann, the nickname "Duchess" or "Duchy" stayed with her. Gladys had the baby about three weeks before Maxene and Levy returned to California. When Levy first saw the infant, he was unimpressed and became nervous about fatherhood. Gladys told him if he didn't want the baby, she would keep her. Levy and Maxene took the baby home, and some months later when Gladys asked Levy if he wanted to return the baby, he replied, "Over my dead body."

Both Maxene and Levy had made commitments before the baby arrived. Levy had business on the East Coast and Maxene had a six-week USO tour beginning in early July. Maxene hired an African American couple to care for her new daughter. Two years later when she and Levy adopted a son, a Hungarian couple became the children's caretakers and were with them until they left home.[110]

In late 1944, the USO ordered the Andrews Sisters to take physical examinations in preparation for assignment to an overseas tour. After initially failing the exam because of a minor urinary disorder they shared, the sisters altered their diets and passed the next one with flying colors. But it was six months later, after the surrender of Germany, before they were finally called to report for overseas duty. Olga Andrews initially opposed the USO tour because of dangers she thought it entailed; when she learned her daughters didn't know where they were going or exactly how long they'd be gone, she was even more concerned.

But the sisters were determined to go, and in June they reported to the USO in New York where they received a battery of inoculations, and were sent to pick up their USO uniforms at Saks Fifth Avenue—a fashion step above the designers of most military uniforms. When told they must audition before acceptance by the USO, the sisters balked and said their professional reputation precluded auditions. The USO relented. Still not knowing their overseas destination, they were taken to Fort Dix, New Jersey, where they boarded an Army Air Corps plane in the middle of night. Since their clothing issue was woolen, they assumed they were headed north, but en route they learned they were headed for summertime Italy.

After a refueling stop in Newfoundland, they flew across the Atlantic to Morocco where they landed at Casablanca. As they sweltered on the tarmac in

Lou Levy was the Andrews Sisters' longtime manager—as well as the husband of Maxene—and arguably the individual most responsible for their successful career. He is pictured here in 1946 with Aleda Ann Levy, the daughter he and Maxene adopted. (Gladys Leichter Collection)

their winter uniforms, a young major stuck his head inside the passenger door and asked: "Which of youse guys are the Andrews Sisters?" The sisters, the only women on the flight, identified themselves and were told to deplane. They were escorted to a waiting jeep and after a drive through the desert, they ended up at a desolate military installation where several thousand GIs gave them a noisy welcome. Maxene remembered her first encounter with military protocol:

> We were late, so they'd already been waiting in the tent, where it must have been 120 degrees. They had their full uniforms on, jackets and all, so Patty said, "Look, we're here to have a good time. Why don't we take our jackets off." So they did, and we did, and they loosened their ties, and it was great until about the middle of our second song, when suddenly it got very quiet … we saw a man walking down the stage … who turned out to be the CO [Commanding Officer]. He asked the men, "Who told you to take off your jackets?" Then he turned to us and said, "As long as I am the CO, I'll give the orders here," and he had everybody put everything back on. We learned something that day: The Army had the last word.[111]

Without rehearsal or rest from the flight, they did two shows in the 120 degree temperature, after which they returned to Casablanca. During their two-day stay in Casablanca, they did eight more shows and managed to work in a tour of the city. When the major escorted them to their hotel after their final show, a telegram awaited him. He read the telegram, became concerned, and told the sisters they must take the next plane to Naples. They hurriedly packed and were whisked to the airport where a plane awaited them. On the plane, the sisters discovered their stop in Casablanca was unscheduled. The major had intercepted them so they could entertain his troops. The brass in Naples learned what happened and ordered the sisters to leave Casablanca immediately. *Variety* carried a different version of the incident:

> Andrews Sisters, now overseas for the USO, were kidnapped a week or so ago during their stay in Casablanca. Trio, standing outside their hotel, were approached by two GIs who informed the girls "the CO wanted to see them." They hopped in a jeep and found themselves later before 1,500 GIs for whom they promptly staged an unscheduled show.[112]

En route to Naples, they made an unscheduled stop at Oran where the first GI to greet them was literally "the boy next door," a young man who lived next to their childhood home at 1600 Lyndale in Minneapolis. Once in Naples, the sisters soon learned they were in the United States Army for the duration of their tour. They were required to travel in Army transport and wear their military uniforms when outside their personal living quarters or when not performing. They could have no visitors backstage or in their private quarters. Visits to the enlisted men's recreation and mess halls were mandatory, but under no circumstances could they perform at an officers' party, dance, or club. British character actor Arthur Treacher joined the sisters in Naples and became a member of their troupe. They were not overly fond of him and thought he was somewhat of a prima donna who preferred the British Officers' Club to mingling with the GIs.

One day the sisters took a midday walk in the neighborhood where they stayed. It was a hot day and they loosened their neckties, unbuttoned their collars and draped their wool jackets over their shoulders. A young officer approached them and dressed them down royally for being out of uniform. On

In June 1945, the Andrews Sisters reported for USO duty overseas. Assigned woolen clothing, they assumed they were going someplace cold, but once on the plane they learned they were headed for summertime Italy. LaVerne and Maxene relax in the Army Air Corps plane that transported them across the Atlantic. (Robert Boyer Collection)

another occasion, because of a delayed plane, the sisters were four hours late for a performance. A general called them in and threatened to send them before a court-martial board on charges of insubordination, even though their tardiness was no fault of their own.

In late July, LaVerne wrote to her longtime friend Florence Hannahan from Rome and provided some personal insights about their tour:

> We've been over here for ten days…. This nation is so poor and filthy. Soap is $5.00 a bar. The only type of people here are the rich, the poor and the Pope, whose robes are gold and jewelry. Also the Sultan in Casablanca who has nothing but filthy, diseased Arabs as his subjects. They are taxed for wearing clothes, shaving, etc. In Italy shoes cost $80.00 a pair. Flo, you couldn't believe it. The Italians in Naples live like animals…. Don't be disgusted with me [for not writing] but have been so busy. The gals say hello.

> Love, LaVerne

> P.S. Of course we are here working and entertaining. It is a great thrill. Don't know how we'll be able to put up with civilization again.

Maxene, Patty, and LaVerne Andrews arrive in Italy for their USO tour. One of the first persons they met in Italy was literally "the boy next door," a young man who lived next to them in Minneapolis when they were kids. (Robert Boyer Collection)

Most of the sisters' experiences in Italy were pleasant. Each week, they received an allotment of nine bottles of beer. According to Maxene, none of them drank at that time, so they cooled the bottles in their toilet tanks and gave them to the GIs who visited them on the steps of their quarters each evening. One morning they were awakened in their Rome hotel by singing. They went to the window and saw below about fifty Italians welcoming them with "Beer Barrel Polka" in Italian. The sisters were scheduled for only one show a day, but they frequently did four or five, and sometimes more. If two or three GIs wanted them to sing, they sang for them and before long an audience congregated to hear more songs. They also visited the GIs' favorite restaurants where they entertained requests from the men. One day they did five shows at a huge racetrack in southern Italy, built by Mussolini for the 1940 World's Fair which never took place, to a combined audience of 70,000.

A GI later remembered seeing the sisters in Italy:

> In a Quonset hut in Casserta, Italy, jammed to the rafters with homesick GIs these gals came on stage singing "The Boogie Woogie Bugle Boy of Company B." The place literally went wild, and at least three soldier boys, perched on cross

Many of the sisters' shows in Italy were in remote army camps on makeshift stages pulled by trucks. Here they join Arthur Treacher on such a stage surrounded by GIs. The sisters received many kindnesses from the GIs and had fond, lifelong memories of the tour. (Author's collection)

> beams, tumbled to the floor from excitement. And when Patty went into her solo, pandemonium broke loose. If ever three gals brought to the GI the feeling of home, it was the Andrews Sisters. They knew how to communicate from the stage.... After the show they devoted all their attention to a lingering crowd of soldier boys.[113]

On two occasions, GIs tried to talk Maxene into taking their gambling winnings back home to their families—to no avail. "Rum and Coca-Cola" was the most requested song from the GIs. Frequently, they sent new lyrics backstage for the sisters to sing that were usually so obscene or so anti–CO that the sisters were unable to comply. Years later, Maxene fondly remembered the many kindnesses of the GIs:

> Every audience lived up to the reputation that USO audiences had—the best any entertainer or singer ever performed for. The small groups of only three or four that we sang for obviously couldn't make the noise that a thousand could, but we could still see and feel their enthusiasm and appreciation.
> The guys seemed to sense that we were on the same wave length as they were.

Although many of the sisters' USO shows in Italy were on makeshift stages, others were in large arenas. Here they entertain a stadium filled with GIs. *The New York Times* claimed the Andrews Sisters entertained 180,000 GIs during their overseas tour. (Author's collection)

As a result, they went out of their way to show us every respect and to give us every consideration, such as the time we arrived at a new stop on our tour and there waiting for us on the back of a flatbed truck were three combat helmets. One contained hot water, one held cold water, and the third had soap chips. These things were rare, almost nonexistent, and the soldiers were sharing these scarce items with us so we could enjoy the luxury of washing briefly with warm water and soap.

At another stop, a small group of grateful GIs traded three cases of pineapple juice to some English soldiers for one case of White Horse Scotch. We used the Scotch as a way of saying thank you when somebody did something extra nice for us. Once we poured some of it out to a few guys who somehow managed to come up with three fresh eggs for us, something you rarely saw over there.[114]

On one occasion, the Andrews Sisters refused to perform until a group of

The Andrews Sisters sign autographs on dollar bills for GIs during their 1945 USO tour in Italy. (Robert Boyer Collection)

African American musicians who preceded them in the show were seated in the front seats normally reserved for such performers. Maxene sensed the men were not being seated because of their race. The sisters had a half-hour standoff with a lieutenant until he finally acceded to their demands and the show went on.

A Hollywood scriptwriter could not have written a better finale for the Andrews Sisters' last show in Italy. Maxene told it best:

> We did many of our shows at the depots where all the guys were shipped out after a long, bloody, and hard war in Europe. Our last show was packed with eight thousand GIs, and it was the unhappiest audience you ever saw. Those guys knew they were being shipped out to another long, bloody, and hard war, the one in the Pacific with Japan. Some of them hadn't been home for four years. We were just trying to put them in good spirits.

Patty was doing a scene with Arthur Treacher when a soldier motioned me offstage and said he had a very important message for Patty to read to the audience. I started to laugh. The GIs were always pulling tricks on me, and this probably was another one. But the soldier saw I was still suspicious, so he said, "I'm not kidding. It's from the CO."

I told him I couldn't do it in the middle of the show, but he pleaded with me saying, "You're going to get me into trouble."

So I took the paper and walked out onto the stage without reading it, thinking that now I was the one who was going to get into trouble—with Patty, Treacher, and the CO, too. When I got out there, Patty was expressing the same kind of objections to me that I had expressed to the GI, but she finally gave in.

Then Patty told the GIs, "Look, there's a big joke going on up here. I have a note *supposedly* from the CO." Without looking at it first, she read it out loud. It announced the end of the war with Japan.

There wasn't a sound in that whole depot. Patty wasn't sure of just what had happened, so she looked at the note again. Then she looked at me. It was beginning to dawn on her that the message really was on the level. This was V-J Day.

She looked out at the audience again and said, "No, fellas—this *is* from the CO. This is an announcement that *the war with Japan is over*. You don't have to go to the Pacific."

With that, she started to cry. So did I. So did LaVerne. Still, there was no reaction from the audience. Patty said it again: "This is the end! This is the end!"

Suddenly all hell broke loose. Those GIs yelled and screamed. We saw a pair of pants and a shirt come down from the rafter where men were crammed together above the stage, followed by a human being. He fell on the guys sitting in the audience, but he didn't care and neither did his human cushions.

Then Patty asked the GIs, "Do you want to go out and get drunk? Or do you want to see the show?"

The audience hollered back, "We want to see the rest of the show!"

So we finished. Aware that this was a moment in history, we kept our act short. After all, this was both our last performance of World War II and our first performance in the new world of peace.[115]

On August 14, following the atomic bombing of Hiroshima and Nagasaki, Japan accepted the surrender terms of the Allies and the formal surrender ceremonies were held September 2, 1945. Estimates of World War II casualties range from 35,000,000 to 60,000,000 lives.

A very shattered world waited rebuilding when the Andrews Sisters departed Italy for New York City.

CHAPTER NINE

1945–1947

And if you haven't heard of the Andrews Sisters, you're either dead or you just don't get around much anymore.[1]

As soon as the Andrews Sisters returned home from their USO tour, they resumed their radio show. The fall show, which began August 26, was essentially the same format as the previous season except Gabby Hayes left the cast to fill a movie contract, probably to Maxene's relief. Curt Massey, a Bing Crosby–like baritone who had joined the show the previous spring and carried it through the summer, stayed on for the fall show, which was called *Eight-to-the-Bar Ranch*. The program still aired on Sunday afternoon, but was now broadcast from New York. A *Variety* reviewer liked the show's music, but not much else:

> The show consists of good music, sprightly vocals and tired dialog. It hasn't much to recommend it as something to wait for weekly in its present state, except for those who follow the Andrews Sisters.... For a program sponsored by a nationally known product it's pretty weak construction.... However, the musical portion of this show was very listenable.... Andrews trio sounded good on every contribution. For some reason their singing is better.[2]

The sisters took their radio format to New York's Paramount Theater in early September for a four-week engagement at $20,000 per week, their highest pay at the theater. *Variety* was not enthusiastic about the western setting, and *The Billboard* also offered a lukewarm review:

> Show is pretty much corn thruout, but it is slick, commercial corn and it gets pretty good reactions from the capacity mob of payees.
>
> After a brief intro by Vic Schoen's ork, Andrews lasses amble on for a pair of

225

oldies and some comedy. The oldies don't set the house on fire, and the comedy is very, very feeble.... Andrews close singing ... a version of "Rum and Coke" which they do well but which they purport to be something special written for them by servicemen. They encore with the usual "requested" medley of past hits. It is sad to report they are still using the nasty nose-wiping bit of business, which doesn't belong on fem performers.[3]

It is unclear what the "nasty nose-wiping bit of business" was that offended the reviewer when used by "fem performers." Possibly it was the mouth-wiping routine Patty occasionally used during "Bei Mir Bist Du Schoen": after singing the more fricative lyrics of the song, she sometimes wiped her mouth with her hand and attempted to dry it on Maxene or LaVerne. Would it have been less offensive if used by male performers? Probably so, given the gender climate of the times. Despite the critics' disappointment in the show, the customers came and the opening week brought in the second highest box office in the city.[4] During the third week of the Paramount engagement, Patty became ill and guests were called in to substitute for the sisters. Maxene acted as emcee, but Curt Massey, Martha Raye, and Louis Jordan filled in for the trio.[5] In the past when Maxene or LaVerne was ill, Patty carried on with the remaining sister or by herself—an illustration of her central role in the trio.

Although the war was over and the sisters were busy at the Paramount Theater, they didn't forget their fans in the military. They continued to visit military hospitals, and when the *Queen Mary* docked in New York City on September 28 with 14,662 troops aboard, the Andrews Sisters were there to welcome them home with songs. They continued to laud their USO tour to reporters, and could not understand complaints lodged by other performers, such as Frank Sinatra, about bad treatment overseas. They said the GIs were the easiest audience to please compared to audiences at home: "The expressions on a GI's face are wonderful; here, it's 'try and please me.'" A *New York Times* story claimed they entertained 180,000 troops during their tour. The sisters said they never stopped singing "Rum and Coca-Cola," which they called "the national anthem of the GI camps."[6]

Apparently the critics weren't the only ones who thought the western format wasn't working on the sisters' radio show. A new program premiered on CBS October 3 called *The Nash-Kelvinator Musical Show Room*, "starring the Andrews Sisters." A *Variety* reviewer couldn't say enough good things about it:

> First nice thing to say about Andrews Sisters Show is that it is just that—the Andrews Sisters—and a show. No long-winded intros, no orchestral preludes, not even an opening commercial, but—zip!—the gals themselves, right smack at you with one tune, and then throwing them off, number after number, at staccato rate, with only a couple of guest spots and mid-commercials for respite.
>
> Not too much small talk between numbers, nary weak chatter or feeble gags to horse up the program, but tunes, good rhythm tunes, danceable tunes, happily sung and snappily played. Which is what the customers expected. The sisters go to it with vim, enthusiasm and the ease of long experience and ensemble work, and brother, the program sparkles ... Nash-Kelvinator got off to a good start, thanks to the Andrews girls.[7]

When the war was over, the Andrews Sisters did not forget their many fans in the military. On September 28, 1945, they took a break from their show at the Paramount Theater in New York to welcome home 14,662 GIs as they disembarked the *Queen Mary*. (Robert Boyer Collection)

Metronome restrained its usual venom for things Andrews, and gave the show a few backhanded compliments: "Whether or not you care for the program depends on your feeling for the Andrewses. I'm agin 'em, but the tunes they sing and those done by Curt Massey are well chosen, with suitable brassy backgrounds by Schoen; Patty is a capable MC, and the others throw in a comment or two."[8]

I listened to most of the programs of the new Andrews Sisters show. Compared to the original *Eight-to-the-Bar Ranch*, *The Nash-Kelvinator Musical Show Room* was a vast improvement, fast paced and strictly musical. The bad jokes and corny western setting were gone. The regular personnel of the new program included the Andrews Sisters, Curt Massey, a male singing group called the Ambassadors, and Vic Schoen and his orchestra as well as announcer Andre Baruch, later replaced by Harlo Wilcox when the show moved to the West Coast. Each week, a special guest received the "Green Room Award" for his or her contribution to the world of entertainment. Typically, the show began with a number by the entire cast. A song by the Andrews Sisters followed which usually segued into a romantic ballad by Curt Massey. The sisters then returned with another song before the first commercial. After the commercial, the sisters sang a recent release, and then the special Green Room guest was introduced. After some introductory chitchat, the guest performed a number associated with him or her, which might be a song, a comic routine, or a scene from a play. For example, Sophie Tucker sang "Some of These Days," Abbott and Costello did their "Who's on First" routine, and stage actress Jane Cowl staged a scene from the melodrama *Smiling Through*. Sometimes the guest simply performed, sometimes briefly interacted with the Andrews Sisters and Massey, or more rarely sang with the sisters. After the special guest, the sisters sang another song before the second commercial. Following the commercial, Patty and Massey sang a romantic duet, and the program ended with another number by the entire cast. Andre Baruch or Harlo Wilcox handled the commercials and shared the emceeing with Patty and Massey. Maxene and LaVerne were rarely heard except, of course, in the musical numbers. On October 10, the sisters' old vaudeville partner Joe E. Howard received the Green Room Award. The award was presented to the Andrews Sisters during a special show aired from the Nash-Kelvinator dealers' convention in Detroit November 21 when the show was on its way to the West Coast.

The *Nash-Kelvinator Musical Show Room* was a program of music—introductions and chitchat were kept to a minimum. Andrews Sisters fans were pleased because it allowed them to hear the sisters sing different versions of their old standards, such as "Bei Mir Bist Du Schoen" which they sang, arguably better than the original, on the November 28 show. Also, the sisters sang currently popular songs they never recorded, as well as special arrangements with Curt Massey and the Ambassadors, and less frequently with the Green Room Award guests. Many of the numbers are still very listenable and some of the sisters' unrecorded songs are regrettably unavailable elsewhere, such as "Let It Snow," "If I Could Be with You," and "Come to Baby, Do." The initial bars of "In Apple Blossom Time" opened the show, introduced the segments, and closed the show. Special guests included some of the great names in show business, such as Xavier Cugat, George Jessel, Jane Froman, Sophie Tucker, Rudy Vallee, Carmen Miranda, Ethel Merman, Mills Brothers, Abbott and Costello, Hoagy Carmichael, and Nat Cole. The *Nash-Kelvinator Musical Show Room* remained on the air through March 1946 when the sponsors announced they were taking a "new approach to radio" with a revision downward in program budgeting[9]—which apparently meant the Andrews Sisters had become too expensive.

The Andrews Sisters repaid Frank Sinatra for his earlier guest spot on their show by appearing in mid–November on his *Songs by Sinatra*. The show began with a song by Sinatra (backed by lots of squealing from his adoring female fans) followed by a brief skit between him and Patty that ended in a duet "A Kiss Good Night." Later in the show the sisters sang "Begin the Beguine" and joined Sinatra in a skit about shows at the Paramount that included a medley of songs, the cleverest of which was an Old Gold cigarette commercial (Sinatra's sponsor) and a Kelvinator refrigerator commercial (the sisters' sponsor) sung to the tune of "Rum and Coca-Cola." The show concluded with "Empty Saddles," a Sinatra-Andrews duet.

In early October 1945, the Andrews Sisters radio show was reworked into *The Nash-Kelvinator Musical Show Room* "starring the Andrews Sisters." Each week a special guest was awarded the "Green Room Award" for his or her contribution to the world of entertainment. Above the sisters greet Xavier Cugat as special guest and winner of the weekly award. (Robert Boyer Collection)

The Andrews Sisters recorded only ten songs in 1945, but seven of them made the charts. The controversial "Rum and Coca-Cola" (twenty weeks) was the big seller and remained number one for ten weeks. "Along the Navajo Trail" (eleven weeks) was another western hit with Bing Crosby; the sisters and Crosby scored again with "Ac-Cent-Tchu-Ate the Positive" (nine weeks), an upbeat novelty number. "The Blond Sailor" (eight weeks) was another war-themed song about a sailor who left his sweetheart behind. "The Three Caballeros" (five weeks), from the Disney film of the same name, was yet another Andrews-Crosby collaboration, this time with a Latin beat. "Corns for My Country" (one week), was a patriotic number the sisters sang in *Hollywood Canteen.* "One Meat Ball" (one week), the flip side of "Rum and Coca-Cola," poignantly told the story of a little man who could afford only one meatball for dinner.[10]

At the beginning of 1946, the Andrews Sisters and Lou Levy formed the Eight-to-the-Bar Ranch Corporation. The sisters and Levy were the four directors of the corporation, each with a 25 percent share. The corporation was the employer of the Andrews Sisters, who agreed to assign their earnings, at a minimum of $500,000 per year, to it for the next seven years.[11] The arrangement resulted in reduced personal income taxes for the sisters, but their later tax problems with the Internal Revenue Service suggest it was not as successful in reducing taxes as they hoped.

Make Mine Music, the first of two animated Disney films for which the Andrews Sisters sang, was released in mid–April 1946. The film was a potpourri of ten cartoons set to different musical styles ranging from jazz to classical and performed by a variety of artists, including the Andrews Sisters, Benny Goodman, Dinah Shore, and Nelson Eddy. The Andrews Sisters sang "Johnny Fedora and Alice Blue Bonnet," a song about two hats on display in a store window that, after falling in love, were sold, separated, and eventually reunited. *Variety* liked the film and noted: "One of the cutest spots is the saga of 'Johnny Fedora' and 'Alice Blue Bonnet,' flirtation skimmers in next door shop-windows, which are torn asunder but finally reunited on the ears of a drayhorse. Disney and his corps of animators ... have weaved a warm romance about the male and female chapeaux, which the Andrews Sisters vocally interpret in usually tiptop manner."[12] The *New York Times* reviewer, of course, liked the film less well and poked predictable barbs at the Andrews Sisters: "And a silly romance between two hats is sketched to the Andrews Sisters' warbling of 'Johnny Fedora and Alice Bluebonnet.'"[13] The film did well at the box office.

About the time *Make Mine Music* hit the theaters, the Andrews Sisters were preparing for another tour. Despite the bad reviews of their *Eight-to-the-Bar Ranch* radio program and Paramount show, the sisters decided to take the show on a seven-week tour of the Northwest (beginning in San Diego) that included San Francisco, Portland, Seattle, Spokane, and Vancouver.

The Andrews Sisters were changing the composition of their theater shows, in keeping with the demise of vaudeville-style programs. Rather than one of several featured acts on the bill, the sisters were now putting on the entire show with their own cast. Bands no longer traveled with them, but rather Vic Schoen brought along a core of musicians, usually a drummer and pianist, and hired others to create a band along the way to take care of musical matters.

The road show was billed as the "8 to the Bar Ranch Musical Rodeo." The sisters received 50 percent of the gross, but equally important they were testing the show for possible use in a film for United Artists.[14] *Variety* reported they were working on a deal with Gene Autry, popular singing cowboy B-movie actor, to co-star with him in a picture of the same title as their show.[15] The picture never materialized. The sisters opened their tour in San Diego May 14, and were in San Francisco the following week where a local critic was no more impressed by the western format than his East Coast colleagues were:

> Well, the Andrews Sisters hit town again yesterday ... and nothing has changed except their hair-dos.... They are still the juke-box queens of America, they have a well-paced, entertaining show and a nice, easy informality in their own renditions.... For some obscure reason, however, they've elected ... wrapping up the production Western-style by dressing in ranchhouse skirts and blouses, bringing the Red River Valley boys and cow-singer Johnny Bond into the act and calling the whole thing "8 to the Bar Ranch." ...The Sisters make some concession to the Western theme by singing "Don't Fence Me In," and then regain

The Andrews Sisters' voices provided narration in two Walt Disney animated films, namely *Make Mine Music* (1946) and *Melody Time* (1948). Above the sisters sing "Johnny Fedora and Alice Bluebonnet" for *Make Mine Music* against a background of animation panels from the film. ©Disney Enterprises, Inc.

their reason [with] a medley of tunes which have droned from every music box in the land over a period of years.... And don't think the audience doesn't love every move they make, because it does.[16]

San Franciscans turned out for the show and the opening box office was only $500 short of Frank Sinatra's gross a few weeks earlier.[17]

Portland hosted the sisters next. The live shows of Mae West and Gypsy Rose Lee and the opening of Howard Hughes' controversial film *The Outlaw* with Jane Russell didn't make a dent in the audiences that lined up to see the Andrews Sisters. Portland liked the sisters and a local reporter described them as "the friendliest girls you ever could meet."[18] The sisters took time out to autograph their latest Decca records at a local department store and then hosted a boogie woogie contest following their final show.[19]

Seattle was next on the itinerary where they packed the Orpheum Theater with enthusiastic audiences, especially "hundreds of soldiers and sailors, with whom the Andrews Sisters stand ace high."[20] A local critic noted:

> Recorded or filmed, but especially in person, the Andrews Sisters are simply murder.... The delighted audience of bobby soxers and a representative delegation from the United States Navy was solidly underscored by the approval of the less colorful citizenry, who may not be quite as hep, but know good vaudeville when they see it.[21]

According to *Variety*, the sisters set an all-time box office high at Seattle's Orpheum Theater.[22] After Seattle, the sisters took their show to Spokane where a prudish reviewer would have liked the show better if it "hadn't been spotted with numerous instances of inelegant humor." Nonetheless, it was "a pleasant hour of songs of the ingratiating swing trio, with Vic Schoen's band giving out good boogie-woogie and four other acts contributing bits." He thought the sisters were "far better looking behind footlights than through the camera."[23] The sisters wrapped up their Northwest tour in Vancouver.

In mid–June, the Andrews Sisters were back in Los Angeles where they appeared on *Radio's Biggest Show*, an annual variety show that featured comic skits, popular music, and occasional theater pieces from Broadway. Among the guests were Bob Hope, Dennis Day, Eddie "Rochester" Anderson, Ginny Simms, and Ray Noble and his orchestra. The sisters sang their new release, "Atlanta, GA," appeared in a skit with Bob Hope who joined them in "Sonny Boy," and closed the show with Hope's signature song "Thanks for the Memory."

In mid–August the sisters were in Atlantic City for a week at the Steel Pier where they were backed by a bass, drum, and piano trio. Not only were big bands on the way out, but equally important the sisters had become too expensive for theaters to back them with a large group of musicians. A *Variety* reviewer caught the show that played to capacity audiences:

> Andrews Sisters ... first appearance in Atlantic City in five summer seasons.... Expertly paced by Patty Andrews, they give out with many of the numbers which have delighted radio, record, juke box and vaude audiences all over the country, mixing their songs up nicely with bits of comedy for solid results.... Girls

have lost nothing since their last appearance here, before the war. Their timing is split-second, their vocaling still a delight.[24]

LaVerne later told a reporter about their Steel Pier appearance: "Wonderfully stimulating—the eastern theatrical public…. No one in show business should be without it too long. You can dry up in too much California sunshine."[25]

Patty and LaVerne briefly visited Minneapolis and Mound on their way from Atlantic City to Chicago, where Maxene joined them at the Chicago Theater. A Minneapolis reporter noted: "On their arrival at the airport the other evening it took them about 20 minutes to kiss everybody all around, especially the two bachelor uncles, Ed and Pete Sollie, whom they're visiting at Mound. Also to greet them were Ma and Pa Andrews, who have been here for the last two weeks, arriving by motor from California."[26]

LaVerne, always the clothes-horse, told the reporter she planned to go into the clothing business "in her old age" and described some of the sisters' new outfits: "our new little white gabardine dressmaker suits, and the short chiffon evening dresses made up in both light blue and rose that we're wearing for our stage appearances." She assumed the role of proud aunt when she talked about Maxene's baby daughter Aleda: "Just imagine … she's only 15 months and she not only walks and talks but can blow her nose and combs her own hair."[27] Patty and LaVerne took a busman's holiday one evening when they joined an old friend on stage who was singing at a Minneapolis nightspot. Two days later, the sisters joined Maxene at the Chicago Theater for a two-week stay. The Andrews Sisters wrapped up the forty-seven-minute review:

> LaVerne, Patty and Maxene Andrews launched themselves with "Beat Me Daddy." Girls threw in some comedy which, of course, wasn't up to their singing … Drew a heavy round of applause after each rendition. Maxene's body twists and LaVerne's dumb act caused twittering, and Patty's twisted arm routine done with synchronized sound effects from the ork went well with the payees. Sisters did three encores and applause continued after the curtain fell.[28]

A *Variety* reviewer also thought their comedy routine needed some work.[29] Nonetheless, their show led the city's box offices and topped an all-time high for the Chicago Theater.[30]

A few months previously, the Andrews Sisters' cousin Gladys Leichter and her brother Ed Moberg were marking days off the calendar. The date was approaching when their youngest brother Jerome, who was adopted out of the family when his mother died in childbirth, would reach his twenty-first birthday. His siblings had always wanted to contact him, but their father insisted they wait until he was twenty-one, at which time he would tell them where Jerome lived.

Gladys began the search. She learned her brother was raised in Marshalltown, Iowa, and his adoptive parents had kept his first name Jerome, or Jerry, but his last name was now Myhr. She discovered he was currently in the Army and stationed in Germany. Gladys contacted him and after convincing his superiors they were his biological siblings who were trying to reconnect with him, he was given a leave to return home and meet his family. Jerry Myhr didn't know

The Andrews Sisters frequently appeared on radio and shared guest slots with comedian Bob Hope. Here they try to make him into a "fourth" Andrews sister during rehearsals for Walgreen Drug Stores' 45th anniversary radio show in June 1946. (Robert Boyer Collection)

he had siblings and was elated to learn about his birth family. The reunion was, of course, an emotional one, but happy for all. During the course of it, Myhr learned that the Andrews Sisters were his first cousins. Needless to say, he was surprised to discover he was related to the top singers in the nation, but the story took another surprising twist when he told his siblings about seeing the Andrews

Sisters perform at Long Beach, California, when he was graduating from Navy boot camp. He was the sailor Patty Andrews selected from the audience for a new uniform. After completing his Navy service, he had joined the Army and was stationed in Germany. Jerry Myhr eventually married a German woman, returned to the United States, and became part of his birth family.[31]

In July 1946, the Andrews Sisters recorded "Rumors Are Flying" with Les Paul, a talented guitarist known to a small circle of fans. The sisters were initially reluctant to record with Paul, having heard he was a prima donna and not interested in working behind "girl singers." Events turned out otherwise. Far from causing problems, Paul created a relaxed atmosphere. "He loved to joke around," Maxene remembered, "but it never cost us any production time."[32] Released in September 1946, "Rumors Are Flying" quickly climbed to the top of the charts, and both the sisters and Paul received critical praise.[33] Paul's unique talent impressed Lou Levy, the sisters' always-savvy manager. To give "Rumors Are Flying" an even bigger boost, Levy decided to use Les Paul and his trio as the opening act on the Andrews Sisters' next road tour. "Watching his fingers work was like watching a locomotive go," Levy said. "People hadn't seen anything like that before. He was one of a kind, perfect for the girls."

Les Paul's attitude toward the Andrews Sisters was more respectful than that of most male musicians, who usually denigrated their talent. He admired the sisters' commercial success and welcomed the opportunity to study them at close range. In November 1946, the Andrews-Paul entourage left Los Angeles for Cincinnati's Albee Theater, the first stop on a tour that would take them to Detroit, Philadelphia, Providence, New York, and Boston, a trip reminiscent of the sisters' demanding road tours of the past. When not traveling by train for hundreds of miles at a stretch, they did five or six shows a day between films, often beginning well before noon and ending after midnight. In between, they made radio appearances and gave newspaper interviews. "We were young, blessed with boundless energy, and incredibly naïve," Maxene remembered. "It was a murderous schedule, but it was standard in the industry. We all did it."

Les Paul and his trio served not only as the Andrews Sisters' opening act but also as their rhythm section. This simplified matters for Vic Schoen. In the past, he hired local musicians at each stop and taught them the show's material, an exhausting process he repeated three or four times a month. Paul's trio provided a strong foundation for the changing roster of musicians. Maxene recalled:

> It was a cinch to go out and sing after Les's act.... We could just walk out and lay on top of what he'd already started. And it was wonderful having him perform with us. He'd tune in to the passages we were singing and lightly play the melody, sometimes in harmony. He made it much easier for us to enjoy what we were doing because he really propelled us along. We'd sing these fancy licks and he'd keep up with us note for note in exactly the same rhythm. He was totally attuned to what we were doing, almost contributing a fourth voice. But he never once took the attention away from what we were doing. He did everything he could to make us sound better.

   Paul's sense of humor sometimes livened up the performances. One evening he wrote "Paul Weston," a popular orchestra leader of the time, on a piece of cardboard and surreptitiously hung it on Vic Schoen's back shortly before Schoen went onstage. Schoen didn't understand why the audience began laughing when he turned to direct the orchestra. Once he figured it out, he vowed to get back at Paul. A few nights later, he fastened a rope to the stool Paul used during performances. In the middle of one of Paul's solos, Schoen and two musicians slowly began pulling the stool into the wings. Paul continued to play as though nothing out of the ordinary was happening while the audience roared.[34]

   During Thanksgiving week, the Andrews Sisters and Les Paul were in Cincinnati where they capped the city's box offices and almost set a record at the Albee Theater.[35] In early December, they led the Detroit box offices at the Downtown Theater.[36] A week later they were in Philadelphia at the Earle where a *Variety* reviewer caught their act which included a segment of songs made famous by Al Jolson, who was enjoying a comeback of sorts after the release of the film *The Jolson Story*:

> Looking nifty in blue costumes, the Andrews gals start things off dynamically with a snappy rendition of "Show Business," followed by a contrasting number, good old-fashioned "Jingle Bells."
>   These gals, who've been around for years, still pack plenty of punch, and put over their stuff in the style that made them top-notchers. Patty handles most of the comedy patter, but sister LaVerne gets laughs with her so-called poetry, while Maxene gets them too with her clever mugging.... [Their] clowning up of a medley from "The Jolson Story," with special emphasis on their handling of "Sonny Boy" really wows the customers. Tricky costume effect is achieved for this number with the girls donning tuxedo coats, white collars, flowing red ties and white gloves.[37]

The next week Providence fans saw the sisters' show, and in mid–December they were back at the New York Paramount where they once again led the city's box offices.[38] Lou Levy bumped the little-known Clooney Sisters (Rosemary and Betty) from the Paramount bill, apparently thinking one sister act was enough. The *Variety* reviewer thought the bill still had too many acts, but he liked the "confident and brimming with poise" Andrews Sisters.[39] *The Billboard*'s reviewer liked the show too, but was a bit prudish about one of Patty's routines:

> Top attraction is the Andrews Sisters, who are in practically the entire show. They bounce in and out, do their specialties ... with Les Paul and his trio and manage to gather plenty of sock mitting and some healthy yocks for their routines. In the song department the gals were in the groove all the way. This time they came up with a comic routine based on the Jolson Story and a medley of tunes associated with Jolson. It also gave them a chance to use that routine Sonny Boy, now being peddled by plenty of comics. The stuff got juicy laughs ... It was spoiled, however, by Patty's crossed legs, I-gotta-go bit. Routine is good enough without it. Patty also stretched her paralytic arm bit to a point of embarrassment. Latter is good for a quickie.[40]

This was the Andrews Sisters' last date at the Paramount Theater.

Les Paul's biographer claimed that after Paul's tour with the Andrews Sisters, he arrived at a crossroads in his career, as had the sisters some years previously when they decided to go for the popular audience. Paul's most successful records for Decca were the ones he recorded with the Andrews Sisters and Bing Crosby. During the tour "he had watched from the stage as the Andrews Sisters' ecstatic fans danced in the aisles to the up-tempo beat of novelty numbers like 'Rum and Coca-Cola' and 'Boogie Woogie Bugle Boy.' But when he and his trio played their jazz songs, only a few people in the audience responded. Paul realized that people preferred songs with melody that they could hum and tap their feet to."[41]

Les Paul, like the sisters, chose the commercial route. Within a short time, he and his new wife Mary Ford became the top musical team in the business with their succession of hit records featuring multi-track recordings of Ford's voice and Paul's guitar. These hits began a small revolution in pop music. Les Paul eventually faded from the pop music scene, but he never lost his following of jazz devotees. He is still one of the most respected men in the music business for both his technical and musical innovations.

During 1946, the Andrews Sisters recorded twenty-one songs. Decca increasingly paired them with its other artists. They had already scored big hits with Bing Crosby. Hoping for a repeat, the Kapps paired the sisters with Dick Haymes, Decca's answer to Frank Sinatra. Also during the year, they again sang with Crosby, and joined for the first time popular folksinger Burl Ives, guitarist Les Paul, black jazz pianist Eddie Heywood, and the perennially popular Guy Lombardo and his Royal Canadians. Twelve of their records made the charts. "South America, Take It Away" (nineteen weeks) with Bing Crosby, about the rigors of Latin dancing, was their big hit of the year and another million seller for the team. "Rumors Are Flying" (thirteen weeks) with guitarist Les Paul was one of the most popular songs of 1946. "Money Is the Root of All Evil," recorded the previous year spent five weeks on the charts. "House of Blue Lights" (five weeks), with Eddie Heywood's jazz orchestra, provided a glimpse of a southern jazz dive. "Winter Wonderland" (four weeks) and "Christmas Island" (four weeks) with Guy Lombardo were sides of the same record and destined to become traditional holiday fare for America. "Route 66" (two weeks), with Bing Crosby again, traveled the famous highway from Chicago to Los Angeles, well known to show biz people. "Patience and Fortitude," "Coax Me a Little Bit," and "I Don't Know Why" each charted for one week.[42]

In *The Billboard*'s survey of the top music and musicians of 1946, the Andrews Sisters came in second as the "Year's Top Selling Singing and Instrumental Groups Over Record Counters."[43] Two of their songs, "South America, Take It Away" (with Bing Crosby) and "Rumors Are Flying" (with Les Paul) were among Decca's top eight selling records for the year.

After a Christmas break, the sisters and Les Paul were back together again in mid–January 1947 at the RKO Theater in Boston where the customers gave them "a wow reception plus a beg-off."[44] In late February, they appeared together on Bing Crosby's radio show. The chief reason for the sisters' presence was to plug *Road to Rio*, the new Crosby-Hope "Road" film in which they made a cameo appearance. They sang their recent hit with Crosby "South America, Take It Away" as well as their song from *Road to Rio*, "You Don't Have to Know the Language."

In early March, the Andrews Sisters headlined the Flamingo, the newly renovated nightclub-casino-hotel owned by the infamous mobster Bugsy Siegel in the postwar desert boomtown Las Vegas. To the north, Reno was still the gambling and entertainment capital of Nevada, but as people continued to pour into southern California, Las Vegas obliged the newcomers by offering entertainment across the state line. Nightclub venues would increasingly provide employment for the Andrews Sisters as live entertainment continued to fade from the movie houses. Maxene recalled their first Vegas engagement:

> We played Bugsy Siegel's Flamingo, but you never called him "Bugsy." It was always "Benny." He was a very handsome ... murderer. His girlfriend was staying there, Virginia Hill. We'd see her out at the pool and chitchat. But we kept our distance from "the boys." [45] ...That's when Las Vegas was small and delightful. The money was good. The top salary was $12,500 a week, that was damn good money then. [46]

Later in the month, the Andrews Sisters teamed with Dick Haymes and Bing Crosby for two songs from Irving Berlin's Broadway hit *Annie Get Your Gun*. "There's No Business Like Show Business" and "I Can Do Anything You Can Do Better" didn't do too well on the charts, but they gave music fans an opportunity to hear Decca's top recording artists on one disc. *Down Beat* gave the songs a chilly review and didn't bother to note the sisters' role in the recording. [47] *Metronome* didn't like the record either, especially the inclusion of the sisters. [48] It was the first time Crosby and Haymes sang together. The "Show Business" number was the only recording of the song to chart, albeit briefly, and is still one of the best recordings of that perennially popular song. Maxene did not have fond memories of the recording session with Haymes:

> The only artist we had problems with was Dick Haymes.... I guess maybe they figured we were a strange act to work with because we didn't read music. So, when we would come into the recording session, we would have the secretary type out all of the lyrics and type out the direction of how it would go. In other words, if Dick started the song, it would be "Dick" and then it would be the lyrics of the song, and then it would be "Dick and Patty" and so on. And nobody ever [disagreed]. Crosby said, "Anything the girls want to do." Dick counted lines, he was a line counter. So, he ruined a wonderful recording session that we could have had with "There's No Business Like Show Business" because he made everybody change things in it. [49]

The sisters would record additional songs with Haymes and eventually sing with him on the radio show *Club 15*.

In mid–March, the Andrews Sisters joined a host of other Hollywood celebrities, including Bob Hope, Jack Benny, Al Jolson, Cary Grant, Benny Goodman, Gene Kelly, Dorothy Lamour, and Frank Sinatra, to raise money for the Damon Runyan Memorial Fund for cancer research. The benefit was held at the Paramount Theater in Los Angeles, which premiered *My Favorite Brunette* with Bob Hope and Dorothy Lamour. [50]

At the end of the month, the sisters made the first of four consecutive weekly appearances on *Your Hit Parade*. Originating in Hollywood and broadcast overseas by the Armed Forces Radio Service, the popular CBS Saturday night radio program showcased the seven most popular songs in the nation. *Your Hit Parade* eventually acquired a regular cast of singers, but at the time the sisters joined it, special guests appeared to sing the country's most popular songs. Regulars included announcer Del Sharbutt, a vocal group called the Hit Paraders, and Mark Warner and his orchestra. In addition to the top ten songs, *Your Hit Parade* "extras" were added to help fill the time slot. I located only two *Your Hit Parade* programs featuring the Andrews Sisters, and one of these was incomplete. The sisters sang several "extras," including such past hits as "Bei Mir Bist Du Schoen," "Beer Barrel Polka," and "Rhumboogie." In addition they sang some of the currently popular songs, including "Linda" and "Managua, Nicaragua." Other singers featured with the sisters were Beryl Davis, an English import, and Andy Russell, a briefly popular toothy crooner.

The sisters engaged Les Paul and his trio again for shows in San Francisco and Chicago. In mid–April they opened at the Golden Gate Theater in San Francisco where they were guaranteed $15,000 plus a split of anything over $34,000.[51] The sisters hit a slow time in the city and the box office didn't top $30,000, which was, nonetheless, the highest in the city.[52] A local critic noted, "They are mistresses of the ad lib, both active and spoken, and, although the business is corny, it's of the best."[53] Another added: "The easy harmony on which they have built their reputation has become even smoother."[54] After San Francisco, they traveled to the Oriental Theater in Chicago where a *Variety* reviewer caught their show: "The Andrews Sisters top a compact, smooth running revue that is a click from the start.... Dressed alike in black draped suits of gabardine with shimmering blouses, gals follow with ... usual sock returns and a begoff."[55] The box office was disappointing in Chicago too. The show brought in a weak $38,000 compared to the previous fall when the sisters drew a $90,000 box office.[56]

In early June, the Andrews Sisters joined Bing Crosby again, this time to record "The Freedom Train" by Irving Berlin—a red, white, and blue recording session that lacked only Kate Smith and apple pie for completion. Irving Berlin happened to be at Decca Studios the day Crosby and the sisters recorded his song. Maxene remembered: "We didn't get to know him too well ... We talked about the song with him. Then we listened to an hour of him talking about himself."[57] Sponsored by the American Heritage Foundation, the Freedom Train was a museum on wheels of the most important documents of the United States. The train was scheduled to visit all forty-eight states and give Americans a chance to view "about 100 documents of American history upon which the development of democracy and civil rights is based" and to rededicate themselves to the importance of freedom and the principles of the Constitution.[58] It was partly a reaction to the threat of post-war communism and other "isms" perceived as threats to the United States. Berlin assigned all his proceeds from the song to the American Heritage Foundation. Other recordings of the song were made, but the Andrews-Crosby version was the only one

During an April 1947 engagement at the Golden Gate Theater in San Francisco, the Andrews Sisters took in a show at Finocchio's, the famous female imper-sonator club. Left to right: Patty Andrews, Cal Gooden, LaVerne Andrews, Vic Schoen, Tommy Rundell, Les Traxler and his wife Arlene Traxler, cousin of the Andrews Sisters. Maxene, tired after the theater performance, did not join the group. (Arlene Traxler Collection)

to chart, albeit for only a week, and was used in the soundtracks of the major newsreels promoting the Freedom Train.

In late July the sisters began a four-week nightclub engagement at the Riv-iera in Fort Lee, New Jersey, at $12,500 plus percentages above $70,000. Ten years previously, before they were nationally known, the sisters played the Riv-iera for $200 a week. A *Variety* story claimed it was "their first café date in the N.Y. vicinity and the second of their career"—apparently meaning their "first" since they became big stars because they certainly played many nightclubs in their early career. A *Variety* reviewer caught their show and noted: "Andrews Trio, in addition to superior harmonics, have for some time developed an excel-lent comedy sense.... Their ... comedics ... add a deal of lustre to what was once purely a singing turn.... Their act and biz when caught indicates that they'll hold up as café draws as long as bonifaces are willing to pay their salary."[59]

On October 1, 1947, the Andrews Sisters resumed their radio career when they joined Bob Crosby's *Club 15*, a fifteen-minute early evening, five-nights-weekly show on CBS. Crosby appeared every night. The Andrews Sisters appeared Monday, Wednesday, and Friday, and the Modernaires joined Margaret Whiting on Tuesday and Thursday. *Variety* liked the show, as did *The Billboard*:

Working the club formula ... the soupmakers sew it up for all practical purposes by a happy mating of talent. Bob Crosby is, as always, a smooth, easy-going emcee who additionally does a capable job of baritoning a ballad. Abetted on the MWF stanzas by the Andrews Sisters, still the No. 1 fem songselling trio, the show falls pleasantly on the ear. Production caught showed smart pacing in that it avoided monotony in tune selection and mixing up its vocal talent (Crosby solo, Andrews threesome, Crosby-Patty duet, etc).... The Vic Schoen influence, of course, is evident in the girls' handling of their material and backing, tho the general musical backgrounding here is excellently supplied by Jerry Gray and a studio ork.... This 15-minuter could easily get to be a habit with plenty of pop music devotees.[60]

Club 15 was successful from its beginning and would be the sisters' longest running radio show—they joined it October 1, 1947, and departed March 23, 1951. Patterned after Perry Como's *Chesterfield Supper Club*, *Club 15* was a fast-paced program of popular music sponsored by Campbell Soups. Bob Crosby was joined each evening with announcer Del Sharbutt and Jerry Gray and his orchestra. Vic Schoen did all the Andrews Sisters' arrangements and their pianist Wally Weschler and drummer Irv Cottler joined the orchestra on the sisters' nights. Crosby explained the show: "We offer nothing but entertainment ... no messages up our sleeves, just music, fun, and laughter."[61]

The fast-paced program began with opening bars of the Campbell Soups commercial "Mmm Mmm Good," and then Del Sharbutt announced "Welcome to Bob Crosby's *Club 15*" or "We take you to *Club 15*." Sounds of people chatting in a nightclub were heard as the announcer continued: "Fifteen minutes of the best in popular music." More Campbell Soups commercial bars segued to the announcer: "Starring the Andrews Sisters, Margaret Whiting, the Modernaires, and Jerry Gray and his orchestra. Brought to you by Campbell Soups." Then, depending on the night, either the Andrews Sisters or the Modernaires sang the Campbell Soups commercial that is still around.

Greetings to the audience from Bob Crosby led to the introduction of the first song, usually a number by him and the Andrews Sisters. Next came some fast comic chitchat between Crosby and Patty, often corny or bad (or both) but so fast that it didn't matter. Crosby then sang a ballad followed by a Del Sharbutt commercial. A song by the Andrews Sisters came next, frequently one of their current releases. After more banter between Crosby and Patty, the two sang a duet, usually light and comic. The Andrews Sisters then sang another song before more comic chitchat between Crosby and Patty, which led to a commercial—and the show was over. Sometimes as many as six songs were packed into the fifteen minutes, but more typically it was four or five songs with a couple of quick comic sketches and two commercials.

The show worked well for the Andrews Sisters because it allowed them to showcase their new releases to a nationwide audience three times a week on one of the nation's major radio networks. In addition, the show was aired on the Armed Forces Radio Service, minus commercials, to a large military audience. On one show, not typical, the sisters sang four of their current releases. Such exposure replaced the grueling tours that comprised so much of their early career. They could live at home in Los Angeles with occasional record-

Club 15 was the Andrews Sisters' longest running radio show. They joined the show in September 1947 and left in March 1951. Above they rehearse a show with host Bob Crosby and other unidentified cast members. (Robert Boyer Collection)

ing sessions to keep the hits coming. Their major public appearances were limited to the summer months when they took a hiatus from *Club 15* and played venues on the East Coast or went abroad as in 1948. The sisters once told reporters they made $5000 a week for the show and rehearsed five hours a day to produce five new arrangements a week.[62] They arrived at the studio at 11:00 A.M. and rehearsed until show time, four-and-a-half hours later. One writer estimated the combined staff time for a fifteen-minute broadcast was sixty hours. Following the broadcast, there was an "aftershow" where new routines were tried out and old ones repeated before the studio audience.[63]

Club 15 worked for the Andrews Sisters' fans, too. They could hear the sisters sing slightly different versions of their recorded songs as well as renditions of current hits they never recorded. During one program the sisters sang "Tennessee Waltz" with LaVerne carrying the lead, one of the few times she sang lead. The music was almost always contemporary and only rarely did the sisters sing their old hits. Periodically, the program had a theme, such as country, western or Gay Nineties, but even these programs used as many current hits as possible.

For the most part, the comic repartee between Patty and Bob Crosby was light and forgettable, but occasionally a skit was genuinely funny, such as one when Patty and Crosby ran into a beer wagon while singing "Bicycle Built for Two," a humorous skit featuring clever puns on names of popular beer brands followed. Crosby and Patty played two recurring Brooklyn characters, "Oil" (Earl) and "Moitle" (Myrtle), to the delight of the audience. In the comic routines, often three or four characters each had a single fast line that led to a punch line—often bad, but quick and painless.

The duets between Crosby and Patty were good. They worked well together and their ad-libbing added to their comfortable relationship. Unfortunately, they recorded only two songs together, "You Was" and "The Pussy Cat Song," a minor hit about two cats in love. Maxene and LaVerne did little more than sing. The show's ambiance was relaxed and comfortable, and reminiscent of that between brother Bing and the sisters, good friends having fun singing together.

Metronome didn't get around to reviewing *Club 15* until the following spring, but even the magazine-that-loved-to-hate-the-Andrews Sisters liked it:

> Sometimes helped, sometimes hindered by a breezy script, Bob comes off best on the nights that the Andrews girls are present. Their cheerful roars when they join him in a song make a reasonable facsimile of the records they've done with Bing; the exchange of chatter between Bob, the brash Patty and the none-too-bright character LaVerne assumes is sometimes highly amusing. The ballad solos by Bob and the Andrews solo specialties are not so diverting.... Margaret Whiting has developed a raucous radio voice and personality, evidently an attempt to keep up with Patty's uninhibited yells, but it is entirely lacking the Andrews sense of humor.... The Modernaires are in there only to sing with Bob ... and to sing the "Mm'mm, good!" commercial to which Patty, Maxene and LaVerne give such a zestful rendition the other nights.[64]

Carroll Carroll, one of the writers of *Club 15*, later remembered the Andrews Sisters in his autobiography. His reminiscences provide insights into the sisters at this stage of their lives:

> At the time we started "*Club 15*," with the Andrews Sisters, they were the most thoroughly kidded women this country had ever seen, including the Cherry Sisters who couldn't sing at all but tried.... Like so many show biz folk, the girls felt that the only way to keep themselves from squandering their money, or lending it to their friends, and yet making it work for them as part of their professional wardrobe, was to buy diamonds, which, in case of an emergency, are always hockable. These Patty, Maxene, and LaVerne wore all the time.
>
> It was a little shocking to see them show up for a morning rehearsal, wearing rehearsal clothes, but with their arms weighted down with hundreds of carats.... LaVerne, perhaps the sweetest but also the least gifted of the three girls, physically and otherwise, was responsible for most of the laughs, although Patty was supposed to be the comic. But you couldn't make up the kind of things LaVerne said.
>
> One morning she showed up not feeling very well—and morning was about eleven thirty. The moment she started to sing, she realized what had to be done and she stopped and took a solemn oath. "I am never," she said, "never going to drink again! Never! From now on nothing but champagne!" ... It was also

LaVerne Andrews and her fiancé Lou Rogers pose for a nightclub photographer with Helen Sothern (left), Puddy Sothern (second from right), and the Andrews Sisters' uncle Pete Sollie, circa 1947. Pete was very proud of his famous nieces, occasionally visited them, and attended their performances. Their other uncle, Ed Sollie, was no less proud of them, but he never visited them and only occasionally saw them perform when they visited Minneapolis. (Gladys Leichter Collection)

> LaVerne, with a rock pile of bracelets on each arm, who said, "I don't know why my arms get so tired."[65]

On October 19, 1947, Patty Andrews married Marty Melcher, who would become one of the most disliked men in Hollywood. She was twenty-nine years old, although the announcements claimed she was twenty-seven. The wedding was held beside a gardenia-covered swimming pool at Maxene's home. Patty was attended by her sisters, and Lou Levy served as best man. Only members of the couple's immediate family were invited to the ceremony, which was conducted by a municipal judge.[66]

Marty Melcher first appeared in the Andrews Sisters' lives in 1942 when their manager Lou Levy was called for induction into the army. Levy arranged for Melcher to manage the Andrews Sisters during his stint in the military. Levy knew Melcher from his music publishing business where he worked as a "song plugger," an agent who sold songs to singers and record companies. When Levy flunked his physical exam and resumed management of the sisters, the Andrews Sisters' career was perhaps spared serious financial problems, given the way Melcher later mishandled other entertainers' careers and finances. Melcher became road manager for the trio while Levy continued as their general manager from his New York and Los Angeles offices. As early as May 1942, an item in *Down Beat* claimed Patty was romantically involved with Melcher.[67] Bernie Woods, a friend of the sisters, remembered Melcher's wooing of Patty:

> Marty Melcher was a song plugger and he apparently suffered it as a means to a better end ... The end arrived in the late 40s. The Andrews Sisters at that point were top level stars and their selling price to theaters was so high that they could not work as an individual act in conjunction with a Big Band. Therefore they had to "own" the entire presentation.
>
> Levy put together a complete package starring the Andrews plus one or two acts he bought, and backed the whole thing with an orchestra ... The final touch was to add Melcher as "Road Manager." Melcher wasted no time. Patty Andrews wasn't married. Melcher took dead aim and in the space of the six or eight weeks the package was on the road, he had Patty's head spinning. She was the focal point of the Andrews trio and already a very wealthy gal. She succumbed to Melcher's blandishments and at the end of the tour they were married.
>
> Patty was in seventh heaven. She and Melcher settled in the Hollywood area, where each of the Andrews girls owned a home. For a long time the marriage seemed idyllic.[68]

Woods' chronology is a bit off and the sisters did not each own a home in Hollywood—Patty and LaVerne still lived with their parents. Woods described Melcher: "He was the epitome of the tall-dark-and-handsome and he knew it well. He had an ego a mile wide and a nasty disposition to match."[69] Doris Day, whom Melcher would later marry, said he was "a tall, well-built man with brown hair, gentle brown eyes, even features, ... a good smile with good teeth" and an "easygoing, amusing manner."[70] Melcher was Jewish, Peter Andrews' second Jewish son-in-law, probably not entirely to his liking if we can believe his first Jewish son-in-law Lou Levy.

Others concurred with Woods' assessment. Melcher's one-time business partner described him: "What you've got to realize, to understand Marty, is that he worshiped money. It was his god, and it was all that he was really focused on ... To accumulate money was Marty's drive from the moment he hit Hollywood until the day he died."[71] Music producer Sam Weiss said: "I don't know anybody who liked Marty. Not even his own family."[72] Actor James Garner agreed: "I never knew anyone who liked Melcher."[73] Singer Gordon McRae summed up his assessment of Melcher: "But one thing for sure, he brought all of us [Melcher's clients] a lot of misery."[74] Band leader Les Brown said: "Marty Melcher was an awful man, pushy, grating on the nerves, crass, money-hungry ... We used to call him Farty Belcher."[75] Weiss and Brown both claimed Melcher's only interest in Patty was her money. Gladys Leichter remembered him as initially charming, but very controlling.[76]

But Patty Andrews was unaware of this dark side of Marty Melcher, or chose not to see it, as she fell in love and married him.

Shortly after Patty's marriage, Maxene Andrews and her husband Lou Levy adopted their second child, a baby boy. He was named Peter after Maxene's father, uncle, and grandfather.

In early December, *Road to Rio*, another of the popular "Road" pictures with Bing Crosby, Bob Hope, and Dorothy Lamour, was released. The Andrews

The Andrews Sisters joined Bing Crosby for "You Don't Have to Know the Language" in *Road to Rio* (1947), one of the popular "Road" films starring Bing Crosby, Bob Hope, and Dorothy Lamour. The sisters' cameo appearance was probably added to cash in on the current string of hit records they were enjoying with Crosby. (Robert Boyer Collection)

Sisters received prominent billing for their cameo role. The film is about two con men (Hope and Crosby) who leave the United States for Brazil to escape their romantic and financial entanglements. En route to Rio, Crosby unaccountably happens upon the Andrews Sisters in the ship's nightclub where they join him in a fun "You Don't Have to Know the Language" song and dance routine. Dressed in fashionable dark suits and white blouses designed by Edith Head, the sisters give one of their best film appearances. Their number is totally irrelevant to the plot and was doubtless added to cash in on the string of hits they were enjoying with Crosby.

For a change of pace, *Down Beat* did not pan their song, but said, "The Andrews Sisters, for all the attention they get, could have stayed at home."[77] *Metronome* actually complimented the Andrews Sisters, perhaps for the first time, saying they "actually help along" the song with Crosby—although they were credited with the wrong song.[78] Their cameo still adds sparkle to a film that has not weathered the years well, despite its box office success at the time. This film began an association with fashion designer Edith Head that the sisters would sustain for several years.

In 1947, the Andrews Sisters recorded a staggering forty-eight songs, over half of them in late November and December in anticipation of another musicians' strike scheduled for the beginning of 1948. Decca didn't want to get caught short on recordings as they had in the 1943–44 strike. The record company continued to pair the sisters with other artists, including Bing Crosby, Dick Haymes, Carmen Cavallaro, and Danny Kaye. Nineteen forty-seven brought twelve charted hits for the Andrews Sisters, five of them with Bing Crosby. "Near You" (seventeen weeks) was one of the year's most popular songs; "Tallahassee" (ten weeks) with Bing Crosby was a paean to Florida's capital city. "On the Avenue" (four weeks) was a mellow song about lovers strolling down the avenue. "Your Red Wagon" (three weeks) offered little sympathy to complainers. "Christmas Island" (two weeks) returned to the charts for the holidays. "The Lady from 29 Palms" (two weeks) exposed a slightly shady lady from the southern California desert town. "Jingle Bells" (two weeks) and "Santa Claus Is Comin' to Town" (one week), both with Bing Crosby, also returned for the holidays. "Civilization" (one week), with Danny Kaye, disdained life in the postwar world. "The Freedom Train" (one week), a burst of patriotism reminiscent of some of the sisters' wartime songs, was another collaboration with Bing Crosby. "There's No Business Like Show Business" (one week), Irving Berlin's show business anthem, brought the sisters together with Bing Crosby and Dick Haymes. "How Lucky You Are" charted for one week as well.[79]

In *The Billboard*'s 1947 music poll, the Andrews Sisters were number two in the "Year's Top Selling Singing and Instrumental Groups Over Record Counters." Their biggest hit of the year was "Near You"; it and "Civilization" were among Decca's top twelve selling records for the year.[80] "Near You" appeared fourteen in *The Billboard*'s list of the thirty-five top selling records.[81]

The Andrews Sisters' popularity in post-war America was undiminished.

CHAPTER TEN

1948–1949

There is a warmth of feeling to their demeanor and a great sense of fun ... [The Andrews Sisters] bring to the stage a delicious sense of knowing just what is wanted in the way of entertainment.[1]

The year 1948 began with another musicians' strike. After the fourteen-month strike of 1943–44, the record companies were better prepared and had backlogged recordings in the event of another long strike. During November and December 1947, the Andrews Sisters recorded thirty-one songs to carry them through a possibly long strike. Their last recording session was December 31, the eve of the strike.

One of the problems faced by record companies during the strike was their inability to cash in on hit songs by recording other versions. In order to jump onto the bandwagon of a hit tune, the companies became ingenious. In March, Decca was the first major company to record when it discovered that harmonica players were not union musicians. The Harmonica Gentlemen backed the Andrews Sisters on "Heartbreaker" and the frenetic "Sabre Dance." Woody Herman's instrumental version of "Sabre Dance" was entering the charts and both songs were selling well at Lou Levy's Leeds Music Corporation, doubtless the reason for the recording session. Prior to the release of the disk, Leeds ran an ad in *Variety* announcing that the Andrews Sisters would introduce "Sabre Dance" on *Club 15*: "Vocal Velocity—7 Syllables a Second! Listen to the Andrews Sisters Slash All Records for Super-Sonic Singing Speed when they introduce the exciting lyric to SABRE DANCE!"[2] Decca expected "Sabre Dance" to be the hit side, but it charted only three weeks while "Heartbreaker" charted five.

Columbia released a Kay Kyser recording of "The Woody Woodpecker Song" based on the popular cartoon character. As it climbed the charts in June, Decca again called in the Harmonica Gentlemen to back the Andrews Sisters and Danny Kaye for a version that made a small splash on the charts.[3] Other companies subsequently recorded during the strike with a capella arrangements as well as recording sessions in England, where the Andrews Sisters would eventually record.

In early May, Lou Levy bought a full-page ad in *Variety* to promote the Andrews Sisters' current activities. The eleven stories on the page claimed: 1) Campbell Soups renewed their contract for *Club 15*; 2) the sisters were scheduled to sail on the *Queen Elizabeth* in mid–July for a four-week engagement at London's Palladium Theater; 3) Danny Kaye, who recently played the Palladium, said: "If I went over as big as I did, believe me, the Andrews Sisters will fracture 'em"; 4) Princess Elizabeth (later Queen Elizabeth) was a collector of American pop music including "a collection of Andrews Sisters' platters that experts believe to be the most complete of any outside the states"; 5) the sisters were in the process of preparing a TV pilot that they would show prospective sponsors in the fall; 6) the Andrews Sisters were scheduled to appear at New York's Roxy Theater before leaving for London; 7) the sisters sang the story of "Little Toot" in the recently released Disney film *Melody Time*; 8) the sisters' recent record, "Sabre Dance" and "Heartbreaker," was on its way to becoming as successful as their current hit "Toolie Oolie Doolie"; 9) Decca president Jack Kapp claimed the Andrews Sisters' string of hits was "one of the greatest success stories on records"; 10) the sisters succeeded in show business because "they have developed a polished style which is slanted to John Q. [Public] and appeals to folks of all ages and musical likes"; and 11) some of the recent successful recordings of the sisters featured Bing Crosby, Dick Haymes, Guy Lombardo, and Danny Kaye.[4]

During all this activity, the Andrews Sisters rented an office suite in Hollywood which they used for rehearsals and other business matters. Their cousin Gladys Leichter acted as receptionist/secretary, answered fan mail, and generally took care of the day-to-day office matters, and occasionally met some of the sisters' collaborators. She remembered Danny Kaye fondly as a "nice man" who was always pleasant and often funny. She also met Bing Crosby and like many others, thought he was aloof and somewhat of a loner. She sometimes dealt with the "song pluggers" who brought potential songs for the sisters to record. She remembered one day when a bare-footed, longhaired young man wearing only trousers and a rope belt came in with a song he wanted the sisters to record. Mostly to get him out of the office, Gladys told him she would give his song to the sisters. The sisters decided against the song, but Nat Cole liked it. "Nature Boy" became one of the major hits of 1948 and boosted Cole's very successful career.

In early June, *Melody Time*, another animated Disney film, was released and marked the last film effort of the Andrews Sisters. The seven stories of the film were sung by such talents as Roy Rogers, Frances Langford, and Dennis Day. The Andrews Sisters sang a ten minute segment called "Little Toot," the story of a mischievous little tugboat who disgraced his father with his childish pranks, and then redeemed himself by saving a floundering ship at sea. The music was unremarkable but it narrated the appealing story cleverly.

Maxene remembered the Disney films fondly: "I loved the Disney pictures … It was quite an experience. On the wall at the studio they had the whole story in picture form. Two songwriters played the score and Walt Disney explained it to us. It was a whole new thing for Disney. We sang the narrative. It was very exciting working with Disney—he was such a gentleman."[5]

In general, *Melody Time* holds up well, and the story of "Little Toot" is as appealing today as when it originally appeared fifty-some years ago. *Variety* reported: "'Little Toot,' fable of a baby tugboat in New York harbor is colorful and engrossing. Andrews Sisters give it popular vocal interpretation."[6] The *New York Times* liked it better than *Make Mine Music*, but noted: "The Andrews Sisters sing the story [of 'Little Toot'] not very excitingly."[7] *Metronome* dourly reported: "The Andrews Sisters sing a silly song about a tugboat."[8] The public liked the film and it was a box office success.

While *Melody Time* was hitting the screens, the sisters headed east for another stint at New York's Roxy, where they joined an impressive bill that included an ice skating revue and two new comedians named Dean Martin and Jerry Lewis who would soon surpass Abbott and Costello as America's most popular comedy team. *Variety* liked the sisters' show—which was not new—and wrote good things about their comedy routines. *The Billboard* was even more enthusiastic:

> If the first part of the show was fine, the latter half was dynamite. The Andrews Sisters, with Vic Schoen in the pit, did an outstanding job. Their songs consisted of current pops and medleys of some of their oldies. Tho warbling was excellent, it was Patty Andrews' comedy bits that broke up the house. Her deformed-arm bit, delivered with perfect timing, got tremendous yocks. The trio's new routine, a hokey Jolson medley in make-up, was a delight. They wrapped it up with the Sonny Boy bit, with Patty as the precocious kid, and ran off to an uproarious hand.[9]

The sisters' Roxy show topped the city's box offices.[10]

The Roxy engagement was cut short, however, when Patty, Maxene, and LaVerne learned their mother suffered a cerebral hemorrhage at the family home in Brentwood. The sisters flew to California and were at their mother's bedside with their father when she died in Santa Monica Hospital on July 3, 1948. Maxene later said her mother's death was one of two occasions when she saw her father cry, the other being President Franklin Roosevelt's death. Services were conducted for Olga Sollie Andrews in the Village Church at Westwood, California. Her age was mistakenly reported as fifty and fifty-two in her obituaries. She was at least ten years older.

The death of their mother was a deep personal loss for the Andrews Sisters. Maxene told a reporter, "When Mama died that was a great shock—she'd always been there if I had a problem."[11] Olga was very close to her daughters, a closeness that was doubtlessly intensified by the early deaths of her own three sisters. Her daughters were certainly her daughters, but they also became the sisters she lost. Olga was a rather reserved woman, but one who generated affection from those around her. Virtually everyone I interviewed who knew her remembered her as a warm, kind woman. Her niece said she was happiest when she was home with her family and cooking for a house full of people.[12]

Olga was no shrinking violet. Against her family's wishes, she married Peter Andrews. She was a large woman and carried additional pounds most of her life. She had very poor eyesight, was probably legally blind, and wore thick glasses, which she always removed when a camera was near. Olga was her daughters' staunch ally during those bleak years when they were trying to break into show business and Peter was certain they would be better off taking secretarial courses back in Minneapolis. Patty once told a reporter regarding her parents' differing views on their daughters' show business aspirations, "At one time we thought our mother and father were going to break up over it."[13] Olga's homespun wisdom served her daughters throughout their lives. "She was a very wise woman," Maxene remembered. "Mom believed in the law of retribution. She thought we all get back what we give."[14] Olga did not lack a sense of humor. Once when the family was on one of their many road tours, they stopped at a small restaurant for lunch. Olga played an Andrews Sisters song on the juke box, and turned to the waitress and said, "You know ... I can't stand those Andrews Sisters. Listen to that!" The waitress replied, "Ain't they terrible? That's the worst singing I ever heard."[15]

Olga believed in her daughters' talent, and without her support and faith, they probably would never have made it. Even after they became international stars, she and Peter routinely chaperoned them to their engagements and traveled with them on tours. LaVerne was still living with her parents at the time of Olga's death and Patty had just moved out the year before to marry.

Olga left her entire estate, including the residence at 430 North Saltair, which was apparently in her name, to her husband Peter, except for $100 to each of her daughters. In the event that Peter predeceased her, she decreed that LaVerne receive one-half share of the house with Maxene and Patty each receiving a quarter share. If Patty or Maxene predeceased Olga, their share would go to LaVerne. Her personal property was equally divided among her daughters.[16]

Olga's death was the beginning of the breakup of the tight little group that accounted for the Andrews Sisters' success. The group would continue to dissolve.

In mid–July, still grieving their mother's death, the Andrews Sisters sailed for England for their four-week engagement at the Palladium in London. They had planned to take their mother with them to England, and then travel on to Norway so she could visit her homeland—a desire she had often expressed.[17] They received special clearance from the British Musicians' Union to bring three musicians with them, namely Vic Schoen, their longtime music director, Tommy Rundell, their drummer, and Wally Weschler, their pianist, a man who would gain prominence in the story of the Andrews Sisters.[18] Jack Kapp, president of Decca Records, and Lou Levy, their manager, were also aboard the ship. During the voyage, Kapp presented the sisters a "Million Record Club" award that acknowledged the Andrews Sisters' five records that sold over a million copies: "Pistol Packin' Mama," "Don't Fence Me In," "South America, Take It Away," "Jingle Bells"—all with Bing Crosby—and "Rum and Coca-Cola."[19]

The Andrews Sisters knew they had many fans in Great Britain, but they were unprepared for the enthusiastic audiences that greeted them in London. Their records had always sold well in Britain, where they were as popular as in the United States. In addition, they received some of the appreciation Britain reserved for Americans as allies who helped them defeat Germany in the recent war. Most American entertainers were enthusiastically received at the Palladium, but several commentators claimed that the reception given the Andrews Sisters topped Danny Kaye's, which had been considered the greatest ever. Reviews of their shows were universally positive, as witnessed by a *London Times* review:

> Their names are Patty, Maxene, and LaVerne, and they do not live in a treacle well. They live, for many of us, as voices on a gramophone record, voices that sing together in the accepted popular manner, but with such rhythm and smartness and such odd additions to the usual power of the human voice that quite ordinary popular songs become a pleasure to hear. So strong is custom that the Andrews Sisters in person seem, at first, unnecessary appendages to the familiar and engaging noises. But on the stage they are all three so wholehearted and unspoilt and determined to please that it is impossible not to like them; and they evidently enjoy themselves. Even though their pranks are not original, the essential part of their performance is never for a moment neglected ... and they are at home on the stage as only true music-hall performers can be. With the Andrews Sisters there, the Palladium becomes a party.[20]

England's prime music magazine *The Melody Maker* began its glowing review of the show: "Three nice people took London by storm on Monday night—the Andrews Sisters.... It isn't only their world-famous singing that makes these girls a "must" ... it is also their charming stage-deportment, their delightful sense of comedy, and an easy and friendly manner that won all hearts the moment they stepped on the stage."[21]

The American reviews were equally enthusiastic. *Variety* saw their opening show and wrote: "For three quarters of an hour trio sang merrily along at the mike, and if audience had had its way would have stayed on indef ... It was not just the singing of popular hits that made the audience yell for more, but their natural charm, their good sense of fun and, above all, their sincerity and honest desire to please."[22] *The Billboard* also reviewed the show glowingly: "Patty, Maxene and LaVerne sang, clowned and danced their way to the loudest burst of hands ever heard here.... The only hitch in their act came when a young girl climbed over the pit to get an autograph. This brought other youngsters to the front and nearly stopped the act until the management called a halt."[23] Even *Down Beat*, never a fan of the Andrews Sisters, carried a long story about their enthusiastic reception by the Brits and claimed Princess Margaret saw their show: "The girls' act was a smashing success from beginning to end, which only came because the theater made a ruling to finish by a certain time.

In July 1948, the Andrews Sisters sailed to England for a month-long engagement at the Palladium in London. The sisters were unprepared for their enthusiastic reception by the Brits. Several reviewers said no other American performers had been so enthusiastically received. Their musical director Vic Schoen accompanied them and led the Palladium orchestra. (Robert Boyer Collection)

... But if past closing nights are anything to go by, they'll be at the Palladium very late on their last night in London."[24]

    Variety reported that the sisters encored for fifty-five minutes at their opening show, and sixty-five minutes at their second one.[25] *The Melody Maker* praised Vic Schoen's role in the sisters' success as "the brilliant American musician who is responsible for all the girls' arrangements. He was given a very nice and well-deserved tribute by the Sisters." The magazine later carried a feature story on Schoen entitled "The Musical Spark-Plug of the Andrews Sisters."[26] In addition to the Palladium shows, the sisters did four Sunday afternoon performances at music halls in the London area.

    The Melody Maker interviewed the sisters about their tourist experiences. They said they had problems translating pounds into dollars and frequently overpaid and overtipped. They respected Britain's regard for tradition but added, "Tradition's fine, so long as it doesn't strangle you." To cope with the food shortages in postwar Britain, they brought a hundred pounds of steaks, but the hotel cooling system malfunctioned and they all spoiled. When asked how they found the food in Britain, they quipped, "It's pretty difficult, but we

Decca increasingly paired the Andrews Sisters with its other singers, probably hoping to find a combination as lucrative as the Andrews-Crosby pairing—or hoping that fans of both parties would boost record sales. The sisters made several records with Dick Haymes, but only "Teresa" made the charts and only for a week. Burl Ives, one of the first folk singers to invade popular music, joined the sisters for two sides: one of them, "Blue Tail Fly," charted for a week. In early March 1949, musical comedy star Dan Dailey signed a Decca contract and his first recording date was with the Andrews Sisters: "Take Me Out to the Ballgame" and "In the Good Old Summertime" didn't make the charts, but they provided some good summertime listening for America. The sisters sang with the legendary Al Jolson on his radio show in early February 1949. They would later record with him: "Old Piano Roll Blues" and "Way Down Yonder in New Orleans" never charted but the record preserved for posterity some rollicking music by two of the century's greatest acts.

Danny Kaye was one of the sisters' successful pairings. In early spring 1948, their song "Civilization" filled the airways and juke boxes. Following its success, Decca released a second record by the sisters and Kaye, "It's a Quiet Town" and "Big Brass Band from Brazil," neither of which charted. They would record two more records together, but neither had the success of "Civilization." The sisters once told reporters about their recording sessions with Kaye:

> On or off sessions—[he] clowns all the time. Recording "Civilization" was a panic. From the moment he entered the studio he was a one-man riot. Usually it takes us about two hours to make two sides: with Danny it took six. With Danny everything happens. In our "It's a Quiet Town" record the routine called for a terrific yell—a natural for Danny. Stepping back to avoid shattering he collapsed over a table full of hot coffee. That yell was so loud we had to cut another master. Danny always said to us: "Never mind how you sing, gals, let it stink so long as it's got the spirit."[49]

Maxene remembered a recording session when Kaye's demanding wife and manager, Sylvia Fine, was present. During sessions when Fine was not present, they "zipped right through it and it was wonderful." But during this session, which Maxene does not identify, Fine was present:

> It took us six hours to do one side one time … Danny did everything, he lay on the floor, he got under the microphone. And Sylvia was in the control room. They had signals, if you wanted Danny to do something, whatever the signals were, that he wouldn't do it or he would do it. But six hours for one side! Decca almost died, and the terrible thing about it is that the records didn't sell.[50]

Vic Schoen recalled the session, too, and remembered Sylvia Fine as "the iron butterfly in the velvet glove."[51]

Carmen Miranda was the only woman the Andrews Sisters joined in the recording studio. Their first collaboration, "Cuanto La Gusta," charted for fourteen weeks in 1948. They later recorded "The Wedding Samba" which made the charts for three weeks. Patty and Maxene were once asked about Carmen Miranda's temperament. Patty said, "Obviously, Carmen had a tempera-

During the post-war period, Decca increasingly paired the Andrews Sisters (from left: Patty, Maxene and LaVerne), with its other artists. In February 1949, they joined musical comedy star Dan Dailey in the recording studio for the first time for "Take Me Out to the Ballgame" and "In the Good Old Summertime." They knew Dailey from their movie-making days at Universal when he appeared with them in *Give Out, Sisters*. (Robert Boyer Collection)

ment—that is, if by temperament you mean fire and spirit." Maxene added, "In the Hollywood sense, which substitutes the word for tantrums induced by a swollen head, she had none."[52] Patty told another reporter who asked her what it was like to work with Carmen Miranda:

> Fantastic ... the sessions were wonderful. She was such a vivacious person. In fact, when she did the "Eight to the Bar Ranch Show" with us, we would take one of the songs we do and sing it with the guest star; we had a big record hit out called "Scrub Me Mama" ... and she did it with us, but it was kind of crazy because ... on the broadcast [when] she said "Scrub Me Mama," it would come out "Screw Me Mama."[53]

Maxene remembered: "It was fun singing with her ... because she was so eager to get the American words out, and sometimes it didn't work too well."[54]

In spring 1949, the Andrews Sisters made their first venture into "pure" country music, called "hillbilly" then, with popular country singer Ernest Tubb. Maxene recalled that Tubb was so tall that she and her sisters had to stand on boxes to reach his height for singing.[55] The sisters had recorded country songs before, such as "Pistol Packin' Mama," but only after they were reworked for mainstream consumption. "Bitin' My Fingernails and Thinking of You" and "Don't Rob Another Man's Castle" were unadulterated "hillbillly" since Tubb wouldn't make any concessions to pop style. A later writer described the Andrews-Tubbs effort: "Probably the weirdest combination of this era was Ernest Tubb trying to mesh his nasal, somewhat flat and toneless voice with the Andrews Sisters' precision harmonizing."[56] Maxene remembered the session with Tubb:

> He sang different than anybody I've ever heard ... He sang the melody of the song, but the timing was different. It wasn't like we were used to—you sing eight bars, and then you sing eight bars, and then you sing eight bars. Not with him. He just sang eight bars, 10 bars, 11 bars, and then stopped, whatever it was. So, we'd just start to follow him ... and we made the records and forgot about them, and then got paid on 750,000 records sold that never came above the Mason-Dixon Line![57]

Ernest Tubb remembered the recording session also:

> I wasn't gonna sing and try to make a pop record with their music—they had to sing and make a country record with me ... I had the sheet music, and really I learned the thing by ear—I learned it from a record—and I wasn't singing from the copy. And they were singing note for note off the sheet music, and finally they said, "We got two different tunes here." I said, "You better change y'all's, then, cause I can't read that thing." So Patty just threw the music away and said, "Let's learn it from Ernest." So they learned the way I was doing it and they did it.[58]

Tubb was mistaken in thinking the sisters were "singing note for note off the sheet music" since only LaVerne could read music. Arranged by Vic Schoen and backed by the Texas Troubadours, the Andrews Sisters received top billing for the songs. Although the record was made to cover Eddy Arnold's hit "Don't Rob Another Man's Castle," it was "Bitin' My Fingernails and Thinking of You" that made the country charts and became one of the top country songs of the year. The sisters would later record several sides with popular country singer Red Foley, but none of them made the charts.

Vic Schoen, who did all the arrangements for these collaborations, remembered the sessions: "My assignment in those cases was never to lose the Andrews Sisters flavor with whomever we might record."[59]

Maxene Andrews was granted an interlocutory divorce from Lou Levy on March 11, 1949. Maxene blamed the dictates of their separate careers for the divorce—her career kept her in Hollywood while Levy's kept him in New York City. She also told the judge that Levy insisted on occupying a separate bedroom.[60] Maxene was granted custody of their two adopted children, Aleda and Peter.

Despite the divorce, Levy continued as manager of the Andrews Sisters.[61] Maxene explained to a reporter: "We love our work too much to break up, and each of us has too great an investment to sacrifice it. We sisters are a corporation, with Lou and each of us owning an equal amount of stock."[62] In an interview with Levy and the sisters, Levy said no "dame" or "guy" was involved in

The Andrews Sisters made their first foray into "pure" country music—called "hillbilly" then—with popular country singer Ernest Tubb in February 1949. Their collaboration of "I'm Bitin' My Fingernails and Thinking of You" became one of the top-selling country songs of the year. (Author's collection)

their separation. Maxene added, "Between the two of us, it was business continually and no time for anything else."[63] Levy was not exactly telling the truth when he said no "dame" was involved, and Maxene apparently didn't realize that he had time for something else. Levy, in fact, was involved with another woman.[64] Either the newspapers didn't know about the affair or chose not to report it. A year later, March 15, 1950, Maxene was granted a final divorce.

Maxene continued to live at Frog Hollow Farm, the twenty-acre home near Chatsworth where she and Levy lived with their two children and the Hungarian couple who served as housekeepers and baby-sitters. A feature story about the home noted, "Simplicity and utility keynote the Chatsworth farm home of Songstress Maxene Andrews." At the time, she had four dogs and two horses. Her favorite activities were horseback riding, swimming, and long hikes. One of her hobbies was furniture-making in her woodworking shop in the garage. The main house was described as "country barn architecture" and included redwood paneling, open beam ceilings, and a six-by-five feet flagstone fireplace. An eight-feet, wine-red Moroccan leather couch, deep green draperies, and antique cherry furniture highlighted the interior. "Conversational antiques" scattered throughout the house included "fine pieces of copper ware, antique silver jewel boxes, an ancient pair of Rockingham wine jugs, and a fascinating group of Meissen ware pug dogs." Among her "cherished" possessions were a "set of white and blue Royal Crown Derby ware and Royal Copenhagen ware, plus scintillating cut-crystal stem ware of excellent design and quality." A guesthouse above the connected garage served as living quarters for the housekeepers.[65]

Maxene hobnobbed with some of the Hollywood set. Her cousin Gladys Leichter remembered meeting Rock Hudson, June Allyson, and Lucille Ball at her home. Ball and her husband Desi Arnaz lived near Maxene and frequently dropped in. Gladys remembered when Ball borrowed a fur coat from Maxene and slinked down the stairs to show it off. When Ball became pregnant with her first child, Maxene hosted a baby shower for her. Maxene once recalled playing canasta with Ball. She made a bad play and Ball chastised her: "She reamed me out. I think I cried all the way home. She acted things out funny, I thought at first it was a joke, but she was serious."[66] Maxene remembered Arnaz's womanizing. Maxene, LaVerne, and Lou Rogers were once invited to the Arnaz home for a New Year's Eve dinner. When they arrived, only Ball was present. The hours ticked by and she kept insisting Arnaz would arrive momentarily. He finally arrived at about one in the morning, and despite attempts by the Andrews to liven up the party, the situation was strained. On another occasion, Ball invited Maxene to go for an automobile ride with her; Maxene thought she was looking for Arnaz.[67] The sisters all knew Ronald Reagan, but LaVerne and her husband socialized with him more than the others did.

The career of the Andrews Sisters suffered another loss in the spring of 1949. Jack Kapp, president of Decca Records, had a stroke in a taxicab in New York City on March 25. Upon reaching his home, the cab driver helped him inside the house where he died shortly thereafter. He was only forty-seven years old.[68] Kapp's brother Dave was in a taxicab twelve years earlier when he first heard the Andrews Sisters sing on the radio and later auditioned them for Decca.

Jack Kapp was born into the record business. His father was a record salesman, and from him, Kapp learned the business end of the recording industry as well as an ability to forecast hit records. He became a talent scout for Brunswick Records and soon earned a reputation for discovering songs that

Maxene Andrews poses for the photographer with her children Aleda Ann Levy and Peter Todd Levy, the two children she and Lou Levy adopted. Circa 1949. (Author's collection)

became hits. He helped develop the careers of Bing Crosby, the Boswell Sisters, and Guy Lombardo among others. He took several artists from the Brunswick label to Decca, when he founded a branch of the British company in the United States in 1934. Part of Decca's success was the thirty-five-cent record Kapp introduced in 1934, a price considerably lower than the seventy-

five cents of the major labels, as well as its focus on the jukebox as a major disseminator of records. Kapp's addition of the Andrews Sisters to the Decca label in late 1937 was an important boost to its growing financial success. Only four years after its formation in the United States, Decca's sales reached a close second to RCA Victor.

Kapp was an innovator. Under his guidance, Decca was the first record company to issue albums of Broadway shows, such as *Oklahoma*, as well as albums of classical drama, such as *Medea*. He trekked into the backcountry of the eastern seaboard and Deep South to record indigenous American music. In his later years, Kapp became a spokesman for American music, which he viewed as "an emissary of peace and worldwide understanding" and lectured at colleges and clubs throughout the country.[69]

Jack Kapp always had a special fondness for the Andrews Sisters, not only because he helped launch their career, but also because they were among the artists responsible for Decca's success. He, Lou Levy, and Vic Schoen selected most of the sisters' songs and he arranged their picture-making stint with Universal. The sisters were equally fond of Jack Kapp. Maxene once remarked: "We were all madly in love with him. He was really quite a wonderful man."[70] Kapp was one of the helmsmen of the Andrews Sisters' career, and the second such person in their intimate professional and personal family to die within a year. Maxene later said, "All the years that Jack lived, there wasn't anything that you wanted to talk to him about that you couldn't get to him. He was that kind of man ... Unfortunately, I judged everybody else in business by him, and it was a very unfortunate thing to do."[71]

In early June, the sisters took their summer leave from *Club 15* and headed east with Vic Schoen for an engagement at the Roxy Theater in New York. Their opening show received an enthusiastic review in *The Billboard*, although the reviewer thought it began slowly:

> The Andrews Sisters drew a cold audience ... opening night and the gals did everything but throw Patty into the orchestra pit to raise the temperature. The sisters are real troupers, so when they swung into "Riders in the Sky," the ice began to melt fast.... The act hasn't changed much since the last time around. The gals clown as much as ever and Patty's slick timing and uninhibited mugging are still the best things in the act.[72]

One of the sisters' lesser-known songs made the news while they were at the Roxy. "Ho-Ho-Kus, N. J." didn't make the charts, but it was a big hit in its New Jersey namesake. The twenty-two members of the town's chamber of commerce alternated in calling disk jockeys in northern New Jersey and New York to request the Andrews Sisters' recording of the song. Prominent window displays of the record filled the downtown area, and the promotion heads of Leeds Music, publisher of the song, and Decca Records were made honorary citizens.[73] The Andrews Sisters were invited to a special block party in Ho-Ho-Kus. A police escort helped them make it to the town for a quick appearance between shows at the Roxy in New York. Profits from the event went to the town's Youth Council.[74] Lou Levy was keeping the sisters' names in the presses.

After the Roxy, the sisters took their show to Baltimore's Hippodrome, their first appearance there in seven years. The reviewer liked the show and again singled out Patty "whose clowning throughout provides maximum humor and skillful pacing."[75] In late July, the Andrews Sisters and Schoen were at the Chicago Theater where they headed the bill. A reviewer noted they included more comedy, with "slapstick" consuming twelve of their twenty minutes.[76] The Andrews Sisters cancelled their last week in Chicago, claiming that Patty needed a rest,[77] most likely because she separated from husband Marty Melcher on August 2.

The following month, rumors circulated that the Andrews Sisters were breaking up their act. To squelch the rumors, Lou Levy told *Variety* "The Andrews Sisters are the female Jolsons of this era and will have just as long a life in showbiz." He noted that the sisters had six years remaining on their Decca contract (they actually had less than five) and were mutually contracted to each other for the next seven years through their Eight-to-the-Bar Ranch Corporation. In addition they had over a million dollars in contracted bookings.[78]

Club 15 returned to the air in September with Dick Haymes replacing Bob Crosby as host. In addition to the Andrews Sisters, Evelyn Knight and the Modernaires were again on the show. Decca artists now comprised the entire cast and one writer speculated they would use the show to push their own recordings and test public reaction to new numbers for future recordings. *Variety* still liked the show:

> Dick Haymes, Andrews Sisters, Evelyn Knight and the Modernaires and Jerry Gray's orchestra ... present a tasty dish of musical entertainment nicely spliced by light and bright wordage that covers a point without smothering or getting in the way of tunes.
> While [Haymes is] superior to Bob Crosby, last season's emcee, as a singer, he's not quite the glib helmsman that Crosby proved himself ... Nevertheless, Haymes does a solid job alternating on pops and standards with the consistent tune-punching of the Andrews Sisters, who seem to get better and better as they go along.[79]

In early October, Campbell Soups asked Decca to produce an album at reduced royalties by the *Club 15* cast, which would serve as a giveaway contest gimmick on the radio show.[80] An album based on *Club 15* was eventually made by Decca; whether it was the one requested by Campbell is unclear. It featured eight songs and was performed live on two segments of the show and then given a month-long promotion. Andrews Sisters songs were "Wunderbar" and "Adieu," both with Dick Haymes, and "He Rides the Range."[81] The popularity of *Club 15* was such that Walt Disney chose the program to introduce the score of his new animated film *Cinderella*. The Andrews Sisters and Dick Haymes introduced three songs, and the following evening, Haymes, Evelyn Knight and the Modernaires introduced three more.[82]

In early October, Campbell Soups hosted a special employees' party in Washington, D.C., which included the stars of *Club 15*. On October 10, Patty, Maxene, and LaVerne Andrews flew from California to New York City on their

way to the party. When they arrived in New York, they learned that their father had suffered a stroke while playing poker with friends in Laguna Beach. His niece Gladys Leichter accompanied the ambulance that took him to a hospital in Los Angeles. The sisters and Lou Levy caught a midnight flight back to Los Angeles, but Peter Andrews died before they arrived. Newspapers reported his age as 65.[83]

Peter Andrews had never recovered from his wife's death. Gladys Leichter, who frequently visited Peter to keep him company when the sisters were on the road, said he was depressed and lonely after the death of his wife. He sometimes reminisced about his early days in the U.S. during her visits, but he never mentioned his youth or family in Greece.[84]

The sisters' bond to their parents was perhaps greater than that of most women their age. The early years when the family wandered together in search of the big time cemented them in ways most families never experience. Understandably, Peter was protective of his family as they moved among strange towns and the sometimes strange people in the dives where he normally would not have allowed his daughters. It was the Depression years with millions of people out of work, some desperate in those unsettled times. A Greek man was expected to protect his family, especially the female members. If he seemed overprotective, and at times controlling, there were cultural reasons for his behavior—both in his native Greece and the desperate times in which he found himself in his new homeland. Lou Levy certainly found Peter to be controlling: "[H]e thought he owned the act … he never said, 'My daughters' act.' 'My act' … he said. It was his act, not mine, not the girls."[85]

After the sisters' big break with "Bei Mir Bist Du Schoen," Peter and Olga wisely realized their daughters needed professional management. They had been actively involved in their daughters' early career, finding bookings and lodging, and dealing with technical crews, musicians, and publicity. It could not have been easy for them to relinquish those responsibilities when Lou Levy, Vic Schoen, and the Kapp brothers took over the Andrews Sisters' career. Peter was prepared to pass on the professional chores, but he was not ready to release his hold on his daughters' personal lives. From today's perspective it seems incredible that when the sisters were in their twenties, they were still not allowed to date unless chaperoned—but it is again important to remember Peter's Greek background. An anthropological discussion of traditional Greek attitudes toward women offers insights: "[T]he girl places a heavy burden on the [Greek] family, in terms … of the constant vigilance that must be kept to see that she does not bring dishonor to the family. Her very nature has to be protected, which is one of the major reasons for her dependence upon men."[86]

Within such a cultural context, Peter's behavior is more understandable. When the sisters returned to Minneapolis before their fateful plunge back into New York that led to "Bei Mir Bist Du Schoen," they sought Peter's permission to return to New York, even though they were all of legal age. If we believe Maxene, he didn't want them to marry until they were forty. And if we believe her again, the sisters received small weekly allowances from their parents when they were making thousands of dollars a week. Maxene once told a reporter,

Peter Andrews jokingly referred to the many women in his family as "my harem."
Here, shortly before his death in 1949, he poses with his famous daughters and
his niece Gladys Leichter. (Gladys Leichter Collection)

"Maybe that sounds strange ... but the fact is, we were very sheltered, the
Andrews Sisters. Our life was the family."[87]

Gladys Leichter remembered her Aunt Olga and Uncle Peter: "They were
strict [with the sisters]. I think they were afraid of losing the girls to husbands
and they wouldn't continue the act ... I think Pete thought they had it, and he
was going to see that they kept it ... He lived like a king in the end. He didn't
work and dressed to the teeth and drove Cadillacs. And he was a gambler. He
played poker. That was his game and he loved it."[88]

Maxene had problems with her father, probably because she shared his
aggressive, assertive personality but not his traditional Greek views of women.
She was the first of the sisters to break away from the family when she eloped
with Levy, but she was afraid to tell the family about her marriage for two
years. Patty tried to break away when Maxene did, but was unable to do so.
She returned to live with her parents until she was twenty-nine, marrying Marty
Melcher just one year before her mother's death. LaVerne was especially close
to Peter and she continued to live with him after her mother's death, and after
her own marriage.

LaVerne was executor of her father's estate. Peter left half the family residence to LaVerne and the other half to Maxene and Patty. In the event of

LaVerne's death prior to distribution of the estate, her share would be equally divided between Patty and Maxene. In case Patty or Maxene died before the estate's distribution, their shares would be equally divided between the surviving sisters. The remainder of Peter's property was divided equally among his three daughters.[89]

Although it was the last of the major record companies to allow its records on the air in the late 1930s, Decca became very aggressive about promoting its potential hits to radio disk jockeys. In early September 1949, Dave Kapp, head of Decca Records Artists and Repertoire, sent over a thousand letters to disk jockeys across the country telling them about the Andrews Sisters' latest record "I Can Dream, Can't I?" and "The Wedding of Lili Marlene."[90] The letter was probably unnecessary. "I Can Dream, Can't I?" became one of the year's biggest hits.

In early November, "I Can Dream, Can't I?" reached the number one spot on the charts and became a million seller for the sisters. A departure from the usual Andrews Sisters fare, the song was mostly a solo by Patty and in keeping with the lush, romantic ballads of the era backed by orchestra and chorus. It was also the beginning of a solo career for Patty. Observers suggested that Patty herself was pushing for this, but in reality virtually all the sisters' songs were still dictated by Decca. Patty explained: "Dave Kapp decided that he wanted me to do a solo, and so he came up with this song ... that he loved. It was one of his favorite songs." She denied she had intentions of going solo at the time.[91] However, a story in *Down Beat* claimed Decca was planning more solos for Patty and she was pursuing personal appearances as a single. She would, however, continue to sing with her sisters.[92]

In early December 1949, the *Minneapolis Tribune* published a feature story on the Andrews Sisters. The writer claimed the sisters were never successful in drawing large audiences for their hometown performances, although their records, movies, and radio appearances were popular with the locals. Much of the interview was familiar material about their career, but some of it offered insights into their personal lives.

> As sisters they get along exceedingly well. Largely because one doesn't try to dominate the other or interfere in any way in any of the other's personal life. They're three individuals living individual lives, but tied together by bonds of family, friendship and business interests.... Through the years there has never been any serious outcropping of temperament among them.... Each girl admits, though, that she sacrificed certain phases of social life and even some romantic interests through the years when they were trying to reach the top.... There were times when those sacrifices were pretty trying, too. But they agreed that that was the only way that they could ever hit the top....
>
> Two of the girls have personal extravagances. LaVerne spends most of her money on clothes and as a result is the best-dressed sister. As a matter of fact, she is one of the best-dressed women in Hollywood.... Maxene spends most of her money on her home and foreign cars. Right now she's driving a high-powered English sports car.... She has a tailored wardrobe. Goes in mostly for suits.... Patty is the thriftiest of all....
>
> All important business decisions for the trio are made by unanimous vote.

Maxene has authority to decide the smaller matters.... Radio and records tie as
the greatest source of their income.... The girls have progressed every year since
they started. Each year has been better than the one before and the constant
increase of royalties makes 1950 loom as their biggest.

About once a year the girls manage to discard the worrisome mantle of fame
to become kids again at Mound on Lake Minnetonka, where they visit an uncle
in his country store.[93]

The year 1949 was another bumper one of recordings for the Andrews Sis-
ters. They recorded thirty-seven songs, but only six of them made the charts.
"I Can Dream, Can't I?" (twenty-five weeks) was the sisters' biggest hit. It was
Patty's song backed by Maxene, LaVerne, and the orchestra and chorus of Gor-
don Jenkins. "Charley, My Boy" (four weeks) was a bouncy number with Russ
Morgan and his orchestra. "More Beer" (three weeks) offended a Canadian
minister when it was played prior to the radio broadcast of a religious program.
"She Wore a Yellow Ribbon" (two weeks) was a march-like song, again with
Russ Morgan and his orchestra. "The Wedding of Lili Marlene" (two weeks)
told the next chapter in the life of the famous World War II heroine. "I'm Bitin'
My Fingernails and Thinking of You" (one week) was the sisters' foray into
pure country music with Ernest Tubb. "Christmas Island" (one week), recorded
in 1948, made it back to the charts for the holidays.

The late 1940s brought great diversity to America's popular music scene.
During most of the 40s, popular music was still segregated into styles that
reflected regional and ethnic tastes, such as hillbilly (country), western, folk,
jazz, blues, and Latin. Although African American musicians participated in
mainstream pop music, some major record companies still produced the so-
called "race" series records that featured non-mainstream African American
musical styles. Any regional or ethnic songs that made it big in mainstream popular music had been reworked for popular consumption. The Andrews Sisters
had many such successes, including "Say Si Si," a wannabe Latin number,
"Shortenin' Bread," a traditional African American song rearranged for swing,
and "Pistol Packin' Mama," a reworked cover of a "hillbilly" hit.

During the war years, musicians, songwriters, producers, and listeners
were personally exposed to the musical diversity of America in ways that
resulted in new musical tastes and trends after the war. American men, and to
a lesser degree American women, were shipped around the world during that
global conflict. Within the United States, men, women and entire families left
homes where they'd lived for generations to travel hundreds or even thousands
of miles cross-continent to war-related jobs. People were thrown together with
ethnic groups they knew only from stereotypes, if at all. Some chose to remain
in their new homes after the war, while many others returned home with new
musical tastes.

The decline of the big bands was part of the music change also. The war
drastically altered the big bands. Many dissolved because their musicians were
drafted into the military, but those that survived became larger. The affluent
war years allowed additional members and movement about the country despite
wartime restrictions on travel. However, the postwar economic slump could not

handle the expensive big bands. As the bands diminished, the "boy" and "girl" singers featured by the bands gained prominence until, ultimately, vocalists dominated popular music. Frank Sinatra was perhaps the best known of the "boy" singers to emerge from the bands. Other names that emerged were Doris Day, Jo Stafford, Tony Bennett, and Tony Martin.

Following the war, Los Angeles became an increasingly important satellite of the New York recording industry as pop music expanded its repertoire. Regional music, such as country, western, and folk began to enter mainstream pop music. Jazz and blues had helped create the swing era, and during the war years, country and western frequently penetrated the pop scene. In the late 1940s and early 1950s, fresh, new voices like Frankie Laine, Tennessee Ernie Ford, Burl Ives, Kay Starr, and the Weavers brought new sounds to pop music in such songs as "Mule Train," "Riders in the Sky," "Sixteen Tons," and "On Top of Old Smokey"—popular songs that mixed pop, country, western, and folk. Throughout the 40s, as the "race" records began to disappear, African American styles increasingly entered mainstream pop music with singers like Louis Jordan and his rhythm and blues hit "Is You Is or Is You Ain't My Baby?", a song the Andrews Sisters and Bing Crosby covered into a hit of their own. As the 1950s began, other African American R and B singers, such as Fats Domino, Muddy Waters, and the Orioles, made the charts and added their sounds to this rich musical blend to help pave the way for rock and roll, which would forever alter the course of American popular music.

The hits of the Andrews Sisters during the post-war period reflect these diverse developments in pop music. Decca's pairing of the sisters with other artists allowed them to take new directions—and assured sales to two sets of fans. Among the sisters' hits from this period were an impressive array of musical styles: jazz ("The House of Blue Lights" with Eddie Heywood 1946), calypso ("His Feet Too Big for De Bed" 1947), polka ("Toolie Oolie Doolie" 1948), classical ("Sabre Dance" 1948), folk ("Blue Tail Fly" with Burl Ives 1948), Latin ("Cuanto La Gusta" with Carmen Miranda 1948), country ("I'm Bitin' My Fingernails and Thinking of You" with Ernest Tubb 1949), western ("Quicksilver" with Bing Crosby 1949), march ("She Wore a Yellow Ribbon" with Russ Morgan, 1949), and ballad ("I Can Dream, Can't I?" 1949).[94]

CHAPTER ELEVEN

1950–1953

The Andrews Sisters are ... the most listened to women in all history.[1]

—Voice of America, 1951

The Andrews Sisters moved promisingly into the second half of the twentieth century with three songs on *Variety*'s January chart of top songs. *The Billboard*'s music survey of 1949 ranked them the number one singing group, thanks largely to their big seller "I Can Dream, Can't I?,"[2] which was sixth in retail sales for the year.[3] For the first time they appeared among "The Year's Top Selling Folk Artists" with their Ernest Tubb collaboration "I'm Bitin' My Fingernails and Thinkin' of You," which was number nine in both retail sales and jukebox plays.[4]

While the Andrews Sisters' career was promising at the beginning of 1950, Patty Andrews' marriage to Marty Melcher was not. The marriage had begun on a happy note, at least for Patty. According to one observer: "Patty was in seventh heaven [after the wedding]. She and Melcher settled in the Hollywood area.... For a long time the marriage seemed idyllic. But Melcher was apparently looking for greener fields."[5] A year after his marriage to Patty Andrews, Melcher confided to a columnist that all was not well with the marriage: "I wish you wouldn't quote me, but you know it's a very tough problem to be married to an act. Say you're at home at night, and you're in a romantic mood. You're feeling mellow. And you're just ready to go into a clinch, and she says, 'Where are we booked for next week?' It's not conducive to happy married life."[6]

As noted earlier, few people in Hollywood had good things to say about Marty Melcher. Music producer Sam Weiss remembered: "Patty was just as nice a gal as you'd ever want to meet, great gal, everybody loved her, but Marty stepped all over her, got everything he could out of her, and when he had a chance to better himself with a new client, Doris Day, who was starting to be big stuff at Warners, Marty couldn't get rid of Patty fast enough."[7] Les Brown claimed Melcher "lived off Patty Andrews; then, when Doris [Day] came along and looked like a better ticket, he glommed onto her."[8] Bernie Woods also said Melcher began his affair with singer/actress Doris Day while still married to Patty:

> Melcher knew Doris from his song plugging contacts with [Les] Brown.... To start with, she was a much more delectable dish than Patty and, with any luck, figured to become a bigger star.... Melcher revised his sights and took dead aim on Doris, while he was still married to Patty.... Melcher began staying out late, at first, then started an all-night routine. His new alliance permeated Hollywood gossip. Patty, genuinely in love with him, went berserk. According to the stories that seeped east she would drive to Doris's house in the wee hours, pound on the door and demand Melcher come home. She tried everything to keep the home fires burning, to no avail.[9]

The gossip that "seeped east" to Woods was probably fueled by an incident reported by music producer Sam Weiss:

> I knew Doris [Day] very well from my band connections ... and that meant seeing a lot of Marty once he moved in on Doris.... I got a call from Doris's mother one night. "Sam," she said, "I'm scared to death. I'm alone in the house and Patty Andrews is at the door yelling that she wants to get at Marty. She's mad as hell."
> "Hold on, Alma," I said, "don't open the door, I'll be there right away."
> "She's going to kill somebody," Alma said. "She's yelling terrible things."
> "Don't open the door."
> I parked about a block from the house and snuck around through the backyard to have a look. Patty was on the porch with someone, and she had a baseball bat in her hand. She was spitting fire. There was no doubt, from the way she was swinging that club, she meant to use it.... Patty left after an hour or so, and it was true that Marty and Doris were on a legitimate publicity mission, but the fact was that the only thing Marty loved was money. He loved Patty's money until Doris's money came along and then, because there was more of it, he loved Doris's money more.[10]

Years later, in her autobiography, Doris Day claimed she did not become romantically involved with Melcher until he was separated from Patty. She recalled a conversation with him when he was her agent:

> "I'm having a pretty rough time in my own marriage. It's been going downhill for a long time. Patty and I just aren't getting along anymore" [said Melcher] ...
>
> He never mentioned his marriage again, but it wasn't long afterward that he moved out of his house and took an apartment by himself. At the time a lot of people jumped to the conclusion that his leaving Patty was motivated by an affair he was having with me. Not so. There was absolutely nothing between us when Marty left Patty. But I heard that Patty was very angry for a while ...
>
> I felt bad about Patty. I liked her very much and I knew she still loved Marty

but I also knew that no third person ever breaks up a marriage. A person does not leave a good marriage for someone else. But I heard that Patty suspected that Marty and I were having an affair and that that was why he moved out. I never saw her after that, until years later, so there was no chance to discuss it with her. Anyway, what is there to discuss? No amount of denial by "the other woman" can ever allay the angry suspicions of a wife. But I did feel very bad about Patty.[11]

On February 2, 1950, Patty Andrews sued Marty Melcher for divorce. The brief complaint charged that Melcher caused her "grievous mental suffering." Patty asked for no alimony or community property, but requested restoration of her maiden name.[12] She charged that her husband "did not come home nights and, when he did, refused to tell her where he had been." An insensitive judge jokingly challenged her to "sing her way out of this one" as she took the witness stand. Patty nervously replied, "I can't."

Patty and Melcher were married October 19, 1947, and separated August 2, 1949. The divorce was granted March 30, 1950.[13] Melcher married Doris Day the following day.

The Andrews Sisters bought a two-page spread in the April 1, 1950 issue of *The Billboard* to acknowledge arranger Vic Schoen's central role in their successful career. The first page, a letter from manager Lou Levy, detailed the many different kinds of hit songs Schoen had arranged for the sisters over their thirteen-year association and concluded: "There has never been another singing act and arranger associated with so many song hits of so many different types."[14] The facing page, headlined "He's Our Boy, Vic!," featured a picture of the sisters standing around a seated, pipe-smoking Vic Schoen. The background was filled with titles of the sisters' hit records. A note at the bottom, signed by the sisters, thanked Schoen for arranging and conducting their Decca recordings, their personal appearances, and their songs on *Club 15*.[15] The reason for this outpouring of sentiment was not stated—probably another Levy maneuver to keep the sisters in the news.

Levy concocted a novel gimmick to plug the summer release of the sisters' "There Will Never Be Another You" and "Can't We Talk It Over?" He sent postcards to disc jockeys across the country with the simple message: "Dear _____, There Will Never Be Another You—Can't We Talk It Over?" Signed: "PLM [Patty, LaVerne, Maxene]." He then sent the postcard to New York music agents at their home addresses.[16] According to *Variety*, some agents' wives thought their husbands were having affairs. The resulting publicity was exactly what Levy had in mind. The songs, however, were not big sellers. Both were similar in tempo and mood to the sisters' recent romantic ballads "I Can Dream, Can't I?" and "I Wanna Be Loved." The public apparently had had enough of such songs from the Andrews Sisters.

In late June, after wrapping up another season of *Club 15*, the Andrews Sisters were back on the road. Their first stop was the Chicago Theater with their *Club 15* sidekick Bob Crosby where a *Variety* reviewer noted their act had less comedy, which he thought was a good move. They added a number to their routine called "What's Gonna Be with Teevee?," a musical exploration of what they might do on television,[17] the medium that was quickly supplanting radio as America's chief source of home entertainment. In mid-July, the sisters took their show to New York's Roxy Theater where a reviewer singled out Patty's crucial role: "Patty Andrews, as usual, holds down the pivot spot with some standout vocal solos and her freewheeling body movement, double-takes and gagging." He thought the Andrews Sisters were a natural for the new medium of television.[18]

After the Roxy engagement, the sisters returned to the West Coast for two weeks at San Francisco's Fairmont Hotel, another venture into nightclubs as the movie theaters continued to cut back on live entertainment. They pulled in unprecedented numbers and were well received by a local reviewer who thought they were great in the nightclub setting.[19] Following their San Francisco engagement, Lou Levy ran a full-page ad in *The Billboard* that featured glowing reviews by local critics, including a letter from the Fairmont Hotel president who said the sisters' engagement was the most successful in the hotel's history.[20]

After their San Francisco engagement, the sisters began their fourth season on *Club 15*. Bob Crosby was back on the show as host, having replaced Dick Haymes the preceding February. In late August, *Variety* reviewed the show, finding it still had "good bop music and pleasant comedy."[21] Campbell Soups later announced it was considering *Club 15* for a television format,[22] but this never transpired. The sisters took a brief hiatus from the show in early September for two days at the California State Fair, which commemorated California's centennial. Bob Crosby and Dick Haymes, singing partners from *Club 15*, participated in the festivities as well.[23]

In November, the sisters taped several *Club 15* shows so they could fill an engagement at the posh Chase Club in St. Louis. Their hour-long show of current hits, past hits, and comic routines received favorable reviews.[24] They later ran a full-page ad in *Variety* of excerpts from reviews of their show, including a picture of them on a TV screen tearing through the center of the page. The reviews highlighted the sisters' stage personalities—a critical ingredient for television success:

> They revive a tradition that many thought had died with Jolson—the tradition that heart, warmth, personality, and the ability to keep an audience crying for more long after most entertainers would have worn out their welcome is every bit a part of their success as the talent for which they are famous. The ability to mingle emotion, laughter, high professional pace and a feeling of intimacy with the audience is rare—and these girls have got it.[25]

Lou Levy was obviously gearing the sisters for television. In early December, a *Variety* story announced they were being considered as a two-week replacement for Milton Berle's television show while he was on vacation. Had they been chosen (they were not), it would have marked the Andrews Sisters' first video appearance.[26]

The Andrews Sisters were not the only ones thinking about television. Virtually everyone in show business realized it was the wave of the future and tried to find a niche in the new medium. Television had been around since the early

Publicity photograph of the Andrews Sisters (from left: Maxene, Patty and LaVerne), circa 1950. (Author's collection)

1930s, but prior to World War II it was an experimental novelty that broadcast very limited programs in New York City, Chicago, and Los Angeles. Technological innovations during the war advanced the fledgling medium dramatically, and by the late 1940s it became a commercially viable alternative to radio—and some thought movies.

Radio reigned supreme as America's home entertainment during the 1930s and 1940s, but by the end of that decade it was seriously challenged by television. The earliest television shows were transfers from radio, such as *Our Miss Brooks*, *The Life of Reilly*, *Amos and Andy*, and *The Lone Ranger*—not to mention the many daytime soap operas that quickly became television staples. Popular radio personalities such as Jack Benny, Bob Hope, George Burns and Gracie Allen moved into the new medium with few changes in their personae.

In addition to the many comedies, adventure programs, and detective shows, television spawned some successful variety shows, which in many ways were a continuation of the vaudeville tradition. The most popular of such shows was the long running *The Toast of the Town*, which eventually became *The Ed Sullivan Show*, named after its famous host. Each Sunday evening in New York City, Sullivan hosted a variety of acts including singers, jugglers, animals, dancers, magicians, contortionists, trapeze artists, clowns, scenes from Broadway shows—anyone and anything that would entertain the millions of Americans who religiously watched the show each week. Sullivan ushered in new talent like Elvis Presley and the Beatles and gave old warhorses like Sophie Tucker and Maurice Chevalier some twilight curtain calls. Other variety shows featured weekly guests with ensemble regulars, such as *Your Show of Shows* with Sid Caesar and Imogene Coca and Milton Berle's *Texaco Star Theater*. Virtually all of these early variety show hosts were weaned in vaudeville and they continued much of that tradition into the early years of television.

As television became increasingly popular and widespread, fears grew that the new medium would totally eclipse radio and film. It did not, of course, even though it certainly changed their courses. Radio became increasingly recorded music and news while Hollywood made some significant changes, like 3-D movies, to attract people back to the theaters they abandoned in the early days of television. The Andrews Sisters had successfully tackled vaudeville, radio, films, records, and personal appearances. Now they were gearing up to take on television.

In October, the governor of the Territory of Hawaii—in hopes of boosting tourism—mailed 2,000 copies of "Mele Kalikimaka," the Hawaiian Christmas song recently recorded by the Andrews Sisters and Bing Crosby, to disk jockeys across the country "urging them to spin the platter in behalf of the Hawaiian people."[27] The song never made the charts, but it became part of America's traditional Christmas music.

During 1950, the Andrews Sisters recorded forty-three songs, a bumper year and second only to 1947 when they were stockpiling for the impending musicians' strike. Seven of these recordings made the charts: "I Wanna Be Loved" (twenty-one weeks), their big winner and another hit solo by Patty with LaVerne and Maxene on back-up; "Quicksilver" (seventeen weeks), a western-style song with Bing Crosby; "Have I Told You Lately That I Love You?" (four weeks), the flipside of "Quicksilver," also with Bing Crosby; "A Bushel and a Peck" (four weeks), from the hit Broadway musical *Guys and Dolls*; "The Wedding Samba" (three weeks), another successful pairing with Carmen Miranda; "Can't We Talk It Over?" (one week), a romantic ballad backed by Gordon Jenkins and his orchestra; and "Merry Christmas Polka" (one week), a holiday charter with Guy Lombardo and his Royal Canadians.[28]

The Andrews Sisters ranked number nine in retail sales for 1950 in *The Billboard*'s annual survey of popular music. The same survey listed the sisters'

"I Wanna Be Loved" seventeen in the retail sales for the year and "I Can Dream, Can't I?" nineteen.

The Andrews Sisters would never again make such a list.

Since the Andrews Sisters' last movie, *Melody Time*, rumors had circulated about film possibilities for the trio. In May 1946, *Variety* reported they were working on a deal with Gene Autry, popular B film cowboy singer, to co-star with him in a picture based on their *Eight-to-the-Bar Ranch* radio show. A month later, Lou Levy announced the sisters had bought the film rights to "In Apple Blossom Time" and would make a film by that title starring themselves. In 1947, Levy told reporters that during the sisters' trip to England, they would negotiate with a British film company about a picture. Again in 1949, Levy said the sisters had contracted a film with Gene Autry. A year later, he announced he had signed with RKO Pictures for the rights to *Flying Down to Rio*, which would debut the following year on Broadway starring the Andrews Sisters, after which it would become a film. None of these rumors materialized into a film.

Films may have been out for the Andrews Sisters, but television was very much on their minds and Lou Levy began exploring possibilities. In spring 1948, the sisters announced they were preparing a TV pilot, which would be shown to prospective sponsors in the fall. The following spring, they made themselves available for television at $3,000 per appearance. In early 1950, they added a new number to their act called "What's Gonna Be with Teevee?" which explored possibilities they could fill in the new medium. In July, Levy announced the sisters planned to make "two 30-minute film shorts on the Coast to showcase their own ideas for a video format." The shorts would cost about $50,000, but were being designed for theater distribution in case a television sponsor didn't pick them up.[29] Nothing more was heard of the venture.

In February 1951, *Variety* again announced the Andrews Sisters were making a pilot film ("a situation layout with plenty of room for vocal routines") that would hopefully lead to a television series. In order to devote all their energies to the new medium, the sisters would leave *Club 15* in late March after three and a half years on the radio show.[30] Campbell Soups wanted to keep the sisters and offered them an adjusted schedule or a television program, which they declined. *Down Beat* claimed it was the first time "a major musical attraction with a high rating in radio has deserted that medium in favor of TV."[31]

A television pilot eventually emerged from all this activity. Entitled *Hollywood Music Shop* and identified as "A Lou Levy Presentation," the film opened with the Andrews Sisters' voices singing "Pennsylvania Polka" over scenes of traffic in Los Angeles. The camera honed in on the sisters in a convertible— Maxene driving, Patty in the middle, and LaVerne in the passenger seat. Credits gave the Andrews Sisters top billing with starring slots to Buddy Ebsen, Marvin Kaplan, Claude Straud, Donald McBride, and Ray Walker. Other credits included Vic Schoen, music arranger and conductor; Alex Gottlieb, producer and writer; and Jean Yarbrough, director. After the credits, the sisters arrived at their music shop where the film is set.

Even in the context of the television situation comedies of the early 1950s, the pilot was terrible. The sisters played themselves. LaVerne resurrected her dimwitted man-hungry character; Patty's energies circulated around her attempts to extract a marriage proposal from her investment savvy but socially naive boyfriend; and Maxene took whatever lines were offered. Buddy Ebsen played a hayseed cowboy who was tied up and kissed by LaVerne when he wandered into the shop. The dialog was tired and the humor worse. Even the musical numbers were a bit worn. In addition to past hits such as "Pennsylvania Polka," "In Apple Blossom Time," and "I Can Dream, Can't I?," the sisters sang a satirical song called "Hawaii," which was not as funny as intended. "Get Out Those Old Records" added some freshness to the musical offerings, which were only slightly relevant to the plot. The most creative part of the enterprise was when the sisters sang pitches to potential sponsors to the tunes of "Bei Mir Bist Du Schoen" and "Good, Good, Good."

After years of complaining about the bad films Universal Studios forced on them, it is ironic that when the sisters had free creative rein with manager Lou Levy and musical director Vic Schoen, they came up with such a bad pilot. Perhaps they thought their names and songs would carry the show. Not so. No one bought the pilot.

As the sisters waited for something to break for them on television, they continued radio appearances. In early February, they joined NBC's *The Big Show*, advertised as "90 minutes of the most scintillating personalities in the entertainment world." Tallulah Bankhead was the unlikely host of the event. Other guests included Judy Garland, Gordon McRae, Groucho Marx, Joan Davis, Meredith Wilson, Dean Martin, and Jerry Lewis. The sisters sang their standard medley of hits and concluded with "I Can Dream, Can't I?" Later in the show they joined Bankhead and Marx in a spoof on commercials, participated with the entire cast in singing Valentine greetings, and then joined the cast again for a sign-off song.

In spring 1951, the Andrews Sisters finally made it to television. Their voices had debuted on television three years earlier on *Hollywood Star Varieties* as the "Three Hepcats," puppets that pantomimed one of their recordings.[32] Their first live television appearance was a cameo on the *Frank Sinatra Show* on March 3. A skit featured Sinatra and guests Perry Como and Frankie Laine lip-synching an Andrews Sisters recording. The camera panned to the sisters sitting in the audience looking outraged. They left their seats, went onstage and belted Sinatra, Como, and Laine with their purses, and indignantly exited.[33] The following night the sisters appeared on the *Colgate Comedy Hour* with Tony Martin. *Variety* reviewed them favorably and thought they could handle television:

> Andrews Sisters displayed their fine harmonics in a medley of their record hits during the last 15 years, finaleing with "I Can Dream, Can't I?" They also evidenced an acceptable flair for comedy in a mildly funny bit about three femme soldiers. Show, which marked their video debut, was to have served as a TV showcase for their talents. Judging from their work, they can carry a program neatly if provided with the right guests and production.[34]

The Billboard also thought the sisters had what it took for television.[35]

I remember walking through a cold March rain to a friend's house to see the Andrews Sisters' first television appearance on one of the few TV sets in the little town where I lived. I was an unsophisticated fourteen-year-old, but I remember thinking their "boy rangers" comedy routine was embarrassingly bad. It was not a promising television debut in my young opinion. Two days later, the sisters appeared on *Texaco Star Theater* with Milton Berle and guests Eddie Fisher and Robert Alda. Again, *The Billboard* liked them.[36]

On March 21, the Andrews Sisters appeared for the last time on *Club 15*, after three and a half years on the popular radio show, in order to devote their energies to television. The final show, called "The Andrews Sisters Story," was a prolonged medley of their many hits. Bob Crosby concluded the show with "So Long, It's Been Good to Know You" and the sisters joined him in "May the Good Lord Bless and Keep You." Giselle McKenzie eventually replaced the Andrews Sisters on the show, which continued for several more years.

Following their exit from *Club 15*, the sisters were back at the Flamingo Room in Las Vegas. *Variety* gave them a good review and singled out Patty for "her almost unpredictable comedics or serioso warblings." The reviewer thought their "Boy Rangers" comedy routine was weak and the only "let-down" in the show.[37]

About a month later, the Andrews Sisters received a rousing welcome home when they returned to Minneapolis for an engagement at the Builders' Show, their first hometown appearance in seven years. They rode on floats in a parade through downtown streets with Mayor Eric Hoyer leading the procession. Lou Levy was also in town and filmed the sisters' activities for a proposed screen biography.[38] The sisters' uncles Pete and Ed Sollie closed their grocery store in Mound "for the first time in its 40-year history" and rode in a convertible in the parade.[39]

Levy pulled out the stops to publicize the Andrews Sisters' return to Minneapolis. A woman columnist described the sisters' wardrobes and noted their preference for diamonds: Maxene kept hers locked up; Patty sported a six-and-a-half-carat ring; and LaVerne wore a platinum ring of twelve carats and a bracelet of twenty-one carats. LaVerne's wardrobe included four furs: a long mink coat fashioned by Dior, a silver blue mink stole, a straight mink stole, and a white mink cape striped in black.[40] A roving reporter for a local newspaper asked the sisters, "Do You Sing in the Bathtub?" Maxene and Patty admitted they did, but LaVerne said she didn't.[41] The sisters were featured in three different ads in the *Minneapolis Morning Tribune*, one for a dairy and two for a photo supply company. They visited a hospitalized friend from their school days where a photographer conveniently photographed them for a local newspaper.[42] A feature story described their visit to their uncles in Mound. The visit was obviously staged, but nonetheless the story sheds some personal light on the sisters and their uncles:

> At least once a year, the singing Andrews Sisters descend upon Mound ... and Sollie's grocery store to visit their two bachelor uncles—Pete Sollie, 74, and his brother, Ed, 69.
>
> I went out last week to witness the sisters' most recent homecoming ... It went about like this:

> Arrive Sollie grocery, small one-story building on the edge of Lake Min-
> netonka, early afternoon ... Maxene, in mink coat, arrives first. Yells "Uncle
> Pete!" Hugs, kisses him. Pete—short, heavy, with thinning gray hair—beams ...
> Patty, LaVerne arrive in second car. Patty, in sporty red and gray outfit, grabs
> Pete, hugs him, says, "How ARE you, Uncle Pete?"
> LaVerne hugs Pete, says hello, runs hand through his hair, says "I tell you, my
> uncle never has gray hair."
> Patty heads for meat case, cuts slice luncheon meat, chews on it. "This place'll
> ruin our diets," says LaVerne, grabbing package cookies.
> "Where's Uncle Eddie?" yells Patty. "Still in bed?" Pete says, "I just sent Char-
> lie over to get 'im." Patty says, "Let's go over."
> Patty, LaVerne run across street, walk into dark, cluttered house. Girls call
> Uncle Ed. "I'm getting all dressed up!" he yells from upstairs.
> Patty sniffs air, makes face. Stage-whispers, "Old potatoes in the basement!"
> Girls yell to Ed to hurry, walk through house, look in drawers and closets, exam-
> ine knick-knacks and antiques.
> "All this stuff would be just crazy in my house!" exclaims Patty.
> Ed—tall, white-haired man—finally comes down. He's wearing large fake nose
> and phony horn-rim glasses. Both girls hug him, scream with delight. "Waaal,
> how the hell are ya!" says Patty, slapping him on back. Girls drag Ed back to
> store.
> They present him and Pete with tiny roulette wheel, stacks of silver dollars
> from Las Vegas, assorted novelties.
> Girls make sandwiches. Pete makes coffee. LaVerne says, "What do you do
> with a mink coat in here?" She tosses it on pop cooler. Ed opens beer. Cus-
> tomers slip in, take care of selves. Girls settle down for afternoon.[43]

Pete and Ed Sollie were proud of their singing nieces and posted their pictures throughout the Sollie Brothers Store. When she was alive, Olga Andrews
often invited her brothers to New York and later Los Angeles to visit the family and see the sisters perform. Pete occasionally accepted the invitations and
enjoyed basking in his nieces' fame. However, Ed, a tall, quiet man, seldom left
home and was unimpressed by the fame of his nieces.[44]

After their hometown engagement, the Andrews Sisters took their show to
Loew's Capitol Theater in Washington, D.C., where one reviewer thought they
"look better than ever, and ... seem to have shed many of their zany antics to
make for a smoother more sophisticated act ... Teamwork is top drawer, and
routine is chosen with an eye for every type of fan."[45] While in D.C., the sisters joined a host of other celebrities for the National Celebrities Golf Tour-
nament Show in Constitution Hall. After D. C., they were back at the Roxy
Theater in New York City. Both *The Billboard* and *Variety* liked the show. *Variety* was impressed by their evolving showmanship and gave a good review of
their act, singling out Patty's central role:

> It's by now an old story that the Andrews Sisters have emerged from a straight
> singing trio to a prime entertainment unit. They've kept pace with changing
> modes with constant refurbishing of material, and Patty is just about reaching
> her apex as a good comedienne. Latter is a great focal point for the trio and she
> paces the girls to top mittings....
> In addition [to their standard songs], they've concocted a bright spoof on the
> wives of the top cowboy filmsters, including a sequence wherein they don horse

outfits and the equines appear to be doing the chirping. Another top song is "Hawaii," which they build up into one of their biggest numbers. The girls do extremely well for themselves at this house. Vic Schoen's batoning during their stand gives them solid musical backing.[46]

While the sisters were at the Roxy, another change occurred in the personnel of their career. Dave Kapp left Decca records after a long dispute with the chief executive of the company.[47] Kapp was head of the Artists and Repertory Division, and the Andrews Sisters had worked directly with him from the beginning of their association with Decca. About the time of Kapp's departure, Maxene left the sisters' engagement at the Roxy to undergo unspecified surgery in Santa Monica, California. Her surgeon announced she would recover in time for the Andrews Sisters' upcoming engagement at the London Palladium in late July. Meanwhile, Patty and LaVerne completed the Roxy date as a duo.[48]

In August, the Andrews Sisters were back at the Palladium in London, hoping to repeat the kudos they won in 1948. Accompanying them were conductor and arranger Vic Schoen, drummer Irving Cottler, pianist Wally Weschler, who was now Patty's fiancé, and manager Lou Levy. The sisters told reporters that one reason for their visit was to gain experience in British variety halls in preparation for "a series of eight one-hour television shows on NBC, with $200,000 in the offing"—another venture that never materialized.

An advance story said the sisters' act would "feature four or five solo vocals by Patty, now making an individual name for herself in the states as a solo record artist." Maxene, who bought a Healey and a Jaguar during her 1948 visit, told reporters she planned to buy another Jaguar. After their British engagements, the sisters said they would travel to France for roles in a film called *Baby Beats the Band*, which would have both English and French soundtracks[49]—yet another venture that never got off the ground.

The sisters opened at the Palladium and received a good review in *Variety*, which also summarized their show:

> The Andrews Sisters ... opened to a rousing reception and have every prospect of being a sellout ... Act, which runs just under an hour, certainly makes a striking pitch for visual appeal, and contains a wealth of those comedy pranks for which the trio is noted. There is a healthy mixture of new tunes and old faves, and a big batch of requests is neatly disposed of by a bunch of chorus snippets ranging from "Bei Mir Bist Du Schoen" to "Roll Out the Barrel."
>
> To open their show they have a special, "Back Again," which expresses their sentiments in a very acceptable way. They then go into a good calypso routine before coming across with their first comedy hit, "Didn't Know the Gun Was Loaded." From there the show really gets into its stride, with trio obviously more relaxed after the warm and immediate audience response. Two or three more numbers together, and then three solos from Patty which clicks strongly ... The other two take over with a first-rate comedy hit, "Why Give all the Solos to Patty." And finally, the trio, together again to score with one laughmaker after another, starting with a brilliant deadpan version of "Hawaii" going on to "Boy Rangers of America," and finishing with "Girls of the Golden West," a good satirical lyric on the wives of three western heroes. Victor Schoen, who conducts

In August 1951, Maxene, Patty and LaVerne were back at the Palladium in London where they once again scored high with British audiences as they performed throughout England and Scotland. Above they pose for a photographer upon their arrival in the United Kingdom. (Author's collection)

the Skyrockets orch on stage, does an excellent job of batoning and insures the required split-second timing.[50]

The Billboard's reviewer caught their Palladium act also. He was not impressed with their comedy, but reviewed them with great affection. He, too, singled out Patty's preeminent role in the act and thought the sisters were preparing for television. He concluded: "They are mercifully free from glamorous affectations and are, in brief, three jolly good sorts who make it seem a privilege to be alive."[51] The British music magazine *The Melody Maker* liked the show too, and credited Vic Schoen for a good deal of the show's success.[52] A reviewer for the *London Times* was less enthusiastic. He liked the comic number about Hawaii, but said, "The rest of their new programme, which lasts a whole hour, is perhaps not quite so successful, and it would be sad to think that their act was really losing the apparent lightness and spontaneity which made it so welcome at the Palladium three years ago."[53]

After the Palladium, the sisters moved on to the Empire Theater in Glasgow where they performed at double prices on a percentage deal. When they arrived in Glasgow, a song named "The Gathering of the Clans" was written especially for them and they bought it on the spot to feature in their show.[54] A surprise appearance in the audience by Broadway star Mary Martin, in London for *South Pacific,* delighted fans at one of the performances.[55] Glasgow loved the sisters. A reviewer wrote: "Few turns have won the audience as quickly as the Andrews Sisters ... They have rhythm, perfect harmony, humor, and ... enchanting personality ... They are better on the stage than on the screen."[56]

The sisters managed to work in a tour of the Scottish Highlands after their Glasgow date. In the little village of Grieff in Perthshire, they met the bard of the MacMillan clan, who sang for them in Gaelic. The always savvy Lou Levy, traveling with them, optioned sixteen of the bard's ballads.[57] While in Scotland, the sisters each bought kilts of the Andrews tartan complete with jackets, shirts, socks, and shoes[58]—apparently a concession to their Scottish admirers and not their ancestry, since their last name came from Ellis Island, not Scotland.

Birmingham was next. The audiences adored them and a reviewer noted: "Good looks have nothing to do with it. None of the three would claim to be a beauty. But the things that really matter are there abundantly ... Sentiment, comic touches, the song with the gay twinkle ... all have their place."[59] The sisters were equally enthusiastically received at Blackpool and Manchester. Before leaving Great Britain, the Andrews Sisters recorded a forty-five minute radio program called *Au Revoir to Great Britain* that included songs associated with the towns they visited. Vic Schoen directed a thirty-piece orchestra for most of their songs, but for their Edinburgh number the sisters were backed by Scottish bagpipes[60]—a combination that would have sent their nemeses at *Down Beat* and *Metronome* over the top. While in Great Britain, the sisters recorded two sides, "Love Is Such a Cheat" and "Lying in the Hay," neither of which charted.

The most noteworthy feature of the Andrews Sisters' trip to Great Britain was the departure of their musical director Vic Schoen. The sisters' relationship with Schoen had been deteriorating for some time. Schoen told it best:

> It was very slow deterioration ... because it held together somehow. It wasn't very comfortable, and by 1951 it had all gone to hell, everything. That's when I left them. It was the house of hostility, and there was a reason for it, as I understand now, but at the time I couldn't see a reason.
>
> Somehow, what had worked for so long, I guess, nearly 17 years—they began to think that those old ways were no longer working ... That is, Lou Levy had sort of become an enemy, and I had become an enemy, and there's no logic to any of it. But Patty married our piano player, who was then a guy named Walter Weschler, and he had ambitions, I guess, to be their everything, manager and creator from that point on. I know it sounds like a lousy script.
>
> It was so bad, it was so uncomfortable. It seemed that this thing should break up, but we didn't know how to do it. They could never fire me for some reason or another, and I could never say, "I quit." But it happened. It happened for the silliest reason. I was going with a lady named Kay Starr. We were playing in Scotland. Kay flew over and was in the wings while they were on, and she stuck her head out, not intending to be seen, but somebody saw her, and it interrupted their whole performance. [People] started yelling for Kay, and Kay had to come out and take a bow, and they tore me up one side and down the other. I had nothing to do with it, and still it became my problem.
>
> I guess that was the reason everybody needed to say, "Okay, let's forget this thing." I went back to New York, and because of that event, Kay and I didn't talk for a long time ... Then I found I had the chance to go with NBC and do the Dinah Shore television show. So, I did that. I wouldn't have done it, I wouldn't

have left if things were as they were because it's not my style to just quit 'cause there's another job. I would never do that.[61]

A *Variety* story reported: "The parting was amicable, with Schoen planning to go out on his own in the platter and video fields."[62] A story in *The Billboard*, however, suggested the parting was less than amicable: "Schoen, who flew back here early this week from London, broke with the trio in the midst of their current theater tour in England. Schoen said that the split had been brewing for several months and that he already had formulated tentative plans for himself."[63] *The Melody Maker* opined: "It is almost certain that Wally Weschler, who has been pianist with Vic and the Andrews Sisters for some years, will take over as MD [musical director]."[64]

Another of the nails that held the Andrews Sisters' career together departed.

The sisters left London for a holiday in Paris where Patty announced her engagement to Wally Weschler, pianist for the Andrews Sisters. Lou Levy also went to Paris after the British tour and quietly married an interior decorator from New York. *The Melody Maker* described him as the "American millionaire song publisher."[65]

The departure of Vic Schoen from the career of the Andrews Sisters was a significant loss for the trio. Schoen had arranged virtually every song the Andrews Sisters recorded, and directed most of the orchestras that backed them. In addition he was musical director of their personal appearances, radio programs, and most of their films.

Born in Brooklyn in 1916, Schoen was a self-taught musician who began playing the trumpet in New York City nightclubs while still in high school. His talent for arranging soon surfaced as he worked with bands around New York. He entered the Andrews Sisters' lives as a nineteen-year-old youth whose musical talents so impressed Leon Belasco that he hired him in 1936 to help move his band into the swing era with the Andrews Sisters as featured vocalists. Lou Levy had an ear for the songs that fitted the Andrews Sisters' style, but Vic Schoen had a knack for arranging them in ways that sold to the public. Schoen and Levy were probably the most significant ingredients in the Andrews Sisters' success and it is no coincidence that the sisters' career began to turn downward when Schoen, and, later, Levy departed.

During his years with the Andrews Sisters, Schoen arranged for other artists as well, including band leaders Glen Gray, Fred Waring, Glenn Miller, Jimmy Dorsey, Tommy Dorsey, Benny Goodman, and Count Basie, and vocalists Danny Kaye, the Weavers, Bing Crosby, Ella Fitzgerald, and Patti Page. He wrote popular music, like "Amen" (sung by the Andrews Sisters in *What's Cookin'?*), as well as serious music, like "Stereophonic Suite for Two Bands."[66] Schoen composed movie scores for Paramount and Universal, including the Andrews Sisters' movies and two of the popular "Road" pictures starring Bing Crosby and Bob Hope. During the early 1940s, *Metronome* frequently reviewed his arrangements, and critics routinely singled him out as a major ingredient in the sisters' success.

Following the Andrews Sisters' 1951 tour of the United Kingdom, they traveled to Paris where Patty announced her engagement to Wally Weschler, pianist for the sisters the previous seven years. They were married the following Christmas. (Author's collection)

After Schoen left the Andrews Sisters, he reunited with Kay Starr for a marriage that lasted a year. He had a successful career in television where he composed for series such as *The Dinah Shore Show* and *The Shirley Temple Show*, as well as specials for Bing Crosby, Danny Kaye, Ethel Merman, and others.[67] Schoen's successful career after he left the Andrews Sisters suggests he could have directed them into the new music of the 1950s and 1960s.

In late September the sisters opened for a week at the Latin Casino in Philadelphia, where both fans and critics enthusiastically received them. The show was the same as their Palladium act, and once again, Patty was singled out for her key role: "Patty carries the ball, both vocally and in the comedy department ... [She] is just about sensational in her solo turn ... Her's is sheer vocal impact, plus great artistry and a highly personal style."[68] After they closed in Philadelphia, they went to New York for *The Frank Sinatra Show*, their sixth television appearance of the year. Other guests were Perry Como and Frankie Laine. The sisters sang "The Peony Bush," a comic number from their current act and joined Sinatra in clown suits for a circus number. A reviewer noted: "Como, Laine and the Andrews Sisters naturally handled their vocal chores expertly, but all of them surprised with the fine way they participated in the skits."[69] In early December, the sisters appeared again on Sinatra's show.

After Dwight Eisenhower's election to the presidency in November, United Press issued a short news story that announced the Andrews Sisters offered to buy President Harry Truman's piano when he moved from the White House for $5,000 and guaranteed the piano "would never fall into the hands of rival politicians."[70] Although the sisters' tight knit community of support was unraveling, Lou Levy was still keeping them in the news.

On Christmas Day 1951, Patty Andrews married Wally Weschler, pianist for the Andrews Sisters the previous seven years, and since Vic Schoen's departure, their musical director. The civil ceremony was a family affair held at LaVerne's home with Maxene as maid of honor and Lou Rogers as best man. It was the second marriage for Weschler also,[71] whose divorce was recently finalized from singer Sue Allen with whom he had an infant daughter. Following the wedding, the sisters opened their third date at the Flamingo in Las Vegas—a combined honeymoon/work date for Patty and Weschler.

The Andrews Sisters recorded thirty-one songs in 1951, ranging from country to Latin, but only three of them made the charts, one a solo by Patty. "Sparrow in the Treetop" (fifteen weeks) with Bing Crosby, a folk-like song, was their biggest hit. "A Bushel and a Peck" (four weeks) came from the Broadway musical *Guys and Dolls*. Patty's cover of Nat Cole's "Too Young" entered the charts for six weeks.[72] First time collaborators included Tommy Dorsey, who accompanied Patty's solo "I Used to Love You"; Desi Arnaz, who sang with the sisters in "Old Don Juan"; and country singer Red Foley, who recorded eight songs with them in Nashville. After Vic Schoen's departure, several different orchestras backed them, including Gordon Jenkins and Guy Lombardo.

In the first issue of 1952, *Variety* published a list of the best selling records of 1951. For the first time since they skyrocketed to fame with "Bei Mir Bist Du Schoen" in 1938, the Andrews Sisters did not have a song on the annual list.

The tight little group that nurtured the Andrews Sisters for so many years continued to disintegrate as tensions mounted between the sisters and Lou Levy. The sisters had managed to maintain their business relationship with Levy after his divorce from Maxene, and several times in interviews they claimed he was still a member of their family. It is unclear what contributed to

As television became the chief source of home entertainment in the early 1950s, the Andrews Sisters guest-starred in the new medium. In early Marxh 1952, they appeared on Frank Sinatra's television show where they participated in a circus skit with Sinatra and an unidentified guest. (Robert Boyer Collection)

the deterioration of the professional relationship, but the divorce was no doubt an ingredient. As already noted, Vic Schoen claimed Patty's husband, Wally Weschler, was another ingredient: "Lou Levy had sort of become the enemy, and I had become an enemy ... But Patty married our piano player ... Walter Weschler, and he had ambitions, I guess, to be their everything, manager and creator from that point on."[73]

Rumors surfaced periodically that the professional relationship with Levy was ending. In late February 1952, *The Billboard* reported that the Andrews Sisters had acquired a new business manager who would handle financial matters for them.[74] A week later a news story announced that the sisters had signed with Music Corporation of America, who would handle their future bookings on radio, television and personal appearances for the next three years. The story noted the sisters had been "pretty dormant" and the MCA deal appealed because it offered them "some lush radio and TV as well as personal appearances."[75] When Levy was asked if he had left the Andrews Sisters, he denied it. He said he was still their personal manager and retained 25 percent interest in their Eight-to-the-Bar Ranch Corporation. He said he arranged the hookup with MCA for booking purposes.[76]

Despite Levy's claims, the sisters were obviously dissolving the relationship. In early June, they initiated a legal twist to get their money out of the Eight-to-the-Bar Corporation, which they owned with Levy. The sisters sued the corporation to recover funds, which they had given the firm, as well as record royalties, which the firm controlled. They stated that on January 1, 1946, they entered into an agreement with the corporation to give it all their royalties from Decca Records. The corporation was then to pay them $50,000 each at the rate of $10,000 annually. Patty claimed the corporation owed her $44,265; LaVerne asked for $42,254; and Maxene demanded $71,130, which included a $9,000 loan she made to the corporation. The suit was served to Patty, president of the corporation. She, with the support of Maxene and LaVerne as officers and directors, failed to file an answer to the complaint, thereby assuring a default judgment in favor of the sisters.[77]

Levy, never one to sit back quietly, responded to the sisters' action by filing suit against them. He accused them of abusing their authority in the Eight-to-the-Bar Corporation as illustrated in their recent default award from the corporation. Furthermore, he said they refused to assign their yearly earnings of $500,000 to the corporation as agreed under the seven-year contract dated to January 1, 1946. He asked the court to appoint a receiver to take over the assets of the corporation pending trial of his suit. He further asked that the sisters be ousted from the corporation and charged with "fraudulent and dishonest" behavior for planning to enrich themselves at the expense of the corporation.[78] When the press asked the sisters about Levy's suit, they called it "ridiculous and amusing." They elaborated:

> Mr. Levy might very well learn a few things about abusive authority during the course of the coming trial. We are perfectly willing to have the courts review our conduct connected with corporation affairs providing they also review his. Mr. Levy's chief complaint it appears is that he still wants 25% of our combined gross earnings. Our complaint is an explanation to us of our gross earning of approximately $500,000.[79]

In a separate action, Levy filed another suit in Superior Court in early July 1952 asking for $500,000 in damages against the sisters as individuals. He requested a complete accounting of money the sisters allegedly diverted from the Eight-to-the-Bar-Ranch Corporation since January and an injunction to restrain them from rendering their services to any employer but the corporation. He also asked the court to set aside the recent default judgment of $157,630 against the corporation in favor of the sisters.[80]

In late March 1953, Lou Levy lost his suit against the Andrews Sisters. The Superior Court judge denied his request that a receiver take charge of the corporation's assets. Levy claimed the sisters had failed to collect $29,217 from the estate of their deceased parents, although that amount was owed the corporation. The sisters countered that Levy was president of the corporation at the time of their parents' deaths and, consequently, he was the one who failed to collect the amount. The sisters also said they owed none of their earnings to the corporation since they had made no commitments through the corporation, but rather had retained a new agent who was paid from their personal accounts. The judge decided there was no evidence that the Andrews Sisters were "embezzling the company's funds" and denied Levy's request.[81]

In September 1953, Lou Levy once again brought legal action against the Andrews Sisters. He claimed that when he founded Blossom Music Corporation with the sisters, they agreed to pay $11,500 for 50 percent of the corporation with the other half owned by Leeds Music Corporation of which Levy was president. The sisters, however, paid only $1,500 and Levy was demanding payment of the balance.[82] I found no outcome to the suit.

Some years later, Maxene claimed she and her sisters received nothing from the music publishing business they built with Levy: "With him [Levy] we had built our own music company into an empire, with nothing but a handshake between us. Very sad, about five years ago Lou sold that company for five million dollars to MCA and we got none of it. All we'd had was that handshake and 75% of what we'd recorded belonged to the music company. It was a blow to me."[83]

Maxene's claim is questionable. The sale she mentioned was the sale of Levy's entire music publishing interests, not just Blossom Music which he owned with the Andrews Sisters. Levy claimed the sale was a fair arrangement since he received none of the recording royalties from the sisters' ongoing sales after they dissolved the corporation: "It has never been printed that when I walked out of the act, I gave them every song ... I could have owned my 25 percent of all the mechanical royalties they got for the next 30 years."[84]

Lou Levy was the last departing ingredient of the recipe that created the remarkable career of the Andrews Sisters. Perhaps he, more than any other individual, was responsible for their success. Leon Belasco once said, "Personally, I have no love lost for Lou Levy, but if there is anyone who is really responsible for their success, it's only Lou Levy."[85]

Levy was one of several Jews who played important roles in the lives of the Andrews Sisters. Their musical director Vic Schoen was Jewish as were the Kapp brothers who oversaw their career at Decca. Nate Blumberg, president of Universal Studios, who orchestrated their movie career, was also a Jew. Their first hit song, "Bei Mir Bist Du Schoen," was written by a Jewish composer. Both Maxene and Patty had Jewish husbands. Maxene once said not entirely inaccurately, "If it hadn't been for the Jews, the Andrews Sisters wouldn't be here today."[86]

Obviously, the talent of the sisters was essential to their success, but the greatest talent will go nowhere if it doesn't have the proper promotion. Levy was the right promoter and always found ways to keep the Andrews Sisters in the public eye during the years he managed them. He arranged their first Decca recording session, chose most of the songs they recorded, negotiated their movie contracts, booked them into theaters and clubs throughout the country, put them on radio and eventually got them their own shows, sent them to Europe with the USO, found TV appearances for them, and generally kept their names in the news.

Levy was often jokingly called "the fourth Andrews Sister."[87] He once explained to a reporter how well he knew the sisters: "I brought them back three hats from Paris. I knew which hat each one would pick. I threw them on a bed, and said, 'each one pick out your hat.' I guessed right."[88]

Lou Levy grew up in New York's tough Lower East Side and once told a reporter, "[I] had to fight my way—now I can't stop punching."[89] He was a small man, once described as "a half-pint, bright-faced, restless go-getter"[90] and elsewhere as "a young nervous wreck."[91] His hyper energy served the sisters well. He began his career in entertainment as a dancer, won several contests in New York City, and toured vaudeville with an up-and-coming comedian named Bob Hope. He and his female dance partner hit the road with dance bands, playing one-nighters and theaters.[92] Through his contacts in show business, he became attracted to the music publishing business. He began as an agent for songwriters but soon realized that publishing offered more rewards and founded his own company, Leeds Music. He initially promoted his songs through elevator operators and shoe shine boys who worked in the building that housed Irving Berlin's music company, a sheet music publishing company, and Decca Record Company. He paid the shoe shine boys to sing his songs as they worked—in hopes that someone riding the elevator or having his shoes shined would hear and like the songs. Louis Armstrong heard one of Levy's songs, liked it, and eventually recorded it for Decca, which began a tie-in with the record company that served Levy so well. Levy first heard the Andrews Sisters on the radio with Leon Belasco at the New Yorker Hotel, but by the time he got down to see them they had moved on to the Edison Hotel with Billy Swanson:

> I went over there to see them, and I asked a fellow where I could find the Andrews Sisters. Patty Andrews was sitting next to him. I knew it was her, but she pushed him and he said, "Oh, they're not here right now." I said, "Too bad, because I'm looking for them. I want to see if I can get them an audition with Decca Records." Then Patty jumped up and said, "I'm Patty Andrews!"
>
> I became their manager, booked them into the famous Catskill resorts. And here were these little Catholic girls, father was Roman Catholic and mother was Lutheran, all wore crosses, singing up in the Catskills, and singing a song in Yiddish![93]

An interesting footnote is that although Levy eventually married into the Andrews family, he apparently never knew they were Greek Orthodox, rather than Roman Catholic.

During the years Levy managed the sisters, Leeds Music, his music publishing company, became one of the largest in the country as it bought up other companies and developed subsidiaries. According to him, he published "about 200 songs and records that were colossal hits."[94] He dabbled in other entertainment fields, such as legitimate and musical theater, and managed a few other acts, including the Ames Brothers, but the Andrews Sisters was his most successful and most enduring. His company published the early songs of Henry Mancini and the first songbook of Bob Dylan, and he helped further the careers of Eddie Fisher, Bobby Darin, Woody Herman, Steve Lawrence, and Petula Clark.[95] Levy picked up the American rights to two of the Beatles' earliest successes, "I Want to Hold Your Hand" and "P.S. I Love You."

Levy eventually reestablished an amiable relationship with the Andrews Sisters, although they never again worked together professionally. After his divorce from Maxene, he married twice and had a son, Leeds, by his second wife. In 1987, Levy received the Songwriter's Hall of Fame Abe Olman Award for excellence in music publishing. He was on the board of directors of the American Society of Composers, Authors and Publishers (ASCAP) from 1958 to 1970. In 1990, an editorial in *Sheet Music* magazine opined: "When people speak of stories behind the songs, and of people behind the songs, they will inevitably speak of Lou Levy. Lou has been, and continues to be, a giant of the music industry. He has discovered more hit song, songwriters, performers, than anyone I could ever name."[96]

In early March 1952, as their relationship with Lou Levy deteriorated, the Andrews Sisters visited Hawaii after appearing again on Frank Sinatra's TV show. An island showman, Fred Matsuo, was booking top name entertainment into the islands and the sisters were first on the bill. Matsuo had met the sisters during their USO tour in Italy when he was with the famous 442nd Regimental Combat team composed of Japanese-Americans. He told them when the war was over, he would book them for a Hawaii engagement. Their contract called for six shows at McKinley Auditorium in Honolulu.[97]

When the sisters arrived in Honolulu, they were greeted at the airport by sixteen Belgian soldiers, fans who wanted to meet them. The sisters told reporters: "For a while we thought we weren't in Hawaii ... because we certainly didn't expect to be greeted by Belgian soldiers."[98] During one of their shows at McKinley Auditorium, Patty introduced actor John Wayne from the audience, who created mild pandemonium with the crowd. While in Honolulu, the sisters guest-starred on the popular radio show *Hawaii Calls*, broadcast from the Banyan Court of the Moana Hotel in Waikiki. Following the sisters' contracted engagements, they visited Army, Navy and Marine bases and hospitals throughout the islands.[99]

When Patty returned home from Hawaii, she discovered an unlikely fan letter. An eighty-nine-year-old man who described himself as "an ardent fan and loaded with stocks and bonds" told Patty he wanted to give her a gift of $187,000. He continued: "For years I have been collecting your phonograph records ... I have received mountains of enjoyment from them ... Since my only real enjoyment has been listening to your music and singing, I want to leave you, Patty, so pretty, so unspoiled, a sum of $187,000 in cash—$10,000 to be used in Operation Bunny."[100] The letter was signed simply "Stanley" of Whittier, California, and was sent to Patty in care of "Operation Bunny," a venture sponsored by the Andrews Sisters to raise funds for Easter gifts for women in the armed forces. The writer "outlined a classified ad" which Patty was instructed to place in the previous Sunday's newspaper. The note, however, was received too late for her to comply. No follow-up story appeared about the outcome of the proffered gift.

Their records weren't making the charts anymore, but the Andrews Sisters' personal appearances still pleased the crowds and critics. In early April, the sisters returned to vaudeville routines sandwiched between movies at Seattle's Polomar Theater where *Variety* caught their act and liked them: "The

Andrews Sisters work all through this 60-minute bill, socking over songs, patter and humor for tremendous response."[101] After Seattle, they moved on to Vancouver for a two-week stay at Amato's Theater Café. Then it was back home to Los Angeles where a reviewer was enthusiastic about their late April show at the Ambassador Hotel's Cocoanut Grove, which netted the third highest gross in the club's history:

> Girl trios have come and gone in droves since the Andrews Sisters catapulted to popular acclaim. Their supremacy is still unchallenged. For the better part of an hour, the girls harmonize, clown and generally entertain this uppercrusty trade ... No longer do the sisters rely on straight singing although the blend of their voices is still a rich embroider of melody. Not with Patty around, who is a great comedic talent to supplement her lead singing. She's a hoyden at heart and never misses a chance to break up Laverne and Maxene with her cutup capers.[102]

The Billboard thought they were somewhat bombastic for the nightclub setting—a holdover from their theater days—but gave them a good review anyway, and added: "In addition to top drawer voice blending, gals are visual performers and knock out the crowd with their zany and uninhibited antics and rib tickling asides."[103]

In early June, the Andrews Sisters were back in San Francisco at the Warfield Theater, which they rechristened "Bombsville" after a week of low attendance. Three young girls, however, did their best to boost attendance. For several nights, they sat in the front row, dressed alike. The Andrews Sisters couldn't help but notice them and after inviting them backstage, they discovered the young girls were the Paris Sisters who had aspirations of becoming a singing trio. The Andrews asked them to sing on stage and they obliged with a version of "Rum and Coca-Cola," their first public performance. The Paris Sisters went on to a successful, albeit not spectacular career. While in San Francisco, the Andrews Sisters participated in a benefit at the Presidio army base that was broadcast to the Letterman Veteran's Hospital's "bedside network" and the Armed Forces Radio Service.[104]

Later in the month, they opened at the Amphitheater in Winnipeg, Canada, for a week, and then headed south for a thirteen-day stint at the Baker Hotel's Mural Room in Dallas. At the end of the month, the sisters guest-starred on Jo Stafford's *Time for a Song*, a radio show hosted by Stafford and broadcast by Radio Luxembourg in Belgium.[105] In mid–July, they were back at the Flamingo in Las Vegas for two weeks. In late August they returned to San Francisco, this time at the Peacock Court in the Mark Hopkins Hotel. A reviewer was impressed by their show, which increasingly included more than just singing, in some ways a return to their vaudeville days but also in the direction of television:

> This booking is solid evidence that the Andrews Sisters can adapt themselves to almost any show biz phase and come off with flying colors. It also indicates that the gals will be able to meet further challenges, including video, their declared next goal. Current stand shows them moving over to eye-value appeal from chiefly ear-value and easing into the odds-and-ends of visual presentation, over and above their song salesmanship, with considerable impact. In this séance

When the Andrews Sisters performed at the Warfield Theater in San Francisco in June 1952, they noticed three young girls dressed alike sitting in the front row. They invited the girls backstage and discovered they were the Paris Sisters, Albeth (left), Priscilla, and Sherell (right), who aspired to become a singing trio. The following night the Paris Sisters appeared on stage and sang the Andrews Sisters' wartime hit "Rum and Coca-Cola." (Robert Boyer Collection)

the emphasis is on movement, chatter and even hoke to ballast their song-festing. The development of a gimmick to provide continuity, which will register via the TV tubes, is still a must, but there is no doubt they are on the right track and can manage the hurdle with further experimentation. Those who have been accustomed to the Sisters as chiefly platter and ether chirpers will have an adjustment to make; but, as happened at this opener, it won't take long until they succumb and find it easy-to-take entertainment and a yard wide ... Piano accomp by Wally Weschler is a feature in itself.[106]

Another review of the show said Lou Rogers, husband of LaVerne, was business manager of the trio and Wally Weschler, husband of Patty, was their conductor and arranger."[107] While the Andrews were in San Francisco, Decca Records invited local disc jockeys to a cocktail party for them at the Mark Hopkins Hotel.

In early September Patty's husband, Wally Weschler, was in the Los Angeles news when his first wife, Sue Allen Weschler, took him to court for more child support for their two-year-old daughter. She claimed Weschler was making considerably more money now that he was musical director of the Andrews Sisters' act, and consequently could afford additional child support. Patty denied in court that Weschler was the sisters' musical director—a denial that does not jibe with other claims—and said he was simply their pianist. When asked if he held a financial interest in the Andrews Sisters' act, Patty responded, "If I'm a good business woman he probably won't ever have an interest in the Andrews Sisters." Weschler told the judge that he and Patty agreed at the time of their marriage that "his property and earnings are his own and that hers are her own and separate" and that they had always maintained separate bank accounts. Weschler claimed his expenses were actually greater since his marriage and he was no longer able to afford the original $200-a-month child support. The judge refused to raise or lower the amount.[108]

In October, Decca released the last recording Bing Crosby and the Andrews Sisters would make together, "South Rampart Street Parade" and "Cool Water." *Variety* gave it a lukewarm review.[109] Predictably, *Metronome* did not like the sisters' part of the record and offered one of its most vitriolic reviews of the trio:

> I'm sorry, but I just can't take those sisters. I know they hate me for it, but there's something about concentrated, unshaded shouting that will always strike me as being completely unmusical. It's a shame that they had to interfere here, because musically speaking, Bing and Matty Malneck's [sic] jumping Dixieland band had a fine side going as they strode down the Street together. But those kibitzers from the side lines! And there was a nice warm mood going on Cool till the gals started polluting that water. That's just not music, that's all.[110]

I disagree with *Metronome* and think "South Rampart Street Parade" is one of the enduring songs of the Andrews-Crosby collaborations. The sisters' seasoned brassy voices become loud instruments within the equally loud, brassy Matty Matlock Dixieland jazz band. Perhaps more than any other song they recorded, their performance illustrates their early claim that they wanted their voices to sound like three trumpets. Indeed their raucous rendition backed by the Matlock band almost blasts Crosby out of the record. Steve Allen, who wrote the lyrics for the song, said the Crosby-Andrews recording was "the biggest thrill" of his songwriting career.[111] "South Rampart Street Parade" never made the charts, but it is still good Dixieland listening.

In early November, the sisters were back at the Cocoanut Grove in Los Angeles where they once again packed the house to good reviews. *Variety* liked their show but thought their comedy was a bit weak.[112] *The Billboard* was enthusiastic about both:

> The Andrews Sisters have the most potent act this reviewer has seen them work in eight years of catching the Decca stars. Up to now, Patty has pretty much carried the comedy load with good assists from her two sisters but now they have full-fledge comedy routines built on their harmony vocals. They kid their poodle cuts in a wonderful number which closes big with the aid of a tiny French poodle, around whom the last verse and chorus are built. In a closer, they trot out Strobe, hokey horses for a wonderful parody on the wives of famous horse opera stars… Patty, one of the ablest comediennes ever, has reached a point, where she burlesques her old standard comedy and the effect is great.[112]

The sisters were in Toronto at the end of the month where the Canucks embraced them as warmly as did the Angelinos.[114] They finished the year at the

Sahara in Las Vegas where they again wowed the crowds and the critics: "Patty, LaVerne and Maxene have a well-defined niche in Vegas, yet never overplay their good fortune by turning out the same song etchings with each return."[115]

In 1952, the Andrews Sisters recorded twenty-nine songs, including an album of Hawaiian songs with Alfred Apaka. None made the charts.

The sisters began 1953 with a mid–January appearance on Milton Berle's *Texaco Star Theater* where they joined Berle and fellow guest Molly Goldberg in skits and sang "The Anniversary Waltz" and "Sonny Boy." The second song was an extension of a Texaco commercial with ventriloquist Jimmy Nelson, the highlight of the show and one of their cleverest television appearances. Maxene and LaVerne acted as mannequins to Nelson's ventriloquism in the commercial, and Patty joined them as a third mannequin in the "Sonny Boy" routine. Years later, Nelson remembered: "It remains one of the most hilarious moments of early TV and, in fact, was screened this year [2000] at the annual Ventriloquist's Convention to enthusiastic response!"[116] He remembered the Andrews Sisters' appearance as his "very favorite" and "an outstanding bit of live television."[117] Nelson worked with many celebrities on the Milton Berle show but regarded the Andrews Sisters' professionalism as "the top of the line." "Others paled by comparison," he said.

Later in the month, the sisters were back in Canada, this time in Montreal at the Normandie Room in the Mt. Royal Hotel. Their opening was delayed three days as Patty recovered from a bout of flu. An enthusiastic audience attended their first night:

> [T]he Sisters prove conclusively why they've been ranking faves for more than a decade ... and their somewhat rowdy but personable approach to both the clientele and their singing is surefire. Experience, which they have plenty of, has taught them how to out-heckle the hecklers, bandy a fast ad lib and still keep overall pacing and showmanship at top level.[118]

After their Montreal engagement, the Andrews Sisters headed a vaudeville bill at the National Motor Show in Toronto. According to an item in *Down Beat*, each ordered a new Cadillac and they bought a Studebaker for their agent and a Chevrolet for their manager.[119] From Canada, the sisters traveled to San Francisco to join an Armed Forces Benefit Stage Show. Upon arrival, they discovered the publicity, staging and scheduling of the event were badly mismanaged, so they pitched in to save the show from total disaster. Wally Weschler rehearsed a hastily formed orchestra and Patty took over as emcee for the all-military amateur show. A grateful organizer of the event wrote: "For a rare display of great showmanship, I humbly bow to Patty, LaVerne and Maxene Andrews ... other performers under similar circumstances would have nixed the ordeal."[120]

The Andrews Sisters continued to pack in audiences at their personal appearances and the critics generally liked what they saw and heard, but major problems were afoot in their professional and personal lives. Their recording career was stalemating. During 1951, they recorded thirty songs and only three made the charts. In 1952, none of the twenty-nine songs they recorded charted. In 1953, they recorded only eight songs and none charted. In 1951, they made eight television appearances; in 1952, they appeared on television only twice; and in 1953, once again they made two television appearances.

Various factors were at play. The popular romantic ballads of the day were sung better by such singers as Doris Day, Kay Starr, Jo Stafford, and Patti Page. The novelty songs that provided so many of the sisters' past successes were becoming passé, and they were having trouble finding a niche in the contemporary music scene. Perhaps most importantly, they no longer had Lou Levy to provide the cream of the new song crop as it passed through his music publishing business. Nor did they have Vic Schoen to arrange their songs in ways that appealed to the public. Wally Weschler, Patty's husband, had taken over these chores and he didn't have the ins or the talent the sisters needed at this critical stage of their career.

Patty increasingly dominated the act. From the beginning she was singled out as the chief talent of the trio, the spark that made it happen. She was a singer, a comedienne, a dancer, and an emcee—an all-around entertainer. As her solos hit the charts, Maxene and LaVerne were relegated to backup singing. Decca increasingly recorded her without her sisters. Maxene later said with some resentment: "Patty was the spokeswoman. It started by design, then it got out of hand, if you know what I mean. There were times LaVerne and I would talk to each other just so we could convince each other we could still talk."[121]

It was obvious that Patty was moving toward a solo career, and perhaps the only people surprised by her announcement in spring 1953 that she was going solo were her sisters Maxene and LaVerne. Her decision apparently came after Maxene and LaVerne refused to give her and Weschler a bigger piece of the act's income. In an interview at Ciro's nightclub in Los Angeles, LaVerne pulled no punches about who she thought was responsible for it all:

> Patty hasn't spoken to Maxene or me in three months ... I called her on Good Friday but she hung up the phone. Her husband told her to hang up on me. And she did ... Wally's done terrible things to us ... We always pooled our earnings. Now he wants a separate deal for Patty. And he wants to run the act ... He's broken us up. We three were always close. Maxene is my best friend. And Patty ... Patty isn't really mad at me. She just does whatever he tells her to do ... If mamma was alive ... this wouldn't have happened. Mamma would know how to handle it ... Patty was the baby and she was always the favorite. Ever since mamma died, she's been going to a psychiatrist ...
>
> Wally said he wanted Patty to have a third of the act but he didn't want her to pay the expenses. It isn't fair. You'd think she'd realize it's not fair ... He doesn't understand what he's done to us ... I cry every night ... I shouldn't come out, because I cry in front of people. I just can't get used to the idea. God blessed us with such a talent. We were one of the greatest acts in the world ... Now we're through.[122]

In a separate interview, Maxene minimized the separation and said that LaVerne tended to be a "sentimentalist" and when problems couldn't easily be solved among the sisters she "considers everything futile." Maxene admitted they were having problems, but insisted the act would not break up. When asked about LaVerne's claim that Patty hadn't spoken to her sisters in three months, Maxene said: "I wouldn't say we haven't been speaking but we certainly haven't seen much of her in the last three months." A source "close to the sisters" summed up the situation: "Patty's husband is Wally Weschler, the pianist and arranger for the act. He wants an increase in salary. The other sisters are battling it because they don't think it is good business at this time." The story reported that the sisters had turned down several $20,000-a-week jobs in Las Vegas because of their dispute. Maxene concluded: "We feel that we should get this business settled before we go on the road again ... I suppose it means just a series of business conferences where first one gives a little and then the other. Eventually it will be settled and everybody will be happy."[123]

While Patty was threatening to go solo, Maxene was testing some new musical waters too. She later told a writer:

> The first time Patty left the act, Frank Loesser was writing a show called "Most Happy Fella" ... I got a call one day from Frank Loesser, and I thought he made a mistake. I thought he wanted Patty and he got me instead. He asked me to come over ... I went over ... and he told me that he was writing this show, and would I be willing to work with the piano player and the music? I was so flattered, and I said, "Of course, I would, Frank." So, for ... every day, five days a week, eight o'clock in the morning, I was over at his house, sitting with the pianist and going over the music...
>
> One day—and it was a hot, hot day—I walked in. I had heels on, and I took my shoes off, sat down at the piano, and I rubbed my feet. I thought I was talking to the piano player, and I said to him, "Ooh, my feet, my poor, poor feet," and Frank wrote a song called "Ooh, My Feet, My Poor, Poor Feet" and he wrote in a part for me...
>
> We went over to Gold Star recording company, and we made the records for him to take to New York.[124] Then ... he asked me if I'd done any Broadway show, and I said no. So, he booked me in the tent up at Sacramento, which at that time was a very big place to go. Many of the big producers were breaking in their shows up there...[125] Frank came up, and I guess he liked what he saw. He brought me to New York, and ... I auditioned five times for him ... But we both decided that the part was too much for me ... So, I didn't get the part, and I wasn't unhappy about that.[126]

In June, the Andrews Sisters called a truce of sorts, most likely because of contractual obligations. A Hollywood columnist noted: "The Andrews Sisters have made up, kissed, and cut their first record since the big blow-up."[127] In early September, they were back at the Flamingo in Las Vegas—even Vic Schoen rejoined their act:

> The Andrews Sisters are in business again, filling the Flamingo Room with the solid, satisfactory aura that comes from good old established showmanship. Reconciliation after their brief breakup can hardly come under the heading of a "new act" since there is nothing added to the old standards. Their turn is a rundown of their disk hits—which the paying customers don't find hard to take ... The backing by Vic Schoen was his usual ace job with the sister team.[128]

While in Las Vegas, the sisters joined other celebrities to help the Ritz Brothers, costars of their first film, celebrate their twenty-fifth anniversary in show business.[129] They also joined the Mills Brothers and Martha Raye in a fundraiser for a new parochial school. Shortly after the engagement, Vic Schoen was seriously injured when he lost control of his car outside Las Vegas. He eventually recovered but his condition remained critical for several days.

Later in the month, the sisters signed with a new personal manager and told a reporter that "talk of a splitting of their act is not true."[130] However, an item in the column of gossipmonger Louella Parsons in late October suggested they were still having problems. Parsons claimed that Patty was offered a starring role in a Broadway musical and would probably take it. When Patty appeared at a conference to meet with Maxene and LaVerne, she brought her attorney and stated her demands, which were not specified.[131]

In early November 1953, King Paul and Queen Frederika of Greece arrived in the United States for a state visit. After charming the East Coast, the royal couple traveled cross-country to San Francisco and then to Los Angeles where they arrived at Union Station. Angelinos rolled out the red carpet for the king and queen, who greeted the locals in a parade through downtown L.A. On the Saturday night of their visit, members of Los Angeles' glitteratti honored them at a banquet at the Ambassador Hotel's Cocoanut Grove. Actor Dick Powell hosted the entertainment segment of the banquet, which included the Andrews Sisters, Eartha Kitt, Frankie Laine, Danny Thomas, and the band of Harry James. The sisters and the other entertainers were formally presented to the royal couple after the program.[132]

The mayor and several councilmen later expressed unhappiness with the choice of entertainers for the king and queen. One councilman complained that the show was "good enough for the Burbank Theater [a local burlesque house] but not for royal performance ... If they'd sung those songs anywhere else there'd have been a raid. Andrews Sisters sang two nice songs then went into their saloon routine." The American Guild of Variety Artists provided the entertainment free, but its West Coast head said it would not do so again because of the complaints. The show's producer said the Greek royalty wanted to see American entertainment and the performers were representative of popular American entertainment. The Andrews Sisters, he said, were not only among the top singers of the nation, but also of Greek descent and therefore appropriate for the show.[133]

On November 11, shortly before entertaining the Greek royalty, the Andrews Sisters made their last record for Decca Records—almost exactly sixteen years after their first recording date for the company. The sisters recorded only eight songs in 1953. One of them, "Fugue for Tin Horns," was noteworthy because it was the sisters' only recording that featured solos by Maxene and LaVerne. That wasn't enough, however, to attract listeners; neither it nor the other seven records entered the charts.

CHAPTER TWELVE

1954–1956

Patty Andrews of the famed Andrews Sisters has announced her intention to try her wings as a solo performer.[1]

In early February 1954, *Down Beat* ran a brief story that announced Patty Andrews planned to pursue a solo career without her sisters.[2] Maxene and LaVerne were unprepared for her decision. According to Maxene: "She never even came to LaVerne and me and said, 'I want to try it alone.' We read about it in the newspaper."[3] She told another reporter, "It left us way out in left field."[4]

Patty may not have announced her plans to Maxene and LaVerne, but they surely realized she was headed in that direction. Their brief separation six months previously must have alerted them to Patty's unhappiness with the status quo. Patty's first solo song was cut way back in spring 1937 when the sisters recorded for Brunswick with Leon Belasco. She didn't solo again until 1948 when she and Bob Crosby cut "The Pussy Cat Song," which hit the charts for a short time. That record was followed by one with Bing Crosby ("Be-Bop Spoken Here") in 1949 and then three with Dick Haymes in late 1949 and early 1950, none of which made the charts. The last two big hits of the Andrews Sisters, "I Can Dream, Can't I?" and "I Wanna Be Loved," were solos by Patty backed by Maxene and LaVerne. "Andrews Sisters" was on the label of both records, but everyone knew they were Patty's songs. In 1950, she soloed with Danny Kaye on "Orange Colored Sky." She soloed again with Bing Crosby in 1951 ("If I Were a Bell") and with country singer Red Foley for four sides. In 1951, she cut four sides by herself, including "Too Young," her only single to hit the charts. In 1952, she cut three more sides alone, and in 1953, she produced two sides without her sisters.

Years later, Patty claimed she was not pushing for a solo career at this time, but rather was recording the songs Decca wanted recorded. Such was probably the case. Lou Levy and the Kapp brothers had always chosen the sisters' songs in the past, and most likely the new Decca executives were doing the same. The sisters had a contract with Decca and since their trio numbers weren't selling, the Decca execs apparently thought Patty might be able to chart some songs on her own. Unsubstantiated rumors claim that because all of Patty's solos were recorded under the Andrews Sisters' contract, Maxene and LaVerne collected royalties on them. If so, this doubtless added to Patty's dissatisfaction.

In late 1951, *Down Beat* announced Decca was grooming Patty for solo work, but nothing suggested the trio would dissolve. The story noted the parallel between Patty Andrews and Connee Boswell who became one of Decca's top singers after the Boswell Sisters retired as a trio.[5] Judy Garland, Jo Stafford, and Rosemary Clooney were other singers who became stars after leaving their sisters.

Although only one of Patty's solo records, "Too Young," hit the charts, she was certainly aware that her solos of "I Can Dream, Can't I?" and "I Wanna Be Loved" made those records big sellers. And she was also aware that the current songs the Andrews Sisters recorded together were not doing too well. Increasingly, reviewers singled her out for her solos and comedic talents. She must have known throughout their career that she was the chief talent of the trio as well as the adhesive that made it work. On the few occasions when she was ill, engagements were cancelled or substitutes brought in. If Maxene or LaVerne were ill, the show went on with Patty and the other sister making it happen. As early as 1938, shortly after the success of "Bei Mir Bist Du Schoen," rumors circulated that Universal Studios wanted Patty to sign a contract with the studio, but she did not want to leave her sisters.[6] And even before that, according to the sisters' cousin Gladys Leichter, Larry Rich was interested only in Patty for his vaudeville show, but Olga Andrews would not let her go without her sisters. The sisters' longtime manager Lou Levy once said:

> At the time I built the act, I built it around one girl: Patty Andrews. She was the soloist, and, I used to call her, the star.[7] ... Patty was a great, great tap dancer.... Patty could have been a great dancer. Patty could have been one of the great comediennes in the musical theater. I always thought I would go on with her and without the girls, 'cause I felt she had all the ingredients to make up a star. She could dance, she could take a joke, give a joke, fall on her face. She was a great, great piece of talent. Where she got lost ... [ellipses in original] someday I'll tell the true story. Until then, I'll just tell [you] she was a fantastic performer.[8]

So long as the sisters were topping the charts, there was no reason to alter the chemistry that brought them success. But as Patty became increasingly responsible for their successful records and their combined efforts were going nowhere on the charts, Patty thought more of trying it on her own as their current Decca contract expired. And if we can believe Maxene, Patty's husband Wally Wechsler was an important factor in her decision. In later years, Maxene told a reporter: "We [Patty and Maxene] have always been very close, but alienation started when she married this man [Weschler] she is married to now. It started in slowly but it began to build up. After about two years, he started this isolation bit. We were never invited to the house and that kind of thing."[9] In an undated radio interview, probably in the mid–1980s, Maxene said, "We got along beautiful, but we had our ups and downs. When husbands started coming in, we had our trouble … Patty's husband was trying to get Pat out as a single. Pat was put in a difficult emotional position. I never wanted to get involved in their marital position."[10]

When the trio separated in spring 1953, LaVerne made it quite clear to a reporter that Wally Weschler was the chief reason for the break-up.[11] As noted, Vic Schoen also suggested Weschler was partly responsible for the changes in the trio: "Patty married their piano player … and he had ambitions, I guess, to be their everything, manager and creator from that point on."[12] A columnist claimed Patty announced at the time she quit the act that "she'd net more money as a single and she wanted to be on her own."[13] Her husband, Wally Weschler, added: "We just felt Patty had gone as far as she could with the girls. You have to grow in a career."[14]

A news story reported, "The trio broke up when Patty demanded more than one-third of the singing fees for the trio."[15] Patty apparently felt it was time for more money for her greater contribution to the trio's success. Years later, when the Andrews Sisters were reunited, Patty was candid on Johnny Carson's show when he asked the sisters about their split. She said: "We split the money three ways now. I thought I'd let you know what we were fighting about."[16] Another news story about their split reported that Patty resented LaVerne and Maxene treating her "like a baby."[17] Maxene remembered the difficult years leading to their split:

> We were so used to Vic [Schoen] because he was such an integral part of us that when he left us we were kind of lost … and then, at that point, we got no help from Lou [Levy], who was fighting his own battles, and I got tired of the fight. This wasn't what success was supposed to be. By that time, I think we were getting to the edge of being burnt out. We'd had it. We'd worked awfully hard in our career, and we were blessed because we felt that we had really created a successful life for ourselves to give us everything we wanted, to take care of our parents and there wasn't anything else.[18]

The death of their parents was probably a factor in the sisters' split as well. So long as the parents were alive, it seems unlikely Patty would have left the trio. In varying ways, the parents controlled the sisters their entire lives. Except for the 1940 gun incident, there's no indication that Patty or the others ever challenged that control. But things were different now that the parents were out of the picture. Their longtime musical director Vic Schoen observed: "They had a very sheltered life and they always wanted to break loose. And when they did, after their parents died, it seemed to me that they were so filled with guilt that they began taking it out on each other. They were always squabbling."[19]

When asked about her estrangement from Patty some years later, Maxene said, "For all our teen years, the three of us were connected at the hip. But as we got older, we talked less and less to each other about our personal feelings.

Obviously somewhere along the line, something was festering in Patty."[20] Elsewhere Maxene said: "But we never had a real fight ... except in 1954. And we broke up. None of us knew exactly why. But we were certainly under a lot of pressure. Our parents had both died. I was getting a divorce. Everything kind of fell apart, so we said 'Bye-bye.'"[21]

Patty reflected on the breakup in later years in two different interviews: "And it's funny, you know, because when we came to that breaking point in 1954, we sort of ... we got to the point where we just couldn't work together anymore. And that was it. We were, like, at each other's throats every minute."[22] She told another reporter: "We were sisters, but so totally different.... There were times when we would be singing together for nights but not speaking for days offstage. You'd go out to take a bow and turn around and a sister wouldn't be there—she'd be up in her dressing room."[23]

In early 1954, Patty began developing her solo act with her husband Wally Weschler. They tried out the act in Detroit in early June. Later that month, they were in Las Vegas, familiar territory when Patty was with her sisters. *Variety* gave her act a good review but thought she shouldn't have included Andrews Sisters songs:

> Patty Andrews proves she can do a single in her first solo try since the breakup of the Andrews Sisters. Most of the special material is good but she perhaps mistakenly rakes up some nostalgics ... to bring up the image of the Three Andrews gals doing those tunes, and alone Patty must suffer by the comparison.
> The star gets the 40-minute act on the road with "An Orchestra Behind Me and an Audience Out There" ... "Rampart Street Parade," is solid and with Maxene and LaVerne would have been a smasher ... Blonde belter scores with "I Can Dream, Can't I?" ... Husband Wally Weschler is a strong act-factor at the piano ... and he propels the bombastic Andrews girl in a stint which, given a little experience, can emerge as a solid nitery bet.[24]

In a rare display of enthusiasm for anything Andrews, *Down Beat* published a good review of Patty's show: "Billed as the surprise act of the season, vivacious Patty Andrews lived up to the advance buildup ... Patty took the audience by storm and led them through several clever special material type numbers ... Patty's flair for comedy was ably displayed ... another top rate single act was added to show business."[25] *The Billboard* was less impressed with Patty's new act: "The show this week bills Patty Andrews' act as her first solo performance away from her famous sisters, and with husband Walter Wechsler, she manages to turn in a pleasing act, but one needing polish ... She relies on a group of numbers the trio made famous, but of course, the familiar harmonizing is missing, even tho a bit of comedy is thrown in for diversification."[26]

Years later, when asked what it was like doing a solo act, Patty replied: "Horrible. It was ... like I couldn't keep my balance. I was always in the middle [and] my sisters weren't there. It was terrible. In fact, Stanley Tawn and my husband wrote me a song when I was doing a single. And it was called 'It's Tough, Mighty Tough to Do a Single When You've Been a Trio All Your Life.' And really it was true."[27]

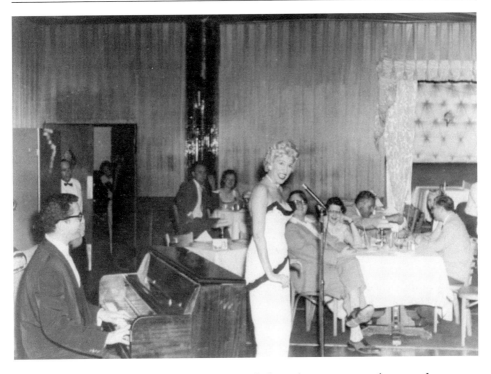

In early 1954, Patty Andrews announced that she was pursuing a solo career without her sisters. Above, she sings at an unidentified club with her husband, Wally Weschler, accompanying her on the piano. Shortly thereafter, Patty signed a contract with Capitol Records and made a series of singles on her own. (Author's collection)

LaVerne and husband Lou Rogers saw Patty's show in Las Vegas. Afterward, LaVerne sent a note to Patty telling her she had seen the show, "but there was no reconciliation, not even a meeting between the sisters."[28]

In late June, the *Los Angeles Times* announced that Patty Andrews was scheduled to co-star in a film called *Three Charms* about an American vaudeville trio touring England. Vivian Blaine, best known for her Broadway role in *Guys and Dolls*, would be one of the trio members with the third, a male, to be announced. Patty's husband Wally Weschler was scheduled to write the musical score for the film, which would begin production in three months. Nothing further, however, was heard of the venture.[29]

In late July 1954, Patty announced she was exploring television because she wanted "to expand." Within a week, she and Bob Crosby, her colleague from the *Club 15* radio days, were scheduled to make a musical comedy pilot, which CBS-TV planned to release in the fall. Again, no such show ever materialized. She told a reporter her single act was a success and not one customer asked her about Maxene and LaVerne. Patty likened the Andrews Sisters' split to that of the Marx Brothers: "They were great together, but you can do just so much, and then Groucho went out on his own … We'd done everything … Toured Europe, done movies, records, we could go no farther. I'd sung with my sisters since I was a kid of 12. Doing a single gives me a chance to do something new. Any girl who has sisters would understand."[30] When the reporter mentioned that the greatest applause during her Las Vegas engagement came when she sang Andrews Sisters songs, Patty replied: "Well, people know I'm an Andrews sister ... I'll always be remembered for that."[31]

While Patty was putting her new act together, LaVerne and Maxene were looking for another sister. They planned to resume nightclub dates as the "Andrews Sisters with _____."[32] They began looking in March and were still searching in early June when they told a reporter about their difficulties finding a singer to replace Patty. They had spent six weeks auditioning singers who responded to an ad in a trade publication. Maxene said when they placed the ad, they decided they'd listen to every singer who wanted to audition: "We haven't forgotten how hard it was for us to get a hearing when we were kids. So we've heard hundreds—and most of them pretty good. Some even great. But finding someone to take Patty's place—that was a problem." LaVerne's husband Lou Rogers, "longtime managerial aide to the girls," was "now the chief worrier about the details of relaunching the Andrews Sisters with a new 'sister' in place of Patty."

Maxene and LaVerne declined to discuss the sisters' split and voiced no ill will toward Patty. LaVerne said, "Patty not only carried the lead but also did those great solo passages ... We wish her all the success possible." Maxene told another reporter:

> We've had our arguments and beefs, but I think they were minor compared to how much we were together.... We still love each other.... We worked together for 21 years, seeing each other all the time. Patty felt she wanted to be on her own, and I understand. After all, she's been with us since she was 11 years old and every girl wants to raise a family and live where she wants to and do things on her own.... It'll seem odd without Patty, I guess. It's like losing an arm.[33]

When Leon Belasco, an important influence on the sisters' early years, was asked about their split, he replied: "I know these kids—and they're really still kids—all they have to do is sit down somewhere by themselves with their memories and talk it over. A lot of their old fans who remember that rousing, lusty beat they put in everything they did, and to whom they will not be the same without Patty, hope they will try it."[34]

In early July, Maxene explored musical theater with a supporting role in a one-week run of *One Touch of Venus* at Sacramento's light opera series "Music Circus." A reviewer liked her performance:

> Another newcomer is Maxene Andrews, on her own after many years of leading [sic] that famous sister act. If Miss Andrews is waiting for a green light to get going as a musical comedy performer, she has got it. Her acting as the wise talking secretary, Molly, is natural, forceful and likeable, and her two songs, only one of which is worth her talents, are delivered with a fine Andrews beat.[35]

In early October, Patty made a radio guest appearance on *The Dennis Day Show* where she sang "South Rampart Street Parade" and "Ain't We Got Fun," and participated in two skits. She then took her new act to Reno's Mapes Skyroom where both she and her husband Wally Weschler were favorably reviewed, although the reviewer missed Maxene and LaVerne for some of the songs:

> Since it was always the high voice of Patty Andrews during the reign of the Andrews Sisters which most identified the trio, customers give approval to old Andrews Sisters hits when Patty trots them out. Even "Apple Blossom Time" sounds about the same, although missing a couple of voices. But where the sisters are missed most is on the fast numbers ... ballad-wise, Miss Andrews misses none ... And of course, "I Can Dream, Can't I?" gets unanimous consent ... Accompanist-husband Walter Weschler traces some wonderful backdrops on the keyboard. And as a straight man he's funny.[36]

Patty's busy schedule caught up with her in Reno where she entered a hospital for observation. Her husband said she was suffering exhaustion from her steady grind of nightclub appearances.[37]

Ironically, as Patty was doing her solo act and Maxene and LaVerne were about to debut their new act with another "sister," it seemed their stiffest competition would come from a record by the original Andrews Sisters. A recently released Decca record cut three years previously by Red Foley and the Andrews Sisters, "She'll Never Know," had moved to ninth place in Decca sales in late October.[38] The song, however, never made the charts.

Maxene and LaVerne were inactive, but they had not abandoned their plan to continue without Patty. *Variety* announced that English singer Dorothy Squires would join Maxene and LaVerne the following month after completing an engagement at the Palace Theater in London.[39] Meanwhile, in early November, Maxene and LaVerne made a guest television appearance on *The Red Skelton Show*. In a skit with the sisters, Skelton tried to find a replacement for Patty and ended up wearing a blond wig as he sang with Maxene and LaVerne. Patty was not amused. Her attorney notified Skelton that Patty objected to the lampoon of the sisters' feud and said she "frankly did not think the burlesque funny." Skelton told the press, "What's the matter with Patty? Has she lost her sense of humor?"[40]

Meanwhile, the sisters' personal relationship continued to deteriorate. On May 28, 1954, Patty Andrews filed a suit asking the Superior Court to force her sister LaVerne to give an accounting of their mother's estate. The suit stated that LaVerne was administrator of the $40,650 estate of Olga Andrews, who left half the estate to LaVerne and the other half in equal shares to Patty and Maxene. Most of the estate consisted of the family home then occupied by LaVerne. Patty wanted the property divided so she could receive her share.[41]

In early November, Patty filed another suit against LaVerne in Superior Court in Long Beach, California. The courtroom was packed with spectators. Dressed in "a spectacular white mink coat and red polka dotted white gloves," Patty was accompanied by her attorney and husband Wally Weschler while LaVerne was backed by her attorney and sister Maxene, a volunteer witness. Patty demanded that LaVerne provide an accounting of their father's estate and that she be cited with contempt for failing to distribute the property of their mother's estate. Patty produced a list of itemized contents—appraised at $200,000—of her late parents' Brentwood home. LaVerne said the valuation

While Patty Andrews was pursuing a solo career, Maxene (left) and LaVerne continued the act as a duo. They guest-starred on Red Skelton's television show where Skelton donned a wig and filled in for the absent Patty. (Robert Boyer Collection)

was a gross exaggeration and the contents were worth only about $10,000, the house itself about $60,000. Patty admitted that she had received eight furs and other articles owned by her mother as gifts from her father, but she wanted an accounting of the entire personal property so she could receive her fair share.

The judge ruled that the accounting of the father's property had been filed and would be heard at a later date. LaVerne and Maxene both told reporters they were confident the property had been equitably distributed.[42]

No follow-up story appeared regarding Patty's demand for an accounting of their father's property, but in early March, the court denied her petition against LaVerne regarding their mother's property. Ten days later a news story reported that Maxene and LaVerne filed suit against Patty in Superior Court seeking a court order "against Patty for the return of that part of the estate already distributed to her under their mother's will" so the court could then distribute the estate equitably among the sisters.[43] The attorney for Maxene and LaVerne said he hoped the complaint would lead to an amicable settlement of differences among the sisters. Apparently such was the case; nothing further was reported of the suit.

In early December 1954, Maxene and LaVerne joined singer Billy Daniels, Dave Barry, and the Spence Twins for an eleven-day Australian tour of Sydney, Melbourne, and Brisbane. If audiences liked them and if they enjoyed performing as a duo, Maxene and LaVerne planned to pursue the act without adding another "sister."[44] In Sydney, they told a reporter "they were sad that their 'baby sister' Patty no longer sang with them because her husband objected."[45] Their portion of the show was a medley of past Andrews Sisters hits. A friend of Maxene later recalled the memories of the tour she shared with him: "Maxene said that they performed in 'boxing rings' and they were constantly rotating before the audience. She said they sang the 'old Andrews Sisters' songs swapping harmony and lead parts, and had a ball. They loved Australia."[46]

Maxene and Laverne returned from Australia shortly before Christmas, and on December 22, headlines across the nation announced that Maxene Andrews attempted suicide by taking an overdose of sleeping pills. Reports varied as to what really happened. Maxene's housekeeper told reporters her employer had been "brooding a lot over trouble with her sister Patty."[47] She said Maxene seemed very depressed as she trimmed a Christmas tree with her children before going to bed. About 2 A.M. Maxene called the housekeeper and told her she had taken too many sleeping pills. Another story claimed the housekeeper had a "hunch" something was wrong and went to the house to discover Maxene unconscious on the kitchen floor. The housekeeper called Gladys Leichter, who called an ambulance. LaVerne rushed to the hospital with her husband Lou Rogers, who told reporters that trouble in the family caused Maxene's despair.

LaVerne later told reporters that Maxene had not attempted suicide, but rather she was "completely exhausted … She just had to get some sleep. The housekeeper found her unconscious and rushed her to the hospital and in the excitement said Maxene must have taken 18 pills. Later she remembered there were only five pills in the bottle." LaVerne added, "Maxene loves life too much to end it."[48] Police, however, told reporters Maxene took eighteen pills in a "suicide attempt."[49] Maxene later said she took only two sleeping pills, washed them down with scotch and then became violently ill.

LaVerne and Maxene took their act to Australia in December 1954 for an eleven day tour of Sydney, Melbourne, and Brisbane. Upon their arrival, they were interviewed by an unidentified reporter. Although Australian crowds received them warmly, the sisters did not continue their act when they returned to the United States. (Robert Boyer Collection)

Maxene's cousin Gladys Leichter did not believe Maxene attempted suicide. She remembered that Maxene returned from the trip exhausted and took a couple of sleeping pills, washing them down with scotch. She passed out and her housekeepers became frightened when they found an empty pill bottle on the table and called Gladys and her brother.[50]

Patty was appearing in Las Vegas when she heard the news about Maxene. She told a reporter that she planned to call Maxene, but added, "this does not mean a reconciliation."[51] She told another reporter: "I called LaVerne as soon as I heard about this ... and she says Maxene's condition is good. I'm satisfied the accident was not of a serious nature ... I will naturally be very happy to assist the members of my family ... I don't know why this should happen. What could make her do a foolish thing like that? Our singing together again would not solve the problem."[52]

Maxene denied she attempted suicide and told reporters, "I did not try to kill myself. I'm living my own secluded life and I'm extremely happy. I'm in a good financial position and my two children have an excellent relationship with their father."[53] She said she was exhausted from the Australia trip and had never fully recovered from her 1951 surgery, which was exacerbated by a strenuous thirty-five pound weight loss diet the previous summer. Maxene told her version of the incident:

> LaVerne and I had returned from our trip to Australia last Saturday. I had gone 30 hours without sleep ... Yesterday I took the children shopping and got a tree. I had a heavy day. When I returned home I had a few drinks and then we had dinner ... I took two sleeping pills which I washed down with a drink of scotch ... I was nervous. I sat down to watch television. I became violently ill—so sick I wanted to die. I remember walking outside to the driveway and calling Bill and Vera [Zsiga, her housekeepers]. That's all I remember until this morning.[54]

Maxene was released from the hospital after her stomach was pumped. Her doctor said she was exhausted, overwrought, and suffering from a "mild nervous breakdown."[55]

Maxene revealed a great deal about her personal life in subsequent interviews, but she never again mentioned the sleeping pill incident.

In late March 1955, Patty made her New York debut as a solo performer at the Latin Quarter. A reviewer gave her show cautious approval, but thought she had too many special novelty numbers and not enough ballads; nonetheless, the reviewer noted, "Patty Andrews makes a very auspicious local café debut ... [and] is an excellent showman with a fine, professional sense of comedy and timing."[56] Another critic was more enthusiastic about the show and summarized its contents which included no Andrews Sisters songs:

> Miss Andrews has become a skilled performer on her own, armed with some excellent material. She can punch, relax and clown all over the floor as well ... Her clown bit at the closer is her major opus.
>
> She climbs into clown rig in front of the audience, whitens her face and delivers the antics that makes for what is almost a show-stopping mitt. Walter Weschler ... accomps her at the piano and sometimes takes the place of the other two sisters in giving her some comedic assists. His lifts, though, are generally confined to his handling of the musical chores; and he gives the turn considerable pacing.
>
> It is still difficult for Miss Andrews to break the association of so many years. That the act has reached a high patina is readily seen, but more important, Miss Andrews gives the impression that she has the capacity to attain depth, which is still a major measure of greatness. She's on the right track, it seems.
>
> Her material is well selected, and gives the impression of variety. She can shift easily from a ballad to a comedy number ... Weschler breaks it up with a bit of boogie-woogie ivorying which gives his wife time to catch her breath. This is Miss Andrews' first time around as a single in New York. With her firm foundations, she'll be back and probably with more stature.[57]

The following month *Variety* carried a full-page ad for Patty Andrews' act. Surrounding her picture were glowing quotes from various critics, and a bottom note announced she was scheduled to guest star on *The Jimmy Durante Show* on NBC-TV.[58]

In May, Patty Andrews signed a contract with Capitol Records.[59] Released in June, her first Capitol recording was "Where To, My Love?" and "Without Love." Neither side went anywhere on the charts.

In late August, Patty was in the news when she cancelled an engagement at the Chez Paree in Chicago over a billing row. The Chez Paree, the premier nightclub in Chicago at the time, typically booked two major acts. Outside the club, one act was advertised on one side of the marquee and the second act was advertised on the other side. The two acts alternated opening the show. Patty was unhappy with the arrangement. Wally Weschler, her accompanist-manager-husband, claimed Patty's agency misrepresented the terms of the contract for the engagement. He said Patty normally received 100 percent "sole star billing but the contract for this date … reads only 100% equal billing." Patty was unwilling to share billing with ventriloquist Jimmy Nelson who also claimed his contract guaranteed 100 percent sole billing.[60] She told a reporter, "There are two stars in this show and there's only room for one … Jimmy and I are getting top billing. In show business the gauge is by the customers that come to see you. We don't know whether the customers are coming to see us or to see Nelson."[61] Patty left Chicago for New York where she planned to read for the lead in Anita Loos' musical *Amazing Adele*.[62] She did not get the part.

In early September, Capitol released Patty's second record, "Suddenly There's a Valley" and "Booga-Da-Woog." Other versions of "Suddenly There's a Valley" hit the charts, but Patty's did not. Nor did its flip side.

In late September, Patty Andrews was back in Reno at Mapes Skyroom where *Variety* once again liked her act:

> Patty Andrews … is no longer simply a singer. She's a one-woman road show, complete with trunk for quick changes on stage.
> Building steadily through a series of "acts," Miss Andrews romps, belts and croons as if each number is the climax—and just about each one is … But production items are the big business. An original number by husband—accompanist Walter Weschler dolls her up like Sadie in floppy hat, parasol and boa. This is "The Rain Came Down," done with humor and abandon … She moves smoothly … into her finale, a song-talk about women seeking fame. This is propped by a trunk which suddenly appears. She opens it, steps behind, and with a circus band behind her, makes up into an authentic clown.[63]

A reviewer who saw her show at Ciro's in Hollywood in mid–October was guardedly enthusiastic:

> Miss Andrews has developed a comedy turn that has plenty of exuberance, but she still needs to smooth some rough edges for best results. Singer wisely eschews the tender ballads for the comedics and much of the material has zing. But there's a tendency to mouth the lyrics too rapidly … She clowns with husband-accompanist Wally Weschler, who has his own keyboard spotlight stint, and builds to a walloping finale in "Lady Clown."[64]

In early November, Patty's third Capitol record was released, "The Rains Came Down" and "I'll Forgive You." The first song, written by her husband Wally Weschler, was used successfully in her nightclub act, but it didn't go anywhere on the charts. Ditto the flip side.

In January 1956, Patty was back in Las Vegas, this time at the Riviera where she shared the bill with three other acts, including a family of chimps. They were having trouble pulling in customers when a reviewer caught the show: "Patty Andrews is the bigger name draw in Vegas … but even her appeal will not bring in big demands for tables these four frames. There is no overabundance of spenders around to fill each nitery room, and some spots will be left on the short end. This looks like one of the places."[65]

The following month, Capitol Records placed a full-page ad in *The Billboard* announcing Patty Andrews' new recording "I Never Will Marry" and "Daybreak Blues." It was reviewed in the following issue: "The theme [of 'Daybreak Blues'] depicts the letdown after a night of frivolity. An engaging lyric and relaxed performance ... Folk flavored item ['I Never Will Marry'], with chanted choruses in a construction to 'Old Smokey.' Thrush sings it simply and with effect."[66] The record did not chart.

After Maxene and LaVerne's tour to Australia and Maxene's bout with sleeping pills, the two sisters ended their pursuit of a career together. LaVerne took a sabbatical from show business, but Maxene went to New York to study theater. Her coach encouraged her to pursue a solo act and got her an audition at the Blue Angel club.[67] Maxene remembered:

> I did a bang-up audition ... one of the owners adored me. I got a two-week engagement. I was afraid that everybody would think they were going to hear Patty ... So for identity I thought it would be amusing to open with the first 16 bars of "I'll Be With You In Apple Blossom Time" in harmony. Then I stopped and said, "I can't sing any more of the song because the rest of the harmony is my sisters." But nobody laughed, and after a few nights I asked for a release.[68]

Variety published a kind review of what was apparently not a great show:

> Maxene Andrews, one of the Andrews Sisters when it was a trio, worked under that tag when it shrunk to a duo after Patty Andrews went into business for herself. The soeurs are now fragmentized into three singles....
>
> Miss Andrews' current date shows an unfamiliarity on two points, working solo and in a small room, but she indicates that once she attains a little more authority on both scores she'll be able to set up shop in virtually any pop vocal situation.
>
> She has come equipped with standards and special material, which serve her needs well. Her exit tune is a rib on Bridey Murphy which has strong qualities, and there's another on not wanting a big wedding—"just a wedding"—that also hits it excellently with the crowd. Current catalog puts a stress on personality.
>
> Miss Andrews handles her tunes well, despite the fact that she's on unfamiliar ground. Her pops hit the mark and, at this point, she passes muster. However, she should gather strength with each succeeding engagement.[69]

Maxene did not enjoy singing alone. She said she kept trying to sing harmony, but there was no one to harmonize with. She later admitted, "after the second night I lost interest."[70] When she closed at the Blue Angel, she did not book elsewhere.

Meanwhile, the ice began to thaw between Patty and her sisters.

Professionally, none of the sisters was setting the world on fire. Patty's solo career was going nowhere. Reviewers generally liked her show, but they almost always compared her to the trio. She was an Andrews sister, and her early act included some of the old numbers because that's primarily what the audiences came to hear. Had she never been an Andrews sister, few probably would have come to hear her. Patty's Capitol recordings never caught on either. They are as listenable today as many of the songs from that era, but the public didn't buy them, probably for the same reason her live performances were not great successes. Maxene later commented that Patty was unsuccessful singing alone, not for any lack of talent, but because "the public was not ready to accept the split of the Andrews Sisters."[71] She told another reporter, "The public wasn't ready for just one of us. We were a household word as sisters, as a family, and the public seemed to resent any squabbling or a separation."[72] And still elsewhere she said, "The public loved the Andrews Sisters, and they put their blinders onto Patty's talent."[73]

Maxene and LaVerne's try as a duo didn't work either. In the public mind, the Andrews Sisters were Patty, Maxene, and LaVerne, not just Patty and not just Maxene and LaVerne. Maxene's flirtation with a solo career bombed, and coincided with the sisters' move toward reconciliation. LaVerne was also apparently ready to become an Andrews sister again; those many years performing before an adoring audience were pulling her back. Maxene summed up the years apart: "It just didn't work out for any of us."[74]

Money was perhaps the most important factor that brought the sisters back together. The incomes of Maxene and LaVerne virtually disappeared when the trio split and Patty's was considerably reduced. When the sisters played Las Vegas a year before their split, they received $15,000 a week. When Patty played there alone, she received $1500 a week.[75] It didn't take an economist to determine the sisters were financially better off as an act. Patty once quipped to a New York reporter who asked her about the sisters' reunion, "Money is thicker than blood."[76] Years later when they were guests on *The Tonight Show*, Johnny Carson asked them about their split. Patty jokingly said, "You know that old bit about the family stays together ... well, if it wasn't for the loot."

Beyond the professional and financial incentives for reuniting, strong emotional reasons must have been at play also. Given the weighty influence of their parents and their role in the early years of their act, the sisters must have felt guilt, and perhaps a sense of betrayal to their parents, when they broke up. Maxene once said her mother always told them, "Sisters stay together. Have love. It will be your strength"—perhaps remembering the early loss of her own three sisters. LaVerne acknowledged the sisters' bond: "We've been together since childhood, missed meals together, huddled together in the same bed as scared and worried kids. We'd been together so long we worked as one person; we thought identically; even made the same mistakes simultaneously. There was a blending, our voices balanced perfectly."[77]

After they got back together, the sisters all agreed that splitting was one of the best things that happened to them. Patty told a reporter, "We had worked so hard we never had time for our personal lives ... We even spoke like a trio."[78] Elsewhere she said that when they got back together "we were able to look at problems and situations and see how ridiculously small they were and that they didn't mean anything. And when we got together in 1956 up until the time that LaVerne passed away, that's the only time that we really enjoyed our work."[79] LaVerne told a reporter:

We had spent 14 years getting in each other's way and living each other's lives ... Trouble was inevitable. It hung around us day and night ... We worked so hard we had no time to make friends, build happy marriages—or even have any hobbies. So it was only natural our chief pastime was getting in each other's hair ... There are so many points on which we would advise any young entertainment group—sisters or not—just starting out ... First would be don't spend too much free time with each other ... Think as individuals ... Patty, Maxene and I aren't the least bit alike personally. We have different tastes different kinds of friends.[80]

In early 1956, Jonathan Productions, an independent film production company, explored the idea of a film based on the lives of the Andrews Sisters. Hollywood gossip writer Hedda Hopper claimed a film about the Andrews Sisters was "signed up." Actresses would portray the sisters and lip-synch their songs.[81] David Susskind, who bought the rights for the proposed film, was instrumental in bringing the sisters back together—even though the film never materialized. At the time, Patty was not speaking to Maxene and only occasionally to LaVerne. LaVerne remembered: "A strange thing happened during those discussions with David Susskind ... We discovered we actually were enjoying each other's company. By then each of us had settled private lives so returning to our career seemed a logical move."[82]

The CBS network was also instrumental in bringing the sisters back together when the network asked them to appear on a television special called *Shower of Stars*. The sisters apparently decided to use the show to test the waters for a possible reconciliation. Telecast February 16, 1956 (Patty's 38th birthday), and billed as "A musical review of your favorite 'million-record' stars," the show also featured Frankie Laine, Georgia Gibbs, Rudy Vallee, Red Skelton, Gary Crosby, and Gene Austin. Skelton introduced the sisters and said Maxene flew in from New York and Patty came from Las Vegas to join LaVerne in Los Angeles for the occasion. He claimed each song in the medley was a Gold Record for the sisters, whereas in fact only three of the seven songs they sang were million sellers. Patty soloed "I Can Dream, Can't I?" and joined her sisters for "Bei Mir Bist Du Schoen," "South America, Take It Away," "Don't Fence Me In," "In Apple Blossom Time," "Pennsylvania Polka," and "Beer Barrel Polka." The sisters appeared svelte in matching pastel street-length gowns with cinched waists and flaring skirts. Their stage personae revealed no evidence of their two-and-a-half year feud. Maxene remembered that when they appeared for the rehearsal, the music began and they sang together "as if we'd never been parted."[83] LaVerne claimed that after their appearance, they received 2,000 letters from fans urging them to reunite.

The Andrews Sisters decided to bury the hatchet.

On June 4, 1956, Patty, Maxene, and LaVerne Andrews hosted a press luncheon at the famous Brown Derby restaurant in Hollywood to announce their reunion. The theme of the reunion was "Bury the Hatchet," and the luncheon was concluded with a cake topped by a partially buried hatchet. The next day, newspapers across the country carried a photo of the sisters with their "bury the hatchet" cake and a brief story of their reunion that reported "they will return together to the singing, acting and recording career that earned them eight million dollars before they parted in anger three years ago,"[84] perhaps the chief incentive for their reunion. As a nineteen-year-old college student, I remember seeing the photo of the sisters cutting the cake, and feeling a warm happiness that my favorite singers were back together. Millions of other Andrews Sisters' fans must have felt the same way. At the luncheon, the sisters announced a new contract with Capitol Records and their initial recording session the following week. The Flamingo in Las Vegas would host their reunion show at the end of the month and they were scheduled for a TV special in the fall, which never materialized.[85]

The *Variety* story that announced the Andrews Sisters' reunion was located directly above a column called "Top Talent and Tunes." The top singer of the week was a young man named Elvis Presley who had three songs in first place, "Heartbreak Hotel," "I Want You, I Need You," and "My Baby Left Me." A new music called "rock and roll"—increasingly synonymous with this new singer—had crept into the popular music scene since the sisters separated some two and a half years previously. The top songs of the day were sung by a collection of strange bedfellows including Elvis Presley, Perry Como, Bill Haley, Peggy Lee, Pat Boone, Little Richard, Doris Day, the Four Lads, and the Chordettes. Most considered the new music a "craze," another of those occasional fads that upset the pop music scene a season or so before going away. "Rock and roll" was not going away, however. It would change the course of the history of popular music—and would exclude the Andrews Sisters.

Other trios of singing sisters were filling the public's need for sister groups when the Andrews Sisters reunited, especially the Fontane Sisters and the McGuire Sisters. Bea, Margie, and Geri Fontane (their family name was actually Rosse) learned harmony from their choir director mother in New Milford, New Jersey, where at an early age they began singing in public. In the late 1940s, their NBC radio show was broadcast from New York and they made several guest appearances on Perry Como's *Chesterfield Supper Club*, which they eventually joined as regulars. When Como moved to television, the Fontane Sisters moved with him and began recording with him on RCA, a combination reminiscent of Bing Crosby and the Andrews Sisters.[86] They eventually left Como and charted a string of hits on their own, including "Hearts of Stone," "Seventeen," and "Lonely Days and Lonely Nights." When the Andrews Sisters reunited, the Fontane Sisters were familiar names on the charts.

Even more popular were the McGuire Sisters—Phyllis, Dorothy, and Christine. Weaned on the music of their ordained minister mother's church, the sisters' big break came when they appeared on Kate Smith's radio show for eight weeks in 1952. Shortly thereafter they won first place on the *Arthur Godfrey's Talent Scouts* television program. Invited to sing on Godfrey's morning show for a week, they ended up staying on *The Arthur Godfrey Show* for six years. The McGuire Sisters first made the charts in 1954, and by the time the Andrews Sisters reunited, their many hits included "Sincerely" and "Goodnight Sweetheart, Goodnight," and they were the top female singing group in the country. By chance, they appeared at the Brown Derby the day the Andrews

In early June 1956, the Andrews Sisters hosted a "bury the hatchet" press party at the famous Brown Derby restaurant in Hollywood to announce their reunion after a two-and-half-year separation. (Author's collection)

Sisters announced their reunion. The two trios met and confessed admiration for one another.[87]

As announced at their reunion luncheon, the Andrews Sisters opened at Las Vegas' Flamingo in late June. Patty's husband Wally Weschler resumed his triple role as musical director, piano accompanist, and personal manager. The

Andrews Sisters' new show opened with "I Was Born to Be with You" to let the audience know the sisters had resolved their differences. They then segued into a medley of former hits as they joked about their recent feud. Patty sang her traditional lead, but the show differed from earlier ones in that Maxene and LaVerne also each had solos. Maxene sang "I Could Have Danced All Night" from the currently popular Broadway musical *My Fair Lady* (starring a new Andrews name), and LaVerne sang "Walk Hand in Hand with Me." Apparently part of the sisters' new arrangement gave Maxene and LaVerne more of the spotlight. The show ended with each sister attempting to sing solo unsuccessfully until the others joined to properly conclude the song.[88] A reviewer who saw their show thought they were still top entertainers:

> The Andrews Sisters return together to the nitery biz with a four stanza turn at the Flamingo, and as far as the fans are concerned, the trio sums it up in their opening shot, "I Was Born to Be with You." Gals never sounded better and there's no reason why they should not resume their role among the surefire regulars on this gold-dust circuit ... They place emphasis on their avowed pledge that the "war" is over when they take time out to kid the woes that befall an act such as their's when they're split apart. During latter ... each takes a solo turn at it, failing to register until joined by the remaining pair. Exaggerated though it may be, it's nonetheless so true.[89]

Patty later remembered, "[W]hen we started the act again, it was like being reborn."[90] She told a reporter at the time, "Most of the audience was in tears, and so were we."[91] Maxene recalled: "When we got back together people cried and came backstage to tell us to never fight again and always stay together."[92] LaVerne told a reporter: "It just wasn't wanting to sing together again, [it was that] the public never wanted us to break up."[93] And the sisters were doubtless happy with the checks that began coming in again.

In October, Capitol Records carried a full-page ad in *The Billboard* to announce the Andrews Sisters' first new record since their reunion, "Crazy Arms" and "I Want to Linger," backed by an orchestra conducted by their former musical director Vic Schoen. A reconciliation of sorts had occurred with this old collaborator as well. Schoen would occasionally work with the sisters in the future, but never on a permanent basis. "Crazy Arms" was a popular hit on the country charts, but the Andrews Sisters' version went nowhere. Nor did its flip side.

In late November, the sisters replaced Vic Damone who bowed out of a scheduled three week date at the Moulin Rouge in Hollywood.[94] A reviewer noted: "And they come up with a socko show with all the old Andrews fervor. It's like the old time religion, a refreshing look at real talent after all the rock and roll gaff that's been sluffed off as talent."[95] A couple weeks later they ran a two-page ad in *Variety* with their picture surrounded by excerpts from reviews of their show. The reviews were, of course, all glowing and several claimed the sisters were better than ever.

In December 1956, the film biography of the Andrews Sisters proposed by David Susskind was still in the works. According to a news story, Susskind

Three months after their reunion in 1956, LaVerne (left), Patty and Maxene were back in the recording studio—this time with Capitol Records. Their first Capitol release was "Crazy Arms" and "I Want to Linger"—neither of which made the charts. The sisters would never again have a hit record. (Robert Boyer Collection)

and his partner planned to spend two million dollars on the film if they could find a major studio to finance and release it. Susskind, who owned the film rights to the story, said, "It's going to be a very hard-hitting film" along the lines of *I'll Cry Tomorrow*, the story of alcoholic Lillian Roth. A one-hundred

LaVerne, Maxene, and Patty Andrews give it their all in a rehearsal session at
the Moulin Rouge in Hollywood, November 1956. Occasionally the sisters would
not be speaking offstage, but onstage they always displayed the fun and intimacy
that endeared audiences to them. (Author's collection)

page script had been completed which the sisters had not seen. Susskind bought
the story from the sisters for a flat fee and a percentage of the profits. Under
the terms of the contract, the sisters had no say about how they were portrayed
or who portrayed them—a provision insisted upon by the sisters "so there
wouldn't be any further inter-family squabbling," according to Maxene. Patty
added, "If we had the right to change the story, we might insist on changing
the meatiest part of it. And we don't want to do that. We want it to be factual."

Susskind said the handling of Peter Andrews would be one of the "hard-
hitting elements" of the film. He continued: "Their father was a very power-
ful patriarch, and ran the girls with an iron hand. He was a Greek, and it was
the only way of life he knew." Susskind planned to rewrite the 1940 gun incident with Peter: When Maxene told her father she planned to marry Lou Levy,
he belted her across the mouth, got a gun, and went out looking for Levy. New
York police picked him up and jailed him before he found Levy. Susskind said,
"Each of the girls, in their romantic life, seemed to be searching for an image
of their father. I hate to get Freudian about this, but parents do have an inor-
dinate influence on children." He added, "As you know the girls have had some
unhappy marriages. We aren't going to pull any punches in that part of the

story." Susskind said the picture would spare no details when it came to telling about the sisters' recent split. Actresses rumored to play the sisters were Eva Marie Saint as Patty, Susan Hayward as Maxene, and Donna Reed as LaVerne. Maxene said, "They can't put three glamour girls in there. The public knows our faces too well." She continued, surely jokingly, "I think Lauren Bacall would be good for me."[96]

Nothing further was heard of the proposed film. Most likely, Susskind was unable to find financial backing.

CHAPTER THIRTEEN

1957–1968

I love the Andrews Sisters ... The girls may not be as pretty as the McGuire Sisters or as young as the Lennon Sisters, but they can still back any trio into a corner when it comes to standing up and belting out a song.[1]

Nightclub dates, television appearances, and unsuccessful records characterized the decade of the Andrews Sisters' career that spanned the late 1950s to the late 1960s—and the decade's end brought the death of LaVerne Andrews.

The sixties was one of America's most creative periods for pop music and totally changed the direction of the genre, but the Andrews Sisters did not participate in that creativity. They occasionally dabbled in current songs, but for the most part their act became increasingly nostalgic, relying on hits from their Decca days—whether in the nightclub or on the television screen. The sisters still lived in southern California, with occasional forays back east for nightclub and television appearances. In the sixties, however, they increasingly stayed home on the West Coast as television shifted from New York to Los Angeles, and Lake Tahoe and Las Vegas expanded as entertainment centers.

I uncovered little about the private lives of the sisters during this period. They pursued their individual lives independently and saw one another primarily at rehearsals, recording sessions, and when they hit the road for personal appearances. LaVerne continued to live with her husband Lou Rogers in the Andrews family home in Brentwood. They acquired a retail liquor store which Rogers managed in a mini shopping mall that they eventually bought. Several people told me that LaVerne developed a serious drinking problem during this period, but few wanted to discuss it. Sometime during the decade,

Maxene sold her small ranch and moved to Encino where Patty also lived with her husband Wally Weschler, who continued in his tri-part role of manager-arranger-accompanist.

Their records didn't make it to the charts anymore, but the Andrews Sisters' fans still flocked to their personal appearances—and the critics continued to give them good marks. In early August 1957, the sisters were at the Beverly Hills in Newport, Kentucky, where a *Variety* reviewer noted that their act consisted of "a half-hour cycle of pops, highlighted by a medley of their disk clicks ... Attractive in matched pink-plumed gowns, the sisters blend expert routines with solo and ensemble chirping."[2]

The sisters were back on the West Coast in early September where they opened in Reno with the same show. A reviewer reported: "The identifying sound of the threesome hasn't changed."[3] While at Palm Springs' Chi Chi in late January 1958, a reviewer heeded their costumes and additional pounds almost as much as their music.

> [T]he Andrews Sisters ... appeared in huge, flaming red coats of slipper satin that would be great as a style to glamorize pregnant little mamas ... Halfway through they toss away their carmine cloaks and reveal themselves in lace frocks studded with rhinestone over faintly tinted pink slips. In a second showing they change to blue frocks plug and sing snips of their new disks, convincing the house that when it comes to harmonizing and original styling, no singing group can top them.
>
> They pull out some high stools ... and try some harmonizing sitting down. They sing just as well either way but they are so well nourished that this sort of relaxation involves risks that may send them all to slenderella mornings if they don't watch out.[4]

From Palm Springs, the sisters flew to Miami for their first appearance in that city where a reviewer liked their show and noted "their look is now on the matronly side."[5] In March, they headlined Hollywood's Moulin Rouge, and in late June, they were in Cincinnati. Their act now included an audience sing-a-long and a 1920s flapper segment that would remain a staple for their remaining career:

> In rolling out ... their many other hits of yesteryear, the Andrews trio maintains solid going over a 33-minute route by injecting rousing capes polished with clever stepping and production routines. Gals are dazzling in sequined gowns of yellow, green and blue which allow onstage changes for clowning in sack effects and reduced lengths for Charleston dance takeoffs. Have the tablers joining in an illuminated song-slide novelty of "Show Me the Way to Go Home."[6]

In early October the Andrews Sisters were back yet again at The Flamingo in Las Vegas, this time sharing the bill with the Mills Brothers. A reviewer reported: "They generate the same excitement and popularity as they did in those wild wonderful years before rock and roll and Presley."[7] The sisters returned to Vegas at the Sahara Hotel to close out 1958 and usher in 1959.

Late 1950s costumes of the Andrews Sisters that led one reviewer to suggest they would "be great as a style to glamorize pregnant little mamas." The cloaks covered other dresses that were revealed later in their act. (Author's collection)

In late February 1959, thcy took their show to Harrah's in Lake Tahoe, which was becoming an important entertainment center in northern California. They shared the bill with an up-and-coming comedy team named Rowan and Martin, who in a few years would revolutionize television with their *Laugh In* variety show: "The Andrews, who need simply to walk on for approval, had

The Andrews Sisters share a cramped dressing room as they apply makeup prior to a personal appearance circa 1958. (Robert Boyer Collection)

the tablers from their initial offerings to the last."[8] The sisters joined other celebrities on June 13 at the Shrine Auditorium in Los Angeles at a benefit for the Del Mar Child Care Service. Shortly after the benefit, they opened at New York's Latin Quarter, their first foray into the Big Apple in ten years. New Yorkers gave them a warm welcome back as enthusiastically reported by a reviewer who was especially impressed by their staging:

> The Andrews Sisters have come back to New York … with a crackerjack turn … The past decade has matured this pop vocal trio into a highly savvy combo that knows how to parlay music, nostalgia and comedy into a whammo payoff … It's a great songbook and this trio delivers in a highly listenable style doubly welcome in its contrast with the contemporary vocal groups riding the rock 'n' roll breakers.
>
> But even more important than their singing is the staging of the act. It's loaded with nifty pieces of business which look so casually inserted and ad libbed but which … made it a standout sight-and-sound turn. After opening with a group of the old disk hits … the gals go into a quick gown change for their piece de resistance, a rundown of tunes from the 1920s … With Patty in the pivot slot, the short-skirted trio performs the jazz age numbers with a dash and humor.[9]

The Andrews Sisters ham it up backstage with comedian Jack Durant and singer Johnny Ray in June 1959. The sisters were in New York at the Latin Quarter, their first engagement in the city in ten years. (Robert Boyer Collection)

The sisters traveled north to Montreal where the Canucks liked them as much as the New Yorkers did: "They still bring a whole powerhouse of energy to their act and after all these years, they still give the impression of getting a naïve and girlish kick out of what they do for a living ... The Andrews, good show people, and ever ready to please an audience, oblige, and the result is nostalgic musical journey back into the recent past of popular music."[10] After Montreal, the sisters were in Washington, D.C., at the New Lotus Club where a reviewer reported: "It's a high spirited romp through musical nostalgia, performed with zest and a fine flair for fun."[11] Concluding a glowing review, another reviewer wrote: "Let's face it, these dolls ARE show business."[12] In late August, the sisters took their show to Atlantic City, site of many performances during their early road days. While at the 500 Club, they left their signatures, handprints, and footprints in cement in the "Sidewalk of Stars" in front of the club.[13] During October and November, they played dates in Boston, Pittsburgh, and Cincinnati before returning home to California.

After a holiday break, the Andrews Sisters opened in early January 1960 for two weeks at the Blue Room in the Hotel Roosevelt, New Orleans—one of their regular venues since their first appearance there with Leon Belasco in 1937. A critic concluded his enthusiastic review: "The sisters wear well, and with everything else said and done, the show is a darned good one."[14] In early February, they were back in Las Vegas for a four-week run at The Riviera sharing the marquee with Dennis Day. The usual accolades greeted them as they won over the Vegas crowd.

The Andrews Sisters headed for London in December to wrap up the year and usher in 1961 at the Talk of the Town, their first visit to England in nine years. Before their arrival, Patty gave a telephone interview to a British music magazine and expressed the Andrews Sisters' dislike of rock and roll: "We think the quality of the American Hit parade is very bad." She mistakenly predicted that rock was "rapidly on the way out in the states" and added, "Fortunately, people are going over to a better type of music." She promised Londoners a very different act from the Andrews Sisters, and said there would be no rock music. She also said the Andrews Sisters would cut several records while in London.[15] The Brits came out to see them, and as in the past, they liked them:

> The three sisters have a natural flair for showmanship. Their act gives an impression of spontaneity, despite its split-second precision, and though their routine is 45 minutes of unabashed corn, it has a gaiety and vivacity that lifts it out of the ordinary ... The girls are in good form, sing well and clearly, and harmonize to perfection.[16]

On New Year's Day, the sisters took their act to *Sunday Night at the London Palladium,* a London television show.

The sisters returned home and didn't hit the road again until July when they opened at the Cal Neva Lodge in Lake Tahoe. In late September, they were at Las Vegas' the Thunderbird where they told a reporter they'd still like to do a Broadway musical. The good reviews continued for their act: " Experience has saturated the Andrews Sisters with showmanship savvy which keeps the trio a top-level attraction—in fact the individual voices seem better than ever, and their harmony is second to none ... At the first show they were having so much fun—and so was the audience—they ran about half hour overtime."[17] This was the Andrews Sisters last engagement in Las Vegas as a trio.

Following their Vegas engagement, the sisters returned home to southern California, which was tinder dry after a long, hot summer. In early November, one of California's infamous fires began in the San Fernando Valley. It quickly grew out of control and moved toward Sepulveda. The morning of November

6, the Andrews Sisters had planned a rehearsal in the family home where LaVerne lived with her husband. Patty called LaVerne and said she was unable to come because roads were closed and people were urged to stay home. LaVerne was watching the progress of the fire on television, but didn't think her home was in danger. However, early afternoon, she called Patty in a panic and said she had been ordered to evacuate the house because the fire had moved from Sepulveda and threatened the Bel Air area where the Andrews family home was located. Maxene learned of the danger, called LaVerne and told her to put the silver in the swimming pool along with anything else that could survive the water. LaVerne did so and as the fire approached, she and her husband abandoned the house after taking what few valuables they could pack into the car. The fire quickly spread to the Andrews property and the storm created by the heat was so charged that the house literally exploded, completely destroying it and everything within. Maxene had prepared scrapbooks of the scripts of the Nash-Kelvinator radio shows to give Patty and LaVerne for Christmas, but they were lost with other mementoes of their career—including clippings and photos their mother began collecting when they were children.[18]

The fire was one of California's great disasters in terms of property loss, second only to the 1906 San Francisco earthquake. The conflagration consumed 456 homes, including those of Burt Lancaster, Joan Fontaine, Zsa Zsa Garbor, and Joe E. Brown.[19] The loss of their family home was a great blow to the sisters, especially LaVerne. She and her husband eventually rebuilt on the property.

In February 1962, the sisters went to the Chi Chi in nearby Palm Springs where another reviewer noted their extra pounds: "The Andrews Sisters seem to be developing more bounce to the ounce (and more ounces, too) as time goes by. Bounciest of them all is blonde Patty. But all three of them are in there pitching and they never sang better than they are singing this week ... They gave a gay, lively and tireless hour of top entertainment."[20] In March, they were back at the Hotel Roosevelt in New Orleans. *Variety* caught their act during an evening of mishaps: "The Andrews Sisters ... captivate firstnighters with a musical turn that's shrewdly devised and projected with know-how ... Gals took a couple of mishaps in stride at opener. At times they either lost the stage lights or got too much light, and another time a busboy dropped a tray full of dishes."[21] In May, the sisters reunited with Vic Schoen in New York at the International where some of the music industry people of their era saw their opening show. The good reviews continued for the Andrews Sisters, still popular despite their additional pounds and paucity of recent hits:

> The Andrews Sisters will bring in a lot of business from those who fondly remember the '40s. The kids may not recall what this shouting is about, but they must certainly be able to discern the showmanship of a peak Tin Pan Alley period. One odd facet of this preem is the turnout of the song-pluggers of the era in remembrance for what the girls did for the music of their day.
>
> The ladies are still vital and vivid, albeit a bit heavier, to be ungallant about it. Their pipes and harmonies are still vibrant, and Patty's sense of comedy has not diminished. Neither has the showmanship of all the girls ... this occasion

also reunites them with their longtime conductor Vic Schoen ... It's a moment of great recollection of a time when Broadway, bands, the music business and entertainment generally were swinging. The trip through nostalgia is bound to be a lure in this spot.[22]

This engagement marked the sisters' last date in New York as a trio. In June they were back on the West Coast "Clowning and singing with a strong accent on nostalgia" and packing them in at San Diego:

Patty is spokesman for the trio ... her patter having the breezy informality of a conversation under the hair dryer. Mainly the talk is self-spoofing as to age, weight, girdle problems, wigs ("You should see this hair of mine on the dresser") et al. It's woman to woman chatter and the femmes in the audience screech with delight ... It's surefire stuff accomplished with a compelling, ageless blend of the wholesome and the earthy.[23]

In August, the sisters were at the Nugget in Sparks, Nevada. In mid–November, they took their act to Houston's the Shamrock where yet another reviewer noted their additional pounds: "The Andrews Sisters have remarkably the same harmony that made them disc starts of the 40s and other than an extra pound here or there, little seems to have changed. Most of the auditors came prepared for nostalgia, and wisely, for it flowed like wine."[24]

In late February 1963, the sisters shared the bill with Little Bertha, a baby elephant, at the Nugget in Sparks, Nevada: "Trio continues to work with much rapport, much vigor, much enthusiasm, and it's all infectious ... opening night house was adequate evidence the three have lost no popularity in these parts."[25] In August, back at the Hotel Roosevelt in New Orleans, another reviewer noted their additional pounds, which, however, he thought detracted nothing from their performance: "Bouncy trio have added a few ounces to the waistlines, which they spoof good-naturedly, but they never sang better than they are now singing ... It's a gay, lively and tireless 50 minutes of entertainment that appeals to the entire family."[26]

While in New Orleans, the Andrews Sisters learned that their eighty-seven-year-old uncle Pete Sollie died in a nursing home in Mound, Minnesota from diabetes. Their other uncle, Ed Sollie, suffered heart problems but he continued to operate the Sollie Brothers Grocery Store in Mound after Pete's death. However, the following spring on April 2 at age 81 he died while sleeping in his rocking chair in the kitchen of the family home. Both brothers were buried in Mound Union Cemetery beside their mother and father. Although the brothers operated their little store in Mound for over forty years, they were not good business men. They extended credit to customers and accumulated debts, which the auction of their estate could not pay off. Their outstanding debts were paid by their nephews and nieces.[27] The Andrews Sisters would occasionally still visit Mound, but their family ties to the little town ended with their uncles' deaths.

The Andrews Sisters' first engagement of 1964 was at Vancouver's The Cave where still another reviewer noted their additional pounds but liked what he saw and heard.[28] The sisters' extra pounds were still being noted when they appeared in July again at New Orleans' Hotel Roosevelt.[29] In October, they returned to the Nugget in Sparks where a reviewer liked them but thought their show needed updating.[30]

In late February 1965, the sisters were back at the Hotel Roosevelt in New Orleans for Mardi Gras: "Everything the sisters three ... do seems so easy, yet it's a product of skill, show business savvy and natural ability ... This trip, Patty injects a bit of audience participation fun by involving ringsiders in the twist and other new dances for top results."[31] On April 1, they opened once again at the Nugget in Sparks, Nevada, where they shared the bill with popular comedian George Gobel.[32] In late June, the Roostertail in Detroit hosted the sisters where a reporter interviewed them about their many years in show business. As many before him, the reporter was impressed by their outgoing personalities. They told him they made $1.8 million in a single year at the height of their career, but said they didn't go in for investments, which they considered a man's world. However, Maxene added, "They won't have to run any benefits for us."[33]

The sisters were quiet until mid–May 1966, when they appeared for the first time at Harvey's in Lake Tahoe where the usual accolades followed their show.[34]

The Andrews Sisters packed the clubs with their personal appearances, but they were reaching an even greater audience with their guest appearances on popular television shows. In the late 1950s when television was still centered in New York, their TV appearances coincided with their club engagements on the East Coast. Their act fit easily into the popular variety shows of the period, such as those hosted by Perry Como, Steve Allen, and the legendary Ed Sullivan. As television settled into the West Coast, the sisters stayed home and appeared on such TV staples as *The Dean Martin Show*, *The Tonight Show*, and *The Sammy Davis, Jr. Show*.

The Andrews Sisters guest-starred on *The Perry Como Show* with fellow guests Tony Bennett and Ernie Kovaks in late February 1957. Dressed in flamboyant ostrich-feather dresses, the sisters sang a medley of past hits, and joined Como in a skit that segued into a clever version of "Rum and Coca-Cola." They later appeared as marionettes with their strings pulled by puppeteers Como, Kovaks, and Bennett as they danced and sang "The Andrews Sisters Puppets" to the tune of "Pennsylvania Polka." One of the backup singers on the show was an attractive young woman named Joyce DeYoung, a long-time fan of the sisters, who would play a prominent role in their career ten years later.

In early March, the sisters appeared on *The Steve Allen Show* via remote from the new Sheraton Hotel in Philadelphia where they headlined the opening show. Dressed in slimming black dresses, the sisters opened with "Born to Sing for You," then sang a medley of their hits, and closed with "No Baby," their sole venture into rock and roll via their recent Capitol release.

The Julius LaRosa Show was their next guest appearance in mid–July. In order to form a trio for the show, LaRosa announced three ticket stub numbers and asked the holders of the tickets to come upstage. The holders were, of course, the Andrews Sisters who came from the audience. Dressed in full skirted black dresses with low bodices and decked in diamond earrings, neck-

A 1957 publicity photograph of the Andrews Sisters in the pink-plumed gowns they wore in their current nightclub act. (Robert Boyer Collection)

laces, and bracelets, the sisters sang two songs. "Of Thee I Sing" was accompanied by a dance routine, and "Stars, Stars" was introduced as their most recent Capitol release. The sisters appeared on Ed Sullivan's popular Sunday night variety show, *The Toast of the Town*, in mid–September. They sang "By His Word," their new Capitol release, and wrapped up with a medley of past hits. In early October, they joined *The Big Band*, a special show hosted by popular singer Patti Page. The sisters sang the predictable medley of hits and Patty sang "You Must Have Been a Beautiful Baby" with fellow guest Jack Leonard.

The Andrews Sisters made it to TV only once in 1958 when they joined the summer show of Bob Crosby, their old friend from *Club 15* radio days. However, during a gig at New York's Latin Quarter in June 1959 they made a flurry of television appearances, including *The Jimmy Rodgers Show, Ray Bolger's Washington Square, What's My Line?* where they appeared as "mystery guests," and *Masquerade Party* where they disguised as the Marx Brothers. While in New York, they told a reporter they had only two remaining unfilled ambitions—a Broadway show and their own television show.[35]

The Andrews Sisters had not yet lain to rest plans for their own television show. In October 1959, they announced they would spend their own money on a television pilot and three subsequent episodes to sell to a network. The show would be a situation comedy tentatively titled *The Collectors* in which the sisters would play three women who operated a bill-collecting agency. Maxene explained: "We figured ... that such a move is the most positive way to show sponsors and the public that we mean business. They'll figure if we have enough faith in our own ability to put up our own savings, then we must feel sure we can handle the job." LaVerne continued: "We decided on this move ... because we sat down one night and asked ourselves: 'Where do we go from here?' TV was the one immediate answer ... We've had just about all we can take of traveling and night clubs. During our last trip out we worked 53 straight days without a single night off."[36] All three sisters were interviewed for the story and emphasized the personal harmony in their lives since the 1954 split. Patty told the reporter: "It's wonderful to think of ourselves as partners again and to know that when we get together socially it's because we honestly want to."

To my knowledge, the TV pilot was never made. If it was, a sponsor never picked it up. This was the Andrews Sisters' last try for their own television show. A few months later, a *New York Times* story announced that the Internal Revenue Service was suing the Andrews Sisters for $230,424 in back taxes for the years 1949 to 1953.[37] Most likely, the sisters shelved their plan for the personally financed television pilot in light of the IRS suit. I found no follow-up story about the outcome of the suit.

The Andrews Sisters wrapped up their East Coast tour with an appearance on a television special called *The Golden Circle* telecast November 25, 1959. The show was a salute to twenty-five years of popular music hosted by Steve Lawrence and Eydie Gorme with guests Frankie Avalon, Nat Cole, the Mills Brothers, and Rudy Vallee. The sisters sang their usual hits medley and Steve Lawrence joined them in "South America, Take It Away." They then sang a "White Christmas" finale with the entire cast.

The sisters took a hiatus from television in 1960, but appeared on *Sunday Night at the Palladium* on New Year's Day 1961 while in London at the Talk of the Town. The year 1962 witnessed only Patty Andrews on television as a guest panelist on the popular *What's My Line?* in mid–April. The sisters' next TV appearance was *The Joey Bishop Show* in November 1963. Bishop would later have a talk-show format, but at this time his show was a situation comedy. The typically weak situation involved the sisters' visit to Bishop and his attempt to sing with them. During the course of the skit, which Patty dominated, they sang

On March 3, 1957, the Andrews Sisters appeared on *The Steve Allen Show* in a live remote from Philadelphia where they were part of the opening of the new Sheraton Hotel. Throughout the 1950s and 1960s, the sisters appeared on many of the major television variety shows. (Robert Boyer Collection)

"In Apple Blossom Time" and "Bei Mir Bist Du Schoen." The sisters' additional pounds were unsuccessfully disguised with dark dresses and loose fitting jackets in the early scenes. Later, balloon skirts were equally unsuccessful in narrowing their waists and hiding their hips.

The sisters took another hiatus from television in 1964, but made two television appearances in early 1965. In mid–January they joined Art Linkletter's *House Party* where they chatted with Linkletter and sang a medley of their hits. They made their first appearance on Johnny Carson's popular *The Tonight Show* on February 1, 1965. Instead of the usual medley of former hits, they opened with a medley of current songs, including "We Got a Lot of Living to Do," "My Favorite Things," and "I Left My Heart in San Francisco." They joked about their ages and reminisced about their USO tour during World War II. When asked when they started singing together, Patty quipped, "When was the Boston Tea Party?" The sisters had a good time. Carson joined them in their comic version of "Sonny Boy." They wrapped up the show with a medley of their polka hits, including "Strip Polka" and Patty's burlesque routine. Carson joked, "The only singing group I know that may be closed down."

In mid–November 1963, the Andrews Sisters (Patty, left, Maxene and LaVerne) appeared on *The Joey Bishop Show*. In their television appearances, they usually sang a medley of their past hits and a currently popular song, and then joined the host in a skit. (John Tyler Collection)

Following a New Orleans engagement in early March, the sisters appeared again on *The Tonight Show* with Johnny Carson in New York City. They made the predictable quips about their longevity in show business and their additional pounds—Patty said they liked to share the bill with Bertha the elephant because she made them look small. Their musical contribution to the show was a swing-style, ten minute hootenanny with audience participation that began with "One More River to Cross" and incorporated a medley of their hits. It was perhaps their most original television number and captured the sisters' great rapport with their audiences. During the week of August 2, the Andrews Sisters co-hosted the syndicated *The Mike Douglas Show*. They made their third and final appearance on *The Tonight Show* with Johnny Carson in early October 1965 and reminisced with fellow guest Jerry Lewis about their time together at the Roxy Theater in New York. The Andrews Sisters guest-starred for the first time on Dean Martin's popular television variety show, *The Dean Martin Show*, in early December 1965. They opened with their nightclub medley of current hits and Martin later joined them in a medley of their past hits.

In March 1966 the Andrews Sisters made perhaps their most memorable television appearance when they joined *The Sammy Davis, Jr. Show*. Davis introduced them with new lyrics to their old hit "Three Little Sisters" as "Three Famous Sisters." Dressed in flamboyant flapper garb, they performed the 1920s segment of their nightclub act. Later in the show, they joined Davis' other guests, the Supremes, to swap hits. As the Supremes sang snippets of Andrews Sisters' hits, the sisters responded in kind with the Supremes' hits. The two groups concluded the show with an abbreviated rendition of "The Birth of the Blues." Supremes Mary Wilson fondly remembered the session:

> We liked one another immediately ... In rehearsals we had a great time. They taught us their parts and how to sway gently, and we taught them our routines. If someone made a mistake, everyone on the set would crack up. In fact some of the goofs were so funny—especially when they would tackle our choreography—that Sammy would make them repeat the mistake for anybody who dropped by. We seemed to be laughing the whole time.[38]

The Andrews Sisters would make only two more television appearances.

The Andrews Sisters continued to record throughout most of this period, albeit not too successfully. None of their Capitol releases made the charts. Capitol also featured them on three LP albums, a format that would become their staple when they joined Dot Records after the expiration of their Capitol contract.

In early March 1957, *Variety* reviewed the Andrews Sisters' first Capitol LP, *Andrews Sisters in Hi-Fi*, a collection of their former hits for which they brought in Vic Schoen.[39] *Variety* liked the LP, which apparently sounded better in 1957 than it does today. The songs are in similar tedious tempo at a pace suggesting the sisters were eager to wrap up the recording session and get out of the studio as quickly as possible. They lack the swing of the original recordings and the sisters' voices have an edge that soon becomes irritating. The album may have entertained an audience that never knew the original songs, but to the Andrews Sisters' old fans it must have been disappointing.

In mid–May 1957, *Variety* gave a lukewarm review of the sisters' latest Capitol single: "'Give Me Back My Heart' has a likeable latino beat which the Andrews girls turn into a pleasant platter. 'Stars, Stars' gives the girls an okay showcase for their bouncy harmonizing style."[40] The record went nowhere.

Another of their Capitol singles was briefly reviewed in late August: "'By His Word' is a bright religioso effectively belted by the Andrews Sisters. 'I'm Goin' Home' is an okay ballad."[41] Again, the public was not receptive. Capitol released an Andrews Sisters Christmas record in November 1957, "Silver Bells" and "A Child's Christmas Song." "Silver Bells" never successfully competed with the many other versions of that perennial favorite, and "A Child's Christmas Song" is notable only because of the brief solos by Maxene's ten-year-old son Peter.

The Capitol singles of the Andrews Sisters were promising and possibly with perseverance and better material, they could have made it to the charts again in the early days of rock and roll—as did some of their contemporaries, such as Perry Como and Doris Day. Their contributions to cha-cha ("Torrero"), rock and roll ("No Baby"), and country-western ("Sunshine") were as good as many that were offered at the time. Years later Maxene reflected on why their Capitol records were unsuccessful:

> We had all the respect in the world for Voyle [Gilmore, production manager of Capitol], but he lacked leadership with us ... I think most every artist at that period of time needed some leadership as to the kind of music they're doing— is this the right song?—listening for a piece of music for us. We couldn't do all of that. Somebody had to be on the lookout for the Andrews Sisters, and we were not getting that at Capitol. There was no direction. None whatsoever. And we were used to a lot of direction. At Capitol, we were just floundering.
>
> We knew the interest that Decca had in the Andrews Sisters ... So, we knew because of that interest that they would want the best for us. But when we went to Capitol, there was no such feeling, and it wasn't until much later that we realized one of the reasons that Capitol wanted us is they wanted the backlog, they wanted to re-record our hits. They wanted it for their library.[42]

In later years, Patty admitted to a reporter that the sisters had trouble finding a niche in the new rock music of the 1950s: "Well, when rock came in, I didn't care for it. Because I remember when we were working, we were trying to find pop tunes to sing, and we couldn't find anything because it didn't have any lyrics ... nothing made any sense. There wasn't anything that we could do that lent to harmony. So we kind of stayed away from it."[43]

Capitol released a second LP album of Andrews Sisters' songs in fall 1957. Unlike the first one, this was not a re-recording of their earlier hits, but rather gave the sisters an opportunity to test new musical waters. Entitled *Fresh and Fancy-Free* and ably backed by Billy May and his orchestra, the album included such popular standards as "You Do Something to Me," "Tea for Two," and "Younger Than Springtime." The selections allowed the sisters to explore ballads they never tried during their heyday at Decca and they brought a fresh approach to the songs. Unlike their traditional harmonic arrangement broken by Patty's short solos, virtually all the songs were sung ensemble. *Fresh and Fancy-Free* used the distinctive harmony of the Andrews Sisters on popular standards in an upbeat mode. *Variety* reviewed the album favorably: "Here's more evidence that the Andrews Sisters still know how to set up a song. Repertoire is tip notch, and they swing 'em out in catchy musical style set down by Billy May's arrangements."[44] Maxene later told a friend that the album did not sell well, despite its enthusiastic reception by critics.[45] Probably for that reason, the sisters did not continue in this new direction. With more perseverance, however, they probably could have found a niche in the current popular music field and wouldn't have been fated to sing their old hits the remainder of their career. Unfortunately, they didn't have a Vic Schoen or Lou Levy to help guide them into the next chapter of American popular music. Capitol was not up to the task.

In spring 1958, Capitol released another Andrews Sisters' LP album called *The Andrews Sisters Sing the Dancing 20's* with orchestration once again provided by Billy May. It is unclear whether the album evolved from the flapper segment of the sisters' nightclub act, or the album inspired the club segment. The anthology is a collection of twelve songs from the 1920s backed by a twenties-style jazz band. The album was a good idea: the Andrews Sisters' style fits many of the songs of the twenties. The individual songs and arrangements are good, but when placed together in one LP, they begin to sound alike and become predictable. Greater variety was needed in the selection of material. The twenties produced some good songs, such as "Makin' Whoopie," "My Blue Heaven," "Bye, Bye Blackbird," and "April Showers," but most of them are not found in this album. Short solos by the sisters could have added variety to the arrangements, but only two of the songs have solos by Patty. On two other songs, band members assist the sisters on choruses for a welcome break. Two of the better offerings are comic numbers, "Don't Bring Lulu" and "Last Night on the Back Porch." Once again the sisters lacked a Lou Levy or a Kapp brother to direct them to the right songs and a Vic Schoen to arrange them in a listenable manner. Most of the distinctive Andrews style was missing from the album, and any number of female trios could have sung the songs as well— if not better.

In summer 1959, the sisters made their only recording for Kapp Records, a new company founded by Dave Kapp, their old friend from Decca days. Their Capitol contract had expired, but the two sides for Kapp ("I've Got to Pass Your House" and "One, Two, Three, Four") went nowhere and the company moved in directions that did not include the Andrews Sisters. While in London for an engagement at the Talk of the Town, the sisters recorded two sides for English Decca ("Sailor" and "Goodnight and Sweet Dreaming"). Neither side went anywhere.

In late 1961, the Andrews Sisters began recording for Dot Records, owned by Paramount Pictures. When Dot was founded in the early 1950s, many of its hit singles made the charts; however, when the sisters joined the record company, it was known for its LPs of past greats, such as Tony Martin, Lawrence Welk, Mills Brothers, and Louis Prima. The Andrews Sisters eventually recorded eight LP albums and three singles for Dot. Three albums were re-recordings of their early Decca hits.

The first of these, released in October 1961, was called *The Andrews Sisters Greatest Hits*, arranged and conducted by Billy Vaughn. This is probably the sisters' best collection of previously recorded hits—and certainly their best Dot album. Unlike their Capitol album of previous hits, which tried to update

In 1958, the Andrews Sisters recorded an LP of 1920s songs called *The Andrews Sisters Sing the Dancing 20's.* Shortly thereafter they incorporated several songs from the album into a flapper segment of their nightclub act that remained a staple until they retired. (Robert Boyer Collection)

the old songs with new arrangements, this collection was true to the original arrangements but the instrumental backgrounds and rhythm patterns were updated. Traditionalists will prefer the original swing backgrounds, but nonetheless the album captured the fun and *joie de vivre* of the Andrews Sisters' early songs. It was a promising start with their new record company.

Great Golden Hits. The Andrews Sisters was released by Dot Records in late September 1962. Vic Schoen was called in to arrange and conduct this LP collection of former hits. Unlike the Capitol album of previous hits that also brought Schoen and the sisters back together, this was not an attempt to recreate the original recordings. Some of the originals were sung with Bing Crosby and Al Jolson, but Schoen rearranged them for the sisters to sing alone. Even the sisters' original songs were rearranged. It seemed a good idea, but it didn't work. The arrangements were not good. Probably because of the placement of mikes, LaVerne's contralto, which normally provided a cushion for the sometimes shrillness of Patty and Maxene is difficult to hear. The sisters sound like three tough broads with hard voices parched by too much living.

In early June 1963, Dot Records released *The Andrews Sisters Present,* an album of recent hit songs of the period including "I Left My Heart in San Francisco" and "Puff, the Magic Dragon." These were other singers' hits and all were done better by the other singers. The songs are unimaginatively arranged and unimaginatively sung. At the bottom of the barrel is "Still," a recitation of saccharine lyrics by Patty backed by Maxene and LaVerne. Again LaVerne's contalto does not come through to cushion the occasional brassiness of Patty and Maxene. A refreshing exception to the bad songs in this collection is "The Doodle Song" which has no lyrics, only the sisters harmonizing with "doodle doodle doodle" to the very good piano of Wally Weschler and combo. It is perhaps the best song the sisters recorded for Dot and reveals they had not lost their touch if provided decent material.

The Andrews Sisters Greatest Hits, Volume II, backed by Allyn Ferguson and orchestra, came out in late September 1963. Another cover of their Decca hits, the songs were familiar but the Ferguson arrangements and some of the lyrics were new. For the most part, the new arrangements and new lyrics were not improvements over the old ones. Although claiming to be the sisters' greatest hits, two of the songs ("You Are My Sunshine" and "Three Little Fishies") were never recorded by them previously.

Another album of other singers' hits, *The Andrews Sisters Great Country Hits*, was released in early June 1964. The selections in this album are good, including such standards as "Ragtime Cowboy Joe," "Cold, Cold Heart," and "Wabash Cannon Ball." Perhaps better than any album, this one illustrates that good selections don't work without good arrangements. To their detriment, the sisters avoided the traditional arrangements. A very predictable guitar-strumming background, occasionally varied with deep-toned twangs, almost drowned the sisters' brassiness. This album converted no one to country music or the Andrews Sisters. *Variety* liked it better than I did: "The girls deliver in simple, unaffected style and have come up with a pleasant LP. Its mood isn't nearly as country as the material, but rather is molded for a broader pop market. As such, it registers successfully in this groove. The oldies still score and the three femmes remain strong purveyors of tunes."[46]

In late April 1965, Dot released *The Andrews Sisters Go Hawaiian*, perhaps the nadir of the sisters' recording career. Under the best conditions, popular Hawaiian music soon surfeits. This LP album contains such standards as "My Little Grass Shack," "Sweet Leilani," and "Beyond the Reef" with uninspired arrangements conducted unimaginatively by Pete King with twanging ukuleles and tired harmonizing by the sisters three. One wonders why the album was ever released. It's difficult to believe many people bought it, and those who did were probably turned off the Andrews Sisters and Hawaiian music for life.

None of the Dot releases caused any excitement on the charts. When asked about the Dot years, Maxene replied:

> Not good ... I wish I could say they were wonderful, but this is getting into the thing [of] "what to do, what to do with the Andrews Sisters," and I think Randy [Woods, the head of Dot Records] was really trying to find something that we could do. I don't know who it came from to do the Hawaiian tunes, but it really wasn't good.
>
> Nobody there ... at Dot or Capitol, knew how to handle the Andrews Sisters,

and when I say "handle," I'm talking about material. We really had nobody looking out for songs, and we had enough to take care of our own end. The song thing, that was Lou's job. The background arrangements was Vic Schoen's job.[47]

Dot Records was scratching the bottom of the barrel looking for things to do with the Andrews Sisters when they came up with *The Andrews Sisters: Favorite Hymns* in late 1965. Perhaps that is why Dot released the LP album through its subsidiary company, Hamilton Records. Using the sisters' sound and style might have provided some interesting results for such old Protestant warhorses as "The Old Rugged Cross," "Nearer My God to Thee," and "Whispering Hope." However, tedious arrangements and a groaning organ made sure that didn't happen.

In summer 1966, the Andrews Sisters celebrated LaVerne's 55th birthday on July 6 in New York City. LaVerne was ill and had been feeling unwell for some time. When the sisters returned to Los Angeles in September, she consulted her physician and a series of tests revealed she had liver cancer. LaVerne, however, did not know the seriousness of her illness. Maxene told a friend, "We played the game ... when she asked what was wrong with her, we told her she had a severe case of hepatitis. We don't think she ever knew [she had cancer]."[48]

At the time of her diagnosis, LaVerne had developed a serious drinking problem. Maxene told a reporter that her sister had lost interest in the act and was drinking heavily.[49] The sisters' cousin Gladys Leichter remembered that LaVerne often suffered nervousness prior to personal appearances, and Maxene, too, once expressed concern about LaVerne's growing anxiety. LaVerne once acknowledged nervousness and insomnia prior to radio appearances. To ease her discomfort, she began taking a drink or two before performances. Her drinking got out of hand and developed into serious alcoholism.[50] Her brother-in-law, in fact, thought she died from sclerosis of the liver from drinking: "That's what it was, sclerosis of the liver—there's no question."[51] Her death certificate reported a malignant liver tumor as the cause of death, but her drinking probably exacerbated the condition.

Ironically, LaVerne and her husband owned a liquor store in Los Angeles. After Rogers stopped playing trumpet, he was unemployed for some time. LaVerne became embarrassed about her husband's unemployment, and asked her cousin Gladys Leichter for help. At that time, the Leichters owned a retail liquor store and offered LaVerne and her husband half-ownership. They eventually bought out the Leichters and also purchased the small mini-mall where the liquor store was located. Gladys remembered that the store was an easy way for LaVerne to get alcohol.[52]

The Andrews Sisters appeared again on *The Dean Martin Show* in late September 1966, but the show had been taped some months previously. Others on the show included Duke Ellington, Lainie Kazan, Tim Conway, and Les Brown and his band. The Andrews Sisters opened with "What Now My Love?" followed by "That's How Young I Feel." Martin joined them for a medley of their combined hits and they joined the entire cast with Duke Ellington at the piano for a concluding, swinging medley of "It Don't Mean a Thing," "Hold Tight," "Hubba, Hubba, Hubba," "The Music Goes 'Round and Around," and

"Swinging Down the Lane." A month later, the sisters appeared on *The Mike Douglas Show*, also taped some weeks previously. This was the final television appearance of the original Andrews Sisters.

In early October, exploratory surgery revealed that LaVerne's cancer was inoperable and incurable. She returned to her home in Brentwood and the care of her husband Lou Rogers. Gladys Leichter frequently visited her cousin and remembered that LaVerne always asked her to bring doughnuts, a craving she had during her illness. Even Gladys was not initially told LaVerne had cancer; only late in her illness did Maxene reveal the truth.

A singer named Joyce DeYoung was invited to fill LaVerne's place in the trio. A fan of the Andrews Sisters for many years, DeYoung first saw them at Baltimore's Hippodrome Theater when she was a teenager during the war years. She met them in February 1957 when they appeared on *The Perry Como Show* where she was a singer. Eight years younger than Patty, DeYoung was no new-comer to show business, having appeared as a regular on such popular televi-sion shows as *The Fred Waring Show, The Perry Como Show*, and *The Garry Moore Show*. In addition she worked as backup singer with Dinah Shore, Danny Kaye, Jerry Lewis, Henry Mancini, and Jim Nabors. Nor was the Andrews act the first sister act DeYoung joined. In spring 1955, she filled in for a departing sister with the DeMarco Sisters where she remained a year. DeYoung also sang background for scores of records with many prominent singers.

Joyce DeYoung met the Andrews Sisters again in spring 1966 when she was singing with Jim Nabors in Tahoe. One evening after a set, Nabors sug-gested she and other members of the act go across the street to hear the Andrews Sisters, whom he knew. Following the show, they went to the sisters' dressing rooms and DeYoung was introduced to them—they did not remember her from their earlier appearance together.[53]

A few months later, in fall 1966, Wally Weschler contacted Joyce DeYoung and invited her to sing with Maxene and Patty Andrews. Patty remembered: "My husband went scouting for a replacement and so did a friend of Max-ene's. They both came up with the same suggestion—Joyce. Happily, she knew and liked our style and was able to fall right in with it."[54] Weschler did not tell DeYoung why she was being auditioned for LaVerne's place in the act and DeYoung did not ask. She later said, "I wondered why ... I didn't know LaVerne was sick. And he never told me."

Joyce DeYoung was elated at the opportunity to sing with the sisters. She met with Patty and Maxene, who did not remember their earlier meetings, and sang several songs with them. The sisters liked the blend of their voices. Since Patty and Maxene did not read music, no written vocal parts were available for DeYoung to study so she played old Andrews Sisters records to learn LaVerne's harmony. It was easy for DeYoung to sing with the sisters, having been a group singer her entire career:

> I learned on my own because I sang harmony all my life and knew how to blend. The rest I learned from playing their records over and over. As for choreogra-phy, all Patty and Maxene had to teach me was their special bow. Being onstage was nothing new to me—having been in show business for many years. The three

LaVerne, Patty and Maxene sang on *The Dean Martin Show* in September 1966, the final television appearance of the original Andrews Sisters. LaVerne reveals the illness that would eventually take her life. (Robert Boyer Collection)

of us just seemed to hit it off ... and they said my voice did not change their sound.[55]

DeYoung sang two one-night engagements with the sisters in fall 1966, including the Hollywood Palladium. They also sang a commercial for Franco-American Pizza, which played several months on television. During her time with the Andrews Sisters, DeYoung was contracted for each engagement rather than given a third of the act's earnings.

Prior to LaVerne's diagnosis, the Andrews Sisters had agreed to perform at a children's Christmas show at the Beverly Wilshire Hotel in Los Angeles sponsored by the Goldiggers Crippled Children Society, one of LaVerne's favorite charities. Patty and Maxene honored the commitment and planned the show without LaVerne, who was still ambulatory but very ill. LaVerne accompanied her sisters and sat in the front row. When Maxene and Patty began the opening number, LaVerne stood up and said, "I can't let them do it alone." She went to the stage and joined them for the entire show. It was her final performance.[56]

Joyce DeYoung remembered when she met LaVerne for the first time. Patty drove her to a fitting session for gowns for the act.

> After the fitting, we were driving home and Patty said, "Would you mind if we stop at LaVerne's house? She wants me to do her hair." I said, "Of course not." We got to LaVerne's and she got out of the car and said, "I won't be long." She went into the house, and I was still sitting in the car. I think she still wanted to protect LaVerne and not have it known that she was ill. A few minutes later Maxene came to the door—she had arrived earlier—and said "Come on in." I went into the house and sat down. One of the sisters said, "LaVerne wants to come into the living room." As soon as she walked in, I knew immediately she was very ill.[57]

DeYoung suspected LaVerne was dying of cancer, having seen her own father succumb to the disease. The family never wanted the public to know the seriousness of LaVerne's illness, probably because she herself did not know. DeYoung assumed that was why she was not told of LaVerne's illness.

In early 1967, Patty, Maxene, and Joyce DeYoung began performing regularly as the Andrews Sisters. No announcements were made to audiences to explain DeYoung's presence, although reviewers commented on the substitution.

LaVerne remained in the family home in Brentwood, where her condition deteriorated. When Patty, Maxene, and Joyce DeYoung opened at Harvey's in Lake Tahoe in early May 1967, LaVerne sent them flowers and congratulations. She contracted pneumonia on Sunday, but called her sisters in the evening to wish them a successful engagement. The next morning, a telephone call from home informed Patty and Maxene their sister had died.

LaVerne Andrews died at 8:30 A.M. May 8, 1967, at her Brentwood home with Lou Rogers, her husband of nineteen years, at her bedside. According to her death certificate, death was caused by "primary adenocarcinoma of the liver"; a malignant tumor on the liver. Notices of LaVerne's death appeared in newspapers throughout the country and around the world, including the *London Times* and the *New York Times*. Her age was variously reported as fifty-one, fifty-four, and fifty-five. She was, in fact, two months shy of her fifty-sixth birthday at the time of death.

A memorial service was held for LaVerne Andrews at the Church of the Recessional, Forest Lawn Memorial Park in Glendale, California, on May 12—

When LaVerne retired because of illness, Maxene (right) and Patty asked Joyce DeYoung (left) to join their act. DeYoung's voice blended perfectly with Maxene and Patty and she began performing with them in fall 1966. (Author's collection)

the day of her cousin Gladys' birthday. Joyce DeYoung remembered the service as particularly sad, not only because of the relative youth of LaVerne but also because it signified the end of one of America's legendary entertainment acts. The service was packed with Hollywood celebrities, friends, and relatives as recorded strains of the Andrews Sisters' songs filled the chapel. Among the

The last photograph of the original Andrews Sisters. LaVerne (right) died of cancer within months of this photograph. (Robert Boyer Collection)

"Honorary Casket Bearers" were Governor Ronald Reagan, David Kapp, and Lou Levy. "In Apple Blossom Time" was played by organist Robert Crowley. LaVerne's remains were placed with those of her parents, Peter and Olga Andrews, at the Great Mausoleum in Forest Lawn Memorial Park. Her name appears on the plaque beneath her parents' names as "LaVerne Rogers" and her birthdate is listed as 1916; she was, in fact, born in 1911.

LaVerne's will was dated November 26, 1960. The dutiful daughter to the end, she provided one thousand dollars for maintaining flowers at the memorial plaque of her mother and father "for a period of five years, or such additional period as said sum will permit." She left a ring of diamonds set in platinum to her niece Aleda Ann Levy, and noted that she had already given her nephew Peter Todd Levy "a valuable watch." The remainder of her estate was left to her husband Louis Ruggiero, "also known as Lou Rogers." In the event her husband predeceased her, she decreed that all her jewelry, furs, and personal effects go to the Golddiggers Crippled Children's Society. The remainder of her estate was to be divided as follows: 20 percent each to Patty and Maxene; 20 percent to Father Daniel Renaldo, a lifelong friend of Lou Ruggiero and also a close friend of LaVerne; 10 percent each to her niece Aleda Ann Levy and her nephew Peter Todd Levy; and 5 percent each to Patrick

Smith, Steven Smith, Diane Smith, and Geffrey Smith, children of friends. Should any of the beneficiaries die without issue before the distribution of the will's bequest, their shares would be equally divided between Patty and Maxene.

LaVerne's estate was appraised at $103,726. Her most valuable assets included the diamond ring she willed to her niece, appraised at $2,500, a 1967 Cadillac automobile appraised at $6,600, and "unearned royalties to become due under contract with Decca Records" appraised at $10,000. She owned jointly with her husband real estate appraised at $65,000 and twenty shares of stocks in Western Harness Racing Association appraised at $2,550. Additional assets were surprisingly absent from her estate.[58]

Dot Records apparently cleaned out its closet of unissued Andrews Sisters songs for the album *The Andrews Sisters: Great Performers*, released on May 19, eleven days after LaVerne's death. The liner notes reported: "This album contains some of the last recordings ever made by the original Andrews Sisters." None of these songs, including "Dixie," sung as a regimental march, and "A Man and a Woman," vocalized sans lyrics, had been issued before—for good reason. The arrangements are tedious and the sisters' voices are in bad form, a sad way for the Andrews Sisters to conclude their thirty-year recording career.

Maxene and Patty were grieved by LaVerne's death, but they continued their contracted engagements with Joyce DeYoung. Even without those obligations it would have been difficult for them to stop being the Andrews Sisters. Maxene remembered: "Even when LaVerne died, we were still working. We were a group image and also a family, so it wasn't easy to break up."[59] Patty and Maxene did not break up the act, for reasons that are contradictory in the literature. In an interview shortly after LaVerne's death, Patty told a reporter, "We didn't even consider folding up after our sister's death. When LaVerne was ill, she made it clear she wouldn't like that ... We also wouldn't know what to do with ourselves if we didn't continue working. When you start as young as we did it becomes so much a part of your life that you'd be lost without it."[60] A news story shortly after LaVerne's death claimed a "spokesman" for the sisters said, "LaVerne insisted that her sisters continue the act and still bill themselves as the Andrews Sisters."[61] However, in later years, Patty and Maxene both said they sought another singer to complete the trio in order to fulfill contracted commitments made prior to LaVerne's death. Joyce DeYoung assumed the act would continue indefinitely.

In July 1967, Patty, Maxene, and Joyce DeYoung traveled to Denmark for a month-long engagement at Tivoli Gardens in Copenhagen. *Variety* gave their show a brief review:

> The Andrews Sisters draw considerable crowds at the Tivoli-Varleteen's height-of-the-season program. Their show is over-long, almost one hour, but once nostalgia has been shattered by Maxene and especially Patty's antics, everybody in the big house settle down to joyous guffawing. Joyce de Young, who has taken LaVerne's place, seems to be left rather out of the fun though.[62]

This was the only reviewer who thought DeYoung did not blend into the act. Perhaps he saw an off-night, or perhaps he had an off-night.

Joyce DeYoung enjoyed the Tivoli engagement, despite the rigorous schedule of sixty-two shows during the thirty-one day stay. Her friendship with Maxene deepened as they explored Copenhagen. Gladys Leichter, Maxene's guest
during the engagement, joined them on their forays. They visited museums,
explored shops, and toured the Royal Copenhagen China factory at Maxene's
insistence. Patty and her husband Wally Weschler joined them at times, and at
other times explored the city on their own. The Danes loved the Andrews Sisters and the press generously covered their visit. They appeared on a popular
variety show on local television before returning to the United States.

In late August, Patty, Maxene, and Joyce were at the Hotel Roosevelt in
New Orleans—a favorite venue of the Andrews Sisters—where a reviewer felt
DeYoung blended perfectly into the act:

> Joining sisters Patty and Maxene this trip is Joyce de Young, who fits in as if she
> were part of the original act ... Dressed in wild green outfits with skirts resem-
> bling umbrellas, matching shoes, mesh stockings, beads and headbands, the
> bouncy, madcap trio serves a highly pleasing meal of harmony, rhythm and fun.
> Stanza, timed at 61 minutes, embodies much of their old material ... They also
> give a refreshing interpretation of newer tunes such as "San Francisco" and "A
> Man and a Woman" ... Patty (who handles the chatter and comedy) wins plau-
> dits with a stripper carbon. Many requests from the cheering audience for their
> evergreens suggest the Andrews Sisters need no change in vocal selections or
> routines.[63]

While in New Orleans, the Andrews Sisters also headlined a benefit show sponsored by the Police Mutual Benevolent Association for widows and orphans of
deceased police officers.[64] The sisters were interviewed during their stint in
New Orleans. Maxene and Patty told the reporter that when LaVerne became
ill they hired Joyce DeYoung until she could return to the act. Patty said, "We
weren't certain how or if we'd be accepted without the original group ... And
we weren't certain at that time if we would continue without LaVerne. It wasn't
an easy decision to make." They said the public reaction to Joyce's substitution for LaVerne was so positive, they decided to continue after LaVerne's
death. The reporter noted that Joyce was about the same height and color as
LaVerne. Patty added, "She even has the same habits LaVerne had ... LaVerne
used to go up to her room after a show and write or read until morning. She
loved to sleep late each day. Joyce has both those habits too."[65]

Joyce DeYoung remembered that audiences loved the Andrews Sisters. She
had fond memories of her time with Patty and Maxene:

> I liked both of the sisters and they were very nice to me ... One time Patty called
> and said, "Come on over to the house and watch the Academy Awards with us."
> So there we sat all evening—Patty, Wally and I—watching the Oscars in their
> den ... Patty worried when I had a cold ... And Patty and I went to see Robert
> Goulet's act in San Francisco—just the two of us. When we weren't perform-
> ing, I usually saw more of Maxene. Maxene was single and would invite me over
> for dinner or to a party ... And both girls liked to laugh. They both had hearty
> laughs, as you can tell from the videos and audios ... I enjoyed the whole expe-
> rience so much.[66]

In late October, the Andrews Sisters appeared on *The Joey Bishop Show*, their first television appearance since LaVerne's death. They opened the show with a medley of current songs, and then sang "Bei Mir Bist Du Schoen" with Bishop. They closed with "In Apple Blossom Time," requested by Bishop because it was his favorite song. Following their appearance on Bishop's show, the trio flew to Jackson, Mississippi, for a Democratic Party fund-raiser.

In early November, the Andrews Sisters arrived in Montreal for two weeks at the Queen Elizabeth Hotel where Patty told a reporter they were still approached by autograph hunters: "But they don't want them for themselves. They want them for their mothers or fathers. And we're bracing ourselves for the day when they ask for them on behalf of their grandmothers or grandfathers." When asked when the Andrews Sisters began singing together, Patty quipped, "When was Lincoln shot?"[67] In late November, they appeared with Lena Horne on Dean Martin's television show. They sang the predictable medley of former hits with Martin, and then dressed in hobo outfits for a clever number called "The Idle Rich" with Horne and Martin. Harvey's at Lake Tahoe hosted them for a twelve-day holiday engagement that ended New Year's Day 1968. A reviewer liked their show:

> The trio, outfitted in outlandish but wildly appropriate spearmint chiffon with matching slippers and hippie mesh stockings, are as fresh as the day they recorded their first big hit ... Joining the sisters Patty and Maxene is newcomer Joyce DeYoung. Joyce fits the original Sisters exactly as if she were a kissing cousin. With her, the trio seems like they always were—swaying, bouncing, joking, walking in time and bowing in unison. [68]

In late January, the Andrews Sisters played Bimbo's in San Francisco. A reviewer noted that a "cute newey" replaced LaVerne, but thought the Andrews Sisters were still "tops in talent, poise and the natural ability to please the public."[69] A few weeks later, they returned to the city for an appearance on Gypsy Rose Lee's locally produced syndicated television show. In mid–February, they were back on the Joey Bishop television show with guests Eddie Fisher and Connie Stevens. The sisters sang "The Song Is You," and Joey joined them with "South America, Take It Away." A month later, they were back on Bishop's show again with a medley of their polka hits, which segued into Patty's stripper routine for "Strip Polka." Bishop went drag in a pink dress and blond wig as Patty to join Maxene and Joyce for "In Apple Blossom Time."

A month later, the Andrews Sisters appeared on the Woody Woodbury television show with guest Frankie Avalon who claimed his mother rocked him in his cradle while listening to the sisters' "Beer Barrel Polka." The sisters talked about their trip to San Francisco and noted that people didn't recognize them anymore. A man sitting next to Patty on the plane said, "I hear they have the Andrews Sisters on the plane. Where do you think they put them?" Patty responded, "Right here!" Maxene was at the Valhalla Restaurant in Sausalito and asked a busboy to tell Sally Stanford, the legendary ex-madam restaurateur, that Maxene Andrews was there. The busboy looked all over the restaurant and returned to tell Maxene he had searched the restaurant but didn't see Maxene Andrews anywhere.

Joyce DeYoung, Maxene, and Patty appeared on *The Dean Martin Show* with fellow guest Lena Horne in late November 1967. In hobo costumes, they sang "The Idle Rich" with Martin and Horne. (Author's collection)

In early May, Patty Andrews appeared alone on the *Joey Bishop Show* for a short-notice engagement which Maxene and Joyce were unable to fulfill. She sang selections from *Mame* and *Hello, Dolly!*, which settled well with her seasoned brassy delivery. One observer noted that her performance was like an audition for a Broadway role.

But all was not well with the reconfigured Andrews Sisters. One day during a break from the road in spring 1968, Maxene invited Joyce DeYoung to lunch at her home in southern California. Midway through lunch, Maxene told DeYoung she would soon be leaving the act. The announcement completely surprised DeYoung, who had no idea Maxene was dissatisfied. Maxene did not say why she was leaving, but DeYoung later surmised it was because of mounting tensions with Patty and her husband, Wally Weschler, over finances and control of the act.

In July, Patty, Maxene, and Joyce DeYoung were back at Lake Tahoe's Harvey's for their last engagement. The crowd still liked their act:

> The Andrews Sisters again document durability with an anthology of tunes they introduced ... and it's obviously what the customers came to hear ... With annotations vis-à-vis trio's longevity in show biz, Patty ... concedes the years have

altered appearances; the 45-minute session, however, gives no suggestion of loss in enthusiasm ... The harmonizing and stylized arrangements continue to please; auditors continue to assure the threesome the Andrews way with a song is classic and enduring.[70]

On July 23, 1968, at Harvey's in Lake Tahoe, Joyce DeYoung sang for the last time with Patty and Maxene Andrews.[71] The Andrews Sisters had entertained America and much of the rest of the world for almost forty years.

CHAPTER FOURTEEN

1968–1974

Death and bitterness have split up one of the most successful acts in show business history—the Andrews Sisters.[1]

In early August 1968, Maxene Andrews called a press conference in Carson City, Nevada, to announce her retirement from show business and the beginning of her new job as dean of Tahoe Paradise College, a small liberal arts college at Lake Tahoe. When asked about Patty, she said her sister would continue performing and added, "I think she wants to do some Broadway musicals."[2]

Maxene's children were young adults now and she had few family demands. Her son Peter was a senior at the University of Southern California. Her daughter Aleda was married and also living in southern California. During the mid-1960s, the Andrews Sisters had regularly appeared at Lake Tahoe. Maxene, especially, found the forests and open spaces of the Tahoe area increasingly appealing as the smog and sprawl of Los Angeles grew increasingly unappealing. She had spent more time at Tahoe than the other sisters, and enlarged her circle of friends among local residents.

Through her new friends, Maxene met a real estate investor who recently founded Tahoe Paradise College, a four-year liberal arts school occupying a former motel and still seeking accreditation. She was originally invited to become a trustee of the college and then to join the faculty and teach music. When she revealed she couldn't read music and therefore couldn't teach it, she was asked what she'd like to teach. She suggested speech and drama, an interest dating to her New York days after the trio split in the early 1950s when she studied drama. She joined the college faculty in 1968 as speech instructor, became sponsor of the student council, was soon promoted to dean of women, and eventually took over the vice presidency in charge of planning and development—impressive positions for a high school dropout. She bought a home on a hill behind the college, "a charcoal gray and dusty pink house with a fireplace in the middle of the living room,"[3] and settled into her new life.

Shortly after her appointment, a reporter interviewed her and described the middle-aged woman he met: "She lights a Silva-Thin, a dime-sized diamond sparkling on her right hand. She has sensible square fingered hands. Her zingy navy brass-buttoned suit is designed after a French sailor's uniform. Her tawny hair is cropped pixie short. The attentive brown eyes survey you from behind oversized spectacles, the voice that belted the songs is eager, throaty."[4] When the reporter asked Maxene how she ended up in academe after so many years in show business, she replied:

> When LaVerne died, I just wasn't interested in singing any more. And, after all, we'd gone on longer than most… Why am I here? That's what I said to myself when this job came right out of left field. I would never have thought of it in my whole life. We'd worked the Tahoe area for years and last year they asked me to be a college trustee, then this summer—dean. The idea of the challenge got to me and I became fascinated with the school … all classes are in seminar. After I decided, I had the worst case of stage fright I've ever had. I couldn't sleep. I was a little nauseous, you know the feeling. And the doubts! But I find I'm more equipped than I ever dreamed I would be.[5]

The following September found Maxene in New York making the rounds of the music industry to raise funds for the school. She told a reporter, "It's a whole new world … Working and living and studying with young people is the biggest kick I've ever had. It beats a million seller."[6] Maxene was attempting to raise a million dollars to enlarge the campus and faculty of Tahoe Paradise College. She was unsuccessful. In fact, the college folded the next year after the founder's death and so did Maxene's academic career.

Following her foray into academe, Maxene remained in Tahoe, became interested in group therapy, and joined a foundation that worked with drug addicts and delinquents.[7] Sometime during this period, she began working for Bravo, a new brassiere manufacturing company. She was scheduled to do advance publicity for the product and receive a percentage of the profits; however, the company folded along with Maxene's brassiere career.[8]

Maxene was ready to leave show business after LaVerne's death, but Patty was not. She told a reporter, "You couldn't get me out of show business with a crowbar." [9] She continued solo engagements in southern California and made occasional television appearances, including *The Donald O'Connor Show* (March 1969) and *The Joey Bishop Show* (August 1969).

Patty appeared with Lucille Ball on *Here's Lucy* in late October 1969. In the TV episode, Patty went to Ball's employment agency to hire two women to portray her sisters for an Andrews Sisters Fan Club reunion. Ball took the assignment for herself and her daughter Lucie Arnaz, but on the night of the show, she accidentally broke the records they planned to lip-synch. So in 1940s drag, complete with big hair, they sang the songs live: "Bei Mir Bist Du Schoen,"

The Andrews Sisters retired as an act in 1968 after Maxene decided to leave show business. Patty, however, continued to perform and made several guest appearances on television. One of her memorable appearances was on *Here's Lucy* in October 1969. In the episode (from left), Lucille Ball and Lucie Arnaz sang with Patty as Maxene and LaVerne while Desi Arnaz, Jr., assumed a Bing Crosby role. (Robert Boyer Collection)

"Pistol Packin' Mama," and "In Apple Blossom Time"—with occasional assistance from Desi Arnaz, Jr., as Bing Crosby. Patty later said: "I loved working with Lucy. And that little Lucie was so talented! This was one of my favorite television appearances, and Lucy told me it was the favorite *Here's Lucy* show she'd done up to that point." Lucie Arnaz remembered the show fondly as well: "Patty Andrews is a great broad, a fabulous broad. She had a great sense of humor, and of course we got to sing all those wonderful harmonies."[10]

In 1970, Patty had a cameo role in *The Phynx*, a movie starring a number of former "greats," including Ruby Keeler, Martha Raye, Busby Berkeley, and Edgar Bergen, who participated in a spy-spoof plot about a criminal gang that kidnapped famous people and held them for ransom. The movie was released briefly, withdrawn and never released again—apparently it was not good. Patty told an interviewer, "The money was so great, and for two days work, which was no bother, I didn't have to learn any music, no big dialogue or anything."[11]

Patty continued to make occasional television appearances and pursued her solo act in nightclubs. She told a reporter that she initially tried to break away from the Andrews Sisters image and excluded their songs from her act. But she soon discovered that audiences wanted to hear the Andrews Sisters' songs and she enjoyed singing them, so she put them back in.[12] In October 1970, popular comedienne Carol Burnett featured a segment on *The Carol Burnett Show* in which she portrayed the Andrews Sisters and sang all three separately filmed parts of "Boogie Woogie Bugle Boy." At the end of the show, Burnett introduced Maxene in the audience.

In early 1971, Patty Andrews rode the nostalgia wave that was sweeping the nation when she joined a World War II–type musical called *Victory Canteen* at the Ivar Theater in Hollywood. Based on music by brothers Richard and Robert Sherman, Oscar winners for their *Mary Poppins* score, the show was a light, sentimental glance at the music and times of World War II and ran for six months in Hollywood before moving to San Diego for another successful run. The show was well received by the critics.[13] Patty played the part of "Mom Davis" who managed a homefront USO canteen in a small town in Indiana. When asked why she was attracted to the part, Patty replied: "I've never done a book show before … I'm not worried about it, though. I was always the one doing the talking when the Sisters worked and that was like doing a show. Musically, too, I'm right at home. This is a play about the '40s and canteen life. Well, let me tell you, we lived it."[14]

Maxene became the show's camp follower. On opening night, she bought the first two rows of seats in the theater and invited twenty of Patty's friends to the performance. She remembered, "And the opening night we all sat there and when she walked on that stage I thought she was going to faint when she saw us all."[15] Patty told an interviewer: "She [Maxene] was here front row center opening night. She's seen the show at least twenty times. Oh, and the kids [performers] just love to have her out there because she is the biggest laugher, and the one who really enjoys it, you know, more than anybody."[16]

During *Victory Canteen*, Patty told a reporter that she wished Maxene would return to the act with her: "I wish Maxene would come back to work.

We could get another girl and go back on the road. My life is show business. I told my husband the other day that, despite our beautiful home, when I'm in a hotel lobby that's where I'm really at home. After all, that's where I was brought up."[17]

In late June 1972, Maxene came out of retirement and joined Patty on a special salute to the pop music of the 20th century on *The Merv Griffin Show*. They sang a medley of Andrews Sisters hits and then reminisced with Griffin about their career. Their singing voices were seasoned and brassy and LaVerne's cushioning contralto was noticeably absent.

In April 1973, millionaire (and future presidential candidate) H. Ross Perot entertained eighty-five Green Berets who made a daring and controversial raid on a North Vietnamese prison camp to rescue prisoners. Perot flew all the men and their wives (or significant others) to San Francisco and put them up at a plush Nob Hill hotel. The men were featured in a Friday ticker tape parade through San Francisco's financial district with John Wayne, star of the then-popular movie *Green Berets*, leading the parade. That evening a banquet honored the men and featured an appearance by Nancy Reagan, wife of California's governor, and entertainment by Patty and Maxene Andrews, Clint Eastwood, and Red Skelton.[18] Why the Andrews Sisters were invited to join this conservative, hawkish group is unclear: there's no indication they shared their political views and they were musically anachronistic for the GIs of the 1970s. Perhaps they were favorites of H. Ross Perot, the man who footed the bill.

Victory Canteen and Patty Andrews came to the attention of Kenneth Waissman and Maxine Fox, producers of the highly successful Broadway musical *Grease*, a nostalgic look at the 1950s. They bought the rights to *Victory Canteen*, changed the name to *Over Here!*, and had the entire show rewritten for the Andrews Sisters, not just Patty. Maxene was plotting the next chapter of her life when she was approached to do the show. She explained why she decided to try Broadway: "I was really content being away from show business, I simply had no idea of ever getting back into that rat race. I'd had it. But of all the things that we had done, we had never done a Broadway show. Pure and simple, no one had ever asked. So when this came along, I said OK."[19]

At about this time, a brassy young singer was beginning to make waves in the pop music scene. Bette Midler, a Jewish girl from Hawaii, was well known among the gay and counter culture worlds of New York City where she got her start singing in the Continental Baths, the notorious gay bath house. She developed a following in the gay underworld, but made her big splash in mainstream pop music with a recording of "Boogie Woogie Bugle Boy," the 1941 hit of the Andrews Sisters, which climbed to number eight on the charts in July 1973. Midler copied the Andrews Sisters' arrangement and sang all three parts. As the record climbed the charts, a new awareness of the Andrews Sisters and their music spread among a younger generation at about the time *Over Here!* was getting ready for Broadway.

Maxene was in a beauty parlor when she first heard Midler's recording on the radio: "I thought, my God—they're playing our record of 'Boogie Woogie Bugle Boy' ... then it got to the release, and I thought, 'That's not Patty singing.'

That's when people started telling me about this girl called Bette Midler."[20] Patty and Maxene both liked the Midler recording, and first met the young singer when she performed to a sold-out concert at Universal Studios Amphitheater in Los Angeles in 1973. Midler learned that the sisters were in the audience and urged them to come on stage to join her in "Boogie Woogie Bugle Boy." To the audience's delight, they did so and "received a tidal wave of applause as these two legendary figures sang with a contemporary superstar."[21] Maxene remembered the occasion: "It afforded me an opportunity to meet her when she first appeared at the Universal Amphitheater. I think she is absolutely wonderful. I had never seen a performer work like that. To be very truthful, I had never seen anybody so trashy in my life. But it was such great humor. Afterward, we went backstage to meet this lovely lady who, at least with us, was nothing like that."[22] Maxene continued: "And she locked the door and turned around and said, 'Now that I've got you in here, what else have you got that I can steal?' Unfortunately we didn't happen to have our albums with us—or our list."[23] Patty later told an interviewer: "Look at what 'Boogie Woogie Bugle Boy' did for Bette Midler and look at what she did for us ... She's great and marvelous, and picked a very difficult song and did it very well." MCA, owners of the Decca catalogue, reissued the original Andrews Sisters "Boogie Woogie Bugle Boy" in late June, and then released a double-LP album of Andrews Sisters hits in September to capitalize on the popularity of the Midler recording.[24]

The idea for *Over Here!* came when producers Kenneth Waissman and Maxine Fox heard tapes of the big band–style music that Richard and Robert Sherman wrote for *Victory Canteen*. When approached by the producers, the Sherman brothers were persuaded to use the music as the basis for a big Broadway musical. The project took some eighteen months to develop. After Patty and Maxene were signed, the producers recruited Tom Moore to direct, Patricia Birch to choreograph, and Will Holt to write the libretto. Among the young dancers and singers of the cast were some talented, unknown youth who would go on to successful careers, including Treat Williams, John Travolta, Beth Fowler, Jim Weston, and Marilu Henner. Years later, Patty told a reporter that she knew John Travolta was destined for stardom when he frequently upstaged her in *Over Here!*: "He was very creative and tried to make his part outstanding. He'd make something out of nothing ... He'd do little shticks that weren't anywhere in the script and a few times he went right in front of me. Or when I would be doing an exit he would suddenly walk in front of me or something ... John was very ambitious without being aggressive—and he was a very sweet person."[25]

Before going to New York for *Over Here!* rehearsals, Maxene made a trip to Minneapolis in mid–October for a reunion at North High School, the school she attended before hitting the road with her sisters and Larry Rich in 1931. The school was scheduled for demolition and the special reunion brought together alumni, Maxene and actor Robert Vaughn being the most famous. Maxene substituted for a no-show master of ceremonies.[26] Back in Hollywood a week later, Maxene joined Patty at a benefit luncheon held at the Century

In spring 1973, a young singer named Bette Midler recorded the Andrews Sisters' 1941 hit "Boogie Woogie Bugle Boy" which climbed the charts in early July. The popularity of the song generated a new interest in the Andrews Sisters. Above Maxene (left) and Patty talk with Midler (center) after her concert at the Universal Amphitheater in Hollywood in 1973. (Author's collection)

Plaza sponsored by the St. Nicholas Greek Orthodox Ladies Guild of Northridge.[27] The following month they joined other celebrities at the Hollywood Palladium in a show commemorating the *Command Performance* Armed Forces Radio Service shows of World War II.

While Maxene was in rehearsal for *Over Here!* a story appeared in a trade publication announcing that she and Emily Stevens had formed the Andrews—Stevens Production Company with plans to do motion picture, television, and theatrical productions. Their initial project would be a film and television series based on Maxene's autobiography followed by "other projects including a mini-series of TV specials beginning with Andrews and following with other stars; a romantic drama by Gertrude Walker; and a 1930s musical by Stevens and Walker, aimed for a New York opening late this year."[28] Maxene had returned to show business in a big way. Nothing further, however, was heard of any of these proposals.

Over Here! appeared in the midst of a nostalgic wave in American pop culture and was part of a string of Broadway successes starring actresses/singers in their middle years, such as *Applause* (Lauren Bacall), *Coco* (Katharine Hepburn), *Follies* (Alexis Smith), and *No, No, Nanette* (Ruby Keeler).

One of the several young cast members in *Over Here!* who went on to successful careers was John Travolta, shown above in a number with Patty Andrews.
(Robert Boyer Collection)

Over Here! is set during World War II aboard a troop train traveling cross-
country, carrying soldiers to the East Coast for embarkation to the European
war. Assorted civilian passengers are onboard also, including Pauline and
Paulette De Paul (Maxene and Patty Andrews), a sister singing team in charge
of the train's canteen who are looking for a third singer to form a trio. They

meet a woman on the train named Mitzi (Janie Sell), a former German cabaret singer, and unbeknownst to all, a Nazi spy. The sisters decide that her voice is perfect to complete their trio act. As the train moves across country, musical numbers reminisce about World War I ("Hey, Yvette!/ The Grass Grows Green"), recall a popular Saturday-night dive ("Charlie's Place"), warn about the dangers of VD ("The Good Time Girl"), criticize the segregated military ("Don't Shoot the Hooey to Me, Louie"), and bemoan the passing of the good old days ("Where Did the Good Times Go?"). The De Paul sisters get their big chance to sing on a nationwide radio broadcast from the train with Mitzi, who has surreptitiously inserted a Morse-code message into their song. A young recruit deciphers the message and suspicion falls on Mitzi's loyalty. When they question her, she tries to prove her American patriotism by reciting Joe DiMaggio's batting average, Kentucky Derby winners, and other bits of Americana. She overdoes it, however, when she sings the second chorus of "The Star Spangled Banner"—no true American knows that. Fortunately, the broadcast with Mitzi's message was not aired, and all ends well for everyone—except Mitzi. *Over Here!* premiered in Philadelphia in early 1974 to an enthusiastic audience. Cast member Jim Weston remembered the opening night's conclusion:

> They told all of us to stay on stage after the curtain call. We didn't know what they had planned. After the curtain call, the curtain went up again. The entire audience was veterans, people who had been through the war, or fans of the Andrews Sisters. Patty came out and said, "Would you like to hear some of the old songs?" And the audience erupted with cheers. The sisters sang a medley of their old songs, and the last thing they sang was "I'll Be with You in Apple Blossom Time." And the whole audience began to sing along. And I tell you, I have goose bumps right now just remembering it. We were crying, the audience was crying. And I thought, oh man, this show's a hit! They did it that night to see what would happen, and it never came out of the show.[29]

After a bit of reworking, *Over Here!* moved on to Broadway where it opened at the Shubert Theater March 6. From the beginning, it was a hit with audiences and received good reviews from the critics, including the following from *The New York Times*:

> Now the Andrews Sisters ... are back in town ... Against all the promptings of what would normally have been my better judgment, I warmed to the show enormously. As a musical it is preposterously bad, but also preposterously engaging and, in its way, devilish clever ... The music and lyrics by Richard M. Sherman and Robert B. Sherman (they sound like tanks that rode with Patton) are almost as disarmingly simple. They are all pastiche songs that you almost recognize but don't quite. Everything sounds perfectly in the period of World War II with boogie-woogie still eight to the bar, that old close harmony vocalizing ... and the big band sound...
>
> Everything seems nostalgically authentic, from the tackiness of the scenery and costumes to the high-key patriotism and the homespun sophistication of the humor. The show does capture the hayseed heartiness of a nation at war that was forever embalmed in the films, radio shows and records of the era ... Only now and then does a new consciousness break in—when we find Patty Andrews singing a song warning against V.D. ... or a suggestion of black and

Patty (left) and Maxene became stars again in the successful Broadway show *Over Here!* which opened on March 6, 1974. The show was a nostalgic look back at the World War II years with original music reminiscent of the era. (Robert Boyer Collection)

white inequality in that army of the people ... Undeniably, this is a show the pure in mind will have to make allowances for—it is not only corny, it is even intended to be corny—but most will find the allowances well worth making....

Incidentally, the show's best part comes after the final curtain. Maxene and Patty come on looking tremendously awful in glitter costumes. Patty says casually: "Do you want to hear some of the old ones?" And you do! And they sing, and sing and sing.[30]

Other critics liked the show too, especially the performances of Patty and Maxene. One wrote: "The two have added a little weight but no excess musical tissue, and the drillmaster finger-wagging, the clockwork footwork, and the upstage sashays are as meticulous as the compact, easy-to-take harmonies."[31] Another said: "[A]nd everybody adores the Andrews Sisters ... The moments really cherished by the audience, which by no means consists entirely of the groupies of 1944, come when all is over bar the encores ... The Andrews Sisters, by their own admission, well on the wrong side of 50, come on arm in arm with a sackful of their golden oldies ... Their first appearance on the Broadway stage looks like being a long one."[32]

Following the opening night performance, the cast of *Over Here!* gathered

Janie Sell (left) joins Patty and Maxene for "The Big Beat" in *Over Here!* The show was nominated for several Tony Awards but only Sell won as "Best Supporting Actress in a Musical." (Robert Boyer Collection)

at Sardi's nightspot to celebrate with Broadway luminaries such as Ethel Merman, who joined Patty and Maxene for some brief vocalizing, and Angela Lansbury, who was having her own Broadway success with a revival of *Gypsy*. According to a New York columnist, Maxene left the celebration in anger because she claimed she brought friends for whom there were no accommodations. When Patty was asked about the incident, she brushed it off: "It was probably first night excitement." She later said regarding the opening: "Everything went just right. Our girdles were on straight and everything."[33]

The success of *Over Here!* and Bette Midler's revival of "Boogie Woogie Bugle Boy" created a renewed interest in the Andrews Sisters. MCA, owners of Decca, released a two-record LP album of Andrews Sisters hits, Dot reissued three of its Andrews Sisters albums, Capitol reissued two of its Andrews Sisters albums, and British Decca released albums abroad. The cast album of *Over Here!* (excluding the post curtain concert) was released May 1, 1974. *People* magazine's premiere issue on March 18, 1974, featured a photo of Patty and Maxene onstage in *Over Here!*

Over Here! received several TONY nominations, but won only "best supporting actress in a musical" for Janie Sell who played Mitzi. Patty, Maxene, and cast members performed the title number "Over Here!" on the televised TONY awards show April 21, 1974, in the Shubert Theater where the show was running. In early September, Patty, Maxene and the *Over Here!* cast appeared on *The Andy Williams Special* television show to perform the title song and "Charlie's Place."

Patty (age 56) and Maxene (58) Andrews recorded the cast album of *Over Here!* in 1974, the last time they recorded together. (Robert Boyer Collection)

Patty and Maxene enjoyed doing *Over Here!* Maxene explained:

> It's interesting—I had a certain dream about what a Broadway show is like. But it's no different from doing those 6 shows a day at the N.Y. Paramount, except now you only do one show a night. Still, every night I look forward to doing the show, because it's always a different audience, and because I enjoy the people in the show—we have a marvelous group—and because it's the one thing I've never done ... Those aftershows are a kick in the head ... It's like the N.Y. Paramount all over again. All those young people out there, and people our age who we're taking back—they're standing in the aisles, they're swinging, they're dancing, and I think it's absolutely marvelous! And now I'm beginning to understand what it all meant to people in those days.[34]

Compared to their earlier performances, they thought the musical theater was easy. Maxene told a reporter: "This is a breeze! ... Only eight shows a week! We used to do seven shows a day, 45 weeks of the year. One Labor Day at the Steel Pier in Atlantic City we did 11 shows, each 25 minutes long with 15 minutes between shows." Patty added: "This is what London is like ... When we played the Talk of the Town on Piccadilly Circus, we did one show a night and had Sundays off. This is the only way to do show business."[35]

Although *Over Here!* was a look back at the 1940s, the Andrews Sisters were very much in touch with the pop music of the day. Maxene told a reporter: "They've got great songs now ... Like 'Sing a Song' or 'We've Only Just Begun.' The Burt Bacharach–Hal David stuff is perfect for us. And the Beatles. 'Yesterday' and 'Let It Be.' 'Let It Be' could have been a gasser for us. So could 'Tie a Yellow Ribbon.' And 'Gypsy Rose' is a dynamite song."[36] Patty said, "I like Blood, Sweat and Tears. And I'm crazy about the Carpenters. And I love everything that Burt Bacharach writes, and Hal David."[37]

Rex Reed was one of the last writers to interview Maxene and Patty together. He talked to them while they were doing *Over Here!* and still speaking to one another. Much of what they told Reed about their careers had been told many times to other reporters, but their repartee is worth repeating here. Reed prefaced his interview: "It's been a long trip from bandstands to Broadway, but the Andrews Sisters have never changed. Talking to them in Maxene's hotel suite last week was like being in a cage with two jitter-bugging magpies. Everything they do is punctuated with rhythm and sometimes it's hard to tell where one begins and the other ends."

> We made 10 movies, recorded 1,000 songs—double that for flip sides—and out of that we got 19 gold records in 20 years [said Maxene]. And let me put it to you this way—we only got about 50 good songs out of it all. The rest were dogs. We hated the movies.
>
> Yeah [said Patty]. Everybody else got Alice Faye and Betty Grable in Technicolor. We got Carmen Miranda and Abbott and Costello. We were the queens of the B's. But we were unique.
>
> Let's face it [said Maxene]. The reason all this stuff is coming back is because of Bette Midler's record of "Boogie Woogie Bugle Boy."
>
> Yeah [said Patty]. That word "camp" doesn't bother us. We think it's very funny.
>
> I hate that word "nostalgia" though [said Maxene]. They don't call Rem-

brandt's painting nostalgia. Anything good is gonna last, honey. I don't care if they say I'm 86 years old.

Well [said Patty], aren't you, boobie?

No, I'm 92 ... My sister Patty might be [a millionaire], but not me.

Oh, the crying towel! [said Patty]. She's always broke. She goes out and buys a new Mercedes, then says "I can't pay the taxes on my 10 acres in Malibu." You know the type.[38]

The conversation gives a feel for the sisters' interaction with one another, or at least the one they wanted to show the public, but it contains a few errors of fact. The Andrews Sisters made eighteen, not ten movies; they recorded 605 songs rather than 2,000; they received seven, not nineteen gold records; and they never made a movie with Carmen Miranda, although they recorded with her. Also, some might question whether the Andrews Sisters' music is comparable to Rembrandt's paintings.

Cast member Jim Weston had good memories of his time with the Andrews Sisters in *Over Here!* "I have nothing but great things to say about them ... Their musicianship was superb ... when we first heard them sing, it sounded like there were three of them ... They were real pros and I always had fun with them. Patty was more of a show business personality ... She was sort of larger than life ... Maxene was a little quieter."[39] Weston remembered that Patty posted pictures of the sisters in her dressing room, including several of LaVerne.

Beth Fowler, who acted as stand-by for Patty and Maxene, also remembered the professionalism of the sisters: "They were pros. I remember saying to Maxene one time, 'I've never seen singers work so easily.' She said, 'Honey, you do twelve shows a day in Atlantic City when you're sixteen years old and you learn to work easy.' I may have the numbers wrong, but I remember the thrust of it. They knew how to turn it out."[40] Fowler knew Maxene better than Patty.

> I really didn't know Patty at all. I only knew the persona she presented to the company. I knew there was a lot going on with Patty that we didn't really see. We just saw the results of it. Her husband was on the premises all the time, in her dressing room, which was a great source of distress to her. She didn't seem to interact with anybody else whereas Maxene mixed more easily with company members. She was more affable. If someone had a party after the show some night, she'd be there. She would come, have something to eat and drink, sing and horse around. Patty would never show up at anything like that. Maxene was one of the guys.[41]

Over Here! looked like a long Broadway run. The audiences liked it, the critics thought it was ok, and the public lined up to see it. Audiences ranged from the World War II era crowd to young people who were discovering the Andrews Sisters through Bette Midler's "Boogie Woogie Bugle Boy." One evening a group of German tourists packed the house and joined the sisters for their post-curtain medley of hits.[42] No one believed it was a great show, but it was a fun show, a warm, fuzzy backward look into a past that never was. After it exhausted the New York audience, a road show was planned for the legions of Andrews Sisters fans throughout the country waiting to see it. Unfortunately, that never happened.

Things were fermenting backstage.

On Christmas Eve, the performance was wrapping up and cast members were looking forward to a Christmas party in the Green Room. Beth Fowler, who was stand-by in case Patty, Maxene, or Janie Sell became ill, was sipping champagne and trimming a Christmas tree with the show's hairdresser in the Green Room as the show was in its final numbers on the stage above them. Suddenly, a stage manager rushed into the room and said to Fowler, "You've got to finish the show! She won't finish the show!" Fowler asked, "Who won't finish the show?" The stage manager said, "Patty," and rushed upstairs with Fowler. Understandably, Fowler had vivid memories of the evening.

> I didn't have my own costume. All I had were shoes. There was no time to put me in a wig because Patty literally walked off after the ballad and locked herself in her dressing room. And they had to beg and plead and bang on the door to get her to open the door so they could have her costume for the finale which they gave to me. They pinned me into it with big safety pins—both sisters were considerably larger than I was. I had the microphone in my hair—they fluffed my hair and I put some lipstick on. And they put the wire down my back and strapped on an Eveready battery pack. In those days, the battery pack for the microphone was really substantial and you'd wear it inside your thigh or somewhere … There was a big staircase on the set for the last number. We'd go up and hit the top of the stairs and then run down to the edge of the apron where we'd start to sing "The Big Beat." I met Maxene at the bottom of the stairs for the number. Maxene knew nothing about Patty. She looked at me and said, "What the heck is this?" I said, "Patty can't finish the show." She said, "Oh, my God. O.K."
>
> We made it to the top of the stairs and at that point I realized the battery pack had slipped between my knees. By the time I got down to the edge of the apron it was swinging between my calves. My microphone was dead. The only ones who knew it were me and the stage manager and probably the first six rows. We were OK at the top of the song, but when we split up, we were supposed to sit on the drums and kick them with our heels. Since my microphone was dead, I ignored my choreography and followed Maxene and sang over her shoulder or into her chest so I could be heard through her microphone.
>
> When the number was over, Maxene went stomping into the wings, turned around and looked at me like I was out of my mind. I didn't say a word, but just pointed between my knees. She saw the battery pack, burst out laughing, and said, "You've got to do the third act with me." I said, "I can't. I don't know those words." She said, "You've got the best teacher in the world. C'mon kid, you're going to sing with me." And that was the beginning of our fun. We had a lot of fun together.[43]

In later interviews, Maxene claimed Patty did not finish the performance because she became ill.

> While we [Patty and Maxene] were in "Over Here," we never had an angry word or an angry scene … We got along beautifully. But by the end of the run, it was starting. On Christmas eve, Patty got ill and walked off the stage in the middle of a scene. She went to her dressing room, got dressed in her street clothes and just sat there. Her understudy finished the show, and afterward I went to her dressing room to see her. Her husband, Walter Weschler, was there. He pushed me out of the door. "Get out of here," he said. "She's no longer your sister."[44]

Beth Fowler, however, had a different understanding of the incident:

> What I was told was this. Our drummer was really tops. But he had to leave the show for a commitment in Florida and found a substitute drummer to fill in. The cast was having trouble working with this new drummer. Before "The Big Beat" number, Wally [Weschler] was in Patty's dressing room complaining about the drummer and tempi, and yelling at Patty to speak up, to not do this, not do that, saying her performance really stank. He undermined her whole confidence. She was very upset herself because she was enough of a musician to know the drummer was off. Sure things were not a hundred percent right, but you know Christmas Eve on Broadway—who the heck cared? Everybody was having a great time. Patty was just beside herself. She couldn't go on and locked herself in her dressing room.[45]

This was the beginning of the deep rift that would separate Patty and Maxene the remainder of their lives.

Over Here! suddenly closed on January 4, 1975, in the midst of controversy and confusion. The producers blamed Patty and Maxene, claiming they wanted more money and made unreasonable demands, and immediately canceled the national tour. The Andrews Sisters blamed the producers, claiming they had mismanaged the show from the beginning and were now using them as scapegoats to protect themselves from their investors. Cast member Beth Fowler remembered when she learned the show was not going on the road:

> One night a message was sent through the company informally that there was going to be a company meeting during the third act while the sisters were on stage. Maxine and Ken [the producers] wanted to speak to the company to tell them what was happening because stories had appeared in the newspapers about problems in the show ... We were in the Green Room downstairs and Ken was making this speech to the company. Suddenly in the doorway appeared Maxene and Lynda Wells [Maxene's manager]. Maxene said, "Well, I understand there's a company meeting. As far as I know, I'm a member of the company." She and Patty had learned about the meeting and agreed that Patty would do the third act solo and Maxene would come down to see what the hell was going on. So Ken just kind of calmed down his language, but what he was saying was that the sisters' demands were so high that they could not meet them. Economically speaking, it was not feasible—it didn't make sense for them to do a tour because nobody would be making any money except the sisters.[46]

The company of *Over Here!* was taken aback by the announcement. Members had started packing, apartments were sublet. They thought the road show was a *fait accompli*.

When the press announced the show's closing, New Yorkers flocked to the theater to catch the final performances. Cast member Jim Weston remembered closing night: "At our closing performance they had to open the doors of the Shubert Theater out on to the street. There were so many people wanting in. They all came because they heard we were closing. People in front of the theater spilled onto the street. The manager said, 'Oh to hell with it! Open the doors. Just let it play.' Mobs of people were out on Shubert Alley and 44th Street peering in trying to see the show, everyone cheering. It was really quite something."[47]

In the producers' press release of complaints against the Andrews Sisters, they claimed the sisters had signed a two-year contract, which included the producers' option to send them on a national tour within that two-year period. The press release continued: "However, in spite of this contract, both Patty and Maxene have been demanding more money. Maxene sent the producers a doctor's note saying that she is too sick to perform on tour. However, according to management, a follow-up call made by her attorney stated that in spite of the letter, Maxene Andrews would be healthy enough to perform if she were given additional monies by the producers."[48]

Patty refused to issue a statement regarding the producers' claims on the advice of her attorney, but typically, Maxene had plenty to say. She began by claiming the press release was "an outrageous lie." She then revealed the basis for some of the friction between her and Patty as well as some of her ongoing health problems with her knees and legs:

> My sister gets thirty-five hundred dollars a week and seven percent of the show; and I get twenty-five hundred dollars a week and three percent of the show after the show makes $60,000. That was a stupid contract on the producers' part, but if I hadn't agreed to work for less money there wouldn't have been a show in the first place. I did agree, because that's how badly I wanted to do it.
>
> This is the first time we have ever worked under an unequal salary, but Patty's husband negotiated her deal. They asked me to take a cut in my percentages to get the show on the road, and I agreed … giving them twenty thousand a week more to spend on production costs. All I asked was that they make it up to me by helping to pay for my medical expenses on the road. What it amounted to was four hundred dollars a week toward my doctor bills. I agreed to a cut in percentage, and I agreed to take no raise in salary, and all I wanted was some financial aid to pay the doctors in every city who would have no medical history of my case. All through the show I have spent a fortune through cortisone shots in my legs, acupuncture, and therapy at paraplegic hospitals, and every time the doctor ordered me to leave the show, I refused. It was only right that I ask for some medical compensation on the road since I was going to get less money anyway, and the crazy fact is, the producers' lawyers agreed. In twenty-five minutes, they had worked out my road deal. In the meantime, I learned they had gone over to see Patty and her husband to play one sister against the other. At the same time, I learned they had financial trouble with the stage designers' union and the rumor was that the scenery was too expensive to take on the road. So they used the sisters as excuses for the blame. Now, they have a two-year contract with us. Even if we have been difficult and asked for more money, as they claim, why didn't they just take us into Equity arbitration and force us to go on the road? They were holding all the cards. They simply are not telling the truth.[49]

Maxene's claim has validity. The sisters were bound by contracts to do the road show and if they truly balked, the producers could have taken them to court. No one was taken to court. A news story claimed the New York run of *Over Here!* had recouped only $250,000 of its $650,000 investment.[50] Most likely the producers realized they could not make enough on the road to recoup the investment and consequently cancelled. The demands the producers attributed to the sisters are not in keeping with the professionalism the Andrews Sisters displayed throughout their long careers.

Maxene claimed the producers delayed finalizing their road contract until December 16 when they approached them with a contract

> ...demanding that we retract all doctors' claims, agree to do all publicity, make the third act at the end of the show where we do our old hit songs a definite part of each performance, and sign our consent before curtain time, or the tour would be canceled ... We had one hour to decide. It was seven o'clock at night, we couldn't reach our lawyers, and naturally we didn't sign. So they made an announcement over the loudspeakers that the cast must meet in costume after the show and the Andrews Sisters were not invited. I went to the meeting anyway and Ken Waissman said, "Get out, you're not wanted here!" The cast was stunned. So I got up and said fine, but first I want to talk to the cast. I explained that we loved them all and were very sorry the show was not going on the road, but it had nothing to do with us. The entire cast applauded and I left ... Every member of the cast has come to me since and personally apologized for the rudeness of the producers.[51]

Wally Weschler, Patty's husband and business manager, shared Maxene's outrage and called the producers' accusations "the dumbest I've ever heard of." He added that the producers had forty weeks of bookings for a national tour that would give them a potential gross of four to five million dollars. He concluded: "The Andrews Sisters are well, healthy and very anxious to make this tour. Perhaps the producers can explain to their investors why this tour is not going on. We have no explanation. In fact, we are shocked, disappointed and feel sorry for the whole cast."[52] Additional details of the differences between the Andrews Sisters and the producers of *Over Here!* are discussed in Rex Reed's accounts of the incident.[53]

Maxene suggested she and Patty were having personal difficulties because of their unequal salaries:

> The biggest mistake is that we were both represented separately, not as an act ... and it cannot go on this way. Maybe the time has come to go our separate ways. But it was immoral for Waissman and Fox to pit one sister against the other. They created the problem by negotiating separately at the beginning, and we never got together to iron it out. So now there is friction. We've always had different life-styles, different friends, different tastes offstage. The only thing we had in common is our work.
>
> We've survived. We overcame seventeen rotten pictures at Universal, World War Two, all the bad pressings Decca turned out that turned into gold records anyway, husbands and ex-husbands, bad publicity, and amateur Broadway producers. The only people who love us are the people. They just keep on coming.[54]

Maxene was overly optimistic. The Andrews Sisters would not survive the incident.

The following spring Patty Andrews and her husband Wally Weschler asked Actors Equity Association to appeal their decision to deny arbitration on Patty's claims against Kenneth Waissman, producer of *Over Here!* Among her grievances were calculation of the box office, the sale of souvenir albums in the lobby, use of Patty's picture on the cast album cover, request that she be paid her weekly salary for the road show that was cancelled, and the unauthorized use of her likeness on tee shirts sold in the lobby. The appeal was denied by Actors Equity, which stated in its memo:

> Each of the claims had been brought to our attention by Mr. Weschler during the run of the show. On numerous occasions he phoned ... to register his complaints that his wife's contract was being breached. Unfortunately, we were unable to persuade him that the breaches he was alleging were not breaches, but legal acts on the part of the management ... These claims arise from ignorance of theatrical practice and customs. Mr. Weschler has been repeatedly informed that he is off base. He has stubbornly refused to accept this fact and has now retained a lawyer to pursue his allegations.[55]

A year after *Over Here!* closed on Broadway, it opened at the Playhouse on the Bergen Mall in Paramus, New Jersey, in late January 1976 with a cast that included Margaret Whiting, popular singer from the 1940s, Dolly Jonah, wife of the author of the book for *Over Here!*, and Maxene Andrews.[56] Maxene said she hoped this would be the first of a number of out-of-town appearances.

Maxene told a Los Angeles columnist that "Patty just didn't feel like going on the road at this time." She added, "I want to quash all those stories that the Andrews sisters fought more than they sang. Patty, LaVerne ... and I never had any fights among us. But there were husbands you know."[57] A few days later, Patty wrote to the columnist to assure him that she was still in show business:

> Enjoyed reading your column about my sister Maxene and the road show of "Over Here." The reason I would not be interested in going on the road is because I've done the show on Broadway successfully for over a year and the excitement is gone. I am more enthused over starting the New Year with several new and exciting projects and I wouldn't want any of your many readers to get the impression that I've retired.
>   In fact, I'm looking forward to 1976 as the happiest time of my life. Thank you and a happy New Year to you too. Love and kisses, Patty Andrews.[58]

The revival of *Over Here!* ran only three weeks in Paramus and did not go elsewhere. *Over Here!*, however, continues to be performed in stock.

The rift that developed between Maxene and Patty Andrews during *Over Here!* and separated them the remainder of their lives has never been fully explained. The Christmas Eve incident when Patty refused to do the final number and Wally Weschler would not allow Maxene in Patty's dressing room appears to have been the proverbial straw that broke the relationship. Thereafter, the sisters tolerated one another during performances, but did not speak off-stage.

The estrangement between the sisters had deep roots, some no doubt going back to their childhood. Others stemmed from the 1954 break up of the Andrews Sisters when both Maxene and LaVerne claimed Wally Weschler was the key ingredient in Patty's decision to leave the act and pursue a solo career. Tensions between Maxene and Patty ripened after LaVerne died when Joyce DeYoung joined the act. DeYoung thought the main reason Maxene decided to leave the act was because of the increasing control Patty and Weschler demanded.[59] The unequal salaries in *Over Here!* were doubtless another irritant to Maxene. Rumors claimed Patty wanted to do the show herself, but the producers didn't want her without Maxene. Perhaps the higher salary mollified her. But the personality conflict between Maxene and Weschler was the critical factor in the estrangement—they simply did not like one another, and Patty sided with her husband.

After *Over Here!* closed, the sisters saw one another on only three occasions. Patty visited Maxene after her heart surgery in 1982, but Maxene was too ill to interact with her. They appeared together in 1987 when a star was presented to the Andrews Sisters on the Hollywood Walk of Fame. They were on stage together in 1992 at the premiere of *Company B,* the dance program based on their World War II songs, but they did not speak to one another.

In an interview during *Over Here!*, Maxene revealed that her personal relationship with Patty was not close: "We think the same way musically, but our taste in clothes, friends—our lifestyles are completely different. We had to learn to respect this. We've been together eight weeks rehearsing this show. Offstage, we've never seen each other socially. Onstage, it's as tho we've never been apart."[60] In another interview during the same period with both sisters, they emphasized their separateness and their growing impatience at always being lumped together:

> We're not glued together! [said Patty] When our fans used to see one of us, they'd always ask, "Where are your sisters?" Every time we got an award, it was just one award for the three of us ... [Maxene said] We have individual personalities that we've never been given a chance to exploit. When we started rehearsing "Over Here!" ... the director was surprised at the way I read my lines. "You don't sound like Patty," he said. "I'm not Patty!" I told him.[61]

Over Here! cast member Jim Weston remembered, "People told me they weren't getting along, but I honest to God never personally saw that. I was never aware of it during the run of the show."[62] However, when Beth Fowler was asked if she was aware of friction between the sisters during the show, she replied:

> Never on stage that I know of. You'd never see any friction between them. They went through periods when they were fine together. You'd hear them chatting backstage and everything was very sisterly-like on the intimate level of casual conversation. But then there was the other stuff when evidently there was a great deal of stress and competition between them. I think it was exacerbated by the stress of Patty's husband prodding her. I always felt that he always wanted her to be the star ... My opinion is that if Wally [Weschler] hadn't been around they would have been fine.[63]

Various versions of the rift appeared in the press, most of them in interviews with Maxene. She told a reporter in 1977: "We just aren't together, that's all ... People keep asking where the other Andrews sister is ... They expect us to eat, sleep, rest and spend all our time together. Each of us is different, but some people won't accept that."[64] Several months later, Maxene told a reporter that Patty "balked" about taking *Over Here!* on the road. "Now she isn't speaking to me any more; the only contact I have with her is through rumor. It's very painful; I would talk to her, but she doesn't want to talk to me."[65] The following year, Maxene told an interviewer who asked her about the estrangement:

It's nothing in my part ... I love my sister. I'm dismayed. We were much closer together than either of us was with LaVerne. Patty has never said to me, "This is the reason we're estranged." It's puzzling ... I'm no longer angry about my split with Patty. I'm no longer hurt. Some day Patty will know the truth. If I were to say, "Patty, I pray for you every day," she'd laugh at me. But I do.[66]

In 1980, not having spoken to Maxene for five years, Patty still had bitter feelings and blamed her sister for the *Over Here!* cancellation. She told a reporter:

Maxene started having private meetings with the producers ... I was never included. She wanted to renegotiate the contract. After several of those meetings, they posted the closing notices. I can't put up with Maxene's dirty tricks anymore. Her greed was the cause of all the troubles. When you have a family that has sisters, and one sister is jealous, there's got to be problems. Maxene and I will never get back again. What else can I say?[67]

A week later, Maxene was interviewed about Patty's statement and she had plenty to say:

I called her up two years ago, and she told me in no uncertain terms that if I ever called her up again, she'd sue me. Then, she hung up. That's the last time we spoke ... I love Patty very much. We are the only two left in the family. I really don't know what's bugging her. She said I had met privately with the producers [of *Over Here!*]? Not so.

Yes, I was getting less than Patty but I didn't meet with anybody, unless she was present, too. This mention of greed is upsetting, since Patty was making more than me. She got $3,500 to $4,000 per week, plus 9% of the gross. I got $2,500, plus 3%. That's the only way she would do the show. But I never asked for more. Maybe I should have.

When asked if Patty's husband was to blame for the estrangement, Maxene replied, "I think a great deal has to do with that ... He was never fond of me or LaVerne. He always got on the extension when we talked on the phone." She continued: "I simply cannot understand this childlike attitude on her part. I have never been jealous of her, as she claims. The only jealousy that may exist must be on her part. We always made Patty the star. We never wanted to do solo acts, except Patty." Maxene said she only wanted "Patty to be happy. She's my kid sister and from the bottom of my heart I love her very much." When asked if they would work together again, she said, "From my part, I see no reason why not. I have no ax to grind. There is no feud on my side. But right now, I can't communicate with her."[68] Later in the year, Maxene told a reporter that if her mother were alive she would be horrified at the split. "We've gone through so much. These years, we should be enjoying together. Pat and I."[69]

Maxene discussed the estrangement with another reporter a year later, and added that she did not understand what happened: "It's very foolish. I'm not angry or hurt anymore but I can't imagine what's making her do this. And believe me, it's what she wants, not me. She was never like this when we were three kids growing up."[70] Maxene was now pursuing a successful solo career, and said she began performing alone for "the simple reason that Patty refuses to work with me." She acknowledged that she and Patty did not speak to one another and added "this is not my choice" but rather because of "outside elements influencing Patty that I don't want to talk about."[71]

In a subsequent interview in *Newsweek*, Maxene said the falling-out occurred when she refused to let Wally Weschler share LaVerne's royalties and earnings, which apparently meant that Weschler wanted an equal share of the act for management as Lou Levy had in the past. "Patty told me that not only did she not want to work with me anymore, but she didn't want to talk to me anymore." Maxene claimed she last heard from Patty three weeks previously when a Los Angeles club billed Maxene's one-woman show as "Maxene, The Andrews Sister." Patty sent a telegram to the club threatening legal action if the line was not removed.[72] The billing was subsequently changed to "Maxene, An Andrews Sister."

Two months later, *Newsweek* published a letter from Wally Weschler refuting Maxene's claim: "Your report ... contains an inaccuracy. It is a matter of record that LaVerne Andrews's money goes, and has always gone, directly to her estate. It is also a matter of contract that all money earned by the Andrews Sisters is paid directly and equally to the three sisters. I do not get paid one penny from these sources, nor have I ever asked to be paid from them."[73] Maxene later confirmed Weschler's claim and suggested that some of Patty's resentment may date to when Maxene was married to Lou Levy and they took in half the earnings of the Andrews Sisters:

> There were reports in the media that it had to do with my refusal to let Patty's husband, Walter Weschler, who was our piano accompanist, share LaVerne's royalties and earnings. That information was incorrect. All money earned by LaVerne is paid into her estate. I honestly don't know what Patty's problem is. Perhaps it dates back to the beginning when we started under the management of Lou Levy. The agreement at that time was that we shared all earnings, split four ways. Then I married Lou Levy, so the two of us brought down 50 percent of the earnings. But that was a contractual agreement since Lou was our manager and certainly earned his share. I really don't understand why Patty is so angry at me. But I wish we could become reconciled. I really miss her a great deal.[74]

In 1985, Maxene again told a reporter she had no idea why Patty did not speak to her and that her estrangement from Patty was "the biggest pain in my entire life. She actually is all I have left. I would do anything if I could bridge whatever the problem is." When the reporter reached Patty and her husband by phone to comment on the estrangement, both declined to comment.[75]

In fall 1987, MCA arranged dedication ceremonies for a star to the Andrews Sisters on the Hollywood Walk of Fame. For the first time since *Over Here!* Patty and Maxene consented to interviews for the same article—albeit separately. When asked about their estrangement, Maxene responded that the split was the result of too many years of working too closely together.[76] She speculated that it would have been healthier for all concerned if the trio had broken up earlier to find their own identities. "It's a natural period of growth," she said. "We just started a little too damn late in life."[77] When Patty was asked about the estrangement, she was less conciliatory and "her warmly coquettish manner turned suddenly cold." She told the reporter: "Well, the story is like this, you see. Ever since I was born, Maxene has been a problem, and the problem hasn't stopped. I don't know, maybe you can call it a sister rivalry." When she was told Andrews Sisters' fans would be unhappy to hear this, she responded: "People don't care. When I start singing the Andrews Sisters songs, they don't give a damn whether I talk to my sister or not." She continued more magnanimously: "I'm not going to do anything or say anything to destroy that image that the people love. I hear that from the people that they love the Andrews Sisters and it's a joy to them. Who am I to take that away from them?"[78]

Maxene commented on the estrangement again in an interview the following year: "In a sense, I guess you could say Patty and I are estranged, though I know that she loves me and she knows that I love her." She continued to explain that after *Over Here!*, Patty's husband told her, "Patty wasn't going to work with me anymore." Maxene believed that Patty and her husband had been planning to work without her all along. She continued in a philosophical vein: "But I don't think it's a bad thing that we go our separate ways now. We needed to find out who we were as individuals, and I tell everyone that my success today is all due to my brother-in-law kicking me out of the nest. It was the best thing that could have happened to me."[79]

The following year, Maxene told a reporter: "You know, I just want my relationship with her again, because we have always been very close, but alienation started when she married this man she is married to now ... It's just one of those things, and I guess it'll take the Lord to straighten it out." [80] In 1993, Maxene reiterated that Weschler was the main reason for her estrangement from Patty: "It's because of her husband ... He's a fighter for control. Unfortunately, she's married to him."[81]

Gladys Leichter, the sisters' cousin, also believed the estrangement was due to Maxene's unwillingness to give in to Weschler's demands. Specifically, she said Maxene told her that Weschler wanted a third of the Andrews Sisters' income. Gladys added, "He's not a family man. He thinks our family is after something, that they want something from the girls ... I never wanted anything. I was proud of them because they were so successful ... I couldn't understand where he got the idea the family wanted anything from them."[82] Gladys remembered that Maxene was frequently distressed by her alienation from Patty. She recalled Maxene crying and saying she didn't understand why Patty behaved as she did. "It caused Maggie a great deal of grief in her later years."[83]

Gladys never had a falling out with Patty, but in later years when she tried to contact her, she received no response to her letters.[84]

I talked to many friends of Maxene and none remembered her saying an unkind word about Patty—however, several admitted she had no love for Wally Weschler.

Patty gave considerably fewer interviews than Maxene and consequently her view of the estrangement is less well known.

CHAPTER FIFTEEN

1975–1987

Maxene Andrews is a classy, gracious, energetic talent whose stage presence is an honor to experience.[1]

Patty Andrews has no problem charming an audience either, as she moves around the stage with ease like the seasoned pro she is.[2]

When Maxene Andrews came out of retirement for *Over Here!*, she didn't realize she would be performing the remainder of her life. She told a reporter in 1972, "I have always felt oppressed except when I was singing. Now I don't sing and I never feel anything but free ... I don't miss the act for one minute. I no longer need it. I'm free."[3] After *Over Here!*, however, she changed her mind. The stage increasingly became a necessary ingredient to Maxene's happiness and she performed almost to the day of her death.

In fall 1975, after *Over Here!* closed the previous January, Maxene tried a one-woman show again, this time at the Spindletop in New York where she was asked to open the club:

> I was flattered that I was asked to open a new club ... And they were not asking Patty; they were asking Maxene. I asked a friend to get some songs together for me. He gave me some 1940's songs and some contemporary songs, but none of them had anything to do with Maxene Andrews or the Andrews Sisters. I went into the room ignorant of what Maxene should do. I stuck it out for two weeks but I felt unqualified to do a single.[4]

She told a reporter: "I missed my sisters terribly, and I really missed the harmony when I found out how difficult it was to be a solo singer."[5] She told another reporter:

I know a lot of people will think I'm doing this because I was envious of Patty, who always got to do the solos. Actually, that was the only way it could have worked when we were together. Patty never did have an ear for harmony ... She sent me a long letter for my opening. It was full of news and all that. And at the end, she said "Just remember, I'll be standing beside you, no matter what. But this time the spotlight will be on you."[6]

Maxene's reference to "a long letter" from Patty is puzzling—considering the sisters were not speaking to one another at this time. Maxene's performance was well received by *Variety*:

Andrews still recalls how a tune should be delivered ... She is paying more attention to the meaning of a tune rather than its rhythmic aspects. Also to be reckoned with is her maturity. At this stage in her life ... the slower and more meaningful aspects of a song are more becoming to her and more in keeping with her abilities.

There are times that she has to explain away a frog in her throat ... Also there was a natural degree of nervousness on her preem night and her fumbling of the mike was a manifestation of that state.

Andrews' style and catalog have relevancy to today. She recalls moments from the sisters' vast catalog of hits, but there are also moments from contemporary writing. In all, she does more than try to live up to a memory. It's another bag for her.[7]

Maxene's former husband and manager Lou Levy was in the opening night audience. Beth Fowler, Maxene's stand-by during *Over Here!*, took in the show one evening. Maxene spotted her in the audience, called her on stage, and asked her to tell the story of her dead microphone when she stood in for Patty on Christmas Eve.[8]

Despite the good reviews, Maxene put her one-woman show on hold for awhile. In summer 1976, she played the lead role of Sally Adams, "the hostess with the mostest," in *Call Me Madam* for a two-month run at the Coachlight Dinner Theater in East Windsor, Connecticut. She told a reporter she much preferred working in the musical theater to movies, which she found dull. She claimed she had offers to star in television situation comedies, but had not found one to her liking.[9] She apparently never found one to her liking; she never appeared in one. During summer 1978, Maxene played the grandmother in the musical *Pippin* for one-week runs in Akron, Dayton, and Ivoryton, Connecticut. She sang the showstopper "No Time at All," but it was a promising, young lanky dancer named Tommy Tune who stole the show.[10]

When Maxene was in New York during winter 1978, an agent who had been urging her to continue her solo act took her to see Geraldine Fitzgerald's one-woman show at the Roundabout Theater. Maxene liked Fitzgerald's show, but she was even more taken by her piano accompanist, a young man named Phil Campanella:

I'd been telling [the agent] that I needed somebody to work with—someone at the piano who was musically creative ... After the show, we had dinner with Miss Fitzgerald and I was introduced to Phil. I told Lynda Wells, my manager, "I want to work with that young man" ... I'm a great believer in God ... I feel my life is being directed. It was like a miracle. A few months later, I found ... that Phil wanted to work with me.[11]

Maxene and Campanella discovered that their personalities and music meshed well together. They put together an act in five weeks and presented it as a semi-autobiographical sketch of Maxene with ample assistance from Campanella. It was the ingredient Maxene was looking for. Probably one reason it worked so well was that Maxene no longer felt alone on stage. Campanella, an accomplished musician, composer, and comedian gave her the backing and security her sisters provided in earlier years. They first tried the act in a gay club on Fire Island near New York City called The Monster. Maxene remembered the engagement:

> The stage was about the size of a pillow and they had a big, old, ugly upright piano filling most of it—I had to lay over the top of the piano to duet with my accompanist ... [The enthusiastic applause] was just great and something I really needed to get me started ... I got over that terrible feeling of shyness that night. You know, that feeling of "maybe I'm not good enough" or "maybe it wasn't really me they wanted." All of those terrible thoughts that come into your mind. But from the reaction I got that night, I got over those feelings and knew that we really had something.[12]

After their enthusiastic reception at Fire Island, they tried another gay venue, this one at Provincetown where the show was extended a second week. Maxene liked her gay audiences: "They're wonderful. Gay audiences are the most receptive and the most loyal—when they like you, *they like you.* They're also quite important in the business side of show business because of their influence on the record industry, especially in the disco market ... And of course, it's the gay audience that's keeping the nightclub and cabaret world alive."[13] Maxene told another reporter: "I'm still absolutely elated! I haven't been having so much fun in ages!"[14]

In mid–September 1979, Maxene was in San Francisco at the Plush Room where a critic reported she had "plenty of moxie and class." He thought the organization of the show could use some changes, but overall reviewed the show favorably.[15] One evening's audience was delighted when Joyce DeYoung was called from the audience to join Maxene on stage.

I saw Maxene's show in San Francisco. She had already played a week to appreciative audiences when I caught her last set on a rainy, cold Thursday night. Only four people were in the audience. Maxene, the consummate performer, was undaunted by the small audience and belted out her songs with accompanist Phil Campanella as if it were the packed Paramount of her earlier years. I thought her non–Andrews Sisters songs were best; her medley of Andrews hits was intended to touch memories and did no more than that. Her final number, "Where Did the Good Times Go?" sung to changing images of the Andrews Sisters' career on a screen above and behind her, was moving without becoming sentimental. It was a good show, not because she was an Andrews sister but because she and Campanella knew how to entertain an audience.

Variety caught Maxene and Campanella in Los Angeles in late September. This time the reviewer was disappointed because the show consisted entirely of songs made famous by the Andrews Sisters. He felt Maxene "still has a capable, even elegant voice" but her "patter was too feigned." The reviewer thought Campanella "was very talented both vocally and on piano, and provided some needed comic relief."[16] A reviewer for the *Los Angeles Times* viewed the show differently. He liked the selection of songs as well as Maxene's wit:

> The set, full of oldies ... was good entertainment. It worked, however, because it was Maxene Andrews singing those songs. A 61-year-old unknown doing the same set in the same way would have been much less interesting.
>
> It would be silly to expect her voice to be the finely tuned instrument it was years ago. It naturally shows signs of wear but isn't brittle or creaky. There is plenty of warmth and some strength in it. This cagey veteran has too much savvy to apply her fragile voice to demanding songs. Her style is very casual and her material suits that style.
>
> A large part of Andrews' appeal was her wit. At every opportunity she would deliver one-liners that were usually on target. The audience kept trying to treat her reverently, like some prized relic, but she refused to take herself that seriously. Her humor sliced through all that weighty reverence and toppled the pedestal on which the audience was trying to place her.[17]

In mid–October, *Newsweek* carried a story about Maxene's new solo career. The story noted that Maxene had performed to audiences ranging from "60-year-old nostalgia buffs to teen-agers turned on by Bette Midler's revival of 'Boogie Woogie Bugle Boy.'" Maxene told the reporter: "Don't use the word comeback about me ... I feel like I'm a new act ... I find more freedom in working alone ... I can sing songs I couldn't sing when we were a trio. We did no sad songs—we were known as the Happy Girls." She summed up her feelings about her present life: "I am having more fun now than I ever had because I am no longer competing ... I am not looking for success—I've had that. I am just looking to do my thing."[18]

In November, Maxene was in New York where *The New York Times* liked her show too, and singled out Phil Campanella as a critical ingredient in its success:

> It is a skillfully constructed act, and Miss Andrews moves through it with genial, unpretentious friendliness ... Her pianist, Phil Campanella, is a straightman, a singing harmonizer, an occasional soloist and an accomplished comedian ... He gives Miss Andrews something to play against and is so effective in his various roles—initially in unobtrusive fashion but building into a full-fledged partner—that he deserves equal billing for his contribution to an act that sets Miss Andrews apart from any other contemporary singers.[19]

Perhaps the most memorable evening of this engagement was when Vet Boswell of the Boswell Sisters showed up for Maxene's show. It was the first time the two seasoned singers met.[20]

For the next four years, Maxene took her show cross-country. I found no bad reviews. The following excerpts are typical of the critical acclaim she received wherever she appeared:

> HOLLYWOOD: There really is no business like show business and Maxene Andrews' exclusive solo engagement at the Studio One Backlot lent the most charming acknowledgment possible to that theme ... Maxene Andrews is a classy, gracious, energetic talent whose stage presence is an honor to experience.[21]

WASHINGTON, D.C. Maxene Andrews ... offered a program ... that included, predictably and rewardingly, reminiscence and re-creation. But she made it clear that she was also going to sing "some of the songs I was not able to sing as one of the Andrews Sisters."[22]

SPRINGFIELD, MASS. Maxene Andrews is a surprisingly strong solo act. The steely-edged, pop-style voice of limited upper range is still strong, vibrant, and accurate of pitch. But more important than the voice is the personality. She comes over as a friendly, out-going human being out to share a couple of hours with friends.[23]

BIRMINGHAM. Miss Andrews, one of the world famous Andrews Sisters who sang their way into the hearts of millions, entered more than a few hearts on her own as she took the crowd back to a time when high school girls wore bobby socks ... But the crowd saved its biggest ovation for her final song, "Where Did the Good Times Go?" As Miss Andrews sang the tender lyrics, a movie projector showed pictures of the Andrews Sisters as they were years ago.[24]

SAN FRANCISCO. Maxene ... is now a hearty blonde matron in her 60s, finally front and center but holding her own as a solo act and—well, just plain nice lady ... When she strolls on in green caftan, she looks like your Aunt Bea about to sing "Happy Birthday" ... You go to see Maxene Andrews out of some nagging curiosity, but you go away charmed and warmed at the sight of the old wartime trouper still calmly doing her thing, a Rosie the Riveter of song ... Even at her most sentimental, Maxene never seems to be wallowing in the past so much as winking at it.[25]

PORTLAND. What pulls the whole thing off is it's not nostalgia ... but the way Ms. Andrews sings those songs and the manner in which Campanella plays piano and takes part in them, the show comes down as an exercise in timeless entertainment ... The show is a must see.[26]

DURHAM. A good, solid, not-too-sentimental voice, a charm that may come from not having been a "star" on her own all these years and a sense of entertainment that never seems to misfire make Maxene's act work. All that plus Phil Campanella, who is young and funny and plays piano honky-tonk or sweet.[27]

INDIANAPOLIS. It's not often that a performer in this city gets a genuine, spontaneous standing ovation. But Maxene Andrews was given two ... She remains in lusty voice and radiant health, with a sunny disposition and outgoing personality that literally captivates her listeners. And she still has that rhythm.[28]

Maxene worked other engagements into her schedule as she moved around the country with her one-woman show. In mid–January 1980, she joined a cast of World War II entertainers at New York's Roseland Ballroom in *G. I. Jive*, a three-hour musical tribute to the performers who boosted the morale of servicemen during the war years. Filmed for PBS television broadcast, the show included singers Hildegard, Maxene Sullivan, Cab Calloway, and hosts Van Johnson and June Allyson. The following March, Maxene sang at a benefit in Luchow's Restaurant in New York with Martha Schlamme, Eartha Kitt, and Geraldine Fitzgerald to raise money for the CSC Repertory Company, an off-Broadway theater group devoted to preserving the classics.[29] In late June, she participated in a big band festival at the Bottom Line in New York where she

Throughout the 1980s and into the 1990s, Maxene toured her critically acclaimed one-woman show throughout the United States. She is pictured here in an appearance with the Kay Kyser orchestra at Chatham, New Jersey, in February 1988. (Joseph Klenner Collection)

and Phil Campanella opened for the Glenn Miller orchestra. After the festival, Maxene traveled to the Deep South where she joined another celebration of big band music, this one at the Boutwell Auditorium in Birmingham, Alabama. Always savvy to the importance of publicity, Maxene gave interviews wherever she performed. She was obviously enjoying her new career:

> I see women my age who look ten years older and it's because they have resigned themselves to being "old." I want to tell them to put on their make-up and get out in the world and enjoy life! ... I've tried this retirement business, and it's not for me ... It sounds great until you try it. You think "Look, I can go out and play golf and I can sleep as late as I want to." It doesn't work that way. If the good Lord gives us our health, I think it means that we've got to get out in the world and DO something...
>
> [Young people] come to the performance knowing more about the Andrews Sisters than I do! ... We recorded maybe 2,000 songs, and some of them were not all that well known ... but these young people know about them. In fact, I've started a list of the obscure songs that they request and have started doing a medley of them in the act![30]

In August 1980, the *Hollywood Reporter* announced that Maxene Andrews donated "more than 500 recordings of original radio broadcasts by the Andrews Sisters" to the University of California at Los Angeles radio archives. The collection included the Nash-Kelvinator shows aired on ABC from 1944 to 1946 as well as many of the *Club 15* shows aired from 1947 to 1951 on CBS.[31] Maxene was back in San Francisco in late October 1981 where her Halloween show sponsored an "Andrews Sisters look-alike contest" in the Plush Room at the York Hotel.[32] In early May the following year, Maxene joined other entertainers at a benefit at Warner Theater in Washington, D.C., sponsored by the Federal City Performing Arts Association to raise funds for rebuilding Wolftrap, a performing arts venue in Vienna, Virginia, that was destroyed by fire. Maxene was back in San Francisco in July to perform with the San Francisco Symphony Pops Orchestra. She sang a medley of Andrews Sisters' hits as part of a salute to MGM musicals and the big-band sounds of the 1940s.[33]

Maxene continued to travel the nation with her one-woman show and audiences continued to like it. She received one of her best reviews at Evanston, Illinois in August 1982:

> Maxene Andrews' ... performance was a joyous, magical retrospective that excelled technically and artistically ... She exuded confidence and poise from the instant she took the stage ... Hers was a warm and intimate show, accented with gentle humor and occasional reminiscence about the old days ... She was charming and inviting, her manner that of a favorite aunt showing her prized possessions to a few close friends ... Andrews covered a crowd-pleasing medley of the trio's biggest hits ... It was a nice finale to a sweet, sharing show, delivered by a woman clearly at peace with her work and herself.[34]

Maxene's pace finally caught up with her. One evening after a performance in Evanston, she and her companion/manager Lynda Wells returned to their hotel. In the lobby, Maxene suddenly felt unwell. Her condition persisted, and they decided a visit to a nearby hospital was in order. They walked the few blocks to Northwestern Memorial Hospital because Maxene wanted the fresh air and exercise. The emergency room personnel examined her and while waiting for the results, she suffered a massive heart attack. The attendant staff unsuccessfully attempted to revive her and was about to conclude she was dead.

Maxene remembered later that as the staff frantically tried to revive her, she saw a long tunnel with a bright light and familiar faces at its end. She was floating above her own funeral—"all this at the same time, which doesn't make much sense but where I was it doesn't have to," she said. A big band was playing and a crowd of happy people was singing "When the Saints Come Marching In." Meanwhile, as the emergency room staff was about to give up attempts to revive her, Maxene stirred and in a very frail, but discernable voice she began singing "When the Saints Come Marching In."[35] The next day, Lynda Wells announced that Maxene was forced to postpone several performances but would return to work "on a less demanding schedule."[36]

Maxene told a reporter that Patty never visited her during her hospitalization. Several months later, however, when Maxene underwent quadruple bypass surgery, Patty and her husband visited her: "When I was in the hospital, she and Walter came to see me three times, but I don't remember because I was so sick … I was told Patty held my hand for five minutes and Walter stood in the background and watched … Once I was well enough to receive visitors at home, Patty never came or called. But because of those visits at the hospital, I know she loves me."[37]

After her bypass surgery, Maxene's doctor told her she would never sing again. Maxene was not convinced: "I couldn't believe I was hearing what he said. I didn't think a heart had anything to do with vocal cords." She was determined she would sing again: "I had a desire to continue singing … It's the only thing I know how to do. Singing is my whole life." Five weeks later Maxene Andrews was singing on a Denver stage.[38]

While Maxene was hospitalized for her heart attack, her manager/companion Lynda Wells had difficulty seeing her because hospital policy allowed only relatives to visit critically ill patients. Shortly thereafter, Maxene legally adopted Wells to avoid such problems in the future.[39]

In early January 1983, Maxene sang with the Los Angeles Pops Orchestra at the season's opening concert with a heart monitor slung over her shoulder. She "brought down the house with sentimental applause" when she sang a medley of Andrews Sisters hits. A reviewer noted that she sang with "verve and maturity."[40] In October, Maxene appeared at Kathy Gallaher's in Los Angeles, her first cabaret date since her bypass surgery. *Variety* thought her performance was undiminished by her illness and her show had lost none of its charm: "Andrews Sister Maxene is … marking her return to performing after heart bypass surgery … Andrews looks in fine fettle, is obviously in fine voice and her 65-minute show is a lot of fun: "nostalgia" without cloying schmaltz, thanks in great part to Andrews' lively, infectious wit … Andrews keeps the perspective on target and it's part of the genuine charm of the show."[41] A *Los Angeles Times* reviewer liked the show too—although he wasn't too wild about the songs of the Andrews Sisters: "Though she's in her late 60s, Andrews is hardly a conservative little old lady. She's chic, hip and very witty. That heart attack she suffered last year apparently hasn't slowed her down at all."[42]

In February 1985, Maxene told a Philadelphia reporter "I was 69 my last birthday [she was now telling her true age], but I feel like I'm 29 ... I just never think of myself as 'old,' you know? What is that wonderful line in the show? Oh, yes. 'Old age is 15 years from now.'" She was being interviewed about her performance in the musical *Taking My Turn*, "an exuberant celebration of aging and old age" that ran for nine months off-Broadway the previous year. Critics liked the show, but New Yorkers didn't line up for it, so now it was on the road to see what it could drum up. The cast of four men and four women, most of them in their 60s, presented monologues and songs. Maxene explained, "There's no real story line, but each segment is a musical celebration of the views these real people have about getting older." Maxene played Janet, a widow of two years, who was afraid to face life alone.[43] The show moved on to New Haven after which Maxene departed. She flew to India to join the *Queen Elizabeth II* for an onboard concert, disembarked in South Africa and flew back to New York. "That's a long way to go for a one-night concert," she acknowledged.[44]

In summer 1985, Bainbridge Records released *Maxene, An Andrews Sister.* The LP was Maxene's first recording date since *Over Here!* some eleven years previously, and consisted primarily of her concert songs of the past six years. Bette Midler wrote for the album liner: "Whether singing solo or singing her own harmonies, Maxene Andrews is always divine. How wonderful to hear this voice again."

The album was a mix of new and old songs, with emphasis on the old. Maxene sang "In Apple Blossom Time" and a medley of hits in concession to the Andrews Sisters. The remainder of the songs was Maxene Andrews. Novelties such as "Mama Llama" and "Show Me the Way to Go Home" were balanced by ballads like "How Deep Is the Ocean?" and "Remember"—perhaps the most haunting and successful of the selections. Maxene's voice worked for the songs. It was the seasoned, experienced voice of Maxene Andrews and that was why people bought the LP.

When the album was released, Maxene was interviewed at her home in Encino, California, with her "two pound Yorkshire terrier named Slippers in her lap." The reporter noted three automobiles, all belonging to Maxene, parked in front of the house with personalized license plates: "BMBDS," "BWBB," and "ABT OC." He recognized the first as "Bei Mir Bist Du Schoen" and the second as "Boogie Woogie Bugle Boy," but the third one stumped him. When asked to explain, Maxene replied, "'Apple Blossom Time,' of course." Most of the interview was about the career of the Andrews Sisters, but at the end the reporter asked Maxene about her estrangement from Patty. "Her eyes welled up" as she said: "This is the biggest pain in my entire life. She actually is all I have left. I would do anything if I could bridge whatever the problem is."[45]

During the late 1970s and early 1980s, Maxene Andrews gave a series of interviews that revealed where she was at that time of her life. Reporters liked her. One said, "Maxene ... is a marvelous story-teller, witty and articulate."[46]

Another observed, "I found Maxene Andrews to be a vital, shrewd, clear-headed, vastly intelligent lady—earthy, honest, and far more than just one-third of a singing trio."[47] Another said, "Maxene is an all-out, world-class talker, whose sharp eye and sharp intelligence shine through the carefully worked surface of her wonderful personality."[48] And still another described her as a "non-smoking, nondrinking, vegetarian, 61-year-old born-again Christian."[49] Maxene's drive impressed one reporter: "I got a sense of the woman's determination, vitality, and most important, her courageous drive toward the independence and self-realization that comes from starting over again after being famous for something you no longer are."[50] Elsewhere, she was described as "a vital and robust woman in her 60s, with twinkling eyes and a lived-in, honest face."[51]

In the late 1970s, Maxene became a born-again Christian. During a period of spiritual searching, she tried her father's Greek Orthodox religion and her mother's Lutheranism but neither provided satisfying answers to her questions. Born-again Christianity did. In 1981, she discussed her religion:

> I became a born-again Christian three years ago ... I've always been a Christian, but the difference is, I re-dedicated my life to Jesus. It was like re-affirming everything I've always believed in. There have been bad connotations to being born again in terms of Anita Bryant, Jerry Falwell and the Moral Majority. But my own faith is a very warm, humane, non-judgmental kind of spiritual renewal which goes into every aspect of my life. I sing a lot, pray a lot, and hallelujah a lot because I feel that as Americans, we have a lot of blessings to be thankful for.[52]

Following her heart attack and bypass surgery, Maxene's born-again Christianity resurfaced. She made two appearances on *The 700 Club*, hosted by conservative televangelist Pat Robertson. I was able to locate only an audiotape of her second appearance on July 14, 1983.

After an introduction featuring film clips, recordings, and the usual misinformation about the number of films, recordings, and gold records of the sisters, Maxene told Robertson of her conversion. She believed God pulled her through her illnesses, which was his way of telling her to slow down. Maxene said she was now "singing for the Lord" and doing church concerts after a successful one at Riverside, California, where she introduced "beautiful, original Christian songs." She told Robertson that she suffered shyness her entire life until her escape from death and her reconversion to Christianity. Now that she had "met the Lord," she was no longer shy. She made the dubious claim that she and Patty had reconciled since her heart attack when Patty came to visit her frequently. She said her life was free of stress, she was happy, her children were happy, she was no longer shy, she was friends with Patty, and she "owed it all to the Lord." Maxene's interview concluded with a tired medley of Christian "praise songs" she previously recorded for the show—unremarkably selected and even less remarkably arranged. I could find no reviews of Maxene's church concerts.

When asked about her religion six years later, Maxene replied:

It's made a tremendous difference in me ... It has made me see values that I guess I knew about but never paid much attention to when I was younger, and it's put me more at peace with myself. It's given me a greater understanding of self-forgiveness and forgiving others ... And I am much more tolerant of things, and I'm learning the great value of a thing called love, which has many different meanings ... the love I have for myself is not the same love I would have for my animals, and the love for myself and the animals is not the same love I would have for a lover, and it's really made a whole new world for me ... I think that being privileged to be able to sing all my life has been one of the great blessings that the Lord has given me, and I constantly bless Him and thank Him for that because I know a lot of people who work at jobs that they loathe. That has never been one of my problems.[53]

During her exploration of spirituality, Maxene once told a reporter that she sometimes sensed the spirit of her deceased sister LaVerne. She attributed the success of *Over Here!* to LaVerne: "We really missed LaVerne but we soon began to realize that she was right up there with us ... One night she literally pushed me on stage and I fell on my you-know-what ... All of a sudden I had a vision of LaVerne. I knew that she was laughing, too. She had the most marvelous laugh and she loved to play jokes." Once during rehearsal, the director ordered a medical bag to serve as a prop. The one that arrived was stamped with the letters "L. A. R." which Maxene interpreted as initials for "LaVerne Andrews Rogers." Maxene once experimented with recording songs in which she sang all three of the Andrews Sisters' parts. She was able to sing her own part and Patty's, but when it came to LaVerne's she was apprehensive: "But the moment I heard the two parts together, it came to me. I knew that LaVerne was in that booth with me and that she had come through again for me."[54]

Maxene enjoyed her new career as a solo performer. She told a reporter:

After being a part of a trio for so many years ... the whole feeling of it is completely different. I'm a fledgling leaving the nest ... I think my voice is more mellow now, and I certainly know a lot more about what the lyrics mean. I can be myself without compromising with other people on which offers to accept and what wardrobe to wear, and I can sing a lot of songs that I would not have been able to sing as one of the Andrews Sisters.

While other kids were enjoying these things, we were out singing. Of course, I loved it, but I missed what the other kids were doing ... Now, I'm getting a taste of all that freedom. I'm finally enjoying my teen age, and I think it's great to be a teen-ager with so much experience behind you.

But you can't help feeling that you have talents outside of singing harmony, and that's what I'm working on now. At first, I was afraid that the solo act might be a real disaster, but the audiences have been good to me—and anyway, I thought I had to try...

When it's going right ... there is a magnetism, an electric current between you and the audience that is the greatest high in the world. I can't understand why people in show business feel that they need drugs, or even booze, when they can get a high like that ... And I can't understand why people my age feel that they have to feel old.[55]

Maxene occasionally mentioned her children in interviews. In 1965, her twenty-year-old daughter was a receptionist in a Burbank radio station. Her son played piano and guitar and was scheduled to attend the University of Southern California in the fall. Maxene said, "It's a constant fight to keep him out of the music business. Once he gets his education, I'll help him."[56] In early 1972, Maxene told a reporter, "My kids, Aleda and Peter, and I have gone through a lot together, and now I can say that we're really friends."[57] In 1974, she told another reporter that her son "skis 24 hours a day" and her daughter was an artist who lived with her husband in Santa Monica.[58] Five years later she reported that her son and daughter were in the construction business together in Utah and were never reared "in any kind of theatrical atmosphere."[59] She told another: "If there's anything I regret … it's that I didn't spend more time with my kids when they were little. I was traveling so much. I had a wonderful Hungarian couple who worked for me 35 years take care of them. They were like the kids' grandparents. The kids are wonderful now."[60] When asked about her career once, she said, "I would love to have been closer to my children."[61] In another interview she said, "I've raised two children, did the best I could with them, they seem to be well-adjusted, and they're leading their own lives now. Pat and LaVerne never had that itch."[62]

I interviewed several of Maxene's friends, and none remembered her talking about her children. Her son Peter attended the Army and Naval Academy at Carlsbad, which his parents thought might lead to Annapolis, but after Carlsbad, Peter apparently had enough military and opted for the University of Southern California.[63] Maxene once told a reporter that she had established trusts for her children "so when they are 40 they won't have any great problem."[64]

Regarding marriage, Maxene told a reporter:

> I've always felt that it was very necessary for both my sisters to be married … But I think I was born free. I think it's something we owe to ourselves. We have responsibilities we certainly cannot shirk, but I feel we also have a responsibility to ourselves, and there's a kind of freedom that's necessary to all of us. That's why I've never remarried. I love the idea of being able to pack up and go whenever I want to. I love the feeling of freedom, as long as it doesn't hurt anyone or obstruct anything.[65]

She made observations about her personal growth. She once said, "Now I can look back at a lot of things I used to cry over, and I can laugh about it. So it wasn't that bad, I guess."[66] A few months later she said, "But when LaVerne died [after her mother died], then I *really* felt I was on my own. I had to make decisions, and I've made some very bad ones. But that's the only way I've been able to learn. I've found a whole new freedom."[67] She told another reporter: "Life is much smoother and peaceful today … I'm out of the rat race and living in Encino [California] with three dogs in a lovely home."[68]

In September 1979, she confided to a San Francisco reporter: "I have very few of what I could call friends in show business. I find it very difficult to carry on any kind of intelligent conversation with them—all they want to know is, 'What have you been doing lately?' She added: "It has been my dream for years to retire here and become the naughtiest little old lady on Telegraph Hill."[69] A month later, she said she was about to embark on a cruise ship where she would

Lou Levy and Maxene Andrews at the graduation of their son Peter Levy from the Army and Navy Academy at Carlsbad, California, in June 1965. (Gladys Leichter Collection)

entertain en route to Bermuda and told a reporter: "I don't think people should be forced into retirement … It's not right to pick an arbitrary age and say to you, 'Okay, that's as far as you can go.'" She summarized her approach to life: "Never stop growing."[70] In early October, she told a reporter in Washington, D.C., "I'm having the time of my life." Then she added, hinting at some of the difficulties of being part of a trio: "I can make my own decisions about where I want to go or what I want to wear or what I want to sing without worrying about what my sisters will think, without living a life of compromises. Now the decisions are mine."[71] The following month she told a *New York Times* reporter: "I'm not going to compete with anyone. My days of competition are over. I'm having a great time, and I want my audiences to have a good time."[72]

In the late seventies, Maxene became interested in nutrition. She gave up red meat, alcohol, coffee and salt and ate only natural foods, and consequently lost thirty pounds in five weeks. She said: "I call it a kind of detoxification diet … I feel like a million dollars and I'm rarely tempted to cheat. It solves a lot of the problems about getting older, like exhaustion, hypertension and depression."[73]

In 1985, Maxene repeated her appreciation of gay audiences: "Gay audiences have been wonderful to me over the years. And it's a joy to work for them because they are so up on everything. They're sharp. I have a rather peculiar sense of humor, which I find that the average public doesn't get. But gay audiences understand my kidding around; that makes it so much easier and more enjoyable to work."[74]

Patty Andrews opted for a quieter life than her sister Maxene and gave considerably fewer interviews. Consequently, less is known about her later years. She occasionally emerged from her private life for television shows and personal appearances.

During *Over Here!* in 1974, Patty told an interviewer that she and her husband, Wally Weschler, sold their home in Encino, California, before going to New York but planned to return to California after the show and buy a new home: "Wally and I love California ... we like that type of life ... we live very quietly. Wally plays golf and every now and then, maybe, once in a blue moon I'll play golf ... we live a very sane type of life. We have our dog and ... we like the simple life."[75]

After *Over Here!* closed, Patty and her husband returned to southern California and bought a home. In early January 1974, Patty appeared on a television special, *One More Time*, and sang "Bei Mir Bist Du Schoen" with the then-popular Pointer Sisters. In September 1977, she told a reporter that she was writing the "real" story about the Andrews Sisters: "Patty, who refuses to say her age, and her manager-husband are working on the book in their Encino [California] home while they try to negotiate a deal for a new Broadway show." No Broadway show materialized and so far no book has been published. She had just finished taping seven sessions of *The Gong Show*, a popular lowbrow TV show and was rehearsing a show she hoped to take to Las Vegas.[76] The following month, Patty told a reporter she was planning a trip to Nashville "to cut a country-western album." The album never materialized. She had recently cancelled a tour to Australia when she learned her sixteen-year-old dog would be subjected to a long quarantine. Like Maxene, Patty had a life-long love for dogs. When not on the road, Patty said: "I do charity work for churches and children's hospitals ... I also help with a home for retired actors in Woodland Hills." In addition, she enjoyed needlepoint and crewel, and golf with her husband.[77]

A year later, Patty was in the news when she filed a lawsuit against NBC. She claimed an NBC crew caused her to fall and injure her leg during a taping of *The Gong Show* when she was a panelist the previous season.[78] Later that fall, Patty appeared as a celebrity judge on another lowbrow game show, *The $1.98 Beauty Show*, a half-hour beauty/talent show that awarded winners $1.98 for their efforts.

In March 1980 Patty was back in New York with a one-woman show, at Les Mouches, where a *Variety* reviewer caught her act. He thought she was depending too much on the Andrews Sisters and not utilizing her own potential:

> In her current cabaret act, one of the two surviving Andrews Sisters unfortunately displays too much Andrews and too little Patty. Comprised of a nostalgic view of the vocal trio's career, the act quickly reveals that much of the material's appeal was due to the ensemble effects created by the sisters, and doesn't hold up that well for a solitary singer.
>
> Andrews tends to make the entire act seem like one long medley and this proves to be musically self-defeating, as she rarely gives herself the time or space

In early January 1974, Patty sang "Bei Mir Bist Du Schoen" on the television special *One More Time* with the then popular Pointer Sisters, two of whom—Anita and Bonnie—are shown here. (Robert Boyer Collection)

to show what she can do as an individual. From the glimpses one gets of her vocal potential, the act is depriving the audience of a great deal, as the singer has a marvelously expressive, bluesy quality to her upper register, and can really start cooking when she begins to get into a song.

Her sense of phrasing is also not to be underestimated, as her great skill at handling both words and music shows how aware she is of how a line should go, as well as how to deliver it just so. Andrews has no problem in charming an audience either, as she moves around the stage with ease like the seasoned pro she is.[79]

Two New York reviewers, one for the *Daily News* and the other for the *Times*, reviewed the shows of both Patty and Maxene in early 1980, and both reviewers preferred Maxene. The *Times* reviewer wrote: "Maxene presents a comfortable, middle-aged personality and a warm, pure-toned voice. Patty has a glittering surface. She wears a tightly curled blond wig, a black spangled jacket with black tie, white shirt and black pants. She projects a show-business hipness, punching out one-liners often more notable for their lack of taste than for their wit." He also felt that Patty relied too much on the old Andrews Sisters hits whereas Maxene explored new material.[80] After a career of being reviewed as the prime mover of the Andrews Sisters, the review could not have sat well with Patty.

The following year in November 1981, back in Los Angeles, Patty joined

Della Reese, Eartha Kitt, and Lainie Kazan in a show called *Swingin' Singin' Ladies*. The show was part of a nostalgia wave that brought various once-big stars out of mothballs, perhaps the most successful of which was *4 Girls 4* that resurrected Helen O'Connell, Margaret Whiting, Rosemary Clooney, and Rose Marie after years of inactivity. A reviewer thought the talent in *Swingin' Singin' Ladies* was good, but the show didn't quite work:

> We were seeing four medium-size to big cats up there, and they belonged together only to the extent that [the] producers had come upon four as a magic number.
>
> The ladies represent four decades of popular music, from Patty Andrews' WWII favorites to Lainie Kazan's more or less contemporary selections ... Kazan sings old standards, and Andrews' sings "New York, New York" and "I Can Do That."
>
> The lines therefore blur. The evening feels like four showroom acts that have been inadvertently hooked onto the same train. With close-cropped, curly blond hair, and wearing a sequined jacket over gray slacks, Andrews sings her songs straight ... Lines such as "Tell me girls, do you still get headaches?" don't play the Hartford as well as they might in Fontana, but her "Beer Barrel Polka" (anyone who tries a polka nowadays deserves some sort of note), "Don't Sit Under the Apple Tree" and "Apple Blossom Time" together suggest America's last age of innocence ... "Swingin' Singin' Ladies" is an entertainment which it's designed to be. Despite the glitzy title, it could have been a good deal larger.[81]

Variety also thought the music was good, but didn't think the format worked: "None of the four works together, so it's more like two mini concerts, with an opener and the featured player. What priorities, if any, producers ... employed are not evident."[82]

The engagement concluded on a sour note. The producers ended up $130,000 in the red and were unable to pay the singers for the show's final week. They planned to book the show into other cities and pay the stars from the first proceeds of future engagements, but the singers filed grievances with the state labor commission and the show never traveled beyond Los Angeles.[83]

The following August, Patty appeared at Holiday House in Pittsburgh in a show called *Great Ladies of the Silver Screen* with a new cast of old timers, namely Mamie Van Doren, Vivian Blaine, Kathryn Grayson, and Dorothy Lamour. A *Variety* reviewer liked the performances, but thought the classical voice of Grayson was out of place in the show which overall was too long and lacked a finale. Of Patty's performance he wrote: "Patty Andrews came on for a triumphant closer. She sang most of the songs she recorded with her sisters, starting with 'Bei Mir Bist Du Schoen' and winding up with 'Apple Blossom Time.'"[84]

In November, Patty was back at Holiday House with still another seasoned cast in a show called *Great Stars of the Silver Screen*. Men were added to the cast this time which included Gordon McRae, Morey Amsterdam, Roberta Sherwood, Gloria DeHaven, and Forrest Tucker. It was another nostalgia package which the reviewer thought was too long. He summed up Patty's segment of the show: "Patty Andrews was in the closing spot and repeated the success of her last visit here with a similar package. She brought back all the Andrews

Sisters hits time would allow and received strong mitting on the first bars of each song, exiting to a standing ovation."[85] The production also played in Miami.

In March 1985, Patty appeared on the Merv Griffin television show in the curly blond wig, dark sparkly top, and dark pants that became her trademark costume in her later years, to sing a medley of songs from *Brigadoon.* A few days later, she was in a television special called *In the Swing*, a tribute to the swing era hosted by Steve Allen. She sang "Boogie Woogie Bugle Boy," a rousing version of "South Ram-

Throughout the 1970s, 1980s and early 1990s, Patty Andrews appeared in concert and on television, frequently accompanied by her pianist husband Wally Weschler. Circa 1980. (John Sforza Collection).

part Street Parade," and a strained "I Can Dream, Can't I?" Patty played an unlikely venue when she performed at Boscov's department store in Camp Hill, Pennsylvania (near Harrisburg), in mid–November 1985. The following October, she sang in concert with Les Brown and his band at the Hollywood Palladium where she was awarded the USO Lifetime Achievement Award.[86] It is unclear from the story whether Maxene and LaVerne were also given awards.

In mid–January 1987, Patty Andrews played her first Atlantic City casino date at Resorts International Hotel Casino. While there, she learned that a recent poll of World War II veterans voted the Andrews Sisters the most popular act of that era. "Number one ahead of Bob Hope," she said proudly. "I'm still in shock over that." Contrary to what she told an earlier interviewer,[87] she said she felt no nervousness on stage the first time she appeared without her sisters: "I did all the solo work and used to emcee the shows over the years, so performing alone wasn't something new to me." She explained the nature of her show: "I do a lot of contemporary music during the first part of the show … The second half, though, is devoted to the music of the Andrews Sisters. Plus, I do a little dancing and talk to the audience. I do it all." She added that she preferred the backup of a big band, but acknowledged that music synthesizers certainly had their uses in the contemporary music scene.[88] She told another reporter: "I've kept going even though LaVerne died and Maxene dropped out ... I enjoy singing and I love people. Wherever I go, there's always some G.I. who saw us at the front or fell in love to our music."[89] Patty was surely aware that Maxene had not "dropped out" but rather was having a very successful solo career. When asked about a possible reconciliation with Maxene, she was conciliatory: "Yes, it would be nice ... We have these differences, like all families, but I would like to iron them out and get back with Maxene again. Maybe this year ... well, who knows."[90]

Like Maxene, Patty occasionally performed on cruise ships. In 1983, she did a Caribbean cruise on the S.S. *Norway* and in 1986 she joined a New Year's cruise to Hawaii. In early May 1989, she sailed on the Holland-American ship S.S. *Rotterdam* and entertained passengers en route to Venezuela. Two passengers recalled meeting her in letters to me, and were impressed by her warmth and friendliness.

In fall 1988, Patty toured with the Glenn Miller band in England and the United States. While in the San Francisco Bay Area, she appeared on *Good Morning Bay Area* with her husband Wally Weschler, Della Reese and the Modernaires. She reminisced about the swing era, sang "Boogie Woogie Bugle Boy," and led the audience for "In Apple Blossom Time."

CHAPTER SIXTEEN

1987–2002

I take great pleasure, on this the 50th anniversary of the Andrews Sisters ... in presenting the Department of Defense Medal for Distinguished Public Service to Ms. Maxene Andrews, to Ms. Patty Andrews and, posthumously to Ms. LaVerne Andrews.[1]

—Caspar W. Weinberger

The Defense Department of the United States of America belatedly recognized the Andrews Sisters' career-long contribution to entertaining servicemen and women by awarding them the Pentagon's highest civilian honor, the Medal for Distinguished Public Service.

In early April 1987, San Francisco hosted a four-day festival called "Army Days 87," celebrating the Army's history of service to the citizens of San Francisco and the Bay Area and the bicentennial of the signing of the United States Constitution. During the festival, Maxene Andrews sang a twenty-minute medley of Andrews Sisters hits in an evening concert at the Masonic Auditorium that also included musical numbers by the United States Army Band and Chorus. At a reception the following day at San Francisco City Hall, hosted by Mayor Dianne Feinstein, Maxene and her sisters were awarded the Medal for Distinguished Public Service by a representative of the United States Defense Department.[2] The award was signed by Caspar W. Weinberger, Secretary of Defense, and read:

> For extremely meritorious service from 1937 to the present, during which time the efforts of the Andrews Sisters have contributed to the morale and well being of millions of servicemen and women. Maxene, Patty and LaVerne Andrews performed for troops throughout the United States [and] in Europe during World War II. Their untiring efforts played a major role in maintaining the morale of

both our fighting men and their loved ones on the home front. Maxene and Patty have continued to provide service to Veterans and service members to this day, by extensively touring, visiting, and performing in, Veterans hospitals across the country. The Andrews Sisters have demonstrated, during the critical World War II era, and for a half century, a great devotion to American service members and to our nation. Their patriotism and service to their country and countrymen reflect great credit upon themselves, their profession and the United States of America.

I take great pleasure, on this 50th anniversary of the Andrews Sisters, and on the occasion of Army Days 87 in San Francisco, in presenting the Department of Defense Medal for Distinguished Public Service to Ms. Maxene Andrews, to Ms. Patty Andrews and, posthumously to Ms. LaVerne Andrews.[3]

A slightly different version of the above was awarded each sister individually. Patty was invited to the ceremony, but declined to attend. She later received her award in southern California from a representative of the Defense Department, where Lou Rogers accepted LaVerne's posthumous award.[4] The recognition of the sisters' military contributions coincided with the fiftieth anniversary of "Bei Mir Bist Du Schoen," the song that catapulted them to national fame.

Another belated recognition came to the Andrews Sisters some five months later on October 1, 1987, when the Hollywood Chamber of Commerce awarded them a star on Hollywood Boulevard's famous "Walk of Fame." Maxene claimed they were offered a star previously, but declined because "The idea of having your name embedded in the sidewalk so people could walk on it and spit on it was rather distasteful to us." The sisters apparently accepted the recognition this time because it coincided with MCA's release of a sixteen-song compact disc, *The Andrews Sisters 50th Anniversary Collection.Volume One*. Maxene and Patty agreed to appear together for the ceremony and gave separate interviews to the *Los Angeles Times* for the occasion.[5]

The day began with a 6.1 earthquake that rocked Los Angeles and led an observer to note: "Suspicions were high that LaVerne was indeed with us and, at least for a day, the three sisters were once again united."[6] As a crowd gathered on Hollywood Boulevard, the sisters' recording of "Bei Mir Bist Du Schoen" entertained over a p.a. system. A small raised platform served as stage for the event that was emceed by Johnny Grant, chairman of the Walk of Fame Committee. Patty and Maxene stood to the left of the stage appearing slightly uncomfortable together.

The two sisters were called to the podium and received several citations, including one from the Los Angeles Board of Supervisors that proclaimed October 1, 1987, as "Andrews Sisters Day" in Los Angeles. Others included tributes from the Human Relations Committee of Los Angeles, the United States Senate, and California Governor George Deukmejian. Lou Rogers was invited to the stage to accept LaVerne's award. Vic Schoen was also called forward to extend his congratulations. When the sisters were introduced, Patty jokingly referred to the earthquake and said, "The rumbling was really Maxene and I on the telephone with each other." The sisters embraced as Maxene kissed Patty on the cheek. The uninformed observer would never have guessed the sisters had not spoken in nearly thirteen years—their fifty-five years before audiences paid off. Maxene told the crowd she and Patty had a lot of love between them as well as their share of fights, but concluded, "When you're sisters, you're sisters." She then passed the mike to her "baby sister."

Patty joked about the sisters' early review that called them "a Chinese puzzle set to off-key music" and gave appropriate thanks to the people responsible for the event, especially her "ever loving husband, Mr. Walter Weschler," who was "most instrumental" in making the fiftieth anniversary CD happen. The emcee asked the sisters to sing "Beer Barrel Polka," his favorite Andrews Sisters song. Patty and Maxene complied with a brief chorus, the last time they would sing together. Roses were presented to the sisters and they left the stage to unveil the star on the nearby sidewalk. Each sister was then presented a star and a third was given to Lou Rogers for LaVerne. Patty and Maxene posed separately for press photos and then gave separate interviews to TV's *Entertainment Tonight.*

Maxene was in the news again in November 1988 when the *Chicago Tribune* interviewed her about her new job as hostess for a series of "California Stardust Memories" tours. The tours were scheduled to include a "Stage Door Canteen" party on the back lot of Universal Studios in Los Angeles, a visit to Howard Hughes' plane the *Spruce Goose,* and a concert by Maxene Andrews. Much of the interview dealt with the Andrews Sisters' career, but some of it revealed the current Maxene. In retrospect, she said she realized that the rift with Patty, painful though it was, led to her career as a solo performer. As always, Maxene had opinions to share. She repeated her dislike of the word *nostalgia*: "I personally don't like that word ... It has a connotation of being old, and to me, that era is not old, because the most creative music and the most fun movies came out of that period of the late 1930s and the 1940s. We had come through a terrible depression, but we were coming out of it, and the whole atmosphere of the country was like we were all holding hands, embracing each other. That whole period was about hope, working together to win."

Regarding contemporary entertainers, she said, "The money they get today still stuns me ... Stars today make as much money in one night as we made in a year." She admitted that she continued to make "a healthy living" from the royalties of the Andrews Sisters' old recordings. Her favorite contemporary performers included Barry Manilow, Neil Diamond, Carly Simon, and the Judds. She didn't understand why contemporary performers dressed and made-up so outrageously for stage performances, perhaps forgetting the camp costumes she and her sisters donned for some of their films. She described her life as very full and said she was in the process of moving from Los Angeles to "the open spaces north of Sacramento." "All my friends think I'm crazy ... But I need the space," she explained. "I enjoy being at home out of the limelight ... Actually, my whole life I have been terribly shy, and I never have gotten over it. I'm fine in a one-on-one situation, but when I get in a crowd, I want to run."[7] During her visit to Chicago, Maxene appeared on *Lifestyle,* a local television show. She reminisced about her career and was entertained by Stardust, a female trio that performed Andrews Sisters songs in the Chicago area.

The following fall, Maxene was a guest on Sally Jessy Raphael's television show with other seasoned singers Phyllis McGuire (of the McGuire Sisters), Sylvia Sims, and Helen O'Connell. She told the predictable stories about the early years of the Andrews Sisters and reminisced about the war years, claiming they did no more than other entertainers in entertaining the troops.

In fall 1991, audiences were once again packing concert halls to hear the music of the Andrews Sisters. The sisters were in the news again, but with a difference this time. The music was recorded and the occasion was a dance program by Paul Taylor, one of America's foremost choreographers.

Taylor was hired to choreograph a dance for the Houston Ballet. He told an interviewer that he left the first rehearsal with no idea as to where the dance was going. When he approached his apartment, he saw an old album of Andrews Sisters songs in a trashcan. It brought back memories of hearing the Andrews Sisters for the first time when he lived in a residence hotel in Washington, D.C., in the late 1930s. In the basement was a canteen with a jukebox and a small dance floor. "I remember going down there one time ... and the place was empty. I put a nickel in the jukebox and heard the Andrews Sisters for the first time." Almost fifty years later, Taylor was trying to come up with an idea for a new work but the muses weren't speaking until he saw the album in the trashcan. He went to his record collection and played "this old record of the Andrews Sisters I put on whenever I want to feel good, and I couldn't think of anything else I'd rather use."[8]

The resulting dance piece that Paul Taylor choreographed was *Company B*, based on World War II songs of the Andrews Sisters, first performed by the Houston Ballet. Taylor then transferred it to his own dance company and presented it at New York's City Center Theater in October 1991. The dance was later featured in the Paul Taylor Dance Company's tour the following winter. A critic described the dance: "Set to nine songs by the Andrews Sisters, *Company B* evokes the exuberant rhythms of the '40s as well as the grim and persistent shadow of war. But even more vividly, it honors Taylor's magnificent dances."[9] Another opined: "Taylor has reacted not only to the style and structure of the Andrews Sisters' recordings but to the culture that produced it."[10] Critics liked *Company B*, including the following one:

> In "Company B," Taylor throws off the robe and slides into his dancing shoes. The relief is palpable as he allows his dancers to adopt a style—knee-swiveling, 1940s jitterbugging—that has its own vibrant associations. He also appreciates the hard hum of the Andrews Sisters: the lack of sentimentality, the sexual knowing, the gutsy, hopped-up beat. The songs are a syncopated joyride of swift stops and cliff-hanging enjambments. Time is their theme: time running out, lengthening and lost. In other words, wartime...
>
> "Company B" opens and closes with the song "Bei Mir Bist du Schon" ... Within that musical frame Taylor's work spins out a series of solo, duet and ensemble pieces requiring an all-American hubris, a spit-shine denial.
>
> The men get the showstoppers. "Tico-Tico," an ode to a clock that won't tick fast enough to the 8 o'clock mark, is a star turn ... "Boogie Woogie Bugle Boy," mainly a series of leaps large and small, flies like a flag. It clearly demands a ballet technique, one with plenty of elevation and snap ... "Oh Johnnie, Oh Johnnie, Oh!," a dance for [a male] and seven females, is a top-speed lascivious reading...
>
> The quieter pieces focus on the absent "you" in many of the songs, and at

these points "Company B"'s grief creeps forward. Taylor's use of silhouette to present his darker motifs is deftly aided by ... ingenious lighting [that] throws the upstage into an eerie sepia tinted twilight zone that grants the dancers their anonymity. In an incomparable moment ... the male half of the duet "There Will Never Be Another You" takes leave of his girlfriend by retiring toward the back, where a line of men march in stiff, slow, nightmare silhouette. As he crosses into the dark, he quietly takes on their tin-soldier angles. We understand that he is already gone.

"I Can Dream, Can't I?" is an agitated reverie featuring [a woman dancer], behind whom two men move left to right in mirror step, a backdrop to her longing. Suddenly, one turns to confront the other. An inch further apart and the gesture would be meaningless; as it is, we realize why [the woman] will never win her man...

"Company B" makes no obvious judgments, no politically correct points. It simply swoops into the '40s and, in the most glancing, ghostly of ways, invokes the present. When Taylor's men crumple to the ground they are falling in love and in battle—a double entendre that, in the age of AIDS, conveys a third association. Romantic love and physical appetite, the brio of youth as much as its dangerous attractions, course through "Company B"'s veins. Could there be a world without such destruction? This dance might answer, "dream on."[11]

Taylor took artistic license in using some pieces that were not World War II songs—in fact only three of the songs were recorded by the Andrews Sisters during the war years, namely "Pennsylvania Polka" (1942), "Tico Tico" (1944), and "Rum and Coca-Cola" (1944). Three were recorded before the war: "Bei Mir Bist Du Schoen" (1937), "Oh, Johnny! Oh, Johnny! Oh" (1939), and "Boogie Woogie Bugle Boy" (1941). Two were recorded after the war: "I Can Dream, Can't I?" (1949) and "There Will Never Be Another You" (1950).

Maxene first learned of Taylor's project when she received a call from the director of special projects at MCA, which owned the Andrews Sisters' Decca recordings. He told her that he had received an unusual request from a ballet company asking for some Andrews Sisters music to use in one of its productions. He knew ballet companies didn't have much money and asked Maxene what she thought he should do. Maxene was intrigued by the project and asked MCA if they could arrange for the ballet company to use the music for a limited time without charge. That was the last she heard of the project until some months later when she received an invitation to Paul Taylor's *Company B* at the Kennedy Center in Washington, D.C. Maxene continued the story:

> I took my manager and two fellas I know very well ... I was kind of on pins and needles. I had no idea what Paul was going to do with the music. As long as he didn't ask me to put a tutu on. At this stage, it would have to be a tu-four, darling. I was as nervous as if I was going to have to get up and do a performance myself, but when it came on I can't tell you how thrilled I was. I'm so used to people getting up and doing the Andrews Sisters' cutesies, putting their finger in the air and jitterbugging.
>
> I wasn't surprised [that Taylor saw a darker side to the songs] ... I was entranced with having it explained in dance. There was a dark side to the period, even though the whole country banded together and pitched in like a wonderful love-in. And Paul did it so clearly and so seamlessly. You knew the darkness was there, but no one thing stood out.[12]

Patty Andrews reportedly cancelled her scheduled appearance at the premier when she learned that Maxene would be there.[13]

President George Bush and First Lady Barbara Bush saw the performance of *Company B* at the Kennedy Center and invited Maxene and her companion/manager Lynda Wells to the White House. The president had meetings to attend and met his guests only briefly, but Mrs. Bush gave them an extensive tour of the presidential residence. She told Maxene that prior to the opening curtain of *Company B*, the president scanned the audience to see if he could locate Maxene Andrews.[14] He, along with many other veterans of World War II, fondly remembered the Andrews Sisters and their music.

Maxene became a camp follower of *Company B*. After seeing its premiere at Kennedy Center in June, she traveled to Houston for its premiere there where Patty also appeared despite Maxene's presence. They attended the premiere separately and were called to the stage for the curtain call—all nine of them. A *New York Post* columnist noted: "On stage they were separated by six dancers. To make certain they never even glanced in one another's direction, let alone inadvertently accidentally faced one another, they backed up inch by inch on stage rather than turn their bodies around to actually see where they were walking."[15] Maxene told her version of the sisters' appearance: "I heard that Walter made demands that Patty would come only if she walked out from the opposite side of the stage from me and she couldn't speak to me or be photographed with me ... And that's what happened. Patty didn't even acknowledge me on the same stage. It hurt so bad I left the stage in tears."[16] This was the last time the sisters saw one another.

Maxene later attended *Company B*'s opening performance by the Paul Taylor Dance Company in New York at City Center Theater where she briefly danced with Taylor during the curtain calls of the opening night.[17] The following summer Maxene and accompanist Phil Campanella fronted the Paul Taylor Dance Company in the Arts and Events Program series at the World Financial Center in New York. A reviewer liked what he heard and saw:

> The redoubtable Miss Andrews got the evening off to a fine start with a rollicking performance of the Andrews Sisters classic "Bei Mir Bist Du Schoen" ... Interspersed among the many songs was wry commentary on the "bad movies" and great songs and singers Miss Andrews and her sisters, Patty and LaVerne, were associated with in their long career. The patter had most of the megawatt sparkle of Miss Andrews's stage presence, and the singer shepherded her audience through the performance with the amusing air of an indulgent mother giving her charges their marching orders ... [T]he evening ended with a performance by the dances of Mr. Taylor's recent "Company B," which is set to some of the Andrews Sisters' most popular songs. A deserved hit, the dance reveals the easily forgotten musical artistry of the singers.[18]

Maxene saw the San Francisco Ballet perform *Company B* in February 1993. She later told a reporter: "I feel so lucky, what with this piece and the concerts. These are the happiest years of my life. I am more interesting, and more interested—in things and people. I've been singing for such a long time, too, only never better than now."[19] "Bette [Midler] brought the Andrews Sisters into the 70's ... Now I think Paul will bring us into the 90's."[20] In March

1994, the Paul Taylor Dance Company performed *Company B* to appreciative audiences in the Andrews Sisters' hometown Minneapolis.

Company B continues on dance companies' repertoires. I saw it performed by Ballet Arizona in Tucson in fall 2000 and again in spring 2001 by the Paul Taylor Dance Company in San Francisco. Despite the many good reviews I'd read of the dance, I wasn't sure a ballet company could handle that many Andrews Sisters songs without redundancy. I was pleasantly surprised. The songs were varied enough to maintain musical interest and the dancers captured the moods of youth and love against the backdrop of an ever-present war.

On New Year's Eve 1991, Patty Andrews made one of her occasional public forays when she appeared in the King Orange Jamboree Parade in Miami, hosted by Burt Reynolds and Loni Anderson for television audiences. Introduced by Reynolds as "a member of one of America's most treasured singing groups," Patty was perched on a float called "Treasure the Child" that consisted of a gigantic orange flanked by waving children. Looking good in her short curly blond wig, a loose glittery cerise top, and black trousers, she sang a subdued version of "South Rampart Street Parade," which was irrelevant to the float's theme, but perhaps appropriate to the parade that wended through New Year's Eve revelers.

A story about the Andrews Sisters appeared in the July 21, 1992, issue of *Globe*, a supermarket tabloid. Lots of people probably read it—many told me about it and the rumors it spawned about Maxene—but reference to the story has never appeared elsewhere in print to my knowledge. The headline read: "SOUNDS OF SILENCE: QUESTION: Why haven't the boogie-woogie Andrews Sisters spoken for over 20 years? ANSWER: Maxene's gay & Patty's furious!"

With quotes from an unnamed "pal" of the sisters, the story claimed that Patty disapproved of Maxene's "lesbian" relationship with her manager Lynda Wells and that—as well as disagreements about money during *Over Here!*—was the reason for their long estrangement. According to the story "Maxene has a live-in lesbian lover—and straitlaced Patty despises her sister's gay lifestyle." An "insider" was quoted as saying: "Patty's always worried what people would think if they knew Maxene had a female lover." The story, which is filled with inaccurate information, concluded with statements from Maxene, including: "I tried to patch things up years ago, only to have Patty hang up on me … In fact, one time I called her and she told me that if I ever called again, she'd sue me! That's the last time I tried to fix things between us."[21]

Exactly one week later, a story appeared in the *National Enquirer*, another purveyor of sensational journalism. This story was an "Exclusive Enquirer interview" with Maxene Andrews entitled "Andrews Sister in desperate bid to end 17-year family feud." The story was about Maxene's anguish over her estrangement from Patty and her desire for reconciliation. She told the reporter: "This breakup has left me so depressed I can't even talk about Patty without crying." She claimed that Patty's husband Walter Weschler was the chief reason for the estrangement: "For years Walter had wanted to take control of us, but I wouldn't allow it … Then he said that if he couldn't be in charge, the Andrews Sisters would never sing again. But I stood up to him … After that disagreement, Patty stopped speaking to me. I have no problem with her. But Walter is keeping us apart. He won't let her talk to me … I pray for God to end my heartache. If I could reach Patty, I'd tell her: 'I'm sorry for whatever I may have done to you. I miss you. I love you. And I want to be friends and sisters again—before it's too late.'"[22]

When contacted by the reporter, Patty said: "The trouble is with Maxene. It's a personal thing with her attitude and just the way she is. Mainly, she doesn't get along with my husband Walter. But that's her problem and her fault, not his." The story made no mention of Maxene's relationship with Lynda Wells or her alleged lesbianism. It appears that the story was Maxene's way of letting the tabloid-reading public know why she and Patty were estranged—Wally Weschler, not lesbianism.

Sensationalism aside, it is certain that Maxene's relationship with Lynda Wells—whether lesbian or otherwise—was not the critical issue in her estrangement from Patty. The problems between the sisters began long before Maxene met Wells, and the chief problem was the personality clash between Maxene and Weschler.

Maxene met Lynda Wells when she was teaching at Tahoe.[23] After Maxene's return to the stage for *Over Here!*, Wells and other friends urged her to pursue a solo career. Wells was, in fact, producer of Maxene's one-woman show. According to Maxene's cousin Gladys Leichter, Maxene adopted Wells after her hospitalization following her heart attack so she could make future decisions regarding Maxene's care.

Virtually everyone I talked to agreed that Wells was a critical ingredient in Maxene's latter day happiness and success. Gladys Leichter remembered that Wells took very good care of Maxene, made sure she ate, exercised properly, and took her medicines.[24] Joyce DeYoung said Wells was extremely solicitous about Maxene and cared for her in her later years.[25] Beth Fowler, who knew Wells and Maxene during *Over Here!* remembered: "She was a bubbly, vivacious, very positive spirit. She kept Maxene's spirits up. She adored Maxene and did everything she could to make her comfortable and happy."[26] Lynda Wells had obviously become the most important person in Maxene's life, and was partly responsible for her buoyant later years when she blossomed in ways she never could as an Andrews sister.

Several times, Maxene Andrews told reporters she was writing a book. An item appeared in February 1976 claiming she had received "a hefty check for her recently completed *Andrews Sisters* biography to be published by Putnam in the fall."[27] In 1977, an interviewer noted she was "working on the second editing of her book, tentatively titled 'An Andrews Sister.'" Maxene told a reporter about the genesis of the book: "I remember, it was on July 16 in the year LaVerne died [1967] … I was in Houston, and I woke up at 3 A.M. and something was telling me to write a book. I finished it 11 years later—I'm not really a writer, and I didn't want to hand the writing over to anyone else, but I think it's a good book and I think it will be published."[28] (Maxene confused her places: On July 16 the year of LaVerne's death she was in Copenhagen, not Houston.) A few months later she told a reporter, "It isn't a book on the Andrews Sisters but on my life as one of the Andrews Sisters."[29] The following year, she told another reporter that her autobiography would be published "within the year." "I started it on July 16, 1967, so you see how difficult it has been for me. I would put it away for a year at a time."

As she continued with the book, she said it became a form of therapy that helped relieve guilt feelings about her relationship with her father. "I hadn't realized we were so much alike. I wish it wasn't too late to tell him."[30] Elsewhere, she said writing the book also helped her understand her feelings toward her mother and sisters.[31] In March 1981, she talked to another reporter about her book:

> I think it might be valuable as a record of the old days—a kind of "The Way We Were" of the period between 1938 and 1951.
>
> There's been a lot of interest shown by publishers who want me to dish dirt, to portray my sisters as monsters. I won't do that because they were not and are not monsters of any sort.
>
> What I want to capture is a portrait of the Andrews Sisters as little girls growing up in Minneapolis and sharing the spotlight with ... the other show biz greats we performed with.
>
> That era was innocent, wholesome, patriotic and very exciting. But maybe those values aren't saleable in today's market. It's too bad, I think.[32]

In early 1985, she was still talking about her autobiography—and her dispute with a publisher: "The publisher told me there wasn't enough sex or gossip in the book, so I took it back, and keep it in a trunk ... I told him I'm never going to write gossipy trash. When I think the time is right, I'll take it out of the trunk and get it published elsewhere."[33]

The autobiography Maxene wrote was never published. She told her cousin Gladys Leichter that publishers weren't interested in the book because she "didn't have enough smut in it." Her cousin read the manuscript and thought Maxene had been very selective in what she chose to remember.[34]

The book Maxene finally wrote was *Over Here, Over There—The Andrews Sisters and the USO Stars in World War II*, co-written with Bill Gilbert and published in 1993. A memoir of the Andrews Sisters' activities during World War II within the context of an informal history of the USO, the book was not the autobiography Maxene talked about. In the preface to *Over Here, Over There*, Maxene and Bill Gilbert explained their reason for writing the book:

> This book represents our best efforts to tell the reader about this unique chapter in American history and in the history of show business, told by the entertainers who lived those four years themselves.... This book is a history of those times and the men and women in show business who were part of them.... It is a tribute—to every member of the entertainment profession in World War II and to the American people, over here and over there, in their audiences.

In addition to library research, the book was based on interviews with sixteen entertainers who performed in USO shows during the war. Patty Andrews was not among those interviewed. The dedication of the book read: "To Patty and LaVerne with Love and to the GI Audiences of Each of America's Wars." The book is a collection of Maxene's reminiscences of the war years, interviews with other USO entertainers, and historical tidbits about the USO and events of World War II. Its most important contributions are the reminiscences of Maxene and other entertainers; the accounts of political and military events are a bit lightweight. The book was not widely reviewed, but a brief review in *Booklist* concluded: "Though the authors' reminiscent tone and nostalgic anecdotes leave a saccharine aftertaste at times, you can't help but be moved by—and secretly wish for a return to—the simple charm and wide-eyed hope that symbolized a generation."[35] Few who lived through the deprivations of the Great Depression and the horrors of World War II would agree they were a generation of "simple charm and wide-eyed hope"—and even fewer would want to return to those days. I found no sales figures for the book, but it was not a best seller.

Maxene appeared around the country on radio and television, and in bookstores to plug her book. On June 11, 1993, she was introduced on *Good Morning America* with film clips about the sisters' activities in World War II. She then reminisced about the war years and told stories from her book. The following day, she was on *Talk Live* with Michael Feinstein to plug her book. She claimed the Andrews Sisters still sold over a million CDs and tapes a year. When asked her views about the recent decision to exclude openly gay people from the military, she replied she thought it was ridiculous to exclude them and opined that someday the policy would be as shameful as that segregating African Americans during World War II. In late June, Maxene was in Minneapolis still plugging her book. She told a reporter she lived in northern California with "her daughter, Lynda Wells, who also is her manager, in a house of dogs, cats and other creatures."[36] She said, "I wanted to do [the book] for years ... but I could never find the right writer, someone who felt as I did about the story." Bill Gilbert saw her on a television show about World War II entertainers and telephoned her. "We talked and I could tell he understood what I felt about it." When the reporter noted that Maxene was kind to everyone she mentioned in the book, she shrugged and said, "That's the way I am." As Maxene met and remembered people from her childhood years at the book-signing session, the reporter observed: "Maxene Andrews, at 77, is one of those people who seem able to recall every event of their lives, every person they've met."

After Minneapolis, Maxene went to Chicago, the next stop on her book tour, where a reporter from the *Chicago Tribune* interviewed her at the Hard Rock Café. As usual, she offered her views on a variety of topics, frequently revealing her generation gap.

> **Language**. Have you noticed that everyone today is an "actor"? ... No one is an "actress" anymore. Our language has gotten out of hand. As has so much in this country.
>
> **Contemporary music**. This isn't music—it's noise ... Go ahead, hum what you just heard, I dare you. I don't know, I used to think I knew a lot about music ... Well, this, too, shall pass ...
>
> **Contemporary youth**. See, that's another thing that stuns me about the youth of today. There are no surprises in life anymore. I mean, sex is right out there in the open, and so are dirty words. Why? We have a beautiful language. I don't enjoy going to a movie and listening to four-letter words. And I'm no prude about that ... Sometimes I get the feeling that the young generation is angry. It's almost like they're trying to get back at us for something, although they've had the best of it ... Maybe that's the problem. Hate has become very popular. You have the

feeling the young people hate the old people, and a lot of the old people resent the young people.[37]

In mid–August, Maxene appeared on CBS's *Sunday Morning* to talk about her book. She claimed she never listened to the old Andrews Sisters records, not because she was not proud of them but rather because her life had moved away from that music and time.

In June 1994, Maxene Andrews participated in events commemorating the 50th anniversary of D-Day, the Allied invasion of Europe that led to the defeat of Germany in World War II. En route to Normandy from Montreal on the *Royal Viking Sun,* she gave a concert accompanied by Phil Campanella that included a special appearance by her long-time friend June Allyson. During the voyage, three of the Andrews Sisters' old movies (*Buck Privates, In the Navy,* and *Hollywood Canteen*) were shown on closed circuit television and in the ship's theater.

Following the ceremony at Normandy where President Bill Clinton and other dignitaries spoke, Maxene visited the American Cemetery. When she left the cemetery, a woman approached her and said, "We wish you had been up there singing for us today, because, if it hadn't been for you girls and your music, many of the young men I nursed simply wouldn't have made it. You gave them a sense of happiness and hope, and I'll be forever grateful."[38] Maxene appeared on *Larry King Live,* reminisced about the war years, and fielded questions from listeners. During her interview with King, Maxene repeated the usual interview stories and told him: "Today, I was walking alone in the cemetery, and someone asked me if I had anyone buried here. I told her the truth. I said, 'All of them. You can't entertain thousands of soldiers without feeling that they all belong to you.'"

While Maxene was in Normandy, Patty Andrews joined other performers in "An Evening to Remember," a D-Day commemorative at Wolftrap, an outdoor performing arts center in Vienna, Virginia near Washington, D.C. She sang "Don't Sit Under the Apple Tree" and coaxed a reluctant audience to join her for "In Apple Blossom Time."

In early 1995, Maxene appeared in a revival of *Follies* in Houston and Seattle, which included former stars Virginia Mayo and Edie Adams. A Seattle reviewer saw the show in late April and liked it, but regarding Maxene's role he simply wrote: "Maxene Andrews, 79, formerly of the Andrews Sisters sings 'Broadway Baby.' Fun!"[39]

The following summer, Maxene traveled to Hawaii for ceremonies and festivities commemorating the 50th anniversary of the end of World War II. Her meeting with President Bill Clinton and First Lady Hillary Clinton was the highlight of the trip. She told a reporter: "Bob Hope, the President and First Lady and I sang 'America the Beautiful,' and it was very moving ... It was a very warm experience for me to be there because I met a lot of the boys—I still call them boys even though they are getting old—that we worked for 50 years ago. We cried a little, we laughed a lot, and I just wonder where all that time went."[40]

I saw Maxene in the parade that wended through Waikiki. She rode in the back of a convertible equipped with sound equipment that played the Andrews

Sisters' recording of "Boogie Woogie Bugle Boy" to appreciative crowds that enthusiastically applauded her along the parade route. That evening she appeared with Bob Hope at a big band dance in a hangar at Hickam Air Force Base.

Later that summer, Maxene was in California and visited her cousin Gladys Leichter. Gladys remembered:

> The last time I saw Maggie ... we had lunch together. And when she left, she took me in her arms and said, "Glad, I'm going to New York, but I'll keep in contact with you. And if there's anything you need, you let me know." She always worried that I might need something ... She was a little bit shaky, she had a little palsy. She knew it. She said, "I'm getting old. I'm getting shaky."[41]

Maxene was on her way to New York to join the cast of yet another musical. This one was called *Swingtime Canteen*, "a 1940s-style musical" playing off-Broadway at the Blue Angel nightclub with drag performer Charles Busch. Maxene joined the cast for a month in late September and *USA Today* reviewed her performance:

> Andrews' role is mainly an extended cameo: She drops into the middle of the show claiming that her flight was so bad she aged 50 years, then sings a medley of her hits.
>
> But this isn't a case of a veteran performer keeping up with young, hip colleagues. Her free-and-easy ad-libbing style keeps other performers on their toes and the audience guessing what will happen next. She makes no apologies: "Isn't it wonderful?" ... she has only the deepest respect and affection for the veterans of the war, who still come backstage after a show. She sometimes remembers them: "I'll say, 'Gosh, the face is very familiar but when I saw you the last time, you were only 17 years old!' We cry a little bit. Tell jokes. And I still call them 'boys.'"[42]

Maxene completed her month in *Swingtime Canteen*. She was scheduled to perform in early November at four sold-out concerts at Leisure World in Laguna Hills, California, and at the Academy Plaza Theater in North Hollywood, following which she would return to *Swingtime Canteen* in December.

In late October, Maxene Andrews, Lynda Wells, and two friends went to Cape Cod for a well-deserved vacation. Prior to her departure, Maxene visited her terminally ill former husband and manager Lou Levy. After a few estranged years following their divorce and Levy's departure from the sisters' career, Maxene and Levy resumed their relationship as good friends. During her first day on the cape, she signed autographs for young fans at a local bagel shop where a picture of the Andrews Sisters adorned a wall. The following day, Maxene suffered a massive heart attack at the vacation home she rented in Orleans on outer Cape Cod. She was rushed to Cape Cod Hospital in Hyannis, Massachusetts, where she was pronounced dead at 4:20 A.M. October 21, 1995. She was 79 years old.

Maxene's longtime companion Lynda Wells told the press: "She went out like a supernova because she never stopped ... When she started new careers at ages most people are thinking about retirement, she showed us that no matter what you want to do, it's never too late."[43] Actress June Allyson, Maxene's friend of fifty years, said: "Mackie was the best friend anyone could have ... But she's not gone. She's right here in my heart. Although the world will miss her so much, she'll still be here with us because the brightest star you'll see shining

The caption on page 407 is for a photo that I submitted which was not put into the book. The correct caption for the picture that actually is on this page is: Maxene and Charles Saunders, a longtime friend and fan of the Andrews Sisters in New York City in September 1995. Maxene died a month after this photograph was taken. (Courtesy Everett Searcy)

My photograph was taken on 17 September 1995 outside the Blue Angel Theatre in New York where Maxene was appearing with female impersonator Charles Busch in *Swingtime Canteen*:

Maxene and Charles Busch, with whom she appeared in *Swingtime Canteen* at the Blue Angel in New York City in September 1995. Maxene died a month after this photograph was taken. (Joseph Klenner Collection)

in the sky will be Mackie."[44] Milton Berle also offered a press statement: "When it comes to harmony, I always considered the Andrews Sisters the best trio of voices blending ever ... They had dedication and perfection. They always worried about perfection. They were real troupers."[45] A reporter attempted to reach Patty by telephone, but her husband Wally Weschler said she was "too emotional to speak." When asked about the sisters' estrangement, he replied, "We wished it could have been otherwise, but it's one of those sad things."[46]

Friends of Maxene remembered her in interviews with me. Ken Petrack said: "She was like a mother, like a grandmother. She had no pretenses—none whatsoever, despite her fame. She was very basic, very down-to-earth. She was a wonderful woman. If you met her, you would never guess this was Maxene Andrews ... Maxene never said anything derogatory about anybody."[47] Ray Hagen remembered Maxene: "Kinda funny. Tough ... Very savvy ... very loose

... very difficult at times but so am I, who isn't? ... very bright woman ... very curious woman ... very much into finding out about a lot of areas of life that I don't think Patty was interested in. I think she was a much more rounded person than Patty."[48] Joyce DeYoung recalled, "She was a straight shooter ... loved to joke, laughed a lot. She could also be very firm in her feelings about people ... She had a lot of friends ... I liked her so much."[49]

A memorial service was held for Maxene Andrews October 29, 1995, at 6 P.M. at the Blue Angel nightclub in New York City where she had recently performed in *Swingtime Canteen*. "Sing a Tropical Song," one of the sisters' early hits, was sung a cappella by two male friends of Maxene followed by a medley of Andrews Sisters hits. Several people offered reminiscences of Maxene, including her longtime accompanist Phil Campanella. Ninety-plus-year-old Gerald Marks, composer of "All of Me," sang the song in memory of Maxene, whom he remembered as a "real lady." Maxene's longtime companion Lynda Wells read a letter from an ailing Lou Levy who was unable to attend the ceremony as well as letters from Bill Clinton, President of the United States, and William Perry, Secretary of Defense. A flag in Maxene's name was presented to Lynda Wells by a color guard and "Taps" was played. Photographs of the Andrews Sisters were projected onto an American flag screen as Maxene's recorded voice sang "Where Did the Good Times Go?" The final musical number was "Boogie Woogie Bugle Boy" sung by a female trio. Lynda Wells and Phil Campanella concluded the service with thank yous to the assemblage and good-byes to Maxene.[50] Donations were directed to "The Singer's Forum Maxene Andrews Scholarship Fund" and "The Maxene Andrews Fellowship at the Save a Heart Foundation."

A second memorial service was held for Maxene on November 3 in southern California at the Lakeside Country Club in Burbank at 7 P.M. Recorded music of the Andrews Sisters played to the packed service. June Allyson and others reminisced about their friendships with Maxene.[51]

Patty Andrews did not attend either of the memorial services for her sister. One of the attendees reflected: "Even in death she couldn't come. Everybody was talking about it." Nor did Maxene's adopted daughter Aleda and son Peter attend either service.

Maxene's remains were cremated. Columnist Rex Reed reported a final twist in the estrangement between Patty and Maxene: "Just recently, Patty was still insisting her sister owed her $5 million, so on the way to the crematorium, Mackie's adopted daughter, Lynda, enclosed two things in the box with the body of Maxene Andrews—a pack of her favorite Carefree sugarless gum, and a check for $5 million made out to 77-year-old Patty—and said, "Burn this!"[52] Maxene's ashes were scattered in the Pacific Ocean and in Lake Minnetonka at Mound, Minnesota.

Maxene's name was added to the Andrews memorial plaque at the Great Mausoleum at Forest Lawn, Glendale, California, with her parents and sister LaVerne. "Andrews" appears at the top of the simple marker and beneath it is listed: "Ollie B. 1898–1948." "Peter 1890–1949." "LaVerne Rogers 1916–1967." "Maxene Anglyn Andrews 1916–1995." A blank space follows Maxene's name, presumably for Patty. The last line on the marker reads, "The Andrews Sisters." Only Maxene's birth date is correct.

In an interview that appeared nine months before she died, Maxene told a writer:

> The wonderful thing was that we [sisters] were together for so many years ... You know, we were never separated: We dressed together, we slept together, we ate together, we roomed together, we went shopping together and of course we rehearsed together. It's wonderful from where I stand right now. I have nothing to regret. We got on the carousel, and we each got the ring, and I was satisfied with that. It's funny because I feel more of a success today than I ever did, and it isn't what I'm doing, it's how I'm living.
>
> There's nothing I would do to change things if I could ... Yes, I would. I would wish I had the ability and the power to bridge the gap between my relationship with my sister Patty. I haven't found the way yet, but I'm sure that the Lord will find the way.[53]

In a will dated August 7, 1990, Maxene left all of her "tangible personal property" to Lynda Wells. The residue of her estate was given to the Maxene Anglyn Andrews Trust, the trustors of which were Maxene and Lynda Wells. Thus, the entire estate went to Lynda Wells in trust. A disinheritance clause in the will read:

> I have intentionally made no provision in this Will for my sister, PATRICIA MARIE ANDREWS WESCHLER, my brother-in-law, MELVIN WALTER WESCHLER, or any person not specifically named, whether claiming to be an heir of mine or not. I have intentionally omitted to provide herein for any of my other heirs living at the date of my death.

According to Gladys Leichter, Maxene's adopted children, Aleda and Peter, had received insurance policies from Maxene earlier. They were estranged from Maxene at her death, both apparently having felt abandonment during their childhood when so much of their mother's time was consumed by her career.[54]

On October 26, 1995, five days after Maxene's death, Lou Rogers, LaVerne's husband, died in Camarillo, California, of complications from Alzheimer's disease. Maxene had remained friends with Rogers and his second wife, Jean, and visited him in the hospital the previous summer.

Ten days after Maxene's death, October 31, 1995, Lou Levy, Maxene's former husband and the Andrews Sisters' longtime manager, died of congestive heart failure. The obituaries of Maxene and Levy appeared side by side in *Variety*.

Vic Schoen, former music arranger for the Andrews Sisters, died January 5, 2000, of pneumonia in Corona del Mar, California. He was 83 years old.

Gladys Leichter, cousin of the Andrews Sisters, died at her home in Apple Valley, California, on May 11, 2002, of a heart attack one day before her 87th birthday. Her ashes were scattered in Lake Minnetonka with those of her beloved cousin Maggie.

In late May 1998, an article by Patty Andrews appeared in the *Los Angeles Times* entitled "Bugle Boys of Company B Died to Keep America Free." She reminisced about the Andrews Sisters' activities with the USO and the troops they entertained. It was, however, primarily a plug for public support

Patty Andrews, looking great at 84, with Stephen Fratallone, publisher of Internet magazine *Jazz Connection*, and her husband Wally Weschler at the Big Band Academy of America annual reunion in March 2002. Patty and her husband currently live in retirement in Northridge, California. (Courtesy Stephen Fratallone)

for a World War II Memorial on the National Mall in Washington, D.C. The article later appeared in other newspapers throughout the country.[55]

Patty Andrews currently lives in retirement with her husband Wally Weschler in Northridge, California. President Bill Clinton invited her to attend groundbreaking ceremonies for the World War II Veterans' Memorial on the Washington Mall, November 11, 2000, followed by lunch at the White House. Still recuperating from a leg injury sustained a year previously, Patty was unable to attend.[56]

On Christmas Day 2001, Patty Andrews and Wally Weschler observed their fiftieth wedding anniversary. Patty told a reporter that she admired "all those kids who are going overseas to entertain our troops."[57] Capitol Records' sixtieth anniversary party in spring 2002 brought Patty and her husband from their home, as did the nineteenth annual Jivin' Jacks and Jills reunion in October 2002.

In spring 2002, *Sisters of Swing*, a musical play based on the Andrews Sisters' career, opened to good reviews in St. Paul, Minnesota. One of the writers telephoned Wally Weschler about the show and later told a reporter: "Weschler showed little interest and seemed overly protective of his wife."[58]

Afterword

I wonder if those girls had any idea of the amount of happiness
they brought to so many people with their singing.[1]

The Andrews Sisters are part of musical Americana. Their voices are
among the most recognizable musical sounds of the 20th century, along with
such legendary singers as Al Jolson, Louis Armstrong, Ethel Merman, Billie
Holiday, the Mills Brothers, Frank Sinatra, and Ella Fitzgerald. For over sixty-
five years, they collectively and individually entertained America. Their career
began in the waning years of vaudeville, zenithed during the Golden Age of
Hollywood and radio, and twilighted into the early years of television. Their
names were household words and their faces familiar friends to the nation. Initially, their songs appealed to the youthful jitterbugs of the late 1930s, but they
eventually won over other generations as they expanded their musical repertoire. They began as a singing act but soon became an entertainment and many
reviewers noted that if you'd only heard the Andrews Sisters on record, you
had no understanding of them as entertainers. They sang, danced, joked, and
mugged their way into the hearts of America.

The Andrews Sisters were one of America's images of family, an image
that was especially cherished during the dark days of World War II. Non-threat-
ening to everyone, they were three homely, likeable sisters of poor immigrant
parents who made it to the big time. Mom and pop escorted them to and from
their successful engagements. They all lived together in Hollywood and gathered each Sunday for a home-cooked dinner by mom in a house she cleaned
herself. Papa was the kindly patriarch who kept his family of women in line.
How American can you get? They were right up there with Bing Crosby, Kate

411

Smith, Irving Berlin, American flag, and apple pie. Singer Rosemary Clooney remembered when Paramount Studios rewrote her family history to make it more respectable: "In this airbrushed version of my family history, my Aunt Ann hadn't died of a drug overdose on the floor of a public hospital. She had simply 'died, very suddenly, at the age of twenty-four, while listening to the Andrews Sisters on the radio.'"[2] A death can't get more respectable than that.

The Andrews Sisters' songs are still very much around. By early 2003, over 100 CDs of their songs had been issued since 1987, most containing the same core of popular titles. CD liners and feature stories often claim total record sales of sixty to ninety million for the sisters, but the range is so great that the figures are not meaningful. I have read undocumented claims that the sisters currently sell over a million CDs annually.

The Andrews Sisters' voices are among the defining sounds of the 1940s and consequently filmmakers frequently use their songs to evoke the period. *Red Sky at Morning* (1970), *The Brink's Job* (1978), and *1941* (1979) all used Andrews Sisters songs to help set scenes. "A Zoot Suit for My Sunday Gal" provided background music throughout much of the Latino film *Zoot Suit* (1981). "Shoo Shoo Baby" helped set a World War II barracks scene in the critically acclaimed *A Soldier's Story* (1984). The BBC-TV miniseries *The Singing Detective* (1986) used Andrews Sisters and Bing Crosby songs in episodes of the popular show. Woody Allen's *Radio Days* (1987) featured "Pistol Packin' Mama" by the sisters and Bing Crosby. The concluding scene in the Robin Williams movie *Jakob, the Liar* (1999) was a young Polish girl's fantasy of the Andrews Sisters singing "Beer Barrel Polka" as Allied troops arrived to rescue a trainload of Jews destined for the death camps. *Catch Me If You Can* (2002) set a Christmas scene with "Mele Kalikimaka" by Bing Crosby and the Andrews Sisters.

Various vocal groups around the country continue the Andrews Sisters tradition. A trio called "Sister Swing" currently performs Andrews Sisters songs throughout northern California. A theater group called "For Sentimental Reasons" has recreated a 1940s radio show for audiences in Massachusetts, and reports that the Andrews Sisters are their most popular request.[3] In April 2000, the Universal Amphitheater in Hollywood premiered *Burn the Floor*, a salute to ballroom dancing that included Andrews Sisters look-alikes lip-synching the original "Boogie Woogie Bugle Boy." In September 2001, three seasoned singers donned World War II military garb to portray the Andrews Sisters at a concert called "Salute to the Greatest Generation" at the National D-Day memorial in Bedford, Virginia.[4] In early 2002, the World War II era *Stars and Stripes Revue* in Clearwater, Florida, starred big band singer Connie Haines and included three singers in WAC uniforms as the Andrews Sisters. Stockbridge, Massachusetts, hosted *A Saint She Ain't* in summer 2002, a musical show about wartime Hollywood that opened with a number by wannabe Andrews Sisters. In spring 2002, *Sisters of Swing*, a musical based on the lives and songs of the Andrews Sisters, played to appreciative audiences and good reviews in St. Paul. The show was so well received that it was brought back for a summer run in 2003, and plans to go on the road in 2004.

Many of the films of the Andrews Sisters are still around. The sisters appeared in eighteen films, eight of which were big box office successes. The three films they made with Bud Abbott and Lou Costello were the top moneymakers of 1941 for Universal Studios. The sisters' appearance in *Follow the Boys* helped make that another box office hit for Universal. *Hollywood Canteen* was the fourth biggest film for Warner Brothers in 1944, and *Road to Rio* was Paramount's top film in 1947. Both *Make Mine Music* and *Melody Time* were big money makers for Disney. All of these films, plus *Private Buckeroo*, are currently available on videocassette or DVD and regularly appear on television's classic movie channels.

For years, the Andrews Sisters have inspired drag impersonators. The earliest documented drag of the Andrews Sisters was that of the Ritz Brothers in the film *Argentine Nights* (1940), perhaps the only scene in the movie that is still funny. Other celebrity drags of the sisters include Frank Sinatra, Frankie Laine, and Perry Como and the even more unlikely combo of Bob Hope, Sammy Davis, Jr., and Jonathan Winters. A history of gays in the military claims that the Andrews Sisters, Carmen Miranda, and Gypsy Rose Lee were the most popular drag impersonations by GIs during World War II.[5] Films featuring Andrews Sisters drag include *The Ritz* (1976) and *Privates on Parade* (1982). In spring 1998, a show opened in San Francisco called *The Andrews Sisters at the Hollywood Canteen*. Three men in drag impersonated the Andrews Sisters and sang some of their best-known songs. The show sold out during its four-week run, and after touring other cities, returned to San Francisco for a successful summer stint.[6] A drag show called *Christmas with the Crawfords* became an annual holiday event in San Francisco for several years in the late 1990s. Set in Joan Crawford's home on Christmas day, the all-male show starred various Hollywood guests who dropped by to visit Crawford, including the Andrews Sisters who sang a medley of their songs. The show played in New York Off-Broadway in December 2001 and 2002. Maxene and Patty once told an interviewer they enjoyed the drag impersonations of the Andrews Sisters. Maxene said they were "fun" and added, "You better have a sense of humor ... because if you don't have a sense of humor, you ain't gonna get through this life."[7]

The Andrews Sisters have made it to the Internet with their own website, albeit with limited and occasionally misleading information. On any given day, the Internet auction site eBay has over 400 Andrews Sisters items for sale ranging from 78s, LPs, 45s, and CDs of their songs to movie posters, record dusters, photographs, autographs, and sheet music with cover pictures of the sisters. Items offered during the past few years include: clocks and wrist watches with Andrews Sisters pictures on their faces, a mousepad featuring a photo of the sisters, Andrews Sisters fan letters, marionettes of Patty and Maxene (with no mention of what happened to LaVerne), a beach towel and T-shirt with pictures of the Andrews Sisters, a ticket to the sisters' *Club 15* radio program, a matchbook with a cover picture of the Andrews Sisters, Andrews Sisters dolls dressed in khaki, outline drawings of the hands of Patty and Maxene, Andrews Sisters postcards, a fake million dollar bill illustrated with a picture of the

Andrews Sisters, and items from the estate sale of Maxene Andrews. In 1998, an on-line university with headquarters in the Caribbean offered two courses on the Andrews Sisters—"The History of the Andrews Sisters" and "The Music of the Andrews Sisters."

Postage stamps have featured images of the sisters. In 1991, Grenada issued stamps with pictures of World War II performers to commemorate the fiftieth anniversary of the USO. The Andrews Sisters (misspelled "Andrew") were among those featured. In 2000, Gambia issued a stamp of the Andrews Sisters (also misspelled) in commemoration of the centennial of radio.

Although the Andrews Sisters did not make it to wax at Madame Tussaud's wax museum in New York City, a life size photo of them in WAC uniforms covers the wall behind the Glenn Miller mannequin. *Goldmine* magazine announced the first group of inductees into the Vocal Group Hall of Fame at Sharon, Pennsylvania, in September 1998. The Andrews Sisters were among those selected by *Goldmine*'s staff and readers for the 1940 decade.[8]

All the houses once inhabited by the Andrews family in Minneapolis are now gone. LaVerne's birthplace was demolished to become part of an industrial park. Maxene's birthplace is an empty lot, and a brick apartment house replaced the building where Patty was born. The Andrews family home at 1600 Lyndale Avenue North was torn down some years ago to give way to a low-income housing development. Peter Andrews' old restaurant on Hennepin Avenue is now a gay bar, and the Orpheum Theater where the sisters made their stage debut has been renovated for live stage shows.

A few people in Mound, Minnesota, know that the Andrews Sisters once lived in their little town, but most do not. Mound is now an affluent suburb of Minneapolis, and Lake Minnetonka is still a popular recreation destination. The Sollie family home was demolished some years ago to make way for a VFW lodge. The building that housed the grocery store of Pete and Ed Sollie still stands but now houses accounting and income tax offices. Chapman's Casino, where the sisters once bowled and roller-skated, is long gone and its site is a public beach park.

The people in Mound may have forgotten the Andrews Sisters, but the sisters still have many devoted fans across the nation who remember them. While researching this book, I sent letters to various publications asking readers to share their memories of the Andrews Sisters. I received almost a hundred letters, several of which led to important interviews. What impressed me most about the responses was the great warmth and affection the writers held for the Andrews Sisters. Many letters were from fans who remembered them during World War II, but others were from younger people who knew only their music. The following reminiscences are typical of the many memories people shared with me.

> There are very few of us World War II veterans who don't have a special place in our hearts and memories for Patty, LaVerne and Maxene Andrews. Their willingness to go everywhere to entertain our troops endeared them to all our servicemen and women. I still have some of their songs on tape.[9]

I heard about the Andrews Sisters when I was a kid of five or six. I remember riding my tricycle around the table in our kitchen while my mom was busy cooking. She had an album of her favorite singer, Bing Crosby, on the record player, and I discovered he was singing with the Andrews Sisters. I also remember, when I got a little older, watching Abbott and Costello's movie *Buck Privates* and discovering "those sisters" were in that movie too. They were an energetic and engaging act. I remember this period as a much warmer and simpler time than that in which we now live. And I liked the music better. [10]

I was a child during World War II when the Andrews Sisters were at the height of their popularity. I remember how with no real involvement in the plot they would turn up in various musical movies to sing a few numbers. Those were also the heydays of the musical movie star Betty Grable, who was blonde and beautiful and famous for her gorgeous legs. The Andrews Sisters seemed so plain next to glamorous actresses like her; yet, when Patty, Maxene and LaVerne sang their close harmony, they usually exhibited much more talent than the often-vapid beauties. [11]

I remember when the Andrews Sisters visited us at Highland Elementary School in East Oakland, California, in 1940 or early 1941. They called a surprise school assembly in the auditorium and lo and behold the Andrews Sisters came and sang. Needless to say, that made quite an impression on us, being the first celebrities most of us ever saw in person. I don't know the circumstances of their visit but I'm sure it was voluntary on their part. Having seen them and being impressed by their visit at an early age always made them special entertainers in my eyes. We saw them in movies, heard their songs on the radio and played their songs on juke boxes. They were a pleasant relief from all the stress and hardship that the war imposed on the nation. [12]

I saw in person the Andrews Sisters in a theater in Oakland in 1943 just before going into the Air Force. I can still remember the sound, they gave it their all and the audience responded. Who could forget the songs? My favorite was "Rum and Coca-Cola"—the song and the booze. Ah, those were the days. [13]

In World War II, I spent some time in Stalag One up near the Baltic Sea. After about six months, the Red Cross sent us a phonograph with some records. Among them was an Andrews Sisters platter, I think with Bing Crosby. Darned if I can think of the name of it, but it sure sounded good and reminded us POWs of better times. [14]

We were three girls, not yet teenagers, in the 1940s. We were very poor, lived in a small mid–Minnesota farming town. My mother saw to it that we went at least once a week to the local movie theater. That, and reading any book we could, brought the world to us. So we met the Andrews Sisters via the motion picture. We enjoyed their lively singing and knew if the "sisters" were in a movie, we would like it. Since we, too, were "three sisters" we enjoyed them all the more. I can hear and see them in my mind as I write this—they are singing "Boogie Woogie Bugle Boy." [15]

Don't even think of publishing a biography of those joyful gals without including a CD of their hits. After Pearl Harbor, millions of us were in the service or in defense jobs and the Andrews Sisters' music was certainly part of what the USA meant to us. [16]

I was a preteen New York City schoolboy during World War II. My pals and

I rarely missed a Saturday matinee at the local movie house. And we enjoyed it all with the exception of overly romantic movies and music. We derisively termed such entertainment "mushy stuff." Imagine however our surprise and delight when Maxene, LaVerne and Patty appeared on the American scene and screen with their bouncy free for all rhythms. I can't imagine any musical group more American, more spirit-lifting, more necessary in anxiety troublesome 1940s. I couldn't begin to tell you how many nickels me and my chums shoved into a Wurlitzer jukebox next to the neighborhood soda fountain to hear play after replay such Andrews Sisters tunes as "Straighten Up and Fly Right" and "Pistol Packin' Mama." And I couldn't begin to tell you how much they meant to America during my boyhood years—though I've tried.[17]

In World War II, I was a dance band singer and a jitterbug queen in England and I worshipped the three sisters. I knew every note of every arrangement and still play their records quite regularly. At our "Vets" meeting in a large seafront ballroom once a month we play World War II songs as "background" music and when it's one of theirs, we all sing along! My "gang" there are all ex-musicians and entertainers and we all know quality when we hear it! Tell any "Vets" you know that we love them all, and that we'll be with them in a permanent "Apple Blossom Time."[18]

I lived in the Lake Minnetonka, Minnesota, area during and after World War II. As a high schooler in the 40s, I was an avid roller skater at the Mound-Glenisle Casino. The Andrews Sisters had an uncle who had a small grocery store near the Casino. They would come out to visit their uncle. On occasion, the sisters came down to the Casino and visited with us "kids." I roller-skated with two of the sisters a few times. They weren't too great on skates, but had fun. They were great people and had done a lot for our war effort. I still enjoy their great music.[19]

I was a young girl living in Columbus, Ohio, when the Andrews Sisters appeared at a downtown theater in what was called a stage show then. I only remember going one day as I had to ride the streetcar a long way but I sat there through several consecutive performances and completely enjoyed all of them. Afterward I went out back with several other people and when we asked for autographs they very nicely obliged. I still remember how nice they were and to this day I still once in a while play some of their music.[20]

I was coming back from Korea in 1952. I was coming down the gangplank of the ship and lost my footing and one of the Andrews Sisters caught me in her arms. She hugged me really hard and told me how good it was to have me back. I told her she had no idea how good it was to be back home. The other sisters came up and hugged me also. We talked for a short time and then I continued on to the bus. I have never forgotten that special homecoming, and how warm and caring those women were. There were bands there, many officers, generals and the like. Reporters were flashing bulbs all over the place and there was a general air of excitement—and for me, relief and joy. Those multi-talented and caring women made a lasting impression on me. I am now seventy-two years old and I still remember the looks on their faces and the smells in the air. It was the smell of freedom.[21]

It had to be sometime in 1956 or 1957, as I was serving in the US Air Force at the Edwards AFB in Southern California. Most GIs had little money toward the end of the month and Special Services sometimes came up with entertainment. The deal was that you had to put on your Class "A's" (dress uniforms), and board a bus, destination unknown. If I had only known what was ahead, I would have begged, borrowed, or stolen a camera and recorded the best act I ever saw. We were dropped off at the Brown Derby Restaurant in LA, saw the Andrews Sisters. They gave a nonstop flawless performance, for what I guess was over an hour on stage. I remember that the girls looked a bit older than I thought they would but then I remembered that they had performed for GIs during World War II and Korea. Their age, (hell, they had to be near 40), did not diminish their talents or energy. The joint really was jumping. Even the waiters were smiling and keeping the beat. I feel so very lucky to have this memory, as now I'm 65, and am pleased you'll be writing about these great ladies.[22]

When I was a youngster, my parents took me into New York City to see the play *Over Here!* It starred the Andrews Sisters and a much younger and slimmer John Travolta before he became a star. I still remember the show; lots of energy and enthusiasm from all, including the aging sisters. After the show was over, the two came out and sang a bunch of their old songs to the delight of all of us. Even though I was about ten at the time, I enjoyed it immensely. Little did I know that I was really seeing something that was very, very special.[23]

I add my personal note to this medley of memories. Throughout my life, the energetic, happy songs of the Andrews Sisters have helped me through some difficult times. Whenever I need a lift, I still play their songs, and before long a smile takes over my face, my feet start tapping and my fingers snapping—and the world becomes a happier, better place.

Thanks LaVerne. Thanks Maxene. Thanks Patty. We owe you big time.

APPENDIX 1

Discography

The number of songs recorded by the Andrews Sisters is greatly exaggerated in the literature. With typical hyperbole and questionable numbers, Maxene once told a reporter, "We made 10 movies, recorded 1,000 songs, double that for flip sides, and out of that we got 19 gold records in 20 years ... And let me put it to you this way: we only got about 50 good songs out of it all. The rest were dogs."[1]

According to my calculations, the Andrews Sisters recorded at least 605 songs as a trio—perhaps more. Patty recorded forty-three songs without her sisters and Maxene recorded fifteen alone. Patty and Maxene recorded five songs together. Of the 605 songs the Andrews Sisters recorded, 113 made *The Billboard*'s weekly charts of the top thirty most popular songs—twenty-three of these were with Bing Crosby. Two of Patty's recordings without her sisters also made the charts.

The literature is filled with inaccuracies regarding the number of Andrews Sisters records that sold over a million copies on initial release. CD booklets frequently claim the sisters had nineteen million-sellers, or Gold Records, a number often claimed by Maxene too. In 1954, Decca Records celebrated its twentieth anniversary and in both *Variety*[2] and *Down Beat*,[3] the company released a list of its records that sold over a million copies. Seven records by the Andrews Sisters made the list, four of

them with Bing Crosby: "Pistol Packin' Mama" (1943) with Crosby, "Jingle Bells" (1943) with Crosby, "Don't Fence Me In" (1944) with Crosby, "Rum and Coca-Cola" (1945), "South America, Take It Away" (1946) with Crosby, "Christmas Island" (1946), and "I Can Dream, Can't I?" (1949). The article specifically stated that "Bei Mir Bist Du Schoen" was not a million-seller, despite frequent claims in the literature to the contrary.[4] Of the four Decca albums that sold over a million copies, *Merry Christmas* by Bing Crosby included "Jingle Bells" and "Santa Claus Is Coming to Town" with the Andrews Sisters; both were originally released in 1943.

Two Andrews Sisters recordings were inducted into the Grammy Hall of Fame, namely "Bei Mir Bist Du Schoen" in 1996 and "Don't Fence Me In" (with Bing Crosby) in 1998. In March 2001, "Boogie Woogie Bugle Boy" was number 6 in a list of 365 songs chosen by "politicos, artists, music industry execs, teachers, journalists and students" as the most important popular songs of the past century. Voters were asked to bear in mind the "historical significance of song, artist and record." The survey was part of a joint project by the Recording Industry Association of America and the National Endowment of the Arts designed for teaching American students about the history of popular music.[5]

I know of no tabulation of total sales

of Andrews Sisters recordings. Given the many times some have been reissued on CD, several have probably passed the million mark by now. The first Andrews Sisters CD was issued in 1987. By late 2003, over 100 CDs of their songs had been issued—most containing the same core of popular titles. CD liners and feature stories often claim total record sales of sixty to ninety million for the sisters, but the range is so great that the figures are not meaningful. I have read claims that the sisters currently sell over a million CDs annually, but the figure is backed by no citation.

The sisters were always reluctant to name their favorite song. Patty once said, "It's like a mother with five children. You can't say what's your favorite."[6] But elsewhere, both Maxene and Patty admitted "In Apple Blossom Time" was their favorite. Maxene explained: "Because it's a song that wears well. There aren't that many songs that wear well for so many years ... I think my least favorite song is 'Rum and Coca-Cola,' because I find it monotonous and yet it was our biggest seller."[7] Patty said "The Cock-eyed Mayor of Kanakakai" was her least favorite song.

The list of Decca recordings below is drawn from Michel Ruppli's *The Decca Labels: A Discography*, Volumes 1, 2, 3, 5, and 6 (Westport: Greenwood Press, 1996). Vic Schoen and orchestra accompany all Decca recordings unless otherwise indicated.

Beginning in 1943 and continuing throughout that decade, the Armed Forces Radio Service issued a series of 33⅓ records, or transcriptions, called "Basic Musical Library" to its bases around the world. The "P" series of the library included popular recording artists of the era. Forty-eight songs by the Andrews Sisters appeared in this series—and possibly more since the source I located listed only the first 1000 records in the series.[8] These songs were taken from the Andrews Sisters' *Eight-to-the-Bar Ranch* radio show and from their Decca recording sessions; however, some of the songs were from radio show rehearsals and some of the Decca songs were takes that were never issued—perhaps all were from these rehearsals and unissued takes. Because it is unclear which songs were from rehearsals and unissued takes and therefore not released elsewhere, I have listed all the Andrews Sisters' songs that appeared in the Armed Forces Radio Service Basic Musical Library since they were issued as separate recordings. All the recordings were with Vic Schoen and his orchestra unless otherwise noted.

This discography lists only the original recordings of the Andrews Sisters. If songs were recorded more than once, each recording is listed. Dates are recording dates, not release dates. I have not attempted to list all the albums, cassettes, 8-tracks and CDs that have reproduced the original recordings.

I wish to acknowledge the assistance of Robert Boyer and Everett Searcy in the compilation of this discography.

Brunswick Recordings

1. Wake Up and Live (with Leon Belasco and Orchestra). Brunswick 7872. New York, March 18, 1937.
2. Jammin' (with Leon Belasco and Orchestra). Brunswick 7863. New York, March 18, 1937.

Decca Recordings

3. Why Talk About Love? Decca 1496. New York, October 14, 1937.
4. Just a Simple Melody. Decca 1496. New York, October 14, 1937.
5. Nice Work If You Can Get It. Decca 1562. New York, November 24, 1937.
6. Bei Mir Bist Du Schoen. Decca 1562. New York, November 24, 1937.
7. Joseph! Joseph! Decca 1691. New York, February 21, 1938.
8. Ti-Pi-Tin. Decca 1703. New York, February 21, 1938.
9. Shortenin' Bread. Decca 1744. New York, February 22, 1938.
10. It's Easier Said Than Done. Decca 1691. New York, February 22, 1938.
11. Where Have We Met Before? Decca 1703. New York, February 22, 1938.
12. Ooooooo-Oh Boom! Decca 1744. New York, February 22, 1938.
13. Says My Heart. Decca 1875. New York, June 4, 1938.
14. Oh! Ma-Ma! Decca 1859. New York, June 4, 1938.
15. Pagan Love Song. Decca 1859. New York, June 4, 1938.

16. I Married an Angel. Decca 1912. New York, June 4, 1938.

17. Oh! Faithless Maid. Decca 1875. New York, June 4, 1938.

18. From the Land of the Sky-Blue Water. Decca 1912. New York, June 4, 1938.

19. Tu-Li-Tulip Time. Decca 1974. New York, July 27, 1938.

20. Sha-Sha. Decca 1974. New York, July 27, 1938.

21. Love Is Where You Find It. Decca 2016. New York, August 6, 1938.

22. When a Prince of a Fella Meets a Cinderella. Decca 2016. New York, August 6, 1938.

23. One-Two-Three O'Leary. Brunswick 02837. New York, August 6, 1938.

24. Lullaby to a Jitterbug. Decca 2082. New York, September 8, 1938.

25. Pross-Tchai. Decca 2082. New York, September 8, 1938.

26. Hold Tight, Hold Tight (with Jimmy Dorsey and Orchestra). Decca 2214. New York, November 21, 1938.

27. Billy Boy (with Ray McKinley, vocalist, and Jimmy Dorsey and Orchestra). Decca 2214. New York, November 21, 1938.

28. Begin the Beguine (with Bob Crosby's Bob Cats). Decca 2290. New York, February 6, 1939.

29. Long Time No See (with Bob Crosby's Bob Cats). Decca 2290. New York, February 6, 1939.

30. You Don't Know How Much You Can Suffer. Decca 2414. New York, March 31, 1939.

31. Rock, Rock, Rock-A-Bye Baby. Decca 2414. New York, March 31, 1939.

32. Beer Barrel Polka. Decca 2462. New York, May 3, 1939.

33. Well, All Right. Decca 2462. New York, May 3, 1939.

34. The Jumpin' Jive. Decca 2756. New York, September 15, 1939.

35. Chico's Love Song. Decca 2756. New York, September 15, 1939.

36. Ciribiribin (with Bing Crosby and Joe Venuti and Orchestra). Decca 2800. New York, September 20, 1939.

37. Yodelin' Jive (with Bing Crosby and Joe Venuti and Orchestra). Decca 2800. New York, September 20, 1939.

38. Oh, Johnny! Oh, Johnny! Oh!. Decca 2840. New York, November 9, 1939.

39. South American Way. Decca 2840. New York, November 9, 1939.

40. Say "Si Si." Decca 3013. New York, February 7, 1940.

41. Let's Have Another One. Decca 3013. New York, February 7, 1940.

42. I Love You Much Too Much. MCA-908. New York, February 7, 1940.

43. The Woodpecker Song. Decca 3065. New York, February 21, 1940.

44. Down by the O-Hi-O. Decca 3065. New York, February 21, 1940.

45. Rhumboogie. Decca 3097. New York, March 23, 1940.

46. Tuxedo Junction. Decca 3097. New York, March 23, 1940.

47. The Cockeyed Mayor of Kaunakakai. Decca 3245. New York, April 23, 1940.

48. Let's Pack Our Things and Trek. Decca 3245. New York, April 23, 1940.

49. Oh, He Loves Me. Decca 3310. Los Angeles, July 7, 1940.

50. Hit the Road. MCA-908. Los Angeles, July 7, 1940.

51. I Want My Mama. Decca 3310. Los Angeles, July 7, 1940.

52. Ferry-Boat Serenade. Decca 3328. Los Angeles, July 15, 1940.

53. Hit the Road. Decca 3328. Los Angeles, July 15, 1940.

54. Johnny Peddler. Decca 3553. New York, August 3, 1940.

55. Beat Me, Daddy, Eight to the Bar. Decca DL-8360. New York, August 3, 1940.

56. Beat Me, Daddy, Eight to the Bar. MCA-908. New York, August 3, 1940.

57. Pennsylvania 6-5000. Decca 3375. New York, August 28, 1940.

58. Beat Me, Daddy, Eight to the Bar. Decca 3375. New York, August 28, 1940.

59. My Love Went Without Water (Released in South Africa only). Decca SA-1873. New York, August 28, 1940.

60. Mean to Me. Decca 3440. New York, September 5, 1940.

61. Sweet Molly Malone. Decca 3440. New York, September 5, 1940.

62. I Love You Much Too Much. Decca 18563. New York, September 5, 1940.

63. In Apple Blossom Time. Decca 3622. New York, November 14, 1940.

64. Scrub Me, Mama, with a Boogie Beat. Decca 3553. New York, November 14, 1940.

65. You're a Lucky Fellow, Mr. Smith. Decca 3599. Los Angeles, January 2, 1941.

66. Bounce Me, Brother, with a Solid Four. Decca 3598. Los Angeles, January 2, 1941.

67. Boogie Woogie Bugle Boy. Decca 3598. Los Angeles, January 2, 1941.

68. Boogie Woogie Bugle Boy. MCA-908. Los Angeles, January 2, 1941.

69. I, Yi, Yi, Yi, Yi (I Like You Very Much). Decca 3622. Los Angeles, January 7, 1941.

70. Yes, My Darling Daughter. Decca 3599. Los Angeles, January 7, 1941.

71. Aurora. Decca 3732. New York, March 18, 1941.

72. Music Makers. Decca 3732. New York, March 18, 1941.

73. Lonesome Mama. Brunswick 03416. New York, March 18, 1941.

74. Daddy. Decca 3821. Los Angeles, May 21, 1941.

75. Sleepy Serenade. Decca 3821. Los Angeles, May 21, 1941.

76. Helena. Decca 18563. Los Angeles, May 29, 1941.

77. Sonny Boy. Decca 3871. Los Angeles, May 29, 1941.

78. Gimme Some Skin, My Friend. Decca 3871. Los Angeles, May 29, 1941.

79. Jealous. Decca 4019. New York, July 28, 1941.

80. For All We Know. Decca 4094. New York, July 28, 1941.

81. Honey. Decca 4008. New York, July 30, 1941.

82. The Nickel Serenade. Decca 3960. New York, July 30, 1941.

83. Jack of All Trades. Decca 4097. New York, July 30, 1941.

84. The Booglie Wooglie Piggy. Decca 3960. New York, July 31, 1941.

85. I Wish I Had a Dime. Decca 3966. New York, July 31, 1941.

86. Why Don't We Do This More Often? Decca 3966. New York, August 4, 1941.

87. Elmer's Tune. Decca 4008. New York, August 4, 1941.

88. Rancho Pillow. Decca 4019. New York, September 10, 1941.

89. At Sonya's Café. Decca 18312. New York, September 10, 1941.

90. Elmer's Tune. MCA 2-4093. New York, September 26, 1941.

91. Any Bonds Today?. Decca 4044. New York, October 8, 1941.

92. The Shrine of Saint Cecelia. Decca 4097. New York, November 15, 1941.

93. Chattanooga Choo-Choo. Decca 4094. New York, November 15, 1941.

94. Tica-Ti-Tica-Ta. Brunswick 03337. New York, November 15, 1941.

95. I'll Pray for You. Decca 4153. New York, December 27, 1941.

96. He Said—She Said. Decca 4153. New York, December 27, 1941.

97. Boolee Boolee Boon. Decca 18319. Los Angeles, January 26, 1942.

98. A Zoot Suit for My Sunday Gal. Decca 4182. Los Angeles, January 26, 1942.

99. What to Do. Decca 4182. Los Angeles, January 26, 1942.

100. Three Little Sisters. Decca 18319. Los Angeles, April 4, 1942.

101. Don't Sit Under the Apple Tree. Decca 18312. Los Angeles, April 4, 1942.

102. That's the Moon, My Son. Decca 18398. Los Angeles, April 23, 1942.

103. When Johnny Comes Marching Home Again. Decca 18533. Los Angeles, April 23, 1942.

104. Six Jerks in a Jeep. MCA-908. Los Angeles, April 23, 1942.

105. You're Just a Flower from an Old Bouquet. MCA-908. Los Angeles, May 28, 1942.

106. Pennsylvania Polka. Decca 18398. Los Angeles, May 28, 1942.

107. I've Got a Gal in Kalamazoo. Decca 18464. Los Angeles, July 17, 1942.

108. The Humming Bird. Decca 18464. Los Angeles, July 17, 1942.

109. Strip Polka. Decca 18470. Los Angeles, July 17, 1942.

110. East of the Rockies. Decca 18533. Los Angeles, July 22, 1942.

111. Mister Five-By-Five. Decca 18470. Los Angeles, July 22, 1942.

112. Massachusetts. Decca 18497. Los Angeles, July 22, 1942.

113. Here Comes the Navy. Decca 18497. Los Angeles, July 22, 1942.

114. Pistol Packin' Mama (with Bing Crosby). Decca 23277. Los Angeles, September 27,1943.

115. Vict'ry Polka (with Bing Crosby). Coral (E) CPS-91. Los Angeles, September 27, 1943.

116. Vict'ry Polka (with Bing Crosby). Decca 23277. Los Angeles, September 27, 1943.

117. Jingle Bells (with Bing Crosby). Decca 23281. Los Angeles, September 29, 1943.

118. Jingle Bells (with Bing Crosby). MCA 2-11503. Los Angeles, September 29, 1943.

119. Santa Claus Is Comin' to Town (with Bing Crosby). Decca 23281. Los Angeles, September 29, 1943.

120. Shoo-Shoo Baby. Decca 18572. Los Angeles, October 5, 1943.

121. Down in the Valley. Decca 18572. Los Angeles, October 5, 1943.

122. Tico Tico. Decca 18606. New York, March 7, 1944.

123. There'll Be a Jubilee. Decca 18581. New York, March 7, 1944.

124. Sing a Tropical Song. Decca 18581. New York, April 4, 1944.

125. Bei Mir Bist Du Schoen. Decca DL-5120. New York, April 4, 1944.

126. Rhumboogie. DL5120. New York, April 4, 1944.

127. Straighten Up and Fly Right. Decca 18606. New York, May 2, 1944.

128. Red River Valley. Decca 18780. New York, May 2, 1944.

129. In Apple Blossom Time. Decca 23608. New York, May 2, 1944.

130. A Hot Time in the Town of Berlin (with Bing Crosby). Decca 23350. New York, June 30, 1944.

131. Is You Is Or Is You Ain't My Baby? (with Bing Crosby). Decca 23350. New York, June 30, 1944.

132. Don't Fence Me In (with Bing Crosby). Decca 23364. Los Angeles, July 25, 1944.

133. Don't Fence Me In (with Bing Crosby). MCA-908. Los Angeles, July 25, 1944.

134. The Three Caballeros (with Bing Crosby). Decca 23364. Los Angeles, July 25, 1944.

135. Don't Blame Me. Decca 23827. Los Angeles, August 24, 1944.

136. Corns for My Country. Decca 18628. Los Angeles, August 24, 1944.

137. Lullaby of Broadway. Decca 23824. Los Angeles, August 24, 1944.

138. Smile! Smile! Smile! (with Dick Haymes). Decca 23412. Los Angeles, August 31, 1944.

139. Great Day (with Dick Haymes). Decca 23412. Los Angeles, August 31, 1944.

140. I'm in a Jam (With Baby). Decca 18628. New York, October 18, 1944.

141. One Meat Ball. Decca 18636. New York, October 18, 1944.

142. Rum and Coca-Cola. Decca 18636. New York, October 18, 1944.

143. There's a Fellow Waiting in Poughkeepsie (with Bing Crosby). Decca 23379. Los Angeles, December 8, 1944.

144. Ac-Cent-Tchu-Ate the Positive (with Bing Crosby). Decca 23379. Los Angeles, December 8, 1944.

145. The Blond Sailor. Decca 18700. Los Angeles, June 26, 1945.

146. Lilly Belle. Decca 18700. Los Angeles, June 26, 1945.

147. Along the Navajo Trail (with Bing Crosby). Decca 23437. Los Angeles, June 29, 1945.

148. Good, Good, Good (with Bing Crosby). Decca 23437. Los Angeles, June 29, 1945.

149. Happy, Happy, Happy Weddin' Day (with Bing Crosby). MCA2-11503. Los Angeles, July 3, 1945.

150. Betsy (with Bing Crosby). Decca 24718. Los Angeles, July 3, 1945.

151. The Welcome Song. Decca 18726. New York, September 4, 1945.

152. Put That Ring on My Finger. Decca 18726. New York, September 4, 1945.

153. Money Is the Root of All Evil (with Guy Lombardo and his Royal Canadians). Decca 23474. New York, November 15, 1945.

154. Johnny Fedora and Alice Blue Bonnet (with Guy Lombardo and his Royal Canadians). Decca 23474. New York, November 19, 1945.

155. Patience and Fortitude. Decca 18780. Los Angeles, December 26, 1945.

156. Coax Me a Little Bit. Decca 18833. Los Angeles, March 7, 1946.

157. Atlanta, Ga. Decca 18833. Los Angeles, March 7, 1946.

158. Her Bathing Suit Never Got Wet. Decca 18840. Los Angeles, March 7, 1946.

159. Avacado. Decca 18840. Los Angeles, March 18, 1946.

160. Azusa. Decca 18899. Los Angeles, March 25, 1946.

161. Three O'clock in the Morning. Decca 27432. Los Angeles, May 8, 1946.

162. I Don't Know Why. Decca 18899. Los Angeles, May 8, 1946.

163. That's My Home (Released only in Argentina). Odeon 286856. Los Angeles, May 8, 1946.

164. Route 66 (with Bing Crosby). Decca 23569. Los Angeles, May 11, 1946.

165. South America, Take It Away (with Bing Crosby). Decca 23569. Los Angeles, May 11, 1946.

166. Rumors Are Flying (with Les Paul). Decca 23656. Los Angeles, July 22, 1946.

167. It's a Pity to Say Goodnight (with Les Paul). MCA 02-11708. Los Angeles, July 22, 1946.

168. Them That Has—Gets (with Eddie Haywood and Orchestra). Decca 23656. Los Angeles, July 26, 1946.

169. The House of Blue Lights (with Eddie Heywood and Orchestra). Decca 23641. Los Angeles, July 27, 1946.

170. A Man Is a Brother to a Mule (with Eddie Heywood and Orchestra). Decca 23641. Los Angeles, July 27, 1946.

171. Christmas Island (with Guy Lombardo and His Royal Canadians). Decca 23722. New York, September 30, 1946.

172 Winter Wonderland (with Guy Lombardo and his Royal Canadians). Decca 23722. New York, September 30, 1946.

173. The Coffee Song. Decca 23740. New York, October 3, 1946.

174. A Rainy Night in Rio. Decca 23740. New York, October 3, 1946.

175. My Dearest Uncle Sam. Decca 23824. New York, October 3, 1946.

176. His Feet Too Big for De Bed. Decca 23860. Los Angeles, February 26, 1947.

177. Jack, Jack, Jack (Cu-Tu-Gu-Ru). Decca 23860. Los Angeles, February 26, 1947.

178. Anything You Can Do (with Bing Crosby and Dick Haymes). Decca 40039. Los Angeles, March 19, 1947.

179. There's No Business Like Show Business (with Bing Crosby and Dick Haymes). Decca 40039. Los Angeles, March 19, 1947.

180. Go West, Young Man (with Bing Crosby). Decca 23885. Los Angeles, March 26, 1947.

181. Tallahassee (with Bing Crosby). Decca 23885. Los Angeles, March 26, 1947.

182. The Turntable Song. Decca 23976. New York, May 26, 1947.

183. The Lady from 29 Palms. Decca 23976. New York, May 26, 1947.

184. The Freedom Train (with Bing Crosby). Decca 23999. New York, May 29, 1947.

185. Sweet Marie (with Carmen Cavallaro and Orchestra). Decca 24102. New York, May 29, 1947.

186. On the Avenue (with Carmen Cavallaro and Orchestra). Decca 24102. New York, May 29, 1947.

187. Near You. Decca 24171. New York, August 4, 1947.

188. How Lucky You Are. Decca 24171. New York, August 4, 1947.

189. Civilization (Bongo, Bongo, Bongo) (with Danny Kaye). Decca 23940. Los Angeles, September 27, 1947.

190. Bread and Butter Woman (with Danny Kaye). Decca 23940. Los Angeles, September 27, 1947.

191. The Blue Tail Fly (with Burl Ives). Decca 24463. Los Angeles, October 7, 1947.

192. I'm Goin' Down the Road (with Burl Ives). Decca 24463. Los Angeles, October 7, 1947.

193. Your Red Wagon. Decca 24268. Los Angeles, October 30, 1947.

194. Don't Worry 'Bout Strangers. Decca 24533. Los Angeles, October 30, 1947.

195. Carioca. Decca 27757. Los Angeles, November 4, 1947.

196. Too Fat Polka. Decca 24268. Los Angeles, November 4, 1947.

197. Apalachicolo, Fla. (with Bing Crosby). Decca 24282. Los Angeles, November 25, 1947.

198. You Don't Have to Know the Language (with Bing Crosby). Decca 24282. Los Angeles, November 25, 1947.

199. How Many Times? Decca 24426. Los Angeles, November 26, 1947.

200. Some Sunny Day. Decca 24426. Los Angeles, November 26, 1947.

201. Cuanto La Gusta (with Carmen Miranda). Decca 24479. Los Angeles, November 29, 1947.

202. The Matador (with Carmen Miranda). Decca 24479. Los Angeles, November 29, 1947.

203. When That Midnight ChooChoo Leaves for Alabam'. Decca 24425. Los Angeles, December 3, 1947.

204. I Want to Go Back to Michigan. Decca 24424. Los Angeles, December 3, 1947.

205. Heat Wave. Decca 24425. Los Angeles, December 3, 1947.

206. Run, Run, Run. Decca 23827. Los Angeles, December 3, 1947.

207. Let a Smile Be Your Umbrella. Decca 24548. Los Angeles, December 10, 1947.

208. Whispering Hope. Decca 24717. Los Angeles, December 11, 1947.

209. Lovely Night. Decca 24717. Los Angeles, December 11, 1947.

210. Beatin', Bangin', and Scratchin' (with Danny Kaye). Decca 24536. Los Angeles, December 12, 1947.

211. Amelia Cordelia McHugh (with Danny Kaye). Decca 24536. Los Angeles, December 12, 1947.

212. Teresa (with Dick Haymes). Decca 24320. Los Angeles, December 13, 1947.

213. My Sin (with Dick Haymes). Decca 24320. Los Angeles, December 13, 1947.

214. A Hundred and Sixty Acres (with Bing Crosby). Decca 24481. Los Angeles, December 17, 1947.

215. A Hundred and Sixty Acres (Parody) (with Bing Crosby). MCA2-11503. Los Angeles, December 17, 1947.

216. At the Flying "W" (with Bing Crosby). Decca 24481. Los Angeles, December 17, 1947.

217. The Money Song. Decca 24499. Los Angeles, December 19, 1947.

218. The Bride and Groom Polka. Decca 24406. Los Angeles, December 19, 1947.

219. Toolie Oolie Doolie. Decca 24380. Los Angeles, December 19, 1947.

220. Big Brass Band from Brazil (with Danny Kaye). Decca 24361. Los Angeles, December 20, 1947.

221. It's a Quiet Town (with Danny Kaye). Decca 24361. Los Angeles, December 20, 1947.

222. Bella Bella Marie. Decca 24499. Los Angeles, December 27, 1947.

223. Alexander's Ragtime Band. Decca 24424. Los Angeles, December 27, 1947.

224. We Just Couldn't Say Goodbye. Decca 24406. Los Angeles, December 27, 1947.

225. I'd Love to Call You My Sweetheart (with Dick Haymes). Decca 24504. Los Angeles, December 31, 1947

226. What Did I Do? (with Dick Haymes). Decca 24504. Los Angeles, December 31, 1947.

227. I Hate to Lose You. Decca 24380. Los Angeles, December 31, 1947.

228. Sabre Dance (with the Harmonica Gentlemen). Decca 24427. Los Angeles, March 23, 1948.

229. Heartbreaker (with the Harmonica Gentlemen). Decca 24427. Los Angeles, March 23, 1948.

230. Put 'Em in a Box, Tie 'Em with a Ribbon (with Danny Kaye and the Harmonica Gentlemen). Decca 24462. Los Angeles, June 4, 1948.

231. The Woody Woodpecker Song (with Danny Kaye and the Harmonica Gentlemen). Decca 24462. Los Angeles, June 4, 1948.

232. You Call Everybody Darling (with Billy Ternent and Orchestra). Decca 24490. London, July 26, 1948.

233. Underneath the Arches (with Billy Ternent and Orchestra). Decca 24490. London, July 26, 1948.

234. More Beer! Decca 24548. Los Angeles, December 14, 1948.

235. Underneath the Linden Tree. Decca 24560. Los Angeles, December 14, 1948.

236. Don't Rob Another Man's Castle (with Ernest Tubb and the Texas Troubadours). Decca 24592. Los Angeles, February 15, 1949.

237. I'm Bitin' My Fingernails and Thinking of You (with Ernest Tubb and the Texas Troubadours). Decca 24592. Los Angeles, February 15, 1949.

238. Take Me Out to the Ballgame (with Dan Dailey). Decca 24605. Los Angeles, February 28, 1949.

239. In the Good Old Summer Time (with Dan Dailey). Decca 24605. Los Angeles, February 28, 1949.

240. I Had a Hat When I Came In (with Dan Dailey). Decca 24610. Los Angeles, March 11, 1949.

241. Clancy Lowered the Boom! (with Dan Dailey). Decca 24610. Los Angeles, March 11, 1949.

242. Hurry! Hurry! Hurry!. Decca 24613. Los Angeles, March 17, 1949.

243. I Didn't Know the Gun Was Loaded. Decca 24613. Los Angeles, March 17, 1949.

244. Malaguena. Decca 24645. Los Angeles, April 4, 1949.

245. Weddin' Day (with Bing Crosby). Decca 24635. Los Angeles, April 14, 1949.

246. Hohokus, N. J. Decca 24645. Los Angeles, April 14, 1949.

247. The Twelve Days of Christmas (with Bing Crosby). Decca 24658. Los Angeles, May 10, 1949.

248. Here Comes Santa Claus (with Bing Crosby). Decca 24658. Los Angeles, May 10, 1949.

249. Only for Americans. Decca 24660. Los Angeles, May 23, 1949.

250. Homework. Decca 24660. Los Angeles, May 23, 1949.

251. Now! Now! Now Is the Time (with Russ Morgan and Orchestra). Decca 24664. Los Angeles, May 25, 1949.

252. Oh, You Sweet One (with Russ Morgan and Orchestra). Decca 24664. Los Angeles, May 25, 1949.

253. I Can Dream, Can't I? (with Gordon Jenkins and Orchestra). Decca 24705. New York, July 15, 1949.

254. The Wedding of Lili Marlene (with Gordon Jenkins and Orchestra). Decca 24705. New York, July 15, 1949.

255. The Windmill's Turning (released only in India). Columbia DB 50278. New York, July 18, 1949.

256. Christmas Candles (with Guy Lombardo and His Royal Canadians). Decca 24748. Los Angeles, July 19, 1949.

257. Stars Are the Windows of Heaven (with Guy Lombardo and his Royal Canadians). Decca 24965. Los Angeles, July 19, 1949.

258. Jolly Fella Tarantella (with Guy Lombardo and his Royal Canadians). Decca 24965. Los Angeles, July 19, 1949.

259. Merry Christmas Polka (with Guy Lombardo and his Royal Canadians). Decca 24748. Los Angeles, July 19, 1949.

260 A Merry Christmas at Grandmother's House (with Danny Kaye). Decca 24769. Los Angeles, September 14, 1949.

261 Wunderbar (with Dick Haymes). Decca 24811. Los Angeles, October 24, 1949.

262. Adieu (with Dick Haymes and Jerry Gray and Orchestra). Decca 24811. Los Angeles, October 26, 1949.

263. He Rides the Range (with Jerry Gray and Orchestra). Decca 24809. Los Angeles, October 26, 1949.

264. Six Times a Week and Twice on Sunday. MCA-908. Los Angeles, October 26, 1949.

265. Open Door—Open Arms. Decca 24822. Los Angeles, November 1, 1949.

266. The Blossoms on the Bough. Decca 24822. Los Angeles, November 1, 1949.

267. Charley My Boy (with Russ Morgan and Orchestra). Decca 24812. Los Angeles, November 3, 1949.

268. She Wore a Yellow Ribbon (with Russ Morgan and Orchestra). Decca 24812. Los Angeles, November 3, 1949.

269. Quicksilver (with Bing Crosby) Decca 24827. Los Angeles, November 25, 1949.

270. Have I Told You Lately That I Love You? (with Bing Crosby). Decca 24827. Los Angeles, November 25, 1949.

271. I See, I See (Asi, Asi) (with Carmen Miranda). Decca 24841. Los Angeles, December 12, 1949.

272. The Wedding Samba (with Carmen Miranda). Decca 24841. Los Angeles, December 12, 1949.

273. Yipsee-I-O (with Carmen Miranda). Decca 24979. Los Angeles, January 6, 1950.

274. Ca-Room-Pa-Pa (with Carmen Miranda). Decca 24979. Los Angeles, January 6, 1950.

275. Can't We Talk It Over? (with Gordon Jenkins and Orchestra). Decca 27115. Los Angeles, January 18, 1950.

276. There Will Never Be Another You (with Gordon Jenkins and Orchestra). Decca 27115. Los Angeles, January 18, 1950.

277. In the Garden (with Victor Young and Orchestra). Decca 14502. Los Angeles, February 2, 1950.

278. Count Your Blessings (with Victor Young and Orchestra). Decca 14502. Los Angeles, February 2, 1950.

279. Softly and Tenderly (with Victor Young and Orchestra). Decca 14509. Los Angeles, February 2, 1950.

280. I Love to Tell the Story (with Victor Young and Orchestra). Decca 14509. Los Angeles, February 2, 1950.

281. Lock, Stock and Barrel (with Bing Crosby). Decca 24942. Los Angeles, February 15, 1950.

282. Ask Me No Questions (with Bing Crosby). Decca 24942. Los Angeles, February 15, 1950.

283. Muskrat Ramble. Decca 24991. Los Angeles, March 10, 1950.

284. Walk with a Wiggle. Decca 24991. Los Angeles, March 10, 1950.

285. Life Is So Peculiar (with Bing Crosby). Decca 27173. Los Angeles, March 24, 1950.

286. High on the List (with Bing Crosby). Decca 27173. Los Angeles, March 24, 1950.

287. I'm Gonna Paper All My Walls with Your Love Letters. Decca 24998. Los Angeles, March 28, 1950.

288. Choo'n Gum. Decca 24998. Los Angeles, March 28, 1950.

289. I Wanna Be Loved (with Gordon Jenkins and Orchestra). Decca 27007. Los Angeles, March 30, 1950.

290. I've Just Got to Get Out of the Habit (with Gordon Jenkins and Orchestra). Decca 27007. Los Angeles, March 30, 1950.

291. Shall We Gather at the River (with Victor Young and Orchestra). Decca 14521. Los Angeles, April 13, 1950.

292. The Ninety and Nine (with Victor Young and Orchestra). Decca 14521. Los Angeles, April 13, 1950.

293. Brighten the Corner (with Victor Young and Orchestra). Decca 14539. Los Angeles, April 13, 1950.

294. Let the Lower Lights Be Burning (with Victor Young and Orchestra). Decca 14539. Los Angeles, April 13, 1950.

295. The Old Piano Roll Blues (with Al Jolson). Decca 27024. Los Angeles, April 18, 1950.

296. Way Down Yonder in New Orleans (with Al Jolson). Decca 27024. Los Angeles, April 18, 1950.

297. Sleigh Ride. Decca 27310. New York, July 17, 1950.

298. The Telephone Song. Decca 27310. New York, July 18, 1950.

299. I Wish I Knew. Decca 27421. New York, July 18, 1950.

300. A Rainy Day Refrain (with Guy Lombardo and his Royal Canadians). Decca 27202. New York, August 2, 1950.

301. The Glory of Love (with Guy Lombardo and his Royal Canadians). Decca 27202. New York, August 2, 1950.

302. Poppa Santa Claus (with Bing Crosby). Decca 27228. Los Angeles, September 7, 1950.

303. Mele Kalikimaka (with Bing Crosby). Decca 27228. Los Angeles, September 7, 1950.

304. Jing-a-Ling, Jing-a-Ling. Decca 27242. Los Angeles, September 15, 1950.

305. Parade of the Wooden Soldiers. Decca 27242. Los Angeles, September 15, 1950.

306. Guys and Dolls. Decca 27252. Los Angeles, September 15, 1950.

307. The Christmas Tree Angel. Decca 27251. Los Angeles, September 20, 1950.

308. I'd Like to Hitch a Ride with Santa Claus. Decca 27251. Los Angeles, September 20, 1950.

309. A Bushel and a Peck. Decca 27252. Los Angeles, September 20, 1950.

310. Ching-Ara-Sa-Sa (with Danny Kaye). Decca 27261. Los Angeles, September 28, 1950.

311. Zing Zing, Zoom Zoom. Decca 27414. Los Angeles, December 14, 1950.

312. A Penny a Kiss, a Penny a Hug. Decca 27414. Los Angeles, December 14, 1950.

313. Between Two Trees. Decca 27421. Los Angeles, December 19, 1950.

314. All the World to Me. Decca 27878. Los Angeles, December 19, 1950.

315. Nobody's Darling but Mine. Decca 27834. Los Angeles, December 19, 1950.

316. I Used to Love You (with Tommy Dorsey and Orchestra). Decca 27700. Los Angeles, January 4, 1951.

317. I Remember Mama. Decca 27537. Los Angeles, January 19, 1951.

318. Love Sends a Little Gift of Roses. Decca 28929. Los Angeles, January 19, 1951.

319. My Mom. Decca 27537. Los Angeles, January 19, 1951.

320. This Little Piggie Went to Market. Decca 28929. Los Angeles, January 19, 1951.

321. Black Ball Ferry Line (with Bing Crosby). Decca 27631. Los Angeles, February 1, 1951.

322. The Yodeling Ghost (with Bing Crosby). Decca 27631. Los Angeles, February 1, 1951.

323. Forsaking All Others (with Bing Crosby). Decca 27477. Los Angeles, February 8, 1951.

324. Sparrow in the Treetop (with Bing Crosby). Decca 27477. Los Angeles, February 8, 1951.

325. Goodbye Darling, Hello Friend. Decca 27834. Los Angeles, March 19, 1951.

326. Gotta Find Somebody to Love. Decca 27569. Los Angeles, March 19, 1951.

327. The Mambo Man (with Sonny Burke and Orchestra). Decca 28483. Los Angeles, April 6, 1951.

328. Old Don Juan (with Desi Arnaz and Orchestra). Decca 28483. Los Angeles, April 7, 1951.

329. Satins and Lace (with Red Foley). Decca 27609. Nashville, April 26, 1951.

330. Bury Me Beneath the Willow (with Red Foley). Decca 29222. Nashville, April 26, 1951.

331. Where Is My Wandering Mother? (with Red Foley). Decca 28163. Nashville, April 26, 1951.

332. I Want to Be with You Always (with Red Foley). Decca 27609. Nashville, April 26, 1951.

333. Hang Your Head in Shame (with Red Foley). Decca 28163. Nashville, April 26, 1951.

334. He Bought My Soul at Calvary (with Red Foley). Decca 14566. Nashville, April 27, 1951.

335. It Is No Secret (with Red Foley). Decca 14566. Nashville, April 27, 1951.

336. She'll Never Know (with Red Foley). Decca 29222. Nashville, April 27, 1951.

339. There Was a Night on the Water (with Guy Lombardo and His Royal Canadians). Decca 27652. New York, June 8, 1951.

340. Dimples and Cherry Cheeks (with Kenny Gardner and Guy Lombardo and His Royal Canadians). Decca 27652. New York, June 8, 1951.

341. Love Is Such a Cheat. Decca 27760. New York, August 16, 1951.

342. Lying in the Hay. Decca 27760. New York, August 16, 1951.

343. Play Me a Hurtin' Tune (with Guy Lombardo and his Royal Canadians). Decca 27910. New York, October 22, 1951.

344. I'm on a Seesaw of Love (with Guy Lombardo and his Royal Canadians). Decca 27910. New York, October 22, 1951.

345. Piccolo Pete (with Sy Oliver and Orchestra). Decca 28481. New York, October 24, 1951.

346. East of the Sun (with Sy Oliver and Orchestra). Decca 28482. New York, October 24, 1951.

347. Dreams Come Tumbling Down (with Sy Oliver and Orchestra). Decca 28116. New York, October 24, 1951.

348. The Three Bells (with Gordon Jenkins and his Orchestra). Decca 27858. New York, October 24, 1951.

349. The Windmill Song (with Gordon Jenkins and Orchestra). Decca 27858. New York, October 24, 1951.

350. Wondering (with the Mellomen). Decca 27979. Los Angeles, January 22, 1952.

351. Poor Whip-Poor-Will. Decca 27979. Los Angeles, January 22, 1952.

352. That Ever Lovin' Rag. Decca 28042. Los Angeles, February 4, 1952.

353. Music Lessons. Decca 28042. Los Angeles, February 4, 1952.

354. Wabash Blues (with Russ Morgan and his Scranton Seven). Decca 28143. Los Angeles, February 8, 1952.

355. Linger Awhile (with Russ Morgan and His Scranton Seven). Decca 28143. Los Angeles, February 8, 1952.

356. Don't Be That Way (with Skip Martin and Orchestra). Decca 28480. Los Angeles, February 11, 1952.

357. Sing Sing Sing (with Skip Martin and Orchestra). Decca 28480. Los Angeles, February 11, 1952.

358. Why Worry? (with George Cates and Orchestra). Decca 28042. Los Angeles, February 15, 1952.

359. I'll Si-Si Ya in Bahia (with Bing Crosby and John Scott Trotter and Orchestra). Decca 9-28256. Los Angeles, February 21, 1952.

360. The Live Oak Tree (with Bing Crosby and John Scott Trotter and Orchestra). Decca 9-28256. Los Angeles, February 21, 1952.

361. Here in My Heart (with Dick Haymes and Nelson Riddle and Orchestra). Decca 28213. Los Angeles, May 1, 1952.

362. I'm Sorry (with Dick Haymes and Nelson Riddle and Orchestra). Decca 28213. Los Angeles, May 1, 1952.

363. My Isle of Golden Dreams (with Alfred Apaka and Danny Stewart and His Islanders). Decca 28294. Los Angeles, May 20, 1952.

364. Nalani (with Alfred Apaka and Danny Stewart and His Islanders). Decca 28294. Los Angeles, May 20, 1952.

365. The Cockeyed Mayor of Kaunakakai (with Alfred Apaka and Danny Stewart and His Islanders). Decca 28295. Los Angeles, May 22, 1952.

366. King's Serenade (with Alfred Apaka and Danny Stewart and His Islanders). Decca 28295. Los Angeles, May 22, 1952.

367. Ke Kali Nei Au (with Alfred Apaka and Danny Stewart and his Islanders). Decca 28296. Los Angeles, May 22, 1952.

368. One for the Wonder (with Nelson Riddle and Orchestra). Decca 28276. Los Angeles, May 26, 1952.

369. Idle Chatter (with Nelson Riddle and Orchestra). Decca 28276. Los Angeles, May 26, 1952.

370. Carmen's Boogie (with Nelson Riddle and Orchestra). Decca 28342. Los Angeles, July 7, 1952.

371. In the Mood (with Nelson Riddle and Orchestra). Decca 28482. Los Angeles, July 7, 1952.

372. Adios (with Skip Martin and Orchestra). Decca 28342. Los Angeles, July 11, 1952.

373. If I Had a Boy Like You (with Skip Martin and Orchestra). Decca 28481. Los Angeles, July 11, 1952.

374. South Rampart Street Parade (with Bing Crosby and Matty Matlock and Orchestra). Decca 28419. Los Angeles, September 5, 1952.

375. Cool Water (with Bing Crosby and Matty Matlock and Orchestra). Decca 28419. Los Angeles, September 5, 1952.

376. No Deposit, No Return. Decca 28492. Los Angeles, October 22, 1952.

377. Fugue for Tin Horns (with Matty Matlock and Orchestra). Decca 28680. Los Angeles, March 23, 1953.

378. Now That I'm in Love (with Matty Matlock and Orchestra). Decca 28680. Los Angeles, March 23, 1953.

379. You Too, You Too? Decca 28773. Los Angeles, June 23, 1953.

380. Tegucigalpa. Decca 28773. Los Angeles, June 23, 1953.

381. My Love, the Blues and Me (with Sonny Burke and Orchestra). Decca 29149. Los Angeles, November 11, 1953.

382. There's a Rainbow in the Valley (with Sonny Burke and Orchestra). Decca 29149. Los Angeles, November 11, 1953.

Victory Discs

Unless otherwise noted, all Victory Discs (V-Discs) are with Vic Schoen and his orchestra. I was unable to locate some dates and record numbers.

383. Medley of Hits (with Mitch Ayres and Orchestra). V-Disc 194A. March 1944.

384. Sing a Tropical Song (with Mitch Ayres and Orchestra). V-Disc 194B. March 1944.

385. Rhumboogie (with Mitch Ayres and Orchestra). V-Disc 194B. March 1944.

386. Boogie Woogie Bugle Boy (with Mitch Ayres and Orchestra). V-Disc 526B. September 25, 1944.

387. Lullaby of Broadway (with Mitch Ayres and Orchestra). V-Disc 358, 128B. September 25, 1944.

388. Is You Is Or Is You Ain't My Baby? (with Mitch Ayres and Orchestra). V-Disc 358, 128B. September 25, 1944.

389. Red River Valley (with Foy Willings and Riders of the Purple Sage). V-Disc 479B. March 18, 1945.

390. The Three Caballeros. V-Disc 452-A, 8. March 25, 1945.

391. Vict'ry Polka. V-Disc 452-A, 8. March 25, 1945.

392. The Blond Sailor. V-Disc 570A. November 7, 1945.

393. Put That Ring on My Finger. V-Disc 570A. November 28, 1945.

394. Money Is the Root of All Evil. V-Disc 579A. December 12, 1945.

395. Down in the Valley.

396. Straighten Up and Fly Right.

397. Don't Blame Me.

398. I'm Gettin' Corns for My Country.

399. Hot Time in the Town of Berlin (with Bing Crosby).

Armed Forces Radio Service Basic Musical Library

400. Down in the Valley. P-217.

401. Lime and Coca Cola. P-217.

402. Bei Mir Bist Du Schoen. P-217.

403. The Three Caballeros. P-217.

404. Here Comes the Navy. P-217.

405. Boogie Woogie Bugle Boy. P-254.

406. A Tisket-A-Tasket (with Arthur Treacher). P-254.

407. One Meat Ball. P-254.

408. Lullaby of Broadway. P-254.

409. The Old Square Dance (with Gabby Hayes and Vera Vague). P-254.

410. Sing a Tropical Song. P-273.

411. I Didn't Want to Love You. P-273.

412. Red River Valley. P-273.

413. Honey, I'm in Love with You. P-273.

414. Good, Good, Good. P-273.

415. June Is Bustin' Out All Over. P-320.

416. One Little Thing at a Time. P-320.

417. Rancho Pillow. P-320.

418. Boogie Woogie Washerwoman (aka Scrub Me Momma with a Boogie Beat) (with Carmen Miranda). P-320.

419. Beer Barrel Polka. P-320.

420. When Johnny Comes Marching Home Again. P-320.

421. Sentimental Journey. P-376.

422. Green Green Hills of Home. P-376.

423. Mean to Me. P-376.

424. Happy, Happy, Happy Wedding Day. P-376.

425. Great Day (Decca Take 4) (with Dick Haymes). P-413.

426. Along the Navajo Trail (with Bing Crosby and John Scott Trotter and Orchestra). P-429.

427. Good, Good, Good (with Bing Crosby and John Scott Trotter and Orchestra). P-429.

428. I Don't Know Why. P-668.

429. South America, Take It Away (with Bing Crosby). P-668.

430. A Man Is a Brother to a Mule (with Eddie Heywood and Orchestra). P-681.

431. A Rainy Night in Rio. P-692.

432. The Coffee Song. P-692.

433. Anything You Can Do (Decca take 2) (with Bing Crosby and Dick Haymes) P-799.

434. There's No Business Like Show Business (with Bing Crosby and Dick Haymes). (Decca take 4). P-799.

435. On the Avenue (with Carmen Cavallero and Orchestra). P-844.

436. Go West Young Man (Decca take 2) (with Bing Crosby). P-844.

437. Tallahassee (Decca take 3) (with Bing Crosby). P-844.

438. The Turntable Song. P-844.

439. How Lucky You Are. P-891.

440. Near You. P-891.

441. Civilization (with Danny Kaye). P-921.

442. Too Fat Polka. P-921.

443. Your Red Wagon. P-921.

444. You Don't Have to Know the Language (Decca take 3). (with Bing Crosby). P-957.

445. Apalachicola, Fla. (Decca take 4) (with Bing Crosby). P-957.

446. Teresa (Decca take 1) (with Dick Haymes). P-961.

447. My Sin (Decca take 2) (with Dick Haymes). P-961.

Capitol Records: Singles

448. Crazy Arms (with Vic Schoen and Orchestra). Capitol 3567. Los Angeles, September 18, 1956.

449. I Want to Linger (with Vic Schoen and Orchestra). Capitol 3567. Los Angeles, September 18, 1956.

450. I'm Going Home (with Vic Schoen and Orchestra). Capitol 3784. Los Angeles, September 18, 1956.

451. Give Me Back My Heart (with Billy Mays and Orchestra). Capitol F3707. Los Angeles, 1957.

452. Rum and Coca-Cola (with Vic Schoen and Orchestra). Capitol 3658. Los Angeles, January 1957.

453. No, Baby! Capitol F3658. Los Angeles, January 23, 1957.

454. Stars, Stars, Stars (with Gordon Jenkins and Orchestra and chorus). Capitol F3707. Los Angeles, January 23, 1957.

455. By His Word (with Gordon Jenkins and Orchestra and chorus). Capitol F3784. Los Angeles, January 23, 1957.

456. Silver Bells (with Lynn Murray and Orchestra and Robert Mitchell's choir). Capitol F3583. Los Angeles, September 24, 1957.

457. A Child's Christmas Song (with Peter Levy, Lynn Murray and Orchestra and Robert Mitchell's choir). Capitol F3583. Los Angeles, September 24, 1957.

458. Alone Again (with Bob Thompson and Orchestra). Capitol CDP-7-94078-2. Los Angeles, November 22, 1957.

459. One Mistake (with Bob Thompson and Orchestra). Capitol F3869. Los Angeles, November 22, 1957.

460. Melancholy Moon (with Bob Thompson and Orchestra). Capitol F3869. Los Angeles, November 22, 1957.

461. Torrero. Capitol F3965. Los Angeles, March 31, 1958.

462. Sunshine. Capitol F3965. Los Angeles, March 31, 1958.

463. I've Got an Invitation to a Dance (with Jack Marshall and Orchestra). Capitol F4144. Los Angeles, December 18, 1958.

464. My Love Is a Kitten. Capitol F4144. Los Angeles, December 18, 1958.

465. E-Ma-Ma (with Jack Marshall and Orchestra). Capitol CDP 7-94078-2. Los Angeles, December 18, 1958.

466. Proper Cup of Coffee (with Jack Marshall and Orchestra). Capitol CDP 7-94078-2. Los Angeles, December 18, 1958.

Capitol Records: Albums

The Andrews Sisters in Hi-Fi. Capitol W-7. Vic Schoen and Orchestra. October 2, 5, 9, 19, 1956.

467. Bei Mir Bist Du Schoen.
468. Beer Barrel Polka.
469. Rum and Coca-Cola.
470. Rancho Pillow.
471. Tu-Li-Tulip Time.
472. Shoo Shoo Baby.
473. Beat Me Daddy, Eight to the Bar.
474. Don't Sit Under the Apple Tree.
475. In Apple Blossom Time.
476. Ti-Pi-Tin.
477. Hold Tight, Hold Tight.
478. Aurora.
479. Boogie Woogie Bugle Boy.
480. Begin the Beguine.
481. Well, All Right!
482. Ferryboat Serenade.

Fresh and Fancy Free. Capitol T-860. Billy May and Orchestra. May 13, 20, June 28, 1957.

483. The Song Is You.

484. You Do Something to Me.
485. Comes Love.
486. Nevertheless.
487. With Every Breath I Take.
488. Of Thee I Sing.
489. Hooray for Love.
490. My Romance.
491. Tea for Two.
492. I Could Write a Book.
493. Let There Be Love.
494. Younger Than Springtime.

The Andrews Sisters Sing the Dancing 20's. Capitol ED 26 0417 1. Billy May and Orchestra. January 2, 16, 1958.

495. Don't Bring Lulu.
496. Me Too.
497. That Naughty Waltz.
498. A Smile Will Go a Long, Long Way.
499. Barney Google.
500. Collegiate.
501. Last Night on the Back Porch.
502. When Francis Dances with Me.
503. Back in Your Own Back Yard.
504. Keep Your Skirts Down, Mary Ann.
505. The Japanese Sandman.
506. Show Me the Way to Go Home.

Kapp Records: Singles

507. I've Got to Pass Your House. Kapp K-309X. October 15, 1959.
508. One, Two, Three, Four. Kapp K-309X. October 15, 1959.

British Decca Records: Singles

509. Sailor. Decca F11316. London, January 1961.
510. Goodnight and Sweet Dreaming. Decca F11316. London, January 1961.

Dot Records: Singles

All of these, except "My Midnight Prison," appear in the Dot albums listed below.

—. Pistol Packin' Mama. Dot 16433. 1962.
—. Ti-Pi-Tin. Dot 16433. 1962.
—. Mr. Bass Man. Dot 16497. 1963.
511. My Midnight Prison. Dot 16497. 1963.

—. Theme from "Man and a Woman". Dot 16962. 1965.
—. Theme from "Come September". Dot 16962. 1965.

Dot Records: Albums

The Andrews Sisters' Greatest Hits. Dot. DLP 3406. Billy Vaughn and Orchestra. 1961.

512. I'll Be with You in Apple Blossom Time.
513. Beer Barrel Polka.
514. Beat Me Daddy, Eight to the Bar.
515. I Can Dream, Can't I?
516. Pennsylvania Polka.
517. Hold Tight, Hold Tight.
518. Rum and Coca-Cola.
519. Down in the Valley.
520. Bei Mir Bist Du Schon.
521. The Shrine of St. Cecilia.
522. Rhumboogie.
523. Joseph! Joseph!

Great Golden Hits: The Andrews Sisters. Dot. DLP 3452. Vic Schoen and Orchestra. 1962.

524. Ti-Pi-Tin.
525. The Old Piano Roll Blues.
526. Near You.
527. Pistol Packin' Mama.
528. Don't Fence Me In.
529. Oh, Johnny, Oh Johnny, Oh!
530. Oh! Ma-Ma!
531. I Wanna Be Loved.
532. Aurora.
533. The Irish Twist.
534. Daddy.
535. Boogie Woogie Bugle Boy.

The Andrews Sisters Present. Dot. DLP 3529. Donn Trenner and Orchestra. 1963.

536. Mr. Bass Man.
537. I Left My Heart in San Francisco.
538. Can't Get Used to Losing You.
539. Gravy Waltz.
540. Still.
541. Those Lazy, Hazy, Crazy Days of Summer.
542. Watermelon Man.
543. I Love You Because.
544. The End of the World.

545. The Doodle Song.
546. Puff , the Magic Dragon.
547. Sukiyaki (My First Lonely Night).

The Andrews Sisters' Greatest Hits, Vol. II. Dot. DLP 3543. Allyn Ferguson and Orchestra. 1964.

548. Don't Sit Under the Apple Tree.
549. Nobody's Darlin' but Mine.
550. In the Mood.
551. Cool Water.
552. Three Little Fishies.
553. Cuanto Le Gusta.
554. Route 66.
555. You Are My Sunshine.
556. Ciribiribin.
557. Sonny Boy.
558. Say Si Si.
559. Sabre Dance.

The Andrews Sisters: Great Country Hits. Dot. DLP 3567. Arrangements by Billy Vaughn and Milt Rogers. (No orchestra listed.) 1964.

560. Ragtime Cowboy Joe.
561. Tennessee Waltz.
562. Your Cheatin' Heart.
563. Sioux City Sue.
564. Mexicali Rose.
565. Jealous Heart.
566. Wabash Cannon Ball.
567. My Happiness.
568. Cold, Cold Heart.
569. Careless Hands.
570. I'm Thinking Tonight of My Blue Eyes.
571. Bouquet of Roses.

The Andrews Sisters Go Hawaiian. Dot. DLP3632. Pete King and Orchestra. 1965.

572. My Little Grass Shack.
573. My Isle of Golden Dreams.
574. Song of the Islands.
575. Drifting and Dreaming.
576. Sweet Leilani.
577. Hawaii.
578. Cocoanut Grove.
579. To You Sweetheart, Aloha.
580. Beyond the Reef.
581. The Hawaiian Wedding Song.
582. Hawaiian Sunset.
583. Blue Hawaii.

The Andrews Sisters: Favorite Hymns. Hamilton (Division of Dot) HL154. Arranged and conducted by Walter Weschler. 1965.

584. Nearer My God to Thee.
585. Fling Out the Banner.
586. I Believe.
587. In the Garden.
588. Beautiful Isle of Somewhere.
589. Whispering Hope.
590. Just a Closer Walk with Thee.
591. Abide with Me.
592. Rock of Ages.
593. Jesus Calls Us.
594. It Is No Secret.
595. The Old Rugged Cross.

Great Performers: The Andrews Sisters. Dot. DLP3807. Arrangements by Arnie Goland, Charles Geran, Vic Schoen, and Billy Vaughn. (No orchestra is identified on album). 1967.

596. A Man and a Woman.
597. Everybody Wants to Be Loved.
598. Theme from "Come September."
599. Is It Really Over?
600. Dixie.
601. Satin Doll.
602. All the Colors of the Rainbow.
603. I Forgot More Than You'll Ever Know.
604. Rose's Theme.
605. Wild Is Love.

Unissued Andrews Sisters Decca Recordings

All with Vic Schoen and Orchestra unless otherwise indicated.

1. Elmer's Tune. New York, August 4, 1941.
2. There Are Such Things. Los Angeles, December 16, 1942.
3. Shoo Shoo Baby. (with Mitch Ayres). Los Angeles, October 5, 1943.
4. Down in the Valley. (with Mitch Ayres). Los Angeles, October 5, 1943.
5. It's Me O Lord. Los Angeles, June 26, 1945.
6. Her Bathing Suit Never Got Wet. (with Guy Lombardo). New York, November 15, 1945.

7. A Rainy Night in Rio. Los Angeles, March 18, 1946.

8. A Man Is a Brother to a Mule. Los Angeles, March 26, 1946.

9. The House of Blue Lights. Los Angeles, March 26, 1946.

10. I'm So Right Tonight. Los Angeles, April 14, 1947.

11. Red Silk Stockings Are Green. Los Angeles, April 14, 1947.

12. Why Am I Always the Bridesmaid? Los Angeles, October 30, 1947.

13. Alexander's Ragtime Band. Los Angeles, November 4, 1947.

14. I'm in Love. Los Angeles, November 13, 1947.

15. Run Run Run. Los Angeles, November 13, 1947.

16. A Hundred and Sixty Acres. (with Bing Crosby). Los Angeles, December 17, 1947.

17. Sweet 'n' Gentle. Los Angeles, December 17, 1947.

18. Mmm-Mmm Good. Los Angeles, December 31, 1947.

19. Malaguena. Los Angeles, December 18, 1948.

20. Take Me Out to the Ballgame. Los Angeles, January 15, 1949.

21. Clancy Lowered the Boom (with Dan Dailey). Los Angeles, February 28, 1949.

22. Hohokus, N. J. Los Angeles, March 17, 1949.

23. Good Times Are Comin.' Los Angeles, April 4, 1949.

24. Jolly Fella Tarentella. Los Angeles, April 4, 1949.

25. There's a Bluebird on Your Windowsill. New York, July 18, 1949.

26. The Windmill Is Turning. New York, July 18, 1949.

27. I Got a Talent (with Gordon Jenkins). Los Angeles, January 19, 1950.

28. Cleanse Me (with Victor Young). Los Angeles, April 13, 1950.

29. Blest Be the Tie That Binds (with Victor Young). Los Angeles, April 13, 1950.

30. Pass the Basket (with Tommy Dorsey). Los Angeles, January 4, 1951.

31. This Little Piggie Went to Market. Los Angeles, January 19, 1951.

32. My Mom. Los Angeles, January 19, 1951.

33. Your Home Is in My Arms (with Victor Young). Los Angeles, March 20, 1951.

34. Sing It in English (with Desi Arnaz). Los Angeles, April 7, 1951.

35. Why Worry. Los Angeles, February 15, 1952.

Patty Andrews Discography

1. There's a Lull in My Life. Brunswick 7872. New York, March 18, 1937.

2. Twilight on the Trail. V-Disc 479B. March 18, 1945

3. The Pussy Cat Song (with Bob Crosby). Decca 24533. Los Angeles, November 22, 1948.

4. You Was (with Bob Crosby). Decca 24560. Los Angeles, January 15, 1949.

5. Be-Bop Spoken Here (with Bing Crosby). Decca 24635. Los Angeles, April 14, 1949.

6. All I Want for Christmas Is My Two Front Teeth (with Danny Kaye). Decca 24769. Los Angeles, September 14, 1949.

7. Why Won't Ya? (with Dick Haymes and Jerry Gray and Orchestra). Decca 24809. Los Angeles, October 24, 1949.

8. Can I Come in for a Second? (with Dick Haymes). Decca 24896. Los Angeles, January 19, 1950.

9. I Oughta Know More About You (with Dick Haymes). Decca 24896. Los Angeles, January 19, 1950.

10. If I Were a Bell (with Bing Crosby). Decca 27232. Los Angeles, September 7, 1950.

11. Orange Colored Sky (with Danny Kaye). Decca 27261. Los Angeles, September 28, 1950.

12. Too Young (with Victor Young and Orchestra). Decca 27569. Los Angeles, March 20, 1951.

13. Unless You're Free (with Red Foley). Decca 28767. Nashville, April 26, 1951.

14. Baby Blues (with Red Foley). Decca 28767. Nashville, April 27, 1951.

15. I'm in Love Again (with Gordon Jenkins and Orchestra). Decca 27635. Los Angeles, May 26, 1951.

16. It Never Entered My Mind (with Gordon Jenkins and Orchestra). Decca 27635. Los Angeles, May 26, 1951.

17. How Many Times? (with Victor Young and Orchestra). Decca 27700. Los Angeles, July 3, 1951.

18. Love Is Here to Stay (with Paul

Nealson and Orchestra). Decca 27845. Los Angeles, October 12, 1951.

19. It's All Over but the Memories (with Paul Nealson and Orchestra). Decca 27845. Los Angeles, October 12, 1951.

20. If You Go (Si Tu Partais) (with Gordon Jenkins and Orchestra). Decca 27913. Los Angeles, December 6, 1951.

21. That's How a Song Is Born (with Gordon Jenkins and Orchestra). Decca 27913. Los Angeles, December 6, 1951.

22. I'll Walk Alone. Decca 28038. Los Angeles, February 15, 1952.

23. That's the Chance You Take. Decca 28038. Los Angeles, February 15, 1952.

24. Goodnight Aloha (with Alfred Apaka and Danny Stewart and His Islanders). Decca 28297. Los Angeles, May 20, 1952.

25. Malihini Mele (with Alfred Apaka and Danny Stewart and His Islanders). Decca 28297. Los Angeles, May 22, 1952.

26. You Blew Me a Kiss (with Vic Schoen and Orchestra). Decca 28492. Los Angeles, October 22, 1952.

27. I Forgot More Than You'll Ever Know. Decca 28852. Los Angeles, August 22, 1953.

28. What Happened to You?. Decca 28852. Los Angeles, August 22, 1953.

29. Dissertation on the State of Bliss (with Bing Crosby and Joseph Lilley and Orchestra). Decca 29537. Los Angeles, December 23, 1954.

30. It's Bigger Than Both of Us (with Jimmy Durante). Decca 29537. Los Angeles, April 21, 1955.

31. When the Circus Leaves Town (with Jimmy Durante). Decca 29537. Los Angeles, April 21, 1955.

32. Without Love (with Nelson Riddle and Orchestra). Capitol 3159. Los Angeles, May 20, 1955.

33. Where to, My Love? (with Nelson Riddle and Orchestra). Capitol 3159. Los Angeles, May 20, 1955.

34. Suddenly, There's a Valley (with Harold Mooney and Orchestra). Capitol 3228. Los Angeles, August 12, 1955.

35. Boog-A-Da-Woog (with Harold Mooney and Orchestra). Capitol 3228. Los Angeles, August 12, 1955.

36. The Rains Came Down (with Harold Mooney and Orchestra). Capitol 3268. Los Angeles, September 16, 1955.

37. I'll Forgive You (with Harold Mooney and Orchestra). Capitol 3268. Los Angeles, September 16, 1955.

38. I Never Will Marry (with Harold Mooney and Orchestra). Capitol 3344. Los Angeles, December 30, 1955.

39. Daybreak Blues (with Harold Mooney and Orchestra). Capitol 3344. Los Angeles, September 16, 1956.

40. A Friendship Ring (with Frank DeVol and Orchestra). Capitol 3403. Los Angeles, March 15, 1956.

41. Music Drives Me Crazy (with Frank DeVol and Orchestra). Capitol 3403. Los Angeles, March 15, 1956.

42. Too Old to Rock-N-Roll (with Frank DeVol and Orchestra). Capitol 3495. Los Angeles, March 15, 1956.

43. Broken (with Frank DeVol and Orchestra). Capitol 3495. Los Angeles, March 15, 1956.

Over Here! SK 32961. Sony Broadway. 1974.

44. The Good-Time Girl. Sony (SK 32961). New York, March 31, 1974.

45. Where Did the Good Times Go? Sony (SK 32961). New York, March 31, 1974.

Maxene Andrews Discography

An Evening with Frank Loesser. DRG5169. 1992. Maxene Andrews' songs were originally recorded in summer 1953.

1. Oooh! My Feet!
2. How's About Tonight?/House and Garden.

Maxene, An Andrews Sister. Bainbridge BT6258. Arranged by Arnold Goland. 1985.

3. I Suppose.
4. Mama Llama.
5. Where Did the Good Times Go?
6. Medley: Bei Mir Bist Du Schoen, Don't Sit Under the Apple Tree, Pennsylvania Polka, Beer Barrel Polka.
7. How Deep Is the Ocean?
8. Show Me the Way to Go Home.
9. In Apple Blossom Time.

10. You're My Everything.
11. Sweet and Low.
12. Nature's Toys.
13. Remember.
14. Fascinating Rhythm.

Over Here! SK 32961. Sony Broadway. 1974.

15. Charlie's Place. Sony (SK 32961). New York, March 31, 1974.

Maxene and Patty Andrews Discography

From the Broadway musical *Over Here!* SK32961. Sony Broadway. 1974.

1. Over Here! Sony (SK 32961). New York, March 31, 1974
2. We Got It!. Sony (SK 32961). New York, March 31, 1974
3. Wartime Wedding. Sony (SK 32961). New York, March 31, 1974
4. The Big Beat. Sony (SK 32961). New York, March 31, 1974
5. No Goodbyes. Sony (SK 32961). New York, March 31, 1974

APPENDIX 2

Songs on *The Billboard* Charts

During their long Decca recording career, the Andrews Sisters achieved top-30 listings on *The Billboard* for 113 of their songs. Patty Andrews charted two songs without her sisters. These numbers are compiled from *The Billboard*'s three Pop Singles charts, namely Best Sellers (in retail stores), Juke Box charts (most popular songs on juke boxes), and Disc Jockey Charts (records most played on the air). The following compilation lists the songs and the number of weeks they appeared on the charts. The number in parentheses is the highest position the song reached in the top 30 weekly listing. This compilation is from *Pop Memories 1890–1954* by Joel Whitburn (1986).

---

1. "I Can Dream, Can't I?" (1949)—25 weeks (1).
2. "Shoo Shoo Baby" (1943)—21 weeks (1).
3. "Don't Fence Me In" (with Bing Crosby) (1944)—21 weeks (1).
4. "I Wanna Be Loved" (1950)—21 weeks (1).
5. "Rum and Coca-Cola" (1945)—20 weeks (1).
6. "South America, Take it Away" (with Bing Crosby) (1946)—19 weeks (1).
7. "In Apple Blossom Time" (1941)—17 weeks (5).
8. "Three Little Sisters" (1942)—17 weeks (8).
9. "Near You" (1947)—17 weeks (2).
10. "Toolie Oolie Doolie" (1948)—17 weeks (3).
11. "Quicksilver" (with Bing Crosby) (1950)—17 weeks (6).
12. "Well All Right" (1939)—15 weeks (5).
13. "Sparrow in the Treetop" (with Bing Crosby) (1951)—15 weeks (8).
14. "Ferryboat Serenade" (1940)—14 weeks (1).
15. "Beat Me Daddy, Eight to the Bar" (1940)—14 weeks (2).
16. "A Hot Time in the Town of Berlin" (with Bing Crosby) (1944)—14 weeks (1).
17. "Cuanto La Gusta" (with Carmen Miranda) (1948)—14 weeks (12).
18. "Vict'ry Polka" (with Bing Crosby) (1943)—13 weeks (5).
19. "Straighten Up and Fly Right" (1944)—13 weeks (8).
20. "Rumors Are Flying" (with Les Paul) (1946)—13 weeks (4).

21. "Yodelin' Jive" (with Bing Crosby) (1939)—12 weeks (4).

22. "The Woodpecker Song" (1940)—12 weeks (6).

23. "Is You Is or Is You Ain't My Baby?" (with Bing Crosby) (1944)—12 weeks (2).

24. "Underneath the Arches" (1948)—12 weeks (5).

25. "You Call Everybody Darling" (1948)—12 weeks (8).

26. "Hold Tight, Hold Tight" (1939)—11 weeks (2).

27. "Aurora" (1941)—11 weeks (10).

28. "Pistol Packin' Mama" (with Bing Crosby) (1943)—11 weeks (2).

29. "Along the Navajo Trail" (with Bing Crosby) (1945)—11 weeks (2).

30. "Bei Mir Bist Du Schoen" (1938)—10 weeks (1).

31. "Say 'Si Si'" (1940)—10 weeks (4).

32. "Tallahassee" (with Bing Crosby) (1947)—10 weeks (10).

33. "Rhumboogie" (1940)—9 weeks (11).

34. "Jealous" (1941)—9 weeks (12).

35. "Strip Polka" (1942)—9 weeks (6).

36. "Ac-Cent-Tchu-Ate the Positive" (with Bing Crosby) (1945)—9 weeks (2).

37. "Boogie Woogie Bugle Boy" (1941)—8 weeks (6).

38. "The Blond Sailor" (1945)—8 weeks (8).

39. "Beer Barrel Polka" (1939)—7 weeks (4).

40. "Scrub Me Mama, with a Boogie Beat" (1941)—7 weeks (10).

41. "The Shrine of Saint Cecelia" (1942)—7 weeks (3).

42. "I Hate to Lose You" (1948)—7 weeks (14).

43. "A Penny a Kiss, a Penny a Hug" (1951)—7 weeks (17).

44. "I, Yi, Yi, Yi, Yi (I Like You Very Much)" (1941)—6 weeks (11).

45. "The Woody Woodpecker Song" (with Danny Kaye) (1948)—6 weeks (18).

46. "Says My Heart" (1938)—5 weeks (10).

47. "Chico's Love Song" (1939)—5 weeks (11).

48. "The Three Caballeros" (with Bing Crosby) (1945)—5 weeks (8).

49. "Money Is the Root of All Evil" (1946)—5 weeks (9).

50. "House of Blue Lights" (with Eddie Heywood) (1946)—5 weeks (15).

51. "Heartbreaker" (1948)—5 weeks (21).

52. "Ti-Pi-Tin" (1938)—4 weeks (12).

53. "Tu-Li-Tulip Time" (1938)—4 weeks (9).

54. "Winter Wonderland" (with Guy Lombardo) (1946)—4 weeks (22).

55. "Christmas Island" (with Guy Lombardo) (1946)—4 weeks (7).

56. "On the Avenue" (1947)—4 weeks (21).

57. "Charley My Boy" (with Russ Morgan) (1949)—4 weeks (15).

58. "A Bushel and a Peck" (1950)—4 weeks (22).

59. "Have I Told You Lately That I Love You?" (with Bing Crosby) (1950)—4 weeks (24).

60. "Nice Work If You Can Get It" (1938)—3 weeks (12).

61. "Lullaby To A Jitterbug" (1938)—3 weeks (10).

62. "Ciribiribin" (with Bing Crosby) (1939)—3 weeks (13).

63. "Pennsylvania Polka" (1942)—3 weeks (17).

64. "Your Red Wagon" (1947)—3 weeks (24).

65. "Sabre Dance" (1948)—3 weeks (20).

66. "More Beer!" (1949)—3 weeks (30).

67. "The Wedding Samba" (with Carmen Miranda) (1950)—3 weeks (23).

68. "Shortenin' Bread" (1938)—2 weeks (16).

69. "I Wish I Had a Dime" (1941)—2 weeks (20).

70. "That's the Moon, My Son" (1942)—2 weeks (18).

71. "Mister Five by Five" (1942)—2 weeks (14).

72. "Here Comes the Navy" (1942)—2 weeks (17).

73. "Route 66" (with Bing Crosby) (1946)—2 weeks (14).

74. "The Lady from 29 Palms" (1947)—2 weeks (7).

75. "Christmas Island" (with Guy Lombardo) (1947)—2 weeks (20).

76. "Jingle Bells" (with Bing Crosby) (1947)—2 weeks (21).

77. "Bella Bella Marie" (1948)—2 weeks (23).

78. "You Don't Have to Know the Language" (with Bing Crosby) (1948)—2 weeks (21).

79. "One Hundred Sixty Acres" (with Bing Crosby) (1948)—2 weeks (23).

80. "The Wedding of Lili Marlene" (1949)—2 weeks (20).

81. "She Wore a Yellow Ribbon" (with Russ Morgan) (1949)—2 weeks (22).

82. "Joseph, Joseph" (1938)—1 week (18).

83. "Sha-Sha" (1938)—1 week (17).

84. "Pross-Tchai" (1939)—1 week (15).

85. "You Don't Know How Much You Can Suffer" (1939)—1 week (14).

86. "Down by the O-HI-O" (1940)—1 week (21).

87. "Hit the Road" (1940)—1 week (27).

88. "Sonny Boy" (1941)—1 week (22).

89. "The Nickel Serenade" (1941)—1 week (22).

90. "Sleepy Serenade" (1941)—1 week (22).

91. "I'll Pray for You" (1942)—1 week (22).

92. "Don't Sit Under the Apple Tree" (1942)—1 week (16).

93. "East of the Rockies" (1943)—1 week (18).

94. "Jingle Bells" (with Bing Crosby) (1943) 1 week (19).

95. "Down in the Valley" (1944)—1 week (20).

96. "Tico Tico" (1944)—1 week (24).

97. "Sing a Tropical Song" (1944)—1 week (24).

98. "One Meat Ball" (1945)—1 week (15).

99. "Corns for My Country" (1945)—1 week (21).

100. "Patience and Fortitude" (1946)—1 week (12).

101. "Coax Me a Little Bit" (1946)—1 week (24).

102. "I Don't Know Why" (1946)—1 week (17).

103. "Civilization" (with Danny Kaye) (1947)—1 week (3).

104. "How Lucky You Are" (1947)—1 week (22).

105. "There's No Business Like Show Business" (with Bing Crosby and Dick Haymes) (1947)—1 week (25).

106. "The Freedom Train" (with Bing Crosby) (1947)—1 week (21).

107. "Santa Claus Is Comin' to Town" (with Bing Crosby) (1947)—1 week (22).

108. "Teresa" (with Dick Haymes) (1948)—1 week (21).

109. "Blue Tail Fly" (with Burl Ives) (1948)—1 week (24).

110. "Christmas Island" (with Guy Lombardo) (1949)—1 week (26).

111. "I'm Bitin' My Fingernails" (with Ernest Tubb) (1949)—1 week (30).

112. "Merry Christmas Polka" (with Guy Lombardo) (1950)—1 week (18).

113. "Can't We Talk It Over?" (1950)—1 week (22).

Charted Songs of Patty Andrews

1. "The Pussy Cat Song" (with Bob Crosby) (1949)—6 weeks (12).

2. "Too Young" (1951)—6 weeks (19).

APPENDIX 3

Radio Appearances

The Andrews Sisters were all over the radio dial. Radio was the chief source of home entertainment during their early career, and from the beginning they had radio spots. In 1938, shortly after their rise to fame with "Bei Mir Bist Du Schoen," they were regulars on two thirteen-week shows out of Chicago sponsored by the Wrigley Company, *Double Everything* and *Just Entertainment*. The following year, they sang on *Honolulu Bound*, also known as *The Phil Baker Show*, for 39 weeks. They ushered in 1940 with thirteen weeks on *Moonlight Serenade* with Glenn Miller. The war years were filled with movie-making and personal appearances that kept the sisters crisscrossing the country, but they managed to work in many guest spots on radio, especially the Armed Forces Radio Service's popular *Command Performance*. In September and October 1943, they appeared weekly on *The Roma Wines Show*, a comedy-variety program. They began 1945 with their own show, *The Andrews Sisters Show* (later renamed *The Nash-Kelvinator Musical Showroom*), which ran for four thirteen-week segments into spring 1946. In fall 1947, they joined *Club 15* for a three-and-a-half-year stay. In addition to these regular shows,

they guest-starred routinely on the popular music and variety shows. Few weeks passed during the late 1930s and 1940s without a radio appearance by the Andrews Sisters.

The following list of radio appearances is doubtless incomplete. Before the Andrews Sisters became nationally known singers in early 1938, they sang with various bands. During this six-year period many of their performances were broadcast on local radio stations. I have not attempted to list these early broadcasts.

I have provided all information that was available to me for each of the following entries. Dates for *Command Performance* and *Mail Call* are recording dates; release dates were frequently several weeks later.

The largest collection of Andrews Sisters radio shows is at the University of California at Los Angeles. In 1980, Maxene Andrews donated several hundred original radio broadcasts of *The Andrews Sisters Show*, *The Nash-Kelvinator Musical Show Room*, and *Club 15* to the UCLA radio archives.

I wish to thank Robert Boyer, Everett Searcy, and Ray Hagen for their contributions to the following compilation.

1931

Nov. 11. The Larry Rich Show was broadcast on a local station from Atlanta's Georgia Theater. This was probably the first time the Andrews Sisters sang on radio.

1937

July 4. *Humke Swing Show.* WMC. Memphis.

Sept. 28. *The Daily Mirror Road to Fame.* The Andrews Sisters appeared with other newcomers on this hour-long musical program featuring promising new talent. WMCA. New York City.

1938

The Paul Whiteman Program.

The National Brewers Association Show.

Jan. 9–Mar. 20. *Double Everything.* Andrews Sisters and special guests. Carl Hohengarten and orchestra. Half-hour musical show broadcast Sunday evening from Chicago. The sisters usually sang two songs during each broadcast. About half their songs were their Decca recordings. CBS.

Mar. 21–July 1. *Just Entertainment.* Andrews Sisters with Jack Fulton and Carl Hohengarten and orchestra. Fifteen-minute musical show broadcast Monday through Friday evening from Chicago. CBS.

Oct. 1. *Avalon Time.* Andrews Sisters were guests with Red Foley, Kitty O'Neil, Phil Davis Orchestra, and others. WMAQ NBC. Chicago.

1939

Jan. 7. *CBS Saturday Night Swing Show.*

Jan. 14–Oct. 4. *Honolulu Bound.* Also known as *The Phil Baker Show.* Half-hour musical/comedy show broadcast weekly Wednesday evening from New York. Andrews Sisters, Phil Baker, Harry von Zell, Harry McNaughton, Johnny Pineapple, and

Eddie DeLange and his orchestra. The orchestra changed over the course of the show.

Dec. 27. *Moonlight Serenade.* Also called *The Chesterfield Show.* Glenn Miller and his orchestra. This premier program was thirty minutes long; subsequent shows were fifteen minutes. CBS.

1940

Jan. 2—Mar. 21. *Moonlight Serenade.* Also called *The Chesterfield Show.* Glenn Miller and his orchestra. Occasional solos by Marion Hutton, Ray Eberle, and Tex Beneke. Announcers Paul Douglas and Ed Herlihy. Fifteen minute program at 10 p.m. on Tuesday, Wednesday, and Thursday. CBS.

Feb. 3. *Martin Block's 5th Anniversary Show.* Glenn Miller and his orchestra, and other guests.

1941

Aug. 14. *The Holland Furnace Show.* Benny Goodman, host. NBC—NFI. Chicago.

Aug. 21. *The Holland Furnace Show.* Benny Goodman, host. NBC—NFI. Chicago.

1942

Apr. 12. *Command Performance.* Gene Tierney, host. Guests: Edgar Bergen and Charlie McCarthy, Sara Berner, Bob Burns, Gary Cooper, Joe Forte, Betty Hutton, Ray Noble orchestra, Raymond Ratcliffe, and Ginny Simms.

July 19. *Star Spangled Vaudeville.* Walter O'Keefe, host. NBC. 8 p. m.

Sept. 27. *Double or Nothing.* Walter Compton, host. NBC. 6 p.m.

Oct. 4. *The Fred Allen Show.* CBS. 9:30 p.m.

Oct. 8. *Stagedoor Canteen Show.* CBS. 9:30 p.m.

Dec. 12. *Command Performance.* Cary Grant, host. Guests: Edgar Bergen and Charlie McCarthy, The Bombardiers, The Charioteers, Gene Krupa orchestra, and Ginny Simms.

Dec. 24. *Command Performance.* "Christmas Command Performance." Bob Hope, host. Guests: Abbott and Costello, Larry Adler, Fred Allen, Jack Benny, Edgar Bergen and Charlie McCarthy, The Charioteers, Bing Crosby, Elmer Davis, Spike Jones and his City Slickers, Kay Kyser and orchestra, Charles Laughton, Alfred Newman and orchestra, Dinah Shore, Ginny Simms, Red Skelton, and Ethel Waters.

1943

Sept. 2. *The Roma Wines Show.* Comedy show starring Mary Astor, Charles Ruggles, Mischa Auer, and Lud Gluskins and his orchestra. Los Angeles. WABC—ABC. 8 p.m.

Sept. 9. *The Roma Wines Show.*

Sept. 11. *Command Performance.* Ginny Simms, host. Guests: Roy Acuff and the Smoky Mountain Boys, Mitchell Ayres orchestra, Pinto Colvig, and Frank Graham.

Sept. 16. *The Roma Wines Show.*

Sept. 23. *The Roma Wines Show.*

Sept. 30. *The Roma Wines Show.*

Oct. 7. *The Roma Wines Show.*

Oct. 14. *The Roma Wines Show.*

Oct. 21. *The Roma Wines Show.*

Oct. 28. *The Roma Wines Show.*

Dec. *A Christmas Package.* Armed Forces Radio Service. Linda Darnell, host. Guests: Fibber McGee and Molly, Bob Hope, Lena Horne, and Ginny Simms.

1944

Mar. 5. *The Philco Radio Hall of Fame.* Gracie Fields, Ilka Chase, and Danny Thomas.

Mar. *Stagedoor Canteen.*

June 24. *Command Performance.* All-Western Program. Bob Hope, host. Guests: Cottonseed Clark, Carole Landis, Riders of the Purple Sage, Roy Rogers, Frank Sinatra, and Meredith Wilson and AFRS orchestra.

June 28. *Mail Call.* Herbert Marshall, host. Guests: Tito Guizar, Gloria DeHaven, Jean Parker, Marjorie Main, Don Wilson, and Harold Peary.

July 15. *Command Performance.* Bing Crosby, host. Guest: Judy Garland and Meredith Wilson.

Aug. *Jubilee.*

Sept. *For the Record.*

Oct. 1. *Philco Radio Hall of Fame.* Ted Husing, Alexander Knox, and Paul Whiteman and his orchestra. Blue Network.

Oct. *On Lower Basin Street.* Johnny Johnston and Paul Lavalle and his orchestra.

Oct 14. *Command Performance.* "Highlights of 1944." Ken Carpenter, host. Guests: Eddie "Rochester" Anderson, Count Basie, Bing Crosby, Tommy Dorsey, Sgt. Ziggy Elman, Judy Garland, Illinois Jacquet, Danny Kaye, Lionel Hampton, Bob Hope, Lena Horne, Groucho Marx, Harpo Marx, Sgt. Ed McKinney, Les Paul, Buddy Rich, Artie Shaw, and Dinah Shore.

Nov. 22. *Mail Call.* Bing Crosby, host. Guests: Garry Moore, Peggy Ryan, The Sportsmen, and Rise Stevens.

Dec. 16. *Command Performance.* Bob Hope, host. Guests: Lauren Bacall, Bing Crosby, Stan Kenton orchestra, and Ann Sheridan.

Dec. Pilot of *The Andrews Sisters Show.* This pilot was almost identical to premier show below, except that guest star was Frank Sinatra instead of Bing Crosby. Wild Bill Elliot was also guest star. 45 minutes.

Dec. 22. *G. I. Journal.* Bob Hope, host. Guests: Connie Haines, Dorothy Lamour, and Louella Parsons.

Dec. 25. *Christmas on the Blue.* Other guests. Blue Network.

Dec. 31. *The Andrews Sisters Show.* Also called *Eight-to-the-Bar Ranch.* Premier show. Half-hour musical comedy. Sunday 1:30 from Los Angeles. Blue Network (ABC). Andrews Sisters, George "Gabby" Hayes,

"Pigmeat" Martin, Vic Schoen and his orchestra, Foy Willing and his Riders of the Purple Sage. Announcer Marvin Miller. Producer Lou Levy. Guest: Bing Crosby. Sponsored by Nash-Kelvinator.

1945

Jan. 7–June 24. *The Andrews Sisters Show.* Also called *Eight-to-the Bar Ranch.* Guests: Abbott and Costello, Robert Benchley, Tom Breneman, Eddie Cantor, Jerry Colonna, Donald Duck and Clara Cluck, Ralph Edwards, Sydney Greenstreet, Bob Hope, Jack Kirkwood, Peter Lorre, Lum and Abner, Marjorie Main, Groucho Marx, Carmen Miranda, Pat O'Brien, Basil Rathbone, Andy Russell, Frank Sinatra, St. Brendan's Boys' Choir, Akim Tamiroff, Arthur Treacher, Vera Vague, and Rudy Vallee. Curt Massey became a regular on the show on June 10.

Jan. 10. *The Eddie Cantor Show.*

Jan. 18. *The Drene Show.* Host Rudy Vallee.

Jan. 25. *The Kraft Music Hall.* Host Bing Crosby.

Jan. 25. *Command Performance.* Frank Morgan, host. Guests: Brenda and Cobina, Nelson Eddy, Frank Sinatra, and Foy Willing and the Riders of the Purple Sage.

Feb. 15. *Command Performance.* "Dick Tracy in B Flat, or For Goodness Sake, Isn't He Ever Going to Marry Tess Trueheart?" Comic operetta based on Chester Gould's comic strip and starring Andrews Sisters, Jerry Colonna, Bing Crosby, Cass Daley, Jimmy Durante, Judy Garland, Bob Hope, Frank Morgan, Dinah Shore, Frank Sinatra, and Harry Von Zell.

Mar. 7. *Mail Call.* Jack Benny, host. Guests: Eddie "Rochester" Anderson, John Brown, Claudette Colbert, Jeannie Crain, Jinx Falkenberg, Paulette Goddard, Sgt. Jerry Hausner, Sgt. Frank Nelson, The Smart Set, and Miguelito Valdez.

Mar. 14. *Mail Call.* Nelson Eddy, host. Guests: Mildred Bailey, Cass Daley, and Jerry Lester.

Apr. 3. *The Bob Hope Show.* NBC.

Apr. 21. *The Andy Russell Show.*

Apr. 26. *The Abbott and Costello Show.*

May. *GI Journal.* Groucho Marx, host. Guests: Lucille Ball, Johnny Weismuller, and Vera Vague.

June 10. *Seventh War Loan Drive.* Don Wilson, host. Guests: Eddie "Rochester" Anderson, Lou Costello, Bing Crosby, Paulette Goddard, and Rise Stevens. Hollywood. Broadcast nationally. Two and half-hours.

June 10. *Walgreen Birthday Party.* Walgreen Drug Stores' 44th Anniversary Show.

June 20. *Mail Call.* Harry Von Zell, host. Guests: Eddie Jackson, Brenda and Cobina, and Ella Mae Morse.

July. *Mail Call.* Guests: Ella Mae Morse, Jimmy Durante, Brenda and Cobina.

Aug. 26–Sept. 23. *The Andrews Sisters Show.* Curt Massey. No guests.

Sept. 6. *Kraft Music Hall.* Bing Crosby, host.

Oct. 14. *The Roma Wine Show.* Mary Astor, host.

Nov. 14. *Songs by Sinatra.* Frank Sinatra, host.

Nov. 17. *Saturday Senior Swing Show.* ABC.

Nov. 28. *Mail Call.* Dennis Day, host.

Oct. 3–Dec. 26. *The Nash-Kelvinator Musical Showroom.* Half-hour weekly musical show. Andrews Sisters, hosts, with Curt Massey, The Ambassadors, Vic Schoen and his orchestra. Each week featured a special guest who was awarded the Green Room Award in recognition of his/her contribution to entertainment. Guests: Abbott and Costello, Jane Cowl, Xavier Cugat, Morton Downey, Jane Froman, Lou Holtz, Joe E. Howard, George Jessel, Ethel Merman, Mills Brothers, Ray Noble, Sophie Tucker, and Rudy Vallee. The show began in New York, moved to Detroit for a November 21 broadcast, and then to Los Angeles. Andre Baruch was announcer in New York, and Harlo Wilcox announced in Los Angeles. Wednesday evening. CBS.

Dec. 13. *Command Performance.* Andrews Sisters, hosts. Guests: Delta Rhythm Boys, Jimmy Durante, Celeste Holm, and Garry Moore.

1946

Jan. 2—Mar. 27. *The Nash-Kelvinator Musical Showroom.* Continuation of 1945 program. Guests: Gene Austin, Kenny Baker, Joe E. Brown, Hoagy Carmichael, The Charioteers, Jerry Colonna, Alfred Drake, Eddy Duchin, Jack Haley, King Cole Trio, Ella Logan, Carmen Miranda, and Al Pearce.

Jan. 10. *Command Performance.* Ken Carpenter, host. Guests: Bud Abbott and Lou Costello, Carmen Cavallaro, Johnny Mercer, The Pied Pipers, Jo Stafford, and Miguelito Valdez.

Jan. 6. *Request Performance.* Guests: Keenan Wynn, Lucille Ball, and Victor Borge.

Spring 1946. *Command Performance.* Dinah Shore, host. Guests: Jimmy Durante and Dave Rose and AFRS orchestra.

Mar. *Mail Call.*

Apr. 6. *Command Performance.* "Army Day Command Performance." Bob Hope, host. Guests: Bing Crosby, Bette Davis, General Dwight Eisenhower, Spike Jones and his City Slickers, Dinah Shore, Frank Sinatra, and Meredith Wilson and AFRS orchestra.

June 18. *Radio's Biggest Show.* Guests: Bob Hope, Frank Sinatra, Frank Morgan, Dennis Day, Eddie "Rochester" Anderson, Eddy Duchin, and Ginny Simms.

June 18. *Walgreen's 45th Anniversary Show.* Guests: Bob Hope, Dennis Day, Ginny Simms, Vera Vague, Eddie Duchin, and Ray Noble and his orchestra.

Dec. 25. *Command Performance.* Guests: Lionel Barrymore, Jerry Colonna, Gloria DeHaven, Jimmy Durante, Linda Darnell, Bob Hope, Frances Langford, Groucho Marx, Garry Moore, Dinah Shore, Vera Vague, and Esther Williams.

1947

Jan. 8. *The Lou Costello Foundation Broadcast.* NBC.

Feb. 27. *Philco Radio Time.* Bing Crosby, host. ABC.

Mar. 22. *Your Hit Parade.* Andy Russell, host. CBS.

Mar. 29. *Your Hit Parade.* Andy Russell, host. CBS.

Apr. 4. *Premier.* Mark Warnow and his orchestra.

Apr. 5. *Your Hit Parade.* Andy Russell, host. CBS.

Apr. 12. *Your Hit Parade.* Andy Russell, host. CBS.

Aug. 13. *Guest Star.* Winn Elliot, host.

Sept. 29–Dec. 31. *Club 15.* Bob Crosby, host. Jerry Gray and his orchestra. Five night weekly fifteen minute musical/comedy show. Andrews Sisters appeared Monday, Wednesday, and Friday. 7:30 EST. Margaret Whiting and Modernaires on Tuesday and Thusday night. CBS.

1948

Jan. 2–June 11. *Club 15.* CBS. Same format as above.

Feb. 17. *Command Performance.* Beryl Davis, host. Guests: Janet Blair, Jerry Colonna, Clifton Finnegan, Harriet Hilliard, Ozzie Nelson, Michel Perriere and AFRS orchestra, and Harry Von Zell.

Sept. 13–Dec. 31. *Club 15.* CBS. Same format as above.

Nov. 25. *Wrigley's Thanksgiving Special.* Guests: Abbott and Costello, Amos and Andy, Gene Autry, Buddy Clark, Arthur Godfrey, Danny Kaye, Dorothy Lamour, Carmen Miranda, Louella Parsons, and Marie Wilson.

Dec. 14. *Command Performance.* Jimmy Wallington, host. Guests: Eve Arden and Gordon McRae.

Dec. 25. *Wrigley's Christmas Special.* Guests: Gene Autry, Bing Crosby, Lionel Barrymore, George Burns and Gracie Allen, Dorothy Shay, Hedda Hopper, Dan Dailey, and Cesar Petrillo and his orchestra.

Dec. 25. *Command Performance.* Guests: Harry Babbitt, Jerry Colonna, Bing Crosby, Cass Daley, Bob Hope, Harry James, Hoosier Hot Shots, Lauritz Melchior, Pied Pipers, and Ann Sothern.

1949

Jan. 3–June 10. *Club 15*. Dick Haymes replaced Bob Crosby and Evelyn Knight replaced Margaret Whiting. CBS.

Feb. 24. *The Kraft Music Hall*. Al Jolson, host. Lou Bring and his orchestra.

Apr. 19. *Command Performance*. Marie McDonald, host. Guests: Bob Crosby and Hal Kantor.

June 19. *Guest Star*. Rebroadcast of earlier *Club 15* show. AFRS.

Sept. 5–Dec. 30. *Club 15*. Same format as above. CBS.

Dec. 7. *The George Burns and Gracie Allen Show*. CBS.

1950

Jan. 2–June 23. *Club 15*. Bob Crosby replaced Dick Haymes as host March 27. Jo Stafford replaced Evelyn Knight. CBS.

Jan. 8. *Guest Star*. Rebroadcast of earlier *Club 15* show. AFRS.

Feb. 22. *The Bing Crosby Chesterfield Show*. John Scott Trotter and his orchestra.

Mar. 29. *The Bing Crosby Chesterfield Show*. John Scott Trotter and his orchestra.

May 13. *Special All-Star Revue*. Guests: Dick Haymes, Steve Allen, Jackie Gleason, Ida Lupino, Ann Miller, and Les Brown and his orchestra.

Aug. 28–Dec. 29. *Club 15*. Same format as above. CBS.

1951

Jan. 1–Mar. 23. *Club 15*. Same format as above. CBS.

Jan. 7. *Salute to Bing Crosby*. Vic Schoen and other guests.

Jan. 19. *Stars on Parade*.

Feb. 11. *The Big Show*. Tallulah Bankhead, host. Guests: Judy Garland, Gordon McRae, Groucho Marx, and others.

Feb. 28. *The Bing Crosby Chesterfield Show*. Guest: Nat King Cole. John Scott Trotter and his orchestra.

Apr. 8. *Hedda Hopper Show*.

Oct. 22. *The Big Show*. Tallulah Bankhead, host. Guests: Fred Allen, Marlene Dietrich, Phil Foster, Benny Goodman, Frank Sinatra, and Margaret Truman.

1952

Mar. 22. *Hawaii Calls*. Honolulu.

June 22. *Time for a Song*. Jo Stafford, host.

1954

Oct. 3. *The Dennis Day Show*. Patty Andrews only.

1957

June 16. *Guest Star*. Armed Forces Radio Service. Mitch Ayres and his orchestra.

Dec. 20. *The Andrews Sisters for Christmas Seals*.

1960

Dec. 4. *In Town Today*. BBC. Interview.

APPENDIX 4

Filmography

Too many people have dismissed and discounted the films of the Andrews Sisters—including the sisters themselves. Certainly, they were not among the great films of the period, but some of them nonetheless represent an important genre, the war escapist film, and some are still entertaining. Movies provided escape from the grim headlines of the war and offered companionship for anxious, lonely wives, parents, and families whose husbands, sons, brothers, and sometimes sisters and daughters were fighting the headline battles. Films, like those of the Andrews Sisters, gave patriotic boosts to the home front, and served as reminders that America was worth the sacrifice of war. The plots were always simple—who wanted complexity with the complex world affairs? And the endings were always happy—too often they weren't outside the theater.

The Andrews Sisters appeared in eighteen films, eight of which were big box office successes. The three films they made with Bud Abbott and Lou Costello were the top moneymakers of 1941 for Universal Studios. The Andrews Sisters' appearance in *Follow*

The Boys helped make that another box office hit for Universal. *Hollywood Canteen* was the fourth biggest film for Warner Brothers in 1944, and *Road To Rio* was Paramount's top film in 1947. Both *Make Mine Music* and *Melody Time* made money for Walt Disney.

The Andrews Sisters' other titles were less successful at the box office, but none of them lost money—a virtual impossibility with the low budgets that financed them. Although the plots are sometimes tedious to view today, the films are nonetheless sparked with good musical numbers by the sisters and occasional good comedy by actors such as Shemp Howard, Mary Wickes, and William Frawley. Nine of the Andrews Sisters' films are currently available on videocassette or DVD and regularly appear on television's old movie channels.

This filmography is taken primarily from *The Motion Picture Guide* (Volumes 1, 3, 4, 5, 6, 7, and 9) by Jay Robert Nash and Stanley Ralph Ross (1985). I was able to view only the musical numbers in *Moonlight and Cactus*. I was unable to view *The Phynx*.

Argentine Nights

1940. Universal Studios. 72 minutes. Black/ white.
Cast: Andrews Sisters (*Themselves*), Ritz Brothers (*Themselves*), Constance Moore (*Bonnie Brooks*), George Reeves (*Eduardo*), Peggy Moran (*Peggy*), Anne Nagel (*Linda*), Kathryn Adams (*Carol*), Ferike Boros (*Mama Viejos*), Paul Porcasi (*Papa Viejos*).

447

Songs by the Andrews Sisters: "Rhumboogie," "Hit The Road," "Oh, He Loves Me," and "Brooklynonga" (with the Ritz Brothers).

Production: Albert S. Rogell (director); Ken Goldsmith (producer); Arthur T. Horman, Ray Golden, Sid Kuller (writers), based on a story by J. Robert Bren and Gladys Atwater; Elwood Bredell (photography); Frank Gross (editor); Sammy Cahn, Saul Chaplin, Sid Kuller, Ray Golden, Hal Borne, Don Raye, Hughie Prince, Vic Schoen (music and lyrics).

Buck Privates

1941. Universal Studios. 82 minutes. Black/white.

Cast: Andrews Sisters (*Themselves*), Bud Abbott (*Slicker Smith*), Lou Costello (*Herbie Brown*), Jane Frazee (*Judy Gray*), Nat Pendleton (*Sgt. Michael Collins*), Samuel S. Hinds (*Maj. Gen. Emerson*), Harry Strang (*Sgt. Callahan*), Nella Walker (*Mrs. Parker II*), Leonard Elliott (*Henry*), Shemp Howard (*Chef*), Mike Frankovitch (*Announcer*), Dora Clement (*Miss Durling*), Jeanne Kelly, Elaine Morey, Kay Leslie, Nina Orla, Dorothy Darrell (*Camp Hostesses*), Don Raye (*Dick Burnette*), J. Anthony Hughes (*Capt. Williams*), Hughie Prince (*Henry*), Frank Cook (*Harmonica Player*), James Flavin, Herold Goodwin (*Sergeants*), Douglas Wood (*Mr. Parker*), Charles Coleman (*Edmunds*), Selmer Jackson (*Captain*), Tom Tyler (*Instructor*), Bud Harris (*Porter*), Al Billings (*Tough Fighter*).

Songs by the Andrews Sisters: "You're a Lucky Fellow, Mr. Smith," "Boogie Woogie Bugle Boy," "In Apple Blossom Time," and "Bounce Me Brother with a Solid Four."

Production: Arthur Lubin (director), Alex Gottlieb (producer), Arthur T. Horman and John Grant (writers), Milton Krasner (photography), Philip Cahn (editor), Nick Caste (choreography), Don Raye, Hughie Prince, Sonny Burke, Neville Fleeson, Albert von Tilzer (music).

In the Navy

1941. Universal Studios. 85 minutes. Black/white.

Cast: Andrews Sisters (*Themselves*), Bud Abbott (*Smokey Adams*), Lou Costello (*Pomeroy Watson*), Dick Powell (*Tommy Halstead*), Claire Dodd (*Dorothy Roberts*), Dick Foran (*Dynmite Dugan*), Shemp Howard (*Dizzy*), Billy Lenhart (*Butch*), Kenneth Brown (*Buddy*), Condos Brothers (*Themselves*), William B. Davidson (*Capt. Richards*), Thurston Hall (*Head of Committee*), Robert Emmett Keane (*Travers*), Edward Fielding (*Commander*), Don Terry (*Floor Manager*), Sunnie O'Dea (*Lancer*), Eddie Dunn (*Ticket Taker*), Ralph Dunn (*Traffic Cop*), Dick Alexander (*Big Bruiser*), Lorin Raker (*Small Meek Husband*), Frank Penny (*Bos'n*), Pat Gleason (*Sentry*), Jack Mulhall (*Lt. Scott*), Mickey Simpson (*Tough Civilian*), Lyle Latell (*Marine*), Chuck Morrison (*Truck Driver*), Lee Kass (*Bandleader*), James Sullivan (*Policeman*), Edna Hall (*Fat Woman*), Claire Whitney (*Gushing Mother*), Joe Bautista (*Mess Boy*), Doris Herbert (*Mother*), Charles Sullivan (*Sailor*), Hooper Atchley, Patsy Obyme, Richard Crane, Douglas Wood.

Songs by the Andrews Sisters: "You're Off to See the World," "Gimme Some Skin," "Hula Ba Luau," and "Starlight, Starbright" (with Dick Powell).

Production: Arthur Lubin (director); Alex Gottlieb (producer); Arthur T. Horman, John Grant (writers), based on a story by Arthur T. Horman; Joseph Valentine (photography); Philip Cahn (editor); John P. Fulton (special effects); Nick Castle (choreography); Gene De Paul, Don Raye (music).

Hold That Ghost

1941. Universal Studios. 86 minutes. Black/white.

Cast: Andrews Sisters (*Themselves*), Bud Abbott (*Chuck Murrary*), Lou Costello (*Ferdinand Jones*), Richard Carlson (*Doctor Jackson*), Joan Davis (*Camille Brewster*), Mischa Auer (*Gregory*), Evelyn Ankers (*Norma Lind*), Marc Lawerence (*Charlie Smith*), Shemp Howard (*Soda Jerk*), Russell Hicks (*Bannister*), William Davidson (*Moose Matson*), Ted Lewis and his Entertainers (*Themselves*).

Songs by the Andrews Sisters: "Sleepy Serenade" and "Aurora."

Production: Arthur Lubin (director); Robert Lees, Fred Rinaldo and John Grant (writers), based on a story by Robert Lees and Fred Rinaldo; Mort Green, Lou Singer, Harold Adamson, Al Jolson, Dave Dreyer, Billy Rose, Andrew B. Sterling, Ted Lewis and Bill Munroe (music and lyrics).

Milton Berle Throws a Party

1941. Columbia Pictures. Screen Snapshots, No. 1. Series 21. 9 minutes. Black/white.

Cast: Andrews Sisters (*Themselves*), Milton Berle (*Himself*), Ken Murray (*Himself*), and the Brewster Twins (*Themselves*).

Song by the Andrews Sisters: "In Apple Blossom Time."

What's Cookin'?

1942. Universal Studios. 69 minutes. Black/white.

Cast: Andrews Sisters (*Themselves*), Jane Frazee (*Anne*), Robert Paige (*Bob*), Gloria Jean (*Sue*), Leo Carrillo (*Marvo*), Charles Butterworth (*J. P. Courtney*), Billie Burke (*Agatha*), Grace McDonald (*Angela*), Donald O'Connor (*Tommy*), Peggy Ryan (*Peggy*), Franklin Pangborn (*Prof. Bistell*), Susan Levine (*Tag-a-long*), Woody Herman and His Orchestra (*Themselves*), The Jivin' Jacks and Jills.

Songs by the Andrews Sisters: "What to Do?" "Amen" (with cast), "I'll Pray for You," "Il Bacio (The Kiss)" (with Gloria Jean), and "Smile, Smile, Smile" (with cast).

Production: Edward F. Cline (director); Ken Goldsmith (producer); Jerry Cady, Stanley Roberts, Haworth Bromley (writers), based on a story by Edgar Allan Woolf; Jerome Ash (photography); Arthur Hilton (editor); Charles Previn (music director); Jack Otterson (art director); Johnny Mattison (choreography).

Private Buckaroo

1942. Universal Studios. 68 minutes. Black/white.

Cast: Andrews Sisters (*Themselves*), Harry James and his Music Makers (*Themselves*), Dick Foran (*Lon Prentice*), Joe E. Lewis (*Lancelot Pringle McBiff*), Jennifer Holt (*Joyce Mason*), Shemp Howard (*Sgt. 'Muggsy' Shavel*), Richard Davies (*Lt. Mason*), Mary Wickes (*Bonnie-Belle Schlopkiss*), Ernest Truex (*Col. Weatherford*), Donald O'Connor (*Donny*), Peggy Ryan (*Peggy*), Huntz Hall (*Cpl. Anemic*), Susan Levine (*Tag-a-long*), The Jivin' Jacks and Jills (*Themselves*)

Songs by the Andrews Sisters: "Three Little Sisters," "That's the Moon, My Son," "Six Jerks In a Jeep," "Don't Sit Under the Apple Tree," "Johnny Get Your Gun Again," and "We've Got a Job to Do" [voices only].

Production: Edward F. Cline (director); Ken Goldsmith (producer); Edmund Kelso, Edward James (writers), based on a story by Paul Gerard Smith; Woody Bredell (photography); Milton Carruth (editor); Harry James (musical director); Jack Otterson (art director); John Mattison (choreography).

Give Out, Sisters

1942. Universal Studios. 65 minutes. Black/white.

Cast: Andrews Sisters (*Themselves*), Dan Dailey, Jr. (*Bob Edwards*), Grace McDonald (*Gracie Waverly*), Charles Butterworth (*Prof. Woof*), Walter Catlett (*Gribble*), William Frawley (*Harrison*), Richard Davies (*Kendall*), Donald O'Connor (*Don*), Peggy Ryan (*Peggy*), Edith Barrett (*Agatha Waverly*), Fay Helm (*Susan Waverly*), Marie Blake (*Blandina Waverly*), Emmett Vogan (*Batterman the Costumer*), Leonard Carey (*Jamison the Butler*), Jivin' Jacks and Jills (*Themselves*), Irving Bacon (*Dr. Howard*), Leon Belasco (*Waiter*), Robert Emmett Keane (*Peabody the Lawyer*), Lorin Raker (*Dr. Bradshaw*), Jason Robards, Sr. (*Drunk*), Duke York (*Louie*), Alphonse Martel (*Headwaiter*), Emmett Smith (*Porter*), Fred "Snowflake" Toones (*Valet*).

Songs by the Andrews Sisters: "New Generation," "You're Just a Flower from an Old Bouquet," "Who Do You Think You're Fooling?" and "Pennsylvania Polka."

Production: Edward F. Cline (director); Bernard W. Burton (producer); Paul Gerard Smith, Warren Wilson (writers), based on a story by Lee Sands and Fred Rath; George Robinson (photography); Paul Landres (editor); Charles Previn (music director); Jack Otterson (art director); John Mattison (choreography); Al Lerner, Sid Robin, Ray Stilwell, Ray Gold, Lester Lee, Zeke Manners, Walter Donaldson, Gwynee and Lucien Denni (music).

How's About It?

1943. Universal Studios. 60 minutes. Black/white.

Cast: Andrews Sisters (*Themselves*), Robert Paige (*George Selby*), Grace McDonald (*Marion Bliss*), Shemp Howard (*Alf*), Walter Catlett (*Whipple*), Buddy Rich and his Orchestra (*Themselves*), David Bruce (*Oliver*), Mary Wickes (*Mike Tracy*), Bobby Scheerer (*Bobby*), Dorothy Babb (*Waitress*), Guss Glassmire, Louis Da Pron.

Songs by the Andrews Sisters: "Going Up," "East of the Rockies," "Don't Mind the Rain," and "Here Comes the Navy."

Production: Erle C. Kenton (director); Ken Goldsmith (producer); Mel Ronson, John Grey (writers), based on a story by Jack Goodman and Albert Rice; Woody Bredell (photography); Vic Schoen (music); Charles Maynard (editor); John Goodman (art); Louis Da Pron (choreography).

Always a Bridesmaid

1943. Universal Studios. 61 minutes. Black/white.

Cast: Andrews Sisters (*Themselves*), Patrick Knowles (*Tony Warren*), Grace McDonald (*Linda Marlowe*), Billy Gilbert (*Nick*), Charles Butterworth (*Col. Winchester*), Edith Barrett (*Mrs. Cavanaugh*), O'Neill Nolan (*Rigsy*), Annie Rooney (*Annie*), Addison Richards (*Martin Boland*), Charles Cane (*Police Lieutenant*), Philip Van Zandt (*waiter*), The Jivin' Jacks and Jills.

Songs by the Andrews Sisters: "That's My Affair," "Thanks for the Buggy Ride," "Ride On," and "Yoo Hoo."

Production: Eric C. Kenton (director); Mel Ronson (writer), based on a story by Oscar Brodney; Louis Da Pron (photography).

Swingtime Johnny

1943. Universal Studios. 60 minutes. Black/white.

Cast: Andrews Sisters (*Themselves*), Harriet Hilliard (*Linda*), Peter Cookson (*Jonathan*), Tim Ryan (*Sparks*), Matt Willis (*Monk*), William "Bill" Phillips (*Steve*), Tom Dugan (*Gruff Character*), Ray Walker (*Mike*), Marion Martin (*Blonde*), John Hamilton (*Caldwell*), John Sheehan (*Raffle Wheel Barker*), Syd Saylor (*Sea Food Barker*), Jack Rice (*Bill*), Emmett Vogan (*Chairman of the Board*), Herbert Heywood (*Pop*), Alphonse Martell (*Pierre*), Mitch Ayres and His Orchestra (*Themselves*).

Songs by the Andrews Sisters: "I May Be Wrong," "When You and I Were Young, Maggie" (abbreviated version), "Boogie Woogie Choo Choo," "You Better Give Me Lots of Lovin', Honey," "Boogie Woogie Bugle Boy" (abbreviated version), "Was There Ever a Woman as Wretched as I?" and a medley of Gay Nineties songs with the cast.

Production: Edward F. Cline (director);

Warren Wilson (producer); Clyde Bruckman (writer), based on a story by Warren Wilson; Jerome Ash (photography); Vic Schoen (music); Edward Curtiss (editor); John B. Goodman (art director); Vera West (costumes).

Follow the Boys

1944. Universal Studios. 122 minutes. Black/white.

Cast: George Raft (*Tony West*), Vera Zorina (*Gloria Vance*), Grace McDonald (*Kitty West*), Charles Grapewin (*Nick West*), Charles Butterworth (*Louie Fairweather*) and others. All-star cast appearing as themselves: Andrews Sisters, Jeanette MacDonald, Orson Welles, Marlene Dietrich, Dinah Shore, Donald O'Connor, Peggy Ryan, W. C. Fields, Arthur Rubinstein, Carmen Amaya and her Company, Sophie Tucker, The Delta Rhythm Boys, Leonard Gautier's Dog Act, Ted Lewis and his Band, Freddie Slack and his Orchestra, Charlie Spivak and his Orchestra, Louis Jordan and his Orchestra, Maria Montez, Susanna Foster, Louise Allbritton, Robert Paige, Alan Curtis, Lon Chaney, Jr., Gloria Jean, Andy Devine, Turhan Bey, Evelyn Ankers, Noah Beery, Jr., Samuel S. Hinds, Louise Beavers, Clarence Muse, Gale Sondergaard, Peter Coe, Nigel Bruce, Thomas Gomez, Martha O'Driscoll, Maxie Rosenbloom, Lois Collier, Elyse Knox, Randolph Scott, Philo McCullough, Agustin Castellon Sabicas.

Songs by the Andrews Sisters: Medley of hits ("Bei Mir Bist Du Schoen," "Well All Right," "Hold Tight, Hold Tight," "Beer Barrel Polka," "Boogie Woogie Bugle Boy," "Pennsylvania Polka," "Strip Polka," and "Vic'try Polka.") and "Shoo Shoo Baby."

Production: Edward Sutherland (director); Charles K. Feldman (producer); Lou Breslow and Gertrude Purcell (writers); David Abel (photography); Leigh Harline (musical director); Fred R. Feitshans, Jr. (editor); John B. Goodman and Harold H. MacArthur (art directors); Russell Gausman and Ira S. Webb (set directors); Vera West and Howard Greer (costumes); John P. Fulton (special effects); George Hale (choreography).

Moonlight and Cactus

1944. Universal Studios. 60 minutes. Black/white.

Cast: Andrews Sisters (*Themselves*), Leo Carrillo (*Pasqualito*), Elyse Knox (*Louis Ferguson*), Tom Seidel (*Tom Garrison*), Shemp Howard (*Punchy*), Eddie Quillan (*Stubby*), Murray Alper (*Slugger*), Tom Kennedy (*Lucky*), Frank Lackteen (*Ogala*), Minerva Urecal (*Abigail*), Jacqueline de Wit (*Elsie*), Mary O'Brien (*Amanda*), Mitchell Ayres and his Orchestra (*Themselves*).

Songs by the Andrews Sisters: "Wahoo," "Down in the Valley," "Sweet Dreams," "Send Me a Man, Amen," "Home," "Sing," and "The Hand Clapping Song."

Production: Edward F. Cline (director); Frank Gross (producer); Eugene Conrad and Paul Gerard Smith (writers); Jerome Ash (photography); Ray Snyder (editor); John B. Goodman and Martin Obzina (art directors); Charles O'Curran (choreography).

Hollywood Canteen

1944. Warner Brothers. 124 minutes. Black/white.

Cast: Robert Hutton (*Slim*), Dane Clark (*Sergeant*), Janis Paige (*Angela*), Jonathan Hale (*Mr. Brodel*), Barbara Brown (*Mrs. Brodel*), Steve Richards and Dick Erdman (*Soldiers on Deck*), James Flavin (*Marine Sergeant*), Eddie Marr (*Dance Director*), Theodore von Eltz (*Director*), Ray Teal (*Captain*), Rudolph Friml, Jr. (*Orchestra Leader*), George Turner (*Tough Marine*). **All Star Cast Appearing As Themselves:** Andrews Sisters, Jack Benny, Betty Brodel, Paul Brooke, Joe E. Brown, Eddie Cantor, Kitty Carlisle, Jack Carson, Carmen Cavallaro and his Orchestra, Joan Crawford, Helmut Dantine, Bette Davis, Jimmy Dorsey and his Band, Faye Emerson, Victor Francen, John Garfield, Golden Gate Quartet, Mary Gordon, Angela Green, Sydney Greenstreet, Alan Hale, Sr., Paul Henreid, Bill Kennedy, Andrea King, Joan Leslie, Peter Lorre, Ida Lupino, Dorothy Malone, Irene Manning, Nora Martin, Joan McCracken, Chef Joseph Milani, Johnny Mitchell, Dolores Moran, Dennis Morgan, Marianne O'Brien, Eleanor Parker, Virginia Patton, William Prince, Joyce Reynolds, John Ridgely, Roy Rogers and Trigger, Rosario and Antonio, S. Z. Sakall, Lynne Shayne, Alexis Smith, Zachary Scott, John Sheridan, Sons of the Pioneers, Barbara Stanwyck, Craig Stevens, Joseph Szigeti, Colleen Townsend, Donald Woods, Jane Wyman.

Songs by the Andrews Sisters: "Hollywood Canteen" (voices only), "Corns for My Country," and "Don't Fence Me In."

Production: Delmer Daves (director and writer); Alex Gottlieb (producer); Bert Glennon (photography); Ray Heindorf (music); Christian Nyby (editor); Leo F. Forbstein (music director); Leo Kuter (art director); Casey Roberts (set director); Milo Anderson (costumes); LeRoy Prinz (choreography).

Her Lucky Night

1945. Universal Studios. 63 minutes. Black/white.

Cast: Andrews Sisters (*Themselves*), Martha O'Driscoll (*Connie*), Noah Beery, Jr. (*Larry*), George Barbier (*J. L. Wentworth*), Maurice Cass (*Papa*), Marie Harmon (*Susie*), Olin Howlin (*Prince de la Mour*), Robert Emmett Keane (*Lawson*), Grady Sutton (*Joe*), Edgar Dearing (*Casey*), Eddie Acuff (*Chauffeur*), Rita Gould (*Fannie*), Charles Jordan (*Bus Driver*), Billy Newell (*Proprietor*), Ida Moore (*Mama*), Jack Rice (*Percy*), Buzz Henry (*Kid*), Virginia Sale (*Umbrella Woman*), Donald Kerr, Eddie Bruce, and Perc Launders (*Onlookers*), Stuart Holmes (*Headwaiter*), Warren Jackson (*Bit Man*), Rena Saunders (*Bit Woman*), Gladys Blake (*Woman-Garter Gag*), Charles Hall (*Window Washer*), Paul Hurst (*Maloney*), Mary McLeod (*1st Usherette*), Nan Brinkley (*2nd Usherette*), Dan Quig (*1st Young Man*), Buddy Wilkerson (*2nd Young Man*), Genevieve Bell (*Dowager*), Kay York (*Bit Girl*), Leslie Denison (*Man*).

Songs by the Andrews Sisters: "Straighten Up and Fly Right," "Sing a Tropical Song," "Is You Is Or Is You Ain't My Baby?" "Dance with the Dolly with a Hole in Her Stocking," and "The Polka Polka."

Production: Edward Lilley (director); Warren Wilson (producer); Clyde Bruckman (writer), based on a story by Warren Wilson; Hal Mohr (photography), Paul Landres (editor); Edgar Fairchild (music director); John B. Goodman (art director); Louis Da Pron (choreography).

Make Mine Music

1946. Disney/RKO. 74 minutes. Color.

Cast (Voices and music): Andrews Sisters, Neslon Eddy, Dinah Shore, Benny

Goodman and his Orchestra, Jerry Colonna, Andy Russell, Sterling Holloway, The Pied Pipers, The King's Men, The Ken Darby Chorus, Tatiana Riabouchinska, David Lichine.

Song by the Andrews Sisters: "Johnny Fedora and Alice Blue Bonnet."

Production: Jack Kinney, Clyde Geronimi, Hamilton Luske, Robert Cormack, and Joshua Meador (directors); Joe Grant (producer); Homer Brightman, Dick Huemer, Dick Kinney, John Walbridge, Tom Oreb, Dick Shaw, Eric Gurney, Sylvia Holland, T. Hee, Dick Kelsey, Jesse Marsh, Roy Williams, Ed Penner, James Bodrero, Cap Palmer and Erwin Graham (writers); Charles Wolcott (music director); Mary Blair, Elmer Plummer and John Hench (art directors); Les Clark, Ward Kimball, Milt Kahl, John Sibley, Hal King and others (animators); George Rowley, Jack Boyd, Andy Engman, Brad Case, Don Patterson (effects animation); Ub Iwerks (process effects); Mique Nelson (color consultant).

Road to Rio

1947. Paramount Pictures. 100 minutes. Black/ white.

Cast: Andrews Sisters (*Themselves*), Bing Crosby (*Scat Sweeney*), Bob Hope (*Hot Lips Barton*), Dorothy Lamour (*Lucia Maria De Andrade*), Gale Sondergaard (*Catherine Vail*), Frank Faylen (*Trigger*), Joseph Vitale (*Tony*), Frank Puglia (*Rodrigues*), Nestor Paiva (Cardoso), Robert Barrat (*Johnson*), Jerry Colonna (*Cavalry Captain*), Wiere Brothers (*Musicians*), Carioca Boys (*Themselves*), Stone-Baron Puppeteers (*Themselves*), George Meeker (*Sherman Malley*), Stanley Andrews (*Capt. Harmon*), Harry Woods (*Ship's Purser*), Tor Johnson (*Samson*), Donald Kerr (*Steward*), Stanley Blystone (*Assistant Purser*), George Sorel (*Prefeito*), John "Skins" Miller (*Dancer*), Alan Bridge (*Ships Officer*), Arthur Q. Bryan (*Mr. Stanton*), Babe London (*Woman*), Gino Corrado (*Barber*), George Chandler (*Valet*), Paul Newlan and George Lloyd (*Butchers*), Fred Zendar (*Stevedore*), Ralph Gomez, Duke York and Frank Hagney (*Roustabouts*); Ralph Dunn (*Foreman*), Pepito Perez (*Dignified Gentleman*), Ray Teal (*Buck*), Brandon Hurst (*Barker*), Barbara Pratt (*Airline Hostess*), Tad Van Brunt (*Pilot*), Patsy O'Bryne (*Charwoman*), Raul Roulien (*Cavalry Officer*), Charles Middle-

ton (*Farmer*), Albert Ruiz and Laura Corbay (*Specialty Dancers*).

Song by the Andrews Sisters: "You Don't Have to Know the Language" (with Bing Crosby).

Production: Norman Z. McLeod (director); Daniel Dare (producer); Edmund Beloin and Jack Rose (writers); Ernest Laszlo (photography); Ellsworth Hoagland (editor); Robert Emmett Dolan (musical director); Hans Dreier and Earl Hedrick (art directors); Edith Head (costumes); Gordon Jennings and Paul Lerpal (special effects); Bernard Pearce and Billy Daniels (choreography); Johnny Burke, Jimmy Van Heusen, Ary Barroso and Bob Russell (music and lyrics); Wally Westmore (makeup).

Melody Time

1948. Disney/RKO. 75 minutes. Color.

Cast (Voices and music): Andrews Sisters, Buddy Clark, Fred Waring and his Pennsylvanians, Frances Langford, Dennis Day, Freddy Martin and his Orchestra, Jack Fina, The Dinning Sisters. (Appearances and voices): Roy Rogers, Luana Patten, Bobby Driscoll, Ethel Smith, Bob Nolan and Sons of the Pioneers.

Song by the Andrews Sisters: "Little Toot."

Production: Clyde Geronimi, Wilfred Jackson, Hamilton Luske, and Jack Kinney (directors); Walt Disney (producer); Winston Hibler, Erdman Penner, Harry Reeves, Homer Brightman, Ken Anderson and others (writers); Winton Hoch (photography); Donald Halliday and Thomas Scott (editor); Eliot Daniel and Ken Darby (music directors); Kim Gannon, Walter Kent, Ray Gilbert, Johnny Lunge, Allie Wrubel, Bobby Worth, Benny Benjamin and George Weiss (music and lyrics).

Film Appearance of Patty Andrews

The Phynx

1970. Warner Brothers.

Cast: Patty Andrews, Joan Blondell, George Tobias, Martha Raye, Fritz Feld, Edgar Bergen and Charlie McCarthy, Busby Berkeley, and others.

Production: Lee Katzin (director).

APPENDIX 5

Television Appearances

This list of television appearances was compiled by the late Charles Saunders, and by Robert Boyer, Everett Searcy, and the author. It is doubtless incomplete because the Andrews Sisters, collectively and individually, occasionally made appearances on local television stations, some of which I have been unable to document.

1951

Mar. 3. *The Frank Sinatra Show* (CBS). The Andrews Sisters made a brief walk-on appearance to attack Sinatra, Frankie Laine, and Perry Como with their purses who were imitating them in drag and lip-synching one of their songs.

Mar. 4. *The Colgate Comedy Hour* (NBC). Co-hosted by Milton Berle and Tony Martin. The Andrews Sisters' official television debut. They sang a medley of their hits and "Girls of the Golden West." Martin and Patty Andrews sang "The Dum Dot Song."

Mar. 6. *Texaco Star Theatre* (NBC). The Andrews Sisters sang "Pennsylvania Polka," "Peony Bush," and "Girls Of The Golden West." Patty Andrews soloed "I Wanna Be Loved," and sang "The Pussy Cat Song" with host Milton Berle and fellow guest Robert Alda.

June 10. *Damon Runyan Memorial Fund* (local show in New York City). Telethon hosted by Milton Berle.

June 12. *Texaco Star Theatre* (NBC). Hosted by Milton Berle.

Oct. 9. *The Frank Sinatra Show* (CBS). The Andrews Sisters sang "The Peony Bush" and participated in skits with fellow guests Perry Como and Frankie Laine.

Oct. 21. *What's My Line?* (CBS). The Andrews Sisters appeared as the show's "mystery" guests.

Dec. 11. *The Frank Sinatra Show*. Other guests included Roger Price, Joan Holloway, and Henry Slate.

1952

Mar. 11. *The Frank Sinatra Show*. The sisters appeared as clowns in a skit with Sinatra.

Nov. 22. *The Jackie Gleason Show* (CBS). The Andrews Sisters sang a medley of their hits, and delivered a singing birthday telegram to Gleason.

1953

Jan. 20. *Texaco Star Theatre* (NBC). The Andrews Sisters sang "Sonny Boy" in a skit with ventriloquist Jimmy Nelson, appeared in comedy skits with host Milton Berle and guest Molly Goldberg, and sang "The Anniversary Song."

Sept. 26. *The Bing Crosby Special* (NBC). Patty Andrews appeared solo. Other guests included Judy Garland, Mary Martin, Bob Hope, and Ethel Merman.

1954

Nov. 2. *The Red Skelton Show* (CBS). Maxene and LaVerne Andrews appeared together after their break with Patty. In one skit, Skelton donned a blond wig to join them as a replacement for Patty.

1955

Apr. 23. *The Jimmy Durante Show* (NBC). Patty Andrews sang "It's Bigger Than Both of Us" with Durante.

Aug. 3. *Frankie Laine Time* (CBS). Patty Andrews sang "Sing! Sing! Sing!" as well as a duet with fellow guest Jack E. Leonard.

Aug. 13. *Swift Show Wagon* (NBC). Patty Andrews appeared on this show hosted by Horace Heidt.

Nov. 16. *The Tennessee Ernie Ford Show* (NBC). Patty Andrews appeared solo.

1956

Feb. 16. *Shower of Stars* (CBS). Although four months away from their official reunion as an act, the Andrews Sisters closed this special hosted by Red Skelton with a medley of their hits. Other guests included Georgia Gibbs, Frankie Laine, and Rudy Vallee.

Oct. or Nov. *Art Linkletter's House Party* (CBS). The first television appearance of the Andrews Sisters after their reunion. They sang their first Capitol recording "Crazy Arms" and "I Want to Linger."

Dec. 10. *It Could Be You* (NBC). No further details on this daytime show.

1957

Feb. 23. *The Perry Como Show* (NBC). The Andrews Sisters sang a medley of their hits. With host Perry Como, they sang "Rum and Coca-Cola" with new lyrics. In a skit, the sisters appeared as marionettes and sang "The Andrews Sisters Puppets" to the tune of "Pennsylvania Polka." Other guests were Ernie Kovaks and Tony Bennett.

Mar. 3. *The Steve Allen Show* (NBC). The Andrews Sisters appeared in a live remote from Philadelphia where they were part of the opening of the new Sheraton Hotel. They sang a medley of their hits, which began with "Born to Be with You," which they changed to "Born to Sing for You." Their segment ended with a lip-synched performance of their single "No, Baby," for which Steve Allen mouthed the words "No, Baby" from New York City.

Apr. 7. *Ray Bolger's Washington Square* (NBC). The Andrews Sisters were guests along with Kay Armand and opera star Salvatore Baccaloni.

July 13. *The Julius La Rosa Show* (NBC). The Andrews Sisters sang "Of Thee I Sing" and "Stars, Stars," their recent Capitol releases.

July 17. *Bandstand* (NBC). No details.

July 27. *The Jimmy Dean Show* (CBS). This show was broadcast live from Washington, D. C. No further details.

Sept. 15. *The Ed Sullivan Show* (CBS). The Andrews Sisters sang "By His Word" and a medley of their hits.

Oct. 9. *The Big Record* (CBS). Patti Page, host. The Andrews Sisters sang a medley of their hits. Patty Andrews sang "You Must Have Been a Beautiful Baby" with Jack E. Leonard. Other guests included Ella Fitzgerald, Les Brown, and Harry Richman.

1958

Aug. 9. *The Bob Crosby Show* (NBC). The Andrews Sisters sang "Feudin' and Fightin'," "Old Man River," "Way Down Yonder in New Orleans," and "Last Night on the Back Porch."

1959

July 7. *The Jimmie Rodgers Show* (NBC).

The Andrews Sisters sang a medley of their hits and "Me Too." Host Jimmie Rodgers joined them in "Boo Hoo."

July 19. *What's My Line?* (CBS). The Andrews Sisters made their second appearance as the show's mystery guests.

July 30. *Masquerade Party* (NBC). The Andrews Sisters appeared disguised as the Marx Brothers—Patty as Groucho, Maxene as Harpo, and LaVerne as Chico.

Nov. 25. *The Golden Circle* (ABC). The Andrews Sisters sang "Bei Mir Bist Du Schoen" and a medley of their hits on this special hosted by Steve Lawrence and Eydie Gorme. Lawrence joined them in "South America, Take It Away." The show concluded with the sisters joining hosts and fellow guests Frankie Avalon, Nat King Cole, Rudy Vallee, and the Mills Brothers in "White Christmas."

1961

Jan. 1. *Sunday Night at the Palladium.* London. At the end of their engagement at The Talk of the Town, the Andrews Sisters appeared on this popular British variety show.

1962

Apr. *What's My Line?* (CBS). Patty Andrews appeared as a guest panelist while the Andrews Sisters were in New York City for an appearance at the International Hotel.

1963

Nov. 16. *The Joey Bishop Show* (ABC). The Andrews Sisters were guests on this situation comedy starring Joey Bishop. They sang "In Apple Blossom Time" and "Bei Mir Bist Du Schoen."

1965

Jan. 19. *Art Linkletter's House Party* (CBS). The Andrews Sisters sang a medley of their hits on the 20th anniversary of this program.

Feb. 1. *The Tonight Show Starring Johnny*

Carson (NBC). The Andrews Sisters sang a medley including "We Got a Lot of Livin' to Do," "My Favorite Things," and "I Left My Heart in San Francisco." Johnny Carson joined them in "Sonny Boy." The sisters concluded with a medley of their polka hits.

Mar. 12. *The Tonight Show Starring Johnny Carson* (NBC). On their second visit to *The Tonight Show*, the Andrews Sisters sang "Bei Mir Bist Du Schoen" and their "One More River" hootenanny, which included "Don't Fence Me In," "Down in the Valley," "You Are My Sunshine," "Blue Tail Fly," "Near You," "Three Little Fishies," and "Old Man River."

Aug. 2–6. *The Mike Douglas Show* (Syndicated). The Andrews Sisters were cohosts for a week.

Oct. 1. *The Tonight Show Starring Johnny Carson* (NBC). The Andrews Sisters sang "One Note Samba," "South America, Take It Away," and "In Apple Blossom Time."

Dec. 9. *The Dean Martin Show* (NBC). The Andrews Sisters sang "Got a Lot of Livin' to Do" and "My Favorite Things." Martin joined them in a medley of their hits plus "That's Amore," "Everybody Loves Somebody," and "Houston."

1966

Feb. 11. *The Jimmy Dean Show* (ABC). The Andrews Sisters sang "In Apple Blossom Time" and a medley of their hits. Dean joined them in "Pistol Packin' Mama."

Mar. 4. *The Sammy Davis Jr. Show* (NBC). The Andrews Sisters, dressed as flappers, sang a medley of 1920 songs including "Collegiate," "Last Night on the Back Porch," and "Don't Bring Lulu." They sang a medley of hits of their fellow guests The Supremes including, "Stop! In the Name of Love," "Baby Love," and "Where Did Our Love Go?" The Supremes responded with a medley of Andrews Sisters' hits. The two trios concluded the show with "The Birth of the Blues."

Sept. 29. *The Dean Martin Show* (NBC). The Andrews Sisters sang "What Now My Love?," "That's How Young I Feel," and a medley with Martin of their combined hits.

They joined Martin and other guests Lainie Kazan, Frank Gorshin, and Tim Conway with Duke Ellington on piano for a medley of swing hits. This was LaVerne's last appearance on network television.

Oct. 27. *The Mike Douglas Show* (Syndicated). The Andrews Sisters sang "Got a Lot of Livin' to Do," "I Left My Heart in San Francisco," "Sabre Dance," and "I Can Dream, Can't I?" This was the last television appearance of the original Andrews Sisters.

1967

July. Television Variety Show in Copenhagen, Denmark. The first television appearance of the Andrews Sisters after Joyce DeYoung replaced LaVerne Andrews. The sisters were appearing at Tivoli Gardens in Copenhagen.

Oct. 24. *The Joey Bishop Show* (ABC). In Joyce DeYoung's American television debut with Patty and Maxene Andrews, the trio sang "Got a Lot of Livin' to Do," "My Favorite Things," "I Left My Heart in San Francisco," "Bei Mir Bist Du Schoen," and "In Apple Blossom Time."

Nov 30. *The Dean Martin Show* (NBC). The Andrews Sisters sang a medley of the trio's hits with Martin. They joined fellow guest Lena Horne and Martin in hobo costumes for "The Idle Rich."

1968

Jan. 20. *The Gypsy Rose Lee Show* (Syndicated). The Andrews Sisters appeared on this talk show while performing at Bimbo's in San Francisco.

Feb. 13. *The Joey Bishop Show* (ABC). The Andrews Sisters sang "The Song Is You" and Bishop joined them for "South America, Take It Away." Other guests were Eddie Fisher and Connie Stevens.

Mar. 13. *The Joey Bishop Show* (ABC). The Andrews Sisters sang a medley of their polka hits. Bishop, in pink dress and blond wig, stood in for Patty and lip-synched "In Apple Blossom Time" with Maxene and Joyce.

Mar. 14. *The Woody Woodbury Show* (Syndicated). As guests on this talk show,

the Andrews Sisters sang "A Man and a Woman" and "Beer Barrel Polka."

May 6. *The Joey Bishop Show* (ABC). Patty Andrews appeared alone when Joyce DeYoung and Maxene Andrews were unable to make the last minute engagement. She sang "Open a New Window," "We Need a Little Christmas," "Mame," "Hello Dolly," and "I Can Dream, Can't I?"

Mar. 27. *The Donald O'Connor Show* (Syndicated). In Patty Andrews' first television appearance after the Andrews Sisters act retired, she sang "I Left My Heart in San Francisco," "South Rampart Street Parade" and joined O'Connor for "Bei Mir Bist Du Schoen."

1969

Aug. 27. *The Joey Bishop Show* (ABC). Patty Andrews sang "South Rampart Street Parade" and "I'll Never Fall in Love Again."

Oct. 27. *Here's Lucy* (CBS). Patty Andrews guest starred in a plot in which she hired "Lucy" (Lucille Ball) and "Kim" (Lucie Arnaz) to help her recreate the Andrews Sisters for a fan club gathering. They sang a medley of Andrews Sisters hit and were joined by Desi Arnaz, Jr. as Bing Crosby.

1970

Oct. 26. *The Carol Burnett Show* (CBS). Carol Burnett sang "Boogie Woogie Bugle Boy" as all three Andrews Sisters. Maxene Andrews was introduced from the audience.

1971

May 10. *It Was a Very Good Year* (PBS). In this nostalgic look at 1945, host Mel Torme' interviewed Maxene Andrews about the Andrews Sisters 1945 USO tour in Italy.

July 4. *The Merv Griffin Show* (CBS). Patty Andrews sang a medley of Andrews Sisters hits and talked about her current role in the musical *Victory Canteen* in Los Angeles.

July 9. *The Virginia Graham Show* (Syndicated). Patty Andrews sang a medley of

Andrews Sisters hits. Other guests: Carol Burnett, Jack Cassidy, and Rex Reed.

1972

June 12. *The Merv Griffin Show* (Syndicated). Patty and Maxene Andrews sang a medley of Andrews Sisters hits. The Lennon Sisters were also guests on the show.

1973

May 17. *The Merv Griffin Show* (Syndicated). Patty and Maxene Andrews sang a medley of their hits. They discussed Bette Midler's recording of "Boogie Woogie Bugle Boy" and their upcoming Broadway show *Over Here!*

1974

Jan. 10. *One More Time* (CBS). Patty Andrews appeared in this special hosted by George Burns to sing "Bei Mir Bist Du Schoen" with the Pointer Sisters.

Apr. 16. *The Today Show* (NBC). Patty and Maxene Andrews were interviewed live, partly about their Broadway show *Over Here!* by Gene Shalit and Floyd Kalber.

Apr. 21. *The Tony Awards* (ABC). Patty and Maxene Andrews sang "Over Here!" with the cast of the Broadway show in which they were currently starring.

July 18. *What's My Line?* (Syndicated). Maxene Andrews taped an appearance as the show's mystery guest for a later broadcast.

Aug. 29. *Geraldo Rivera's Goodnight America* (ABC). Maxene Andrews was interviewed by Geraldo Rivera.

Sept. 1–2. *Jerry Lewis Telethon* (Syndicated). Maxene and Patty Andrews and cast members of *Over Here!* sang selections from the Broadway show.

Sept. 7. *Andy Williams Special* (NBC). Maxene and Patty Andrews and the cast of *Over Here!* sang "Over Here!" and "Charlie's Place" on this special taped at the Ed Sullivan Theater in New York City.

1975

Nov. 3–7. *Showoffs* (ABC). Maxene Andrews was a celebrity player for a week on this charades-type game show hosted by Bobby Van.

1977

Aug. *The Gong Show* (NBC). Patty Andrews began appearing as a celebrity judge on this talent/game show. She was on both the daytime version on NBC and on the nighttime syndicated version. Clips of her appearances were used in the 1980 movie *The Gong Show Movie*.

1978

Fall. *The $1.98 Beauty Show* (Syndicated). Patty Andrews appeared several times as a judge on this talent/beauty show that awarded winners $1.98.

1979

Nov. 15. *Over Easy* (PBS). Maxene Andrews was interviewed by host Hugh Downs. She sang "By Myself" and "There'll Be Some Changes Made."

1980

Jan. 30. *The Dick Cavett Show* (PBS). Maxene Andrews was interviewed by host Dick Cavett. She sang a medley of Andrews Sisters hits and "It Never Entered My Mind."

Mar. 15. *G. I. Jive* (PBS). This special salute to World War II entertainers was taped in Roseland Ballroom in New York City in December 1979 and was shown on PBS stations across the country in March 1980. Maxene Andrews sang a medley of Andrews Sisters hits.

Aug. 21. *Dinah! and Friends* (Syndicated). Maxene Andrews was guest when Dinah Shore taped her show at Resorts International Hotel, Atlantic City. Maxene sang "Where Did the Good Times Go?" and joined Shore for "Beer Barrel Polka."

1981

Oct. *700 Club* (CBN). Maxene discussed her born-again Christianity and sang a medley of Andrews Sisters' hits.

Oct. 6. *Over Easy* (PBS). Maxene Andrews was interviewed by host Hugh Downs and sang "Ac-Cent-Tchu-Ate the Positive" with accompanist Phil Campanella. She reminisced with fellow guest Mary Martin about their voice teacher Helen Fouts Cahoon.

1982

Aug. 16. *Cromie Circle.* Maxene appeared on this local Chicago show hosted by Bob Cromie on WGN.

1983

July 4. *March of Dimes Telethon* (Syndicated). Patty Andrews made a guest appearance.

July 14. *700 Club* (CBN). In a return appearance on this Christian Broadcasting Network talk show hosted by Pat Robertson, Maxene Andrews discussed her by-pass heart surgery and her "born-again" Christian experience. She sang a medley of Christian songs.

Aug. 30. *Entertainment Tonight* (Syndicated). Patty Andrews was interviewed in a segment about female singing groups.

1984

Feb. 22. *Entertainment Tonight* (Syndicated). Patty Andrews was interviewed for a segment called "Hollywood Goes To War."

June 6. *Good Morning America* (ABC). Maxene Andrews and Greer Garson were interviewed about their memories of D-Day, June 6, 1944.

Sept. *Hour Magazine* (Syndicated). Maxene Andrews appeared on the show to cook with host Gary Collins.

1985

Mar. 19. *The Merv Griffin Show* (Syndicated). Patty Andrews sang "It's Almost Like Being in Love."

Mar. 21. *In the Swing* (PBS). Patty Andrews appeared on this special hosted by Steve Allen. She sang "South Rampart Street Parade," "I Can Dream, Can't I?" and "Boogie Woogie Bugle Boy." The show was produced in Hollywood in 1983, and shown on PBS stations around the country at various times.

June 29–30. *March of Dimes Telethon* (Syndicated). Live from Hollywood, Patty Andrews sang a medley of Andrews Sisters songs.

Aug. 12. *Good Morning America* (ABC). Maxene Andrews was interviewed by host David Hartman about her new solo album, *Maxene, An Andrews Sister.*

1986

Mar. 7. *Irving Berlin's America* (PBS). Patty Andrews was among the many stars interviewed on this tribute to songwriter Irving Berlin.

May 26. *Bob Hope's High-Flying Birthday* (NBC). Patty Andrews made a brief walk-on appearance after Bob Hope, Sammy Davis, Jr., and Jonathan Winters appeared in drag to lip-synch the Andrews Sisters' "Boogie Woogie Bugle Boy." This special was taped aboard the *USS Lexington* in Pensacola, Florida.

June 30. *The Merv Griffin Show* (Syndicated). Patty Andrews sang "Boogie Woogie Bugle Boy" on this "Liberty Special" edition of Griffin's talk show.

Dec. 4. *Our World* (ABC). Maxene Andrews was interviewed following an airing of the film footage of the recording session of "Boogie Woogie Bugle Boy" for Victory Discs that took place September 25, 1944.

1987

Oct. 2. *Entertainment Tonight* (Syndicated). A brief segment aired about the Andrews Sisters' star dedication ceremony on Hollywood's Walk of Fame, which took place the previous day. Maxene Andrews and Patty Andrews were interviewed separately.

Nov. 28. *Remembering Bing* (PBS). Patty Andrews was among the celebrities interviewed about Bing Crosby.

1988

May 13. *Good Morning, Bay Area* (KGO). Patty Andrews and her husband Wally Weschler appeared with other guests on this local San Francisco station. Patty sang "Boogie Woogie Bugle Boy" and led the audience in "In Apple Blossom Time."

Sept. 23. *Showbiz Today* (CNN). A feature story about Maxene Andrews was aired to publicize the upcoming PBS program *All Night Strut,* which she hosted.

Oct. 6. *CBS This Morning* (CBS). Maxene Andrews was interviewed by Kathleen Sullivan to promote the upcoming program *All Night Strut.*

Oct. 7. *All Night Strut* (PBS). Maxene Andrews hosted this musical tribute to the music of the 1930s and 1940s.

Nov. *Lifestyle.* Maxene Andrews was interviewed on a local Chicago station about her career. Also on the program was a female trio named "Stardust" who sang Andrews Sisters songs and other songs of the 1930s and 40s.

1989

Mar. 11. *Entertaining the Troops* (PBS). Maxene Andrews was interviewed in this special about the entertainers of World War II.

Sept. 22. *Sally Jessy Raphael* (Syndicated). Maxene Andrews appeared on this talk show with fellow singers Phyllis McGuire, Sylvia Sims, and Helen O'Connell.

1991

Feb. 10. *Entertainment Tonight* (Syndicated). Patty Andrews was interviewed

about entertaining troops during World War II.

Nov. 11. *Stars and Stripes* (AMC). Maxene Andrews was among the stars interviewed for this television special.

Dec. 31. *King Orange Jamboree Parade* (NBC). Patty Andrews sang "South Rampart Street Parade" while riding the Tropicana float in this Miami parade.

1992

Mar. 6. *Those Fabulous Forties* (PBS). Maxene Andrews was interviewed about the music of the 1940s.

1993

June 11. *Good Morning America* (ABC). Maxene Andrews appeared in a taped segment with Joel Siegel, who interviewed her about her book *Over Here, Over There.*

June 12. *Talk Live* (CNBC). Guest host Michael Feinstein interviewed Maxene Andrews about her book *Over Here, Over There.*

Aug. 15. *Sunday Morning* (CBS). Maxene Andrews appeared in an interview with Richard Roth, which was taped at her home in Auburn, California.

1994

June 6. *Larry King Live: D-Day Remembered* (CNN). As part of the 50th anniversary of the D-Day invasion, Maxene Andrews appeared live in Normandy with host Larry King and reminisced about entertaining troops during World War II.

June 9. *An Evening to Remember* (A&E). Patty Andrews was among the stars who performed in this recreation of a 1940s radio broadcast at Wolf Trap Farm Park in Vienna, Virginia, on the 50th anniversary of D-Day. She sang "Don't Sit Under the Apple Tree" and "In Apple Blossom Time."

Notes

Preface

1. Smith, Andrew 1974, 89.
2. Morgan 1934, 15.
3. "Three Zombies of Swing" 1944, 97–98.
4. Harris 1943, 2.
5. "Lampoon Picks Andrews Girls as 'Most Frightening'" 1941.
6. Koll 1939, 45.
7. "Record Reviews. Andrews Sisters" 15 Oct. 1941, 14.
8. Radcliffe 1941, 24.
9. "We Couldn't Believe It!!!" 1948, 28.
10. *Washington Daily Press* 1959.
11. Adams 1951, 44.

One. 1887–1932

1. Gavin 1996, 3.
2. Qualey and Gjerde 1981, 220.
3. Sollie family lore claims that Peter was Sophia's son by a previous marriage (Gladys Leichter interview by author, 2001).
4. Violet Sollie (unrelated to the family of the Andrews Sisters) was told by the Norwegian consul in Minneapolis that Sollie was the name of an area in Homalvik and many immigrants chose that name as a family name when they arrived in the United States (Violet Sollie letter, 4 June 2000). Gladys Leichter, the Andrews Sisters' cousin, thought the family was from an area named "Trona" or "Trunda," names she remembered Maxene mentioning.
5. I could locate no death certificate for Martin Sollie, but his name disappeared from the city directory after 1900.
6. Elydia Sollie, Certificate of Death, 1908.
7. "Peter Solie [sic], Uncle of Andrews Sisters, Dies" 1963.
8. The 1900 Census claimed he spoke English.
9. "Peter Solie [sic], Uncle of Andrews Sisters, Dies" 1963.
10. Mason 1940, 90.
11. Hall 1989, 170–171.
12. Rose 1974, 20. Peter's illiteracy was not uncommon. About a quarter of the Greeks who immigrated to the United States during the first decade of the 20th Century were illiterate (Scourby 1984, 48).

13. Maxene Andrews and Patty Andrews interview by Rex Reed, 1974.
14. Qualey and Gjerde 1981, 233.
15. Saloutos 1981, 472.
16. Saloutos 1981, 477.
17. Ardmore 1974, 89–90.
18. Ruhlmann 1995, 19.
19. Mason 1940, 90.
20. Gladys Leichter interview by author, 2001.
21. Irene Wilmot letter, 4 Oct. 1976.
22. Gladys Leichter interview by author, 2001.
23. Wallace circa 1940.
24. Levy "And Then I Published..." 1990, 60.
25. Ruhlmann 1995, 18; Sforza 2000, 17.
26. Thomas.
27. When Peter Andrews's name first appeared in the Minneapolis City Directory in 1907, he was identified as a "helper" who roomed at the Sollie family address. The next year he lived at the same address, but worked as an "ice cream maker" at Crescent Creamery Company. He worked at the same job in 1909, but lived at 71 Western Avenue (now Glenwood Avenue). In 1910, he was a "laborer" still residing at 71 Western Avenue

at the time he married Olga Sollie. He was not listed in the 1911 city directory, but his daughter LaVerne's birth certificate of that year gave his profession as "ice cream man." The 1912 directory did not list him, but the following year he was again identified as "ice cream maker," but at the Minneapolis Milk Company. From 1914 through 1920, Peter appeared in the city directory as a pool hall operator. His name, but not his profession, was listed in 1921 and he did not appear in the 1922 directory. In 1923 and 1924, Peter was a restaurateur at 422 Hennepin Avenue. In 1925, no occupation was listed for him, but in 1926 he was proprietor of "Andrews Fruit Company." From 1927 until 1932, he operated a pool hall with his partner James Karalis, called "Karalis and Andrews," at 404 West Broadway, Minneapolis.

28. Saloutos 1981, 476.

29. Peter P. Solle [sic], Certificate of Death, 1920.

30. Sophia H. Sollie, Certificate of Death, 1920.

31. Irene Wilmot letter, 4 Oct. 1976.

32. C. Donald Peterson letter, 3 Sept. 1976.

33. Gladys Leichter interview by author, 2001.

34. Helen Klimo interview by author, 2000.

35. Gladys Leichter interview by author, 2001.

36. Bell 1980, F-3, 4.

37. Ruhlmann 1995, 19.

38. Harris 1980, E-13.

39. Weaver 1946, 27.

40. Ardmore 1974, 86.

41. Sidney Stocking interview by Robert Boyer, 1976.

42. Ardmore 1974, 86.

43. Sidney Stocking interview by Robert Boyer, 1976.

44. Harris 1980, E-13; Hall 1989, 170.

45. Weaver 1946, 27.

46. Hall 1989, 170–171.

47. Bell 1980.

48. Gladys Leichter interview by author, 2001.

49. Maxene Andrews interview on *One Night Stand*, circa 1974.

50. Gladys Leichter interview by author, 2001.

51. Smith 1988, 25.

52. Rose 1974, 20.

53. Helen Klimo interview by author, 2000.

54. Marion Robinson Bloomberg letter, 8 Sept. 1976.

55. Irene Wilmot letter, 30 Aug. 1976.

56. Williams and Diehl 1999, 59.

57. Marion Robinson Bloomberg letter, 8 Sept. 1976.

58. Frances Gershowitz Blindman letter, 1976.

59. Harry J. Davis letter, 29 Aug. 1976.

60. E. K. Taylor letter, 29 Aug. 1976.

61. C. Donald Peterson letter, 3 Sept. 1976.

62. Gladys Leichter interview by author, 2001.

63. "Offer Dance Numbers" 1930.

64. Andrews and Gilbert 1993, 9. Copyright 1993 by Maxene Andrews and Bill Gilbert. All rights reserved. Reprinted by permission of Citadel Press/Kensington Publishing Corp. *www.kensington-books.com.*

65. Maxene Andrews interview by Jan Shapiro, 1989.

66. Maxene Andrews interview by Pat Cheffer. 1988.

67. Gladys Leichter interview by author, 2001.

68. "Variety and Picture Bills of the Week" 1931, 8.

69. "Larry Rich" 1934, 3.

70. Maxene Andrews and Patty Andrews interview by Rex Reed, 1974.

71. "Revue Features Song and Dance Numbers" 1931, 6.

72. Rose 1974, 20.

73. Wendeborn 3 April 1981; Rose 1974, 20.

74. Glassner 1974, 25.

75. Ardmore 1974, 89–90.

76. Glassner 1974, 25.

77. Gladys Leichter interview by author, 2001.

78. Forsmark 1983, 4.

79. "Three Zombies of Swing" 1944, 97–98.

80. Sidney Stocking letter, 24 June 1976.

81. Smith 1988, 26.

82. Smith 1988, 26.

83. Bell 1980.

84. Harris 1980, E-13.

85. Wendeborn 3 April 1981.

86. Ruhlmann 1995, 19.

87. "Three Zombies of Swing" 1944, 97–98.

Two. 1932–1934

1. Morgan 1934, 15.

2. "Circuit Vaude Drops 70% During The Last Five Years" 1932, 6.

3. Green and Laurie 1951, 370.

4. Harris 1980, E-13.

5. Ardmore 1974, 89.

6. Maxene Andrews letter, 6 Nov. 1931.

7. LaVerne Andrews letter, 6 Nov. 1931.

8. LaVerne Andrews letter, 6 Nov. 1931.

9. LaVerne Andrews letter, 11 Nov. 1931.

10. Joseph Malmstrom letter, 1 April 2002.

11. Wendeborn 3 April 1981.

12. Hall 1989, 171.

13. Ruhlmann 1995, 19.

14. Ruhlmann 1995, 5.

15. Hall 1989, 171.

16. Ardmore 1974, 89.

17. Grudens 1996, 28–29.

18. Rose 1974, 20.

19. Reed 1974, 6:3.

20. "Sisters Sing Carols" 1931, 14.

21. Weinstock 1940.

22. Harris 1932, 10.

23. Char 1932, 39.

24. Maxene Andrews interview by Jan Shapiro, 1989.

25. Maxene Andrews interview by Jan Shapiro, 1989.

26. "Screen Comedian Is Listed in Leading Vaudeville Act" 1932, D-7.

27. "RKO Proctor's" 1932, 7.

28. LaVerne Andrews letter, 17 April 1932.

29. Maxene Andrews interview by Jan Shapiro, 1989.

30. Ardmore 1974, 89–90.

31. "Knickerbocker Dance Pupils Appear Here" 1932, 14.

32. LaVerne Andrews letter, 28 May 1932.

33. Hill 1932, 10.

34. LaVerne Andrews letter, 8 June 1932.

35. LaVerne Andrews letter, 27 June 1932.

36. "Big Time Vaudeville" 1932, II-7.

37. "Orpheum" 1932, 4.

38. LaVerne Andrews letter, 24 June [July] 1932.

39. Morgan 1932, 10.

40. Kauf 1932, 42.

41. LaVerne Andrews letter, 19 Oct. 1932.

42. Crichton 1939, 44.

43. Ardmore 1974, 90.

44. LaVerne Andrews letter, 19 Oct. 1932.

45. Ardmore 1974, 90.

46. LaVerne Andrews letter, 19 Oct. 1932.

47. Ardmore 1974, 90.

48. Ardmore 1974, 90.

49. LaVerne Andrews letter, 19 Oct. 1932.

50. LaVerne Andrews letter, 19 Oct. 1932.

51. Chic 1932, 32.

52. Maxene Andrews interview by Robert Boyer, 1975.

53. "Fun On Roller Coaster Recalled" 1967.

54. Patty Andrews interview by Richard Lamparski, circa 1972.

55. LaVerne Andrews letter, 23 Nov. 1932.

56. Ardmore 1974, 90.

57. Howard 1956, 104.

58. O'Connor 24 Aug. 1954, A-12.

59. Sidney Stocking interview by Robert Boyer, 1976.

60. LaVerne Andrews letter, circa Jan. 1933.

61. Sachs 1933, 15.

62. Ardmore 1974, 90.

63. "Fun On Roller Coaster Recalled" 1967.

64. Hall 1989, 173.

65. Hagen 1974, 12.

66. When Ted Mack died at 72 in July 1976, an obituary quoted an earlier interview with him when he reminisced about a time when he, his wife and the Andrews Sisters found themselves outside Indianapolis with only twenty-five cents among them. I found nothing about this incident.

67. Unidentified Memphis newspaper 1933, Robert Boyer Collection.

68. "More Stars for Denver's Gayest Night—Wednesday" 1933, 3.

69. "Ted Mack's Wowing 'Em at Denver" 1933, 11.

70. "Ted Mack Is Welcomed Joyously at The Denver" 1933, 14.

71. LaVerne Andrews letter, 15 Dec. 1933.

72. O'Connor 24 Aug. 1954, A-12.

73. O'Connor 24 Aug. 1954, A-12.

74. LaVerne Andrews letter, 16 Jan. 1934.

75. Glassner 1974, 25.

76. Ardmore 1974, 90.

77. Rose 1974, 20.

78. Weinstock 1940.

79. O'Connor 24 Aug. 1954, A-12.

80. Weinstock 1940.

81. Leed 1979.

82. Gladys Leichter interview by author, 2001.

83. *Detroit News* 1934, 11.

84. Hall 1989, 174.

85. Morgan 1934, 15.

86. "Oriental, Chi" 1934, 14.

87. Ruhlmann 1995, 20.

88. Ruhlmann 1995, 20.

89. Manning 1942, 24.

90. Maxene Andrews and Patty Andrews interview by Rex Reed, 1974.

91. Clarke 2000, 47–48.

92. Ruhlmann 1995, 20.

93. Hall 1989, 174.

Three. 1934–1937

1. Ruhlmann 1995, 22.

2. Andrews and Gilbert 1993, 9. Copyright by Maxene Andrews and Bill Gilbert. All rights reserved. Reprinted by permission of Citadel Press/ Kensington Publishing Corp. *www.kensingtonbooks.com.*

3. Patty Andrews interview by Richard Lamparski, circa 1972.

4. "Chi Par Club's Show" 1934, 47.

5. LaVerne Andrews letter, 16 Oct. 1934.

6. LaVerne Andrews letter, 9 Dec. 1934.

7. LaVerne Andrews letter, 17 Dec. 1934.

8. LaVerne Andrews letter, 5 Jan. 1935.

9. Patty Andrews letter, 1 March 1935.

10. Andrews and Gilbert 1993, 85. Copyright 1993 by Maxene Andrews and Bill Gilbert. All rights reserved. Reprinted by permission of Citadel Press/Kensington Publishing Corp. *www.kensingtonbooks.com.*

11. "Chi's Nitery Biz Best Since Boom Times; Town Splurging on Shows" 1935, 49.

12. Manning 1942, 24.

13. LaVerne Andrews undated letter, circa July 1935.

14. Warner 1992, 6.

15. "In New Ringside Floor Show" 1935.

16. Olga Andrews letter, 13 Nov. 1935.

17. Hall 1989, 172.

18. Ruhlmann 1995, 20.

19. Hall 1989, 175.

20. "Fire Razes Mayfair, Leading K.C. Nitery" 1936, 39.

21. "Club Chatter" 1936, 13.

22. "Her Fan Slipped" 1934, 45.

23. "N.Y. Cops Guard Rich Café Patrons" 1936, 11.

24. "Mayfair Club" 1936.

25. "Mayfair" 1936, 42.

26. Dexter 1936, 27.

27. Vic Schoen interview by Robert Boyer, 12 July 1998.

28. Maxene Andrews interview on *One Night Stand*, circa 1974.

29. Vic Schoen interview by Robert Boyer, 12 July 1998.

30. Hoyt 1936, 48.

31. Toulon 1936, 40.

32. "Belasco Opens Pavilion Caprice For Season; Sister Trio Sings" 1936.

33. Boyer 1999, 3-5.

34. Crichton 1939, 16.

35. "Night Club Reviews: Hotel New Yorker, N.Y." 1937, 12.

36. Simon 1937, 22-23.

37. Forsmark 1983, 5.

38. Orodenker 8 May 1937, 11.

39. Orodenker 15 May 1937, 11.

40. Washburn 1937, 5.

41. Lang 1937, 18.

42. Cullum 1937, 10.

43. "Those Rhythm Cry Babies" 1937, 8.

44. Forsmark 1983, 5.
45. Manning 1942, 25.
46. Leon Belasco letter, 1976.
47. Hall 1989, 176.
48. Ardmore 1974, 90.
49. Hagen 1974, 12.
50. "Sister" 1991, 33-35.
51. Ardmore 1974, 90.
52. Ruhlmann 1995, 21.
53. Kenny 28 September 1937, 42.
54. Kenny 4 October 1937.
55. "Café News" 1937, 10.
56. Ruhlmann 1995, 22.
57. Hall 1989, 177-178.
58. Hall 1989, 178.
59. "Sister" 1991, 33-35.
60. Crichton 1939, 44.
61. Weaver 1946, 55.
62. Patty Andrews interview by Richard Lamparski, circa 1972.
63. Ruhlmann 1995, 22.
64. Patty Andrews interview by Richard Lamparski, circa 1972.
65. Ruhlmann 1995, 22.
66. Ruhlmann 1995, 22.
67. Ruhlmann 1995, 22.
68. Ruhlmann 1995, 22.
69. Hall 1989, 179.
70. Ruhlmann 1995, 22, 24.
71. Ruhlmann 1995, 24.
72. Hall 1989, 179-180.
73. Ruhlmann 1995, 24, 26.
74. Levy "How 'Bei Mir Bist Du Schoen' Became a Hit" 1990, 60.
75. Secunda 1982, 148.
76. "Three Zombies of Swing" 1944, 97-98.
77. Crichton 1939, 44.
78. "Sister" 1991, 35.
79. Hall 1989, 180-181.
80. Ruhlmann 1995, 26.
81. Secunda 1982, 152.
82. Ruhlmann 1995, 26.
83. Secunda 1982, 156.
84. "Yiddish Into Navajo" 1938, 46.
85. Secunda 1982, 150.
86. Secunda 1982, 156.
87. Reuter 1938, 76.
88. "The Story of a Song: 'Bei Mir Bist Du Schon' Now Heads Best-Sellers" 1938, 39.

Four. 1938–1939

1. DuBois 1987, 6.
2. Reed 1974, 6-3.
3. Maxene Andrews and Patty Andrews interview by Rex Reed, 1974.
4. Reed 1974, 6-3.
5. Andrews, Maxene 1990, 60.
6. Dubois 1987, 6.
7. Parillo "Wrigley's DOUBLE MINT Gum presents 'Double Everything,'" Undated.
8. LaVerne Andrews letter, 1 Feb. 1938.
9. Reed 1974, 6-3.
10. LaVerne Andrews letter, 17 March 1938.
11. Ruhlmann 1995, 26.
12. Reed 1974, 6-3.
13. Ruhlmann 1995, 28.
14. Maxene Andrews and Patty Andrews interview by Rex Reed, 1974.
15. Parrillo "Wrigley's SPEARMINT GUM presents 'Just Entertainment' Radio Program," Undated.
16. "He Might Say 'Vunderbar!'" 1938, 27.
17. Humphrey 1938, 11.
18. "Just Entertainment" 1938, 35.
19. "Follow Up Comments" 1938, 28.
20. "Current Program Notes" 1938.
21. Clarke 2000, 86.
22. Stowe 1994, 173.
23. Stowe 1994, 173.
24. "The Gal Yippers Have No Place In Our Jazz Bands" 1939, 16.
25. "Are Vocalists Unnecessary?" 1941, 6.
26. "Girl Singers Confess" 1937, 17.
27. "Puttin' on the Ritz" 1940, 24.
28. Reed, 1974, 6-3.
29. Hall 1989, 174.
30. Mazo 1992, 76.
31. Mazo 1992, 76.
32. Maxene Andrews interview by Jan Shapiro, 1989.
33. Andrews, Patty 1987.
34. Andrews, Maxene 1987.
35. Hagen 1974, 17.
36. Hagen 1974, 12.
37. Crichton 1939, 16.
38. Crichton 1939, 16.
39. Maxene Andrews interview by Jan Shapiro, 1989.
40. Torme 1994, 166–167.
41. Parker 1974.
42. Allen 1954, 85.
43. Reed 1974, 6-3.
44. Lawson 22 February 1992, D-1.
45. Gale 1939, 32.
46. Ruhlmann 1994, 20.
47. Hall 1989, 173.
48. "Sister" 1991, 34–35.
49. Andrews Sisters Aug. 1938, 21.
50. Andrews Sisters Sept. 1938, 21.
51. Andrews Sisters Oct. 1938, 15.
52. Hagen 1974, 12.
53. Smith 1974, 110.
54. Parker 1974.
55. "Possibilities" 1938, 4.
56. The King Sisters took a hiatus from show business in the late 1940s to attend to their growing families, but began recording again in the late 1950s for Capitol Records. In the 1960s, they joined their extended musical kin group as The King Family for a series of television specials and an album. They continued to perform into the early 1970s.
57. Andrews and Gilbert 1993, 85. Copyright 1993 by Maxene Andrews and Bill Gilbert. All rights reserved. Reprinted by permission of Citadel Press/Kensington Publishing Corp. *www.kensington-books.com.*
58. "Three Zombies of Swing" 1944, 97.
59. "Paramount, N.Y." 1938, 45.
60. Denis 1938, 20.
61. Ardmore 1974, 93.
62. MacArthur 1938.
63. Frank 1938, 20.
64. Fortune 1938.
65. Scho 1938, 47.
66. "Andrews Sis to Hop to Cleve. From B'klyn Date" 1938, 43.
67. "T. Dorsey-Andrews-'Co-Ed- Big $16,000 In Football Mad Mpls.; 'Drums' $2,000." 1938, 11.
68. Alden 1938, 14.
69. McConnell 1938, 33.
70. Herb 1938, 45.
71. "Andrews Sis Nix Double, Play Theatre with Gray" 1938, 35; Abel 1938, 41.
72. Hobe 1938, 38.
73. Richman 1938, 30.
74. "Trio and Quartet" 1938, 34.

75. Whitburn 1986, 27.
76. Dubois 1987, 7.
77. Dalz 1939, 45.
78. Franken 1939, 10.
79. "Casa Manana, New York" 1939, 20.
80. "Jimmy Dorsey's Birthday Party" 1939, 10.
81. Char. 1939, 37.
82. "Jitterbug Banned on Campus" 1938, 43.
83. Harris 1980, E-13.
84. Andrews and Gilbert 1993, 3–4. Copyright 1993 by Maxene Andrews and Bill Gilbert. All rights reserved. Reprinted by permission of Citadel Press/Kensington Publishing Corp. *www.kensington-books.com.*
85. "Collegiate Choice of Female Vocalists" 1939, 13.
86. Abel 1939, 44.
87. "B'way in Vaude Comeback" 1939, 20.
88. "Andrews-Murray Tie-Up" 1939, 11.
89. "Over a Half Million Records" 1939, 12.
90. "Breese-Andrews Sisters" 1939, 9.
91. Scho 1939, 45.
92. Lehman 1939, 22.
93. "Crosby-Andrews 7G Hot" 1939, 13.
94. Eck 1939, 37.
95. Kany 1939, 54.
96. Koll 1939, 45.
97. Crichton 1939, 44.
98. Hall 1989, 181–182.
99. Laredo 1996, 6.
100. Thompson 1975, 82–83.
101. Stein 1979, 43.
102. "Record Buying Guide" 1939, 70.
103. "Phonograph Records. Bing Crosby with Andrews Sisters" 1939, 14.
104. "Records—News" 1939, 21.
105. "Ellington Cops 1939 Record Honors" 1940, 16.
106. Gold 1939, 46.
107. Honigberg 1939, 24.
108. Franken 6 Jan. 1940, 9.
109. Polic 1997, 22–23.
110. Andrews and Gilbert 1993, 14. Copyright 1993 by Maxene Andrews and Bill Gilbert. All rights reserved. Reprinted by permission of Citadel Press/Kensington Pub-

lishing Corp. *www.kensington-books.com.*
111. Hall 1989, 183.
112. Glassner 1974, 26.
113. Andrews and Gilbert 1993, 14. Copyright 1993 by Maxene Andrews and Bill Gilbert. All rights reserved. Reprinted by permission of Citadel Press/Kensington Publishing Corp. *www.kensington-books.com.*
114. Fuller 1993, E-4.
115. Glassner 1974, 26.
116. Whitburn 1986, 27, 113.
117. "Names in The Swing News" 1939, 5.
118. "Hold Tight"—Here We Go Again" 1939, 13.
119. Ruhlmann 1995, 28.
120. Ruhlmann 1995, 28.
121. Simon and Friends 1979, 14.
122. "Inside Stuff—Music" 1939, 40.
123. Richman 1939, 76.
124. "Record Buying Guide" 1939, 70.
125. Whitburn 1986, 27, 113.

Five. 1940–1941

1. McLellan 1979, E-1.
2. Campbell 1985, 5-C14.
3. Stein 1979, 43.
4. Campbell 1985, 5-C14.
5. Grein 1987, 4.
6. Crandall 1941, 7–9.
7. Katz and Braun 1939, 12.
8. Mason 1940, 90.
9. Maxene Andrews interview by Sally Jesse Raphael, 1989.
10. Ruhlmann 1995, 32; Hopper 1956, 25.
11. Mason 1940, 90.
12. Ruhlmann 1995, 32.
13. Scourby 1984, 13.
14. Mason 1940, 90.
15. "Andrews Sisters' Dad Held on Gun Charge" 1940, 4.
16. "Singing Andrews Sisters Say All Is Harmony in the Family" 1940, 5.
17. "Singers in Discord—Gun Jails Pa" 1940, 3.
18. Ruhlmann 1995, 30.

19. "Love Upsets Trio; Girls Won't Split" 1940, 1.
20. Ruhlmann 1995, 30.
21. Ruhlmann 1995, 30, 32.
22. Ruhlmann 1995, 32.
23. "Love Upsets Trio; Girls Won't Split" 1940, 1.
24. Mason 1940, 90.
25. "No Break-Up for Andrews Sisters" 1940, 13.
26. "Andrews Gals May Break Over PA" 1940, 21.
27. Herb 1940, 46.
28. Franken 9 March 1940, 22.
29. "Good B'way Takes; Miller, Andrews Head for $55,000" 1940, 20.
30. Andrews, LaVerne 1940, 4.
31. Huggins 1940, 16.
32. "Protest Decca Air Ban" 1940, 5.
33. "Decca Okays Radio's Use of Disks" 1940, 31.
34. "Andrews Sisters' Film" 1940, 2.
35. Gold 1940, 47.
36. Green 1940, 24.
37. Glassner 1974, 26.
38. Levy Jan./Feb. 1990, 61.
39. Hall 1989, 185.
40. "Lampoon Picks Andrews Girls as 'Most Frightening'" 1941.
41. "'We'll Scare Those Guys to Death'—Andrews Sisters" 1941, 4.
42. T.M.P. 1940, 25.
43. Walt 1940, 18.
44. "Three Zombies of Swing" 1944, 97–98.
45. McClelland 1978, 365.
46. Hagen 1974, 13–14.
47. Glassner 1974, 26.
48. Patty Andrews interview by Richard Lamparski, circa 1972.
49. Wool 1983, 118.
50 Hall 1989, 185.
51. "Musical Fiesta" 1940.
52. Owen 1940, 22.
53. "Puttin' on the Ritz" 1940, 24.
54. "Andrews Sisters Draw Big" 1940, 19.
55. "Andrews Sisters May Encore in 2d U Pic" 1940, 3.
56. Burm 1940, 24.
57. Carter 1940, 48.
58. Kent 1940, 40.
59. Wood 25 Sept. 1940, 54.
60. Honigberg 1940, 22.

61. Gladys Leichter interview by author, 2001.

62. Gladys Leichter interview by author, 2001.

63. Shal 1940, 46.

64. "'Rockne'—Andrews Scoring $18,500 to Lead Wash." 1940, 11.

65. Wood 30 Oct. 1940, 55.

66. "Krupa-Andrews Top Prov. Attractions" 1940, 25.

67. "Andrews Sisters Bring Down the House" 1940.

68. Whitburn 1986, 27.

69. Mulholland 1975, 56.

70. Mulholland 1975, 61.

71. Hirschhorn 1981, 185.

72. Costello 1981, 57–58.

73. Sackett 1995, 47.

74. Costello 1981, 57–58.

75. Cox and Lofflin 1990, 56.

76. Walt 5 Feb. 1941, 12.

77. "Andrews Sisters' Performance and Songs Fine in U's 'Buck Privates'" 1941, 10.

78. T.S. 1941, 15.

79. "On the Wax" 1941.

80. "Andrews Sisters in New Movie" 1940, 34.

81. "Andrews Sisters, Three Stooges Head Neat Bill" 1941, 8.

82. Weinstock 1940.

83. "Welcome for Andrews Sisters" 1941, 12.

84. "The Andrews Sisters in Minneapolis" 1941, 3.

85. "The Andrews Sisters Come Home" 1941, 7.

86. Rees, 1941, 54.

87. "Stage Shows Again Rescue Chi; 'Mothers'— Andrews-Krupa 45G, 'Suez'— Vaude 22G, H.O.s Strong" 1941, 9.

88. Gold 12 Feb.1941, 40.

89. Cohen 12 March 1941, 47.

90. Cohen 8 March 1941, 23.

91. "Andrews Gals Big 24G in Pittsburgh" 1941, 20.

92. "Arranges a Profitable Mob Scene to Sell Andrews Sisters Discs: First Corners Local Supply" 1941, 40.

93. "'Abbott-Costello', Pic Title" 1941, 1.

94. Walt 4 June 1941,15.

95. Crowther 1941, 29.

96. "Ted Lewis, Andrews Sis Added to A. & C. Film" 1941, 3.

97. Walt 1941, 18.

98. T. M. P. 1941, 13.

99. Smith 1941, 14.

100. Glassner 1974, 27.

101. Cox and Lofflin 1990, 41.

102. Cox and Lofflin 1990, 40.

103. Cox and Lofflin 1990, 41.

104. Gladys Leichter interview by author, 2001.

105. "Top-Rating Pictures for 1940–41" 1940, 24.

106. Manning 1942, 45.

107. "Andrews Sisters Defer on U's Jukebox Picture" 1941, 2.

108. "Gibson-Andrews Girls and Berle" 1941, 2.

109. Andrews and Gilbert 1993, 12. Copyright 1993 by Maxene Andrews and Bill Gilbert. All rights reserved. Reprinted by permission of Citadel Press/Kensington Publishing Corp. www.kensingtonbooks.com.

110. Gioia, 1997, 101.

111. Martin 1938, 5.

112. Shaw 1998, 168.

113. Simon and Friends 1979, 14.

114. Reed, 1974, 6–3.

115. Shaughnessy 1993, 132.

116. Reed 1974, 6–3.

117. "Over a Half Million Records" 1939, 12.

118. Harris 1939, 4.

119. "Record Reviews. Andrews Sisters" 15 Oct. 1941, 14.

120. Levin 15 May 1942, 14.

121. "Record Reviews. Boswell Sisters Album" 1943, 16.

122. "Record Reviews. Andrews Sisters" June 1944, 22.

123. "Record Reviews. Andrews Sisters." July 1944, 22.

124. "Record Reviews. Bing Crosby" 1948, 44.

125. Schaeffer 1956, 24.

126. Marne 1941, 23.

127. "Record Reviews. Bing Crosby—Andrews Sisters—Joe Venuti" 1939, 21.

128. "Record Reviews: Andrews Sisters" 1 Oct. 1940, 14.

129. "Record Reviews. Andrews Sisters" 1 Dec. 1940, 14.

130. "Record Reviews. Andrews Sisters" 1944, 8.

131. "Record Reviews. Andrews Sisters" 26 Aug. 1946, 21.

132. "Record Reviews: Andrews Sisters" 1949, 15.

133. Speegle 1941, 7.

134. "'Draft' Pulls Big 20G in Mild Frisco, Andrews Sis-Fight Pix Terrif $23,000" 1941, 11.

135. "Cut Rates For Service Men Big in S.F." 1941, 37.

136. "Andrews Sisters' $4,984 on Frisco %" 1941, 2.

137. "Philly Picks Up Despite Heat Wave; Andrews Sis-'Widow' Nice $20,000" 1941, 10.

138. Shal 1941, 47.

139. "Andrews, Krupa Near Record in Pittsburgh" 1941, 24.

140. McConnell 1941, 23.

141. Morris circa 1945, m13.

142. Andrews and Gilbert 1993, 20. Copyright 1993 by Maxene Andrews and Bill Gilbert. All rights reserved. Reprinted by permission of Citadel Press/Kensington Publishing Corp. www.kensingtonbooks.com.

143. Ruhlmann 1995, 36.

144. Morris circa 1945, m13.

145. Orodenker 16 Aug. 1941, 12.

146. Honigberg 1941, 23.

147. Gold 13 Aug. 1941, 25.

148. "Andrews Sisters Doubled Salary within One Year" 1941, 21.

149. Andrews and Gilbert 1993, 23. Copyright 1993 by Maxene Andrews and Bill Gilbert. All rights reserved. Reprinted by permission of Citadel Press/Kensington Publishing Corp. www.kensingtonbooks.com.

150. Leath 1941, 17.

151. Carter 1941, 55.

152. Wilson 1974, II-3.

153. Orodenker 2 Aug. 1941, 13.

154. "Another Scoop for Excelsior Park" 1941, 8.

155. "Andrews-Venuti Find $1.10 High" 1941, 4.

156. Gladys Leichter interview by author, 2001.

157. Banks 1945, 6.

158. Gladys Leichter interview by author, 2001.

159. "J. Dorsey, Basie Crack 1-Niter Records; Ditto Krupa, But Storm Clips Weeks" 1941, 31.
160. "Andrews-'Parachute' Hefty $16,000 in Balto" 1941, 15.
161. "Andrews Sisters' 25G Terrific in Boston" 1941, 24.
162. Fox 1941, 46.
163. Andrews and Gilbert 1993, 138. Copyright 1993 by Maxene Andrews and Bill Gilbert. All rights reserved. Reprinted by permission of Citadel Press/Kensington Publishing Corp. *www.kensington.com.*
164. Mori 1941, 22.
165. "Long-Andrews Big $66,000 in N. Y.; Lewis Fair 19G in Philly, Krupa OK 14½ G, L.A., Pastor 14G in Balto" 1941, 42.
166. "Illness Reduces Andrews From Trio to a Single" 1941, 45.
167. Jon 1941, 24.
168. "'Heaven' Plus Andrews Sis-Davis Huge $31,000 For Pitt; 'Badlands' 6G" 1941, 12.
169. "Andrews Sisters on the Cover " 1941, 1.
170. Whitburn 1986, 27–28.
171. Radcliffe 1941, 24.
172. Andrews and Gilbert 1993, 5–6. Copyright 1993 by Maxene Andrews and Bill Gilbert. All rights reserved. Reprinted by permission of Citadel Press/Kensington Publishing Corp. *www.kensington-books.com.*

Six. 1942–1943

1. Rose 1974, 18.
2. "N.Y. Para Half Million" 1942, 1.
3. Speegle 29 Jan. 1942, 7.
4. Green and Laurie 1951, 513.
5. "Glenn Miller's 'Choo Choo' Hits 1,000,000 Mark in Disc Output and May Become All-Time High" 1942, 39.
6. "Top Phono Artists" 1942, 9.
7. Hirschhorn 1981, 201.
8. Crowther 1942, 15.
9. Walt 25 Feb. 1942, 8.
10. G.T.S. 1942, 19.
11. "Andrews Sis-'Spitfire Baby' Terrif $25,000 in Frisco; 'Boots' Trim 12G H.O" 1942, 11.
12. "Andrews Earn Their Top Vaude Salary" 1942, 30.
13. Wern 1942, 46.
14. "Chi Temp. and Biz Warming Up: 'Day'-Andrews Bright $45,000, 'Pulham' Fine 17G, 'Hellz' 2d 13G" 1942, 9.
15. Honigberg, "Chicago" 28 Feb. 1942, 7.
16. "Andrews Sisters Hit Their Top Vaude Pay, $7,750 for Chi Week" 1942, 3.
17. Honigberg, "Chicago, Chicago" 28 Feb. 1942, 18.
18. "'Gesture'-Long-Andrews Sis Pacing Solid Det. $36,000; 'Woman' Lush 15G" 1942, 13.
19. "Andrews Sisters to Coast For 3 U Pix After Vaude, Disc Dates End This Wk" 1942, 3.
20. T. S. 1942, 27.
21. Walt 3 June 1942, 8.
22. Hirschhorn 1981, 208.
23. Abbott 1942, 17.
24. "Lou Levy Due Into U.S. Army July 22" 1942, 43.
25. "Lou Levy Gets 4-F, Resumes Business" 1942, 41.
26. "Lou Levy's Operation" 1942, 41.
27. "Patti Andrews Taken Off Train for Emergency Op at Rock Island, Illinois" 1942, 3.
28. "Patty's 40 Grand Appendectomy" 1942, 1.
29. Ignace 1942, 16.
30. Joyce DeYoung interview by author, 17 Oct. 2000.
31. "'Spy'-Andrew [sic] Sis-Osborne Huge 30G in Hub; 'Crossroads' 40G in 2 Spots" 1942, 16.
32. Poole 1942, 16.
33. Andrews and Gilbert 1993, 54. Copyright 1993 by Maxene Andrews and Bill Gilbert. All rights resersved. Reprinted by permission of Citadel Press/Kensington Publishing Corp. *www.kensington-books.com.*
34. *The Andrews Sisters' Army, Navy and Marines Song Folio* 1942.
35. Levin 1 Aug. 1942, 1.
36. Glassner1974, 26.
37. McClelland 1978, 102.
38. Char 1942, 18.
39. T. M. P. 1942, 22.
40. "Give Out, Sisters" 28 Aug. 1942.
41. "Give Out, Sisters" 5 Sept. 1942.
42. "Andrews Sisters Tired of Turkeys" 1942, 2.
43. "'Major'-Pastor-Andrews, $82,000, Newest Wow in OK N.Y.; 'Serenade' 2nd Nifty $50,000, 'Talk' 3d $90,000" 1942, 9.
44. Hobe 1942, 44.
45. "Herb Ross, Music Machine Operator" 1942, 67.
46. Orodenker 1942, 17.
47. "Andrews Gals Big $30,000 in Philly; Fay's Hit Average" 1942, 14.
48. "'Rangers'-Andrews Sis Big $54,000, Chi Leader; 'Affairs'-Davis Great 26G, 'Done It' $15,500, 'Eileen' 19 _ G" 1942, 9.
49. Loop 1942, 47.
50. "Record Reviews. Andrews Sisters" 15 Sept. 1942, 9.
51. "Inside Stuff—Music" 1942, 43.
52. "Strip Polka" Is First Smash Hit San Ether Help" 1942, 23.
53. Sahu 1942, 22.
54. Monk 1942, 40.
55. "Ambassador Theatre War Workers Show" 1942, D-5.
56. Andrews and Gilbert 1993, 188. Copyright 1993 by Maxene Andrews and Bill Gilbert. All rights reserved. Reprinted by permission of Citadel Press/Kensington Publishing Corp. *www.kensington-books.com.*
57. "Recipe for Success" 1945, 62.
58. Patty Andrews interview by Richard Lamparski, circa 1972.
59. Maxene Andrews interview by Jan Shapiro, 1989.
60. Whitburn 1986, 28.
61. "Decca Is Santa on Bing's 'Xmas'" 1943, 21.
62. Sanjek 1996, 137–138.
63. Rachlin 1981, 192.
64. "400,000 Music Machines" 1940, 1.
65. "Singing Andrews Sisters" 1943, 2.
66. "Andrews Sis. Standoff" 1943, 2.

67. "Andrews Sis Vs. Andrews Sis to Lawsuit Again" 1944, 25.
68. Frohlich 1943, 14.
69. Walt 1943, 14.
70. "Andrews Sisters Net $10,500 in Oakland" 1943, 39.
71. Soanes 1943, B-7.
72. "'Jordon' Plus Andrews Sis-Ayres Fine $17,000 in Omaha; 'Children' 18G" 1943, 11.
73. "Andrews Sis-Ayres Up 'Pittsburgh' to 19,000, Mpls, 'Rhythm' 9 G H. O." 1943, 10.
74. Rees 1943, 40.
75. "Andrew [sic] Sisters 19G Big in Minneapolis" 1943, 16.
76. Adams 1943, 7.
77. "Andrews Sis Up 'Holmes' to Trim $18,000, Indpls" 1943, 9.
78. Kenny 1943, 14.
79. Andrews and Gilbert 1993, 160. Copyright 1993 by Maxene Andrews and Bill Gilbert. All rights reserved. Reprinted by permission of Citadel Press/Kensington Publishing Corp. www.kensingtonbooks.com.
80. Pool 1943, 39.
81. Cohen 1943, 24.
82. "'Saludos'-Andrews-Ayres Wham $28,500 in Cleve." 1943, 12.
83. "Spitalny Smash 48G, Det., Spivak Fine $22,500, Pitts., Andrews Sis-Ayres Big 30G in Hub; Krupa Hot $9,300, 3 Days" 1943, 34.
84. Elle 1943, 46.
85. "Andrews Draw Big $27,900 in Buffalo" 1943, 18.
86. "Andrews Buck Heat, Cop Near-High 10G" 1943, 19.
87. Andrews and Gilbert 1993, 186–188. Copyright 1993 by Maxene Andrews and Bill Gilbert. All rights reserved. Reprinted by permission of Citadel Press/Kensington Publishing Corp. www.kensingtonbooks.com.
88. "New Bills Overcome Heat; Para's Andrews Sis-'Dixie' Big $80,000; MH 105G; Roxy Points to $87,000" 1943, 19.
89. Abel 1943, 46.
90. Denis 1943, 18–19.
91. Ulanov 1943, 32.
92. George Sleder letter, 7 December 2001.

93. "Andrews Sisters" 1943, 4.
94. Wilson 1943, 32.
95. Andrews and Gilbert 1993, 34. Copyright 1993 by Maxene Andrews and Bill Gilbert. All rights reserved. Reprinted by permission of Citadel Press/Kensington Publishing Corp. www.kensingtonbooks.com.
96. Wallace 1943, 139.
97. Hawn 1985, VI-2.
98. Andrews and Gilbert 1993, 5. Copyright 1993 by Maxene Andrews and Bill Gilbert. All rights reserved. Reprinted by permission of Citadel Press/Kensington Publishing Corp. www.kensingtonbooks.com.
99. Andrews and Gilbert 1993, 83. Copyright 1993 by Maxene Andrews and Bill Gilbert. All rights reserved. Reprinted by permission of Citadel Press/Kensington Publishing Corp. www.kensingtonbooks.com.
100. Andrews and Gilbert 1993, 136. Copyright 1993 by Maxene Andrews and Bill Gilbert. All rights reserved. Reprinted by permission of Citadel Press/Kensington Publishing Corp. www.kensingtonbooks.com.
101. Andrews, Maxene "Boogie Woogie Bugle Boy" 1984, 269.
102. Gladys Leichter interview by author, 2001.
103. "Ayres Band Signed for Andrews Sisters Picture" 1943, 15.
104. Wallace 1943, 141.
105. Andrews and Gilbert 1993, 103. Copyright 1993 by Maxene Andrews and Bill Gilbert. All rights reserved. Reprinted by permission of Citadel Press/Kensington Publishing Corp. www.kensingtonbooks.com.
106. Andrews and Gilbert 1993, 79. Copyright 1993 by Maxene Andrews and Bill Gilbert. All rights reserved. Reprinted by permission of Citadel Press/Kensington Publishing Corp. www.kensingtonbooks.com.
107. Weaver 1946, 55.

108. Morris circa 1945, m13-m15.
109. Gordon 1946, 6–7.
110. Gordon 1946, 28.
111. Gladys Leichter interview by author, 2001.
112. Morris 1945, m15.
113. Gladys Leichter interview by author, 2001.
114. Alden 1943, 4.
115. Morris 1945, m13.
116. Gladys Leichter interview by author, 2001.
117. Gordon 1946, 28.
118. Thomas Therault interview by author, 2000.
119. Andrews and Gilbert 1993, 78–79. Copyright 1993 by Maxene Andrews and Bill Gilbert. All rights reserved. Reprinted by permission of Citadel Press/Kensington Publishing Corp. www.kensingtonbooks.com.
120. Andrews and Gilbert 1993, 79–80. Copyright 1993 by Maxene Andrews and Bill Gilbert. All rights reserved. Reprinted by permission of Citadel Press/Kensington Publishing Corp. www.kensingtonbooks.com.
121. Wear 1943, 8.
122. "Bing Over the Line" 1943, 36–37.
123. "'Pistol' in Black Market Demand" 1943, 45.
124. "'Mama' Censored" 1943, 40.
125. Ruhlmann 1995, 38.
126. "Bing First Over the Line" 1943, 36–37.
127. "Crosby-Andrews on 75c Disc Release by Decca" 1943, 35.
128. "Record Reviews. Crosby-Andrews Sisters" 1 Dec. 1943, 8.
129. "Record Reviews. Crosby—Andrews" Dec. 1943, 24.
130. "Crosby-Andrews Duo Is Profit Packin' Pistol" 1943, 62.
131. "WJZ Bans 'Pistol' Disc" 1943, 61.
132. Wells 1943, 98.
133. "Lay That Pistol Down, Babe, Lay That Pistol Down!" 1943, 10.
134. "War Workers Make It 'Piston Packin' Mama'" 1943, 2.
135. Ruhlmann 1994, 16.

136. Hilburn 1997, F-26.
137. Weaver 1946, 55.
138. Fuller 1993, E-4.
139. "Sister" 1991, 34.
140. Andrews and Gilbert 1993, 161. Copyright 1993 by Maxene Andrews and Bill Gilbert. All rights reserved. Reprinted by permission of Citadel Press/Kensington Publishing Corp. *www.kensingtonbooks.com.*
141. Grudens 1996, 30.
142. Henshaw and Jones 1948, 3.
143. Thompson 1975, 237.
144. Ruhlmann 1995, 38.
145. Ulanov 1948, 291.
146. Ruhlmann 1995, 38.
147. Ruhlmann 1995, 30.
148. Elrod 1997; Ulanov 1944, 20.
149. "Top Talent for V Discs" 1944, 10.
150. Sears 1980.
151. *The Andrews Sisters Publicity* 1943–1944.
152. T. S. 1943, 23.
153. Whitburn 1986, 28, 113.
154. Andrews, Maxene, "Maxene Andrews" 1984, 69–71.
155. Andrews, Patty 1998, B-5.
156. "Singer Maxene Andrews dies at 79" 1995, A-13.
157. Hinckley 1993.

Seven. The Andrews Sisters

1. Andrews and Gilbert 1993, 53. Copyright 1993 by Maxene Andrews and Bill Gilbert. All rights reserved. Reprinted by permission of Citadel Press/Kensington Publishing Corp. *www.kensingtonbooks.com.*
2. "Who's Who Among Recording Girl Singers" 1947, 64–65.
3. McClelland 1978, 104.
4. "Three Zombies of Swing" 1944, 97–98.
5. "Laverne Andrews" 1967, 79.
6. Weaver 1946, 27.
7. Woods 1994, 159.
8. Harris 1943, 2.
9. Andrews and Gilbert 1993, 53. Copyright 1993 by Maxene Andrews and Bill Gilbert. All rights reserved. Reprinted by permission of Citadel Press/Kensington Publishing Corp. *www.kensingtonbooks.com.*
10. Wern 1941, 41.
11. McClelland 1978, 102.
12. Andrews and Gilbert 1993, 45. Copyright 1993 by Maxene Andrews and Bill Gilbert. All rights reserved. Reprinted by permission of Citadel Press/Kensington Publishing Corp. *www.kensingtonbooks.com.*
13. Wallace 1943, 140.
14. Torme 1994, 166.
15. "The Andrews Sisters" 1943, 10.
16. Bacon 1952.
17. "Three Zombies of Swing" 1944, 98.
18. "The Andrews Sisters" 1943, 10.
19. Smith 1988, 25.
20. "Sister" 1991, 35.
21. Maxene Andrews and Patty Andrews interview by Merv Griffin, 1972.
22. Terry 1993, 10.
23. Andrews and Gilbert 1993, 52–53. Copyright 1993 by Maxene Andrews and Bill Gilbert. All rights reserved. Reprinted by permission of Citadel Press/Kensington Publishing Corp. *www.kensingtonbooks.com.*
24. Andrews Sisters interview by Johnny Carson, 1965.
25. Bacon 1952.
26. Woods 1994, 160.
27. "The Andrews Sisters" 1943, 10.
28. Terry 1993, 10.
29. Simon and Friends 1979, 14.
30. "Juke-Box Divas" 1941, 36.
31. "The Andrews Sisters" 1943, 10.
32. "Who's Who Among Recording Girl Singers" 1947, 64–65.
33. Yvonne King letter, 26 July 2001.
34. Weinstock 1940.
35. Ruhlmann 1995, 32.
36. Van Horne 1946, 19.
37. Morris circa1945, m14.
38. Weaver 1946, 27.
39. Maxene Andrews interview by Mark Simone, 1992.
40. Andrews and Gilbert 1993, 236. Copyright 1993 by Maxene Andrews and Bill Gilbert. All rights reserved. Reprinted by permission of Citadel Press/Kensington Publishing Corp. *www.kensingtonbooks.com.*
41. Ruhlmann 1995, 30.
42. Stein 1979, 43.
43. Greene 1946, 56.
44. Hagen 1974, 17.
45. Maxene Andrews interview by Jan Shapiro, 1989.
46. Weaver 1946, 27.
47. Maxene Andrews interview by Sally Jessy Raphael, 1989.
48. Ardmore 1974, 90.
49. Morris circa 1945, m15.
50. Andrews, Maxene 1987.
51. Woods 1994, 160.
52. Patty Andrews interview by Richard Lamparski, circa 1972.
53. Ruhlmann 1995, 30.
54. Drewes 1968, 9.
55. Gordon 1949, 33.
56. Gordon 1944, 27.
57. Gordon 1946, 28.
58. Leath 1941, 17.
59. "The Andrews Sisters" 1943, 10.
60. Wilson 16 Nov. 1979, C-3.
61. Morris circa1945, m13.
62. "Juke-Box Divas" 1941, 36.
63. Weaver 1946, 27.
64. "The Andrews Sisters" 1943, 10.
65. Hagen 1974, 17.
66. "Andrews Gals May Break Over PA" 1940, 21.
67. Andrews and Gilbert 1993, 20. Copyright 1993 by Maxene Andrews and Bill Gilbert. All rights reserved. Reprinted by permission of Citadel Press/Kensington Publishing Corp. *www.kensingtonbooks.com.*
68. Andrews and Gilbert 1993, 3–4. Copyright 1993 by Maxene Andrews and Bill Gilbert. All rights reserved. Reprinted by permission of Citadel Press/Kensington Publishing Corp. *www.kensingtonbooks.com.*
69. Soanes 1943, B-7.

70. Patricia Kurzawinski interview by author, 2003.
71. Joyce DeYoung interview by author, 2000.
72. Gladys Leichter interview by author, 2001.
73. "The Andrews Sisters Answer 20 Questions" 1947, 39.
74. Speegle 1 Feb. 1942, 18.
75. Schallert 1944, III-6.
76. "The Andrews Sisters" 1943, 10.
77. Morris 1945.
78. Greene 1946, 55.
79. Van Horne 1946, 17.
80. Larson 1946, 10.
81. Reed 1974, 6–3.
82. Wilson 1974, II-3.
83. McClay 1972, 20.
84. Maxene Andrews and Patty Andrews interview by Rex Reed, 1974.
85. Maxene Andrews and Patty Andrews interview by Merv Griffin, 1972.
86. Ardmore 1974, 93.
87. Andrews and Gilbert 1993, 45. Copyright 1993 by Maxene Andrews and Bill Gilbert. All rights reserved. Reprinted by permission of Citadel Press/Kensington Publishing Corp. *www.kensingtonbooks. com.*
88. "Singer Maxene Andrews dies at 79" 1995, A-13.
89. Van Matre 1988, 10.
90. Kendall 1977, 36–37.
91. Leacock 1998, 12.
92. Frank Lenger letter, 1985.
93. Marion Robinson Bloomberg letter, 1976.

Eight. 1944–1945

1. "Milestones" 1995, 23.
2. Andrews and Gilbert 1993, 52. Copyright 1993 by Maxene Andrews and Bill Gilbert. All rights reserved. Reprinted by permission of Citadel Press/Kensington Publishing Corp. *www.kensingtonbooks.com.*
3. "Andrews, Ayres Hit 50G in Chi; Oriental Weak" 1944, 21.

4. N. G. 1944, 26.
5. Kardale 1944, 12.
6. "Andrews Sis-Ayres Tilt 'Hostages' Big $45,000, Det.;'Woman' Tall 39G" 1944, 16.
7. "Within These 5 Pages Are Listed the Most Generous People in the World" 1944, 27; "American Theatre Wing" 1944, 5.
8. "'Gung Ho,' Giant $16,500, Leads Cincy Pix; 'Criminal'-Andrews Sis Big 28G" 1944, 16.
9. Ring 1944, 20.
10. "'Moonlight'-Andrews Sis-Ayres Sock $31,000, Hub; 'Russia' OK 36G, 2 Spots" 1944, 14.
11. Elle 1944, 16.
12. Abel 29 March 1944, 21.
13. Dunning 1998, 565.
14. "Andrews Sis' 15G Plus % in Chi, Their Tops" 1944, 1.
15. "Andrews Sisters in Their Best Bill Yet" 1944, 6.
16. "Andrews' Pic Plans" 1944, 2.
17. "Andrews Sisters' Saga of D'Attagnan Spirit" 1944, 2.
18. Morris circa 1945.
19. Hirschhorn 1981, 250.
20. "Moonlight and Cactus" 17 Aug. 1944.
21. "Moonlight and Cactus" 16 Aug. 1944, 6–7.
22. "GI's Tab Their Favorites" 1944, 12.
23. "Hi-Schoolers Say James Best" 1944, 12.
24. Wood 1944, 42.
25. Feather 1944, 25.
26. "Sinatra Para. Preem Poor 90G as Bobby Sox Hog Seats; M. H. Opens with Juicy 130G" 1944, 23.
27. "Andrews Sisters Set for Concert Tour at Guarantee of 20Gs on 60% Split" 1944, 41.
28. "Sinatra, Spitalny and Andrews Sisters' Bids Cue Big Concert Biz" 1944, 1.
29. "Andrews Sis Like Concerts, Want More" 1944, 40.
30. Mike 1944, 34.
31. "Chi Marks Time; 'Indemnity'-Andrews Sis Great 57G, 'Neighbor'-'Gay 90's' 15G" 1944, 27.
32. Abel 6 Dec. 1944, 14.
33. Hoopes 1994, 176.

34. "Hollywood Canteen' Selling at 50% Gross" 1944, 5.
35. "Part 3—The Billboard Music Popularity Chart. Record Possibilities" 11 Nov. 1944, 18.
36. "Music News. Bing Crosby—Andrews Sisters" 1944, 8.
37. McBrien 1998, 272–273.
38. Andrews and Gilbert 1993, 161. Copyright 1993 by Maxene Andrews and Bill Gilbert. All rights reserved. Reprinted by permission of Citadel Press/Kensington Publishing Corp. *www.kensingtonbooks.com.*
39. Ruhlmann 1995, 38.
40. Andrews and Gilbert 1993, 161. Copyright 1993 by Maxene Andrews and Bill Gilbert. All rights reserved. Reprinted by permission of Citadel Press/Kensington Publishing Corp. *www.kensingtonbooks.com.*
41. Grudens 1996, 31.
42. Ruhlmann 1995, 34.
43. Andrews and Gilbert 1993, 161–163. Copyright 1993 by Maxene Andrews and Bill Gilbert. All rights reserved. Reprinted by permission of Citadel Press/Kensington Publishing Corp. *www.kensingtonbooks.com.*
44. Morris circa 1945, m14.
45. Morris circa 1945, m14.
46. Andrews and Gilbert 1993, 108–109. Copyright 1993 by Maxene Andrews and Bill Gilbert. All rights reserved. Reprinted by permission of Citadel Press/Kensington Publishing Corp. *www.kensingtonbooks.com.*
47. Maxene Andrews interview by Pat Cheffer, 1988.
48. Grein 1987, VI-4.
49. Andrews, Patty 1987.
50. Weaver 1946, 54.
51. Morris circa 1945, m14.
52. Ruhlmann 1995, 26.
53. Whitburn 1986, 28, 113.
54. "A Roundup of Fun and Song for the New Year!" 1944, 60.
55. "It's 'Andrews Sis Show' Now; Flacks Nixed '8 to Bar'" 1944, 5.
56. Morris circa 1945, m14.
57. Donn 1945, 24.

58. Koshler 1945, 31.
59. Gould 1945, X-7.
60. Ulanov 1945, 26.
61. Walker Undated.
62. "Andrews Gals' Show Getting New Scripters" 1945, 31.
63. "Andrews Sisters, Sponsor Wrangling Over Comedy Lines" 1945, 5.
64. Kiner and Mackenzie 1990, xi-xviii.
65. "Her Lucky Night" 1945.
66. "Andrews Gals Only Bright Spot in Pic" 1945.
67. Cross 1981, 150–151.
68. Hagen 1974, 14.
69. Hagen 1974, 15.
70. Patty Andrews interview by Richard Lamparski, circa 1972.
71. Bacon 15 Jan. 1976.
72. Ruhlmann 1995, 32, 34.
73. Terry 1993, V-10.
74. Andrews and Gilbert 1993, 216. Copyright 1993 by Maxene Andrews and Bill Gilbert. All rights reserved. Reprinted by permission of Citadel Press/Kensington Publishing Corp. *www.kensingtonbooks.com.*
75. Terry 1993, V-10.
76. "Decca's Newest Hit—Rum and Coca-Cola" 1945, 21.
77. "Rum and Coca-Cola" 1945, 38.
78. "Most Spectacular Song Success of the Music Business" 1945, 39.
79. Terry 1993, V-10.
80. Ardmore 1974, 86.
81. Ardmore 1974, 86.
82. Ruhlmann 1995, 40.
83. "Snub 'Rum, Coke'" 1945, 14.
84. "Rum and Coca-Cola Now Okay on NBC; All Nets Pass It" 1945, 4.
85. "Decca 'Rum & Coke' Disc May be Co.'s Bigger Seller Despite Net Ban" 1945, 43.
86. "Feist Beefs on 'Parade' Brushoff of 'Rum, Coke' Tune; Ditto 'Dream'" 1945, 41.
87. "'Rum & Cola' Haunts Phoenix Grille Staff" 1945, 18.
88. Lawson 15 February 1991, E-2.
89. "A Decca 'Rum-Coke' Cut By Calypso Ork" 1945, 14.
90. "Rum & Coca-Cola"

Okay on CBS Now; Still Nix on NBC" 1945, 7.
91. "Rum and Coca-Cola Now Okay on NBC; All Nets Pass It" 1945, 4.
92. "Record Reviews. Andrews Sisters" Feb. 1945, 14.
93. Rooks 1945, 30.
94. Ewen 1966, 334–335.
95. "10 Best Sellers on Coin-Machines" 1945, 44.
96. "Andrews Gals, Miller, Crosby Poll Toppers" 1945, 41.
97. "High-School Music Survey Tab" 1945, 20.
98. "They've Done It Again" 1945, 15.
99. Dunning 1998, 173–174.
100. Mackenzie 1996, 1.
101. Henshaw and Jones 1948, 3.
102. "Dream Cast to Wax 'Dick Tracy' for GI's" 1945, 1.
103. "Andrews Sis 18G 'take' in Record San Diego Wk" 1945, 48.
104. "Drive Starts for Show Biz in Hollywood" 1945, 16.
105. Stein 1979, 43.
106. Gladys Leichter interview by author, 2001.
107. Gladys Leichter interview by author, 2001.
108. "Lou Levys Adopt Baby" 1945, 41.
109. Morris circa 1945, m13.
110. Gladys Leichter interview by author, 2001.
111. Hinckley 1993.
112. "Andrews Sis 'Kidnapping' Gives GIs Ad Lib Show" 1945, 2.
113. Phillips 2003, 19.
114. Andrews and Gilbert 1993, 247–248. Copyright 1993 by Maxene Andrews and Bill Gilbert. All rights reserved. Reprinted by permission of Citadel Press/Kensington Publishing Corp. *www. kensingtonbooks.com.*
115. Andrews and Gilbert 1993, 247–248. Copyright 1993 by Maxene Andrews and Bill Gilbert. All rights reserved. Reprinted by permission of Citadel Press/Kensington Publishing Corp. *www. kensingtonbooks.com.*

Nine. 1945–1947

1. Speegle 1946, 9.
2. Wood 1945, 26.
3. Ross 1945, 35.
4. "N.Y. High; 'Tavern'-Andrews Sis Hot $115,000, 'Grapes' Terrif 125G, 'Glory' Big 20G, 'Fair'-Boswell Lusty 94G, 2d" 1945, 13.
5. "Patti Andrews Ill, So Stars Fill in for Sisters" 1945, 36.
6. "Andrews Sisters Back" 1945, 17.
7. Bron 1945, 30.
8. "Regular Shows—Andrews Sisters" 1946, 49.
9. "Andrews Sis Bowing Out March 27 as N-K Pulls in Horns; Set New Show" 1946, 29.
10. Whitburn 1986, 28, 113.
11. Ruhlmann 1995, 104.
12. Abel 1946, 16.
13. Crowther 1946, 26.
14. "Andrews Sisters to N'west; $$$, Picstuff Test" 1946, 47.
15. "Andrews Sis' '8-Bar' Idea Into Autry Pic" 1946, 3.
16. Speegle 1946, 9.
17. "S. F. Gate Aims at 48G with Andrews" 1946, 45.
18. Larson 1946, 10.
19. Hunt 1946, 7.
20. Sayre 1946, 19.
21. "Theatres and their players" 1946, 11.
22. "Andrews Sisters Left 'Dawn' 34G, Seattle" 1946, 11.
23. M. B. 1946, 5.
24. Walk 1946, 56.
25. Safford 1946, 12.
26. Safford 1946, 12.
27. Safford 1946, 12.
28. "Chicago, Chicago" 1946, 42.
29. Foos 1946, 22.
30. "Chi Hotsy; 'Beaucaire'-Andrews Sis Colossal 90G, 'Loved You' Smash 25G, 'Day' Wham 50G, 'Music' Strong 38G" 1946, 15.
31. Gladys Leichter interview by author, 2001.
32. Shaughnessy 1993, 130.
33. During the same studio date, the sisters and Paul also recorded "It's A Pity to Say Goodnight," but it was not released until 1997 when MCA

issued the complete Decca recordings of Les Paul.

34. Shaughnessy 1993, 132–134.

35. "Andrews Lift 'Miracle' to Wham $35,000 Cincy" 1946, 20.

36. "'Brides'-Andrews Huge $34,000, Det" 1946, 10.

37. Shal 1946, 24.

38. "N. Y. Vamps Till Xmas But 'Heart' Plus Andrews Sis Lofty $80,000; 'Life' Zestful 45G, 'Lady' Hot 62G" 1946, 17.

39. Wood 1946, 42.

40. "Paramount, New York" 1946, 35.

41. Shaughnessy 1993, 136–137.

42. Whitburn 1986, 28, 113.

43. "Winners 1946 Honor Roll of Hits" 1947, 1.

44. Elle, 1947, 55.

45. Terry 1993, V-1, 10.

46. Glassner 1974, 26.

47. "Record Reviews. Bing Crosby, Dick Haymes and the Andrews Sisters" 1947, 15.

48. "Record Reviews. Bing Crosby—Dick Haymes—Andrews Sisters" 1947, 26.

49. Ruhlmann 1995, 104.

50. "Andrews Sisters to Appear at Runyon Fund Benefit" 1947, I-7.

51. "Andrews Sisters Draw 15G Plus % for Frisco Date" 1947, 46.

52. "Andrews Sis Up 'Devil' 30G, Frisco; 'Ramrod' Thin 14G, 'Calcutta' 17G" 1947, 13.

53. Jones 1947, 15.

54. Parmenter 1947, 11.

55. Hunt 1947, 64.

56. "Benny's 113G Vs. Andrews Gals Shatters Chi" 1947, 37.

57. Gavin 1996, 24.

58. "Showbiz As 'Train' Stoker" 1947, 1.

59. Jose 1947, 48.

60. Csida 1947, 12.

61. Fredericks 1947, 36.

62. Henshaw and Jones 1948, 3.

63. Fredericks 1947, 36.

64. B.H. April 1948, 26.

65. Carroll 1970, 257–258.

66. "Patti Andrews Wed to Agent" 1947.

67. "Strictly Ad Lib by the Square" 1942, 4.

68. Woods 1994, 156–157.

69. Woods 1994, 155–156.

70. Hotchner 1976, 123.

71. Hotchner 1976, 175.

72. Hotchner 1976, 218.

73. Hotchner 1976, 218.

74. Hotchner 1976, 236.

75. Hotchner 1976, 238.

76. Gladys Leichter interview by author, 2001.

77. Emge 1948, 8.

78. B. U. 1948, 22.

79. Whitburn 1986, 28, 113.

80. "The Year's Best Selling Popular Retail Records" 1948, 18.

81. "The Year's Top Popular Retail Record Sellers" 1948, 19.

Ten. 1948–1949

1. "We Couldn't Believe It!!" 1948, 29.

2. "Listen to the Andrews Sisters" 1948, 48.

3. "Decca Aboard 'Woodpecker'" 1948, 41.

4. "Andrews—Wow!—Boff!—Socko!" 1948, 64.

5. Ardmore 1974, 93.

6. Brog 1948, 13.

7. Crowther 1948, 28.

8. B. H. July 1948, 26.

9. Smith 1948, 40.

10. "Visitors Boost B'way; 'Regards' Plus Andrews Sis-Martin & Lewis-Iceshow Wow 125G, 'Apache'-Horne Sock 116G" 1948, 13.

11. Ardmore 1974, 94.

12. Arlene Traxler interview by author, 2002.

13. Jones 1956, 1.

14. Kendall 1977, 37.

15. Wallace circa 1940.

16. Ollie Andrews, "Last Will and Testament" 1946.

17. Gladys Leichter interview by author, 2001.

18. "Andrews Sis Get British Clearance For U.S. Musikers" 1948, 38.

19. "Inside Orchestras—Music" 1948, 36.

20. "London Palladium, The Andrews Sisters" 1948, 7.

21. "Andrews Sisters' Dynamic Success at London Palladium!" 1948, 1.

22. Myro 1948, 47.

23. Waggoner 1948, 39.

24. Allen 25 Aug. 1948, 15.

25. "Andrews Sisters' Boff London Hit" 1948, 41.

26. Jones 1948, 2.

27. Henshaw and Jones 1948, 3.

28. "Andrews Sis Record 2 Songs in London" 1948, 34; "Decca Initiates Foreign Waxing" 1948, 14.

29. Allen 22 Sept. 1948, 1.

30. "Last Minute MU Action Stops Andrews' Waxing" 1948, 1.

31. "Andrews Sisters' Special Show for Olympicers at London Palladium" 1948, 45.

32. "Scalpers Got $15-$20 For Andrews Sis' Socko Lond. Palladium Finale" 1948, 44.

33. "Last Minute MU Action Stops Andrews' Waxing" 1948, 1.

34. "We Couldn't Believe It!!!" 1948, 28–29.

35. "Louis Ruggiero" 1995, B-11.

36. Arthur Ruggiero interview by author, 2000.

37. Gladys Leichter interview by author, 2001.

38. Safford 1951, 22.

39. "Disk Executive and Andrews Sister Marry" 1948, I-12.

40. Arthur Ruggiero interview by author, 2000.

41. Arthur Ruggiero interview by author, 2000.

42. Gladys Leichter interview by author, 2001.

43. Stein 1979, 43.

44. Hopper 1948, 8.

45. "Andrews Sis in 5-Yr. Decca Deal" 1948, 43.

46. Whitburn 1986, 28–29.

47. "The Year's Top Singing Instrumental Groups on the Nation's Juke Boxes" 1949, 59.

48. "The Year's Top Selling Singing and Instrumental Groups Over Retail Counters" 1949, 19.

49. Henshaw and Jones 1948, 3.

50. Ruhlmann 1995, 106.

51. Ruhlmann 1995, 106.

52. Gil-Montero 1989, 175.

53. Glassner 1974, 26.

54. Gavin 1996, 29.

55. "Andrews Trio Dip Into Hillbilly Music" 1949, 41.

56. Ward, Stokes and Tucker 1986, 44–45.
57. Ruhlmann 1995, 106.
58. Pugh 1996, 159–160.
59. Ruhlmann 1995, 106.
60. "Maxene Andrews Wins Divorce" 11 March 1949.
61. "Maxene Andrews Wins Divorce" 12 March 1949, 10.
62. Parish and Pitts 1991, 27.
63. Wilson 1949.
64. Gladys Leichter interview by author, 2001.
65. Duggan 1950, VII-4.
66. Brady 2001, 139.
67. Brady 2001, 169.
68. Green 1949, 37.
69. Green 1949, 37.
70. Hall 1989, 181.
71. Ruhlmann 1995, 106.
72. Bundy 1949, 45.
73. "Ho-Ho-Kus, N. J., Plugs Song of Same Name" 1949, 45.
74. "Ho-Ho-Kus Party" 1949, 27.
75. Burm 1949, 48.
76. Greg 1949, 111.
77. "Blair—Blackburns Fill in for Andrews Sis" 1949, 44.
78. "Spikes Rumored Andrews Split" 1949, 21.
79. Wood 7 Sept. 1949, 28.
80. "Kapp to Decide on Giveaway Album" 1949, 40.
81. "Decca, Campbell Soup Set Album on Radio Show" 1949, 1, 16.
82. "Campbell Airshow to Intro Disney's 'Cinderella' Score" 1949, 60.
83. "Tragedy Hits Twice— In Same Way—In Andrews Sisters Parents' Death" 1949, 42.
84. Gladys Leichter interview by author, 2001.
85. Ruhlmann 1995, 32.
86. Scourby 1984, 19.
87. Ardmore 1974, 94.
88. Gladys Leichter interview by author, 2001.
89. Peter Andrews, "Last Will and Testament of Peter Andrews," 1949.
90. "Dave Kapp Personally Takes a Hand to Win Disk Jockey Friends" 1949, 41.
91. Ruhlmann 1995, 108.
92. "Disc Brings Andrews Sister Solo Bookings" 1949, 2.
93. Adams 1949.
94. Whitburn 1986, 29, 113.

Eleven. 1950–1953

1. "Station KXLW" 1950, 56.
2. "Top Singing and Instrumental Groups on Juke Boxes" 1950, 77.
3. "The Year's Top Popular Records" 1950, 14.
4. "The Year's Top Selling Folk Artists" 1950, 19.
5. Woods 1994, 156–157.
6. Hopper 1948, 8.
7. Hotchner 1976, 238.
8. Hotchner 1976, 238.
9. Woods 1994, 157.
10. Hotchner 1976, 126.
11. Hotchner 1976, 122–123.
12. "Patti Andrews Asks Divorce, No Alimony" 1950, III-10.
13. "Andrews Sister Wins Divorce From Manager" 1950, I-2.
14. Levy 1950, 16.
15. "He's Our Boy, Vic!" 1950, 17.
16. "Inside Orchestras—Music" 16 Aug. 1950, 42.
17. Zabe 1950, 47.
18. Herm 1950, 22.
19. Murphy 1950, 44.
20. "Andrews Sisters ... Greatest Business in History of the Fairmount [sic] Hotel..." 1950, 57.
21. Chan 1950, 20.
22. "Campbell Mulls TV'ers on 'Club 15,' 'Double'" 1950, 27.
23. "Icer, Andrews Sisters, Haymes, Bob Crosby Unit to Sacramento" 1950, 66.
24. "Chase Club, St. Loo" 1950, 50.
25. "Station KXLW" 1950, 56.
26. "Andrews Sis, Ritz Bros., Raye May Sub for Berle" 1950, 30.
27. "Gov. of Hawaii Turning Plugger for Native Tune" 1950, 1.
28. Whitburn 1986, 29, 113.
29. "Andrews Sis 50G TV Film Auditions" 1950, 1.
30. "Andrews Sis Quit Radio for Video" 1951, 23.
31. "Andrews Sisters Quit 'Club 15' For TV Show" 1951, 18.
32. "Radio and Television Program Reviews: holiday Star Varieties" 1948, 8.
33. "Television Follow-Up: Frank Sinatra Show" 1951, 30.
34. "Television Follow-Up: Tony Martin" 1951, 30.
35. Csida "Colgate Hour (The Tony Martin Show)" 17 March 1951, 11.
36. Csida, "Texaco Star Theater" 17 March 1951, 11.
37. Will 1951, 46.
38. "Andrews Sisters Given Rousing Welcome on Home Town Appearance" 1951, 63.
39. "Nieces Are in Town" 1951.
40. Safford 1951, 22.
41. "Just Ask: Do You Sing in the Bathtub?" 1951, 6.
42. "The Andrews Sisters" 18 April 1951, 30.
43. Jones 1951, 15.
44. Gladys Leichter interview by author, 2001.
45. "Capitol, Wash" 1951, 22.
46. Jose 1951, 20.
47. "Dave Kapp Exits Decca, Which His Brother Co-Founded 17 Years Ago" 1951, 45.
48. "Maxene Andrews, Okay After Surgery, May Make London Palladium July 30" 1951, 51.
49. "Andrews Sisters Here For $200,000 Television Work-Out" 1951, 7.
50. Myro 1951, 55.
51. Vance 1951, 3.
52. Brand 1951, 2.
53. "The Palladium" 1951, 8.
54. "Scots hustle to write new Andrews Sisters song" 1951, 6.
55. "Mary Martin Surprise Visitor to Andrews Sis" 1951, 2.
56. *Scottish Daily Mail,* 1951.
57. "Andrews Gals Hear Clan Bard Sing" 1951, 17.
58. Mitchell 1967, 35.
59. *Birmingham Evening Dispatch* 1951.
60. "Andrews Sisters to record 45-min. 'Farewell to Britain'" 1951, 6.
61. Ruhlmann 1995, 108, 110.
62. "Schoen, Andrews Sis Split After 16 Years" 1951, 53.

63. "Schoen Quits Andrews Unit; Weighs Plans" 1951, 14.
64. "Vic Schoen Leaves Andrews Sisters" 1951, 1.
65. "Publisher Lou Levy weds in London" 1951, 1.
66. Kinkle 1974, 1712.
67. Jaques Cattell Press 1980, 447; "Vic Schoen; Musical Director for Andrews Sisters" 2000, A-14.
68. Gagh 1951, 65.
69. Stal 1951, 30.
70. "Andrews Sisters Offer Truman $5,000 for Piano" 1952.
71. "Patty Andrews Wed on Coast" 1951, 20.
72. Whitburn 1986, 29, 113.
73. Ruhlmann 1995, 110.
74. "New Front For Andrews Gals" 1952, 1.
75. "Andrews Sign MCA Contract" 1952, 15.
76. "Levy Denies He's Split as Manager of Andrews Sis" 1952, 29.
77. "Andrews Sisters Win 157G Judgment From Their Own Corporation" 1952, 41; "Andrews Trio Pull Legal Coup" 1952, 1.
78. "Levy Asks Court Oust Andrews Sis, Name Receiver for Firm" 1952, 38.
79. "'Amusing,' Comments the Andrews Sisters" 1952, 10.
80. "Lou Levy Launches 500G Suit Vs. Andrews Sisters in Corporation Wrangle" 1952, 39.
81. "Court Rules for Andrews Sisters in Suit" 1953, I-2.
82. "Blossom Music Sues Andrews, Seeking 10G" 1953, 14.
83. Ardmore 1974, 94.
84. Ruhlmann 1995, 110.
85. Leon Belasco letter, 1976.
86. Maxene and Patty Andrews interview by Rex Reed, 1974.
87. "Fourth Sister?" 1945, 15.
88. Wilson 1949.
89. Morris circa 1945, m13.
90. Morris circa 1945, m13.
91. Crichton 1939, 44.
92. Dexter 1941, 32–33.
93. Levy Jan./Feb.1990, 60.
94. Levy Jan./Feb. 1990, 61.

95. Galloway 1995, 82.
96. "Publisher's Desk" 1990, 2.
97. "Andrews Sis First of Hawaiian 100G" 1952, 48.
98. "Andrews Sisters Given Unusual Airport Greeting" 1952, 5.
99. McClay 1952, 15.
100. "Andrews Sister's 'Fan' Would Give Her $187,000" 1952, II-1.
101. Reed 1952, 61.
102. Helm 30 April 1952, 48.
103. Zhito 1952, 15.
104. "In San Francisco" 1952, 26.
105. Gord 1952, 32.
106. Ted 1952, 52.
107. Forrest 1952, G-4.
108. "No Kin of Andrews, Says Ex-Wife of Patty's Mate" 1952, II-1.
109. Gross 15 Oct. 1952, 38.
110. Simon 1953, 27.
111. Laredo 1996, 11.
112. Helm 5 Nov. 1952, 50.
113. Sippel 1952, 15.
114. McStay 1952, 53.
115. Will 1952, 43.
116. Jimmy Nelson letter, 2000.
117. Jimmy Nelson interview by author, 2000.
118. Newt 1953, 54.
119. "Strictly Ad Lib" 1953, 21.
120. "Daily Diary" 1953.
121. Campbell 1985, 5 C14.
122. Coates 1953, 10.
123. "Famed Andrew [sic] Sisters Lack Harmony Now" 1953.
124. In 1992, Maxene's audition tape was released on an album called An Evening with Frank Loesser.
125. I could find no record of Maxene's appearance in Sacramento for summer 1953. She was probably referring to her appearance in One Touch of Venus in Sacramento the following summer.
126. Ruhlmann 1995, 110.
127. Graham 1953.
128. Gould 1953, 55.
129. Las Vegas Morning Sun 1953.
130. "Burton Pilots Andrews Gals" 1953, 22.
131. Parsons 1953.
132. "L.A. Toasts Royal

Pair at Scintillating Banquet." 1953, 10.
133. "Aver 'Command' Show for Greek Rulers Unruly" 1953, 1.

Twelve. 1954–1956

1. "Patti Leaves Again" 1954, 3.
2. "Patti Leaves Again" 1954, 3.
3. Stein 1979, 43.
4. O'Connor 27 Aug. 1954, A-7.
5. "Patti Andrews Gets Buildup As Single" 1951, 19.
6. Orodenker 1938, 16.
7. Ruhlmann 1995, 26.
8. Ruhlmann 1995, 108.
9. Hall 1989, 182.
10. Maxene Andrews interview on One Night Stand, circa 1974.
11. Coates 1953, 10.
12. Ruhlmann 1995, 108.
13. Mosby 18 March 1954.
14. Mosby 29 July 1954.
15. "Maxene Andrews Tried Suicide, Police Say" 1954.
16. Andrews Sisters interview by Johnny Carson, 1965.
17. "Laverne Andrews, 51, Is Dead; Eldest of Andrews Sisters Trio" 1967, 47.
18. Ruhlmann 1995, 110.
19. Simon, George T. and Friends 1979, 13.
20. Stein 1979, 43.
21. Smith 1974, 110.
22. Patty Andrews interview by Richard Lamparski, circa 1972.
23. Smith 1974, 110.
24. Bob, "Patty Andrews" 1954, 50.
25. Lewy 1954, 5.
26. Oncken 1954, 39.
27. Patty Andrews interview by Richard Lamparski, circa 1972.
28. O'Connor 27 August 1954, A-7.
29. Schallert 1954, III-7.
30. Mosby 30 July 1954, 15.
31. Mosby 30 July 1954, 15.
32. "Andrews Sis to Go on Despite Patti Ankling" 1954, 2.

33. Mosby 18 March 1954.
34. English 1954.
35. Glackin 1954, 3.
36. Mark 1954, 61.
37. "Patti Andrews Gets Checkup" 1954, I-18.
38. "Andrews Sisters' Big 'Threat' from Orig. Disks" 1954, 56.
39. "Andrews' New Pard" 1954, 65.
40. "Skelton Skit Miffs Patty Andrews" 1954, 24.
41. "Patti Andrews files will suit against LaVerne" 1954.
42. "Andrews Sisters Tangle in Court" 1954, I-2.
43. "Andrews Sue Over Estate" 1955, 1–15.
44. "Andrews Sis May Stay As Duo Depending on Aussie Aud Reaction" 1954, 41.
45. *Sydney Morning Herald* 1954.
46. Charles Saunders Collection.
47. "Singer Denies She Tried to Kill Herself" 1954, 16.
48. "Maxene Andrews Treated for Overdose of Pills" 1954, 18.
49. "Singer Denies She Tried to Kill Herself" 1954, 16.
50. Gladys Leichter interview by author, 2001.
51. Maxene Andrews Tried Suicide, Police Say" 1954.
52. "Suicide Try Denied by Singer" 1954, 1.
53. "Maxene Andrews Denies Suicide Try" 1954, 1.
54. "Maxene Andrews Denies Suicide Try" 1954, 1.
55. "Suicide Try Denied by Singer" 1954, 2.
56. Francis 1955, 13.
57. Jose 1955, 60.
58. "Patty Andrews" 1954, 57.
59. "Capitol Adds Patti Andrews, Geo. Shearing." 1955, 40.
60. "Patti Andrews Exits Chez Paree in Billing Row" 1955, 59.
61. "Patti Andrews Quits Job Here" 1955.
62. "Patti Andrews Exits Chez Paree in Billing Row" 1955, 59.
63. Mark 1955, 68.
64. Kap 1955, 51.
65. Will 1956, 53.

66. "Reviews of New Pop Records" 1956, 55.
67. Wilson 16 Nov. 1979, C-3.
68. Wilson 16 Nov. 1979, C-3.
69. Jose 1956, 70.
70. Hagen 1974, 16.
71. Stein 1979, 43.
72. Leed 1979.
73. Sternig 1977, 26.
74. Rose 1974, 20.
75. O'Connor 27 August 1954, A-7.
76. *Las Vegas Sun,* 3 July 1956:
77. O'Connor 27 Aug. 1954, A-7.
78. Reed 1974, 6–3.
79. Patty Andrews interview by Richard Lamparski, circa 1972.
80. Heffernan 1959, 18.
81. Hopper 1956, 25.
82. Heffernan 1959, 18.
83. Maxene Andrews and Patty Andrews interview by Rex Reed, 1974.
84. "Hatchet Buried" 1956, 1.
85. "Andrews Sisters (3)" 1956, 41.
86. McKinley 1954, 44.
87. Ames 1956, V-14.
88. "Andrews Sisters Smash Hollywood Record!!" 1956, 40–41.
89. Alan 1956, 53.
90. Reed 1974, 6–3.
91. "Andrews Sisters Launch New Career After Spat" 1956, 24.
92. Stein 1979, 43.
93. "Laverne Andrews, 51, Is Dead; Eldest of Andrews Sisters Trio" 1967, 47.
94. "Andrews Sis Vice Vic" 1956, 48.
95. "Joe Russell" circa 1956.
96. Jones 1956, 1.

Thirteen. 1957–1968

1. Price 1961.
2. Koll 1957, 54.
3. Mark 1957, 63.
4. Soul 1958, 63.
5. Lary 1958, 70.
6. Koll 1958, 70.
7. *Las Vegas Sun* 1958.
8. Long 1959, 55.

9. Herm 1959, 55.
10. "Andrews Sisters at Bellevue in Good, Mellow Performance" 1959.
11. "After Dark: Andrews Sisters at Lotus" 1959.
12. *Washington Daily Press* 1959.
13. Walk 1959, 53.
14. Meyers 1960.
15. "Andrews Sisters slam rock" 1960, 10.
16. Myro 1960, 55.
17. Duke 1961, 70.
18. Saunders, undated.
19. "Hot Spots Checked in Topanga Blaze" 1961, 1.
20. Scul 1962, 55.
21. Liuz 1962, 60.
22. Jose 1962, 173.
23. Don 1962, 59.
24. Skip 1962, 42.
25. Dong 1963, 59.
26. Liuz 1963, 51.
27. Gladys Leichter interview by author, 2001.
28. Shaw 1964, 85.
29. Luiz 1964, 53.
30. Long 1964, 58.
31. Liuz 1965, 66.
32. Long 1965, 58.
33. Barnard 1965, D-12.
34. Long 1966, 61.
35. Kleiner 1959.
36. Heffernan 1959, 18.
37. "U. S. Sues Andrews Sisters" 1960, 90.
38. Wilson, Mary 1999, 185–186.
39. Gros 1957, 42.
40. Schoenfeld 1957, 58.
41. Schoenfeld 1957, 44.
42. Ruhlmann 1995, 111.
43. Patty Andrews interview by Richard Lamparski, circa 1972.
44. "Album Reviews" 1957, 62.
45. Saunders undated.
46. "Dean Martin, Christy Minstrels, Everly Bros., 'Best,' 'Beatle Jazz,' Peggy Lee, Kelly Lester top New LPs" 1964, 42.
47. Ruhlmann 1995, 112.
48. Charles Saunders Collection.
49. Sternig 1977, 26.
50. Gladys Leichter interview by author, 2001.
51. Arthur Ruggiero interview by author, 2000.
52. Gladys Leichter interview by author, 2001.

53. Joyce DeYoung interview by author, 2000.

54. Mitchell 1967, 35.

55. Joyce DeYoung letter, 2000.

56. Maxene and Patty Andrews interview by Rex Reed, 1974.

57. Joyce DeYoung interview by author, 2000.

58. Laverne Andrews "Last Will of LaVerne Andrews Ruggiero" 1960.

59. Reed 1974, 6–3.

60. Mitchell 1967, 35.

61. "New Singer Added to the Andrews Trio" 1967.

62. Kell 1967, 55.

63. Liuz 1967, 59.

64. "Police Variety Show Monday" 1967.

65. Perry 1967.

66. Joyce DeYoung letter, 2000.

67. Mitchell 1967, 35.

68. "Andrews Sisters Swing Into Harvey's for Christmas, New Year Appearance" 1967, 4.

69. "Andrews Sisters Plus David Frye Are Show Stoppers at Bimbo's 365 Club" 1968, 42.

70. Long 1968, 59.

71. Joyce DeYoung continued in show business on *The Carol Burnett Show* as an administrative assistant and occasional background singer where she remained until her retirement in 1980.

Fourteen.
1968–1974

1. Miller 1981, E-8.

2. "An Andrews Sister Takes College Post" 1968, 2.

3. Drewes 1968, 9.

4. Drewes 1968, 9.

5. Drewes 1968, 9.

6. Dexter 1969, 25.

7. "Do You Remember ... The Andrews Sisters?" Circa 1972.

8. Charles Saunders Collection.

9. Wilson 1974, II-3.

10. Fidelman 1999, 246.

11. Glassner 1974, 27.

12. Patty Andrews interview by Richard Lamparski, circa 1972.

13. Thomas Undated.

14. Lieberman 1971.

15. Maxene and Patty Andrews interview by Rex Reed, 1974.

16. Patty Andrews interview by Richard Lamparski, circa 1972.

17. Lieberman 1971.

18. "City Hails the Men of Son Tay" 1973, 3.

19. Hagen 1974, 16–17.

20. Gavin 1996, 6.

21. Mair 1995, 86.

22. Grein 1987, VI-4.

23. Smith 1974, 111.

24. Ruhlmann 1995, 112.

25. Levin 1978.

26. Forsmark 1974, 23.

27. "Andrews Sisters Date" 1973.

28. "Maxene Andrews Joins Stevens to Form Prod. Co." 1974.

29. Jim Weston interview by author, 2000.

30. Barnes 1974, 51.

31. Kerr 1974, II-5.

32. Higgins 1974, 9.

33. "Maxene the Party Pooper" 1974.

34. Hagen 1974, 17.

35. Wilson 1974, II-3.

36. Smith 1974, 110.

37. Patty Andrews interview by Richard Lamparski, circa 1972.

38. Reed 1974, 6–3.

39. Jim Weston interview by author, 2000.

40. Beth Fowler interview by author, 2001.

41. Beth Fowler interview by author, 2001.

42. Beth Fowler interview by author, 2001.

43. Beth Fowler interview by author, 2001.

44. Wilson 1979, C-3.

45. Beth Fowler interview by author, 2001.

46. Beth Fowler interview by author, 2001.

47. Jim Weston interview by author, 2000.

48. Reed 1977, 151.

49. Reed 1977, 151–152.

50. "Patti Andrews Vs. 'Over Here'" 1975, 88.

51. Reed 1977, 152–153.

52. Calta 1974, 18–5.

53. Reed 1975; 1977.

54. Reed 1977, 154.

55. "Patti Andrews Vs. 'Over Here'" 1975, 88.

56. Cook 1976, 75.

57. Bacon 8 Jan. 1976, A-12.

58. Bacon 15 Jan. 1976.

59. Joyce DeYoung interview by author, 2000.

60. Reed 1974, 6–3.

61. Wilson 1974, II-1.

62. Jim Weston interview by author, 2000.

63. Beth Fowler interview by author, 2001.

64. Podesta 1977.

65. Weintraub 1979, C-1.

66. Wilson 1979, C-3.

67. "No Harmony Between the Andrews Sisters" 1980, 9.

68. Roura and Poster 1980.

69. Harris 1980, E-14.

70. Tagashira 1981.

71. Stein 1979, 43.

72. Keerdoja 1979, 21.

73. Weschler 1979, 14.

74. Miller 1981, E-8.

75. Hawn 1985, VI-2.

76. Grein 1987, VI-4.

77. Grein 1987, VI-4.

78. Grein 1987, VI-4.

79. Van Matre 1988, 10.

80. Hall 1989, 182.

81. Terry, 1993, V-10.

82. Gladys Leichter interview by author, 2000.

83. Gladys Leichter interview by author, 2000.

84. Gladys Leichter interview by author, 2000.

Fifteen.
1975–1987

1. Goldin 1979.

2. Roso 1980, 107.

3. "Do You Remember ... The Andrews Sisters?" circa 1972.

4. Wilson 1979, C-3.

5. Stearns 1995, D-4.

6. O'Haire 1975.

7. Jose 1975, 114.

8. Beth Fowler interview by author, 2001.

9. Widem 1976, 22.

10. Lipper 1978, 30.

11. Wilson 1979, C-3.

12. Garfield 1985, 23, 26.

13. Leed 1979.

14. Bell 1980, F-3.

15. Silvert 1979, 56.
16. Neff 1979, 83.
17. Hunt 1979, 26.
18. Keerdoja 1979, 21–22.
19. Wilson 1979, C-3.
20. David McCain letter, 2000.
21. Goldin 1979.
22. Stokes 1979, D-15.
23. Conway 1980, 4.
24. Crenshaw 1980, F-5.
25. Nachman 1981, 40.
26. Wendeborn, 7 April 1981.
27. Smith 1981.
28. Patrick, 1982.
29. Cummings1980, B-4.
30. Bell 1980, F-3.
31. "UCLA archives deposit" 1980.
32. "Maxene Andrews" 1981, 19.
33. Tagashira 1981.
34. Vettel 1982, IV-7.
35. Johnny Gunn letter, 2001.
36. "Singer's condition 'fair'" 1982.
37. Hitchens 1992, 20.
38. Hawn 1985, VI-2.
39. Gladys Leichter interview by author, 2000.
40. Bailey 1983, 2.
41. Kirk 1983, 93.
42. Hunt 1983, 18.
43. O'Reilly 1985.
44. McNally 1985, E-4.
45. Hawn 1985,VI-2–3.
46. Hall 1989, 170.
47. Hagan 1974, 18.
48. "Sister" 1991, 34.
49. McLellan 1979, E-1.
50. Leed 1979.
51. Miller 1981, E-8.
52. Miller 1981, E-8.
53. Hall 1989, 186.
54. Holt 1975.
55. McLellan 1979, E-1.
56. Barnard 1965, D-12.
57. "Do You Remember … The Andrews Sisters?" circa 1972.
58. Wilson 1974, II-3.
59. Stein 1979, 43.
60. Campbell 1985, 5-C-14.
61. Stearns 1995, D-4.
62. Hagen 1974, 17.
63. Gladys Leichter interview by author, 2000.
64. Drewes, 1968, 9.
65. Hagen 1974, 17.
66. Hagen 1974, 18.
67. Ardmore 1974, 94.

68. Podesta 1977.
69. Stein 1979, 43.
70. McLellan 1979, E-1.
71. Weintraub 1979, C-1.
72. Wilson 1979, C-3.
73. Miller 1981, E-8.
74. Garfield 1985, 26.
75. Glassner 1974, 27.
76. Podesta 1977.
77. "Followup" 1977.
78. "Gonged" circa 1978.
79. Roso 1980, 107.
80. Wilson 1980, C-9.
81. Christon 1981, 5.
82. Edwa 1981, 91.
83. Crotta 1981, B-1, 6.
84. Lit 25 August 1982, 85.
85. Lit 17 Nov. 1982, 79.
86. *Hollywood Reporter* 10 Oct.1986.
87. Patty Andrews interview by Richard Lamparski, circa 1972.
88. Spatz 1987, F-7.
89. Chadwick 1987.
90. Chadwick 1987.

Sixteen. 1987–2002

1. Weinberger 1987.
2. "Maxene will sing here for Army Days '87" 1987, B-5.
3. Weinberger 1987.
4. Ken Petrack interview by author, 2000.
5. Grein 1987, VI-1.
6. The Andrews Sisters 50th Anniversary Collection. *Volume II, 1987.*
7. Van Matre 1988, 10–11.
8. Shapiro 1991, 68.
9. Mazo 1992, 72.
10. Jacobs 1991, 21–22.
11. Mazo 1992, 72.
12. Dunning 1991, C-3.
13. "Personalities: Boogie Woogie Redux" 1991, F-3.
14. Robert Boyer letter to author, 2000.
15. Adams 1992, 10.
16. Hitchens 1992, 20.
17. Mazo 1992, 76.
18. Dunning 1992, C-13.
19. "Sister" 1991, 34.
20. Dunning 1991, C-3.
21. Tracy 1992.
22. Hitchens 1992, 20.
23. Robert Boyer letter to author, 2000.
24. Gladys Leichter interview by author, 2001.

25. Joyce DeYoung interview by author, 2000.
26. Beth Fowler interview by author, 2001.
27. *The Advocate* 1976.
28. McLellan 1979, E-1.
29. Leed 1979.
30. Bell 1980, F-3.
31. Cook 1976, 75.
32. Miller 1981, E-8.
33. McNally 1985, E-4.
34. Gladys Leichter interview by author, 2001.
35. Wilkes 1993, 1760–1761.
36. Fuller 1993, E-4.
37. Terry 1993, V-1.
38. Wells 1994, 10.
39. Adcock 1995, C-1.
40. Brozan 1995, A-24.
41. Gladys Leichter interview by author, 2001.
42. Stearns 1995, D-4.
43. Gross 1995, B-1.
44. Gross 1995, B-l.
45. "Maxene Andrews, of Andrews Sisters, dies" 1995.
46. Gross 1995, B-3.
47. Ken Petrack interview by author, 2000.
48. Ray Hagen interview by author, 2000.
49. Joyce DeYoung interview by author, 2000.
50. "Maxene Andrews' Memorial Service" 1995.
51. The Music Corporation of America (MCA) published a memorial to Maxene in several trade publications, which included her picture and the following text: "In Memory of Maxene Andrews Who with the Andrews Sisters Brought Us Hope in Times of Strife and in More Than One Hundred Hits a Legacy of Joy, Success and Variety."
52. Reed 1995.
53. Ruhlmann 1995, 114.
54. Gladys Leichter interview by author, 2001.
55. Andrews, Patty 1998, B-5.
56. Everett Searcy letter, 2000.
57. Archerd 2001, 4.
58. Royce 2002.

Afterword

1. Heuring undated.

2. Clooney and Barthel 1999, 93.

3. Jenna Wimms Hashway letter, 2000.

4. "Concert Coming to D-Day memorial" 2001.

5. Berube 1990, 90.

6. Van Iquity 1998, 24.

7. Maxene and Patty Andrews interview by Rex Reed 1974.

8. "First group of inductees chosen for Vocal Group Hall of Fame" 1998.

9. Stanley T. Andrews letter to author, 2000.

10. David Schuster letter to author, 2000.

11. Bill Scott letter to author, 2000.

12. Al Dias letter to author, 2000.

13. Al Haas letter to author, 2000.

14. Jay Jones letter to author, 2000.

15. Beverly Thun letter to author, 2001.

16. Travis Lafferty letter to author, 2000.

17. Raymond Harvey letter to author, 2000.

18. Dawn Gould letter to author, 2001.

19. Herm Renner letter to author, 2001.

20. Bonnie Carroll letter to author, 2000.

21. Calvin O. Perry, Jr. letter to author, 2001.

22. Gene May letter to author, 2001.

23. David Lebovitz letter to author, 2000.

Appendix 1.
Discography

1. Reed 1974, 6–3.

2. "Decca's One Million Sellers" 1954, 55.

3. "Decca's 'Million' Club" 1954, 6.

4. Sforza 2000, 185; Murrells, 1984.

5. McClintock and Gallo 2001, 1.

6. Grudens 1996, 32.

7. Hall 1989, 182.

8. Kiner and Mackenzie 1990, x–xviii.

Bibliography

Entries that contain "collection," such as "Merle Smith Collection," are newspaper and magazine clippings from private collections that do not have complete bibliographic data.

Abbott, Sam. "Orpheum, Los Angeles." *The Bill-board*, 20 June 1942, 17.

"'Abbott-Costello,' Pic Title." *Variety*, 9 April 1941, 1.

Abel. "Follow the Boys." *Variety*, 29 March 1944, 21.

_____. "Glass Hat, N.Y." *Variety*, 21 December 1938, 41.

_____. "Hollywood Canteen." *Variety*, 6 December 1944, 14.

_____. "Make Mine Music." *Variety*, 17 April 1946, 16.

_____. "Paramount, N.Y." *Variety*, 5 July 1939, 44.

_____. "Paramount, N.Y." *Variety*, 30 June 1943, 46.

Adams, Cedric. "In This Corner." *Minneapolis Star-Journal*, 13 March 1943, 7.

_____. "In This Corner." *Minneapolis Star*, 16 April 1951, 44.

_____. "Three Little Sisters." *Minneapolis Tribune*, 11 December 1949.

Adams, Cindy. "Cindy Adams." *New York Post*, 1 July 1992, 10.

Adcock, Joe. "Cheery Escapism Saves 'Follies' in the End." *Seattle Post-Intelligencer*, 29 April 1995, C-1.

The Advocate. Item about Maxene Andrews' book. February 11, 1976. Everett Searcy Collection.

"After Dark: Andrews Sisters at Lotus." H. M. DC Press, August 1959. Charles Saunders Collection.

Alan. "Flamingo, Las Vegas." *Variety*, 4 July 1956, 53.

"Album Reviews." *Variety*, 16 October 1957, 62.

Alden, John. "Seeing the Movies." *The Minneapolis Tribune*, 15 October 1938, 14.

Alden, Ken. "Facing the Music." *Radio Mirror*, August 1943, 4.

Allen, Rex. "Recording Artists Roster—A Twentieth Anniversary Special." *Down Beat,* 30 June 1954, 85.

Allen, Stuart S. "Andrews Sisters Draw Top Palladium Plaudits." *Down Beat*, 25 August 1948, 15.

_____. "British Musicians Forbidden to Wax with U.S. Artists." *Down Beat*, 22 September 1948, 1.

"Ambassador Theatre War Workers Show." *St. Louis Post-Dispatch*, 21 November 1942, D-5.

"American Theatre Wing." *The Billboard*, 29 January 1944, 5.

Ames, Walter. "Sisters Everywhere! Andrews, McGuires Hold Get-Together." *Los Angeles Times*, 6 June 1956, V-14.

"'Amusing,' Comments the Andrews Sisters." *Variety*, 9 June 1952, 10.

Andrews, LaVerne. "Sing Sing Trend to Swing Reported by Andrews Sisters." *Swing*, February 1940, 4.

Andrews, Maxene. "Boogie Woogie Bugle Boy." In *The Good War* by Studs Terkel. New York: Pantheon Books, 1984.

_____. "How 'Bei Mir Bist Du Schoen' Became

a Hit." *Sheet Music*, September/October 1990, 11, 60.

_____. "Maxene Andrews." *The Atlantic*, July 1984, 69–72.

_____. *The Andrews Sisters 50th Anniversary Collection*. Volume 1. Compact Disc Booklet. MCA Records, 1987.

_____, and Bill Gilbert. *Over Here, Over There*. New York: Kensington Publishing Corporation, 1993.

Andrews, Patty. *The Andrews Sisters 50th Anniversary Collection*. Volume 1. Compact Disc Booklet. MCA Records, 1987.

_____. "Bugle Boys of Company B Died to Keep America Free." *Los Angeles Times*, 25 May 1998, B-5.

"Andrews, Ayres Hit 50G in Chi; Oriental Weak." *The Billboard*, 29 January 1944, 21.

"Andrews Buck Heat, Cop Near-High 10G." *The Billboard*, 3 July 1943, 19.

"Andrews Draw Big $27,900 in Buffalo." *The Billboard*, 29 May 1943, 18.

"Andrews Earn Their Top Vaude Salary." *The Billboard*, 14 February 1942, 30.

"Andrews Gals $30,000 in Philly; Fay's Hit Average." *The Billboard*, 7 November 1942, 14.

"Andrews Gals Big 24G in Pittsburgh." *The Billboard*, 22 March 1941, 20.

"Andrews Gals Hear Clan Bard Sing." *Down Beat*, 30 November 1951, 17.

"Andrews Gals May Break Over PA." *Variety*, 21 February 1940, 21.

"Andrews Gals, Miller, Crosby Poll Toppers." *Variety*, 21 February 1945, 41.

"Andrews Gals Only Bright Spot in Pic." *Hollywood Reporter*, 24 January 1945.

"Andrews Gals' Show Getting New Scripters." *Variety*, 7 March 1945, 31.

"Andrews, Krupa Near Record in Pittsburgh." *The Billboard*, 19 July 1941, 24.

"Andrews Lift 'Miracle' to Wham $35,000 Cincy." *Variety*, 27 November 1946, 20.

"Andrews-Murray Tie-Up." *The Billboard*, 22 July 1939, 11.

"Andrews' New Pard." *Variety*, 24 November 1954, 65.

"Andrews-'Parachute' Hefty $16,000 in Balto." *Variety*, 7 September 1941, 15.

"Andrews' Pic Plans." *Variety*, 24 May 1944, 2.

"Andrews Sign MCA Contract." *The Billboard*, 1 March 1952, 15.

"Andrews Sis-Ayres Tilt 'Hostages' Big $45,000, Det.; 'Woman' Tall 39G." *Variety*, 26 January 1944, 16.

"Andrews Sis-Ayres Up 'Pittsburgh' to $19,000, Mpls; 'Rhythm' 9G H.O." *Variety*, 17 March 1943, 10.

"Andrews Sis Bowing Out March 27 as N-K Pulls In Horns; Set New Show." *Variety*, 27 February 1946, 29.

"Andrews Sis' '8-Bar' Idea Into Autry Pic." *Variety*, 7 August 1946, 3.

"Andrews Sis 18G 'take' in Record San Diego Wk." *Variety*, 23 May 1945, 48.

"Andrews Sis' 15G Plus % in Chi, Their Tops." *Variety*, 3 May 1944, 1.

"Andrews Sis 50G TV Film Auditions." *Variety*, 26 July 1950, 1.

"Andrews Sis First of Hawaiian 100G." *Variety*, 12 March 1952, 48.

"Andrews Sis Get British Clearance for U. S. Musikers." *Variety*, 21 July 1948, 38.

"Andrews Sis in 5-Yr. Decca Deal." *Variety*, 15 December 1948, 43.

"Andrews Sis 'Kidnapping' Gives GIs Ad Lib Show." *Variety*, 25 July 1945, 2.

"Andrews Sis Like Concerts, Want More." *Variety*, 1 November 1944, 40.

"Andrews Sis May Stay as Duo Depending on Aussie Aud Reaction." *Variety*, 8 December 1954, 41.

"Andrews Sis Nix Double, Play Theatre with Gray." *Variety*, 21 December 1938, 35.

"Andrews Sis Quit Radio for Video." *Variety*, 14 February 1951, 23.

"Andrews Sis Record 2 Songs in London." *Variety*, 4 August 1948, 34.

"Andrews Sis, Ritz Bros., Raye May Sub for Berle." *Variety*, 6 December 1950, 30.

"Andrews Sis-'Spitfire Baby' Terrif $25,000 in Frisco; 'Boots' Trim 12G H.O." *Variety*, 4 February 1942, 11.

"Andrews Sis. Standoff." *Variety*, 3 February 1943, 2.

"Andrews Sis to Go on Despite Patti Ankling." *Variety*, 27 January 1954, 2.

"Andrews Sis to Hop to Cleve. from B'klyn Date." *Variety*, 21 September 1938, 43.

"Andrews Sis Up 'Devil' 30G, Frisco; 'Ramrod' Thin 14G, 'Calcutta' 17G." *Variety*, 23 April 1947, 13.

"Andrews Sis Up 'Holmes' to Trim $18,000, Indpls." *Variety*, 31 March 1943, 9.

"Andrews Sis Vice Vic." *Variety*, 21 November 1956, 48.

"Andrews Sis vs. Andrews Sis to Lawsuit Again." *The Billboard*, 25 November 1944, 25.

"Andrews Sister Goes Solo." *The Times—Picayune*, 30 November 1988. Ken Petrack Collection.

"An Andrews Sister Takes College Post." *New York Post*, 10 August 1968, 2.

"Andrews Sister Wins Divorce from Manager." *Los Angeles Times*, 31 March 1950, I-2.

"Andrews Sisters." *The Billboard*, 26 June 1943, 4.

"The Andrews Sisters." *CUE*, 12–29 July 1943, 10.

"The Andrews Sisters." *The Minneapolis Star*, 18 April 1951, 30.

Andrews Sisters. "The Plot's the Thing." *Swing*, September 1938, 21.

_____. "So You Want to Start a Trio." *Swing*, August 1938, 21.

_____. "Three Famous Sisters Tell You About 3 Kinds Of Swing." *Swing*, October 1938, 15.

"The Andrews Sisters Answer 20 Questions." *Radio Life*, 30 November 1947, 7, 39.

The Andrews Sisters' Army, Navy and Marines Song Folio. New York: Leeds Music Corporation, 1942.

"Andrews Sisters at Bellevue in Good, Mellow Performance." Unidentified newspaper, August, 1959. Charles Saunders Collection.

"Andrews Sisters Back." *New York Times*, 21 August 1945, 17.

"Andrews Sisters' Big 'Threat' from Orig. Disks." *Variety*, 27 October 1954, 56.

"Andrews Sisters' Boff London Hit." *Variety*, 4 August 1948, 41.

"Andrews Sisters Bring Down the House." *Atlanta Constitution*, 18 November 1940.

"The Andrews Sisters Come Home." *Minneapolis Star Journal*, 2 February 1941, 7.

"Andrews Sisters' Dad Held on Gun Charge." *Daily Mirror*, 31 January 1940, 4.

"Andrews Sisters Date." *Hollywood Reporter*, 19 October 1973.

"Andrews Sisters Defer on U's Jukebox Picture." *Variety*, 11 June 1941, 2.

"Andrews Sisters Doubled Salary Within One Year." *The Billboard*, 23 August 1941, 21.

"Andrews Sisters Draw Big." *The Billboard*, 17 August 1940, 19.

"Andrews Sisters Draw 15G Plus % for Frisco Date." *Variety*, 9 April 1947, 46.

"Andrews Sisters' Dynamic Success at London Palladium!" *The Melody Maker*, 7 August 1948, 1.

"Andrews Sister's 'Fan' Would Give Her $187,000." *Los Angeles Times*, 9 April 1952, II-26.

The Andrews Sisters 50th Anniversary Collection. Volume II. Compact Disc Booklet. MCA Records. 1987.

"Andrews Sisters' Film." *Variety*, 3 April 1940, 2.

"Andrews Sisters' $4,984 on Frisco %." *Variety*, 2 July 1941, 2.

"Andrews Sisters Given Rousing Welcome on Home Town Appearance." *Variety*, 18 April 1951, 63.

"Andrews Sisters Given Unusual Airport Greeting." *Honolulu Star-Bulletin*, 18 March 1952, 5.

"Andrews Sisters ... Greatest Business in History of the Fairmount [sic] Hotel..." *The Billboard*, 9 September 1950, 57.

"Andrews Sisters Here for $200,000 Television Work-Out." *The Melody Maker*, 28 July 1951, 7.

"Andrews Sisters Hit Their Top Vaude Pay, $7,750 for Chi Week." *Variety*, 4 March 1942, 3.

"The Andrews Sisters in Minneapolis." *Minneapolis Star Journal*, 2 February 1941, 3.

"Andrews Sisters in New Movie." *Down Beat*, 15 December 1940, 34.

"Andrews Sisters in Their Best Bill Yet." *Minneapolis Sunday Tribune*, 14 May 1944, 6.

"Andrews Sisters Launch New Career After Spat." *Portland (Me.) Press Herald*, 12 November 1956, 24.

"Andrews Sisters Left 'Dawn' 34G, Seattle." *Variety*, 12 June 1946, 11.

"Andrews Sisters May Encore in 2d U Pic." *Variety*, 7 August 1940, 3.

"Andrews Sisters Net $10,500 in Oakland." *Variety*, 10 March 1943, 39.

"Andrew [sic] Sisters 19G Big in Minneapolis." *The Billboard*, 3 April 1943, 16.

"Andrews Sisters Offer Truman $5,000 for Piano." 1952 Undated Newspaper Clipping. Robert Boyer Collection.

"Andrews Sisters on the Cover." *Down Beat*, 15 December 1941, 1.

"Andrews Sisters' Performance and Songs Fine in U's 'Buck Privates.'" *The Billboard*, 15 February 1941, 10.

"Andrews Sisters Plus David Frye Are Show Stoppers at Bimbo's 365 Club." *San Francisco Progress*, 17–18 January 1968, 42.

The Andrews Sisters Publicity. Press Book. Fall-Winter, 1943–44.

"Andrews Sisters Quit 'Club 15' for TV Show." *Down Beat*, 23 March 1951, 18.

"Andrews Sisters' Saga of D'Attagnan Spirit." *Variety*, 2 August 1944, 2.

"Andrews Sisters Set for Concert Tour at Guarantee of 20Gs on 60% Split." *Variety*, 27 September 1944, 41.

"Andrews Sisters Slam Rock." *The Melody Maker*, 26 November 1960, 10.

"Andrews Sisters Smash Hollywood Record!!" *Variety*, 19 December 1956, 40–41.

"Andrews Sisters' Special Show for Olympicers at London Palladium." *Variety*, 11 August 1948, 45.

"Andrews Sisters, Sponsor Wrangling Over Comedy Lines." *The Billboard*, 9 June 1945, 5.

"Andrews Sisters Swing Into Harvey's for Christmas, New Year Appearance." *Tahoe*, December 1967, 4.

"Andrews Sisters Tangle in Court." *Los Angeles Times*, 9 November 1954, I-2.

"Andrews Sisters (3)." *Variety*, 6 June 1956, 41.

"Andrews Sisters, Three Stooges Head Neat Bill." *Minneapolis Star Journal*, 2 February 1941, 8.

"Andrews Sisters Tired of Turkeys." *Down Beat*, 15 October 1942, 2.

"Andrews Sisters to Appear at Runyon Fund Benefit." *Los Angeles Times*, 7 March 1947, I-7.

"Andrews Sisters to Coast for 3 U Pix After Vaude, Disc Dates End This Wk." *Variety*, 25 March 1942, 3.

"Andrews Sisters to N'west; $$$, Picstuff Test." *The Billboard*, 4 May 1946, 47.

"Andrews Sisters to record 45-min. 'Farewell to Britain.'" *The Melody Maker*, 25 August 1951, 6.

"Andrews Sisters' 25G Terrific in Boston." *The Billboard*, 18 October 1941, 24.

"Andrews Sisters Win 157G Judgment from Their Own Corporation." *Variety*, 4 June 1952, 41.

"Andrews Sue Over Estate." *Los Angeles Examiner*, 19 March 1955, 1–15.

"Andrews Trio Dip Into Hillbilly Music." *Variety*, 2 March 1949, 41.

"Andrews Trio Pull Legal Coup." *The Billboard*, 7 June 1952, 1.

"Andrews-Venuti Find $1.10 High." *The Billboard*, 13 September 1941, 4.

"Andrews—Wow!—Boff!—Socko!" *Variety*, 12 May 1948, 64.

"Another Scoop for Excelsior Park." *Minneapolis Morning Tribune*, 20 August 1941, 8.

Archerd, Army. "Just for Variety." *Dailey Variety*, 19 December 2001, 4.

Ardmore, Jane. "We Won the War While They Won Our Hearts." *Photoplay*, July 1974, 44, 86, 89–90, 92–94.

"Are Vocalists Unnecessary?" *Down Beat*, 1 February 1941, 6.

"Arranges a Profitable Mob Scene to Sell Andrews Sisters Discs: First Corners Local Supply." *Variety*, 19 March 1941, 40.

"Aver 'Command' Show for Greek Rulers Unruly." *The Billboard*, 21 November 1953, 1.

"Ayres Band Signed for Andrews Sisters Picture." *The Billboard*, 24 July 1943, 15.

B. H. "Melody Time." *Metronome*, July 1948, 26.

_____. "Too Many Cooks." *Metronome*, April 1948, 26.

B. U. "Road to Rio." *Metronome*, April 1948, 21–22.

Bacon, James. "Famous Andrews Sisters 15 Years in Show Business—Still Good Pals." 1952. Merle Smith Collection.

_____. "James Bacon." *Los Angeles Herald-Examiner*, 8 January 1976, A-12.

_____. "James Bacon." *Los Angeles Herald-Examiner*, 15 January 1976.

Bailey, Jeanne. "L.A. Pops Rolls Out the Barrel." *Los Angeles Daily News*, 16 January 1983, 2.

Banks, Dale. "What's New from Coast to Coast." *Radio Romances*, July 1945, 6.

Barnard, Ken. "The Andrews Sisters—Then and Now." *Detroit Free Press*, 28 June 1965, D-12.

Barnes, Clive. "Stage: The Andrews Sisters Return." *New York Times*, 7 March 1974, 51.

"Belasco Opens Pavilion Caprice for Season; Sister Trio Sings." *Cincinnati Enquirer*, 8 October 1936.

Bell, Elma. "After Years as an Andrews Sister, Maxene's a Solo Act." *Birmingham News*, 11 July 1980, F-3, 4.

"Benny's 113G Vs. Andrews Gals Shatters Chi." *The Billboard*, 24 May 1947, 37.

Berube, Allan. *Coming Out Under Fire*. New York: Free Press, 1990.

"Big Time Vaudeville." *Los Angeles Times*, 2 July 1932, II-7.

"Bing First Over the Line." *PIC*, 23 November 1943, 36–37.

"*Birmingham Evening Dispatch*. "Pep, Poise and Personality Plus…" *Variety*, 26 September 1951, 124.

"Blair—Blackburns Fill in for Andrews Sis." *Variety*, 3 August 1949, 44.

"Blossom Music Sues Andrews, Seeking 10G." *The Billboard*, 19 September 1953, 14.

Bob. "Patty Andrews." *Variety*, 30 June 1954, 50.

Boyer, Robert. "The Andrews Sisters—Remembered in Music." *The Song Sheet*, March-April 1999, 3–5.

Brady, Kathleen. *Lucille*. New York: Billboard Books, 2001.

Brand, Pat. "Effervescent Andrews!" *The Melody Maker*, 4 August 1951, 2.

"Breese-Andrews Sisters." *The Billboard*, 19 August 1939, 9.

"'Brides'-Andrews Huge $34,000, Det." *Variety*, 4 December 1946, 10.

Brog. "Melody Time." *Variety*, 19 May 1948, 13.

Bron. "Andrews Sisters Show." *Variety*, 10 October 1945, 30.

Brozan, Nadine. "Chronicle." *New York Times*, 8 September 1995, A-24.

Bundy, June. "Roxy, New York." *The Billboard*, 18 June 1949, 45.

Burm. "Hipp, Balto." *Variety*, 21 August 1940, 24.

_____. "Hippodrome, Balto." *Variety*, 13 July 1949, 48.

"Burton Pilots Andrews Gals." *The Billboard*, 14 November 1953, 22.

"B'way in Vaude Comeback." *The Billboard*, 15 July 1939, 20.

"Café News." *New York Post*, 9 October 1937, 10.

Calta, Louis. "'Over Here!' Tour Is Off in Dispute." *The New York Times*, 21 December 1974, 18–5.

Campbell, Mary. "Glory Days Not Forgotten in Andrews Sister Album." *Chicago Tribune*, 28 November 1985, 5-C14.

"Campbell Airshow to Intro Disney's 'Cinderella' Score." *Variety*, 16 November 1949, 60.

"Campbell Mulls TV'ers on 'Club 15,' 'Double.'" *Variety*, 22 November 1950, 27.

"Capitol Adds Patti Andrews, Geo. Shearing." *The Billboard*, 21 May 1955, 40.

"Capitol, Wash." *Variety*, 6 June 1951, 22.

Carroll, Carroll. *None of Your Business*. New York: Cowles Book Company, Inc., 1970.

Carter. "Steel Pier, A. C." *Variety*, 28 August 1940, 48.

_____. "Steel Pier, A. C." *Variety*, 3 September 1941, 55.

"Casa Manana, New York." *The Billboard*, 25 February 1939, 20.

Chadwick, Bruce. "Go to Resorts—Patti's Over There." *New York Daily News*, unknown date 1987. Merle Smith Collection.

Chan. "Club 15." *Variety*, 30 August 1950, 20.

Char. "Flatbush, B'klyn." *Variety*, 29 March 1939, 37.

_____. "Give Out, Sisters." *Variety*, 2 September 1942, 18.

_____. "Hippodrome." *Variety*, 26 January 1932, 39.

"Chase Club, St. Loo." *Variety*, 22 November 1950, 50.

"Chi Hotsy; 'Beaucaire'-Andrews Sis Colossal 90G, 'Loved You' Smash 25G, 'Day' Wham 50G, 'Music' Strong 38G." *Variety*, 4 September 1946, 15.

"Chi Marks Time; 'Indemnity'-Andrews Sis Great 57G, 'Neighbor'-'Gay 90's' 15G." *Variety*, 8 November 1944, 27.

"Chi Par Club's Show." *Variety*, 11 September 1934, 47.

"Chi Temp. and Biz Warming Up: 'Day'-Andrews Bright $45,000, 'Pulham' Fine 17G, 'Hellz' 2d 13G." *Variety*, 25 February 1942, 9.

Chic. "Grand O. H., N.Y." *Variety*, 25 October 1932, 32.

"Chicago, Chicago." *The Billboard*, 7 September 1946, 42.

"Chi's Nitery Biz Best Since Boom Times; Town Splurging on Shows." *Variety*, 24 July 1935, 49.

Christon, Lawrence. "Four Ladies Swing, Sing at Hartford." *Los Angeles Times*, 14 November 1981, 5.

"Circuit Vaude Drops 70% During the Last Five Years." *Variety*, 12 November 1932, 6.

"City Hails the Men of Son Tay." *San Francisco Examiner*, 28 April 1973, 3.

Clarke, Gerald. *Get Happy*. New York: Random House, 2000.

Clooney, Rosemary and Joan Barthel. *Girl Singer*. New York: Doubleday, 1999.

"Club Chatter." *The Billboard*, 31 October 1936, 13.

Coates, Paul V. "Well, Medium and RARE." *Los Angeles Mirror*, 4 May 1953, 10.

Cohen. "Stanley, Pitt." *Variety*, 12 March 1941, 47.

_____. "Stanley, Pitt." *Variety*, 21 April 1943, 24.

Cohen, Harold W. "The New Films: On the Stage." *Pittsburgh Post-Gazette*, 8 March 1941, 23.

"Collegiate Choice of Female Vocalists." *The Billboard*, 15 April 1939, 13.

"Concert Coming to D-Day memorial." *The Bedford Bulletin*. Bedford, Virginia. 5 September 2001. Everett Searcy Collection.

Conway, Richard. "Maxene Solos in Classy Memoir." *Springfield Daily News*, 26 April 1980, 4.

Cook, Joan. "'Andrews Sound' at the Mall." *New York Times*, 22 January 1976, 75.

Costello, Chris. *Lou's on First*. New York: St. Martin's Press, 1981.

"Court Rules for Andrews Sisters in Suit." *Los Angeles Times*, 24 March 1953, I-2.

Cox, Stephen and John Lofflin. *The Official Abbott & Costello Scrapbook*. Chicago: Contemporary Books, 1990.

Crandall, Robert. "How Love Broke Up the Andrews Sisters." *Music and Rhythm*, January 1941, 7–9.

Crenshaw, Solomon, Jr. "Maxene Andrews Gets Ovations." *Birmingham News*, 12 July 1980, F-5.

Crichton, Kyle. "Sweet and Hot." *Colliers*, 28 October 1939, 16, 44.

"Crosby–Andrews Duo Is Profit Packin' Pistol." *The Billboard*, 20 November 1943, 62.

"Crosby-Andrews on 75c Disc Release by Decca." *Variety*, 13 October 1943, 35.

"Crosby-Andrews 7G Hot." *The Billboard*, 11 November 1939, 13.

Cross, Robin. *The Big Book of B Movies, or How Low Was My Budget*. New York: St. Martin's Press, 1981.

Crotta, Carol A. "'Swingin,' Singin' Ladies' Stars Have a Case of Paycheck Blues." *Los Angeles Herald-Examiner*, 12 December 1981, B-1, B-6.

Crowther, Bosley. "The Screen." *New York Times*, 26 February 1942, 15.

_____. "The Screen." *New York Times*, 28 May 1948, 28.

_____. "The Screen in Review." *New York Times*, 12 June 1941, 29.

_____. "The Screen in Review." *New York Times*, 22 April 1946, 26.

Csida, Joe. "Colgate Hour (The Tony Martin Show)." *The Billboard*, 17 March 1951, 11.

_____. "Network Program Reviews & Analyses: Club 15." *The Billboard*, 18 October 1947, 12.

_____. "Texaco Star Theater." *The Billboard*, 17 March 1951, 11.

Cullum, Charles. *The Dallas Morning News*, 24 May 1937, 10.

Cummings, Judith. "A Tribute to Players Who Pay Homage to Stage Classics." *New York Times*, 24 March 1980, B-4.

"Current Program Notes." *Billboard*, 9 April 1938.

"Cut Rates for Service Men Big in S.F." *Variety*, 25 June 1941, 37.

"Daily Diary." *Los Angeles Herald & Express*, 13 March 1953.

Dalz. "Paramount, Newark." *Variety*, 1 February 1939, 45.

"Dave Kapp Exits Decca, Which His Brother Co-Founded 17 Years Ago." *Variety*, 27 June 1951, 45.

"Dave Kapp Personally Takes a Hand to Win Disk Jockey Friends." *Variety*, 7 September 1949, 41.

"Dean Martin, Christy Minstrels, Everly Bros., 'Best,' 'Beatle Jazz,' Peggy Lee, Kelly Lester top New LPs." *Variety*, 26 August 1964, 42.

"Decca Aboard 'Woodpecker'." *Variety*, 9 June 1948, 41.

"Decca, Campbell Soup Set Album on Radio Show." *The Billboard*, 10 December 1949, 1, 16.

"Decca Initiates Foreign Waxing." *The Billboard*, 7 August 1948, 14.

"Decca Is Santa on Bing's 'Xmas.'" *The Billboard*, 19 June 1943, 21.

"Decca Okays Radio's Use of Disks." *Variety*, 10 April 1940, 31.

"Decca 'Rum & Coke' Disc May Be Co.'s Bigger Seller Despite Net Ban." *Variety*, 14 February 1945, 43.

"A Decca 'Rum-Coke' Cut By Calypso Ork." *The Billboard*, 10 March 1945, 14.

"Decca's 'Million' Club." *Down Beat*, 22 September 1954, 6.

"Decca's Newest Hit—Rum and Coca-Cola." *The Billboard*, 6 January 1945, 21.

"Decca's One Million Sellers." *Variety*, 1 September 1954, 55.

Denis, Paul. "Paramount, N.Y." *The Billboard*, 3 July 1943, 18–19.

_____. "Paramount, New York." *The Billboard*, 23 July 1938, 20.

Detroit News, 15 July 1934. Sports sec., 11. Robert Boyer Collection.

Dexter. "Kansas City." *Metronome*, August 1936, 27.

Dexter, Dave, Jr. "Dexter's Scrapbook." *The Billboard*, 20 September 1969, 25.

_____. "I Won't Hire a Man over 30!—Lou Levy." *Music and Rhythm*, September 1941, 32–33.

"Disc Brings Andrews Sister Solo Bookings." *Down Beat*, 21 October 1949, 2.

"Disk Executive and Andrews Sister Marry." *Los Angeles Times*, 13 November 1948, I-12.

"Do You Remember ... The Andrews Sisters?" circa 1972 Newspaper Clipping. Robert Boyer Collection.

Don. "Roaring Twenties, S.D." *Variety*, 20 June 1962, 59.

Dong. "Nugget, Sparks, Nev." *Variety*, 27 February 1963, 59.

Donn. "Andrews Sisters Show." *Variety*, 10 January 1945, 24.

"'Draft' Pulls Big 20G in Mild Frisco, Andrews Sis–Fight Pix Terrif $23,000." *Variety*, 25 June 1941, 11.

"Dream Cast to Wax 'Dick Tracy' for GI's." *Variety*, 14 February 1945, 1.

Drewes, Caroline. "Maxene Andrews, Swinging Dean." *San Francisco Sunday Examiner and Chronicle*, 27 October 1968, Women Today, 9.

"Drive Starts for Show Biz in Hollywood." *Variety*, 16 May 1945, 16.

DuBois, Pam. *The Andrews Sisters 50th Anniversary Collection*. Volume 2. Compact Disc Booklet. MCA Records, 1987.

Duggan, Shirle. "Family Farm." *Los Angeles Examiner*, 9 April 1950, VII-1, VII-4.

Duke. "Thunderbird, Las Vegas." *Variety*, 4 October 1961, 70.

Dunning, Jennifer. "Paul Taylor Devises Some 40's Nostalgia." *New York Times*, 30 July 1992, C-13.

_____. "Putting Song on Hold for Ballet." *New York Times*, 1 November 1991, C-3.

Dunning, John. *On the Air: The Encyclopedia of Old Time Radio*. New York: Oxford University Press, 1998.

Eck. "State, Hartford." *Variety*, 8 November 1939, 37.

Edwa. "Swingin' Singin' Ladies." *Variety*, 18 November 1981, 91.

Elle. "RKO, Boston." *Variety*, 19 May 1943, 46.

_____. "RKO, Boston." *Variety*, 12 April 1944, 16.

_____. "RKO, Boston." *Variety*, 22 January 1947, 55.

"Ellington Cops 1939 Record Honors." *Metronome*, January 1940, 16.

Elrod, Bruce. *V DISC. A Musical Contribution by America's Best for Our Armed Forces Overseas. Andrews Sisters.* Compact Disc Booklet. IMC Licensing, SA, 1997.

Emge, Charles. "Bing and Bob Clown Musicians in 'Rio.'" *Down Beat*, 28 January 1948, 8.

English, Mary. "Tryout Time for Andrews'." *Down Beat*, 2 June 1954.

Ewen, David. *American Popular Songs from the Revolutionary War to the Present*. Random House: New York, 1966.

"Famed Andrew [sic] Sisters Lack Harmony Now." *Tacoma News Tribune*, 5 May 1953.

Feather. "Andrews—Ayres." *Metronome*, November 1944, 25.

"Feist Beefs on 'Parade' Brushoff of 'Rum, Coke' Tune; Ditto 'Dreams.'" *Variety*, 21 February 1945, 41.

Fidelman, Geoffrey Mark. *The Lucy Book*. Los Angeles: Renaissance Books, 1999.

"Fire Razes Mayfair, Leading K. C. Nitery." *Variety*, 1 July 1936, 39.

"First Group of Inductees Chosen for Vocal Group Hall of Fame." *Goldmine*, 25 September 1998.

"Follow Up Comments." *Variety*, 6 April 1938, 28.

"Followup." *TV Guide*, 21 October 1977. Everett Searcy Collection.

Foos. "Chicago, Chi." *Variety*, 4 September 1946, 22.

Forrest, Gene. "About Town: Andrews Sisters in Peacock Court Tuesday." *San Francisco Call-Bulletin*, 16 August 1952, G-4.

Forsmark, Laird. "School Reunion Brings Back Stars." *Hollywood Studio*, January 1974, 23–24.

_____. "The Story on the Andrews Sisters." Unpublished manuscript. Minnesota Historical Society Library, St. Paul, 1983.

Fortune, Dick. "Trio That Can Sing." *Pittsburgh Press*, 27 August 1938.

"400,000 Music Machines." *The Billboard*, 28 September 1940, 1.

"Fourth Sister?" *The Billboard*, 21 July 1945, 15.

Fox. "Keith's, Boston." *Variety*, 8 October 1941, 46.

Francis, Bob. "Patty Andrews Makes Solo N.Y. Nitery Bow." *The Billboard*, 9 April 1955, 13.

Frank, Morton. "Stanley, Pittsburgh." *The Billboard*, 3 September 1938, 28.

Franken. "Phil Baker." *The Billboard*, 28 January 1939, 10.

_____. "Program Reviews: Glenn Miller." *The Billboard*, 6 January 1940, 9.

Franken, Jerry. "Paramount, New York." *The Billboard*, 9 March 1940, 22.

Fredericks, Tod. "Music 'n' Fun." *Radio Life*, 9 November 1947, 36–37, 39.

Frohlich, Shirley. "Picture Tie-Ups for Music Machine Operators." *The Billboard*, 2 January 1943, 14.

Fuller, Jim. "It's Andrews Sister Now, but She's Still on Road." *Minneapolis Star Tribune*, 22 June 1993, E-1, 4.

"Fun on Roller Coaster Recalled." *Milwaukee Journal*, 17 May 1967. Everett Searcy Collection.

G. T. S. "Film Reviews. 'What's Cookin'.'" *Metronome*, April 1942, 19.

Gagh. "Latin Casino, Philly." *Variety*, 3 October 1951, 65.

"The Gal Yippers Have No Place in Our Jazz Bands." *Down Beat*, 15 October 1939, 16.

Gale, Moe. "Personality on a Platter." *The Billboard*, 23 September 1939, 10, 32.

Galloway, Doug. "Lou Levy." *Variety*, 6 November 1995, 82.

Garfield, Kim. "Maxene Goes Solo." *The Advocate*, 1 October 1985, 22–23, 26.

Gavin, James. *The Andrews Sisters.* Compact Disc Booklet. The Reader's Digest Assn., 1996.

"'Gesture'-Long-Andrews Sis Pacing Solid Det. $36,000; 'Woman' Lush 15G." *Variety*, 18 March 1942, 13.

"Gibson-Andrews Girls and Berle." *Down Beat*, 15 July 1941, 2.

Gil-Montero, Martha. *Brazilian Bombshell: The Biography of Carmen Miranda.* New York: Donald I. Fine, Inc., 1989.

Gioia, Ted. *The History of Jazz.* New York: Oxford University Press, 1997.

"Girl Singers Confess." *Metronome*, January 1937, 17, 37.

"G.I.'s Tab Their Favorites." *The Billboard*, 16 September 1944, 12, 65.

"Give Out, Sisters." *Daily Variety*, 28 August 1942.

"Give Out, Sisters." *Motion Picture Herald*, 5 September 1942.

Glackin, William C. "Music Circus Switches from Sentiment to Humor and Presents Something Different in One Touch of Venus." *The Sacramento Bee*, 6 July 1954, 3.

Glassner, Lester. "The Andrews Sisters." *Andy Warhol's Interview*, IV, October 1974, 24–27.

"Glenn Miller's 'Choo Choo' Hits 1,000,000 Mark in Disc Output and May Become All-Time High." *Variety*, 14 January 1942, 39.

Gold. "Chicago, Chi." *Variety*, 13 December 1939, 46.

_____. "Chicago, Chi." *Variety*, 1 May 1940, 47.

_____. "Chicago, Chi." *Variety*, 12 February 1941, 40.

_____. "Chicago, Chi." *Variety*, 13 August 1941, 25.

Goldin, Ellen. "Maxene Andrews, Studio One Backlot." *The Hollywood Drama-Logue*, Volume X, no. 40, 1979. Ken Petrack Collection.

"Gonged." circa 1978. Everett Searcy Collection.

"Good B'way Takes; Miller, Andrews Head for $55,000." *The Billboard*, 9 March 1940, 20.

Gord. "Time for a Song." *Variety*, 25 June 1952, 32.

Gordon, Shirley. "The Andrews Brothers." *Radio and Television Life*, 10 April 1949, 33, 39.

_____. "Gleesome Threesome." *Radio Life*, 31 December 1944, 27, 31.

_____. "Of Cats and Elephants and 'The Duchess.'" *Radio Life*, 17 March 1946, 6–7, 28.

Gould. "Flamingo, Las Vegas." *Variety*, 16 September 1953, 55.

Gould, Jack. "Three New Programs." *The New York Times*, 7 January 1945, X-7.

"Gov. of Hawaii Turning Plugger for Native Tune." *Variety*, 11 October 1950, 1.

Graham, Sheila. "Hollywood Today." *Tacoma News Tribune*, 20 June 1953.

Green, Abel. "Jack Kapp Brought New Kind of Showmanship to Disk Biz." *Variety*, 30 March 1949, 37.

_____, and Joe Laurie, Jr. *Show Biz from Vaude to Video.* New York: Henry Holt and Company, 1951.

Green, Nat. "Chicago, Chicago." *The Billboard*, 4 May 1940, 24.

Greene, Alice Craig. "The Andrews Sisters." *Swank*, July 1946, 54–57.

Greg. "Chicago, Chi." *Variety*, 27 July 1949, 111.

Grein, Paul. "New Harmony for Andrews Sisters?" *Los Angeles Times*, 1 October 1987, VI-1, 4.

Gros. "Album Reviews." *Variety*, 6 March 1957, 42.

Gross, Jane. "Maxene Andrews, One of Singing Sisters, Dies at 79." *Los Angeles Times*, 23 October 1995, B-1, 3.

Gross, Mike. "Jocks, Jukes and Disks." *Variety*, 15 October 1952, 38.

Grudens, Richard. *The Best Damn Trumpet Player.* Stony Brook: Celebrity Profiles Publishing, 1996.

"'Gung Ho,' Giant $16,500, Leads Cincy Pix; 'Criminal'-Andrews Sis Big 28G." *Variety*, 9 February 1944, 16.

Hagen, Ray. "The Andrews Sisters." *Film Fan Monthly*, July/August 1974, 10–18.

Hall, Fred. *Dialogues in Swing.* Ventura: Pathfinder Publishing, 1989.

Harris, Betsy. "Andrews Sister Back to Indiana Theatre." *Indianapolis Star*, 11 October 1980, E-13–14.

Harris, Ed J. "Swing Concert Is Money Flop, but Artistic Success." *Down Beat*, July 1939, 4.

Harris, Radie. "Hollywood Runaround." *Variety*, 18 August 1943, 2.

Harris, Sidney. "Hippodrome, N.Y." *Variety*, 30 January 1932, 10.

"Hatchet Buried." *Minneapolis Morning Tribune*, 5 June 1956, 1.

Hawn, Jack. "48 Years After 'BMBDS,' Maxene Andrews Is a Solo." *Los Angeles Times*, 14 August 1985, VI-2–3.

"He Might Say 'Vunderbar!'" *Chicago Daily News*, 7 April 1938, 27.

"'Heaven' Plus Andrews Sis-Davis Huge $31,000 for Pitt; 'Badlands' 6G." *Variety*, 26 November 1941, 12.

Heffernan, Harold. "Andrews Sisters Risk Savings to Crash TV." *The Detroit News*, 18 October 1959, 18.

Helm. "Ambassador Hotel, L.A." *Variety*, 30 April 1952, 48.

_____. "Ambassador Hotel, L.A." *Variety*, 5 November 1952, 50.

Henshaw, Laurie and Max Jones. "There's More in the Andrews Than Meets the Ear!" *The Melody Maker*, 21 August 1948, 3.

"Her Fan Slipped." *Variety*, 18 December 1934, 45.

"Her Lucky Night." *Daily Variety*, 24 January 1945.

Herb. "Earle, Philly." *Variety*, 16 November 1938, 45.

_____. "Paramount, N.Y." *Variety*, 6 March 1940, 46.

"Herb Ross, Music Machine Operator." *The Billboard*, 17 October 1942, 67.

Herm. "Latin Quarter, N.Y." *Variety*, 1 July 1959, 55.

_____. "Roxy, N.Y." *Variety*, 26 July 1950, 22.

"He's Our Boy, Vic!" *The Billboard*, 1 April 1950, 17.

Heuring, Harvey. "Nostalgia—The Good Old Days and the Andrew [sic] Sisters." *Record Finder*. Undated. Merle Smith Collection.

Higgins, John. "When You and I Were Seventeen, or Even Younger." *London Times*, 16 May 1974, 9.

"High-School Music Survey Tab." *The Billboard*, 16 June 1945, 1, 20.

Hilburn, Robert. "Andrews Sisters, Crosby Make for Fun Match." *Los Angeles Times*, 14 February 1997, F-26.

Hill, Katherine. "Larry Rich Heads Bill at Orpheum." *San Francisco Chronicle*, 18 June 1932, 10.

Hinckley, David. "Making Her Plea for Harmony." *New York Daily News*, 14 June 1993. David McCain Collection.

Hirschhorn, Clive. *The Hollywood Musical*. New York: Crown Publishing Inc, 1981.

"Hi-Schoolers Say James Best." *The Billboard*, 3 June 1944, 12.

Hitchens, Neal. "Andrews Sister in Desperate Bid to End 17-Year Family Feud." *National Enquirer*, 28 July 1992, 20.

Hobe. "Paramount, N.Y." *Variety*, 28 December 1938, 38.

_____. "Paramount, N.Y." *Variety*, 23 September 1942, 44.

"Ho-Ho-Kus, N. J., Plugs Song of Same Name." *Variety*, 8 June 1949, 45.

"Ho-Ho-Kus Party." *Variety*, 22 June 1949, 27.

"'Hold Tight'—Here We Go Again." *Swing*, May 1939, 13.

"'Hollywood Canteen' Selling at 50% Gross." *Variety*, 13 December 1944, 5.

Hollywood Reporter, 10 October 1986.

Holt, Toni. "'Spirit of Sister LaVerne Guides My New Career,' Says Maxene of the Famed Singing Andrews Sisters." *Tatler*, 7 August 1975. John Tyler Collection.

Honigberg, Sam. "Chicago." *The Billboard*, 28 February 1942, 7.

_____. "Chicago, Chicago." *The Billboard*, 16 December 1939, 24.

_____. "Chicago, Chicago." *The Billboard*, 16 August 1941, 23.

_____. "Chicago, Chicago." *The Billboard*, 28 February 1942, 18.

_____. "Paramount, New York." *The Billboard*, 28 September 1940, 22.

Hoopes, Roy. *When the Stars Went to War: Hollywood and World War II*. New York: Random House, 1994.

Hopper, Hedda. "Andrews Sister Delays Marital Dispute Move." *Los Angeles Times*, 12 November 1948, 8.

_____. "In Hollywood." *San Francisco Chronicle*, 4 June 1956, 25.

"Hot Spots Checked in Topanga Blaze." *Los Angeles Times*, 9 November 1961, 1.

Hotchner, A. E. *Doris Day, Her Own Story*. New York: William Marrow and Company, Inc. 1976.

Howard, Joe. *Gay Nineties Troubadour*. Miami Beach: Joe Howard Music House, 1956.

Hoyt. "Muehlebach Grill." *Variety*, 5 August 1936, 48.

Huggins, Bill. "Andrews Gals, Leonard Band, Lay Huge Egg." *Down Beat*, 15 April 1940, 16.

Humphrey, Harold. "Air Briefs: Chicago." *The Billboard*, 2 April 1938, 11.

Hunt. "Oriental, Chi." *Variety*, 7 May 1947, 64.

Hunt, Dennis. "The Fun of Those Silly Andrews Songs." *Los Angeles Times*, 14 October 1983, 18.

_____. "Maxene Andrews in a Cabaret Mood." *Los Angeles Times*, 27 September 1979, 26.

Hunt, Harold. "In Our Town." *The Oregon Journal*, 3 June 1946, 7.

"Icer, Andrews Sisters, Haymes, Bob Crosby Unit to Sacramento." *The Billboard*, 5 August 1950, 66.

Ignace, John F. "Hippodrome, Baltimore." *The Billboard*, 8 August 1942, 16.

"Illness Reduces Andrews from Trio to a Single." *Variety*, 29 October 1941, 45.

"In New Ringside Floor Show." *Fort Worth Star-Telegram*, 7 November 1935.

"In San Francisco." *Variety*, 4 June 1952, 26.

"Inside Orchestras—Music." *Variety*, 11 August 1948, 36.

"Inside Orchestras—Music." *Variety*, 16 August 1950, 42.

"Inside Stuff—Music." *Variety*, 9 August 1939, 40.

"Inside Stuff—Music." *Variety*, 25 November 1942, 43.

"It's 'Andrews Sis Show' Now; Flacks Nixed '8 to Bar.'" *The Billboard*, 23 December 1944, 5.

"J. Dorsey, Basie Crack 1-Niter Records; Ditto Krupa, but Storm Clips Weeks." *Variety*, 10 September 1941, 31.

Jacobs, Laura. "The Forties and Beyond." *The New Leader*, 2–16 December 1991, 21–22.

Jaques Cattell Press. *ASCAP Biographical Dictionary, fourth edition*. New York: R. R. Bowker Company, 1980.

"Jimmy Dorsey's Birthday Party." *Swing*, April 1939, 10.

"Jitterbug Banned on Campus." *Metronome*, November 1938, 43.

"Joe Russell." *Hollywood Reporter*, circa December 1956. Charles Saunders Collection.

Jon. "Adams, Newark." *Variety*, 19 November 1941, 24.

Jones, Dilys. "Andrews in Sparkling Show." *San Francisco Examiner*, 17 April 1947, 15.

Jones, Max. "The Musical Spark-Plug of the Andrews Sisters." *The Melody Maker*, 7 August 1948, 2.

Jones, Will. "Andrews Sisters Head Right for the Free Lunch." *Minneapolis Tribune*, 15 April 1951, 15.

_____. "Life Was No Song Singing Way to Top." *Minneapolis Sunday Tribune*, 9 December 1956, Feature Section, 1.

"'Jordon' Plus Andrews Sis-Ayres Fine $17,000 in Omaha; 'Children' 18G." *Variety*, 10 March 1943, 11.

Jose. "International, N.Y." *Variety*, 2 May 1962, 173.

_____. "Latin Quarter, N.Y." *Variety*, 30 March 1955, 60.

_____. "Maxene Andrews." *Variety*, 1 October 1975, 114.

_____. "Maxine [sic] Andrews." *Variety*, 25 April 1956, 70.

_____. "Riviera, Fort Lee, N. J." *Variety*, 30 July 1947, 48.

_____. "Roxy, N.Y." *Variety*, 20 June 1951, 20.

"Juke-Box Divas." *Time*, 1 December 1941, 36.

"Just Ask: Do You Sing in the Bathtub?" *Minneapolis Morning Tribune*, 21 April 1951, 6.

"Just Entertainment." *Variety*, 30 March 1938, 35.

Kany. "Colonial, Dayton." *Variety*, 15 November 1939, 54.

Kap. "Ciro's, Hollywood." *Variety*, 26 October 1955, 51.

"Kapp to Decide on Giveaway Album." *Variety*, 5 October 1949, 40.

Kardale, Chick. "Along Chicago's Melody Row." *Down Beat*, 1 February 1944, 12.

Katz, G. and R. Braun. "Patty Andrews Composes Tuneful Little Ditty." *Metronome*, May 1939, 12.

Kauf. "Orpheum, N.Y." *Variety*, 27 September 1932, 42.

Keerdoja, Eileen (with Martin Kasindorf). *Newsweek*, 22 October 1979, 21–22.

Kell. "Tivoli, Copenhagen." *Variety*, 12 July 1967, 55.

Kendall, Robert. "The Amazing Andrew [sic] Sisters." *Hollywood Studio Magazine*, November 1977, 36–37.

Kenny, H. Jr. "Lyric, Indianapolis." *The Billboard*, 3 April 1943, 14.

Kenny, Nick. "Kenny Kandid Kamera." *New York Daily Mirror*, 4 October 1937.

_____. "Nick Kenny Speaking." *New York Daily Mirror*, 28 September 1937, 42.

Kent. "Adams, Newark." *Variety*, 11 September 1940, 40.

Kerr, Walter. "The Andrews Sisters, with Pleasure." *New York Times*, 17 March 1974, II-5.

Kiner, Larry F. and Harry MacKenzie. *Basic Musical Library, "P" Series 1–1000*. New York: Greenwood Press, 1990.

Kinkle, Roger D. *The Complete Encyclopedia of Popular Music And Jazz, 1900–1950*. Volume 3. New Rochelle: Arlington House Publishers, 1974.

Kirk. "Gallagher's, L. A." *Variety*, 12 October 1983, 93.

Kleiner, Dick. "Sisters Want TV Show." New York Press, July 1959. Charles Saunders Collection.

"Knickerbocker Dance Pupils Appear Here." *The Minneapolis Journal*, 8 May 1932, 14.

Koll. "Beverly Hills, Cincy." *Variety*, 25 June 1958, 70.

_____. "Beverly Hills, Newport." *Variety*, 14 August 1957, 54.

_____. "Shubert, Cincy." *Variety*, 22 November 1939, 45.

Koshler, Joe. "Andrews Sisters' Show." *The Billboard*, 20 February 1945, 31.

"Krupa-Andrews Top Prov. Attractions." *The Billboard*, 7 December 1940, 25.

"L.A. Toasts Royal Pair at Scintillating Banquet." *Los Angeles Times*, 15 November 1953, 1, 2, 10.

"Lampoon Picks Andrews Girls as 'Most Frightening.'" *Minneapolis Star*, 27 January 1941.

Lang, Samuel. "Belasco's Band, Show Win Favor." *The Times Picayune*, 17 April 1937, 18.

Laredo, Joseph F. *Bing Crosby and the Andrews Sisters: Their Complete Recordings Together*. CD Booklet. MCA/Decca. 1996.

"Larry Rich." *The Billboard*, 7 July 1934, 3.

Larson, Herbert L. "Song Sisters Just Human." *The Oregonian*, 1 June 1946, 10.

Lary. "Carillon, Miami B'ch." *Variety*, 5 February 1958, 70.

Las Vegas Morning Sun, 15 September 1953. Charles Saunders Collection.

Las Vegas Sun, 3 July 1956. Charles Saunders Collection.

_____, 11 October 1958. Charles Saunders Collection.

"Last Minute MU Action Stops Andrews' Waxing." *The Melody Maker*, 4 September 1948, 1.

"Laverne [sic] Andrews, 51, Is Dead; Eldest of Andrews Sisters Trio." *New York Times*, 9 May 1967, 47.

Lawson, Kyle. "Andrews Reflects on Cheering Troops of Another War." *The Arizona Republic*, 15 February 1991, E-2.

_____. "Andrews Reminisces on Old Days." *The Arizona Republic*, 22 February 1992, D-1.

"Lay That Pistol Down, Babe, Lay That Pistol Down!" *Down Beat*, 15 October 1943, 10.

Leacock, Victoria. *Signature Flowers*. New York: Broadway Books, 1998.

Leath, Linda. "Andrews Girls: Ladies in Wax." *Radio Life*, 3 August 1941, 17.

Leed, Rick. "A Sister Solos." *The Advocate*, 4 October 1979. John Tyler Collection.

Lehman, Phil. "Hippodrome, Baltimore." *The Billboard*, 4 November 1939, 22.

Levin, Gerry. "Andrews Sister: I Knew Travolta Would Be a Star." *National Enquirer*, 12 September 1978.

Levin, Mike. "All Recording Stops Today." *Down Beat*, 1 August 1942, 1.

_____. "Record Reviews. The Andrews Sisters." *Down Beat*, 15 May 1942, 14.

Levy, Lou. "And Then I Published..." *Sheet Music*, January/February 1990, 2, 60–61.

_____. "How 'Bei Mir Bist Du Schoen' Became a Hit." *Sheet Music*, September/October 1990, 11, 60.

_____. "Lou Levy." *The Billboard*, 1 April 1950, 16.

"Levy Asks Court Oust Andrews Sis, Name Receiver for Firm." *Variety*, 11 June 1952, 38.

"Levy Denies He's Split as Manager of Andrews Sis." *Variety*, 27 February 1952, 29.

Lewy, Henry. "Patti Andrews; Hotel Last Frontier, Las Vegas." *Down Beat*, 11 August 1954, 5.

Lieberman, Frank H. "Patti Andrews at the 'Victory Canteen.'" *Los Angeles Herald Express*, 24 January 1971.

Lipper, Hal. "Quest of 'Pippin' Provides Energetic Vaudeville Comedy." *Dayton Daily News*, 19 July 1978, 30.

"Listen to the Andrews Sisters." *Variety*, 10 March 1948, 48.

Lit. "Great Ladies of Silver Screen." *Variety*, 25 August 1982, 85.

_____. "Great Stars of the Silver Screen." *Variety*, 17 November 1982, 79.

Liuz. "Hotel Roosevelt, N.O." *Variety*, 21 March 1962, 60.

_____. "Hotel Roosevelt, N.O." *Variety*, 21 August 1963, 51.

_____. "Hotel Roosevelt, N.O." *Variety*, 8 July 1964, 53.

_____. "Hotel Roosevelt, N.O." *Variety*, 3 March 1965, 66.

_____. "Hotel Roosevelt, N.O." *Variety*, 30 August 1967, 59.

"London Palladium, The Andrews Sisters." *London Times*, 3 August 1948, 7.

Long. "Harrah's, Lake Tahoe." *Variety*, 4 March 1959, 55.

_____. "Harrah's, Lake Tahoe." *Variety*, 25 May 1966, 61.

_____. "Harvey's, Lake Tahoe." *Variety*, 17 July 1968, 59.

_____. "Nugget, Sparks." *Variety*, 14 October 1964, 58.

_____. "Nugget, Sparks." *Variety*, 7 April 1965, 58.

"Long-Andrews Big $66,000 in N.Y.; Lewis Fair 19G in Philly, Krupa OK 14 1/2 G, L.A., Pastor 14G in Balto." *Variety*, 29 October 1941, 42.

Loop. "Chicago, Chi." *Variety*, 11 November 1942, 47.

"Lou Levy Due Into U.S. Army July 22." *Variety*, 15 July 1942, 43.

"Lou Levy Gets 4-F, Resumes Business." *Variety*, 29 July 1942, 41.

"Lou Levy Launches 500G Suit vs. Andrews Sisters in Corporation Wrangle." *Variety*, 2 July 1952, 39.

"Lou Levys Adopt Baby." *Variety*, 6 June 1945, 41.

"Lou Levy's Operation." *Variety*, 11 November 1942, 41.

"Louis Ruggiero." "Obituary." *Ventura County Los Angeles Times*, 28 October 1995, B-11.

"Love Upsets Trio; Girls Won't Split." *Down Beat*, 15 February 1940, 1.

M.B. "Spokane Likes Andrews Trio." *The Spokesman-Review*, 15 June 1946, 5.

MacArthur, Harry. "The Andrews Sisters Score." *Washington Star*, 30 July 1938.

Mackenzie, Harry. *Command Performance, USA!*, Westport: Greenwood Press, 1996.

Mair, George. *Bette: An Intimate Biography of Bette Middler*. New York: Carol Publishing Group, 1995.

"'Major'-Pastor-Andrews, $82,000, Newest Wow in OK N.Y.; 'Serenade' 2nd Nifty $50,000, 'Talk' 3d $90,000." *Variety*, 23 September 1942, 9.

"'Mama' Censored." *Variety*, 1 September 1943, 40.

Manners, Dian. "Men, Maids and Manners." *Down Beat*, 15 January 1944, 8.

Manning, Don. "We Starved Ten Months Out of the Year!" *Music and Rhythm*, January 1942, 24–25, 45.

Mark. "Mapes Skyroom, Reno." *Variety*, 13 October 1954, 61.

_____. "Mapes Skyroom, Reno." *Variety*, 28 September 1955, 68.

_____. "Riverside, Reno." *Variety*, 4 September 1957, 63.

Marne, Geoffrey. "The Wax Works." *Swing*, January 1941, 23.

Martin, Sidney. "How the 'Boogie-Woogie' was Born." *Down Beat*, July 1938, 5.

"Mary Martin Surprise Visitor to Andrews Sis." *Variety*, 15 August 1951, 2.

Mason, Jerry. "I Love You Much Too Much." *Radio and Television Mirror*, May 1940, 20–21, 90.

"Maxene Andrews." *Bay Area Reporter*, 29 October 1981, 19.

"Maxene Andrews Denies Suicide Try." *Los Angeles Examiner*, 22 December 1954, 1, 3.

"Maxene Andrews Joins Stevens to Form Prod. Co." *Hollywood Reporter*, 21 February 1974.

"Maxene Andrews' Memorial Service." Notes. 1995. Robert Boyer Collection.

"Maxene Andrews, of Andrews Sisters, dies." *Minneapolis Star Tribune*, 23 October 1995.

"Maxene Andrews, Okay After Surgery, May Make London Palladium July 30." *Variety*, 27 June 1951, 51.

"Maxene Andrews Treated for Overdose of Pills." *San Francisco Chronicle*, 22 December 1954, 18.

"Maxene Andrews Tried Suicide, Police Say." *Minneapolis Tribune*, 22 December 1954.

"Maxene Andrews Wins Divorce." *Los Angeles Daily News*, 11 March 1949.

"Maxene Andrews Wins Divorce." *New York Times*, 12 March 1949, 10.

"Maxene the Party Pooper." March 1974. Unidentified newspaper clipping. John Tyler Collection.

"Maxene Will Sing Here for Army Days '87." *San Francisco Progress*, 27 March 1987, B-5.

"Mayfair." *Variety*, 3 June 1936, 42.

"Mayfair Club." *Kansas City Star*, 8 June 1936. Robert Boyer Collection.

Mazo, Joseph H. "Swingtime." *Dance Magazine*, January 1992, 76.

McBrien, William. *Cole Porter: A Biography*. New York: Alfred A. Knopf, 1998.

McClay, Georgia. "The Singing Andrew [sic] sisters." *Hollywood Studio*, December 1972, 20.

McClay, Howard. "Andrews Sisters Rock Honolulu." *Los Angeles Daily News*, 26 March 1952, 15.

McClelland, Doug. *The Golden Age of "B" Movies*. Nashville: Charter House Publishers, Inc., 1978.

McClintock, Pamela and Phil Gallo. "List Attunes Youth to Century's Best Songs." *Variety*, 7 March 2001, 1.

McConnell, Rex. "Palace, Akron, O." *The Billboard*, 26 November 1938, 33.

_____. "Review of Unit: Andrews Sisters and Joe Venuti's Band." *The Billboard*, 26 July 1941, 23.

McKinley, Ray. "Biographies of Dot Artists." *The Billboard*, 9 October 1954, 44.

McLellan, Joseph. "Solo Sister." *Washington Post*, 10 October 1979, E-1.

McNally, Owen. "Maxene Andrews Rides Comeback Wave to New Haven." *Hartford Courant*, 8 March 1985, E-4.

McStay. "Casino, Toronto." *Variety*, 3 December 1952, 53.

Meyers, Jim. "Show Hailed at Blue Room." *New Orleans Times-Picayune*, 8 January 1960.

Mike. "Chicago, Chi." *Variety*, 8 November 1944, 34.

"Milestones." *Time*, 6 November 1995, 23.

Miller, Jeanne. "An Andrews Sister Carries on Solo." *San Francisco Examiner*, 9 March 1981, E-8.

Mitchell, Beverley. "Andrews Sisters Get New Partner." *The Montreal Star*, 8 November 1967, 35.

Monk, Herbert L. "Ambassador Stage, Screen Shows All Out for Music." *St. Louis Daily Globe-Democrat*, 21 December 1942, 40.

"Moonlight and Cactus." *Hollywood Reporter*, 17 August 1944.

"Moonlight and Cactus." *Variety*, 16 August 1944, 6–7.

"'Moonlight'-Andrews Sis-Ayres Sock $31,000, Hub; 'Russia' OK 36G, 2 Spots." *Variety*, 12 April 1944, 14.

"More Stars for Denver's Gayest Night—Wednesday." *The Rocky Mountain News*, 18 December 1933, 3.

Morgan, F. Langdon. "Oriental, Chicago." *The Billboard*, 18 August 1934, 15.

_____. "Palace, Chicago." *The Billboard*, 20 August 1932, 10.

Mori. "Paramount, N.Y." *Variety*, 29 October 1941, 22.

Morris, Mary. "The Andrews Sisters at Home." circa 1945, m12-m15. Merle Smith Collection.

Mosby, Arline. "Arline Mosby in Hollywood." *Beverly Hills Newslife*, 18 March 1954.

_____. "Arline Mosby in Hollywood." *Beverly Hills Newslife*, 29 July 1954.

_____. "Patty Andrews to Do Lone TV Act; Wants to Expand." *Las Vegas Review Journal*, 30 July 1954, 15.

"Most Spectacular Song Success of the Music Business." *Variety*, 17 January 1945, 39.

Mulholland, Jim. *The Abbott and Costello Book*. New York: Popular Library, 1975.

Murphy, Edward. "Andrews Sisters Crack $ Record in Coast Hotel Supper Club Bow." *The Billboard*, 19 August 1950, 44.

Murrells, Joseph. *Million Selling Records from the 1900s to the 1980s*. New York: Arco Publishing Company, 1984.

"Music News. Bing Crosby—Andrews Sisters." *Down Beat*, 15 November 1944, 8.

"Musical Fiesta." *Los Angeles Times*, 1 June 1940

Myro. "Palladium, London." *Variety*, 11 August 1948, 47.

_____. "Palladium, London." *Variety*, 8 August 1951, 55.

_____. "Talk of Town, London." *Variety*, 14 December 1960, 55.

N. G. "Chicago, Chicago." *The Billboard*, 22 January 1944, 26.

"N.Y. Cops Guard Rich Café Patrons." *The Billboard*, 19 December 1936, 11.

"N.Y. High; 'Tavern'-Andrews Sis Hot $115,000, 'Grapes' Terrif 125G, 'Glory' Big 20G, 'Fair'-Boswell Lusty 94G, 2d." *Variety*, 12 September 1945, 13.

"N.Y. Para Half Million." *The Billboard*, 3 January 1942, 1.

"N.Y. Vamps Till Xmas But 'Heart Plus' Andrews Sis Lofty $80,000; 'Life' Zestful 45G, 'Lady' Hot 62G." *Variety*, 25 December 1946, 17.

Nachman, Gerald. "Maxene Andrews—Past Master of Song." *San Francisco Chronicle*, 14 March 1981, 40.

"Names in the Swing News." *Swing*, April 1939, 5.

Nash, Jay Robert, and Stanley Ralph Ross. *The Motion Picture Guide*. Vols. 1, 3, 4, 5, 6, 7, and 9. Chicago: Cinebooks, 1985.

Neff. "Studio One, L. A." *Variety*, 3 October 1979, 83.

"New Bills Overcome Heat; Para's Andrews Sis-'Dixie' Big $80,000; MH 105G; Roxy Points to $87,000." *The Billboard*, 3 July 1943, 19.

"New Front for Andrews Gals." *The Billboard*, 23 February 1952, 1.

"New Singer Added to the Andrews Trio." *Montreal Gazette*, 9 November 1967. Joyce De Young Collection.

Newt. "Mt. Royal Hotel, Mont'l." *Variety*, 4 February 1953, 54.

"Nieces Are in Town." *Minneapolis Star*, 14 April 1951. Robert Boyer Collection.

"Night Club Reviews: Hotel New Yorker, N.Y." *The Billboard*, 27 March 1937, 12.

"No Break-Up for Andrews Sisters." *The Billboard*, 2 March 1940, 13.

"No Harmony Between the Andrews Sisters." *New York Daily News*, 28 February 1980, 9.

"No Kin of Andrews, Says Ex-Wife of Patty's Mate." *Los Angeles Times*, 4 September 1952, II-1.

O'Connor, Dick. "Famous Songbirds 7-Year Fight Up Success Ladder Told." *Los Angeles Herald Express*, 24 August 1954, A-1, A-12.

_____. "Patti, the Youngest Sister, Makes Break After Twenty Years." *Los Angeles Herald Express*, 27 August 1954, A-7.

"Offer Dance Numbers." *Minneapolis Tribune*, 21 December 1930.

O'Haire, Patricia. "Half a Sister Act Sinks-or-Swims." *New York Daily News*, 29 September 1975.

"On the Wax." *The Yale Record*, 1941. David McCain Collection.

Oncken, Ed. "Patty Andrews." *The Billboard*, 10 July 1954, 39.

O'Reilly, David. "A Musical Celebrating Old Age." *Philadelphia Inquirer*, 13 February 1985.

"Oriental, Chi." *Variety*, 14 August 1934, 14.

Orodenker, M. H. "Review of Records." *The Billboard*, 8 May 1937, 11.

_____. "Review of Records." *The Billboard*, 15 May 1937, 11.

_____. "Orchestra Notes." *The Billboard*, 5 March 1938, 16.

_____. "Selling Theater." *The Billboard*, 2 August 1941, 13.

_____. "Selling the Band." *The Billboard*, 16 August 1941, 12.

_____. *The Billboard*, 31 October 1942, 17.

"Orpheum." *The Rocky Mountain News*, 15 July 1932, 4.

"Over a Half Million Records." *Down Beat*, August 1939, 12.

Owen, Dean. "Paramount, Los Angeles." *The Billboard*, 27 July 1940, 22.

"The Palladium." *London Times*, 31 July 1951, 8.

"Paramount, N.Y." *Variety*, 20 July 1938, 45.

"Paramount, New York." *The Billboard*, 28 December 1946, 35.

Parish, James Robert and Michael R. Pitts. *Hollywood Songsters*. New York: Garland Publishing, Inc., 1991.

Parker, Jerry. "Andrews Sisters Hope to Ride 'Mini-Revival' Back to Broadway." *Minneapolis Star*, 15 February 1974.

Parmenter, Derek. "Andrews Sisters Well Liked." *San Francisco Chronicle*, 17 April 1947, 11.

Parrillo, Raphaele. "Wrigley's DOUBLE MINT Gum Presents 'Double Everything.'" Wrigley Archives. Undated. Robert Boyer Collection.

_____. "Wrigley's SPEARMINT GUM Presents 'Just Entertainment' Radio Program." Wrigley Archives. Undated. Robert Boyer Collection.

Parsons, Louella. Untitled. *Seattle Post-Intelligencer*, 22 October 1953. Frank Bivens Collection.

"Part 3—The Billboard Music Popularity Chart. Record Possibilities." *The Billboard*, 11 November 1944, 18.

Patrick, Corbin. "Maxene Opens Big at IRT's Cabaret." *The Indianapolis Star*, 3 February 1982. Ken Petrack Collection.

"Patti Andrews Asks Divorce, No Alimony." *Los Angeles Times*, 3 February 1950, III-10.

"Patti Andrews Exits Chez Paree in Billing Row." *Variety*, 24 August 1955, 59.

"Patti Andrews Files Will Suit Against LaVerne." *Los Angeles Daily News*, 29 May 1954.

"Patti Andrews Gets Buildup As Single." *Down Beat*, 16 November 1951, 19.

"Patti Andrews Gets Checkup." *Los Angeles Times*, 12 October 1954, I-18.

"Patti Andrews Ill, So Stars Fill in for Sisters." *The Billboard*, 22 September 1945, 36.

"Patti Andrews Taken Off Train for Emergency Op at Rock Island, Illinois." *Variety*, 1 July 1942, 3.

"Patti Andrews vs. 'Over Here.'" *Variety*, 2 April 1975, 88.

"Patti Andrews Wed to Agent." *Los Angeles Times*, 21 October 1947.

"Patti Leaves Again." *Down Beat*, 10 February 1954, 3.

"Patty Andrews." *Variety*, 20 April 1954, 57.

"Patty Andrews Quits Job Here." *Chicago American*, August 1955.

"Patty Andrews Wed on Coast." *New York Times*, 26 December 1951, 20.

"Patty's 40 Grand Appendectomy." *Down Beat*, 15 July 1942, 1.

Perry, James A. "Great Singers Never Fade Away." *New Orleans States-Item*, 9 September 1967. Joyce De Young Collection.

"Personalities: Boogie Woogie Redux." *The Washington Post*, 19 June 1991, F-3.

"Peter Solie [sic], Uncle of Andrews Sisters, Dies." 1963. Undated newspaper clipping. Gladys Leichter Collection.

Phillips, Frosene. "Frosene on the Scene." *San Mateo County Times*. 26 May 2003, 19.

"Philly Picks Up Despite Heat Wave; Andrews Sis-'Widow' Nice $20,000." *Variety*, 2 July 1941, 10.

"Phonograph Records. Bing Crosby with Andrews Sisters." *Metronome*, December 1939, 14.

"'Pistol' in Black Market Demand." *Variety*, 15 September 1943, 45.

Podesta, Jane Sims. "Gone from the Headlines—But Not Forgotten." *Minneapolis Star*, 22 September 1977.

Polic, Edward F. *The Andrews Sisters with the Glenn Miller Orchestra*. CD booklet. RCA Victor, 1997.

"Police Variety Show Monday." *New Orleans States-Item*, 24 August 1967. Joyce DeYoung Collection.

Pool. "Michigan, Detroit." *Variety*, 7 April 1943, 39.

Poole, Harry. *The Billboard*, 5 September 1942, 16.

"Possibilities." *The Billboard*, 1 October 1938, 4.

Price, Paul. "Dateline LV." *Las Vegas Sun*, 7 October 1961. Charles Saunders Collection.

"Protest Decca Air Ban." *The Billboard*, 30 March 1940, 5.

"Publisher Lou Levy Weds in London." *The Melody Maker*, 30 September 1951, 1.

"Publisher's Desk." *Sheet Music*, January/February 1990, 2.

Pugh, Ronnie. *Ernest Tubb: The Texas Troubadour*. Durham: Duke University Press, 1996.

"Puttin' on the Ritz." *Down Beat*, 1 July 1940, 24.

Qualey, Carlton C. and Jon A. Gjerde. "The Norwegians." In *They Chose Minnesota, A Survey of the State's Ethnic Groups*, edited by June Drenning Holmquist, 220–247. St. Paul: Minnesota Historical Society, 1981.

Rachlin, Harvey. *The Encyclopedia of the Music Business*. New York: Harper and Row, 1981.

Radcliffe, E. B. "Out in Front." *The Enquirer, Cincinnati*, 6 December 1941, 24.

"Radio and Television Program Reviews: Holiday Star Varieties." *The Billboard*, 4 December 1948, 8.

"'Rangers'-Andrews Sis Big $54,000, Chi Leader; 'Affairs'-Davis Great 26 G, 'Done It' $15,500, 'Eileen' 19½ G." *Variety*, 11 November 1942, 9.

"Recipe for Success." *Band Leaders*, January 1945, 62.

"Record Buying Guide." *The Billboard*, 25 November 1939, 70.

"Record Reviews. Andrews Sisters." *Down Beat*, 1 October 1940, 14.

"Record Reviews. Andrews Sisters." *Down Beat*, 1 December 1940, 14.

"Record Reviews. Andrews Sisters." *Down Beat*, 15 October 1941, 14.

"Record Reviews. Andrews Sisters." *Down Beat*, 15 September 1942, 9.

"Record Reviews. Andrews Sisters." *Down Beat*, 1 January 1944, 8.

"Record Reviews. Andrews Sisters." *Metronome*, July 1944, 22.

"Record Reviews. Andrews Sisters." *Metronome*, February 1945, 14.

"Record Reviews. Andrews Sisters." *Down Beat*, 26 August 1946, 21.

"Record Reviews. Andrews Sisters." *Down Beat*, 1 July 1949, 15.

"Record Reviews. Andrews Sisters." *Metronome*, June 1944, 22.

"Record Reviews. Bing Crosby." *Metronome*, February 1948, 44.

"Record Reviews. Bing Crosby—Andrews Sisters—Joe Venuti." *Down Beat*, 15 December 1939, 21.

"Record Reviews. Bing Crosby, Dick Haymes and the Andrews Sisters." *Down Beat*, 16 July 1947, 15.

"Record Reviews. Bing Crosby—Dick Haymes—Andrews Sisters." *Metronome*, September 1947, 26.

"Record Reviews. Boswell Sisters Album." *Metronome*, June 1943, 16.

"Record Reviews. Crosby—Andrews." *Metronome*, December 1943, 24.

"Record Reviews. Crosby—Andrews Sisters." *Down Beat*, 1 December 1943, 8.

"Records—News." *Down Beat*, 15 December 1939, 21.

Reed. "Palomar, Seattle." *Variety*, 16 April 1952, 61.

Reed, Rex. "Andrews Sisters Sounding Sour Notes." *Philadelphia Inquirer*, 5 January 1975.

_____. "On the Town with Rex Reed." *New York Observer*, 13 November 1995. Robert Boyer Collection.

_____. "Those Boogie-Woogie Babies Bounce Back." *Chicago Tribune*, 3 March 1974, 6–3.

_____. *Valentines & Vitriol*. New York: Delacorte Press, 1977.

Rees. "Orpheum, Mpls." *Variety*, 5 February 1941, 54.

_____. "Orpheum, Mpls." *Variety*, 17 March 1943, 19, 40.

"Regular Shows—Andrews Sisters." *Metronome*, January 1946, 49.

Reuter, Maynard. "Weekly Music Notes." *The Billboard*, 12 February 1938, 76.

"Reviews of New Pop Records." *The Billboard*, 18 February 1956, 55.

"Revue Features Song and Dance Numbers." *The Minneapolis Journal*, 14 June 1931, 6.

Richman, Daniel. "Paramount, New York." *The Billboard*, 31 December 1938, 30.

_____. "Record Buying Guide." *The Billboard*, 6 May 1939, 76.

Ring. "Adams, Newark." *Variety*, 22 March 1944, 20.

"RKO Proctor's." *Newark Evening News*, 26 February 1932, 7.

"'Rockne'—Andrews Scoring $18,500 to Lead Wash." *Variety*, 16 October 1940, 11.

Rooks, C. F. C. "Bums and Coca-Cola." *Metronome*, August 1945, 30.

Rose, Frank. "Dancing the 40's Polka." *Zoo World*, 10 October 1974, 18, 20.

Roso. "Patty Andrews." *Variety*, 12 March 1980, 107.

Ross, Paul. "Paramount, New York." *The Billboard*, 15 September 1945, 35.

"A Roundup of Fun and Song for the New Year!" *Variety*, 27 December 1944, 60.

Roura, Phil and Tom Poster. "Sing? Patti, Maxene Don't Even Talk." *New York Daily News*, 7 March 1980. David McCain Collection.

Royce, Graydon. "Andrews Sisters Are a Faded Minnesota Memory." *Minneapolis Star-Tribune*, 12 April 2002.

Ruhlmann, William. *The Andrews Sisters:Their All Time Greatest Hits*. Compact Disc Booklet. MCA Records, Inc., 1994.

_____. "The Andrews Sisters, Three Sides to Every Story." *Goldmine*, 1995, (21): 2: 16–22, 24, 26, 28, 30, 32, 34, 36, 38, 40, 101, 103–104, 106, 108, 110–112, 114, 123, 139, 147–148.

"Rum and Coca-Cola." *Variety*, 10 January 1945, 38.

"'Rum and Coca-Cola' Now Okay on NBC; All Nets Pass It." *The Billboard*, 17 March 1945, 4.

"'Rum & Coca-Cola' Okay on CBS Now; Still Nix on NBC." *The Billboard*, 3 March 1945, 7.

"'Rum & Cola' Haunts Phoenix Grille Staff." *The Billboard*, 17 February 1945, 18.

Ruppli, Michel. *The Decca Labels: A Discography*. Vols. 1, 2, 3, 5 and 6. Westport: Greenwood Press, 1996.

"S. F. Gate Aims at 48G with Andrews." *The Billboard*, 1 June 1946, 45.

Sachs, Bill. "Orchestra Notes." *The Billboard*, 8 July 1933, 15.

Sackett, Susan. *Hollywood Sings!* New York: Billboard Books, 1995.

Safford, Virginia. "Virginia Safford." *The Minneapolis Star*, 27 August 1946, 12.

_____. "Virginia Safford." *The Minneapolis Star*, 17 April 1951, 22.

Sahu. "Ambassador, St. L." *Variety*, 25 November 1942, 22.

Saloutos, Theodore. "The Greeks." In *They Chose Minnesota: A Survey of the State's Ethnic Groups*, edited by June Drenning Holmquist, 472–488. St. Paul: Minnesota Historical Society, 1981.

"'Saludos'-Andrews-Ayres Wham $28,500 in Cleve." *Variety*, 28 April 1943, 12.

Sanjek, Russell. *Pennies from Heaven*. New York: Da Capo Press, 1996.

Saunders, Charles. Undated. "The Andrews Sisters." Unpublished manuscript.

Sayre, J. Willis. "Crowd Greets Andrews Trio." *Seattle Post-Intelligencer*, 7 June 1946, 19.

"Scalpers Got $15–$20 for Andrews Sis' Socko Lond. Palladium Finale." *Variety*, 1 September 1948, 44.

Schaeffer, Dirk. "Footnotes on Jazz." *Metronome*, July 1956, 24.

Schallert, Edwin. "Hotcha Trio Can Laugh at Critics." *Los Angeles Times*, 30 July 1944, III-1, 6.

_____. "Patty Andrews to Star in 'Three Charms'; Hope Starts 'Foy' Next Month." *Los Angeles Times*, 25 June 1954, III-7.

Scho. "Flatbush, B'klyn." *Variety*, 27 September 1939, 45.

_____. "Strand, Brooklyn." *Variety*, 21 September 1938, 47.

"Schoen, Andrews Sis Split After 16 Years." *Variety*, 5 September 1951, 53.

"Schoen Quits Andrews Unit; Weighs Plans." *The Billboard*, 8 September 1951, 14.

Schoenfeld, Herm. "Jocks, Jukes and Disks." *Variety*, 15 May 1957, 58.

_____. "Jocks, Jukes and Disks." *Variety*, 28 August 1957, 44.

"Scots Hustle to Write New Andrews Sisters Song." *The Melody Maker*, 18 August 1951, 6.

Scottish Daily Mail, 14 August 1951. Charles Saunders Collection.

Scourby, Alice. *The Greek Americans*. Boston: Twayne Publishers, 1984.

"Screen Comedian Is Listed in Leading Vaudeville Act." *The Providence Sunday Journal*, 7 February 1932, D-7.

Scul. "Chi Chi, Palm Springs." *Variety*, 14 February 1962, 55.

Sears, Richard L. *V-Discs: A History and Discography*. Westport: Greenwood Press, 1980.

Secunda, Victoria. *Bei Mir Bist Du Schon:The Life of Sholom Secunda*. Weston: Magic Circle Press, 1982.

Sforza, John. *Swing It! The Andrews Sisters Story*. Lexington: The University Press of Kentucky, 2000.

Shal. "Earle, Phila." *Variety*, 2 July 1941, 47.

_____. "Earle, Philly." *Variety*, 9 October 1940, 46.

_____. "Earle, Philly." *Variety*, 11 December 1946, 24.

Shapiro, Laura. "This Time, One from the Heart." *Newsweek*, 11 November 1991, 68–69.

Shaughnessy, Mary Alice. *Les Paul: An American Original*. New York: William Morrow and Company, Inc., 1993.

Shaw. "Cave, Vancouver." *Variety*, 22 January 1964, 85.

Shaw, Arnold. *Let's Dance: Popular Music in the 1930s*. New York: Oxford University Press, 1998.

"Showbiz As 'Train' Stoker." *The Billboard*, 30 August 1947, 1.

Silvert, Conrad. "A Veteran Superstar with Moxie, Class." *San Francisco Chronicle*, 13 September 1979, 56.

Simon, George. "Leon Belasco." *Metronome*, April 1937, 22–23.

Simon, George T. "Record Reviews: Popular. Bing Crosby—Andrews Sisters." *Metronome*, January 1953, 27.

_____, and Friends. *The Best of the Music Makers*. Garden City: Doubleday and Company, Inc., 1979.

"Sinatra Para. Preem Poor 90G as Bobby Sox Hog Seats; M. H. Opens with Juicy 130G." *The Billboard*, 28 October 1944, 23.

"Sinatra, Spitalny and Andrews Sisters' Bids Cue Big Concert Biz." *Variety*, 4 October 1944, 1.

"Singer Denies She Tried to Kill Herself." *San Francisco Chronicle*, 23 December 1954, 16.

"Singer Maxene Andrews Dies at 79." *San Francisco Examiner*, 23 October 1995, A-13.

"Singer's Condition 'Fair.'" *Chicago Tribune*, 7 September 1982.

"Singers in Discord—Gun Jails Pa." *New York Daily News*, 31 January 1940, 3.

"Singing Andrews Sisters." *Variety*, 27 January 1943, 2.

"Singing Andrews Sisters Say All Is Harmony in the Family." *Daily Mirror*, 1 February 1940, 5.

Sippel, Johnny. "Cocoanut Grove, Ambassador Hotel, Los Angeles." *The Billboard*, 8 November 1952, 15, 65.

"Sister." *The New Yorker*, 11 November 1991, 33–35.

"Sisters Sing Carols." *The Des Moines Register*, 22 December 1931, 14.

"Skelton Skit Miffs Patty Andrews." *San Francisco Chronicle*, 5 November 1954, 24.

Skip. "Shamrock, Houston." *Variety*, 21 November 1962, 42.

Smith, Andrew. "Focus on the Andrews Sisters." *Harper's Bazaar*, April 1974, 89, 110–111.

Smith, Bill. "Roxy, New York." *The Billboard*, 3 July 1948, 40.

Smith, Cecil. "Bud and Lou Go Crazy in a Haunted House." *Chicago Daily Tribune*, 7 August 1941, 14.

Smith, Joe. *Off the Record: An Oral History of Popular Music.* Warner Books, 1988.

Smith, R. C. "Andrews Sister Shines Like It Was Yesterday." *Durham Morning Herald*, 18 December 1981. Ken Petrack Collection.

"Snub 'Rum, Coke.'" *The Billboard*, 20 January 1945, 14.

Soanes, Wood. "Andrews Trio Likes to Sing." *Oakland Tribune*, 21 February 1943, B-7.

Soul. "Chi Chi, Palm Springs." *Variety*, 29 January 1958, 63.

Spatz, David. "Patty Andrews Appreciates Old and New." *The Press*, 4 January 1987, F-6, F-7.

Speegle, Paul. "Andrews Sisters Are Stars of Gate Show." *San Francisco Chronicle*, 23 May 1946, 9.

_____. "The Andrews Sisters, Gate Fans Are Clapping Even Before They Sing." *San Francisco Chronicle*, 19 June 1941, 7.

_____. "Pack Up Your Troubles! The Gate's Send Is Solid." *San Francisco Chronicle*, 29 January 1942, 7.

_____. "Sisters Andrews." *San Francisco Chronicle*, 1 February 1942, 18.

"Spikes Rumored Andrews Split." *Variety*, 24 September 1949, 21.

"Spitalny Smash 48G, Det., Spivak Fine $22,500, Pitts., Andrews Sis-Ayres Big 30G in Hub; Krupa Hot $9,300, 3 Days." *Variety*, 19 May 1943, 34.

"'Spy'-Andrew [sic] Sis-Osborne Huge 30G In Hub; 'Crossroads' 40G in 2 Spots." *Variety*, 26 August 1942, 16.

"Stage Shows Again Rescue Chi; 'Mothers'— Andrews-Krupa 45G, 'Suez'—Vaude 22G, H.O.s Strong." *Variety*, 12 February 1941, 9.

Stal. "Frank Sinatra Show." *Variety*, 17 October 1951, 30.

"Station KXLW." *Variety*, 29 November 1950, 56.

Stearns, David Patrick. "Maxene Andrews Swings Solo in Campy Sendup of USO." *USA Today*, 2 October 1995, D-4.

Stein, Ruthe. "The Rift That Split the Andrew [sic] Sisters." *San Francisco Chronicle*, 14 September 1979, 43.

Sternig, Barbara. "Andrews' Sister Maxene, 59: I Want to Sing with Patty Again." *National Enquirer*, 6 December 1977, 26.

Stokes, W. Royal. "Maxene Andrews." *Washington Post*, 11 October 1979, D-15.

"The Story of a Song: 'Bei Mir Bist Du Schon' Now Heads Best-Sellers." *Life*, 31 January 1938, 39.

Stowe, David W. *Swing Changes. Big-Band Jazz in New Deal America.* Cambridge: Harvard University Press, 1994.

"Strictly Ad Lib." *Down Beat*, 25 March 1953, 21.

"Strictly Ad Lib by the Square." *Down Beat*, 15 May 1942, 4.

"'Strip Polka' Is First Smash Hit San Ether Help." *The Billboard*, 17 October 1942, 23.

"Suicide Try Denied by Singer." *Los Angeles Examiner*, 22 December 1954, 1, 2.

Sydney Morning Herald, 2 December 1954. Charles Saunders Collection.

"T. Dorsey-Andrews-'Co-Ed'- Big $16,000 in Football Mad Mpls.; 'Drums' $2,000." *Variety*, 19 October 1938, 11.

T. M. P. "At Loew's State." *New York Times*, 11 October 1940, 25.

_____. "At the Capitol." *New York Times*, 8 August 1941, 13.

_____. "At the Palace." *New York Times*, 28 August 1942, 22.

T. S. "At Loew's Criterion." *New York Times*, 25 June 1942, 27.

_____. "At Loew's State." *New York Times*, 14 February 1941, 15.

_____. "At Loew's State." *New York Times*, 17 December 1943, 23.

Tagashira, Gail S. "An Andrews Sister." *San Jose Mercury News*, 24 July 1981. Ken Petrack Collection.

Ted. "Mark Hopkins, S.F." *Variety*, 27 August 1952, 52.

"Ted Lewis, Andrews Sis Added to A. & C. Film." *Variety*, 9 April 1941, 3.

"Ted Mack Is Welcomed Joyously at The Denver." *The Rocky Mountain News*, 15 December 1933, 14.

"Ted Mack's Wowing 'Em at Denver." *The Rocky Mountain News*, 17 December 1933, 11.

"Television Follow-Up: Frank Sinatra Show." *Variety*, 7 March 1951, 30.

"Television Follow-Up: Tony Martin." *Variety*, 7 March 1951, 30.

"10 Best Sellers on Coin-Machines." *Variety*, 14 February 1945, 44.

Terry, Clifford. "At the Hard Rock Cafe with Maxene Andrews." *Chicago Tribune*, 29 June 1993, V-1, 10.

"Theatres and Their Players." *The Seattle Times*, 7 June 1946, 11.

"They've Done It Again." *The Billboard*, 21 July 1945, 15.

Thomas, Bob. "Places and People." Undated. John Tyler Collection.

Thompson, Charles. *Bing: The Authorized Biography*. New York: David McKay Company, Inc., 1975.

"Those Rhythm Cry Babies." *The Commercial Appeal*, 4 July 1937, 8.

"Three Zombies of Swing." *Newsweek*, 18 September 1944, 97–98.

"Top Phono Artists." *The Billboard*, 17 January 1942, 9.

"Top-Rating Pictures for 1940–41." *Variety*, 3 September 1940, 24.

"Top Singing and Instrumental Groups on Juke Boxes." *The Billboard Juke Box Supplement*, 4 March 1950, 77.

"Top Talent for V Discs." *Metronome*, October 1944, 10.

Torme, Mel. *My Singing Teachers*. New York: Oxford University Press, 1994.

Toulon. "Memphis." *Metronome*, October 1936, 40.

Tracy, Kathleen. "Sounds of Silence." *Globe*, 21 July 1992.

"Tragedy Hits Twice—In Same Way—In Andrews Sisters Parents' Death." *Variety*, 12 October 1949, 42.

"Trio and Quartet." *Down Beat*, December 1938, 34.

"UCLA Archives Deposit." *Hollywood Reporter*, 18 August 1980.

"U.S. Sues Andrews Sisters." *New York Times*, 24 January 1960, 90.

Ulanov. "Mitch Ayres." *Metronome*, August 1943, 21, 32.

_____. "Radio Reviews: Andrews." *Metronome*, April 1945, 26.

Ulanov, Barry. *The Incredible Crosby*. New York: McGraw-Hill Book Company, Inc., 1948.

_____. "V Discs." *Metronome*, May 1944, 20.

Unidentified Memphis Newspaper, 26 October 1933. Robert Boyer Collection.

Van Horne, Harriet. "Cinderella in Triplicate." *Pageant*, March 1946, 17–19.

Van Iquity, Sister Dana. "Andrews Sisters Wow GI's." *San Francisco Bay Times*, 30 April 1998, 24.

Van Matre, Lynn. "Echos [sic]of an Era." *Chicago Tribune*, 20 November 1988, 10–11.

Vance, Leigh. "3 Jolly Good Sorts Are Andrews Ladies, Meaning Sock in London." *The Billboard*, 11 August 1951, 3.

"Variety and Picture Bills of the Week." *The Minneapolis Journal*, 14 June 1931, 8.

Vettel, Phil. "Maxene Andrews in Concert is Joyous, Magical Retrospective." *Chicago Tribune*, 19 August 1982, IV-7.

"Vic Schoen Leaves Andrews Sisters." *The Melody Maker*, 30 September 1951, 1, 7.

"Vic Schoen; Musical Director for Andrews Sisters." *Los Angeles Times*, 10 January 2000, A14.

"Visitors Boost B'way; 'Regards' Plus Andrews Sis-Martin & Lewis-Iceshow Wow 125G, 'Apache'-Horne Sock 116G." *Variety*, 30 June 1948, 13.

Waggoner, Kenneth H. "Palladium, London." *The Billboard*, 21 August 1948, 39.

Walk. "500 Club, A. C." *Variety*, 26 August 1959, 53.

_____. "Steel Pier, A. C." *Variety*, 28 August 1946, 56.

Walker, Evelyn. "I Worked Backstage with the Andrews Sisters." Undated magazine article. Merle Smith Collection.

Wallace, Ed. "Andrews Sisters Beat Life 8 to the Bar." circa 1940. Robert Boyer Collection.

Wallace, Irving. "The Three Jive Bombers." *Coronet*, March 1943, 138–141.

Walt. "Argentine Nights." *Variety*, 4 September 1940, 18.

_____. "Buck Privates." *Variety*, 5 February 1941, 12.

_____. "Hold That Ghost." Variety, 30 July 1941, 18.

_____. "How's About It." *Variety*, 3 February 1943, 14.

_____. "In the Navy." *Variety*, 4 June 1941, 15.

_____. "Private Buckaroo." *Variety*, 3 June 1942, 8.

_____. "What's Cookin'." *Variety*, 25 February 1942, 8.

"War Workers Make It 'Piston Packin'' Mama.'" *Variety*, 1 December 1943, 2.

Ward, Ed, Geoffrey Stokes and Ken Tucker. *Rock of Ages*. New York: Rolling Stone Press, 1986.

Warner, Jay. *The Billboard Book of American Singing Groups*. New York: Billboard Books, 1992.

Washburn, Mel. "Blue Room Show Has No Weak Spots." *The New Orleans Item*, 16 April 1937, 5.

Washington Daily Press, August 1959. Charles Saunders Collection.

"We Couldn't Believe It!!!" *Variety*, 8 September 1948, 28, 29.

Wear. "Always a Bridesmaid." *Variety*, 29 September 1943, 8.

Weaver, Gretchen. "Tunester Three." *Band Leaders*, April 1946, 27, 55.

Weinberger, Caspar W. "DOD Medals For Distinguished Public Service To: Ms. Maxene Andrews, Ms. Patty Andrews, Ms. LaVerne Andrews." Typescript. April 1987. Ken Petrack Collection.

Weinstock, Matt. "A Trio of Cinderellas." 1940. Merle Smith Collection.

Weintraub, Boris. "Maxene Andrews? A Happy Single." *The Washington Star*, 10 October 1979, C-1.

"Welcome for Andrews Sisters." *Minneapolis Star Journal*, 1 February 1941, 12.

"'We'll Scare Those Guys to Death'—Andrews Sisters." *Down Beat*, 15 February 1941, 4.

Wells, Lynda. "D-Day Revisited. The Melodies Linger On." *Sheet Music*, November/December 1994, 6–8, 10.

Wells, Margaret S. "Music in the News." *The Billboard*, 27 November 1943, 98.

Wendeborn, John. "Maxene Andrews Still Answers Call of Road." *Oregonian*, 3 April 1981. Ken Petrack Collection.

_____. "Maxene Program a Must-See." *Oregonian*, 7 April 1981. Ken Petrack Collection.

Wern. "Golden Gate, S. F." *Variety*, 25 June 1941, 41.

_____. "Golden Gate, S. F." *Variety*, 4 February 1942, 46.

Weschler, M. W. "Andrews Revenue." Letters to the Editor. *Newsweek*, 17 December 1979, 14.

Whitburn, Joel. *Pop Memories, 1890–1954*. Menomonee Falls: Record Research, Inc., 1986.

"Who's Who Among Recording Girl Singers." *Metronome*, April 1947, 64—65.

Widem, Allen M. "An Andrews Sister Returns to Stage at the Coachlight." *The Hartford Times*, 25 June 1976, 22.

Wilkes, Mary Frances. "Over Here, Over There: The Andrews Sisters and the USO Stars in World War II." *Booklist* (89), 1993, 1760–1761.

Will. "Flamingo, Las Vegas." *Variety*, 26 March 1951, 46.

_____. "Riviera, Las Vegas." *Variety*, 25 January 1956, 53.

_____. "Sahara, Las Vegas." *Variety*, 31 December 1952, 43.

Williams, Esther and Digby Diehl. *The Million Dollar Mermaid*. New York: Simon and Schuster, 1999.

Wilson, Earl. "Earl Wilson." *Los Angeles Daily News*, 20 June 1949.

_____. "It Happened Last Night." *New York Post*, 30 June 1943, 32.

Wilson, John S. "An Andrews Sister Goes Solo." *New York Times*, 16 November 1979, C-3.

_____. "Bei Him They're Still Schon." *New York Times*, 28 April 1974, II-1, 3.

_____. "Pop: Patti Andrews Solo." *New York Times*, 6 March 1980, C-9.

Wilson, Mary. *Dream Girl & Supreme Faith: My Life As a Supreme*. New York: Cooper Square Press, 1999.

"Winners 1946 Honor Roll of Hits." *The Billboard*, 4 January 1947, 1.

"Within These 5 Pages Are Listed the Most Generous People in the World." *Variety*, 26 January 1944, 27.

"WJZ Bans 'Pistol' Disc." *Variety*, 10 November 1943, 61.

Wood. "Club 15." *Variety*, 7 September 1949, 28.

_____. "Eight to the Bar Ranch." *Variety*, 5 September 1945, 26.

_____. "Flatbush, B'klyn." *Variety*, 30 October 1940, 55.

_____. "Paramount, N.Y." *Variety*, 25 September 1940, 54.

_____. "Paramount, N.Y." *Variety*, 13 September 1944, 42.

_____. "Paramount, N.Y." *Variety*, 25 December 1946, 42.

Woods, Bernie. *When the Music Stopped*. New York: Barricade Books, 1994.

Wool, Allen L. *The Hollywood Musical Goes to War*. Chicago: Nelson-Hall, 1983.

"The Year's Best Selling Popular Retail Records." *The Billboard*, 3 January 1948, 18.

"The Year's Top Popular Records." *The Billboard*, 14 January 1950, 14.

"The Year's Top Popular Retail Record Sellers." *The Billboard*, 3 January 1948, 19.

"The Year's Top Selling Folk Artists." *The Billboard*, 14 January 1950, 19.

"The Year's Top Selling Singing and Instrumental Groups Over Retail Counters." *The Billboard*, 1 January 1949, 19.

"The Year's Top Singing Instrumental Groups on the Nation's Juke Boxes." *The Billboard*, 22 January 1949, 59.

"Yiddish Into Navajo." *Variety*, 19 January 1938, 46.

Zabe. "Chicago, Chi." *Variety*, 5 July 1950, 47.

Zhito, Lee. "Cocoanut Grove, Ambassador Hotel, Los Angeles." *The Billboard*, 3 May 1952, 15.

Interviews

Andrews, Maxene. Interview by Robert Boyer. 1975

Andrews, Maxene. Interview by Fred Hall on radio program *Swing Thing*. WAIT, Chicago. March 1983.

Andrews, Maxene. Interview by Pat Cheffer on television show *Lifestyle*. November, 1988.

Andrews, Maxene. Interview by Jan Shapiro. Typescript of videocassette interview. 20 June 1989.

Andrews, Maxene. Interview by Sally Jesse Raphael on television. 22 September 1989.

Andrews, Maxene. Interview by Mark Simone on radio program *The Mark Simone Show*. WWAM, New York City, NY. July 1992.

Andrews, Maxene. Interview by unknown radio host on radio program *One Night Stand*. circa 1974.

Andrews, Maxene and Patty Andrews. Interview by Merv Griffin on television show *The Merv Griffin Show*. 26 June 1972.

Andrews, Maxene and Patty Andrews. Interview by Rex Reed. Audiocassette. March 1974.

Andrews, Patty. Interview by Joey Bishop on *The Joey Bishop Show*. 6 May 1968.

Andrews, Patty. Interview by Richard Lamparski

on radio program "*Whatever Happened To...?*" circa 1972.

Andrews Sisters. Interview by Johnny Carson on television show *The Johnny Carson Show*. 2 March 1965.

Boyer, Robert. Interview by author. September 2000.

Deniké, Karina. Interview by author. October 2001.

DeYoung, Joyce. Interviews by author. 17 October 2000, 15 November 2000.

Forsmark, Mary Ann. Interview by author. May 2000.

Fowler, Beth. Interview by author. June 2001.

Hagen, Ray. Interview by author. 20 September 2000.

Klenner, Joseph. Interview by author. 10 February 2002.

Klimo, Helen Malliaras. Interview by author. 2 October 2000.

Kurzawinski, Patricia. Interview by author. 19 January 2003.

Leichter, Gladys. Interviews by author. 6 February 2001, 20 February 2001, 24 March 2001.

Nelson, Jimmy. Interview by author. 14 November 2000.

Petrack, Ken. Interview by author. 3 October 2000.

Ruggiero, Arthur. Interview by author. 6 November 2000.

Sabatino, Louis. Interview by author. October 2001.

Schoen, Vic. Interview by Robert Boyer. 12 July 1998.

Stocking, Sidney. Interview by Robert Boyer. 26 June 1976.

Therault, Thomas. Interview by author. October 2000.

Traxler, Arlene Moberg. Interview by author. 15 February 2002.

Weston, Jim. Interview by author. 27 October 2000.

Legal Documents

Andrews, Angelyn. Certificate of Birth. 14 July 1913. Department of Health—Division of Vital Statistics. City of Minneapolis.

Andrews, Angelyn. Certificate of Death. 17 March 1914. Division of Vital Statistics. State of Minnesota.

Andrews, LaVerne. Record of Birth. 6 July 1911. Division of Vital Statistics. State of Minnesota.

Andrews, LaVerne. Certificate of Death. 8 May 1967. Office of the State Registrar of Vital Statistics. State of California.

Andrews, LaVerne. Last Will of LaVerne Andrews Ruggiero also known as LaVerne Andrews. 26 November 1960.

Andrews, Maxine. Record of Birth. 3 January 1916. Division of Vital Statistics. State of Minnesota.

Andrews, Maxene. Will of Maxene Anglyn Andrews. 7 August 1990. Placer County, California.

Andrews, Ollie. Last Will and Testament. 19 September 1946. Los Angeles County Records Center. Los Angeles County, California.

Andrews, Patricia. Record of Birth. 16 February 1918. Division of Vital Statistics. State of Minnesota.

Andrews, Peter. Last Will and Testament of Peter Andrews. 26 September 1949. Los Angeles County Records Center. Los Angeles County, California.

Andrew [sic], Peter and Olga B. Sollie. Application for Marriage License. 6 July 1910. State of Minnesota. County of Hennepin.

Andrew [sic], Peter and Olga B. Sollie. Marriage License and Certificate. 6 July 1910. State of Minnesota. County of Hennepin.

Moberg, Mable. Certificate of Death. 7 July 1925. Division of Vital Statistics. State of Minnesota.

Solle [sic], Peter Peterson. Certificate of Death. 8 February 1920. Division of Vital Statistics. State of Minnesota.

Sollie, Edward E. Certificate of Death. 2 April 1964. Minnesota Department of Health, Section of Vital Statistics.

Sollie, Elydia. Certificate of Death. 31 December 1908. Department of Health—Division of Vital Statistics. City of Minneapolis.

Sollie, Peter. Certificate of Death. 19 August 1963. Minnesota Department of Health, Section of Vital Statistics.

Sollie, Sophia Hoove. Certificate of Death. 24 August 1920. Division of Vital Statistics. State of Minnesota.

United States Census. City of Minneapolis. 1900. 1910. 1920. 1930.

Letters

Andrews, LaVerne. Letter to Florence Hannahan from Atlanta, Georgia. 6 November 1931. Robert Boyer Collection.

Andrews, LaVerne. Letter to Peter and Olga Andrews from Atlanta, Georgia. 6 November 1931. Robert Boyer Collection.

Andrews, LaVerne. Letter to Florence Hannahan from Atlanta, Georgia. 11 November 1931. Robert Boyer Collection.

Andrews, LaVerne. Letter to Florence Hannahan from New York, New York. 5 February 1932. Robert Boyer Collection.

Andrews, LaVerne. Letter to Florence Hannahan from Cleveland, Ohio. 17 April 1932. Robert Boyer Collection.

Andrews, LaVerne. Letter to Florence Hannahan from Seattle, Washington. 28 May 1932. Robert Boyer Collection.

Andrews, LaVerne. Letter to Florence Hannahan from San Francisco, California. 8 June 1932. Robert Boyer Collection.

Andrews, LaVerne. Letter to Florence Hannahan from Omaha, Nebraska. 24 June [July] 1932. Robert Boyer Collection.

Andrews, LaVerne. Letter to Florence Hannahan from San Francisco, California. 27 June 1932. Robert Boyer Collection.

Andrews, LaVerne. Letter to Florence Hannahan from Omaha, Nebraska. 24 July 1932. Robert Boyer Collection.

Andrews, LaVerne. Letter to Florence Hannahan from New York, New York. 19 October 1932. Robert Boyer Collection.

Andrews, LaVerne. Letter to Florence Hannahan from New York, New York. 23 November 1932. Robert Boyer Collection.

Andrews, LaVerne. Letter to Florence Hannahan from New York, New York. Circa January, 1933. Robert Boyer Collection.

Andrews, LaVerne. Letter to Florence Hannahan from Denver, Colorado. 15 December 1933. Robert Boyer Collection.

Andrews, LaVerne. Letter to Florence Hannahan from Chicago, Illinois. 16 January 1934. Robert Boyer Collection.

Andrews, LaVerne. Letter to Florence Hannahan from Toledo, Ohio. 16 October 1934. Robert Boyer Collection.

Andrews, LaVerne. Letter to Florence Hannahan from Louisville, Kentucky. 9 December 1934. Robert Boyer Collection.

Andrews, LaVerne. Letter to Florence Hannahan from Chicago, Illinois. 17 December 1934. Robert Boyer Collection.

Andrews, LaVerne. Letter to Florence Hannahan from Chicago, Illinois. 5 January 1935. Robert Boyer Collection.

Andrews, Laverne. Undated letter to Florence Hannahan. Circa July 1935. Robert Boyer Collection.

Andrews, LaVerne. Letter to Florence Hannahan from Chicago, Illinois. circa July, 1936. Robert Boyer Collection.

Andrews, LaVerne. Letter to Florence Hannahan from Chicago, Illinois. 1 February 1938. Robert Boyer Collection.

Andrews, Laverne. Letter to Florence Hannahan from Chicago, Illinois. 17 March 1938. Robert Boyer Collection.

Andrews, Laverne. Letter to Florence Hannahan from Rome, Italy. July 1945. Robert Boyer Collection.

Andrews, Maxene. Letter to Peter and Olga Andrews from Atlanta, Georgia. 6 November 1931. Robert Boyer Collection.

Andrews, Olga. Letter to Florence Hannahan from Chicago, Illinois. 15 January 1934. Robert Boyer Collection.

Andrews, Olga. Letter to Florence Hannahan from St. Louis, Missouri. 13 November 1935. Robert Boyer Collection.

Andrews, Patty. Letter to Florence Hannahan from Vancouver, British Columbia. 1 March 1935. Robert Boyer Collection.

Andrews, Stanley T. Letter to author. 16 September 2000.

Belasco, Leon. Letter to Robert Boyer. 1976. Robert Boyer Collection.

Blindman, Frances Gershowitz. Letter to Robert Boyer. Undated but known to be from 1976. Robert Boyer Collection.

Bloomberg, Marion Robinson. Letter to Robert Boyer. 8 September 1976. Robert Boyer Collection.

Boyer, Robert. Letter to author. 19 November 2000.

Carroll, Bonnie. Letter to author. 14 September 2000.

Davis, Harry J. Letter to Robert Boyer. 29 August 1976. Robert Boyer Collection.

De Young, Joyce. Letter to author. 27 October 2000.

Dias, Al. Letter to author. 19 November 2000.

Forsmark, Laird. Letter to David McCain. 6 January 1985. David McCain Collection.

Forsmark, Laird. Letter to David McCain. 25 January 1985. David McCain Collection.

Gould, Dawn. Letter to author. 20 April 2001.

Gunn, Johnny. Letter to author. 22 March 2001.

Haas, Al. Letter to author. 12 September 2000.

Harvey, Raymond. Letter to author. 9 November 2000.

Hashway, Jenna Wims. Letter to author. 16 October 2000.

Jones, Jay. Letter to author. 13 September 2000.

King, Yvonne. Letter to author. 26 July 2001.

Lafferty, Travis. Letter to author. 12 September 2000.

Lebovitz, David. Letter to author. 14 September 2000.

Lenger, Frank. Letter to David McCain. 7 December 1985. David McCain Collection.

Malmstrom, Joseph. Letter to author. 1 April 2002.

May, Gene. Letter to author. 24 March 2001.

McCain, David. Letter to author. 29 October 2000.

Nelson, Jimmy. Letter to author. 19 October 2000.

Perry, Calvin O., Jr. Letter to author. 3 December 2001.

Peterson, C. Donald. Letter to Robert Boyer. 3 September 1976. Robert Boyer Collection.

Renner, Herm. Letter to author. 16 February 2001.

Schuster, David. Letter to author. 12 October 2000.

Scott, Bill. Letter to author. 12 September 2000.

Searcy, Everett. Letter to author. December 2000.

Sleder, George. Letter to author. 7 December 2001.

Sollie, Violet J. Letter to author. 4 June 2000

Stocking, Sidney. Letter to Robert Boyer. 24 June 1976. Robert Boyer Collection.

Taylor, E. K. Letter to Robert Boyer. 29 August 1976. Robert Boyer Collection.

Thun, Beverly. Letter to author. 15 February 2001.

Wilmot, Irene. Letter to Robert Boyer. 30 August 1976. Robert Boyer Collection.

Wilmot, Irene. Letter to Robert Boyer. 4 October 1976. Robert Boyer Collection.

Index

Numbers in *italics* indicate photographs